HUMAN
RESOURCES
AND
PERSONNEL
MANAGEMENT

McGRAW-HILL SERIES IN MANAGEMENT

Consulting Editors
Fred Luthans
Keith Davis

HUMAN RESOURCES AND PERSONNEL MANAGEMENT

FIFTH EDITION

William B. Werther, Jr., Ph.D.

Professor of Management
University of Miami

Keith Davis, Ph.D.

Professor Emeritus of Management
Arizona State University

McGraw-Hill, Inc.

New York St. Louis San Francisco Auckland Bogotá Caracas
Lisbon London Madrid Mexico City Milan Montreal New Delhi
San Juan Singapore Sydney Tokyo Toronto

Human Resources and Personnel Management

Copyright © 1996, 1993, 1989, 1985, 1981 by McGraw-Hill, Inc. All rights reserved. Printed in the United States of America. Except as permitted under the United States Copyright Act of 1976, no part of this publication may be reproduced or distributed in any form or by any means, or stored in a data base or retrieval system, without the prior written permission of the publisher.

This book is printed on acid-free paper.

1 2 3 4 5 6 7 8 9 0   DOC DOC   9 0 9 8 7 6 5

ISBN 0-07-069572-5

This book was set in Palatino by Ruttle, Shaw & Wetherill, Inc.
The editors were Lynn Richardson, Dan Alpert, and Laura D. Warner;
the designer was Wanda Siedlecka;
the production supervisor was Denise L. Puryear.
New drawings were done by Fine Line Illustrations, Inc.
R. R. Donnelley & Sons Company was printer and binder.

Library of Congress Cataloging-in-Publication Data

Werther, William B.
   Human resources and personnel management / William B. Werther,
Jr., Keith Davis.—5th ed.
     p.   cm.—(McGraw-Hill series in management)
   Includes bibliographical references and indexes.
   ISBN 0-07-069572-5
   1. Personnel management.   I. Davis, Keith, (date).   II. Title.
III. Series.
HF5549.W4386   1996
658.3—dc20   95-12884

International Edition

Copyright 1996. Exclusive rights by McGraw-Hill, Inc. for manufacture and export. This book cannot be re-exported from the country to which it is consigned by McGraw-Hill. The International Edition is not available in North America.

When ordering this title, use ISBN 0-07-114849-3.

About the Authors

William B. Werther, Jr., is the Samuel N. Friedland Professor of Executive Management at the University of Miami's School of Business Administration, where he was honored with the school's first endowed professorship and a variety of teaching awards. His teaching and research interests include corporate strategy and human resources.

Dr. Werther is an award-winning author. Besides books translated into Chinese, French, German, Korean, Norwegian, Spanish, and Portuguese, he has authored more than eighty articles for *Organizational Dynamics, California Management Review, Personnel Journal, Labor Law Journal,* and other professional journals. His background includes work as a consulting editor to a dozen publishers and editorial board responsibilities for the *National Productivity Review,* the *Journal of Management Development,* and other journals.

Professor Werther stays active as an international corporate and human resource management strategist. His experience includes seminars for business leaders in the Bahamas, Canada, Chile, Germany, Honduras, Mexico, Portugal, and the United States. He has also worked for the White House Conference on Productivity and the American Productivity and Quality Center. His expertise has been sought by the U.S. House of Representatives, the Arizona State Senate, *Fortune, The Wall Street Journal, U.S. News and World Reports,* the *Nightly Business Report* (PBS), and a wide range of organizations, including AT&T, Bell Canada, Ciba Geigy, Citicorp, General Motors, Hershey, Hewlett-Packard, IBM, and NASA. In connection with these activities, Werther has conducted more than 1000 management seminars and workshops.

He has served the professional community as past chair of the Managerial Consultation Division of the Academy of Management. For more than two decades he has been a labor arbitrator for the American Arbitration Association and the Federal Mediation and Conciliation Service. From 1980 to 1982 he chaired the Public Employment Relations Board for the City of Phoenix, Arizona. Additionally, his service includes appointments to boards of directors for nonprofit organizations, and he has served as a gubernatorial appointee to the International Currency and Barter Exchange Committee of Florida. He also works with the legal community as an expert witness in employee relations, wrongful discharge, and economic worth cases. In addition, he regularly holds summer teaching appointments at the Universidad Gabriela Mistral in Santiago, Chile, and the Universidad do Porto in Porto, Portugal.

Werther was an N.D.E.A. Title IV Fellow at the University of Florida, where he earned a Ph.D. in Economics and Business Administration (Phi Beta Kappa) in 1971. Before joining the faculty at the University of Miami in 1985, he was a professor of management at Arizona State University for fourteen years.

Keith Davis is professor emeritus of management at Arizona State University, College of Business, and a fellow in both the Academy of Management and the International Academy of Management. He is the author of prominent books on management and the former consulting editor for 135 books in the McGraw-Hill Series in Management. Before entering the teaching field, Davis was a personnel specialist in industry and a personnel manager in government.

He received a Ph.D. from Ohio State University and has taught at the University of Texas and Indiana University. His fields of work are organizational behavior, human resource management, and social issues in management. Davis has been visiting professor at a number of universities, including the University of Western Australia, the University of Colorado, and the Georgia Institute of Technology. He also has served as a consultant to a number of business and government organizations, including Mobil Oil Company, Texaco, the U.S. Internal Revenue Service, and the state of Hawaii.

Davis is former president of the Academy of Management and has received the National Human Relations Award from the Society for Advancement of Management. He has been a national Beta Gamma Sigma distinguished scholar and is an accredited Senior Professional in Human Resources. In 1992 he received the Distinguished Educator Award from the Academy of Management in recognition of his influence on an entire generation of management practitioners and teachers through his writings and leadership in the field.

Two popular books by Davis are (with John W. Newstrom) *Organizational Behavior: Human Behavior at Work* (9th ed., 1993) and (with William C. Frederick and James E. Post) *Business and Society* (7th ed., 1992), both published by McGraw-Hill. He also has contributed chapters to more than 100 books and is the author of over 150 articles in journals such as *Harvard Business Review, Academy of Management Journal, Management International,* and *California Management Review.* Four of his books have been translated into other languages.

*This book is dedicated to
the late Richard E. Werther
and to Sue Davis*

Contents in Brief

Contents

Preface

We believe that human resource departments play a pivotal and expanding role in shaping the success of domestic and international organizations.

THE AUTHORS

Student and faculty acceptance is the ultimate test of any college textbook. After four editions and hundreds of adoptions and readoptions, *Human Resources and Personnel Management* has passed the test of the marketplace. Perhaps even more gratifying, many students have retained this book for their professional libraries after course completion, suggesting that they, too, found real value in its contents.

Adoptions of the book around the world have been led by the Canadian edition (adapted by Professors Hermann F. Schwind and Hari Das of Saint Mary's University), which expanded its role as the leading human resource textbook in Canada. The Spanish, Portuguese, and French translations—along with the international student edition published in Singapore—gained additional adoptions around the world.

Reviewers tell us that the book's global acceptance can be attributed to its balanced coverage of both theory and practice. Students and instructors tell us it is understandably written and pragmatic in orientation. As we wrote in the preface to the first edition in 1981:

> Although balanced and thorough coverage is the most important feature of the book, we believe that readers and instructors want more than that. Comments from colleagues and students convinced us that an introductory personnel management text must be readable and teachable. It should:
>
> - Capture the interest of readers
>
> - Reflect the flavor and challenges of this exciting field
>
> - Provide instructors with a flexible teaching tool

In the fifth edition we continue to stress the application-oriented approach of previous editions by further expanding the use of "real-life" examples drawn from well-known companies around the world. These examples not only add interest but also provide authentic insights into this dynamic field. And, given the increased globalization of organizations, the discussion of international human resource management is expanded throughout the book. At the same time, we have updated the coverage in every chapter and added more extensive citations for those wishing to explore specific topics in greater depth.

Purpose

Our *premise* is that modern organizations are the most important innovations of our era because their success or failure shapes the well-being of every person on earth. Organizations succeed by effectively and efficiently combining resources to implement their strategies. However, central to any strategy, to any use of resources, are the employees who devise and execute an organization's strategy. Simply put, how well an organization obtains, maintains, and retains its human resources is a major determinant of its success or failure.

The *purpose* of this book is to explain how proactive managers and human resource professionals share their dual responsibility for continuously improving the human contribution to organizations.

Our *focus* is practical. The text presents key concepts, issues, and practices without being encyclopedic. We emphasize applications of theory and practice so that readers gain a useful understanding of human resource management, whether they seek careers as managers or as HR professionals.

Quality and Acceptance

The *guiding principle* that drove this revision was the desire to produce a highly readable book that was clear, interesting, and of high quality. A study by George S. Cole of Shippensburg University, published in the *Academy of Management Review,* compared several leading human resource textbooks, including ours.* It rated an earlier edition of our book as the highest-quality personnel book. The study also found that this book received the *most* favorable reaction from students and had the *highest* proportion of users saying they "certainly would" adopt the book again.

We believe this edition improves on those that came before.

Balanced Coverage and Revision Highlights

The book seeks balanced coverage among traditional topics and emerging challenges. Theory and practice are supplemented with "real-life" examples and research summaries drawn from our experience and the literature. Since this is an introductory book, we assume no prior knowledge of the field by the reader.

The fifth edition contains an extensive content revision to reflect rapid

---

*George S. Cole, "Managing the Human Resources of Work: A Review of Personnel/Human Resource Management Texts," *Academy of Management Review,* October 1985, pp. 881–888.

changes in the field. Greater attention has been paid to the HR department's strategic role as a source of competitive advantage. As a result, we have strengthened the chapter titled "International Challenges," retaining it as Chapter 3 to emphasize the growing importance of international human resource management to many firms.

To keep the text at a usable length while adding new material, the book's nineteen chapters are organized into five parts:

- **PART 1**   **Frameworks and Challenges**
- **PART II**   **Preparation and Selection**
- **PART III** **Development and Evaluation**
- **PART IV**   **Compensation and Protection**
- **PART V**   **Employee Relations and Assessment**

PART I examines different approaches to human resource management and identifies the professional, international, and equal employment challenges within which the human resource function must operate. PART II explores the need for a human resource information system by examining job analysis and design and human resource planning as preconditions for effective recruitment and selection. PART III covers the development and evaluation of human resources in terms of orientation, placement, training, development, performance appraisal, and career planning. PART IV addresses compensation management, including chapters on incentives and gainsharing, benefits and services, and safety, security, and health. PART V concludes with chapters on employee and labor relations. The last chapter addresses the assessment of human resource management and future challenges.

While the structure of the book remains unchanged, readopters of the text will find that we have updated the chapters and added dozens of new, named company examples to reflect the never-ending changes that take place in practice. Additionally, we have recast more than 90 percent of the review and discussion questions, chapter incidents and exercises, chapter objectives, and chapter-opening quotations. We have added coverage of the Family and Medical Leave Act of 1993, along with updates on recent court decisions. In response to user comments, we have expanded our coverage of international developments, diversity, action learning, and future challenges.

Key Pedagogical Features

The fifth edition expands the key features of previous editions. Among the features users and reviewers report as helpful are:

1. *Part openings.* Each of the book's five parts begins with a brief overview of the following chapters and emphasizes the topic's importance to readers.

The graphic model of the book is included to highlight the chapters' relationship to the overall plan.

2. *Real-life examples.* This edition includes more than 200 examples drawn almost exclusively from named companies. Many are new. They demonstrate and reinforce the relevancy of key ideas and practices while increasing reader interest and retention. To provide greater continuity and integration, the same organizations are often used for several examples within a chapter.

3. *Chapter objectives.* Six learning objectives introduce each chapter to highlight its key areas. (These objectives are useful review tools, especially for comprehensive and essay examinations.)

4. *Opening example.* To provide a practical context for the theory and practices discussed in the chapter, each introduction includes an example drawn from a major corporation.

5. *Chapter quote.* Each chapter opens with a quotation or two from a researcher or practitioner. The quotes were selected to stimulate interest in the chapter, underscore the importance of the following content, or offer an interesting counterpoint to conventional wisdom.

6. *Chapter summary.* A brief summary of each chapter is provided at the end to capture the key ideas.

7. *Terms for review.* Following each summary is a list of key concepts mentioned and, as in previous editions, italicized and defined within the chapter. Their number has been expanded in this revision. (Definitions of key terms also appear in the glossary at the end of the book.)

8. *Review and discussion questions.* Each end-of-chapter section includes eight review and discussion questions. These are of two kinds: some request a summary of chapter ideas, while others focus on the application of concepts. More than 90 percent have been revised or replaced.

9. *Chapter incidents.* Classroom-tested incidents emphasize the application of chapter concepts to specific questions. Nearly all have been updated for this edition.

10. *References.* Chapters end with a mixture of classical and current references to allow the reader to explore topics in greater depth and serve as a jumping-off point for course-based assignments. The fifth edition has expanded these references to provide greater detail in documentation.

11. *Glossary.* Since the book is intended as an introduction to the topic of human resources and personnel management, the extensive glossary of earlier editions has been expanded to allow adopters to vary the chapter sequence to suit their personal preferences. (The glossary also serves as a useful review tool for comprehensive examinations.)

Supplementary Materials

A thoroughly updated and comprehensive instructor's manual, with a test bank, is available to adopters to augment the balanced coverage and interest-building features of the book. Users of previous editions report that the manual/test bank was one of the most comprehensive teaching resources available.

Instructor's manual/test bank.   The instructor's manual is a resource book. Section 1 contains a sample course syllabus, alternative course designs, suggested term projects, a film and videotape bibliography with addresses, and other instructional resources. Section 2 offers chapter-by-chapter materials such as lecture notes keyed to chapter outlines, experiential in-class exercises, answers to review and discussion questions, and comments on chapter incidents.

Section 3 contains a detailed test bank made up of about 1000 questions, including true-false, multiple-choice, essay, and other formats drawn from the text. It has been extensively revised and expanded to include materials from this edition. The test bank is also available in computerized form; to obtain a copy, contact your local McGraw-Hill representative.

Videos.   The McGraw-Hill Human Resource Management Video Series offers a range of high-quality programs and is designed to supplement key areas of topic coverage. Teaching notes accompany the videos. Contact your local McGraw-Hill representative for details.

Acknowledgments

The great laboratory of a free economy and the diligent efforts of researchers have created a never-ending stream of innovations. The index identifies those who have contributed the most to our view of human resource management through their research and writings. For many others, unknown to us, who have moved the field forward, we believe this book captures the fundamentals of their creative efforts.

We have also been helped considerably by the support of our schools—the University of Miami and Arizona State University—and by the encouragement of our departmental colleagues. The book also has benefited from our annual international teaching experiences, especially at the Universidad Gabriela Mistral in Chile and the Instituto Superior De Estudos Empresariais of the Universidad do Porto in Portugal.

Our greatest appreciation goes to those who gave so freely of their time and advice; their good counsel enriched the book in many ways. In particular, we are most grateful to John W. Newstrom of the University of Minnesota–Duluth and to William E. Reif of Arizona State University. Along with Fred Luthans of the University of Nebraska, these scholars played an important role in the initiation of this book in its first edition.

Our sincere appreciation also extends to those who have provided many useful comments and suggestions during the course of this book's development through five editions, especially Philip Adler, Jr., Georgia Institute of Technology; George Biles, Robert Morris College; George Bohlander, Arizona State University; Tom Chacko, Iowa State University; Randy L. DeSimone, Rhode Island College; Joseph DiAngelo, Widener University; Diane Dodd-McCue, University of Virginia; Jeremy B. Fox, Appalachian State University; Robert Gatewood, University of Georgia; Joyce Giglioni, Mississippi State University; David A. Gray, University of Texas at Arlington; Richard A. Grover, University of Southern Maine; Jean M. Hanebury, Texas A&M University at Corpus Christi; Stephen Hartman, New York Institute of Technology; Christine L. Hobart, Northeastern University; Wallace Johnson, Virginia Commonwealth University; Thomas Johnston, Nassau County Community College; Paul Keaton, University of Wisconsin–LaCrosse; Richard A. Lester, University of North Alabama; Marvin Levine, Orange County Community College; Robert McGinty, Eastern Washington University; Carl McKenry, University of Miami; Gregory Northcraft, University of Arizona; John Overby, University of Tennessee; Richard J. Randolph, Johnson County Community College; Robert F. Scherer, Wright State University; Lee Stepina, Florida State University; George E. Stevens, Oakland University; Arthur Whatley, New Mexico State University; and Harold C. White, Arizona State University.

We are grateful for their contributions but remain responsible where we failed to heed their advice.

WILLIAM B. WERTHER, JR.
KEITH DAVIS

HUMAN RESOURCES AND PERSONNEL MANAGEMENT

1. **The Human Resource Frameworks**
2. **Environmental Challenges**
3. **International Challenges**
4. **Equal Employment Challenges**

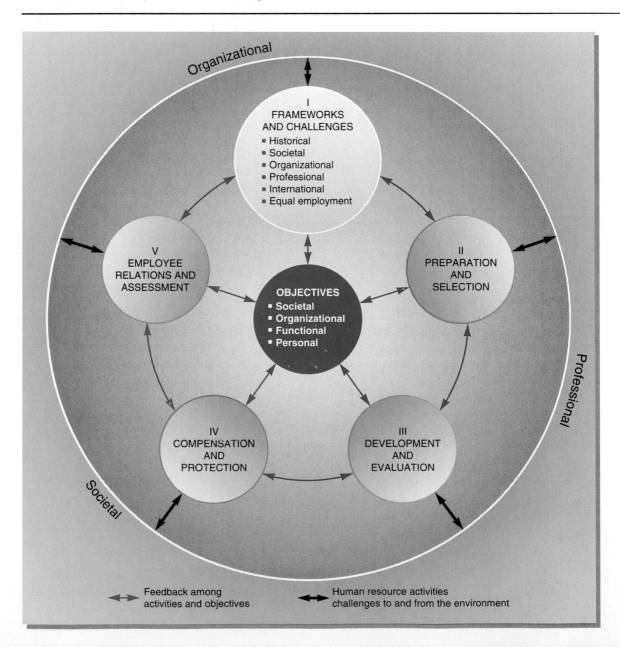

FRAMEWORKS AND CHALLENGES

HUMAN RESOURCE departments exist to help people and organizations reach their goals. Along the way, they face many challenges arising from the demands of the employees, the organization, and society. The domestic and international environments are particularly turbulent because of the growing diversity of the workforce and the globalization of businesses. Challenges also result from ever-changing laws, especially laws that address the need for equal employment opportunity. Within these constraints, the human resource department must contribute to the organization's "bottom line" in ways that are both ethical and socially responsible.

This book's first four chapters explore these challenges and set a foundation on which the rest of the book builds. Your personal success as a manager of people or a specialist in human resources depends on how these challenges are met. You are affected because organizations touch your life every day. How well our organizations succeed also determines your well-being and the well-being of our society.

1

There aren't any easy answers to problems caused for employees by competition and the rapidly changing skills that companies need to survive.
BRIAN O'REILLY[1]

Management . . . must have the support of all employees. I cannot think of anything more important.
ROBERT CRANDALL[2]

The Human Resource Frameworks

CHAPTER OBJECTIVES

After studying this chapter, you should be able to:

1. EXPLAIN the purpose and objectives of human resource management.

2. DIAGRAM the relationships among the key jobs and basic functions of human resource management.

3. DESCRIBE the major human resource management activities.

4. IDENTIFY the central challenge facing our society.

5. EXPLAIN the "dual responsibility" for human resource management shared by managers and professionals.

6. DISCUSS the challenges arising from the globalization of businesses.

A generation ago the shipbuilding, motorcycle, automobile, steel, tire, consumer-electronics, semiconductor, banking, and computer industries of North America were the envy of the world. In recent years, however, each of these industries has encountered relentless challenges from international competitors, particularly those in Japan, South Korea, Taiwan, Germany, and the other European Union nations. These economic pressures will intensify, with even more competition coming from newly emerging competitors in Asia and eastern Europe. The response?

> From Armonk, N.Y., to Zurich, Switzerland, business is on a weight-loss binge. . . . Such domineering presences as IBM and ABB Asea Brown Boveri have shed employees, layers of management, and old ways of doing things. They have reengineered work processes and raised efficiency by creating quality initiatives, multidisciplinary teams of workers, and employee empowerment programs. Strip away the business babble, and it comes down to this: Top-heavy organizations are out. Slender, nimble ones are in.[3]

Global markets

How well any country survives in this global economy depends squarely on the performance of its organizations—private and public. Ultimately, every society's wealth and well-being come from its organizations, which provide the jobs, products, and services needed to sustain a modern industrial or postindustrial nation. By selling more goods and services in global markets, nations are able to earn more wealth for their societies and, in time, increase the standard of living of their citizens.

Organization-based advances

At the same time, organizations are more than vehicles for global competition. Name the greatest accomplishment of the twentieth century. Biogenetic engineering? The moon landing? Computers? The most significant achievement may not even have happened yet. But every major advance in this century shares a common feature: organizations.

> Biogenetic engineering breakthroughs have come from Stanford University and a company called Genentech, among others. The Apollo missions to the moon were made possible by an organization called the National Aeronautics and Space Administration (NASA). Likewise, computers were first developed by Sperry Rand and other organizations. Even on a day-to-day basis, organizations play a central role in our lives. The water we drink, the food we eat, the clothes we wear, and the vehicles we drive come from organizations.

When future historians view our era, they may see twentieth-century organizations as our greatest accomplishment. Certainly they will agree with the essayist who penned these words:

> Organizations are the most inventive social arrangements of our age and of civilization. It is a marvel to know that tens of thousands of people with highly individualized backgrounds, skills, and interests are coordinated in various enterprises to pursue common institutionalized goals.[4]

The term "human resources" refers to the people in an organization. When managers engage in human resource (HR) activities as part of their jobs, they seek to facilitate the contribution people make to achieving an organization's strategies and plans. The importance of HR efforts comes from the realization that people are the common element in every organization; they create the strategies and innovations for which organizations are noted. As a slogan at a Union Carbide plant puts it, "Assets make things possible, people make things happen."

Although human resource activities contribute to an organization's success in a variety of ways, ultimately they must support the company's strategies.[5]

Strategic HR   This "strategic management of human resources" view requires that managers use HR efforts to further the firm's competitive advantage through plans and actions focused on contributing to the economic, or "bottom-line," success of the organization.[6] This contribution must be made in ways that are ethical and socially responsible.

To illustrate the importance of HR activities, this book draws on a variety of "real-life" practices by named companies. Consider the following example which highlights the importance of HR management.

Lawrence A. Bossidy is the chief executive officer of Allied-Signal, a company with sales in excess of a billion dollars a month in automotive, chemical, and other industries. In the early 1990s, Allied-Signal lured him away from his position as vice chairman at General Electric to become CEO at Allied-Signal with a package worth more than $25 million according to *Fortune.*[7]

Allied-Signal   "Bossidy's belief that Allied-Signal needs stronger executive talent has led him to take personal responsibility for the company's human resources—an unusual role for a big-time CEO.

"Bossidy then told his three executive vice presidents and President Alan Belzer to lead teams to prepare detailed plans to improve college recruiting, staffing, career development, and training and education. They benchmarked the best—companies like Corning, Bechtel, Hewlett-Packard, Johnson & Johnson—and held focus groups to learn how employees felt human resources could help their careers more. Says aerospace head Daniel Burnham: '. . . it is the heart of what we do' "[8]

Although Allied-Signal's balance sheet does not list its human "assets," those assets are the backbone of the company. Allied-Signal's leader considers human resources so crucial that he took direct charge of HR activities as part of his turnaround strategy for the company.

▶ The Central Challenge

As the challenges shown in Figure 1-1 become more complex, our society will face further demands to compete globally, feed the hungry, find new energy sources, cure diseases, lower unemployment, and meet other challenges that

Figure 1-1	The Central Challenge to Organizations

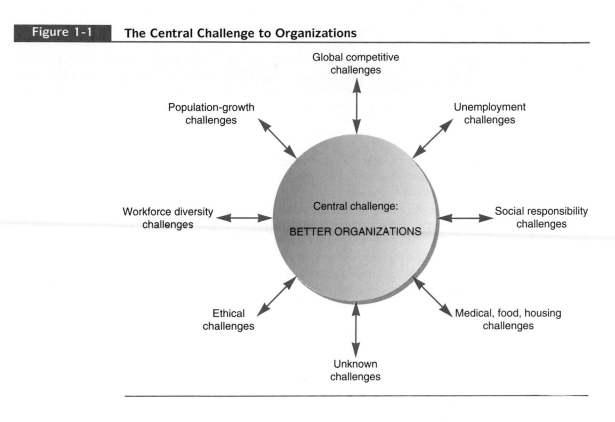

we cannot imagine. We will respond to these challenges through our most creative invention: organizations. The better our organizations work, the more
easily our society can meet these challenges and opportunities. *Therefore, the
central challenge facing our society is the continued improvement of our organizations,
both private and public.*

When public and private organizations improve, society prospers and meets
the challenges shown in Figure 1-1. But how do they improve? Organizations
improve through more effective and efficient use of their resources. *Effective*
means producing the right goods or services that society deems appropriate. In
Allied-Signal's case, this means providing safe and reliable automobile parts,
for example. But Allied-Signal must do more than just the *right things*; it must
also perform its activities in the *right ways*. Since Allied-Signal competes with
other suppliers, it must be efficient to survive. *Efficient* means that it must use
the minimum amount of resources needed to produce its goods and services. If
Allied's people, for example, can do a better job of scheduling its factories and
shipments, the company can serve more customers while using fewer resources.
The result for society is an improvement in this industry's productivity.

Productivity is the ratio of an organization's outputs (goods and services) to
its inputs (people, capital, materials, and energy), as shown in Figure 1-2.[9] Productivity increases as an organization finds new ways to use fewer resources to

Central challenge

*Effective versus
efficient use of
resources*

Figure 1-2	Productivity Defined as a Ratio

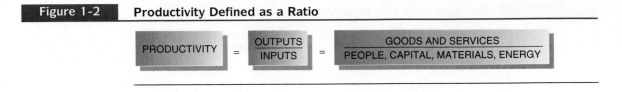

$$\text{PRODUCTIVITY} = \frac{\text{OUTPUTS}}{\text{INPUTS}} = \frac{\text{GOODS AND SERVICES}}{\text{PEOPLE, CAPITAL, MATERIALS, ENERGY}}$$

produce its output. Through productivity gains, managers can reduce costs, save scarce resources, and enhance profits. In turn, improved profits allow an organization to provide better pay, benefits, and working conditions. The result can be a higher quality of work life for the employees, who are more likely to be motivated toward further improvements in productivity.

HR and productivity

HR actions contribute to improved productivity *directly* by finding better and more efficient ways to meet objectives and *indirectly* by improving the quality of work life for employees.[10] Admittedly, managers must deal with trade-offs between employee satisfaction and economic, or bottom-line, results. A high quality of work life alone does not ensure economic success. At the same time, quality of work life and bottom-line gains must be achieved in ways that support the company's strategies, are ethical for the parties involved, and are socially responsible to the larger society.

This chapter begins the explanation of how organizations make these trade-offs through HR activities. It shows the purpose of HR management and explains how it responds with clear objectives and specific activities to improve the productive contribution of people. The chapter ends by describing an overall framework in the form of a model. Later chapters expand the model and provide details.

The Purpose of Human Resource Management

The purpose of human resource management is to improve the productive contribution of people to the organization in ways that are strategically, ethically, and socially responsible. This purpose guides the study and practice of HR management, which is also commonly called personnel management. The study of HR management describes the HR-related efforts of operating managers and shows how personnel professionals contribute to those efforts.

Human resources determine every organization's success. Improving the human contribution is so ambitious and important, however, that all but the smallest firms create a specialized personnel or HR department. It is ambitious because HR departments do not control many of the factors that shape the employees' contribution, such as capital, materials, and procedures. The department decides neither strategy nor a supervisor's treatment of employees, although it strongly influences both. Simply put, the HR department exists to support managers and employees as they pursue the organization's strategies. However, to guide its many activities and support the managers who operate other parts of the organization, HR departments must have objectives.

HR's supporting role

The Objectives of Human Resource Management

Managers and HR departments achieve their purpose by meeting objectives. *Objectives* are benchmarks against which actions are evaluated. Sometimes they are carefully thought out and expressed in writing. More often objectives are not formally stated. Either way, they guide the HR function in practice. Consider the objectives of Hewlett-Packard's founders:

Hewlett-Packard

> When Bill Hewlett and Dave Packard founded the company that shares their names, they wanted to create an environment that allowed employees to undertake creative work. Fearful that a formal personnel department might add a layer of bureaucracy, the company was 18 years old before a formal HR department was created. Even then, reflecting the objectives that the founders set, the HR department was very decentralized.[11]

HR objectives

Human resource objectives not only need to reflect the intention of senior management, they also must balance challenges from the organization, the HR function, society, and the people who are affected. Failure to do so can harm the firm's performance, profits, and even survival. These challenges spotlight four objectives that are common to HR management and form a framework around which this book is written.

Organizational objective. To recognize that HR management exists to contribute to organizational effectiveness. Even when a formal HR department is created to help managers, the managers remain responsible for employee performance. The HR department exists to help managers achieve the objectives of the organization. HR management is not an end in itself; it is only a means of assisting managers with their human resource issues. For example, Hewlett-Packard's HR department found that it could enhance its contribution to the organization through sophisticated information systems that allowed the department to cut $35 million a year from its budget.[12] Simply stated, an HR department exists to serve the rest of the organization.

Functional objective. To maintain the department's contribution at a level appropriate to the organization's needs. Resources are wasted when HR management is more or less sophisticated than the organization demands. Realizing that the HR department had grown too large, Hewlett-Packard changed its ratio of HR staff members to employees from 1 per 53 down to 1 per 75 without violating the company's long-standing "no-layoffs" policy.[13]

Societal objective. To be ethically and socially responsive to the needs and challenges of society while minimizing the negative impact of such demands on the organization. The failure of organizations to use their resources for society's benefit in ethical ways may result in restrictions. For example, society may limit HR decisions through laws that address discrimination, safety, and other areas of societal concern.

Personal objective.   To assist employees in achieving their personal goals, at least insofar as those goals enhance the individual's contribution to the organization. The personal objectives of employees must be met if workers are to be maintained, retained, and motivated. Otherwise, employee performance and satisfaction may decline and employees may leave the organization. In addition to Hewlett-Packard's no-layoff policy, the HR department, for example, also furthers personal objectives. In one instance the HR department helped its technically oriented women network and further their careers by organizing a technical women's conference.[14]

Not every HR decision can meet these organizational, functional, societal, and personal objectives every time. Trade-offs do occur. But these objectives serve as a check on decisions. The more these objectives are met by the department's actions, the larger its contribution will be to the organization's bottom line and the employees' needs. Moreover, by keeping these objectives in mind, HR specialists can see the reasons behind many of the department's activities.

Human Resource Management Activities

To achieve their purpose and objectives, HR departments help managers obtain, develop, utilize, evaluate, maintain, and retain the right numbers and types of workers. As Figure 1-3 shows, these activities meet HR objectives. When these objectives are met, the purpose of HR management is achieved through people who contribute to the organization's strategies and overall goals of effectiveness and efficiency. For these reasons, HR executives play an increasingly important role in the governance of domestic and global companies.[15] Consider, for example, how the former chairman of American Express viewed Irene (Rennie) C. Roberts, senior vice president for human resources:

American Express

"Chief executives have finally come to realize that people are what give you the competitive edge, and we're telling them how to get the right people." AmEx's fast growing subsidiaries . . . need strong, entrepreneurial managers, according to former AmEx Chairman James D. Robinson III. "Rennie Roberts and her staff," he says, serve as "an objective sounding board for an evaluation of people, compensation structures, benefit costs, and work life so that we can attract and hold the people we want."[16]

Key human resource activities.   Human resource activities are actions that are taken to provide and maintain an appropriate workforce for the organization. Not every manager or HR department undertakes every activity discussed in this book. Small companies may not have an HR department, and small employers with HR departments may lack large budgets and adequate numbers of staff members. These departments simply focus on the activities that are most important for the organization. Large departments usually are

Full-service HR

"full-service" ones; they do all the activities shown in Figure 1-3 and described in the following paragraphs.

Figure 1-3

The Response of Human Resource Management to Societal Needs and Challenges

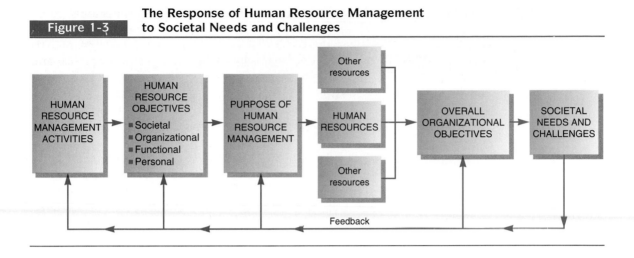

As an organization becomes large, attempts are made to estimate its future HR needs through an activity called *human resource planning.* With an eye toward future needs, *recruitment* seeks to secure job applicants to fill those needs. The result is a pool of applicants who are screened through a *selection process.* This process selects those people who meet the needs uncovered through HR planning.

New workers seldom meet the organization's needs exactly, and so they must be *oriented* and *trained* to perform effectively. As demands change, *placement* activities transfer, promote, demote, lay off, and even terminate workers. Subsequent HR plans reveal new staffing needs. These openings are filled through the recruitment of additional workers and the *development* of present employees. Development teaches employees new knowledge, skills, and abilities, ensuring their continued usefulness to the organization and meeting their personal desires for advancement.

Key HR activities

Then individual performance is *appraised.* Not only does this activity evaluate how well people perform, it also indicates how well HR activities have been done. Poor performance may mean that selection, training, or developmental activities should be revised, or there may be a problem with employee relations.

Employees also must receive *compensation* in the form of wages, salaries, or incentives, along with employee benefits such as insurance and vacations. Some rewards are *required services* dictated by law, such as social security, workers' compensation, safe working conditions, and overtime pay.

HR departments also play an important role in *employee relations,* usually by establishing policies and assisting managers. When employees are dissatisfied, they may band together and take collective action. Then management is confronted with a new situation: *union-management relations.* To respond to collective demands by employees, HR specialists may have to negotiate and administer a labor agreement.

Figure 1-4	The Relation of Activities to Objectives in Human Resource Management

MANAGEMENT OBJECTIVES	SUPPORTING ACTIVITIES
SOCIETAL OBJECTIVE	1. Legal compliance
	2. Benefits
	3. Union-management relations
ORGANIZATIONAL OBJECTIVE	1. Human resource planning
	2. Employee relations
	3. Selection
	4. Training and development
	5. Appraisal
	6. Placement
	7. Assessment
FUNCTIONAL OBJECTIVE	1. Appraisal
	2. Placement
	3. Assessment
PERSONAL OBJECTIVE	1. Training and development
	2. Appraisal
	3. Placement
	4. Compensation
	5. Assessment

Effective HR departments conduct an *assessment* of their effectiveness to assure their continued success. Traditional budgetary limitations are one form of control. Another means of control might be to conduct an evaluation of the effectiveness of each activity in meeting company objectives.

Figure 1-4 matches each activity to one or more objectives. For example, appraisal contributes to organizational, functional, and personal objectives. If an activity does not contribute to one or more of the department's objectives, the resources devoted to that activity should be redirected.

Responsibility for human resource activities. The responsibility for HR management activities rests with *each manager.*[17] If managers throughout the organization do not accept this responsibility, HR activities may be done only partially or not at all. Even when an HR department is created within the organization, both operating managers and HR experts have dual responsibility for employee performance. Individual managers remain involved with planning, selection, orientation, training, development, evaluation, compensation, and other HR activities, even though they may be assisted by experts in the HR de-

Managers' responsibilities

partment. For example, one reason why Hewlett-Packard did not have an HR department during its first eighteen years was that the founders "believed that line managers should care about their people and handle their own personnel issues."[18]

When managers find that HR work seriously disrupts their other duties, that work may be reassigned to another worker or to a specialized department that handles HR matters. This process of getting others to share the work is called *delegation*. Delegation does not reduce a manager's responsibility; it only allows the manager to share that responsibility with others who become accountable. For example, a manager may ask a senior worker to train a new employee. If the new employee makes a costly mistake and the experienced worker lets it pass, the manager will be held responsible for the problems that result. As HR activities become more complex and time-consuming, the need for a separate department may arise.

▶ The Organization of a Human Resource Department

A separate department usually emerges when the expected benefits of a department exceed its costs. Until then, managers must handle HR activities themselves or delegate them to subordinates. When a department emerges, it is typically small and is the responsibility of a middle-level manager. Figure 1-5

Figure 1-5   **The Human Resource Department in a Small Organization**

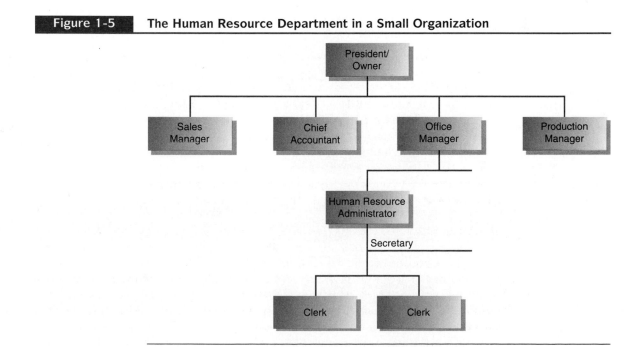

illustrates a common placement of the department when it is first formed. Such departments are usually limited to maintaining employee records and helping managers find new recruits. Whether the department performs other activities depends on the needs of other managers in the firm.

The department becomes more important and more complex as the demands on it grow. Figure 1-6 demonstrates this increased importance by showing the head of the department reporting directly to the company president. Increased importance may be signified by a change in title to vice president, the title used for the top HR officer at Hewlett-Packard, for example. To deal with

Size and specialization

growth and new demands, jobs in the department become more specialized. Often highly specialized subdepartments emerge to provide a wide range of services, as shown in levels II and III of Figure 1-6.

The size of the department varies widely, depending largely on the size of the organization being supported. One study reported a median ratio of 1 human resource staff member per 100 employees in the organization. As was mentioned earlier, Hewlett-Packard's ratio was 1 per 53 in the early 1990s and has since dropped to 1 HR staffer for every 75 employees.[19] The average depart-

HR budgets

ment's budget is 1 percent of a company's operating expenses.[20] Another study suggests that HR departments have been spared the layoffs recently experienced by other departments because of their perceived importance by top management.

| Figure 1-6 | **The Hierarchy of Jobs within a Large Human Resource Department** |

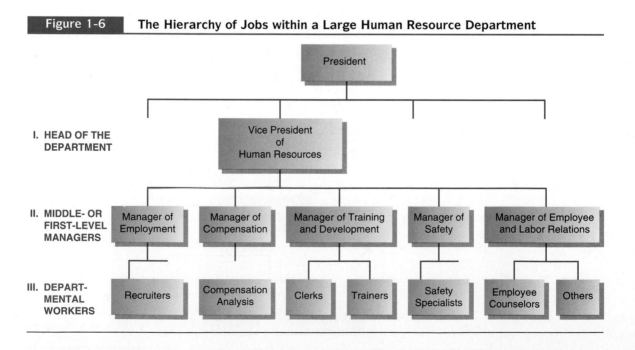

The numbers may reflect the more "strategic" role played by these divisions today, says Lawrence Schein, director of the Conference Board Survey. . . . Top executives look to them for problem-solving techniques. The survey showed, for example, that 90 percent of executives want their personnel divisions to find ways to improve productivity, which has been woefully low throughout the industrial and service sectors. "Companies are obviously hoping that personnel management will provide them with a strong competitive edge," he said.[21]

Departmental Components

The subdepartments of a large, full-service HR department approximately correspond with the activities shown in Figure 1-4. For each major activity, a subdepartment may be established to provide the specialized service. The work of the employment department, for example, involves recruitment and selection. Other divisions in the figure perform the activities their names imply. This specialization allows members of the department to become experts in a limited number of activities.

Activities not shown in Figure 1-6 are shared among the different sections. For example, employment, training, and development sections may share in HR planning and placement. Performance appraisals are used to determine pay, and so the compensation division may assist managers in appraising performance. Required services come under the benefits and safety sections. Control activities, communications, and counseling are divided among all the subdepartments, with employee and labor relations doing most of these tasks. Employee and labor relations sections also provide the official union-management coordination when unions exist. The Delta Air Lines personnel division provides a real-life example, as shown in Figure 1-7.

Key Roles in a Human Resource Department

HR titles

Within the HR department there is a hierarchy of jobs, as shown in Figure 1-6. The top job varies in importance and title in different organizations.[22] When the department first is formed, its head is often called a personnel or human resource manager, director, or administrator. The title of vice president of personnel or vice president of human resources becomes more likely as the department's size, contribution, sophistication, and responsibility grow.[23] If unions make a major demand on the personnel function, the title typically becomes director or even vice president of industrial relations.

Large HR departments have a variety of positions. The manager of employment helps other managers with recruiting and selection. The compensation manager establishes fair pay systems. The training and development manager provides guidance and programs for managers who want to improve their human resources skills. Other activity managers contribute their expertise and

Figure 1-7 Organizational Chart of the Personnel Division of Delta Air Lines

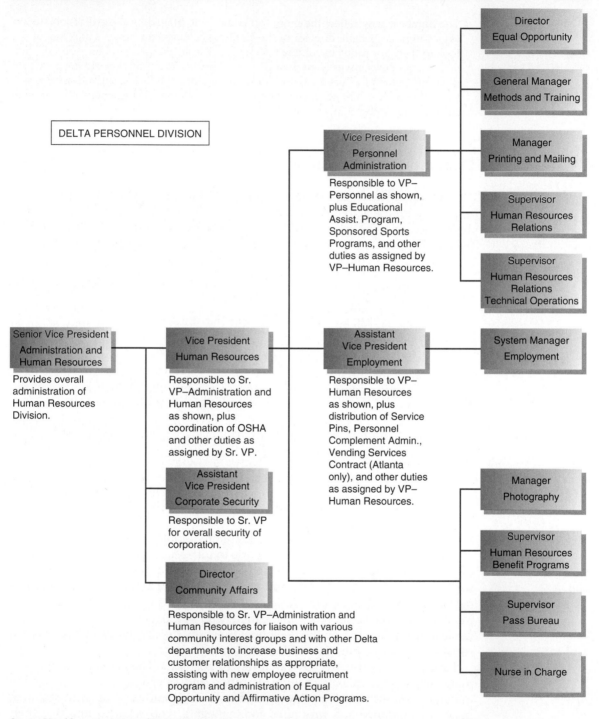

Source: Used by permission of Delta Air Lines.

usually report directly to the head of the HR department. Activity managers may be supported by an assortment of specialists, secretaries, and clerks. These are the people who carry out the department's activities. It is the specialists in large organizations who actually do the recruiting, training, and other necessary tasks. These specialist positions are the jobs in which college graduates often start their careers in HR work.

The Service Role of a Human Resource Department

HR departments exist to assist the organization, its managers, and its employees. HR is a service department. Even when faced with a need to reduce costs, service-oriented HR departments, such as the one at Hewlett-Packard, often seek to substitute computer and information technologies for lower staffing levels as a means of maintaining service to others in the organization.[24]

HR's authority

As members of a service department, HR managers and specialists do not have the authority to manage other departments. Instead, they have *staff authority,* which is the authority to advise, not direct, other managers. *Line authority* is the right to direct the operations of departments that make or distribute an organization's products or service. Those who have line authority are sometimes called line or operating managers. Line managers make decisions about production, performance, and people. They determine promotions, job assignments, and other people-related decisions. HR specialists advise operating managers and other staff managers, who are ultimately responsible for their employees' performance.

Although advisory, staff authority is powerful. When HR advises a manager about an HR issue, that manager may reject the advice. In doing so, however, the manager bears the full responsibility for the outcome. If the results cause employee relations problems, the consequences fall on the manager. To avoid disruptive consequences, managers usually consider the HR department's advice and follow it. As a result, the department has considerable influence in shaping the actions of managers in other departments.

Functional authority

When the cost of not following the HR department's counsel is high, top management may replace staff or advisory authority with functional authority over specific issues. *Functional authority* is the right given to specialists to make the final decision in specified circumstances. In highly technical or routine decisions, functional authority allows the department to make decisions that would otherwise be made by managers in other departments. If, for example, each department manager at Hewlett-Packard made separate decisions about employee benefits, the result would be excessive costs and inequities. Therefore, the right of these managers to determine their employees' benefit package at Hewlett-Packard is given to the HR department by top management. If these managers disagree with the department's actions, they can ask top management to review and even veto those plans. Otherwise, the department makes the decisions about employee benefits to ensure control, uniformity, and the use of its expertise. When given functional authority, the HR department no longer advises: It decides. However, as in all organizational decisions, the use of functional authority is subject to review by top management.

Dual responsibility

The use of line, staff, and functional authority results in a *dual responsibility for human resource management.*[25] Both line and HR managers are responsible for employee productivity and the quality of work life. HR departments are responsible for creating a productive climate by finding ways to enhance the organization's quality of work life through its activities and advice to other managers. Hewlett-Packard, for example, is often rated as one of the best companies to work for in the United States.[26] At the same time, managers are responsible for their employees' day-to-day treatment and for the quality of work life in their departments.

The HR department's size also affects the type of service provided to employees, managers, and the organization. In small departments the manager handles many of the day-to-day activities related to the organization's HR needs. Other managers bring their problems directly to the head of the department, and those meetings constantly remind the HR manager of the contribution that is expected.

In large HR departments, problems are handled by subordinates. Not only do HR managers have less contact with lower-level managers, but others in the HR department become increasingly specialized. At this point HR managers and their subordinates may lose sight of the overall contributions that are expected of them or of the limits on their authority. Instead, experts sometimes become more interested in perfecting their specialties than in asking how they may serve others and further the company's strategic concerns. Or specialists may assume authority that they do not have. When HR professionals make these mistakes, it often results from failing to recognize the connection between different HR management activities.

▶ The Human Resource Management Model

HR management is a system that consists of many interdependent activities. These activities do not occur in isolation; virtually every one affects another HR activity.

In preparing a bid for a construction contract, an estimator miscalculated the staffing requirements. Too many unskilled workers and too few skilled employees were hired. As the expansion of the football stadium fell behind schedule, supervisors tried to get work done more quickly. This speedup led to complaints from the union. Finally, the project manager realized the problem. The manager fired one-third of the unskilled workers and replaced them with skilled cement masons and carpenters. This decision led to legal problems involving unemployment compensation claims, and the higher-paid skilled workers caused the original payroll estimates to be wrong. The HR manager had to intervene. The stadium seats were in place by the first home game, but the contractor lost $385,000 on the job.

As this illustration shows, HR activities are connected. A poor decision about staffing requirements can lead to problems in employment, placement, legal compliance, union-management relations, and compensation. When HR activities are involved as a whole, they form an organization's human resource management system.

A *system* consists of two or more parts (or subsystems) that work together as an organized whole with identifiable boundaries.[27] Examples are numerous. A car is a system composed of subsystems (engine, transmission, radio, and the like). A human body is a system with respiratory, digestive, circulatory, and other subsystems. Cars, people, and HR departments have identifiable boundaries.

As shown in Figure 1-8, each HR activity (subsystem) relates directly to

| Figure 1-8 | The Human Resource Management Model and Subsystems |

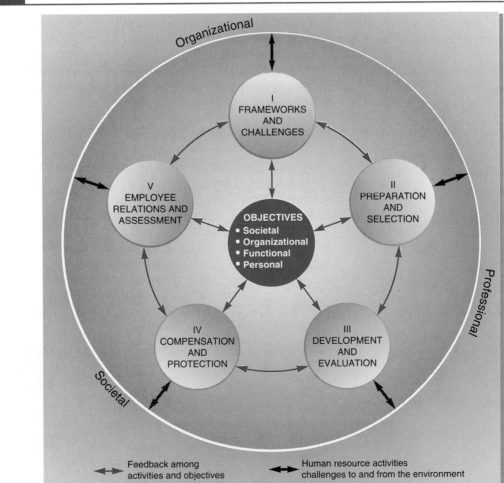

every other activity. For example, the challenges faced by the HR department affect the selection of employees. The selection subsystem influences the department's development and evaluation of employees. In addition, each subsystem is affected by the department's objectives and policies and by the external environment in which HR management takes place, as shown in Figure 1-8.

HR subsystems affect each other, and specialists must remain aware of this interdependency. Perhaps the most effective way to recognize possible complications is through systems thinking. Figure 1-9 provides a simplified visual model for applying systems thinking.[28]

Systems thinking

An applied systems view describes HR activities as taking *inputs* and *transforming* them into *outputs*. Then a manager or an HR specialist checks the results to see if they are correct. This checking process produces *feedback*, which is information that helps evaluate success or failure. In practice, systems thinking helps identify the key variables. After viewing new information as an input, managers of HR specialists decide what the desired output is. Once inputs and outputs are known, decision makers draw on their knowledge of HR activities to transform the inputs into outputs in the most effective way. To verify their success, they acquire feedback about the outcome.

Applied systems thinking

Thinking in terms of systems is useful because it enables one to recognize interrelationships among parts. If one adopts a systems view of HR management, the relationships among activities are less likely to be overlooked. Systems thinking also requires the recognition of the system's boundaries, which mark the beginning of its external environment. The environment is an important consideration because most systems are open systems. An *open system* is one that is affected by the environment. Organizations and people are open systems because they are affected by their environments. HR management is also an open system that is influenced by the external environment. For example, the stadium contractor's organization described earlier is an open system because the society, the organization, and professional HR practices affect the

Open system

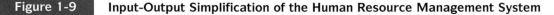

| Figure 1-9 | **Input-Output Simplification of the Human Resource Management System** |

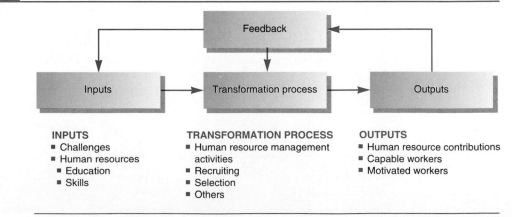

INPUTS
- Challenges
- Human resources
  - Education
  - Skills

TRANSFORMATION PROCESS
- Human resource management activities
- Recruiting
- Selection
- Others

OUTPUTS
- Human resource contributions
- Capable workers
- Motivated workers

way in which the department responds. At the same time, systems exhibit a continual interaction with their environment, even influencing the environment, as the stadium contractor's decision to hire large numbers of skilled workers undoubtedly affected the local labor market.

HR model

The role of major human resource subsystems shown in Figure 1-8 is highlighted by a brief discussion of this model that also serves as a preview of the five parts of this book and their major topics. Each part of the book is identified in the model by a Roman numeral.

I. Frameworks and Challenges

Operating managers and HR experts face many challenges in dealing with people. The central challenge is to assist the organization in improving its effectiveness and efficiency in an ethical and socially responsible way. Other challenges arise from the environment in which organizations operate; changing demands of workers, international and domestic competitors, pressure groups, professional ethics, and government are just a few. Challenges also come from within the organization. For example, managers and other departments compete with the HR department for larger budgets, for a larger share of the organization's resources. Perhaps the most pervasive forces are workforce diversity, international competition, and the legal requirement for equal employment opportunity. Success in advising other managers about these and other challenges depends on continued awareness of the challenges facing both operating managers and HR professionals.

II. Preparation and Selection

HRIS

A solid information base lies at the center of effective HR management. Without accurate and timely information, managers and HR departments are seriously limited in their ability to meet challenges. To build a *human resource information system,* data are gathered about each job and about the organization's future HR needs. Using this information, specialists can advise managers about the design of the jobs they supervise and find ways to make those jobs more productive and satisfying. Estimates of future HR needs allow managers and the department to become proactive in the recruitment and selection of new workers.

III. Development and Evaluation

Once hired, new employees are oriented to the company's policies and procedures. They are then placed in jobs and given the training needed to be productive. With a solid base of information, managers and HR specialists can help determine the needs for orientation, training, development, and career counseling of present employees. As a result of these activities, many job openings can be filled from within rather than by recruiting from outside the firm. The results should lead to a more effective workforce. To evaluate employees, formal performance appraisals are conducted periodically. Appraisals give workers feedback on their performance and can help the manager and the department spot weaknesses.

IV. Compensation and Protection

Equitable compensation is needed to retain and maintain an effective workforce. Employees must be paid a fair wage or salary relative to their productive contribution. When appropriate, incentives may be added. When compensation is too low, turnover and other problems involving employee relations are likely. If pay is too high, the company can lose its competitive position in the marketplace. But modern compensation management goes beyond pay. Benefits are an increasingly important part of every compensation package and must be at a level consonant with employee productivity if the company is to retain its workers and remain competitive. At the same time, the organization needs to protect its workers from occupational hazards. Through health and safety programs, the department not only assures a safe work environment but also keeps the employer in compliance with health and safety laws. All these concerns require specialized knowledge and are largely left to the discretion of the HR department in regard to advising line management.

V. Employee Relations and Assessment

Maintaining an effective workforce requires more than just pay, benefits, and safe working conditions. Employees need to be motivated and satisfied with their jobs. Personal and job-related problems may lead to the need for counseling or discipline. Here again, HR specialists can provide effective programs or specific advice to operating managers. To increase employee satisfaction and organizational productivity, communications are used to keep people informed. When employee relations are ineffective, the employees may join together and form self-help groups called unions. When this occurs, the HR department is usually responsible for dealing with the union. As with any ongoing system, HR departments need to uncover their successes and failures through self-evaluation. Full-service departments regularly conduct audits of their performance and do research to uncover more effective ways to serve the organization. Often this research helps uncover future challenges and predict their impact on the organization and its human resources.

▶ Proactive versus Reactive Human Resource Management

Proactive HR

Using a systems perspective is helpful but insufficient. Managers and HR departments cannot always wait for feedback and then respond. Waiting until an actual problem occurs and then reacting may be inappropriate and costly. *Reactive* human resource management occurs when decision makers respond to HR problems. *Proactive* human resource management occurs when HR problems are anticipated and corrective action begins before a problem arises.

Effective and efficient solutions are generally more likely to be found if managers and HR departments use proactive approaches. By applying systems thinking, managers can take action before serious problems arise. To institutionalize a proactive approach, for example, progressive HR departments even assign community, legislative, and other public affairs functions to members of the department as a means of monitoring the environment for proactive opportunities. This approach improves productivity by minimizing the resources needed to respond to changes in the environment or to produce the organization's goods or services. Furthermore, progressive approaches that are proactive imply superior financial performance.[29] In short, a proactive approach to the management of HR is a major step in enhancing organizational productivity.

▶ Viewpoints of Human Resource Management

HR perspectives

This chapter introduced several ways of looking at HR management that were called viewpoints. These viewpoints provide complementary themes that help managers and HR professionals keep the HR function and its activities in the proper perspective. These underlying themes will be examined throughout the book. They include:

■ *Strategic approach.* HR management must contribute to the strategic success of the organization. If the activities of managers and the HR department do not help the organization achieve its strategic objectives, resources are not being used effectively.

■ *Human resource approach.* HR management is the management of people. The importance and dignity of human beings should not be ignored for the sake of expediency. Only through careful attention to the needs of employees can organizations grow and prosper.

■ *Management approach.* HR management is the responsibility of every manager. The HR department exists to serve managers and employees through its expertise. In the final analysis, the performance and well-being of each worker are the *dual responsibility* of that worker's immediate supervisor and the HR department.

■ *Systems approach.* HR management takes place within a larger system: the organization. Therefore, HR efforts must be evaluated with respect to the contribution they make to the organization's productivity. In practice, experts must recognize that the HR management model is an open system of interrelated parts: Each part affects the others and is influenced by the external environment.

■ *Proactive approach.* HR management can increase its contribution to the employees and the organization by anticipating challenges before they arise. If its efforts are reactive only, problems may be compounded and opportunities may be missed.

Since HR management is an open system, it is affected by the environment in which it is practiced. The historical evolution of HR management and the standards of professionalism in the field help shape that environment, for example. Other challenges arise from society and even from the organization that the department serves. These historical, societal, and professional challenges set the context in which HR management is practiced. Recognition and understanding of these challenges are fundamental to the proper practice of HR management. Each of these challenges is explored more fully in Chapter 2. Chapter 3 will examine international challenges, and Chapter 4 will discuss the challenge of providing equal employment opportunity.

▶ Summary

The central challenge facing society is the continued improvement of our organizations, both private and public. The purpose of HR management is to improve the contribution made by people to organizations.

To carry out this role, managers and HR departments need to satisfy multiple and sometimes conflicting, objectives. Societal, organizational, functional, and personal objectives must be met, but only in a way that is appropriate to the organization being served. These objectives are achieved through a variety of HR activities designed to obtain, maintain, utilize, evaluate, and retain an effective workforce. These activities are the responsibility of all managers in the organization, even though many of them may be delegated to specialists in the HR department.

HR activities can be viewed as a system of interrelated actions. Each activity affects other activities directly or indirectly. Managers and HR specialists view information and human resources as the primary inputs. They transform these inputs through various activities to produce results that help the organization meet its goals and increase its productivity. Ideally, managers and HR experts undertake this role proactively.

▶ **Terms for Review**

Productivity

Purpose of human resource
    management

Delegation

Staff authority

Line (operating) authority

Functional authority

Dual responsibility for human
    resource management

System

Feedback

Open system

Reactive

Proactive

▶ **Review and Discussion Questions**

1. Since HR departments are typically seen as a cost of operations, explain how they contribute to an organization's ability to confront the increased globalization of business now taking place throughout the world.

2. Describe the purpose and primary objectives of an HR department.

3. Why is improved human productivity important to organizations?

4. Explain the relationship between societal needs and the activities of a human resource department.

5. What benefits exist when the HR department is viewed with a systems approach?

6. Why does this chapter emphasize a proactive approach to human resource management?

7. Suppose you worked for Allied-Signal's automobile parts division and the company decided to open a chain of parts stores. Briefly describe what areas of human resource management would be affected if you become the HR manager for the chain.

8. If a bank opened a branch in a distant city, what activities would the HR department need to undertake before a fully operational and staffed branch was ready for business?

▶ Incident 1-1

Hewlett-Packard's Award-Winning HR Department

As has been suggested throughout this chapter, Hewlett-Packard's HR department represents a sophisticated, modern example of the HR function in action. The department is so successful that the *Personnel Journal* awarded it its Optimas Award for general excellence. The award acknowledges that Hewlett-Packard has demonstrated excellence in human resource management and strategy in areas such as providing the company with a competitive advantage, innovation, global outlook, managing change, quality of life, service, and financial impact.

The dilemma faced by Pete Peterson when he became vice president of personnel after a twenty-four-year career in the HR field was how to maintain a high level of HR services to Hewlett-Packard's widely dispersed operations while reducing the department's overall head count. In 1990 the firm had 1800 staff members in the department. Nearly all of the company's 50 divisions and 120 sales offices had HR staff members to assist them. As a result, one concern that Peterson had beyond costs was that many operating managers were depending on the HR function and not growing in their ability to handle employee relations.

The solution Peterson pursued was to strike a new balance between decentralized and centralized HR activities. For example, twenty-six members of the HR department had varying responsibilities for managing disability claims. After the responsibility for these activities was centralized into a disability service center and operating managers were required to submit initial information about claims, managers gained greater control over the claims process. Similar consolidations occurred in connection with medical transactions and relocations.

In a similar manner, the thirteen different personnel office sites around the San Francisco Bay area were consolidated into a Bay Area Personnel Services Regional Center to serve the more than 15,000 Bay Area employees.

By centralizing some activities, the operating managers had to take on greater responsibility for HR activities. But at the same time, the department was able to reduce its budget by $35 million.[30]

1. Assume that you are a manager in an operating department of Hewlett-Packard. What concerns do you think you would have when you learned about the centralization of some HR activities?

2. Even though significant savings resulted from the centralization, what unintentional outcomes might result from this change in the HR systems at Hewlett-Packard?

▶ **References**

1. Brian O'Reilly, "The New Deal: What Companies and Employees Owe One Another," *Fortune*, June 13, 1994, p. 52.

2. Robert Crandall, Chairman, American Airlines, as quoted in Ruth Simon and Graham Button, "What I Learned in the Eighties," *Forbes*, Jan. 8, 1990, p. 103.

3. John Byrne, "The New Headhunters," *Business Week*, Feb. 6, 1990, p. 63.

4. Robert Granford Wright, "Managing Management Resources through Corporate Constitutionalism," *Human Resource Management*, Summer 1973, p. 15.

5. William E. Fulmer, "Human Resource Management: The Right Hand of Strategy Implementation," *Human Resource Planning*, vol. 13, no. 1, 1990, pp. 1–11. See also Cynthia A. Lengnick-Hall and Mark L. Lengnick-Hall, "Strategic Human Resources Management: A Review of the Literature and a Proposed Typology," *Academy of Management Review*, vol. 13, no. 3, 1988, pp. 454–470; and Randall S. Schuler, "Strategic Human Resources Management: Linking the People with the Strategic Need of the Business," *Organizational Dynamics*, Summer 1992, pp. 18–32.

6. John M. Abowd, George T. Milkovich, and John M. Hannon, "The Effects of Human Resource Management Decisions on Shareholder Value," *Industrial and Labor Relations Review*, February 1990, pp. 203S–237S.

7. Thomas A. Stewart, "Allied-Signal's Turnaround Blitz," *Fortune*, Nov. 30, 1992, pp. 72–76.

8. Ibid., p. 75.

9. William B. Werther, Jr., William A. Ruch, and Lynne McClure, *Productivity through People*, St. Paul, Minn.: West, 1986, pp. 3–5. See also Thomas A. Stewart, "U.S. Productivity: First but Fading," *Fortune*, Oct. 19, 1992, pp. 54–57.

10. Paul Michael Swiercz and Barbara A. Spencer, "HRM and Sustainable Competitive Advantage: Lessons from Delta Air Lines," *Human Resource Planning*, vol. 15, no. 2, 1992, pp. 35–46. See also George W. Bohlander and Angelo J. Kinicki, "Where Personnel and Productivity Meet," *Personnel Administrator*, September 1988, pp. 122–130.

11. Adapted from Jennifer J. Laabs, "Hewlett-Packard's Core Values Drive HR Strategy," *Personnel Journal*, December 1993, p. 38.

12. Ibid., p. 40.

13. Ibid.

14. Ibid.

15. Laura M. Herren, "The New Game of HR: Playing to Win," *Personnel*, June 1989, pp. 19–22.

16. John Hoerr, "Human Resources Managers Aren't Corporate Nobodies Anymore," *Business Week*, Dec. 2, 1985, p. 58.

17. Barbara Whitaker Shimko, "All Managers Are HR Managers," *HRMagazine,* January 1990, pp. 67–70.

18. Laabs, op. cit., p. 38.

19. Ibid.

20. "ASPA-BNA Survey No. 53: Personnel Activities, Budgets, and Staffs: 1988–1989," Washington, D.C.: Bureau of National Affairs, June 22, 1989, p. 1.

21. "Personnel People," *The New York Times,* May 11, 1986, sec. 3, p. 1.

22. Dennis J. Kravetz, *The Human Resource Revolution: Implementing Progressive Practices for Bottom-Line Success,* San Francisco: Jossey-Bass, 1988.

23. Dave Stier, "More Use of Human Resource Titles," *Resource,* October 1989, p. 2.

24. Laabs, op. cit., p. 38.

25. Stier, op. cit.

26. Laabs, op. cit., p. 38.

27. Robert Wright, *Systems Thinking: A Guide to Managing in a Changing Environment,* Dearborn, Mich.: Society of Manufacturing Engineers, 1989. For an additional discussion of systems theory, see also Daniel L. Katz and Robert L. Kahn, *The Social Psychology of Organizations,* New York: Wiley, 1966, pp. 14–29.

28. Wright, op. cit.

29. Ilan Meshoulam and Lloyd Baird, "Proactive Human Resource Management," *Human Resource Management,* Winter 1987, pp. 483–502.

30. Laabs, op. cit.

2

We don't believe any company can get along without a well-articulated point of view about tomorrow's opportunities and challenges.
GARY HAMEL and C. K. PRAHALAD[1]

Environmental Challenges

CHAPTER OBJECTIVES

After studying this chapter, you should be able to:

1. **DISCUSS** the evolution of human resource departments.

2. **DEFINE** the external challenges that are reshaping the quality of today's workforce.

3. **EXPLAIN** the manager's and the HR department's role in addressing cultural diversity.

4. **IDENTIFY** the internal organizational challenges to human resource management.

5. **DESCRIBE** how the professionalism of the field of human resource management affects practitioners.

6. **EXPLAIN** the relationship between organizational strategy and human resource policies and practices.

As was discussed in Chapter 1, organizations and their HR departments are open systems and are affected by the environment in which they operate. For managers and HR departments to respond proactively, they must have an awareness of the external, organizational, and professional environments in which they operate. An example of how one company is responding to the challenges in its environment comes from Continental Corp., a $5 billion New York–based insurer with more than 12,000 employees.

Continental Corp.

In the early 1990s Continental undertook a self-study to learn how flexible management was in dealing with employees. Employees reported that the company was fairly rigid, limiting their ability to respond to work and family conflicts. In the words of the CEO, Jake Mascotte, "So much of business is still structured like fourth grade."[2] Mascotte believes that companies that fail to balance business and family issues "may be jeopardizing their future," according to a *Business Week* interview.[3]

Since work and family conflicts distracted employees from their jobs, the company initiated a series of family-oriented programs. Continental eliminated the use of "occurrences," the practice of recording every employee absence and using that record to shape employee evaluations. Another change now permits alternative schedules, providing employees with greater flexibility in balancing their work and family responsibilities.

The results for the company have been a 15 percent jump in productivity and a 50 percent reduction in voluntary employee turnover to under 5 percent a year.[4]

Given the growing diversity among Continental's employees and their diverse expectations about work and family issues, Continental responded proactively to its environment. The company was aware that changes in the external environment meant that it had to adapt its business and HR strategies to a new reality. In doing so, the company and its HR department were meeting, at least partially, the strategic, organizational, departmental, societal, and individual objectives discussed in Chapter 1.

Managers and HR professionals at Continental or at any other company cannot meet the objectives in Figure 2-1 without understanding and being aware of environmental challenges. Two of the most pervasive environmental challenges faced by managers and HR departments are international human resource management and government.

International HR

International human resource management and the strategic viewpoints of many companies are being shaped by competitive pressure from foreign competitors. More and more, executives at major corporations—Procter & Gamble, Ford, Coca-Cola, and others—are expected to have international experience as part of their background.[5] For managers and HR professionals to operate in a global environment, they must be aware of international challenges so that they can make a meaningful contribution to the overall success of the organiza-

**A Model of the Human Resource Management System
and Its Major Environmental Challenges**

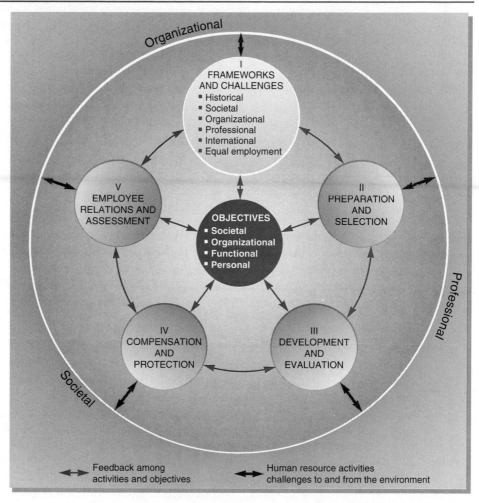

tion's strategies. For example, managers in Europe and Japan lack the flexibility that North American managers have in reducing the workforce through layoffs and discharges.[6] Legal and cultural patterns in those countries restrict the use of mass layoffs. Dealing with the unique challenges posed by global operations has become so important that all of Chapter 3 is devoted to international HR management.

Another pervasive challenge is government. Through laws and regulations, it has such a major impact that Chapter 4 is devoted to just one aspect: equal employment opportunity laws and regulations. Other government challenges

Government
challenge

affect compensation, safety and health, and labor relations. These challenges are discussed in subsequent chapters.

This chapter focuses on the nongovernmental challenges that form the environment in which HR management takes place. These challenges are added to the model of HR management shown in Figure 2-1, which was first presented in Chapter 1. To explain how present-day HR management practices began, the chapter examines the historical foundations of HR management. Then it looks at the challenges that arise from the external, organizational, and professional environments. Throughout the book, these challenges will be reexamined to see how they affect specific HR management activities.

▶ Historical Foundations

The efforts of managers and early HR pioneers led to today's more sophisticated and proactive methods.[7] When this evolution is traced, what emerges is the importance of the field of HR management and how it has been influenced by a changing environment.

Early Causes and Origins

The precise origins of HR management are unknown. Probably the first cave dwellers struggled with the problem of utilizing human resources. Even the Bible records the selection and training problems faced by Moses.[8]

Few large organizations existed during the thousands of years between Moses and the industrial revolution. Except for religious orders (the Roman Catholic Church, for example) and governments (particularly the military), most work was done in small groups. Whether on the farm, in a small shop, or in the home, the primary work unit was the family. There was little need for a formal study of HR management. However, the industrial revolution changed the nature of work. Big coal mines, textile mills, and foundries sprang up in England and later in North America. Expensive facilities, steam engines, and other innovations required large numbers of people to work together to attain economies of scale. Collectively, people were still an important resource, but the industrial revolution meant greater mechanization and unpleasant working conditions for many workers.

HR problems emerged. In the late 1800s some employers reacted to the human problems caused by industrialization by creating the post of welfare secretary. Welfare secretaries existed primarily to meet workers' needs and discourage them from forming unions, sometimes by spying on union sympathizers. Social secretaries, as they were sometimes called, relieved managers from dealing with employees who had personal problems such as education, housing, and medical needs. These early forerunners of HR specialists also sought to improve conditions for workers. The emergence of welfare secretaries before

Small groups

Welfare secretaries

1900 demonstrates that HR activities in large organizations had already become too extensive for operating managers to handle. Thus, social secretaries marked the birth of specialized human resource management, as distinct from the day-to-day supervision of people by operating managers.

Scientific Management and Human Needs

At about the same time welfare and social secretaries began appearing in large organizations, Frederick Taylor and others began advocating the benefits of scientific management. The scientific management movement showed the world that the systematic, scientific study of work could lead to improved efficiency. Arguments for specialization and improved training furthered the need for HR departments.

Primitive HR

At companies such as AT&T primitive personnel departments began to emerge during the first decades of this century and replaced welfare secretaries. These new departments contributed to organizational effectiveness by maintaining wages at proper levels, screening job applicants, and handling grievances. They also assumed the welfare secretary's role of improving working conditions, dealing with unions, and meeting other employee needs.

These early departments were seldom headed by senior executives and were not important parts of the organizations they served. They were record depositories with advisory authority only. At that time, production, finance, and marketing problems overshadowed the role of HR management. The importance of HR departments grew slowly as their contributions and responsibilities increased. During World War I selection tests were developed to match recruits with their roles in the U.S. Army. This led to the industrial use of tests, which continues today and is usually a responsibility of the HR department.

From the end of World War I until the Great Depression in the 1930s, personnel departments—as HR departments were called during that period—played a growing role in handling compensation, testing, unions, and employee needs. The importance of individual needs became even more pronounced as a result of the research studies conducted at Western Electric's Hawthorne plant during this period.[9] These studies showed that the efficiency goals of scientific management had to be balanced against human needs. These elementary observations eventually had a profound impact on the management of people, but the Depression and World War II diverted attention to more urgent matters of organizational and national survival.

Hawthorne experiments

Modern Influences

Citizens lost faith in the ability of business to meet society's needs during the 1930s, and so they turned to government. Government intervened to give workers unemployment compensation, social security, a minimum wage, and the federally protected right to join a union. The government's emphasis was on improving employees' security and working conditions. This outpouring of legislation during the 1930s helped shape the modern role of HR departments by adding legal obligations. Organizations were now pressured by the force of law to consider societal objectives, and this elevated the importance of personnel departments. In practice, these departments were made responsible for discouraging unionization among employees, but with newfound legal protections, unions grew dramatically. These organizing successes startled many leaders into rethinking their use of *paternalism,* the "management-knows-best" approach to emloyee welfare. As a result, personnel departments began replacing paternalism with more proactive approaches that took employee desires into account. When workers did organize, the responsibility for dealing with unions also fell to the personnel department, which was sometimes renamed the industrial relations department to reflect these new duties.[10]

Paternalism

During the 1940s and 1950s personnel departments continued to increase in importance. The recruiting and training demands of World War II added to the credibility of personnel departments that successfully met those challenges. After the war, these departments grew in importance as they contended with powerful unions and an expanding need for knowledge workers such as engineers and accountants. The explosive growth of employee benefits also contributed to the personnel department's importance. At the same time, the widespread understanding of the Hawthorne studies and newer behavioral findings led to concern for improved human relations. These findings helped underscore the importance of sound management practices.

In the 1960s and 1970s the central force shaping human resource management was again legislation, resulting in an HR function that was highly regulated. Laws were passed to eliminate differences in pay between men and women. Laws to end discrimination in employment because of sex, race, religion, national origin, and age were also enacted. Laws addressing safety and health, veterans' status, disabilities, pension laws, and pregnancy were added in the 1970s. These acts gave HR departments a still larger voice—a voice that began to equal those of production, finance, and marketing executives in major corporations.

Legal forces

Figure 2-2 summarizes the key historical developments in the field of personnel management and human resources. As is evident from the figure, many of the historical factors that affected HR management resulted from external changes. Although historical events have shaped the role of HR departments, current challenges from the external, organizational, and professional environments mean that more changes are likely.

▶ External Challenges

Modern organizations exist in a turbulent environment filled with challenges over which an organization and its HR department have little influence. These challenges shape the way the organization operates and thus affect HR policies and practices. For example, after scientists at Western Electric developed the transistor, the management at Motorola opened a research facility in Phoenix, Arizona, to study this new technology. Their successes led Motorola's management to formulate a corporate strategy centered on high technology. From this strategy and its modest research facility, Motorola's operations in Arizona have grown to tens of thousands of employees who have had to be recruited, selected, oriented, trained, compensated, and maintained. As this example illustrates, changes in the external environment, such as a new technology, affect corporate strategy and planning. Less obviously, changing technologies affect the type of workers, their educational preparation, and their performance. Managers and HR departments then respond to these changes and help the organization meet its objectives.

Motorola

Changes in the organization's environment evolve at varying rates. The composition of the workforce changes over many years, for example, while new laws and court rulings seemingly occur overnight. Managers and HR professionals deal with these changes by taking the steps shown in Figure 2-3, constantly searching the environment for changes and evaluating their impact on the organization and the HR function. When noteworthy changes are uncovered through reading, continuing education, or studying company strategy, proactive plans are developed and implemented, as suggested by Continental's effort to create a more flexible work environment for its employees.[11] Common sources of external challenge to the HR department include workforce diversity, technology, economics, and government, which are discussed in the following sections.

Workforce Diversity

The most diverse workforce in the world can be found in North America. Its composition includes people born in North America—almost always of immigrant ancestry—mixed with newcomers from around the globe. Within this diversity of national origins there is an even wider diversity of cultures, religions, languages and dialects, educational attainment, skills, values, ages, races, genders, and other differentiating variables. Knowledge of these variations challenges managers and HR professionals to develop proactive policies and practices.[12] For example, in a study of 1705 respondents, it was found that workforce diversity lowered the psychological attachment of group members to the organization,[13] calling for more proactive efforts by HR departments in the face of increased diversity. Nevertheless, as the president of the Boeing Company observed, "It is only by finding ways to harness the diverse skills of all its employees in the pursuit of mutual goals that a company can achieve its full competitive potential."[14] As suggested by the progressive attitude at Boeing and other employers, managing diversity goes beyond acceptance or toleration. Proactive managers and HR departments value individual diversity because it brings a rich source of innovative perspectives to the company.

Sources of diversity

Research summary

Knowledge about diversity comes from personal observations and from *demography*, the statistical study of population characteristics. Workforce demographics describe its composition: education level, race, age, sex, percentage of

Demographics

gious, or ethnic differences may not permit the same degree of workforce diversity in overseas operations. For example, in most developing countries, Moslem nations, and even advanced economies like Japan, diversity may be resisted through severe limitations placed on women, nonbelievers, or members of specific castes or tribes.[31] Likewise, when transferring foreign nationals to North American assignments, HR professionals must be sensitive to the potential cultural shock inherent in the diverse workforce of the United States and Canada. Many men from the Middle East and the orient, for example, have never been supervised by a woman. Consider the situation Karla Leavelle faces:

7-Eleven

Karla Leavelle is a regional HR manager for the Southland Corp., the parent company of 7-Eleven convenience stores. She handles 811 stores and more than 6700 employees representing 70 different countries of origin.

"Karla Leavelle can tell you a lot about managing foreign-born workers. During the Iran-Iraq War, she had to separate employees from Iran and Iraq who had been working side by side. She had to convince immigrants from Ethiopia and Somalia to throw away food that was one hour too old and didn't meet U.S. health codes."[32]

Technological Challenges

Jobs and job skills are changed by technology. Perhaps the greatest potential impact on jobs since the industrial revolution is artificial intelligence. The industrial revolution allowed people to make greater use of mechanical power—from water wheels and steam engines to nuclear power—to amplify human productivity. Artificial intelligence will give a growing number of workers access to expert systems—computerized programs that capture the knowledge and decision-making approaches of experts. In fact, one estimate suggests, "As many as 90% of all jobs in American organizations will be candidates for augmentation, replacement or displacement by expert systems and other forms of artificial intelligence between the year 2000 and 2005."[33] As the capabilities of artificial intelligence give people and machines greater problem-solving powers, jobs and the skills they require will change dramatically, affecting the employment, training, development, compensation, and employee relations activities of the HR department.[34]

Artificial
intelligence

One of the biggest impacts of technology on human resource management comes from the way in which technology alters industries and lifestyles.

The technology of cars and airplanes modified the transportation industry. Automobile and aviation companies grew, creating a demand for more employees and training. For those already employed by these firms, growth provided promotional opportunities. Railroad companies were affected by the same technology, except that the HR management challenges differed. Revenue lost to cars, trucks, and airplanes limited growth. Advancement opportunities—even employment opportunities—shrank. HR departments in these companies had to reduce the workforce and create early retirement systems.

Automation is another way in which technology affects the field of HR management.

The introduction of computers into banks changed employment needs. Before computers, HR specialists recruited large numbers of unskilled and semiskilled clerks. Computers, however, required highly skilled programmers and systems analysts. Semiskilled employees who could process information into computer-usable form were also needed. Bank systems that could be observed by outsiders changed very little, but the HR departments of banks had dramatically changed their recruiting and training programs.

Robots

One specific form of automation that is likely to have a significant impact on organizations is robotics. As robots become more common and sophisticated, they will affect organizational productivity and the quality of work life for employees. Their increased use seems a certainty since their costs relative to labor costs are declining. The good news is that hazardous and boring jobs will be taken over by robots. Dangerous jobs—such as working with toxic chemicals and paints—will be changed by substituting robots for people. Similarly, highly repetitive assembly tasks increasingly will be taken over by robots during the late 1990s. Productivity and quality are likely to improve, but at what cost?

These changing technologies also will shape the educational preparation of future workers and thus their productivity. For example, recruits who went to poorer school systems may lack the computer literacy of students from wealthier school districts. And as the use of computerization spreads to companies that are increasingly relying on human resource information systems, knowledge of computer technologies will grow increasingly crucial to HR departments.

Worker alienation

The bad news is that HR professionals may have to contend with increased worker alienation since job opportunities may shrink along with opportunities for socialization on the job. High-paying factory work for unskilled and semiskilled employees may become scarce, leading factory workers to accept lower-paid unskilled jobs in the service sector. To use expensive robots effectively, more and more factories may find it necessary to work two or three shifts a day, even on weekends. Perhaps even more important is the trend toward making robots lighter, faster, stronger, and more "intelligent." Artificial intelligence and lower costs will mean more applications for these marvels in service industries, causing even more widespread dislocations.

Economic Challenges

Global competition puts pressure on all the firms in an industry to be more productive. Robots and other technological advances boost productivity, but robots are designed, installed, programmed, and maintained by people. Whether economic challenges become more intense because of robots, artificial intelligence, or foreign competition, HR professionals will need to find more innovative ways to help line managers increase productivity through people.[35]

Business cycles

Over the course of a business cycle, for example, managers and HR departments must adjust to changes in their organizations' business plans. When the economy expands, new employees and training programs are needed. Voluntary departures by employees increase. Pressures for higher wages, better benefits, and improved working conditions also grow. Managers and HR departments must act cautiously, however. Overstaffing, bloated benefit programs, and higher wages become serious burdens when the business cycle turns downward. A recession creates a need to maintain a competent workforce and reduce labor costs. Decisions to reduce hours, lay off workers, or accept lower profit margins involve the advice of HR experts. The more effectively HR departments monitor the economy, the better they can anticipate an organization's changing needs. Sometimes these departments can develop proactive policies that anticipate changes in the business cycle. Motorola provides an example.

Contract labor

Motorola

Motorola uses contract labor to satisfy its human resource needs during periods of peak business activity. *Contract labor* consists of people who are hired and often trained by an independent agency that supplies companies such as Motorola with needed staff for a fee. When Motorola finds that it needs assemblers of electronic components to finish a project, it recruits, hires, and trains most of those people through its own department. But some of the workers it uses are contracted from a temporary help agency that can provide extra staff quickly. These agency workers do not become Motorola employees but work for the agency and are assigned to Motorola to meet the temporary need for more workers. When the project is completed or when the business cycle declines, Motorola informs the agency that it needs fewer of these temporary contract workers. Thus the department can meet the staffing needs of its divisions while providing high levels of employment security to Motorola's employees. Of course, Motorola has less control over the quality of the contract workers, whose loyalty and dedication to the company's objectives may be lower than that of career Motorolans.

This policy of tapping into the *contingency workforce*[36] by using contract labor is another example of how proactive managers and HR departments meet organizational and human needs while remaining sensitive to the firm's economic environment. In Motorola's case, the managers and HR department did not wait for the economy to go up or down before reacting. Instead, these practitioners developed policies that allow their organizations to adjust smoothly to changes caused by technological, economic, and other challenges.

Government Challenges

Federal regulations

Through the enforcement of laws, government has a direct and immediate impact on managers and the HR function. Federal laws regulating the employee-employer relationship challenge the methods HR departments use. Some laws, such as the Occupational Safety and Health Act and the Civil Rights Act, make major demands on HR management. The impact of these laws has helped elevate the importance of HR decisions, as was discussed earlier in this chapter.

Government involvement in the employment relationship is meant to achieve societal objectives—usually the elimination of practices that are considered contrary to public policy. For managers and HR specialists, government involvement requires compliance and proactive efforts to minimize the organizational consequences. Throughout this book, laws related to employment discrimination, compensation, unions, and other issues illustrate the challenges and actions faced by HR departments.

▶ Organizational Challenges

Besides external demands, managers and HR departments find current challenges within the organizations they serve. Internal challenges arise because employers pursue trade-offs among financial, sales, service, production, employee, and other goals. Since HR objectives are just one set among many in the eyes of top management, managers and HR professionals must confront internal challenges while maintaining a balanced concern for other needs. The employer does not exist solely, or even largely, to meet HR objectives. Instead, HR activities exist to assist the organization in achieving its other objectives. Managers and HR departments are faced with several internal challenges from unions, informational needs, organizational character, and conflicts.

Organizational character

Unions

In the HR environment, unions represent an *actual* challenge to unionized companies and a *potential* challenge to companies that are not unionized. In companies with unions, the employer and the union sign a labor agreement that specifies compensation (wages and benefits), hours, and working conditions. This agreement limits the HR activities of supervisors and HR departments. For both, the challenge is to achieve company objectives without violating the agreement.

Two-tier wages

A more recent challenge involves labor costs and competitiveness, especially when unionized firms compete against nonunion ones. Higher union wage rates have caused some employees to negotiate a *two-tiered wage structure* to avoid outright wage cuts and other "givebacks." Current members get the old rate (and maybe a slight raise), but new workers start out at a much lower wage rate. This practice can result in two workers doing the same work at markedly different rates of pay. Besides the challenges of future contract bargaining—discussed more fully in Chapter 18—challenges of motivation, morale, and employee turnover result from two-tiered wage rates.

Spillover effect

Employers *without* unions are affected too. To retain the flexibility of nonunion status, HR departments implement compensation policies, hours of work, and working conditions similar to those found in unionized operations, resulting in what is known as a *spillover effect.* Here the HR challenge is usually determined by top management: try to operate so that unionization is discouraged. For example, major firms in the electronics industry, such as Motorola and Texas Instruments, are mostly nonunion.

Information Systems

Managers and HR departments require large amounts of detailed information. Increasingly, the quality of HR decisions depends on the quality of information. Many HR activities and much effort by HR professionals are devoted to obtaining and refining the department's information base. The information requirements of a full-service department are only hinted at by questions such as:

Information needs

- What are the duties and responsibilities of *every* job in the organization?
- What are the skills possessed by *every* employee?
- What are the organization's future HR needs?
- How do external constraints affect the organization?
- What are the current trends in compensation of employees?

This list could be continued for pages.

Clearly, the acquisition, storage, and retrieval of information present a significant challenge. A key part of the challenge is gaining cooperation from others in the organization who provide the department with much of its information. Responses to HR department questionnaires, supervisors' absentee control reports, and most other sources of HR information come from people outside the department. Line managers may see the department's request for information as far less important than producing and selling the firm's goods and services. To ensure a timely flow of accurate information, HR specialists must not only communicate the importance of their requests but maintain good working relationships with other managers to earn their cooperation.

To store and retrieve information, HR departments increasingly rely on computer-based information systems that store detailed information about employees, jobs, laws, unions, economic trends, and other internal and external factors. But massive information systems challenge the department's ability to safeguard the privacy of employee records. As a manager at a consulting firm specializing in computer security observed:

Employee privacy

> Computer security is more important in the human resource management field than in any other area where computers might be used.
>
> There is an ethical responsibility to protect the individual. But more importantly and certainly more of a problem is the legal aspect of privacy.
>
> I don't know of any state that doesn't have some sort of privacy legislation on the books regarding the confidentiality of . . . personnel records in general. HRM administrators can be held criminally liable if they do not take adequate measures to protect that data.[37]

Organizational Culture and Conflicts

Every employer is unique. Similarities between organizations can be found among their parts, but each organization as a whole has a unique culture.[38] *Organizational culture* is the product of all the organization's features: its people, its successes, and its failures. Organizational culture reflects the past and shapes the future.

Organizational culture

The challenge for managers and HR specialists is to adjust proactively to the culture of the organization. For example, objectives can be achieved in several acceptable ways. This idea, which is called *equifinality,* means that there are usually multiple paths to objectives. The key to success is picking the path that best fits the organization's culture.

 As an HR manager, Aaron Chu feared that his request to hire a training assistant would be turned down. Instead of asking for funds to hire someone, Aaron expressed concern that poor supervisory skills were contributing to employee complaints and resignations. He observed at the weekly management meeting that unskilled replacements could lead to rising labor costs.

Knowing that top management was concerned about remaining a low-cost producer, Aaron was not surprised when the plant manager suggested hiring "someone to do training around here." Aaron got a budget increase for training by adjusting to the organization's culture.

In nearly every organization a few core values or beliefs shape the culture. Sometimes service is highly valued, as at IBM. At other times product innovation is seen as the key to the firm's success, as at the 3M Company. At Emerson Electric and Aaron's firm, it is labor costs. Top management evidently believes that success depends on low labor costs and is willing to support actions that will keep labor costs low. Effective practitioners identify the values or beliefs in their organizations and strive to further those values.

Depending on the culture of the organization and the attitudes of its people, HR challenges may arise from conflicts among groups. Smoking at work is an example. Should smokers' addiction be treated as a disability and accommodated, or should the rights of nonsmokers be paramount? What obligations, if any, does an employer have to address employees' fears of dealing with AIDS-infected coworkers? How do managers and HR departments help reduce the conflict between the stockholders' right to maximize their financial return and the employees' desire for job security, especially during a merger or acquisition? How do employment departments meet the legal requirement to deny employment to undocumented foreign aliens without discriminating against minority citizens under the 1986 *Immigration Reform and Control Act*? These are not hypothetical conflicts; they occur daily in organizations. Managers and HR departments are usually responsible for developing and enforcing policies in these areas.

Smokers and HR

▶ Professional Challenges

Professionalism is another challenge to HR management. HR management skills are too important to organizations and society to be ignored. External and internal challenges require practitioners who are at least minimally qualified. Since the actual capabilities of experts vary widely, the professionalism of the HR management field became a matter of growing interest. The *Society for Human Resource Management* (formerly the American Society for Personnel Administration) took an important step toward building the profession of HR management: certification.

Certification

The society studied the question of certification for a decade. By late 1975 it had established standards and credentials for certification. Experienced practitioners and academics were admitted under a "grandfather" clause that granted them certification on the basis of letters of recommendation and experience. This provision ended after the first year, and credentials are now earned by testing, which ensures a minimum level of competence among those who receive a professional designation from the Society for Human Resource Management (SHRM).

SHRM and professionalism

SHRM created two professional designations, as shown in Figure 2-4. The Professional in Human Resources (PHR) applies to generalists, and the designation Senior Professional in Human Resources (SPHR) applies to generalists

Figure 2-4	**Professional Designations Granted by the Society for Human Resource Management**

SHRM CERTIFICATION

The Human Resource Certification Institute grants certification after an application has:

1. verified current full-time professional exempt experience in the HR field as either a practitioner, educator, researcher or consultant, and . . .

2. passed a comprehensive written examination to demonstrate mastery of the HR Body of Knowledge.

The basic generalist designation

PROFESSIONAL IN HUMAN RESOURCES (PHR)

Four years of professional HR exempt experience

Two years professional HR exempt experience and a bachelor's degree	**OR**	One year professional HR exempt experience and a graduate degree

AND

Pass a comprehensive examination

The senior generalist designation

SENIOR PROFESSIONAL IN HUMAN RESOURCES (SPHR)

Eight years of professional HR exempt experience

Six years professional HR exempt experience and a bachelor's degree	**OR**	Five years professional HR exempt experience and a graduate degree

AND

Pass a comprehensive examination

Source: Human Resource Certification Institute (an affiliate of the Society for Human Resource Management).

---

with more experience. Both designations require that applicants complete a comprehensive test on the following topics:

- Compensation and benefits
- Employee and labor relations
- Selection and placement
- Training and development
- Health, safety, and security
- Management practices

The test for those seeking the SPHR designation is weighted to favor the "Management Practices" section. Testing and certification are handled by an affiliate of SHRM called the Human Resource Certification Institute (HRCI). HRCI also handles recertification, which must take place every three years.

Other Professional Requirements

HR as a profession

Certification does not make HR management a profession. Some argue that the field will never become a profession because there is no common body of knowledge. HR management is not a clearly separate discipline like law, medicine, or economics; it draws on a variety of disciplines. Furthermore, individual practitioners have little control over their activities, and this limits their professionalism. Unlike self-employed physicians or attorneys who are independent decision makers or teachers who have traditionally guaranteed rights under tenure rules, HR experts are dependent on the direction of top management and have few rights. And unlike professions that have legally sanctioned procedures to establish minimum competency, there are no legal certification or licensing requirements in the HR field. Even SHRM's certification program is voluntary. As a result, no standard codes of conduct or ethics are widely recognized. Although Figure 2-5 reproduces SHRM's code, neither practitioners nor the public uniformly supports it. Thus there is little reason for the public to recognize the field as a profession.

While debate will continue over whether HR management is or will become a profession, the field is *becoming* more professional through the leadership of SHRM, more highly educated practitioners, and more advanced university education in HR management. The result is a challenge to every practitioner that goes beyond organizational boundaries: Can the field of HR management become a profession?

▶ Human Resource Management in Perspective

Even though HR management confronts a variety of historical, external, internal, and professional challenges, it exists to further the organization's strategy with maximum effectiveness and efficiency in an ethically and socially responsible way. Research shows, however, that executives and lower-level managers have different expectations about HR activities. Figure 2-6 illustrates the ten most important HR activities as viewed by executives. Note how these perceptions differ from those of lower-level managers. For example, executives and managers rank selection differently. To be effective, HR specialists must determine the areas of concern among the different groups they support.[39] Otherwise, their advisory authority will be less effective and more likely to be ignored.

| Figure 2-5 | Code of Ethics of SHRM |

SOCIETY FOR

HUMAN

RESOURCE

MANAGEMENT

Code of Ethics

As a member of the Society for Human Resource Management, I pledge myself to:

■ Maintain the highest standards of professional and personal conduct.

■ Strive for personal growth in the field of human resource management.

■ Support the Society's goals and objectives for developing the human resource management profession.

■ Encourage my employer to make the fair and equitable treatment of all employees a primary concern.

■ Strive to make my employer profitable both in monetary terms and through the support and encouragement of effective employment practices.

■ Instill in the employees and the public a sense of confidence about the conduct and intentions of my employer.

■ Maintain loyalty to my employer and pursue its objectives in ways that are consistent with the public interest.

■ Uphold all laws and regulations relating to my employer's activities.

■ Refrain from using my official positions, either regular or volunteer, to secure special privilege, gain or benefit for myself.

■ Maintain the confidentiality of privileged information.

■ Improve public understanding of the role of human resource management.

This Code of Ethics for members of the Society for Human Resource Management has been adopted to promote and maintain the highest standards of personal conduct and professional standards among its members. Adherence to this code is required for membership in the Society and serves to assure public confidence in the integrity and service of human resource management professionals.

Source: Reprinted by permission of the Society for Human Resource Management, Alexandria, Virginia.

Figure 2-6	A Comparison of Human Resource Functions as Their Importance Is Perceived by Personnel Directors, Executives, and Managers

| | RANKING BY: | | |
	PERSONNEL DIRECTORS	EXECUTIVES	MANAGERS
Affirmative action/EEO	2	1	1
Recruiting	3	2	2
Wage/salary/administration	1	3	3
Employment selection	27	4	16
Human resource planning	12	5	7
Training/development	23	6	13
Performance appraisal	29	7	12
Orientation	32	8	8
Insurance benefits	5	9	6
Discharges	14	10	14

Source: Adapted from Harold C. White, APD, and Michael N. Wolfe, "The Role Desired for Personnel Administration," *Personnel Administrator,* June 1980, pp. 90–91.

HR as an internal consultant

When policies and practices hinder an organization's success, they must be subordinated to the needs of the organization. As international competitiveness increases, operating managers will rely more heavily on their "people skills" and HR professionals as managers will be forced to deal with downsizing and other changes to their organizations.[40] The success of managers— whether in staff positions or in operating positions—means that the HR department will face even more demands and challenges.

If these challenges are not met, HR management does not achieve its purpose. Perhaps the most rigorous challenges come from the need to understand the international dimension and provide equal employment opportunity. A detailed examination of these challenges in Chapters 3 and 4 reveals how critical the HR function can be to organizations. Other challenges are reviewed in more depth throughout the book.

▶ Summary

The environment in which HR management takes place helps shape the demands on managers and HR professionals. These challenges arise from the historical, external, organizational, and professional demands confronting managers and HR specialists.

The historical challenges began with the industrial revolution, which led to the scientific study of work and workers. As the tools available to managers became more sophisticated, the need for specialists in HR management grew. Early in this century personnel departments emerged to meet these increased demands. Today managers and HR professionals are responsible for dealing with the external, organizational, and professional issues that affect employees.

The external challenges come from several sources: changing technologies, economic cycles, workforce diversity, and government involvement. Each of these factors influences the ways in which managers and HR departments meet their objectives.

Organizational challenges include the elements within the organization that HR management cannot ignore. Unions are an obvious example. They demand that management achieve its economic objectives within the constraints imposed by labor organizations. Even nonunion companies must be aware of actions that can cause workers to unionize. A professionally managed HR department must develop and maintain a sophisticated database to be effective. The need for information and the best way to implement HR activities are also dependent on unique aspects of the organization's culture.

The newest challenge to HR management is professionalism. The important role that HR departments and their members play in modern organizations requires a professional approach and professionally trained people. The growing importance of this function requires practitioners to strive for the high standards that are expected of professionals. The certification program of the Society for Human Resource Management represents a major step in that direction.

If managers and HR departments can successfully meet the environmental challenges discussed in this chapter, they are more likely to contribute effectively to the goals of the organization and its people.

▶ Terms for Review

Paternalism	Spillover effect
Demography	Organizational culture
Guest workers	Equifinality
Participation rates	Society for Human Resource Management
Contract labor	
Contingency workforce	Certification
Two-tiered wage structure	

▶ Review and Discussion Questions

1. Explain how the growing diversity in Continental's workforce contributed to the need for greater flexibility in the company's work rules.

2. As the numbers of workers employed at large firms grew in the 1800s, how did employers respond to employees' needs?

3. Assuming that the trend toward robotics and artificial intelligence continues into the next century, how might managers and HR departments be affected?

4. Why should managers and HR specialists monitor demographic trends?

5. Assuming that the North American workforce continues to become more diversified, how will managers and HR departments be affected?

6. How could the increased professionalization of the HR field benefit HR practitioners and their employers?

7. What is the purpose of a code of ethics such as the one developed by SHRM? Can you suggest any additions to SHRM's code?

8. How do economic cycles affect the HR function? Give an example of an HR policy that takes variations in the economy into account.

▶ Incident 2-1

Technology and HR Management

Electronic technology has reached the point where it is technologically (although not necessarily economically) feasible to provide workers with:

- A computer console and access via Internet to on-line databases via hard (phone) lines or satellite uplinks.

- A television set with hundreds of channels fed by a cable system that allows interactivity via the cable while serving as a visual display for computer outputs and inputs and can double as a two-way video phone.

- A machine connected to the television that permits photocopies of screen information and doubles as a fax machine.

Though the need for special wiring and expensive equipment make such a home setup prohibitively expensive for most white-collar workers, the costs of this hardware and its interconnectivity are likely to decline steadily during the coming years, making such an "at-home" office economically feasible. At about the time this all becomes a reality, serious people will ask, Why do we still follow the primitive ritual of going to work? Why don't we do our jobs at home, since most workers are now white-collar information handlers? Shortly afterward, the practice of going to work, which began with the industrial revolution, will end for many workers. People will still work. Some people will even have to "go to work," especially those who provide services to others in retail establishments. But many clerical, technical, and professional workers will be able to stay at home, plugged into a worldwide information grid.[41]

Assuming that this scenario comes true during your career:

1. What implications does it hold for our culture and society?

2. What are the implications of these changes for operating managers?

▶ **Incident 2-2**

Government Intervention

Since the 1930s the federal government has increased its regulation of the way employers treat employees. Laws have been passed that permit workers to join unions, require employers to pay a minimum wage, ensure a safe and healthy work environment, prohibit discrimination, and restrict the freedom of employers to make HR decisions in other areas.

Some futurists believe that the trend toward increasing government intervention will continue. To support their argument, these thinkers point to efforts to require employer-paid health insurance and to Japan and Europe, where government involvement is far more extensive than it is in the United States and Canada. These people believe that the federal government will require employers to provide even greater job security and improved treatment that will further limit HR decisions.

Other experts think that the trend toward growing government involvement is beginning to end. Complaints about taxes, deregulation of the airlines and other industries, and the demographic trend toward an older population provide the evidence these people cite to support their position. These experts also argue that regulation cannot continue if U.S. and Canadian firms are to remain competitive in international markets.

1. Which trend do you think will occur, and why?

2. If government regulation continues to increase, how will HR departments be affected?

▶ **References**

1. Gary Hamel and C. K. Prahalad, "Seeing the Future First," *Fortune,* Sept. 5, 1994, p. 64.

2. Lori Bongiorno, "Business Is Still Structured Like Fourth Grade," *Business Week,* June 28, 1993, p. 86.

3. Ibid.

4. Ibid.

5. Patrick Oster, "The Fast Track Leads Overseas," *Business Week,* Nov. 1, 1993, pp. 64–68.

6. "Getting Europe Back to Work," *The Economist,* Aug. 28, 1993, pp. 43–44.

7. Peter F. Drucker, "Management and the World's Work," *Harvard Business Review,* September–October 1988, pp. 65–76.

8. Moses was confronted by one of the earliest recorded human resource challenges when Jethro, his father-in-law, advised: "And thou shalt teach them ordinances and laws, and shalt shew them the way wherein they must walk, and the work they must do. Moreover, thou shalt provide out of all the able men . . . to be rulers." Exodus 18:20–21.

9. Elton Mayo, *The Human Problems of an Industrial Civilization,* Cambridge, Mass.: Harvard University Press, 1933. See also F. J. Roethlisberger and W. J. Dickson, *Management and the Worker,* Cambridge, Mass.: Harvard University Press, 1939.

10. James N. Brown, P. Devereaux Jennings, and Frank R. Dobbin, "Mission Control? The Development of Personnel Systems in U.S. Industry," *American Sociological Review,* August 1988, pp. 497–514.

11. Mary Mattis, "New Forms of Flexible Work Arrangements for Managers and Professionals: Myths and Realities," *Human Resource Planning,* vol. 13, no. 2, 1990, pp. 133–145.

12. Geert Hofstede, "Cultural Constraints in Management Theories," *Academy of Management Executive,* vol. 7, no. 1, 1993, pp. 81–93.

13. Anne S. Tsui, Terri D. Egan, and Charles A. O'Reilly III, "Being Different: Relational Demography and Organizational Attachment," *Administrative Science Quarterly,* December 1992, pp. 549–579.

14. Philip Condit, "Workforce Diversity," *American Workplace,* September 1993, p. 3. For another view by a company president and an overview of what Hoechst Celanese Company has been doing in the diversity area, see Faye Rice, "How to Make Diversity Pay," *Fortune,* Aug. 8, 1994, pp. 78–86.

15. Phyllis Barnum, "Misconceptions about the Future U.S. Work Force: Implications for Strategic Planning," *Human Resource Planning,* vol. 14, no. 3, 1991, pp. 209–219. For insights into changing values and attitudes, see Harvey Bunke, "Summing Up," *Business Horizons,* May–June 1994, pp. 1–26.

16. Alan L. Otten, "Young Adults Point Up Growing Diversity," *The Wall Street Journal,* Eastern ed., Dec. 7, 1992, p. B1.

17. Jaclyn Fierman, "The Contingency Work Force," *Fortune,* Jan. 24, 1994, pp. 30–35. See also Mary Rowland, "Temporary Work: The New Career," *The New York Times,* National ed., Sept. 12, 1993, p. 15.

18. Vicki Clark, "Employees Drive Diversity Efforts at GE Silicones," *Personnel Journal,* May 1993, pp. 148–153.

19. Edward L. Hansen, "Companies Add Work/Family Managers and Other New Positions," *William M. Mercer News Release,* July 14, 1993, p. 1. See also Sue Shellenbarger, "Managers Navigate Uncharted Waters Trying to Resolve Work-Family Conflicts," *The Wall Street Journal,* Eastern ed., Dec. 7, 1992, p. B1.

20. Jaclyn Fierman, "Are Companies Less Family-Friendly?" *Fortune,* Mar. 21, 1994, pp. 64–67; Dana E. Friedman, "Work and Family: The New Strategic Plan," *Human Resource Planning,* vol. 13, no. 1, 1990, pp. 79–89. See also Helene Paris, "Balancing Work and Family Responsibilities: Canadian Employer and Employee Viewpoints," *Human Resource Planning,* vol. 13, no. 1, 1990, pp. 147–157.

21. John Schwartz, Dody Tsiantar, and Karen Springen, "Escape from the Office," *Newsweek,* Apr. 24, 1989, pp. 58–60. The trend toward "telecommuters" is likely to increase as the Environmental Protection Agency pressures more firms to comply with the Clean Air Act of 1990 by threatening fines if employers cannot reduce the number of employees who drive to work in cities with heavy air pollution.

22. Jeff Miller and William B. Werther, Jr., "AIDS: The Executive and EAP Implications for the Second Decade," *EAP International,* vol. 1, no. 3, 1993, pp. 14–18; Vivien Chitty, "AIDS and the Workplace: What the Employer Can Do," *Employee Counseling Today,* vol. 4, no. 1, 1992, pp. 8–11. See also Helen Elkiss, "Reasonable Accommodation and Unreasonable Fears: An AIDS Policy Guide for Human Resource Personnel," *Human Resource Planning,* vol. 14, no. 3, 1991, pp. 183–191.

23. "Diversity Management Is a Culture Change, Not Just Training: 1993 SHRM/CCH Survey," *Human Resource Management Newsletter,* Commerce Clearing House, Part II, May 26, 1993, p. 12.

24. A survey of 268 companies by Japan's Ministry of Labor found that these firms were unable to recruit even a fourth of the workers they wanted. Louis S. Richman, "The Coming World Labor Shortage," *Fortune,* Apr. 9, 1990, pp. 71–72.

25. Joel Dreyfuss, "Get Ready for the New York Force," *Fortune,* Apr. 23, 1990, p. 167. See also Philip R. Harris and Robert T. Moran, *Managing Cultural Differences,* 3d ed., Houston: Gulf, 1991.

26. "The Mix of People Coming to America," compiled by the staff of *American Demographics* magazine as reported in *The Wall Street Journal,* Apr. 21, 1989, p. B1. See also Charlene Marmer Solomon, "Managing Today's Immigrants," *Personnel Journal,* February 1993, pp. 57–65.

27. Jaclyn Fierman, "Is Immigration Hurting the U.S.?" *Fortune,* Aug. 9, 1993, p. 76.

28. Ibid.

29. Susan Meisinger, "100th Congress Makes Its Mark," *Resource,* October–November 1988, pp. 1, 7.

30. Diane Crispell, "Workers in 2000," *American Demographics,* March 1990, pp. 36–40. See also Leonard H. Chusmir, "A Shift in Values Is Squeezing Older People," *Personnel Journal,* January 1990, pp. 48–52.

31. "How to Turn Workforce Diversity into a Competitive Edge." *BNA Communicator,* Summer 1990, pp. 1, 5. See also Wayne Wendling, "Response to a Changing Work Force," *Personnel Administrator,* November 1988, pp. 50–54; Jolie Solomon, "Learning to Accept Cultural Diversity," *The Wall Street Journal,* Western ed., Sept. 12, 1990, p. B1.

32. Solomon, op. cit.

33. Robert W. Goddard, "Work Force 2000," *Personnel Journal,* February 1989, p. 66.

34. Ibid. See also Joseph H. Boyett and Henry P. Conn, *Workplace 2000,* New York: Dutton, 1991.

35. William B. Werther, Jr., William A. Ruch, and Lynne McClure, *Productivity through People,* St. Paul, Minn.: West, 1986.

36. Fierman, "The Contingency Work Force."

37. "Securing Computerized Personnel Records," *Resource,* November 1982, p. 2. See also Susana Barciela, "Protecting Privacy at Work," *The Miami Herald,* p. BM–13; "Employers Sued on Privacy Charges," *Resource,* May 1986, p. 15.

38. William B. Wolf, "Organizational Constructs: An Approach to Understanding Organizations," *Journal of the Academy of Management,* April 1968, pp. 7–15. See also Robert Granford Wright, *Mosaics of Organizational Character,* New York: Dunellen, 1975, p. 39.

39. Harold C. White and Michael N. Wolfe, "The Role Desired for Personnel Administration," *Personnel Administrator,* June 1980, pp. 87–98.

40. Wayne F. Cascio, "Downsizing: What Do We Know? What Have We Learned?" *Academy of Management Executive,* vol. 7, no. 1, 1993, pp. 95–104.

41. William B. Werther, Jr., Evan Berman, and Eduardo Vasconcellos, "The Future of Technology Management," *Organizational Dynamics,* Winter 1994, pp. 20–32. See also Lynette Lamb, "The 21st Century Office," *Utne Reader,* March–April, 1994, pp. 42–44.

Unlike industrialized countries, where the population is aging and analysts have projected a shortage of workers in the future, 95 percent of the world's population growth is projected to occur in the developing countries of Asia, Africa, and Latin America over the next 25 years.

CAROL HALL[1]

International Challenges

CHAPTER OBJECTIVES

After studying this chapter, you should be able to:

1. **EXPLAIN** why HR activities are crucial to global firms.

2. **DISTINGUISH** among organizational, legal, cultural, and national assumptions that have an impact on HR practices.

3. **DEBATE** the pros and cons of decentralized HR management.

4. **BALANCE** the advantages and disadvantages of using home-country versus foreign nationals.

5. **LIST** the ways in which the HR function furthers a company's plans for internationalization.

6. **DISCUSS** how diversity may facilitate globalization.

AT&T

When Eric Phillips ended his White House Fellowship two years ago, he was eager to return to American Telephone & Telegraph Co.'s home office in Basking Ridge, N.J., and get his career back on track. Instead, his bosses asked the 10 year AT&T veteran to move to Brussels to manage sales of communication services in Europe. "I didn't want to move my family," says Phillips, 40. "I knew my wife would have to give up a wonderful job. But the company was going global. I had to go."[2]

Chapter 1 stated that the purpose of HR management is "to improve the productive contribution of people to the organization in ways that are strategically, ethically, and socially responsible." As businesses become more global in their outlook, managers and HR departments face new challenges in supporting the objectives of the company and its people, as the concerns of Eric Phillips suggested. Consider the observations of one writer about the international placement of executives:

International placement

There is an alarmingly high failure rate when executives are relocated overseas. This mismatching of executives and foreign subsidiaries is primarily caused by poor or inappropriate selection procedures and inadequate orientation programs. To complicate matters, many executives steer clear of overseas assignments because they feel that their absence from their company's headquarters will hurt their chances for career advancement and that good jobs will not be waiting for them at home when they do repatriate.[3]

International HR management relies on the objectives, practices, and professionalism discussed in Chapters 1 and 2. Job openings must still be filled, but the objectives sought, the practices used, and the challenges faced become more complex. Managers and the HR department are confronted with unfamiliar laws, languages, practices, competitors, attitudes, management styles, work ethics, and more. For example, when Japanese managers are transferred to the United States, they are seldom prepared to recognize that women deserve equal professional opportunities, since women have a different status in Japanese companies compared with those in the United States. At the same time, employees must balance the potential excitement of an international job with unique personal, career, and family complexities. Both employees and the organization also face ethical dilemmas, since foreign cultures and laws may vary widely from standards in the home country.

To respond to these challenges, managers like Eric Phillips and HR departments must be flexible and proactive. The HR department at Dow Chemical provides an example of professional and proactive efforts that meet the needs of the company and its people assigned abroad.

Dow Chemical pursues the selection and orientation of employees for international assignments on an individualized basis. Each international move is considered unique. Candidates are given information about the host country and an intensive two-week course in the language and culture. Even the spouse of a recently returned employee visits with the executive and his or her family to discuss the emotional issues likely to be encountered during an international move.

Dow Chemical

The employee is also assigned a "godfather," a high-ranking staff member in the person's function. They stay in touch, keeping each other informed of activities and career issues. The godfather serves as a mentor and reviews compensation issues. Starting about a year before the employee is to be repatriated to the home country, the godfather begins to arrange for the new job—a position at the same level or a higher level than that which was guaranteed before the employee was sent overseas. Small, informal support groups at Dow help returning employees readjust.[4]

"There is ample evidence that non-U.S. nationals and those who have had overseas assignments do advance to the top. Consider Dow Chemical: Nearly half of the top management team is non-American and more than three quarters, including Chairman Frank Popoff, have had foreign assignments."[5]

International experience is important, and each international move is unique, as the Dow example illustrates. What is not unique, however, is the growing interest in international business. Driven by increased competitive pressures and global opportunities, a growing number of companies are transforming themselves into global players, operating across international borders in search of resources and markets. When this occurs, managers and HR departments must proactively adjust from a domestic to a global perspective that supports the company's strategies. The most visible signs of that adjustment are a variety of programs that assist and inform employees before, during, and after foreign assignments.

Changing
perspectives

This chapter will identify the challenges faced by international HR management. Following the overall structure of this book, the chapter begins with an examination of how the HR management framework (Part I) is affected by assumptions, structure, and employee rights. Then, continuing with structure of the book, international challenges associated with preparation and selection (Part II), development and evaluation (Part III), compensation and protection (Part IV), and employee relations and assessment (Part V) are discussed. The chapter concludes with a look at the special challenges facing managers, HR departments, and international employees. Then, throughout the text, the strategic, policy, and operational implications of international HR are revisited to illustrate the problems domestic firms face when operating internationally and the problems foreign companies encounter when operating in the U.S. environment.

▶ Frameworks and International Challenges

Although the HR functions and activities outlined in Chapter 1 apply to international businesses, professionals must be aware of how international activities affect day-to-day management, the structure of the HR department, and employee rights. Underlying all HR frameworks are assumptions about culture.

Assumptions

Ethnocentrism

Operating managers and HR professionals find that their nationality, training, and experience lead them to make assumptions that are culturally based.[6] The use of one's cultural reference points to evaluate others is called *ethnocentrism*. An ethnocentric view often fails to recognize the viewpoints of others. Ethnocentrism does not apply only to U.S. employees overseas; it also applies to foreign companies when they operate in the United States. For example, consider two fundamental differences between Japanese and American managers.

While Japanese managers believe that "a company exists as much to enhance employee welfare as stockholder welfare, for Americans the firm's goal is to maximize shareholder interests."[7] At the same time, attitudes about individualism are more common in the United States than in Japan, where the culture stresses the harmony of the group, for example.[8]

In Japan, it is culturally acceptable to discriminate in employment on the basis of a person's sex or another non-performance-related criterion.[9] Such discrimination against women is culturally acceptable in many developing nations too. However, as Chapter 4 will show, it is illegal in the United States to discriminate in employment on the basis of race, sex, age, religion, handicap, pregnancy, and national origin if the person can do the job.

Comparisons within Europe and between Europe and the United States also reveal subtle cultural differences.

Research summary

A study among groups of managers at the European Institute of Business Administration (INSEAD) found that more than half the French, Italian, and Japanese managers believed that it is important to have precise answers to most of their subordinates' questions. Americans and Swedes felt that way only 13 percent of the time.[10]

As the researcher observed: "When their responses were analyzed, it appeared that the most powerful determinant of their assumptions was by far their nationality. Overall and across 56 different items of inquiry, it was found that nationality had three times more influence on the shaping of managerial assumptions than any of the respondents' other characteristics such as age, education, function, type of company. . . ."[11]

Research suggests that even mobility is different, with Europeans being less willing to move even within their own national borders to find employment.[12]

Simply put, HR professionals and other decision makers must guard against ethnocentrism by not assuming that their attitudes and values apply universally. Unfortunately, assumptions reinforced by years of experience in the home culture are often difficult to recognize, and this partially explains why more companies expect their senior managers to have gained some international experience. However, the diversity of the North American workforce may be an asset for the United States and Canada to the extent that immigrants and foreign nationals in North American firms may help ease their employers' transition to global operations.

Departmental Structure

As was discussed in Chapter 1, the design of the HR department is strongly influenced by its objectives and practices. When the challenges of international HR management become part of the department's concerns, recruitment, selection, placement, compensation, and other traditional activities continue. The responsibilities for these activities may be handled from the home-country offices, or they may be decentralized to divisional, regional, national, or facility-based offices. Often a matrix management approach is used, with some responsibilities being handled on a centralized basis. For example, relocation policies and executive-level replacement planning are commonly handled at company headquarters. Other day-to-day activities—such as hiring entry-level workers, skills training, and employee relations—are usually handled on a local basis. The degree of centralization or decentralization is shaped by the past practices of the department and the country's culture. For example, in Germany the HR function is typically a lower-level activity, but it is a more important corporate function in the United States and is even more important in Japan. However, the greater the cultural, economic, and political differences, the more a decentralized approach allows for rapid and customized responses.[13] Complex local customs and laws also favor a decentralized approach, allowing the local HR department to adapt its policies and practices to local realities.[14]

Centralization versus decentralization

Employee Rights

Employee rights are a major element in the practice of international HR management. The dominant laws are those in the country where the employee works, regardless of the company's or employee's country of origin. Although ethical managers and socially responsible employers may wish to apply nondiscrimination standards internationally, local customs and laws may make such standards impractical or even illegal. Japanese managers in international firms operating in the United States, for example, are advised not to ask personal questions when interviewing. This practice, which is common in Japan, can lead those not hired to consider such questions as forming the basis for a discrimination suit. As a result, many Japanese firms provide handbooks, videotapes, and seminars to managers who are transferred to the United States.[15] Similarly, mixing different castes or Hindus and Moslems in India may be disruptive to a firm's bottom-line results. To guard against violating local

Ethics and laws

Clashing diversity

laws, companies may find it advantageous to rely on foreign nationals to staff HR positions.[16]

Although employee rights are unique to each country, similarities exist, particularly among members of common trading blocs, such as the European Union and North America. *Codetermination,* for example, gives employees and their unions the right to participate in board-level decisions. Beginning with the *Work Council Act* of 1920, Germany has had a long tradition of worker participation in major decisions. Since World War II, codetermination has spread across Europe. Likewise, laws about worker safety and health are common to all industrial nations. For example, French employers must create nonsmoking work areas, just as many U.S. firms are required to do by local or state law.[17] Laws and court rulings against wrongful discharge limit employers' ability to fire or lay off workers in most developed countries. In Europe, for example, termination and layoff laws are far more restrictive than those in North America. In post–World War II Japan, male workers at large companies typically have been considered to have *lifetime employment* until they reach retirement age, although that trend has been cracking in recent years with layoffs at Japan Airlines and Nissan and with Toyota hiring temporary workers under one-year contracts.

Although a discussion of all the workplace laws and court rulings in every country would fill volumes, it is important for HR specialists to understand the rights of employees in each nation where a company does business. This challenge is often met by hiring local professionals and seeking the advice of international law firms that specialize in work-related laws and employee rights, even though the top positions are often reserved for those from the home country.

When the British firm Grand Metropolitan bought Burger King, it assigned a managing director and human resource officer to Burger King's headquarters in Florida. Grand Met believed it was important to have the senior human resource position filled by a British employee who was familiar with the company culture, especially since Burger King's operations are global, not limited to the United States. However, the remainder of the department is staffed by U.S. nationals who are familiar with the laws and culture of Burger King's major market, the United States.

For the HR departments of U.S.-based firms, however, two important exceptions exist: the Foreign Corrupt Practices Act and the Civil Rights Act of 1991. The *Foreign Corrupt Practices Act* prohibits U.S. firms and their subsidiaries from using bribes or other corrupt practices in foreign countries even if such practices are common in a particular country. The *Civil Rights Act* of 1991 makes it illegal for U.S. employers to engage in employment discrimination against their U.S. employees abroad. Thus, a U.S. firm operating overseas cannot discriminate against a U.S. citizen on the basis of race, sex, age, religion, handicap, pregnancy, and national origin if the person can do the job.

Margin notes: Codetermination · Lifetime employment · Burger King · Foreign corruption law

▶ **International Preparation and Selection**

Home-country nationals

Planning and staffing organizations overseas are crucial activities of international HR management, and the slow growth of workforces in all developed nations makes this activity increasingly important and difficult.[18] Central to preparation and selection activities are the employer's policies about filling openings with foreign nationals or home-country citizens reassigned to an international post. The assignment and movement of a home-country national to a foreign opening means that the person is more likely to be familiar with home-country expectations and the company's practices and procedures. Of course, employing a local foreign national means that the firm is more likely to have someone familiar with local laws and customs. Although each company adjusts its plans to the specific opening, home-country nationals are most likely to be in senior positions, such as the chief HR and managing director roles in the British-owned, U.S.-based Burger King example. When the technologies of products or production processes are complex or unique, home-country experts in design and production are likely to be assigned as senior managers or advisers. As one researcher observed:

> Complexity, political risk, and cultural distance increase the inherent uncertainty . . . in the foreign country and appear best managed with U.S. nationals acting primarily as sources of information and unobtrusive control. While competition also increases the risk . . . it also increases the importance of local nationals as conduits to the local market. . . . The higher the interdependence between the branch and headquarters, the more U.S. nationals . . . manage the inherent uncertainty. Yet, if the main sources of interdependence are within the nation-state, then . . . local nationals can better manage the uncertainty.[19]

International succession planning

Corporate-level HR departments play a particularly important role through their involvement in international succession planning. From the centralized perspective of the organization and its strategies, the head of HR is often given the responsibility for developing replacement plans. Potential successors are identified for all the key positions in the company. Each successor is then evaluated in regard to remaining deficiencies that can be addressed through training and experience. Working closely with top management, the department is able to ensure a smooth flow of qualified internal candidates who are prepared to assume greater responsibilities domestically and internationally.[20] Therefore, recruiting and selection are of particular importance to the staffing process.

International Recruiting

Global organizations need to identify potential applicants for openings both in the home country and abroad. The two sources of candidates are present employees and new hires. The reassignment of present employees offers an opportunity for career development of the employee in addition to filling a job opening, which is why companies such as Dow move key employees all around the world. Although an international assignment often looks attractive to first-time applicants, career, family, language, and cultural considerations may cause more experienced candidates not to apply. Dual-career families, children, and assignments to less developed areas are often significant barriers. For example, the U.S. Department of Labor estimates that 81 percent of all marriages are dual-career partnerships.[21]

A lack of knowledge about internal openings can be a barrier. Some people are reluctant to apply for international jobs because they fear they will lose touch with developments at headquarters, harming their opportunities for career advancement. As a result, many people are forced to rely on an informal network when the HR department does not create systematic linkages among people to overcome these concerns. Consider an example from General Dynamics, a major defense contractor:

William L. Godsey had headed General Dynamics Corporation's European operations in Brussels . . . when he got a call from Frederick S. Wood, a vice president at St. Louis Headquarters. Mr. Wood thought Mr. Godsey should apply for the newly opened job of vice president for international programs at the company's Pomona, Calif., division.

Mr. Godsey did just that. He got the job and a short time later he and his family were winging their way back to the States. "If Fred hadn't called," Mr. Godsey said, "I would never have known the job existed."[22]

To address these and other concerns, companies such as Dow, Ciba-Geigy, and Colgate-Palmolive have created mentor programs to help coach employees and serve as a link to company developments.[23] The HR department may offer incentives and assistance to help overcome these barriers, or the department may need to consider other sources of recruits. Colgate-Palmolive provides an example:

Colgate-Palmolive's senior management noted that the company was having difficulty securing top executive talent for its international operations. Since Colgate's international business is crucial to the company's overall success, management decided to reexamine its recruitment and development practices in this area.

As a result, Colgate developed a new strategy of recruiting students from recognized undergraduate and M.B.A. programs whose experience, education, and language skills demonstrated their commitment to an international career.[24]

Recruiting foreign nationals to apply for work in the home country can be more difficult than seeking applicants in a firm's domestic market. In Japan, for example, many people prefer to work for Japanese companies, especially older and longer-service workers who see resigning to work for others as a sign of disloyalty. Even in developing nations such as Mexico, recruiting people from local firms is viewed as inappropriate.[25] Working for a foreign company even in one's home country may look unattractive. Some people fear a *glass ceiling* above which promotions are reserved for employees from the company's home

Dual careers

General Dynamics

Colgate-Palmolive

Glass ceiling

country. Differences in cultural expectations can be particularly frustrating for women, who may not be considered "appropriate" for senior or professional-level positions by the senior management of an international employer.[26] Although nearly half the senior management at Dow Chemical is non-American and the CEO of Coca-Cola is Cuban,[27] for example, companies from Japan and other countries operating in the United States often exclude U.S. citizens from the top jobs, making recruitment for key jobs even more difficult.[28]

International Selection

As an organization evolves from a domestic to a global company, the selection process follows a similar path of development. The company's initial efforts to operate overseas tend to favor transferring employees from the home country. As the company becomes more international in its scope of operations and out-look, more foreign nationals are hired for positions overseas. As the organization and the HR department gain international experience, the HR department makes fewer distinctions among the nationalities of employees hired to fill openings. As the company matures into a truly global operation, senior managers at headquarters become more diverse in their nationalities, as the mix of executives at Dow Chemical suggests.

The selection of a person to fill an international opening requires the HR department to consider more than just technical or managerial ability.[29] The person's ability to adapt to the company and country cultures is also important.

Research summary Research shows that "maturity and emotional stability" and "technical knowl-edge of the business" are two common factors prized among those selected for international assignments.[30] In looking for someone to assign abroad, to bring to the home country, or to work in the home country for a foreign employer, compatibility with the company culture must be taken into account or a mismatch between the company's and the employee's expectations may result.

Employment opportunities for a spouse, education for the children, and the family's ability to adapt to new surroundings influence whether the placement will be successful. Although these issues are considered during recruitment, the selection process must identify the candidate's chances for success. At the same time, these concerns cannot be used to discriminate against qualified applicants in violation of local laws. Legal constraints and assimilation challenges make in-ternational selection complex. This complexity grows when religious, tribal, lan-guage, and class or caste standards must be applied as selection criteria.

▶ Development and Placement

Once a candidate is selected, he or she needs to be oriented, trained, developed for future responsibilities, and evaluated. Development and placement, as with most other international HR activities, often involve great effort from the HR department and operating managers.

Orientation

Regardless of how qualified job candidates are, newcomers generally need an orientation to the company and their jobs. Research suggests that expatriates from the United States have a high failure rate, with half the firms in one study reporting 10 to 20 percent failures among their international placements.[31] An orientation touches on the policies, place, procedures, and people to be encountered. Unlike new employee orientations that may last only a few hours, international orientations may begin weeks or months before *and* last for weeks after an assignment is made. Although a predeparture orientation is common and important, an on-site orientation after arrival in an international post further enlightens the new hire or transferee.

International openings add culture, language, and other unique aspects to the assignment, requiring insight into local customs, culture, and expectations. Social attitudes toward time and punctuality, power, teamwork, entertaining, cultural taboos, and the use of titles and the degree of formality expected in different social settings are often included in an international orientation. The employee's spouse may be part of the orientation and training, as is the case at Dow Chemical, where both the husband and the wife are allowed to attend a two-week language and culture orientation course.[32] The orientation is likely to include a visit from an employee or spouse who has served in the location. Aside from the personal touch, repatriated families are likely to have keen insights about a particular locale.[33]

Training and Development

Many global firms rely on a series of rotations through different business functions in different countries to help develop managers and professionals into potential executives. Exposure to different functions and cultures produces a broad understanding of the organization and the environments in which it operates. Training and development activities are supplemented with more traditional education and training courses by the HR department, universities, and private trainers. As more companies expand their international involvement, experience abroad will become an even more important development activity.

Large multinational companies such as Hewlett-Packard use annual conferences on technical and managerial issues to bring together key managers and professionals from around the world. These meetings result in the development of informal networks that help tie people to the company regardless of where they work. Companywide training programs are also used to develop people and expose them to others in the firm. An additional benefit of bringing people together for these meetings is the development of a shared culture. Perhaps the most

Overseas failures

Hewlett-Packard

striking aspect of visiting an international Hewlett-Packard facility, for example, is how similar the corporate culture seems to that at Palo Alto, the company's headquarters.

GATT and WTO

The diversity issue will gain importance among international HR professionals. France and the United States, for example, are advocating expanded talks about global labor rights as part of the World Trade Organization that will emerge from the last round of General Agreement on Tariffs and Trade (GATT) talks. At the same time, companies such as Dow Chemical are pushing diversity training abroad, often with the intention of addressing discrimination against foreign women working for U.S. firms.[34] For multinational companies such as Hewlett-Packard and Dow Chemical, orientation and training efforts combined with international job rotation are important ways to build a unified corporate culture that spans the globe.

Evaluation and Career Development

Employees in international operations need to be evaluated and require assistance in career planning. Evaluation is particularly difficult because the person doing the evaluation may be thousands of miles away and may not be familiar with the unique challenges faced by the person who is to be evaluated.

Dow Chemical

At Dow, a senior manager in the same function is assigned to the role of godfather. The employee and his or her mentor (godfather) are expected to keep each other informed about performance and other matters that affect the person's career.[35] The godfather then becomes involved with pay raises and locating a job in the home country when the employee is repatriated.

The unique character of international assignments makes the evaluation and development of those abroad as important as it is difficult. Specific performance expectations not only form the basis for evaluation but also give direction to the expatriate's career development. The development of international managers often relies heavily on rotation into different jobs within and among different countries. Without a godfather or a similar formal or informal mechanism, an expatriate can feel cut off from the company and from his or her career. Since job rotation approaches to development may involve moving people through different countries and different divisions of the organization, the responsibility for tracking, evaluating, and developing overseas personnel often falls to the HR department, regardless of what formal programs may state as their procedures and objectives. Of particular importance to the person and his or her family is compensation, including the expatriation and repatriation benefits that make international assignments a distinctive feature of international human resource management.[36]

▶ Compensation and Protection

Overseas benefits

International compensation and protection go beyond pay and benefits. Pay is expanded to compensate for additional taxes and living expenses. Incentives may be added, especially for assignments in less desirable locations. Supplements may be given to cover the extra costs of educating children, making return trips to the home country, and paying servants' salaries. All these changes must be considered within the context of the foreign culture.[37] Benefits may include a company car, a driver, club memberships, housing, and other "perks" normally reserved for top management. Extensive benefits are particularly common in countries with very high tax rates, since benefits are typically not subject to taxation. Some companies, such as Dow, give explicit job guarantees, assuring the returning employee a comparable or superior job. Or employment contracts may specify pay, benefits, termination bonuses, and other terms and conditions of employment.

Perhaps the most complicated benefit is *relocation assistance.* This company-paid assistance can range from buying the employee's home at its market value to shipping household goods, cars, and other possessions abroad. Figure 3-1 lists some of the concerns faced by a medium-sized company when it places executives internationally.[38] As the figure suggests, the HR department may become involved in shipping family medical and dental records and helping to locate housing, schools, and other needed services.

Figure 3-1	Human Resource Department Issues in International Placement

A *few* of the human resource department's concerns at Ferro Corp., when international placement takes place, include:

- Developing an overseas compensation and benefits plan, taking into account cost-of-living differences and any special needs

- Giving tax advice and financial counseling

- Supervising the sometimes extensive paperwork involved

- Assisting with housing and the selection of good schools

- Helping the employee set up banking accounts and make cash transfers

- Transferring medical, dental, and school records, and assisting with inoculations

- Helping with absentee ballots and international driving licenses

- Providing language training, often through "immersion" courses

- Assisting with moves of household furniture and goods abroad

- Helping the trailing spouse get work permits and jobs abroad, if possible

Source: Adapted from Ellen Brandt, "Global HR," *Personnel Journal,* March 1991, p. 41.

Repatriation

As part of protecting one's career with the company, repatriation of the person back to the country of origin involves many of the same issues involved in sending someone abroad. Additionally, there may not be a clear career path for the person upon his or her return. In fact, there may not even be a specific job in the home country. Effective HR planning by the home-office personnel department requires careful consideration of international succession planning to ensure that international assignments and repatriation to the home country result in meaningful jobs and developmental experiences. When the planning of international placements does not consider eventual repatriation, executives often feel their new jobs are less challenging at the same time that they are trying to make the transition back into the home culture. These feelings may lead returning executives to conclude that their overseas experience may be of greater value to another firm, even a competitor. To the extent that expatriates remain in touch with the company through newsletters, return trips, and contacts with mentors and past colleagues, the repatriation will be more successful. The HR department can make a contribution to the company and the employee by ensuring that international transfers are well planned and facilitated by the department's compensation and benefit plans.

International transfers

▶ Employee Relations and Assessment

Perhaps the most complex area of international HR is employee relations. Managers, whether they are expatriates or foreign nationals, seek the HR department's help in dealing with employees. How well those relations among managers and employees are handled has a direct impact on the organization's ability to execute its strategies. Variations in languages, customs, cultures, laws, employee expectations, competition, and other factors cause all but the smallest international companies to rely on foreign nationals to handle the bulk of international employee relations.

The use of foreign nationals, however, does not mean that the headquarters HR department can abdicate its role. Instead, a matrix arrangement usually finds the local HR office handling the culture-specific tasks of hiring, placing, training, and compensating employees. The home-office department sets broad policies and serves an assessment function to ensure that local offices are in compliance with company policies and procedures.

Assessment and prediction of the performance expatriates and foreign nationals go beyond individual evaluations. The department must assess its entire placement function, including planning, staffing, development, compensation, and support systems for employee relations. Proactive adjustments must be made to ensure effectiveness and efficiency in international HR policies and activities. The execution of international HR functions is an important vehicle for the department to contribute to the organization's strategic success and the needs of its people.

▶ **Challenges of International Human Resource Management**

Beyond the impact on traditional HR activities, international challenges affect the organization in more subtle ways. Perspectives do change. Outlooks become more global as senior-level managers become more aware of international developments. Those in the organization who lack this perspective or are unable to develop it fail to grasp the growing changes in global competition. Strategies and policies become culture-bound and do not benefit from the rich diversity of viewpoints found internationally.

International HR management affects the company and the HR department in countless unforeseen ways. Some of the companywide concerns raised for the department include the challenges of troubleshooting, workplace diversity, and cultural awareness.

International Human Resource Troubleshooting

As with domestic operations, HR problems arise in international operations. In dealing with a labor shortage, an unexpected resignation, or a union problem, international managers may need assistance with specific HR issues. It is unrealistic to expect any single person or department to possess the knowledge and skills needed to address the wide array of HR issues encountered internationally, but the department needs to be able to identify sources of assistance. It must be able to identify people within the company and outside who can provide the expertise needed to address issues that may be specific to an individual culture or country. Developing a worldwide list of lawyers, consultants, and other experts may be the only cost-effective way to prepare for the nearly unlimited range of HR issues that can confront a company.

HR as
troubleshooter

International Challenges and Workplace Diversity

Challenges of workforce diversity are amplified in international HR management. Not only must managers and HR experts contend with diversity in the domestic workforce, globalization means increased diversity both at home and abroad. Compounding this diversity are a growing maze of international alliances among firms, with the key determinant of their success often being how well human resource policies can be integrated and implemented.[39] Diversity increases as foreign nationals are transferred to the home country; it also increases as jobs are transferred to other countries. Compounding this diversity will be immigration from a variety of countries, as suggested by the year's pattern of immigration shown in Figure 3-2. Consider these comments:

Over the next 20 years the working-age population in developing countries will rise by roughly 700 million—just about equal to the *total* current population of North America, Japan, and Western Europe. Says John Sewell, president of the Overseas Development Council, a Washington, D.C., think tank: "The work-hungry multi-

Worker or job
migration

tudes of the Third World will either descend on the developed economies in a flood of immigration, compete with increasing success for the low-skilled and semiskilled jobs that will migrate to them, or most likely, do both."[40]

In dealing with immigrants or foreign employees, managers and HR departments will face even more diversity in the workforce in the coming years.[41] Although some may see these challenges as a threat, they represent an opportunity for developed nations because of the coming labor shortages many may face. Japan's Ministry of Labor reports that a survey of 268 companies has revealed that these firms are already unable to recruit even a quarter of the new workers they would like.[42] In the United States, for example, there will be almost 1 million fewer new entrants into the workforce during each year of the 1990s than there was in the 1980s. And western Europe's workforce is shrinking because of low birthrates, even though political policies have caused unemployment to remain high. Slow growth of the labor force combined with growing numbers of retirees in Japan, North America, and western Europe will require managers and HR departments to seek more foreign nationals at home and abroad.[43]

| Figure 3-2 | **Sources of Immigrants into the United States** |

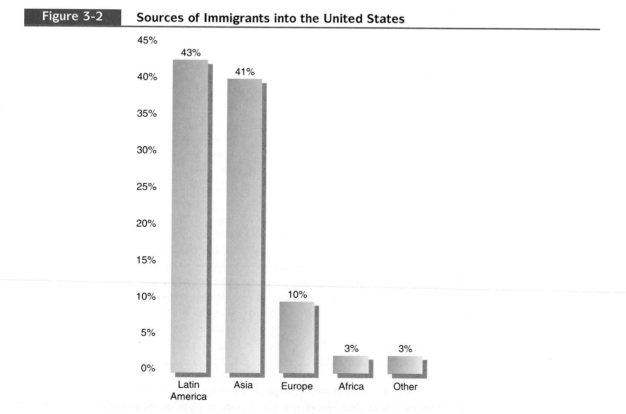

Source: United States Immigration and Naturalization Service, 1988.

The international
"bonus"

In the process of learning about a foreign culture, international managers get a bonus: They become aware of their own cultural values and heritage and may decide to capitalize on or modify some of their accustomed behaviors. Another bonus is the recognition that many cultures coexist in . . . workplaces as well. Changing . . . demographics makes it imperative that these cultural differences be recognized, dealt with, and capitalized on as the work force at home becomes even more richly diverse.[44]

Employers with ongoing diversity programs and those with extensive international operations probably have gained a competitive advantage by being prepared to manage the highly diverse workforce of the twenty-first century.[45]

Cultural Awareness

Managers and the HR department further their contributions to the organization by being informed about cultural differences among the company's international operations. Pilot projects or innovations that have been successful in one country are often duplicated and applied in others. Technically or financially oriented innovators, however, may focus on technological or financial feasibility, unaware of cultural differences that could reduce their success. The department's role is not to object to or block technology transfers or other innovations but to facilitate them. Proactive departments work with operating managers and project leaders to identify solutions to cultural or national differences that may impede a company's strategy.

Changing roles
of women

A specific area where cultural differences commonly affect business plans is the growing cadre of women managers and professionals. In many cultures women are expected to assume traditional, family-centered roles. Developing countries, Moslem-dominated regions, and Japanese companies have not afforded women an equal employment opportunity.[46] In some Moslem cultures, for example, women are discouraged from working side by side with men; in others, tradition defines the jobs a woman can hold.

A company that is dedicated to equal employment opportunity must make international assignments available to women if they are to advance to senior-level positions. Awareness of cultural differences can enable succession planning and other departmental efforts to provide equal employment opportunity for women in ways that are beneficial to the employee's needs and the company's objectives. In fact, equal employment opportunity is so central to the role of HR departments that Chapter 4 is devoted to this challenge.

▶ Summary

International HR management places a wide variety of new pressures on traditional HR activities. At the same time, a manager or department's ability to meet these challenges provides an opportunity to make significant contributions to the company. With better qualified people executing the company's strategy on a global scale, managers can work with the HR department to create a source of competitive advantage for the company.

For managers and the HR department to be a source of competitive advantage, the department generally must evolve to support the organization's transformation from a domestic to an international to a global-oriented company. This evolution requires an awareness of the assumptions and employee rights that are likely to be encountered in the international arena and a rethinking of the department's structure and activities.

Virtually every activity of the HR department is affected directly or indirectly by the internationalization of the firm's business. The need to do international succession planning arises, as do policy decisions about the use of foreign nationals and expatriates in assignments abroad. Internal barriers to international assignments need to be identified and reduced, and the company must identify external sources of needed talent. Then, within a wide range of legal constraints, the HR department must select qualified people who can be assimilated into the company and the local culture.

Orientation, training, and development gain considerably in complexity and importance. The success of a foreign national or expatriate's performance depends heavily on effective placement and development. Compensation becomes more complex too. Adjustments, allowances, and incentives, along with unique benefit packages, add considerably to the firm's compensation costs and the HR department's involvement in customizing individual compensation packages.

Managers and HR departments must assess the effectiveness of their international efforts to ensure effective employee relations. Often the department is called on to serve as a troubleshooter in helping managers address employee relations and other HR issues.

Globalization amplifies the cultural diversity of an organization and requires the members of the HR department to become increasingly aware of cultural differences so that other managers can be properly advised.

▶ Terms for Review

Ethnocentrism	Glass ceiling
Foreign national	Perks
Codetermination	Relocation assistance
Lifetime employment	Repatriation programs
Succession planning	Expatriate
Mentors	Labor shortages

▶ Review and Discussion Questions

1. What objections might you expect to hear from employees about overseas assignments?

2. Assume you are an executive at Dow, overseeing all of its factories worldwide. What actions do you want the HR department to perform so that international assignments are eagerly accepted?

3. Why should Dow's managers and HR department be concerned about the differences in cultural assumptions found around the world? Provide an example of an assumption that differs from those found in developed countries.

4. When an HR department seeks to centralize its operations at headquarters, what benefits does it gain? What risks does it incur?

5. Do you agree or disagree with the following statement? Why? "Since U.S. laws do not apply outside the United States, managers and HR specialists need not worry about U.S. employment laws, though the host country's laws are important."

6. What makes international staffing so complicated?

7. Outline the key factors that need to be considered in developing an international relocation program for a company's employees.

8. Excluding job-related and company-related items, what do you think a foreign national needs to know before moving to your country?

▶ Incident 3-1

ABB Asea Brown Boveri and the Future

ABB Asea Brown Boveri is a $29 billion a year Swedish-Swiss merger company based in Switzerland. The company is a major worldwide producer of transportation and electrical equipment. According to the CEO, Percy Barnevik, "It is a fallacy to think that industry will increase employment overall in the Western world."[47] According to a story in *Fortune*:

> Barnevik foresees "a massive move from the Western world. We already have 25,000 employees in former communist countries. They will do the job that was done in Western Europe before." More jobs will shift to Asia. . . . ABB, which employed only 100 workers in Thailand in 1980 . . . will have more than 7,000 by the end of the century. Barnevik's forecast borders on the apocalyptic: "Western Europe and American employment will just shrink . . . in an orderly way. Like farming at the turn of the century."[48]

1. What implications do Barnevik's predictions hold for the international managers and HR department at ABB?

2. If you were just beginning a career with ABB, what implications would Barnevik's forecast hold for you?

▶ Incident 3-2

Levi Strauss, Global Sourcing, and Ethics

Global companies such as Levi Strauss face several interesting dilemmas. Levi Strauss's single largest market is the United States, but this U.S. company finds that to compete, it must produce about 50 percent of its jeans and other products overseas. Given the labor-intensive nature of many sewing operations, Levi Strauss cannot pay U.S. wage rates, provide workers with expected fringe benefits, comply with numerous labor laws, and still compete.

Levi Strauss is an ethical employer, not wanting to be socially irresponsible as it seeks to create wealth for its owners and satisfy its customers' and employees' needs. In studying the working conditions provided by its 400 international subcontractors, the company found that 25 percent of the employers provided terrible working conditions. For example, its contractors in Bangladesh routinely used child labor, according to *Fortune.*[49]

In response, Levi Strauss developed strict codes of conduct for suppliers, requiring them to provide wages and working standards at least equal to those which prevail in the producer's country. Workweeks are limited to sixty hours, and these standards are enforced by surprise visits from Levi Strauss employees. *Fortune* asked the following questions:

1. "Should U.S. companies justify paying near-starvation wages because that's what the market will bear?"[50]

2. What implications do Levi Strauss's international HR policies and practices have for the company if it allows its subcontractors to exploit foreign workers?

▶ References

1. Carol Hall, "World Trade Organization to Discuss Global Labor Rights," *International HR Update,* April–June 1994, p. 3.

2. Patrick Oster et al., "The Fast Track Leads Overseas," *Business Week,* Nov. 1, 1993, p. 64.

3. Paul L. Blocklyn, "Developing the International Executive," *Personnel,* March 1989, p. 44.

4. Ibid., pp. 44–47.

5. Calvin Reynolds, "HR Must Influence Global Staff Strategy," *HRNews,* March 1991, p. C-1.

6. Geert Hofstede, *Culture and Organizations,* Berkshire, UK: McGraw-Hill International, 1991.

7. Mary Sullivan Taylor, "American Managers in Japanese Subsidiaries: How Cultural Differences Are Affecting the Work Place," *Human Resource Planning,* March 1991, pp. 43–49.

8. Susan Moffat, "Should You Work for the Japanese?" *Fortune,* Dec. 3, 1990, pp. 107–120. See also Deborah L. Jacobs, "Japanese-American Culture Clash," *The New York Times,* Sept. 9, 1990, sect. 3, part 2, p. 23.

9. Steven Greenhouse, "State Dept. Finds Widespread Abuse of World's Women," *The New York Times,* National ed., Feb. 3, 1994, p. 1.

10. André Laurent, "The Cross-Cultural Puzzle of International Human Resource Management," *Human Resource Management,* Spring 1986, pp. 91–102.

11. Ibid., p. 93.

12. Gene Koretz, "Europe's Work Force Isn't Moving with the Money," *Business Week,* June 21, 1993, p. 24.

13. Nakiye Boyacigiller, "The Role of Expatriates in the Management of Interdependence, Complexity and Risk in Multinational Corporations," *The Journal of International Business,* Third Quarter, 1990, p. 373.

14. Anne V. Corey, "Ensuring Strength in Each Country: A Challenge for Corporate Headquarters Global Human Resource Executives," *Human Resource Planning,* March 1991, pp. 1–8.

15. Jacobs, op. cit.

16. Boyacigiller, op. cit.

17. Christine D. Keen, "French Employers Must Create Non-Smoking Work Areas," *HR Update,* January–February 1993, p. 3.

18. Louis S. Richman, "The Coming World Labor Shortage," *Fortune,* Apr. 9, 1990, pp. 70–77. See also Alan Riding, "Now, The Graying of Europa," *The International Herald Tribune,* July 23, 1990, p. 1; Hall, op. cit.

19. Boyacigiller, op. cit., p. 373.

20. James E. McElwain, "Succession Plans Designed to Manage Change," *HRMagazine,* February 1991, pp. 67–71.

21. Calvin Reynolds and Rita Bennett, "The Career Couple Challenge," *Personnel Journal,* March 1991, pp. 46–48. See also Linda L. Ball, "Overseas Dual-Career Family: An HR Challenge," *HRNews,* March 1991, p. C-8; Richard Souders, "HR Exec Best to Design, Manage Compensation," *HRNews,* March 1991, p. C-5.

22. Claudia H. Deutsch, "Getting the Brightest to Go Abroad," *The New York Times,* National ed., June 17, 1990, sect. 3, part 2, p. 25.

23. Blocklyn, op. cit.

24. Ibid., p. 45.

25. Brian O'Reilly, "Doing Business on Mexico's Volcano," *Fortune,* Aug. 29, 1988, pp. 72–74.

26. Banu Golesorkhi, "Why Not a Woman in Overseas Assignments," *HRNews,* March 1991, p. C-4.

27. Reynolds, op. cit.

28. Moffat, op. cit.

29. Raymond J. Stone, "Expatriate Selection and Failure," *Human Resource Planning,* March 1991, pp. 9–18.

30. Rosalie L. Tung, "Selection and Training of Personnel for Overseas Assignments," *Columbia Journal of World Business,* vol. 16, no. 1, 1981, pp. 68–78. See also F. Mueller-Maerki, "Help Wanted: Adam Marx or Karl Smith: A New Breed of Executive for Eastern Europe," *Corporate Issues Monitor,* vol. VI, no. 1, 1991, pp. 1–4.

31. Tung, op. cit.

32. Blocklyn, op. cit., p. 46. See also J. Steward Black and Mark Mendenhall, "Cross-Cultural Training Effectiveness: A Review and a Theoretical Framework for Future Research," *Academy of Management Review,* vol. 15, no. 1, 1990, pp. 113–136.

33. Nancy K. Napier and Richard B. Peterson, "Expatriate Re-Entry: What Do Repatriates Have to Say?" *Human Resource Planning,* March 1991, pp. 19–28.

34. Hall, op. cit.; Joann S. Lublin, "Diversity Training Extends Beyond the U.S.," *The Wall Street Journal,* Eastern ed., July 30, 1994, p. C1.

35. Blocklyn, op. cit.

36. Rosalie L. Tung, "Career Issues in International Assignments," *The Academy of Management Executive,* vol. II, no. 3, 1988, pp. 241–244.

37. Luis R. Gomez-Mejia and Theresa Welbourne, "Compensation Strategies in a Global Context," *Human Resource Planning,* March 1991, pp. 29–41.

38. Ellen Brandt, "Global HR," *Personnel Journal,* March 1991, p. 41.

39. Wayne Cascio and Manuel G. Serapio, Jr., "Human Resources Systems in an International Alliance: The Undoing of a Done Deal?" *Organizational Dynamics,* Winter 1991, pp. 63–74.

40. Jolie Solomon, "Learning to Accept Cultural Diversity," *The Wall Street Journal,* Eastern ed., Sept. 12, 1990, p. B1.

41. Richman, op. cit., p. 70.

42. Riding, op. cit., p. 1. See also "Jobless Europe," *The Economist,* June 26, 1993, p. 17; Carla Rapoport, "Europe Tackles Its Job Crisis," *Fortune,* Oct. 4, 1993, pp. 133–134.

43. William B. Johnston, "Global Work Force 2000: The New World Labor Market," *Harvard Business Review,* March–April 1991, pp. 115–127.

44. Victoria J. Marsick, Ernie Turner, and Lars Cederholm, "International Managers as Team Leaders," *Management Review,* March 1989, p. 47.

45. Brian O'Reilly, "Your New Global Work Force," *Fortune,* Dec. 14, 1992, pp. 52–66.

46. Ball, op. cit.

47. O'Reilly, op. cit., p. 52.

48. Ibid.

49. Brian Dumaine, "Exporting Jobs and Ethics," *Fortune,* Oct. 5, 1992, p. 10.

50. Ibid.

"Glass Ceiling" is the phrase used to describe the artificial barriers, based on attitudinal or organizational bias, that prevent qualified individuals from advancing within their organization and reaching their full potential.
THE GLASS CEILING COMMISSION
U.S. DEPARTMENT OF LABOR

Equal Employment Challenges

CHAPTER OBJECTIVES

After studying this chapter, you should be able to:

1. EXPLAIN the impact of workforce diversity on equal employment and affirmative action.

2. DESCRIBE the scope of each major equal employment law.

3. DISCUSS the relationship among federal, state, and local equal employment laws.

4. EXPLAIN the enforcement procedures used by the Equal Employment Opportunity Commission.

5. DESCRIBE how equal employment laws affect managers and the human resource function.

6. OUTLINE the key elements of an affirmative action program.

Equal employment opportunity (EEO) laws require managers and human resource (HR) departments to provide applicants an equal opportunity for employment without regard to race, religion, sex, disability, pregnancy, national origin, or age. Since many violations of these laws result from failure to inform managers, EEO-related laws are of concern to both operating managers and HR professionals.

These laws have an impact on nearly every HR activity, including planning, recruiting, selection, placement, training, compensation, and employee relations. Although other developed nations have various forms of equal employment opportunity—such as Japan's Equal Opportunity Law, which went into effect in 1986, making men and women "officially" equal—the most extensive laws are found in the United States.[1] To illustrate the scope of these laws, consider how they affected the American Telephone and Telegraph Company (AT&T).

EEO in Japan

AT&T

In the 1970s, the American Telephone and Telegraph Company asked the Federal Communications Commission for approval to increase long-distance telephone rates. The Equal Employment Opportunity Commission (the federal agency that is largely responsible for policing equal employment laws) filed a petition to stop the increases. The EEOC argued that "approval of the rate increase would be both unconstitutional and contrary to the public interest because AT&T had engaged . . . in extensive violations of Federal, State and constitutional prohibitions against job discrimination."[2] This case "was the first government effort to attack all significant patterns and practices of discrimination of a major national employer."[3]

After more than two years of hearings and negotiations—and hundreds of thousands of pages of exhibits, testimony, and statistical data—AT&T negotiated a settlement by outlining a series of actions it would take to remedy the alleged patterns and practices of discrimination. As the federal district court judge who signed the consent decree commented, it was, up to that time, "the largest and most impressive civil rights settlement in the history of the nation."[4]

AT&T and EEO

The consent decree required AT&T to pay some $45 million to affected employees during the first year. Officially, the EEOC estimates that AT&T has spent $100 million in back pay and incentive awards.[5] Not only was money paid to nearly 50,000 AT&T employees who had been financially affected by past practices, AT&T was required to become more aggressive in recruiting, hiring, developing, and promoting women and minority group members. Labor relations problems also resulted when suits were filed by AT&T's unions to protect the seniority rights of employees who did not benefit from the back pay and accelerated training opportunities.

These issues were not resolved quickly. AT&T remained under the consent decree for six years before the EEOC agreed that the company had met most of its equal employment objectives. By the early 1990s minority group members accounted for 21 percent of AT&T's workforce and 17 percent of its managers.[6]

As the AT&T example suggests, most of the aspects of HR management shown in Figure 4-1 are affected by EEO law. Preparation, selection, development, evaluation, and compensation must all be done without discrimination. If past actions have had a discriminatory result, the government can require

| Figure 4-1 | A Model of the Human Resource Management System and Its Major Environmental Challenges |

that corrective action be taken, including affirmative action by the employer to remedy past discrimination. Although equal employment is only one of the challenges listed in Figure 4-1, its impact on HR management may be the most pervasive.

Since regulation of the employment relationship concerns managers and HR practitioners, these individuals have three responsibilities. First, they must stay abreast of new laws, agency decisions, and court rulings; if they do not, their knowledge will become outdated and useless to the organization. Second, they

EEO compliance

must develop and administer programs that ensure the organization's compliance with EEO laws. Failure to do so may lead to discrimination, loss of government contracts, poor public relations, and suits by government agencies or affected individuals, as happened with AT&T. Third, they must pursue their traditional role of obtaining, maintaining, and retaining an optimal workforce. No organization benefits from compliance with EEO laws by hiring poorly qualified workers.

Since EEO laws are a major challenge to HR activities, they are examined in this chapter. The impact of these laws on specific HR undertakings will be discussed throughout the book.

▶ Equal Employment Laws: An Overview

EEO laws seek to outlaw discrimination in employment based on race, color, religion, disability, national origin, sex, pregnancy, or age (over 40). Vietnam-era veterans are also covered under specific conditions discussed later in the chapter.

Origins of EEO

Equal employment constraints have three origins: federal acts, state and local legislation, and executive orders of the president. Each source has similar—and sometimes overlapping—objectives and jurisdictions. As Figure 4-2 implies, coverage overlaps because federal jurisdiction includes only employers whose operations affect interstate commerce, some government agencies, and contractors for the federal government. Employers who do not fall into these categories might discriminate if state and local legislative bodies did not pass fair employment practice laws to fill this void. Executive orders are presidential decrees that affect federal agencies and federal government contractors. To comply with equal employment laws or remedy past discrimination, HR specialists develop affirmative action plans that identify the employer's actions and set a timetable for ensuring compliance with equal opportunity laws.

But before affirmative action programs are reviewed, the three layers of equal employment law will be discussed. The chapter will look at the purpose, prohibitions, enforcement, and implications of these laws as well as major court decisions.

| Figure 4-2 | Types, Sources, Objectives, and Jurisdiction of Equal Employment Laws |

TYPE	SOURCE	OBJECTIVES AND JURISDICTION
FEDERAL ACTS	Passed by Congress and enforced by the executive branch.	To ensure equal employment opportunities with employers involved in interstate commerce, with government agencies, and with most government contractors.
STATE AND LOCAL LAWS (sometimes called fair employment practices)	Enacted by state legislatures or local lawmakers and enforced by state or local executive branches.	To ensure equal employment opportunities within the state or local community.
EXECUTIVE ORDERS	Decreed by the president and enforced by the executive branch.	To ensure equal employment opportunities with federal agencies and with certain government contractors.

▶ Federal Equal Employment Laws

Federal equal employment acts are an important group of laws that form the basis for nearly all attempts to provide equal employment opportunity. Most state and local fair employment practices are modeled after the federal acts listed in Figure 4-3. When conflicts arise among federal laws and other laws, the most demanding law—usually a federal law—dominates. Among federal laws, none is as encompassing as Title VII of the 1964 *Civil Rights Act*, as amended.

Civil Rights Act

Title VII

Title VII of the Civil Rights Act of 1964 and its subsequent amendments form the centerpiece of EEO laws. This act attempts to ensure equal employment opportunity by prohibiting discrimination in hiring, promotion, compensation, and other conditions of employment. As a result, discrimination in employment based on race, color, religion, sex, pregnancy, or national origin is illegal. Sections 703(a) and (d) of the law are presented in Figure 4-4 and discussed below.

Figure 4-3	Major Federal Equal Employment Opportunity Laws	
EQUAL EMPLOYMENT ACTS	**MAJOR PROHIBITIONS**	**JURISDICTION**
TITLE VII OF THE CIVIL RIGHTS ACT OF 1964 As amended in 1972, amended again in 1978 (by the Pregnancy Discrimination Act) and 1991	Outlaws discrimination in employment based on race, color, religion, sex, pregnancy, or national origin.	Employers with fifteen or more employees; unions with fifteen or more members; employment agencies; union hiring halls; institutions of higher education; federal, state, and local governments.
AGE DISCRIMINATION IN EMPLOYMENT ACT OF 1967	Outlaws discrimination against those who are 40 and above.	Employers with twenty or more employees; unions with twenty-five or more members; employment agencies; federal, state, and local governments.
EQUAL PAY ACT OF 1963	Outlaws discrimination in pay based on the sex of the worker.	Employers engaged in interstate commerce and most employees of federal, state, and local governments.
VIETNAM ERA VETERANS READJUSTMENT ACT OF 1974	Outlaws discrimination against Vietnam-era veterans.	Employers with federal contracts of $10,000 or more.

Sources of violations

As sections 703(*a*) and (*d*) indicate, Title VII covers all aspects of the employment relationship, including all actions by an employer that adversely affect an individual's status or opportunities because of that person's membership in a protected group. Title VII specifies the affected classes. Discrimination on the basis of a person's sex, race, or color is the most common violation. However, discrimination because of one's national origin or the national origin of one's parents is also a violation.[7] Laws and amendments passed since 1964 also outlaw discrimination against a disabled person[8] or a pregnant woman,[9] provided that the person can perform the job. Likewise, an employer cannot discriminate because of one's religion.[10] In fact, an employer must accommodate an employee's religious observances or practices as long as they do not impose an undue hardship on the employer.

Favorable discrimination

Discrimination among workers on the basis of their effort, performance, or another work-related criterion remains both *permissible* and *advisable*. Managers and HR specialists are paid to discriminate on the basis of performance but not

| Figure 4-4 | Excerpts of Title VII of the Civil Rights Act of 1964, as Amended |

Section 703(a). It shall be an unlawful employment practice for an employer—

(1) to fail or refuse to hire or to discharge any individual or otherwise to discriminate against any individual with respect to his compensation, terms, conditions, or privileges of employment, because of such individual's race, color, religion, sex, or national origin; or

(2) to limit, segregate, classify his employees or applicants for employment in any way which would deprive or tend to deprive any individual of employment opportunities or otherwise adversely affect his status as an employee, because of such individual's race, color, religion, sex, or national origin.

(*d*) It shall be an unlawful employment practice of any employer . . . controlling . . . training programs to discriminate against any individual because of his race, color, religion, sex, or national origin in admission to, or employment in, any program established to provide apprenticeship or other training.

on the basis of someone's membership in a protected class. EEO laws *do* permit employers to reward outstanding performers and penalize unacceptable productivity. EEO laws require only that rewards and punishment be based on work-related issues—not unrelated issues such as a person's sex, race, or religion or other prohibited criteria. Not only do these laws prohibit intentional discrimination against the members of a protected class arising from evil intent or motive, they also prohibit disparate treatment and disparate impact even when such discrimination is unintentional.

Adverse and
unequal treatment

Disparate treatment. *Disparate treatment* occurs when the members of a protected class receive unequal treatment because of their membership in that class. If AT&T regularly hired female applicants as telephone operators without letting them apply for higher-paid and more skilled craft jobs, the result would be unequal or disparate treatment. Unequal treatment also occurs when different standards are applied to different groups. For example, an employer who refuses to hire a woman with small children because the children may cause her to miss work but hires a man with young children is applying a different standard.

Adverse and
unequal impact

Disparate impact. *Disparate impact* occurs when the results of an employer's actions have a different and negative impact on one or more protected classes. Even if there is no intention to discriminate, when an employer develops a uniform standard and applies it equally to all classes, the results may be discriminatory. Consider the comments of Gerald H. Trautman, former chairman of the board for the Greyhound Corporation, when he observed that the federal government:

Greyhound
Corporation

... went after us in San Francisco to eliminate our safety rule which required any applicant, male or female, for the driver's position to be five foot seven. They took us to court and wanted us to give up the rule. But we finally decided it just wasn't worth the fight. . . . The first four people who were under five foot seven . . . flunked the test. They weren't able to handle the bus. But we don't have that rule anymore.[11]

When a standard discriminates against one or more protected groups, the burden historically falls on the employer to prove that the standard is necessary. At Greyhound, management thought the standard was reasonable since it would ensure that drivers were big enough to change large tires when flats disabled buses. However, the height standard discriminated against women and men of Asian descent, since these groups tend to be shorter than men of European or African heritage. The treatment was equal, but the impact was discriminatory. In *Griggs v. Duke Power Company*,[12] a similar outcome was ruled on by the U.S. Supreme Court.

Duke Power

The Duke Power Company had a long-standing policy of requiring a high school degree for all jobs except those in the labor pool. As a result, the labor pool consisted mostly of men of African-American heritage who were denied an opportunity for better jobs at the utility because they did not have a high school degree. The requirement for a high school diploma and a general intelligence test were challenged in court. Duke Power Company could not show that a high school diploma was necessary to perform many jobs or that the test bore any relationship to on-the-job performance.

Wards Cove
v. Antonio

Albemarle
v. Moody

Regardless of the company's intent, the impact of its actions was ruled to be discriminatory because the degree requirement and the test tended to have an unequal impact on one protected class: African-Americans. The test and degree requirements were disallowed even though they were applied equally to all applicants. In the Griggs and Greyhound examples, the burden of proof fell on the employer. But in 1990 the Supreme Court weakened these standards in *Wards Cove v. Antonio*. There the court held that disparate impact, even if supported statistically, is not a violation if the employer can put forward a legitimate reason or business justification.[13] The burden now falls on covered employees to show that specific practices are discriminatory.

When a disparate impact results—even when business reasons justify the result—the HR department should find other methods. In *Albemarle Paper Company v. Moody*[14] the company used business reasons for its actions. However, the U.S. Supreme Court found that discrimination resulted because the company relied on employment tests that were discriminatory and could not satisfactorily prove that the tests were related to the jobs for which people were being hired. The implication for managers and HR specialists is that all actions must be related to a business purpose and not be discriminatory in intent or result. If job-related actions discriminate against a protected class, those actions should be discontinued in favor of nondiscriminatory approaches.

Even when the overall impact on a protected class is nondiscriminatory, this may not constitute an effective defense against charges of discrimination. In *Connecticut v. Teal* the Supreme Court ruled that every individual employee is protected against discriminatory treatment and practices.

Pregnancy Discrimination Act

Even though pregnancy affects a protected group, the U.S. Supreme Court ruled in *General Electric v. Gilbert*[15] that the denial of pregnancy-related benefits *did not* violate Title VII. Congress subsequently amended Title VII with the *Pregnancy Discrimination Act* of 1978, and employers could no longer require women to take a leave of absence or resign because of pregnancy. As long as the woman was still capable of doing her job, the employer could not discriminate in regard to benefits or other conditions of employment. The implications for pregnancy-related leaves are listed in Figure 4-5.

Harassment. Perhaps the most difficult form of discrimination to deal with is *harassment*. It occurs whenever a hostile work environment is created because of one's membership in a protected group. Sexual harassment is an example. In a survey of 607 women by the National Association for Female Executives, 60 percent reported having experienced sexual harassment.[16] According to the director general of the International Labor Organization based in Geneva, Switzerland:

Sexual harassment

> Research findings in 23 industrialized countries around the globe demonstrated that sexual harassment is a pervasive problem affecting a considerable proportion of working women.[17]

| Figure 4-5 | **Guidelines for Pregnancy Leave** |

The *Pregnancy Discrimination Act* of 1978 amended Title VII of the 1964 *Civil Rights Act*. As a result, covered employers may not:

- Treat disabilities related to pregnancy or childbirth differently from other types of disabilities or medical conditions.

- Use any employment practice that discriminates against applicants or employees because of pregnancy, childbirth, abortion, or a planned adoption.

- Apply leave standards for child care that differ from those for other nonmedical leaves.

- Withhold any fringe benefits to a woman because of an abortion or planned abortion, except that employer-provided health insurance need not cover the expense of an abortion unless performed to protect the mother's life.

U.S. courts prohibit sexual harassment, which has been defined as follows:

Sexual harassment defined

Unwelcome sexual advances, requests for sexual favors, and other verbal or physical conduct of a sexual nature constitute sexual harassment when (1) submission to such conduct is made either explicitly or implicitly a term or condition of an individual's employment, (2) submission to or rejection of such conduct by an individual is used as the basis for employment decisions affecting such individual, or (3) such conduct has the purpose or affect of unreasonably interfering with an individual's work performance or creating an intimidating, hostile, or offensive working environment.[18]

To win a sexual harassment suit, the person being discriminated against "need not prove that his or her tangible productivity has declined as a result of the harassment," Justice Ginsburg wrote in her concurring opinion for the U.S. Supreme Court in *Harris v. Forklift Systems.* All the plaintiff need show is that the harassment changed the working conditions and made "it more difficult to do the job."[19] As one writer observed, "Sexual harassment is not really about sex. It's about power—more to the point, the abuse of power."[20] Moreover, harassment extends beyond sexual harassment and includes harassment based on race, religion, national origin, age, and disability.

The U.S. Supreme Court expanded the concept of harassment to cover "hostile environment," a term that takes us from the casting couch to such offenses as persistent telling of dirty jokes and pin-up girls on factory walls. This enlargement of the law has itself been steadily enlarged by the Equal Employment Opportunity Commission (EEOC), which has issued rulings applying the hostile-environment concept to racial, religious, and national-origin minorities, plus the aged and the handicapped.[21]

One difficulty with allegations of racial or sexual harassment is proof, since cases often hinge on one person's word against another's.[22] As a result, it is believed that most of these offenses go unreported. Another concern is the ease with which harassment can occur, especially when the wrongdoer believes that his or her actions are made playfully or in jest. Even people in nonsupervisory positions should realize that sexual or racial comments may form the basis for legal action regardless of the "actual" intent. Given the reputation and career damage harassment charges can cause, countersuits by those accused are becoming more common.[23]

HR departments usually develop and communicate a strongly worded policy stating that racial or sexual harassment violates company rules. Proactive

Training

departments "are using awareness-training programs to help employees understand the pain and indignity of harassment. Such programs, if they are comprehensive and used aggressively, can be highly effective. The cost ranges from $5,000 for a small company to $200,000 for a large one."[24]

Managers and others who harass employees can expect harsh discipline and often termination of their employment. Finally, the policy directive usually indicates what actions an offended party should take. Strong action is needed by the HR department because of the unfair nature of harassment and the U.S.

Supreme Court's view that the employer can be held liable, as it ruled in *Meritor Savings Bank v. Vinson*.[25]

Exceptions. Although sexual or racial harassment is never permitted, Title VII and the courts do permit some exceptions to equal employment opportunity. These exceptions include bona fide occupational qualifications, seniority systems, preferential quota systems, refusal to hire illegal aliens, and religious organizations as employers.

BFOQ

A *bona fide occupational qualification* (BFOQ) exists when discrimination against a protected group is reasonably necessary to the normal operation of an organization. A preference by the employer or long-standing tradition is insufficient, and race is generally not considered a BFOQ. There must be a "justified business reason." For example, in *Diaz v. Pan American World Airways, Inc.*, Pan Am argued that hiring only female flight attendants was a BFOQ. The courts found no reason why male flight attendants could not perform the same functions and ruled against Pan Am.

Seniority

In labor agreements negotiated between employers and unions, *seniority clauses* are common. These provisions usually require that promotions, pay, and other conditions of employment be preferentially affected by how long a worker has been employed. When the senior workers are predominantly of one race or sex, the application of seniority may lead to a disparate impact on those in protected classes. However, Title VII anticipates this issue with the following section:

> *Section 703(h)*. Notwithstanding any other provision of this title, it shall not be an unlawful employment practice for an employer to apply different standards of compensation, or different terms, conditions, or privileges of employment pursuant to a bona fide seniority or merit system.

In *International Brotherhood of Teamsters v. United States*,[26] the U.S. Supreme Court upheld this section of Title VII, provided that the seniority system was not created to discriminate against a protected class. Furthermore, the seniority system must apply equally to all the people covered by it.

Quotas

A third exception is *preferential quota systems*. These approaches reserve a proportion of job openings, promotions, or other employment opportunities for members of protected classes who might have been discriminated against previously. When an employer recognizes that members of a protected class have unequal representation in a particular job classification, that employer may develop a plan to correct the imbalance. Kaiser Aluminum & Chemical Corporation's Gramercy, Louisiana, plant provides a landmark example.

Kaiser's workforce at the plant was 14.8 percent black, and the labor force in the area was 39 percent black. But in the skilled and higher-paying craft jobs, less than 2 percent of the workers were black. Kaiser's management entered into a nationwide collective bargaining

Kaiser Aluminum

agreement with the United Steelworkers. An on-the-job training program for craft jobs was established. It was decided that the ratio of entry into the program would be one white and one black until minority representation equaled the same percentage of minority group members found in the area's civilian labor force: 39 percent.

Eventually this preferential quota system was challenged in the courts by Brian F. Weber, an employee of the plant who believed the 1:1 ratio discriminated against him. The U.S. Supreme Court ruled in *United Steelworkers of America and Kaiser Aluminum & Chemical Corporation v. Weber* that preferential systems would help undo the effects of past discrimination. Although not every preferential quota approach is sure to be legal, such an approach may offer a defense against allegations of discrimination when its purpose is to remedy past discrimination.[27]

Another exception comes from the *Immigration Reform and Control Act* of 1986. This federal law imposes civil and criminal penalties on employees who knowingly hire illegal aliens. Thus, even though the *Civil Rights Act* prohibits discrimination on the basis of national origin, it does not protect illegal aliens. To comply with the act, HR departments need to verify citizenship or see a work permit from the Immigration and Naturalization Service. Unfortunately, this law has spawned a large market for fraudulent documents in Los Angeles, New York, Chicago, Miami, and other cities with large populations of illegal immigrants, leading one writer to characterize the situation as a "turnstile on our border."[28]

At the same time, employers risk an accusation of discrimination on the basis of national origin if they discriminate against a person because that person has a foreign accent.

Accents and discrimination

Hollis Nurse is a Trinidad-born American who twice called Malaga Bank in Palos Verdes Estates, California, about a bank teller opening, only to be told that the job was filled. But when his friend made similar inquiries on the same day, the job was open.

Then Hollis Nurse realized that his friend spoke without an accent, whereas Hollis himself had one. "Nurse filed a complaint with the Equal Employment Opportunity Commission alleging that the bank discriminated on the basis of national origin. 'It's unfair to judge a person just by the way he sounds,' he charges."[29]

EEO overseas

International employment is covered by Title VII of the *Civil Rights Act* of 1991. Ali Boureslan worked in Dhahran, Saudi Arabia, for Aramco, a U.S. company. He alleged that he was discharged because of his race, religion, and national origin and was harassed by religious, ethnic, and racial slurs.[30] In *EEOC and Boureslan v. Aramco Co.*, the U.S. Supreme Court ruled in 1991 that Title VII does not offer "extraterritorial protection" when U.S. citizens work abroad. Later that year, the 1991 Civil Rights Act amended Title VII with a "provision extending civil rights protection against job discrimination to millions of U.S. citizens working in foreign countries for American-controlled companies."[31] As a result, managers and HR professionals must be concerned about employment laws in dealing with international employees. Not only do most developed nations have detailed employment laws that cover employees working in their countries, a company's ability to attract top international talent is shaped by the treatment it provides its employees. Foreign companies doing business in the United States must comply with U.S. laws regardless of their home-country practices.

Religious discrimination is permitted among churches and other religious organizations for their religion-related employment needs. For example, a Catholic school can discriminate against non-Catholics when hiring instructors to teach classes in relgion.

Employer retaliation. As with most employment laws, it is a separate violation to retaliate *in any way* against those who exercise their Title VII rights. Individuals who file charges, testify, or otherwise participate in a Title VII action are protected by the law. If a supervisor tries to "get even" with an employee who filed charges, the act is violated. The usual remedies are reinstatement (if a discharge was involved) and back pay to cover lost wages.

Enforcement. The five-member *Equal Employment Opportunity Commission* (EEOC) enforces Title VII through its offices in major cities. Congress expanded the authority of the commission by passing the *Equal Employment Opportunity Act* of 1972. Under this act, the EEOC was empowered to initiate court action against noncomplying businesses.

Figure 4-6 summarizes the EEOC's enforcement procedures. Enforcement begins when a charge is filed by the aggrieved person, someone acting on behalf of that person, or one of the EEOC commissioners. In states with fair employment laws, charges can be filed with the state agency. If charges are filed with the EEOC, it defers jurisdiction to qualified state or local agencies for sixty days. These jurisdictions are known as *deferral jurisdictions.*

Deferral jurisdictions

Charges are filed directly with the EEOC in *nondeferral jurisdictions,* or jurisdictions without qualified agencies. The accused parties are notified within ten days by the EEOC once charges have been filed. The EEOC then conducts an investigation and decides whether the charges constitute a violation. If there is reason to believe that a violation has occurred, the EEOC seeks a *conciliation agreement,* which is a negotiated settlement acceptable to the EEOC and all the parties involved. Its acceptance closes the case.

Conciliaton

If conciliation fails, a suit can be brought by the EEOC when the wrongdoer is a private employer or by the U.S. attorney general when the charges are against a public employer. Individuals may file suit within ninety days once a *right-to-sue letter* has been issued by the EEOC. A right-to-sue letter is granted when:

Right-to-sue letter

- The EEOC dismisses the charges.

- No suit is brought after the EEOC fails to obtain a conciliation agreement.

| Figure 4-6 | **EEOC Enforcement Procedure** |

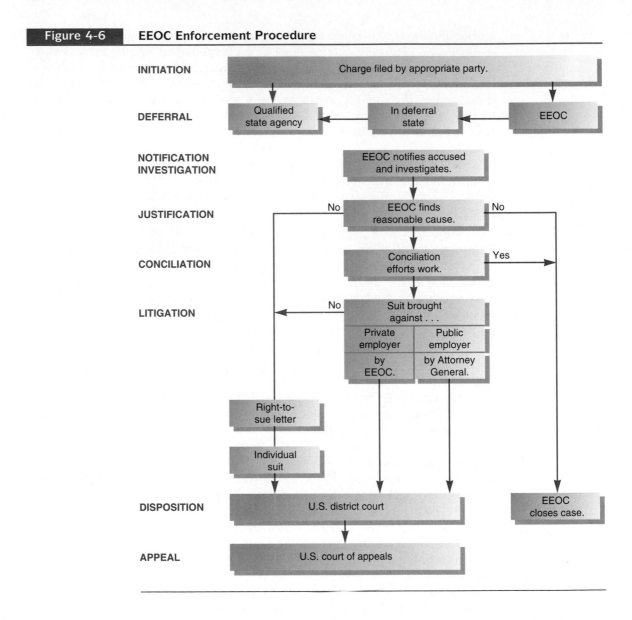

Remedies.   Title VII clearly acknowledges that remedies can include a wide range of penalties.

Court remedies

Section 203(g). If the court finds that the respondent has intentionally engaged in . . . an unlawful employment practice charged in the complaint, the court may enjoin the respondent from engaging in such unlawful employment practice, and order such affirmative action as may be appropriate, which may include, but is not limited to, reinstatement or hiring of employees, with or without back pay (payable by the employer, employment agency, or labor organization that is responsible for the unlawful employment practice), or any other equitable relief as the court deems appropriate.

Whether compliance results from a conciliation agreement or a court order, remedies have similar characteristics. In the example described earlier in this chapter, AT&T agreed to:

AT&T's remedies

■ Cease and desist from practices that caused disparate treatment or impact.

■ Hire, train, and promote those in protected classes who were allegedly discriminated against.

■ Make financial payments to compensate for past discrimination in order to "make whole" those affected.

As the AT&T example points out, remedies typically include an agreement by the company to cease and desist from discriminatory practices. Past patterns and practices of discrimination against entire groups (for example, women and minorities at AT&T) may have to be corrected with affirmative action plans that include special hiring, training, and promoting quotas and programs. If any financially measurable harm has been done to those in protected classes, the employer often must pay financial restitution to "make whole" those who were affected. This requirement entails making up losses suffered because of discriminatory actions. Reinstatement with no loss of seniority and full payment of back wages are common *make-whole remedies* in illegal discharge cases, for example.

Make-whole remedies

Under the Civil Rights Act of 1991, victims of intentional discrimination can pursue punitive damages in addition to compensatory ones. Damage awards can range from $50,000 for employers with 15 or more employees to $300,000 for employers with 500 or more employees, and legal fees can be awarded to the prevailing party. Perhaps most damaging to employers, the burden of proving business necessity as a defense has shifted to the employer when a statistically disproportionate impact on women and minorities is shown by a plaintiff.

Shoney's restaurants

Shoney's, a Nashville-based restaurant chain, employs about 30,000 people in more than 1800 restaurants. For years the company allegedly had a policy of giving African-Americans lower-paying jobs and not allowing more than two African-Americans to wait on customers in any one shift. As a result of an EEOC suit, Shoney's has agreed to pay $105 million to employees and job applicants who claimed they were discriminated against in hiring and promotions and were harassed on the job. The settlement earned Shoney's the dubious distinction, previously held by AT&T, of losing the largest class-action racial discrimination suit in U.S. history.

"The company said . . . it will take an $85.7 million charge in the fourth quarter, wiping out its . . . profits. As many as 75,000 to 80,000 people could be eligible to collect damages.

"Shoney's has agreed to invest $92 million over a three-year period in minority-owned franchises."[32]

Even when no discharges are involved, monetary adjustments may be required to compensate those who were discriminated against. When funds are paid to those affected, the company receives little benefit. Therefore, most HR professionals try to translate the financial penalties into specified amounts that will be spent on training those who were discriminated against. This way the company gets some return for its outlays.

Americans with Disabilities Act

In 1990, Congress passed and the president signed the *Americans with Disabilities Act* (ADA), which prohibits employers from discriminating against the disabled in employment decisions. A disabled person is defined as someone who has a physical or mental impairment that substantially limits him or her in a major life activity. It also includes those who have a record of such impairment. For example, a person who has recovered from a heart attack but is discriminated against would be considered to have a *record* of an impairment. Employers are required to undertake "reasonable accommodations" to adjust the work environment to meet the special needs of the disabled. Installing a ramp for a wheelchair-bound person is one example; providing a no-smoking area for an employee who is allergic to smoke is another.

The law does not require employers to hire a disabled worker unless that person is qualified to do the job. If accommodations would impose an undue hardship on the employer, such as great difficulty or expense, the employer may reject the handicapped person. The law also specifically excludes from coverage current illegal drug users, homosexuals, people with sexual disorders, and compulsive gamblers. Alcoholics and HIV-infected individuals are covered as long as they do not pose a direct health or safety threat to others. Recent court rulings have also extended protection to severely obese individuals.[33]

The differently abled

Simply put, a "differently abled" person cannot be discriminated against in employment if that person can perform the essential job duties when "reasonably accommodated" by the employer. When discrimination does occur, the enforcement provisions of Title VII of the Civil Rights Act will be applied by the EEOC.[34]

EEO lawsuit

The Equal Employment Opportunity Commission's first litigation under ADA resulted in a $572,000 award to a director at a security firm who had been discharged after he was diagnosed with terminal brain cancer.[35]

Age Discrimination in Employment

Equal opportunity is sometimes denied because of age. To prevent age discrimination, the *Age Discrimination in Employment Act* of 1967 was passed by Congress. As amended, it prohibits discrimination against those age 40 and above when a person's age is a factor in employment-related decisions. The 1986 amendments to the act eliminate the mandatory retirement age. In 1990 the law was amended again by the *Older Workers Benefit Protection Act*, which prohibits discrimination in employee benefits. The law specifies that employers use an "equal benefit or equal cost" standard when granting benefits; this requires that older workers receive benefits at least equal to those of younger workers unless the cost of providing for an older worker would be more than that for a younger one. The law also sets minimum standards employers must meet to create valid waivers of age claims, which are often signed by older workers in return for early retirement or other benefits when they leave an employer. When the waivers comply with the act, they shield the employer against age discrimination suits.[36]

Ironically, older workers may be the best employees under some circumstances, especially if the findings of one research project are representative:

Research summary

> A four-year study done among telephone reservationists at Days Inn "found that the older workers were just as efficient as their younger colleagues, cost less to recruit and train, and were far more likely to put up with the demands of the job. After the first year only 29.9% of the youngsters were still around, vs. 87.3% of the employees over 50. Even the seniors' health care costs were about the same as the younger workers'; the authors of the study suggest that's because older workers still on the job rank above average in health and tend to have fewer dependents."[37]

As with Title VII, bona fide accupational qualifications are permitted, but they are extremely limited. For example, a casting director can discriminate against older actors in hiring for children's roles.

Enforcement is handled by the EEOC and follows the procedures outlined for Title VII violations. However, federal law requires that an attempt to achieve voluntary compliance be made by the government before legal action is taken. If voluntary compliance efforts fail, a suit can be filed in federal court. Since courts have wide latitude in deciding remedies and since litigating the issue is expensive even if the company wins, HR departments often find that voluntary compliance is less costly.

Equal Pay Act

The growing number of households headed by women and the obvious discrimination involved in paying men more than women are paid led Congress to pass the *Equal Pay Act* in 1963. This act requires employers to pay equal wages for equal work. Jobs are considered equal when both sexes work at the same place and their jobs demand substantially the same skill, effort, and responsibility and have similar working conditions. When one of these factors differs, the employer is justified in paying different wages. As Figure 4-7 lightheartedly illustrates, the greater effort of Santas justifies a higher wage rate. If male Santas had been paid more than female Santas, a violation would have existed. The figure also shows that equal work is determined by an examination of job duties, not simply job titles.

Santa beats
Easter Bunny

The Equal Pay Act does permit employers to reward workers for seniority, individual merit, and performance. As long as seniority and merit pay differentials are not based on the sex of the worker, they are legal. Companies also can pay employees according to their productivity, paying for each unit produced, for example. As with other employment laws, those who exercise their rights under the Equal Pay Act are protected against employer retaliation.

The Equal Pay Act of 1963 may be enforced by the federal government or state agencies. In the absence of state laws and agencies, the EEOC handles equal pay violations. Its enforcement procedures are the same as those applied in age discrimination cases except that the Equal Pay Act does not require voluntary conciliation before a suit is brought against the employer. Since courts have wide discretion under this act, they have granted back-pay awards to thousands of workers.

Suit summary

A federal court found that the Wheaton Glass Company had violated the Equal Pay Act. The court ordered Wheaton to pay $900,000 in back pay and interest to 2000 female employees.[38]

| Figure 4-7 | **Sad News for the Easter Bunny** |

The Easter Bunny lost its sex discrimination dispute with Santa Claus yesterday.

Because Santa works harder, keeps longer hours and sees more children each year, he's worth 90 cents more an hour than department store bunnies, a California deputy labor commission ruled.

. . . After a two-hour hearing in San Jose conducted by Commissioner Andrew Evans of the state's Division of Labor Standards, . . . he found no evidence of discrimination.

"There are some basic differences in the job," Evans noted. "Santa works harder."

He found that Santa sees more children and is twice as successful as the Easter Bunny in the business of selling parents snapshots of their children on his lap.

However, Evans said, he found that a man or a woman who suits up as Santa earns the same wage; and a male and female Easter Bunny earn equal pay, even though it's less than Santa's.

Source: San Francisco Chronicle, Feb. 25, 1976, p. 5. Used by permission.

Vietnam Era Veterans Readjustment Act

The *Vietnam Era Veterans Readjustment Act* of 1974 is more limited in scope than other federal EEO laws. Its major provisions are summarized in Figure 4-3. As Vietnam-era veterans were discharged from military service, many found it difficult to obtain employment. To assist their integration into the private economy, Congress passed the Vietnam Era Veterans Readjustment Act of 1974. The act requires government contractors with contracts of $10,000 or more to provide equal employment opportunity to Vietnam-era veterans. Violations can lead to the loss of government contracts. HR departments help ensure compliance by actively seeking applications from veterans through contacts at local military bases and work with veterans' affairs offices at large universities.

Honeywell, Inc.

Honeywell, Inc.'s, efforts go even further than the law requires. As a proactive move, the company appointed a "Vietnam veterans program coordinator" to help workers who are veterans deal with psychological problems and advance their careers. The coordinator works to get vets hired, organizes family counseling sessions, and publishes a company newsletter for veterans.[39]

Family and Medical Leave Act

Another employment-related limitation on managers and HR departments comes from the *Family and Medical Leave Act* (FMLA) of 1993. Though not specifically targeted at ending discrimination, this act seeks to assure working Americans the right to take unpaid leave under specified circumstances instead of facing permanent replacement. Interestingly, though many employers in the past would permanently replace an employee who sought extended leave, research suggests that granting leaves may be less costly to the organization.[40]

Required leaves

The FMLA requires employers with fifty or more employees to grant eligible employees up to twelve weeks of unpaid leave during any twelve-month period. Requested leaves must be authorized for the birth, adoption, or placement of a foster child with an employee. Leaves also must be granted when a spouse, child, parent, or employee experiences a serious health condition that prevents the employee from performing his or her job duties. In addition, the employer must maintain the employee's group health-care coverage under the same conditions that would apply if the employee were not on leave. Finally, the employee is entitled to the same job or an equivalent one with equivalent pay, benefits, and working conditions on returning from the leave.[41]

Administered by the U.S. Department of Labor's Wage and Hour Division, the FMLA permits employees to use their leave in one block or intermittently.

▶ State and Local Fair Employment Practices

FEPs

State and local laws, which are often called *fair employment practices* (FEPs), are the second major source of EEO laws. They are limited to employers within the jurisdiction of state or local governments. Although important to the companies that are covered, fair employment practices are too numerous and varied to discuss here in detail. In general, however, their objectives are similar to those of federal acts: to provide equal opportunity. They do this in two ways. One is to extend state or local protection to groups exempted from federal laws. For example, some jurisdictions prohibit discrimination on the basis of marital status or sexual preference.

> The Florida Commission on Human Rights (FCHR) has ruled that a corrections officer was unlawfully discharged . . . on the basis of handicap discrimination. The decision is unusual because the handicap was "transsexualism." The FCHR ruled 8–1 to order reinstatement. The Jacksonville City Council recently approved a settlement agreement in the case which includes reinstatement of the corrections officer and payment of $149,500.[42]

The second way is by sharing jurisdiction with the federal government in deferral jurisdictions. Except in circumstances where fair employment standards cover omissions in federal laws or when federal agencies have agreed to defer to state agencies, federal law is supreme when conflicts exist.

State versus
federal laws

Enforcement and remedies under state and local laws also parallel federal procedures. The administration of these practices is typically the responsibility of state or local fair employment practices commissions, which are normally found in the executive branch of the state or local government. In nearly all situations compliance with federal laws results in compliance with state and local fair employment practices. Nevertheless, experienced managers and HR practitioners stay informed about state and local laws.

▶ Executive Orders

Presidential
prerogatives

The largest employer and consumer in the United States is the executive branch of the federal government. By applying equal employment opportunity standards to itself, it sets an example for other employers.[43] By requiring its contractors to follow equal employment rules, the federal government can influence many employment relationships. Toward these ends, different presidents have issued *executive orders,* as described in Figure 4-8. The purpose and content of these orders parallel the federal equal employment laws already discussed. Like the Vietnam Era Veterans Readjustment Act, executive orders have a narrow jurisdiction, applying only to federal government agencies and contractors.

Figure 4-8	Executive Orders Designed to Ensure Equal Employment Opportunity	

EXECUTIVE ORDER	MAJOR PROHIBITIONS	JURISDICTION
E.O. 11246	Outlaws discrimination in employment based on race, color, religion, or national origin.	Government contractors
E.O. 11375	Revises E.O. 11246 to prohibit sex discrimination.	Government contractors
E.O. 11478	Outlaws discrimination in employment based on race, color, religion, national origin, sex, political affiliation, marital status, or physical handicap.	Government agencies and the U.S. Postal Service
E.O. 11141	Outlaws discrimination in employment based on age.	Government agencies Government contractors

Government Agencies

Federal agencies are required to provide equal employment opportunity, which means they are prohibited from discriminating on the basis of race, color, religion, national origin, sex, political affiliation, marital status, and physical disability under Executive Order 11478. These agencies are also prohibited from discriminating on the basis of age under Executive Order 11141. Under both orders, those who think they have been mistreated may file complaints and have the discrimination ended by the offending agency.

Government Contractors

Managers and HR specialists are affected by executive orders when their employer is a government contractor. Government contractors must abide by all equal employment laws: Title VII of the Civil Rights Act, the Americans with Disabilities Act, the Age Discrimination in Employment Act, the Equal Pay Act, the Family and Medical Leave Act, and the Vietnam Era Veterans Readjustment Act. In addition, they must comply with Executive Order 11246, as revised by Executive Order 11375, which outlaws discrimination that is based on race, color, religion, national origin, or sex. Age discrimination by these employers also is illegal according to Executive Order 11141.

Government contractors are significantly affected by Executive Order 11246. This presidential decree applies to an entire company even though only one plant or division sells to the federal government. The order requires that government contractors take affirmative action—systematic steps to ensure that past discrimination is remedied and that further discrimination does not occur. To enforce this requirement, government contractors must file affirmative action plans with the Office of Federal Contract Compliance Programs (OFCCP), which is in the U.S. Department of Labor. The OFCCP devotes most of its efforts to reviewing contractors' affirmative action plans and visiting sites to interview managerial and nonmanagerial employees. Violation of OFCCP rules and regulations can lead to the loss of government contracts, although this penalty is seldom imposed.

OFCCP

Executive Orders and Equal Employment Laws

Executive orders overlap federal and state acts. This duplication exists for two reasons. First, some federal equal employment acts specifically exempt agencies of the federal government, and state laws do not apply to federal employees. To assure federal employees of equal employment opportunities, executive orders were passed to fill the void. Second, since government agencies and contractors spend public funds, they are subject to close examination. Under executive orders, the federal government can demand compliance whether a charge is filed or not. Compliance before charges are brought against a company often requires government contractors to submit affirmative action programs.

▶ Affirmative Action

Affirmative action programs

Affirmative action refers to employers' efforts to rectify the results of past discrimination. Affirmative action programs are written systematic plans that outline goals for hiring, training, promoting, and compensating groups protected by federal EEO laws, fair employment practices, and executive orders. They exist for several reasons. From a practical standpoint, employers seldom benefit from excluding people who belong to a particular group. Excluding an entire class of workers, such as women or minorities, limits the labor pool from which an employer can draw. And with the growing diversity of the workforce, the majority of applicants will soon come from protected classes. Open discrimination can also lead to negative public relations, boycotts by consumers, and government intervention. To ensure that such discrimination does not occur, employers may develop affirmative action programs voluntarily.

Voluntary compliance is also a practical way to correct past discrimination and avoid costly and time-consuming legal battles. As United Steelworkers of America and Kaiser Aluminum & Chemical Corporation v. Weber illustrated, voluntary affirmative action programs are a legal way to remedy past discrimination. Moreover, the ruling in the Weber case suggests that voluntary plans may constitute a defense against "reverse discrimination" suits when they are based on self-analyses that identify and seek to rectify racial imbalances.

Sometimes compliance is the best course even when a company thinks its past actions were legal because time in litigation, legal costs, and adverse publicity can be minimized. At other times compliance results from a consent decree, which is a legally binding, judicially sanctioned agreement to undertake specific actions. AT&T's massive affirmative action plan began with the consent decree it signed with the EEOC, the Department of Justice, and the Department of Labor.[44]

AT&T was in a delicate position. As the largest private employer in the United States at the time of the suit, it made an attractive target for the government. The EEOC's victory put large and small employers on notice that the government was serious about enforcement. AT&T recognized that its ability to get rate increases on long-distance calls might have been delayed for years if it had fought the EEOC all the way through court appeals.

Since every employer with fifteen or more employees is covered under Title VII of the 1964 Civil Rights Act, as amended, virtually all companies should have some form of affirmative action program. EEOC compliance is usually the responsibility of the HR department, which develops a plan to achieve the organization's affirmative action goals in the least disruptive manner.

Affirmative Action Issues

The design and implementation of an affirmative action plan may lead the HR department to take actions that employees and managers do not like. For example, an aggressive plan may cause managers or the HR department to hire and promote qualifiable workers rather than qualified ones. A qualifiable worker is one who does not currently possess all the required knowledge, skills, or abilities to do a job but through additional training and experience will become qualified. Other employees—such as Brian Weber in United Steelworkers v. Weber—may resent being passed over for a qualifiable worker, especially if they believe themselves to be qualified already. Managers may resent the loss of the authority to make final hiring, firing, and other employment decisions. The issues of reverse discrimination and its impact on management merit further discussion.

Qualifiable workers

Reverse discrimination.   The use of affirmative action plans has led to charges of reverse discrimination against employers. These charges usually arise when an employer seeks to hire or promote a member of a protected class over an equally (or better) qualified candidate who is not a member of that class. For example, if an employer has an affirmative action program that gives preference to women over men when promotions occur, a qualified man may sue the employer and claim that he was discriminated against because of his sex. Since equal employment laws prohibit discrimination on the basis of sex, courts have entertained such suits in the past.[45]

Defense against reverse discrimination

Charges of reverse discrimination put HR departments in a difficult position. On the one hand, the department is responsible for eliminating discrimination. On the other hand, giving preference to the members of a protected class (such as women) raises questions about whether the department is fair. Although preferential treatment will always raise questions of fairness, the U.S. Supreme Court has ruled in *United Steelworkers v. Weber* that such treatment is not discriminatory when it is done to meet the objectives of a bona fide affirmative action program. Even when such programs are voluntary and are not required by law or by the courts, preferential treatment for the purpose of meeting goals is permissible and not in violation of Title VII of the 1964 Civil Rights Act.

Managers' reactions.   The implementation of an affirmative action program may cause managers to feel a loss of authority. They may lose the right to make final hiring and promotion decisions because the HR department may overrule them to achieve the objectives of the plan. In time, supervisors may believe that members of protected classes are getting preferential treatment, and this may cause them to feel resentment. This resentment may be particularly dangerous since supervisory actions are a major cause of EEO violations. If workers also sense an element of reverse discrimination, conflicts may arise and lessen the effectiveness of the work group.

Educating
supervisors

To overcome the potentially damaging side effects of affirmative action plans, HR specialists must educate managers, particularly first-line supervisors. Training programs, seminars, and explanations of HR decisions that affect protected classes must be given to managers. Otherwise, their support and understanding of affirmative action are likely to be low, and as a result the perceived quality of the work environment may decline.

Development of Affirmative Action Plans

Affirmative action plans are situational. Their design depends on the specific discriminatory practices involved. For example, when an employer has a high number of members of a protected class doing a particular job, concentration exists. *Concentration* occurs when the proportion of protected class members holding a particular job is greater than their availability in the labor market. When AT&T signed its consent decree, for example, women represented less than half the labor market but held more than 98 percent of all telephone operator jobs. *Underutilization* is the opposite. It occurs when protected class members are underrepresented in particular jobs compared with their availability in the workforce. The scarcity of women in middle-level management positions at AT&T at the time of the consent decree is an example. Thus the affirmative action strategy used by an organization must consider the extent of concentration or underutilization.

Concentration

Underutilization

The nature of the program also depends on the organization's growth rate. A slow-growing employer uses affirmative action strategies that differ from those of a growth company with greater opportunities for promotion. Similarly, the reasons for an affirmative action plan influence its final form. For example, a large government contractor's program must meet every agency regulation, whereas a totally voluntary program need only meet the employer's objectives and timetable.

Regardless of these situational variables, resistance to the plan is likely on the part of those who fear reverse discrimination and managers who believe that their authority may be diminished. To gain acceptance for the plan, an educational strategy is needed to explain affirmative action to employees and supervisors before the plan is developed and implemented. Preplan development may begin with the creation of an affirmative action advisory committee that includes line managers, workers, and staff members from the human resource department. If it is well chosen, the committee can reflect the concerns of others in the organization. It may even conduct a survey to learn about the perceptions held by others. As they help design the plan, committee members not only increase their understanding of affirmative action but also are likely to educate their peers about the scope, goals, and need for the plan.

Beyond the internal strategies used to educate and win support for affirmative action, HR departments usually follow common steps in developing these plans. The major action steps are summarized in Figure 4-9.

A key aspect of affirmative action planning is overcoming past perceptions. For example, a major problem faced by AT&T was overcoming perceptions that telephone operator jobs were for women and outside repair jobs were for men. To break down these perceptions, AT&T had to exhibit a strong commitment to affirmative action. Managers were evaluated on how well they met affirmative action plans, and the company appointed a high-ranking director to manage affirmative action. The company further publicized its commitment by declaring in its internal and external communications that it was an "equal opportunity employer."

AT&T also followed the other steps in Figure 4-9. It surveyed its workforce to find areas of concentration and underutilization and then developed goals and timetables to systematically correct those situations. AT&T also designed remedial and preventive programs. For example, some equipment used in

---

Figure 4-9   **Major Steps in Affirmative Action Programs**

1. *Exhibit* strong employer commitment.
2. *Appoint* a high-ranking director.
3. *Publicize* commitment internally and externally.
4. *Survey* the workforce for underutilization and concentration.
5. *Develop* goals and timetables.
6. *Design* remedial and preventive programs.
7. *Establish* control systems and reporting procedures.

training and in the field was redesigned to accommodate members of protected classes so that more would successfully complete their training and be promoted. Beyond the reports required by the Equal Employment Opportunity Commission, AT&T developed its own internal reporting and control systems to ensure that affirmative action would become an ongoing way of life and would receive proper visibility within the company.

In reviewing a recent series of U.S. Supreme Court decisions about affirmative action, a monthly newsletter of the Society for Human Resource Management concluded:

> It appears that courts may order, and employers may voluntarily establish, affirmative actions plans, including numerical standards, to address problems of underutilization. Further, these plans need not be directed solely to identified victims of discrimination but may include general class-wide relief for all members of the included class.
>
> While the courts will almost never approve a plan that would result in whites *losing* their jobs through layoffs, the court has apparently sanctioned plans that would impose limited burdens on whites in hiring and promotions.[46]

Merely developing an affirmative action plan may not be enough. Proactive employers not only seek to eliminate concentration and underutilization but try to remove less obvious attitudes and barriers to equal opportunity within the organization. Consider the efforts of the PQ Corporation of Valley Forge, Pennsylvania:

PQ Corporation

The HR department realized that demographic trends all but assured increased competition for highly qualified professional women and minorities. They also realized that stereotypical negative attitudes among some in the firm served as a barrier to the proper advancement of those in protected groups. Although emphasizing demographic trends and the legal repercussions of discrimination helps change attitudes, the department also knew that an important step in the process was "to provide qualified and experienced women and minority candidates."[47]

To eliminate discriminatory attitudes, incidents, and other barriers in staffing decisions by managers, a detailed hiring procedure was developed. This staffing procedure requires an evaluation of the requirements for each job opening. Then, as part of the selection process, the manager has to complete a two-part checklist. The first part asks fourteen questions about each aspect of the selection process, from internal posting requirements to whether qualified minority candidates were available and were interviewed.

The second part of the checklist evaluates the relationship between job criteria and candidates' attributes. These questions force the selection process to focus on a match between job requirements and applicant abilities instead of nonmerit elements or stereotypical attitudes.

"Any program such as this one has inherent risks,"[48] two members of PQ's HR department observed. Not only may such an elaborate effort be resisted by operating managers, an EEO audit of the company's selection process would uncover detailed documentation of any discriminatory incidents that did exist. However, this program forces operating managers to consider skills, not stereotypes. If the HR department can provide qualified candidates, the presence of competent women and minority group members assures, perhaps best of all, the fading away of discriminatory and stereotypical attitudes.

▶ Equal Opportunity in Perspective

Equal employment laws have a broad impact on the practice of HR management. Professionally, the challenge of equal employment gives HR professionals more visibility and power within their organizations. Threats of suits and government investigations and the remote possibility of losing a government contract have caused top management to lend more support to activities that further equal employment opportunity. At the same time, some HR departments have found that their relationships with other managers in the organization can suffer. When managers believe that the HR department's rules prevent them from hiring the best candidates or require them to spend valuable hours completing reports, they question whether the department is truly furthering organizational objectives. In extreme cases the department can be viewed as a hindrance. When this happens, many of the other services provided by the department may be overlooked. As a result, managers may not seek the assistance they need to improve the operation's productivity and the employees' quality of work life.

Help or hindrance

As was mentioned in Chapter 1, the HR department is a service department. It may be required to carry out societal and even organizational objectives that managers do not appreciate and may even dislike. Nevertheless, activities such as assuring equal employment are critical to HR management. What professionals must do, however, is meet their organizational, societal, functional, and personal objectives simultaneously. As illustrated in the model in Figure 4-1, these objectives are at the center of all HR activities. They must be pursued, but care must be taken so that the HR department's pursuit of them causes the least disruption to the organization's performance. One way to minimize such disruption is to consider its impact on the other human resource activities:

EEO's impact

■ *Human resource plans* must reflect the organization's affirmative action goals.

■ *Job descriptions* must not contain unneeded requirements that exclude members of protected classes.

■ *Recruiting* must ensure that all types of applicants are sought without discrimination.

■ *Selection* of applicants must involve screening devices that are valid and nondiscriminatory.

■ *Training and development* opportunities must be available to workers without regard to factors that discriminate.

■ *Performance appraisals* must be free of biases that discriminate.

■ *Compensation programs* must be based on skills, performance, and/or seniority and cannot discriminate against jobholders because of their membership in a protected class.

Virtually every HR activity is affected by equal employment and affirmative action plans.[49] If the equal employment implications are weighed when other activities are undertaken, the need for remedial programs will decline as organizations move closer to complete equal employment opportunity.

Part II of this book addresses the actions HR departments undertake to assure a timely flow of qualified applicants. As the chapters in Part II will reveal, equal employment must be addressed in all phases of the staffing process, especially during the selection process discussed in Chapter 8 and the HR planning process covered in Chapter 6.

▶ Summary

Since government acts with the force of law, it presents a major challenge to the practice of HR management. Its influence comes from laws aimed at the employment relationship. Although most of these laws are limited in scope, they affect virtually every manager and HR activity. It is particularly important to managers because it is often a manager's actions that give rise to alleged violations of equal employment opportunity laws.

The three main sources of EEO laws are federal acts, state and local fair employment practices, and executive orders. The most significant law is Title VII of the 1964 Civil Rights Act, as amended. Along with the Americans with Disabilities Act and the Age Discrimination in Employment Act, it defines the major protected classes. Other federal equal employment laws include the Equal Pay Act and the Vietnam Era Veterans Readjustment Act.

Title VII seeks to eliminate intentional discrimination in employment in addition to employment practices that cause disparate treatment or impact. Racial and sexual harassment also are prohibited.

To eliminate past discrimination and ensure future compliance, most organizations have developed affirmative action programs designed to identify areas of past and present discrimination, develop affirmative goals, and implement corrective programs. Many government contractors develop affirmative action plans to comply with the OFCCP in the Department of Labor.

▶ Terms for Review

Civil Rights Act

Protected group

Disparate treatment

Disparate impact

Harassment

Bona fide occupational qualification

Equal Employment Opportunity
　Commission

Deferral and nondeferral
　jurisdictions

Conciliation agreement

Make-whole remedies

Americans with Disabilities Act

Age Discrimination in Employment
　Act

Executive orders

Affirmative action programs

Qualifiable worker

Concentration

Underutilization

▶ Review and Discussion Questions

1. Given the increasing diversity of the workforce and the slowdown in its growth, how will these social trends affect employers' efforts to provide equal employment opportunities?

2. A hundred years ago the United States was largely a nation of farmers and small proprietors, with virtually all people working in family or small businesses. Today most people work for different types of businesses. How has this social change led to a greater need for equal employment opportunity?

3. Assume that you manage a restaurant and that one of the employees insists on taking off every Saturday, your busiest day, for religious reasons. What does the law require you to do? Under what circumstances would you be required to let the employee have time off? Under what circumstances could you require attendance?

4. Explain the jurisdictions of federal, state, and local equal employment laws.

5. Since Title VII of the Civil Rights Act covers U.S. citizens working overseas, international human resource specialists need to be concerned about equal employment overseas. Do you agree or disagree? Why?

6. Assume you were going to develop an affirmative action plan for your firm. Before studying underutilization and concentration in the firm, how would you plan to win the support of operating managers and supervisors?

7. Why do some firms sign conciliation agreements even though they believe that they have not discriminated?

8. What makes equal employment laws so important to the HR department? How have these laws "benefited" the HR department?

▶ **Incident 4-1**

Southern California Restaurants, Inc.

Two friends, Harry Rodriguez and Saul Goldstein, formed a partnership before opening their first restaurant in Orange County, California, in 1994. The restaurant, Ma's Kitchen, was intended to be a delicatessen. It was an instant success, profitable from its second month. The restaurant did 65 percent of its business in "eat-in" business, 25 percent in "take-out," and 10 percent in catering. Saul and Harry divided their time evenly, with both working in the deli for the busy morning and weekend trade.

After a year they opened a second restaurant in Orange County, Chef Cloe's. This new restaurant was an expensive bistro with white tablecloths, an upscale menu, and prices to match. It too appeared to be a success as 1995 came to a close. On a slow morning in the deli, Harry and Saul discussed their human resource strategies.

"I think we should stay with waitresses in the deli. Most of our customers are businessmen during the week and couples during the weekend," Saul observed. "I think for this price range, people expect to see waitresses."

Harry agreed, adding, "Yes, but for the bistro we need to have waiters to continue projecting the upscale image we need."

One of the waitresses at the deli overheard the owners talking about jobs and the bistro and asked, "Could I work at the bistro? It would be easier for me to get my children off to school, and the tips would be much better."

"No," Saul shot back. "We need to use waiters there because it is more upscale."

Eventually the waitress filed a suit with the EEOC, alleging sex-based discrimination.

When the EEOC investigated, it found that all the table servers at the bistro were men and all the table servers at the deli were women; all the busboys were Mexican-Americans; and all the kitchen help was male, with the relatively highly paid cooks and chefs being white men and the rest of the kitchen help being Mexican-Americans.

1. If you were the field investigator for the EEOC, what examples of concentration and underutilization would you cite?

2. If you were asked by Saul and Harry what to do, what would you recommend?

▶ References

1. David E. Terpstra and Douglas D. Baker, "Outcomes of Federal Court Decisions on Sexual Harassment," *Academy of Management Journal,* March 1992, pp. 181–191. See also Yitchak Haberfeld, "Employment Discrimination: An Organizational Model," *Academy of Management Journal,* March 1992, pp. 161–180.

2. *Equal Employment Opportunity Commission Eighth Annual Report* (Fiscal Year 1973), Washington, D.C.: U.S. Government Printing Office, 1975, p. 25.

3. Ibid.

4. "U.S. Government Finds AT&T in Compliance," *U.S. Equal Employment Opportunity Commission News Release,* 1979, p. 3.

5. *Equal Employment Opportunity Commission Tenth Annual Report* (Fiscal Year 1975), Washington, D.C.: U.S. Government Printing Office, 1977, p. 5.

6. Howard Gleckman et al., "Race in the Work Place: Is Affirmative Action Working?" *Business Week,* July 8, 1991, pp. 56, 58.

7. Catherine Yang, "In Any Language It's Unfair," *Business Week,* June 21, 1993, p. 110.

8. "What ADA Means to You," *Recruitment Today,* Summer 1990, pp. 6–10.

9. David Gold and Beth Unger, "Better Pregnancy Benefit Not Discriminating," *HR News,* January 1990, p. 7. See also David Gold and Nancy Russell, "What Laws Cover Pregnant Workers?" *Resource,* June 1988, p. 3.

10. James G. Frierson, "Religion in the Workplace," *Personnel Journal,* July 1988, pp. 60–67.

11. Gerald H. Trautman, "Greyhound Ain't No Dog," *Arizona,* June 12, 1977, p. 10. According to Charlotte M. Cloninger, director of women's affairs for the Greyhound Corporation, the height rule required applicants to be "more than five-feet, six inches tall."

12. *Griggs v. Duke Power Company,* 401 U.S. 424 (1971).

13. Judith A. Winston and Claudia A. Withers, "A Turn to the Right: Civil Rights in the Supreme Court, the 1988–90 Term," *Legal Report,* Fall 1989, pp. 1–5.

14. *Albemarle Paper Company v. Moody,* 422 U.S. 405 (1975).

15. *General Electric v. Gilbert,* 429 U.S. 125 (1976).

16. Troy Segal, Kevin Kelly, and Alisa Solomon, "Getting Serious about Sexual Harassment," *Business Week,* Nov. 9, 1992, p. 78.

17. "Women's Plight at Work," *The Miami Herald,* Dec. 1, 1992, p. 1C. See also Ted Holden and Jennifer Wiener, "Revenge of the 'Office Ladies,' " *Business Week,* July 13, 1992, pp. 42–43.

18. *Harassment and Pay Discrimination in the Workplace,* Chicago: Commerce Clearing House, 1986.

19. "Excerpts from Supreme Court Ruling on Sexual Harassment in Workplace," *The New York Times,* National ed., Nov. 10, 1993, p. A-14.

20. Anne B. Fisher, "Sexual Harassment: What to Do?" *Fortune,* Aug. 23, 1993, p. 84.

21. Daniel Seligman, "Growth Situation," *Fortune,* Dec. 13, 1993, pp. 195–196.

22. Michele Galen, Zachary Schiller, Joan O'C. Hamilton, and Keith H. Hammonds, "Ending Sexual Harassment: Business Is Getting the Message," *Business Week,* Mar. 18, 1991, pp. 98–100.

23. Kathleen Murray, "A Backlash on Harassment Cases," *The New York Times,* National ed., Sept. 18, 1994, p. F-23.

24. Susan Crawford, "A Wink Here, a Leer There: It's Costly," *The New York Times,* National ed., Mar. 28, 1993, p. 17.

25. "High Court Rules on Harassment," *Resource,* July 1986, p. 2. The U.S. Supreme Court ruling appeared in *Meritor Savings Bank v. Vinson* (1986). Dawn Bennett-Alexander, "Sexual Harassment in the Office," *Personnel Administrator,* June 1988, pp. 174–188.

26. *International Brotherhood of Teamsters v. United States,* 431 U.S. 324 (1977).

27. *Weber v. Kaiser Aluminum and Chemical Corp.,* 443 U.S. 193 (1979).

28. Lizette Alvarez and Lisa Getter, "Turnstile on Our Border," *The Miami Herald,* Dec. 14, 1993, p. 1.

29. Adapted from Yang, op. cit., p. 110.

30. Betty Southard Murphy, Wayne Barlow, and D. Diane Hatch, "Title VII Doesn't Cover Americans Working Abroad," *Personnel Journal,* January 1989, pp. 19–20. See also Asra Q. Nomani, "Racial Slurs: Courts Shoot Down Defenses for Their Use in Workplaces," *The Wall Street Journal,* Eastern ed., June 7, 1994, p. 1.

31. "Rights Enforcement of American Workers Abroad," *HR Update,* November–December 1992, p. 1.

32. Julia Lawlor, "Shoney's Settles Race-Bias Lawsuit," *USA Today,* Nov. 6, 1992, p. 28. The shifting burden of evidentiary standards is discussed in Philip E. Varca and Patricia Pattison, "Evidentiary Standards in Employment Discrimination: A View toward the Future," *Personnel Psychology,* 1993, pp. 239–258.

33. Tamar Lewin, "Workplace Bias Tied to Obesity Is Ruled Illegal," *The New York Times,* National ed., Nov. 24, 1993, p. A-10.

34. J. Freedly Hunsicker, Jr., "Ready or Not: The ADA," *Personnel Journal,* August 1990, pp. 81–83.

35. "$572,000 Awarded under ADA," *Labor Law Newsletter,* April 1993, p. 1.

36. David P. Twomey, *Equal Employment Opportunity Law,* 3d ed., Cincinnati: South-Western, 1994, pp. 123–125. See also Thomas J. Lueck, "Job-Loss Anger: Age Bias Cases Rise in the East," *The New York Times,* National ed., Dec. 12, 1993, pp. 1, 22.

37. Kevin Labich, "The New Unemployed," *Fortune,* Mar. 8, 1993, p. 43. See also Joan L. Kelly, "Employers Must Recognize That Older People Want to Work," *Personnel Journal,* January 1990, pp. 44–47.

38. *Schultz v. Wheaton Glass Company,* 421 F. 2d, 259 (1970).

39. "Veterans' Advocate: A Firm Makes Special Efforts to Solve Vets' Problems," *The Wall Street Journal,* Western ed., Dec. 28, 1982, p. 1.

40. Barbara Presly Nobel, "The Family Leave Bargain," *The New York Times,* National ed., Feb. 7, 1993, p. F-25.

41. John R. Gaffin and Sandra L. O'Neil, "Family and Medical Leave Act of 1993," *Personnel & Labor Special White Paper,* July 1993, pp. 1–2.

42. G. Thomas Harper (ed.), "Fired Transsexual Wins $150K Discrimination Suit," *Florida Employment Law Letter,* 1993, p. 1.

43. The standard the government sets for itself is somewhat tarnished by the fact that Congress generally exempts itself from EEO laws and that enforcement in the federal sectors seems less aggressive than it is in the private sector. See Frank Greve, "Anti-Bias Agencies Ignored Reports of Minority Firings," *The Miami Herald,* Dec. 19, 1993, p. 4A. See also "Exception That Makes Rules," *Time,* Oct. 18, 1993, p. 25.

44. The U.S. Supreme Court has held that a consent decree does not violate Title VII even if the employer agrees to do more through affirmative action than a federal court could require. This holding comes from *Local 93, Firefighters, AFL-CIO v. the City of Cleveland,* Docket Number 84-1999, July 2, 1986. See also Lawrence S. Kleiman and Robert H. Faley, "Voluntary Affirmative Action and Preferential Treatment: Legal and Research Implications," *Personnel Psychology,* vol. 41, 1988, pp. 481–496.

45. K. Dow Scott and Beverly L. Little, "Affirmative Action: New Interpretations and Realities," *Human Resource Planning,* vol. 14, no. 3, 1991, pp. 177–182.

46. "High Court Shifts Direction in Affirmative Action Ruling," *Resource,* August 1986, p. 6.

47. Jeanne C. Poole and E. Theodore Kautz, "An EEO/AA Program That Exceeds Quotas: It Targets Biases," *Personnel Journal,* January 1987, p. 104. See also Dorothy P. Moore and Marsha Hass, "When Affirmative Action Cloaks Management Bias in Selection and Promotion Decisions," *Academy of Management Executive,* vol. 4, no. 1, 1990, pp. 84–90.

48. Ibid, p. 105.

49. Horace E. Johns and H. Ronald Moser, "Where Has EEO Taken Personnel Policies?" *Personnel,* September 1989, pp. 63–66.

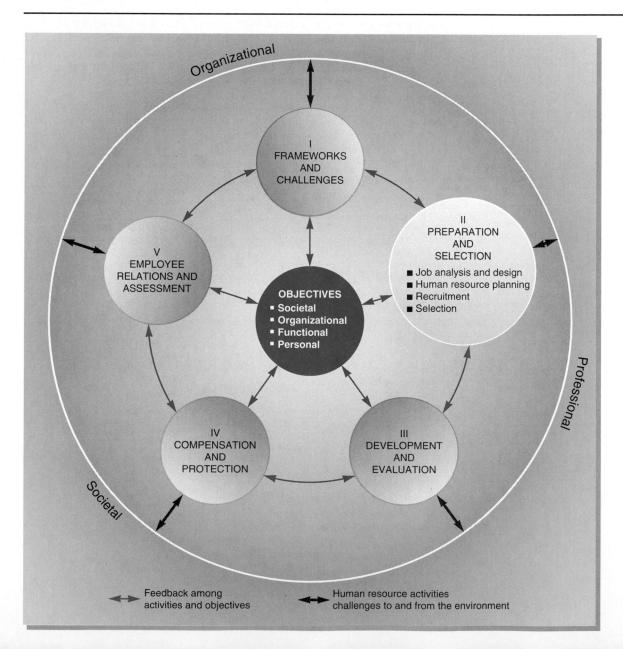

PART

II

PREPARATION AND SELECTION

A N INFORMATION base is central to an effective HR department. The employment process begins with an understanding of the organization's jobs and the plans to fill them. Then the HR department recruits and helps select the people needed to assist the organization in meeting its objectives. Preparation and selection are crucial because an organization can be no better than the people it hires.

The next four chapters discuss the activities used to select employees. You are affected as either a manager or an HR specialist because your success depends on the people you hire. Selection activities may be the most important ones a manager undertakes because good selection decisions help assure good performance. You also are involved in the selection process each time you look for a job.

5

Accurate job descriptions enhance organizational effectiveness.
ROBERT J. SAHL[1]

Job Analysis and Design

CHAPTER OBJECTIVES

After studying this chapter, you should be able to:

1. DISCUSS the foundations of a human resource information system.

2. EXPLAIN how managers and human resource departments depend on accurate job analysis information.

3. LIST the major methods of collecting job analysis information.

4. DESCRIBE the content and uses of a job description.

5. IDENTIFY efficiency and behavioral considerations in the design of jobs.

6. DISCUSS the different job-redesign techniques used to improve the quality of work life.

The environmental, international, and legal challenges discussed in Part I of this book demand a proactive response from managers and the HR department. But for professionals to act in a proactive manner, they must acquire information about the jobs in the organization. A *job* is a pattern of tasks, duties, and responsibilities that can be done by a person. *Job analysis* seeks to study these patterns of activity to determine the tasks, duties, and responsibilities needed for each job.

Job analysis

In small operations needed information may be handled by the memory of managers or reliance on paper files. As the complexity grows, information about jobs and their relationships to applicants, compensation, and other HR matters is typically computerized. For example, a study of 568 firms found that 74 percent use computers to track job applicants,[2] suggesting that those who seek a career in HR management need computerized, data-management skills.[3] The resulting aggregation of data about a company's jobs, when organized into useful and accessible information, forms a cornerstone of a firm's *human resource information system* (HRIS), as shown in Figure 5-1.

HRIS

For the HR department to assist managers with staffing and other HR activities, the HRIS must capture information about jobs and help develop an understanding of job-design principles. However, capturing that information is

Figure 5-1   **The Cornerstones of a Human Resource Information System**

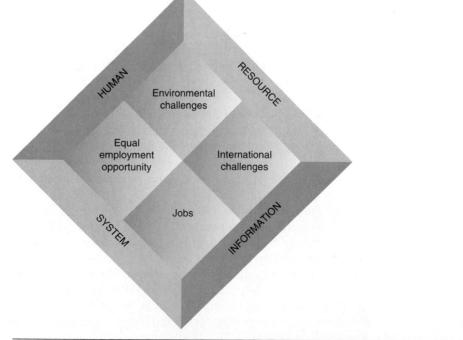

becoming increasingly difficult because the nature of jobs continues to change. In the last century, most jobs were crisply defined sets of tasks that combined to define a specific job. Today's flatter organizations—brought about by the ongoing merger of computer and communications technologies—mean that managers have broader ranges of employees reporting to them. As a result, narrowly defined jobs are giving way to a wider range of responsibilities that permit greater management flexibility in assigning work, making the description and standards of those jobs less precise.[4] In the face of changing patterns of competition, organizational structures, and emerging technologies, well-designed jobs remain at the heart of productive organizations, as the following example suggests.

Shenandoah Life

Shenandoah Life Insurance Company of Roanoke, Virginia, spent $2 million to computerize its claims processing operations. The results? A typical application for a policy conversion still took twenty-seven working days, thirty-two clerks, and three departments to process.

The technology worked, but jobs had to be reengineered before the benefits of automation became apparent. The HR department had to study the clerks' job and add that information to its HRIS. After it applied its job-design knowledge, jobs were regrouped and responsibilities were expanded. As a result, case-handling time fell to two days and complaints practically vanished. Eventually, Shenandoah Life was using 10 percent fewer workers and processing 50 percent more applications.[5]

Armed with an HRIS that detailed the nature of the clerks' jobs, Shenandoah combined that information with an understanding of job design to produce an improvement in performance. Not all attempts to restructure jobs succeed as well as this one did. However, improvements in productivity, quality, and cost often begin with the jobs employees do. But with hundreds or even thousands of jobs, HR specialists cannot know the details of every one. The solution is an effective HRIS that contains detailed information about every job in the organization. With this written or electronically stored information, specialists can quickly learn the details of any job. This knowledge is crucial to the success of an HR department—especially in a large corporation like Shenandoah Life—because it enables specialists to be more proactive, to offer operating managers ways to meet their goals.

HRIS implications

This chapter describes three closely related topics: job analysis information, human resource information systems, and job design. It shows how HR professionals expand the department's information base through job analysis to provide better service to operating managers. Then the chapter addresses the HRIS and its management implications. The chapter concludes by showing how managers and specialists use the HRIS to help design and redesign jobs. Chapter 6 discusses the connection between the HRIS and human resource planning. Subsequent chapters detail other applications of the HRIS.

▶ Job Analysis Information: An Overview

Job analysts

As HR activities grow in scope and complexity, many duties, such as recruiting and compensating, are delegated to the HR department. But HR specialists do not know the details of jobs as well as operating managers do. Knowledge about jobs and their requirements must be collected through a process known as *job analysis,* in which information about jobs is systematically collected, evaluated, and organized. These actions are usually done by HR specialists, called *job analysts,* who gather data about each job but not about every person in the organization.

For example, suppose Shenandoah has fifty accounts payable clerks in its central accounts payable department. Each job is the same since each clerk does the same work: process incoming invoices so they can be paid. The job analyst does not need to study all fifty clerks. Instead, the analyst only needs to review a random sample of those fifty positions. Data collection on a sample of positions for accounts payable clerks generates an accurate information base for all fifty positions. Simply stated, a job analyst can understand an accounts payable clerk's job without studying the tasks of each clerk.

Recorded job information plays a crucial role because it influences most HR activities.[6] Some of the affected areas are listed in Figure 5-2. For example, to match job applicants to openings, HR specialists must know what each job requires. Requirements must be specific enough to enable specialists to recruit

Figure 5-2	**Major Human Resource Management Actions That Rely on Job Analysis Information**

1. *Evaluate* how environmental challenges affect individual jobs.

2. *Eliminate* unneeded job requirements that can cause discrimination in employment.

3. *Discover* job elements that help or hinder the quality of work life.

4. *Plan* for future human resource requirements.

5. *Match* job applicants and job openings.

6. *Determine* training needs for new and experienced employees.

7. *Create* plans to develop employee potential.

8. *Set* realistic performance standards.

9. *Place* employees in jobs that use their skills effectively.

10. *Compensate* jobholders fairly.

EEO caution

those with the needed knowledge, skills, and abilities. Knowledge about cultural, language, and other unique attributes must be captured through job analysis information and made part of the HRIS in internationally oriented firms. Similarly, compensation analysts cannot determine a fair wage or salary without detailed knowledge about jobs. However, unneeded or marginal job requirements may cause the department to reject qualified minority or handicapped applicants, in potential violation of EEO regulations and company affirmative action plans. Perhaps most important, the absence of accurate job analysis information may mislead managers during the hiring process. Simply put, the HR department must formalize the collection, evaluation, and organization of job analysis information to perform its activities and assist managers.

▶ Collection of Job Analysis Information

Analyst preparation

Before collecting the information about specific jobs, employees should be informed about why the job analysis is being done. An explanation of the need for the process and assurances that the outcome will not have an adverse effect on employees may ensure greater cooperation. Otherwise, employees may feel threatened and resist the information collection process.[7] Another important preliminary step is for the job analyst to become familiar with the external environment and the organization: its purpose, strategies, design, inputs (people, materials, and procedures), and outputs (products and services). Familiarity with company, industry, and government reports about the work to be analyzed further equips the analyst to develop useful job analysis information.

Once employees understand the purpose of collecting job analysis information and the analyst is armed with a general understanding of the environment, the organization, the work, and the workers to be studied,[8] analysts:

- Identify the jobs to be analyzed.
- Develop a job analysis questionnaire.
- Collect job analysis information.

Job Identification

Analysts identify the different jobs in the organization before they collect job information. In large companies, analysts may have to construct lists of jobs from payroll records, organization charts, and discussions with workers and supervisors. If job analysis has been done before, analysts may be able to use earlier records to identify many of the jobs in the firm. Competitive pressures are forcing companies to consolidate their job classifications into fewer and broader categories, which simplifies this phase of job analysis.[9]

Questionnaire Development

To study jobs, analysts usually develop checklists or questionnaires; this ensures that the information is collected in a consistent manner for all jobs. Or analysts may elect to use standardized preprinted forms such as the *Position Analysis Questionnaire*[10] (PAQ) or the *Job Element Inventory*.[11] Regardless of what they are called, questionnaires (or job analysis schedules, as they are also known) are used to collect job information. The job analysis schedule uncovers the duties, responsibilities, human abilities, and performance standards of the jobs investigated. It is important to use the same questionnaire for similar jobs. Analysts want differences in job information to reflect differences in the jobs, not differences in the questions asked.

PAQs

After two appliance producers merged, each initially retained its separate HR department and job analysis schedule. As a result, all the production supervisors evaluated on one form had their jobs and pay substantially upgraded because the job analysis schedule suggested that those jobs were of great importance to the success of the company. The supervisors in the other plant had identical jobs but received only modest pay raises.

As this example points out, similar jobs should be studied with identical checklists. This does *not* mean that the HR department is limited to one questionnaire. Job analysts often find that technical, clerical, and managerial jobs require different checklists. Different questionnaires, however, should never be applied to similar jobs.

What are the questions asked in a job analysis questionnaire? Figure 5-3 shows an abbreviated sample form. The major parts are discussed in the following paragraphs.

Status and identification. The first two headings in the figure show how current the information is and identify the job being described. Without these entries, users of job analysis data might rely on out-of-date information or apply it to the wrong job. Since most jobs change over time, outdated information may misdirect other HR activities.

Outdated job information

Job analysis information about the position of billing clerk at Brevard General Hospital had not been collected for three years. This outdated information indicated that bookkeeping experience was the major skill needed. But since the hospital's entire billing system had been computerized recently, bookkeeping skills actually were unimportant. Instead, new billing clerks needed typing skills to enter billing information into the computer.

Figure 5-3   *(continued)*

   3. Experience for this job:

   _____ **a.** Unimportant

   _____ **b.** Includes _____ (months) as (job title) _____

   4. Can training be substituted for experience?

   _____ Yes   How: _____

   _____ No   Why: _____

G. Working Conditions
   1. Describe the physical conditions under which this job is performed. _____

   _____

   2. Are there unusual psychological demands connected with this job? _____

   _____

   3. Describe any conditions under which the job is performed that make it unique.

   _____

   _____

H. Health or Safety Features
   1. Describe fully any health or safety hazards associated with this job. _____

   _____

   _____

   2. Is any safety training or equipment required? _____

   _____

I.   Performance Standards
   1. How is the performance of this job measured? _____

   _____

   2. What identifiable factors contribute most to the successful performance of this job?

   _____

J.   Miscellaneous Comments
   Are there any aspects of this job that should be noted? _____

   _____

   _____

_____   _____

Job Analyst's Signature   **Date Completed**

_____

E. **Responsibility**
   1. What are the responsibilities found in this job, and how significant are they?

	Significance of Responsibility	
Responsibility for:	Minor	Major
a. Equipment operation	_____	_____
b. Use of tools	_____	_____
c. Materials usage	_____	_____
d. Protection of equipment	_____	_____
e. Protection of tools	_____	_____
f. Protection of materials	_____	_____
g. Personal safety	_____	_____
h. Safety of others	_____	_____
i. Others' work performance	_____	_____
j. Other (Specify _____)	_____	_____

F. **Human Characteristics/Job Specifications**
   1. What physical attributes are necessary to perform the job? _____
      _____
      _____
      _____

   2. Of the following characteristics, which ones are needed and how important are they?

Characteristic	Unneeded	Helpful	Essential
1. Vision	_____	_____	_____
2. Hearing	_____	_____	_____
3. Talking	_____	_____	_____
4. Sense of smell	_____	_____	_____
5. Sense of touch	_____	_____	_____
6. Sense of taste	_____	_____	_____
7. Hand-eye coordination	_____	_____	_____
8. Overall coordination	_____	_____	_____
9. Strength	_____	_____	_____
10. Height	_____	_____	_____
11. Health	_____	_____	_____
12. Initiative	_____	_____	_____
13. Ingenuity	_____	_____	_____
14. Judgment	_____	_____	_____
15. Attention	_____	_____	_____
16. Reading	_____	_____	_____
17. Arithmetic	_____	_____	_____
18. Writing	_____	_____	_____
19. Education (Level _____)	_____	_____	_____
20. Other (Specify _____)	_____	_____	_____

| Figure 5-3 | A Job Analysis Questionnaire |

BREVARD GENERAL HOSPITAL

Job Analysis Questionnaire

(Form 110-JAQ)

A. Job Analysis Status
1. Job analysis form revised on _____
2. Previous revisions on _____
3. Date of job analysis for specified job _____
4. Previous analysis on _____
5. Job analysis is conducted by _____
6. Verified by _____

B. Job Identification
1. Job title _____
2. Other titles _____
3. Division(s) _____
4. Department(s) _____
5. Supervisor(s) title _____

C. Job Summary
Briefly describe purpose of job, what is done, and how. _____
_____
_____

D. Duties
1. The primary duties of this job are best classified as:
_____ Medical   _____ Technical   _____ Managerial
_____ Clerical   _____ Professional

2. List *major* duties and the proportion of time each involves:
   a. _____, _____%
   b. _____, _____%
   c. _____, _____%

3. List other duties and the proportion of time each involves:
   a. _____, _____%
   b. _____, _____%
   c. _____, _____%

4. What constitutes successful performance of these duties? _____
_____

5. To perform these duties, how much training is needed for normal performance?
_____
_____

Duties and responsibilities.   Many forms seek information about the purpose of the job, the duties performed, and the way those duties are performed. The specific duties and responsibilities are listed to give a more detailed insight into the position. Questions about responsibility are expanded significantly when the checklist is applied to management jobs. Additional questions map areas of responsibility for decision making, controlling, organizing, planning, and other management functions.

Human characteristics and working conditions.   Besides information about the job, analysts need data about the human qualifications required to perform the job. This section uncovers the particular knowledge, skills, abilities, training, education, experience, and other characteristics that jobholders should possess. Information about the job environment also helps in understanding the job. Working conditions may explain the need for particular skills, training, knowledge, or even a particular job design. Knowledge of hazards allows the HR department to redesign the job or protect workers through the use of training and safety equipment. Unique working conditions influence hiring, placement, and compensation decisions.

Unique needs

During World War II an airplane manufacturer had problems installing fuel tanks inside the wings of the bombers it was building. The crawl space was extremely narrow and cramped. These tight conditions caused considerable production delays. When the HR department learned about this situation, it recruited welders who were less than five feet tall and weighed under 100 pounds.

Performance standards.   The job analysis questionnaire also gathers information about the job standards that are used to evaluate performance. When these standards are not readily apparent, job analysts may ask supervisors or industrial engineers to develop reasonable standards of performance.

Data Collection

There is no best way to collect all the information found on a job analysis questionnaire. Analysts must evaluate the trade-offs between time, cost, and accuracy associated with the use of interviews, panels of experts, questionnaires, employee logbooks, observations, or a combination of these techniques.[12]

Interviews.   Face-to-face interviews are an effective way to collect job information. The analyst has the job checklist as a guide, and interviews allow the interviewer to explain unclear questions and probe into uncertain answers. Both jobholders and supervisors are usually interviewed. The analyst often talks with a limited number of workers first, and then interviews with supervisors verify the information. This pattern ensures a high level of accuracy, though it is time-consuming and costly.

Panel of experts.   Another expensive and time-consuming method is to use a panel or jury of experts. The panel consists of senior job incumbents and immediate supervisors. To get the job analysis information, the analyst conducts an interview with the group. The interaction of the members during the interview can add insight and detail that the analyst might not get from individual interviews. A side benefit of this process can be a clarification of expected job duties among the workers and supervisors who are on the jury.

Mail questionnaires.   A fast and less costly option is a mail questionnaire developed from the job analysis questionnaire. This approach allows many jobs to be studied at once and at little cost. However, accuracy is lower because of misunderstood questions, incomplete responses, and unreturned questionnaires. Supervisors can also be given mail questionnaires to verify employee responses.

Employee log.   An employee log or diary is another option. Workers periodically summarize their tasks and activities in the log. If entries are made over the entire job cycle, the diary can be quite accurate. It may be the only feasible way to collect job information if interviews, experts, and questionnaires are unlikely to capture a complex job.

A New York public relations firm has four dozen account executives, and each handles a bewildering array of activities for clients. Since interviews and questionnaires often overlooked major parts of the job, the HR department suggested a logbook. Most account executives initially resisted, but eventually they agreed to a one-month trial. The HR department obtained the information it wanted, and the account executives learned how they *actually* spent their days.

Shortcomings
of logs

Logs are not popular because they are time-consuming for jobholders and HR specialists. This makes them costly. Managers and workers often see them as a nuisance and resist their introduction. After the novelty wears off, accuracy may decline as entries become infrequent.

Observation.   Direct observation is slow, costly, and potentially less accurate than other methods. Accuracy may be low because the analysts may miss irregularly occurring activities. However, observation is the preferred method in some situations. When analysts question data from other techniques, observation may confirm or remove their doubts. Language barriers may cause observation to be used, especially with workers who speak a foreign language.

Combinations.   Since each method has faults, analysts often rely on combinations. That is, two or more techniques are used concurrently.

A lumber company has six facilities scattered throughout the United States and Canada. Interviewing a few workers and supervisors at each facility was considered prohibitively expensive; relying only on question-

Common approach

naire data was thought to be too inaccurate. Therefore, the HR department interviewed selected employees at the home office and sent questionnaires to other facilities.

HR departments often use multiple approaches even when all the employees are at the same location. When international operations are involved, intercultural differences are more likely to go unnoticed unless analysts use varying viewpoints to collect job analysis information. Besides, combinations can ensure higher accuracy at minimum costs, as the lumber company example implies. Regardless of the technique used, the raw job analysis information is of little value until it is put into a more usable form.

▶ Applications of Job Analysis Information

Job analysis applications

The relationship between the preparation, collection, and application of job analysis information is shown in Figure 5-4. Through the preparation and collection phases of job analysis, HR departments obtain information about jobs. The immediate application of this information transforms it into job descriptions, job specifications, and job standards. Together, these applications of job analysis information become key elements in the department's HRIS, allowing the department to undertake the tasks outlined in Figure 5-2.

Job Descriptions

A *job description* is a written statement that explains the duties, working conditions, and other aspects of a specified job.[13] Within a firm, all the job descriptions should follow the same format, although the form and content may vary among companies. One approach is to write a narrative description in a few paragraphs. Another way is to break down the description into several sub-

Figure 5-4	The Three Phases of Job Analysis Information

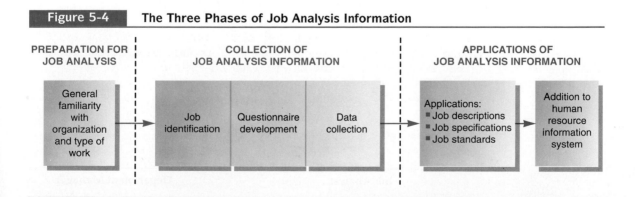

PREPARATION FOR JOB ANALYSIS	COLLECTION OF JOB ANALYSIS INFORMATION			APPLICATIONS OF JOB ANALYSIS INFORMATION	
General familiarity with organization and type of work	Job identification	Questionnaire development	Data collection	Applications: ■ Job descriptions ■ Job specifications ■ Job standards	Addition to human resource information system

parts, as illustrated in Figure 5-5.[14] This figure shows a job description that parallels the job analysis checklist that originally generated the data.

In a job description, the section on job identity may include a *job code*. Job codes use numbers, letters, or both to provide a quick summary of a job. These codes are useful for comparing jobs. Figure 5-6 explains the code used in the U.S. Department of Labor's *Dictionary of Occupational Titles* (DOT). It is an all-numeric code that helps arrange jobs into occupational groups. Once they are grouped, codes can be compared to see the relationships that exist between

DOT codes

Figure 5-5   **A Job Description**

BREVARD GENERAL HOSPITAL

Job Description

Job Title:	Job Analyst	**Job Code:**	166.088
Date:	January 3, 1996	**Author:**	John Doakes
Job Location:	Personnel Department	**Job Grade:**	
Supervisor:	Harold Grantinni	**Status:**	Exempt

Job Summary: Collects and develops job analysis information through interviews, questionnaires, observation, or other means. Provides other personnel specialists with needed information.

Job Duties: Designs job analysis schedules and questionnaires. Collects job information.

Interacts with workers, supervisors, and peers.

Writes job descriptions and job specifications.

Reports safety hazards to area manager and safety departments.

Verifies all information through two sources.

Performs other duties as assigned by supervisors.

Working Conditions: Works most of the time in well-ventilated modern office. Data collection often requires on-site work under every working condition found in company. Works standard 8 a.m. to 5 p.m., except to collect second-shift data and when traveling (one to three days per month).

The above information is correct as approved by:

(Signed)   (Signed)
_____   _____
Job Analyst   **Department Manager**

| Figure 5-6 | Explanation of Job Codes in the *Dictionary of Occupational Titles* |

Each job in the *Dictionary of Occupational Titles* has a six-digit code. The first digit divides all jobs into nine occupational categories.

0.
1. Professional, technical, or managerial occupations
2. Clerical and sales occupations
3. Service occupations
4. Farming, fishery, forestry, and related occupations
5. Processing occupations
6. Machine trades occupations
7. Bench work occupations
8. Structural work occupations
9. Miscellaneous occupations

The second and third digits narrow the occupation to one of 603 occupational groups. For example, a job analyst's code is 166.088. The 1 indicates that a job analyst is a "professional, technical, or managerial occupation." The first two digits (16) indicate "occupations in administrative specializations." The addition of the third digit (166) classifies the job as being in "personnel and training administration occupations." Thus, from the DOT code, the 166 means a professional, technical, or managerial administrative specialization in personnel or training administration.

The last three digits explain the job's relationship to data (fourth digit), people (fifth digit), and things (sixth digit). The job analyst code of 166.088 means that the analysis synthesizes data but has no significant relationship with people or things.

DATA (FOURTH DIGIT)	PEOPLE (FIFTH DIGIT)	THINGS (SIXTH DIGIT)
0. Synthesizing	0. Mentoring	0. Setting up
1. Coordinating	1. Negotiating	1. Precision working
2. Analyzing	2. Instructing	2. Operating-Controlling
3. Compiling	3. Supervising	3. Driving-Operating
4. Computing	4. Diverting	4. Manipulating
5. Copying	5. Persuading	5. Tending
6. Comparing	6. Speaking-Signaling	6. Feeding-Offbearing
7. No significant relationship	7. Serving	7. Handling
	8. No significant relationship	8. No significant relationship

For those familiar with the DOT code, just the six digits of the job analyst's code indicate "a professional, technical, or managerial administrative specialization in personnel or training administration that synthesizes data but bears no significant relationship to people or things."

Source: Dictionary of Occupational Titles (vol. 1), U.S. Department of Labor, 1978, p. xvi.

different jobs. The code also identifies relationships between data, people, and things.[15]

The job identity section of the job description (found in Figure 5-5) contains other useful information:

- *Date.* The date tells subsequent users how old the description is. The older it is, the less likely it is to reflect the current job.

- *Author.* The writer of the description is identified so that questions or errors can be brought to the author's attention.

- *Job location.* The department or departments where the job is located helps identify the job for future reference. Location references may include division, plant, or other organization breakdowns.

- *Job grade.* Job descriptions may include a blank space for adding the job grade or level. This information helps rank the job's importance for pay purposes.

- *Supervisor.* The supervisor's title may be listed to help identify the job and its relative importance.

- *Status.* Analysts may identify the job as exempt or nonexempt from overtime laws.

Job summary and duties.   After the job identification section, the next part of the job description is the job summary, a written narrative that concisely summarizes the job in a few sentences. It tells what the job is, how it is done, and why. Most authorities recommend that job summaries specify the primary actions involved. Then, in a simple, action-oriented style, the job description lists the job duties. Figure 5-5 provides an example of this style.

Since the effectiveness of other HR actions depends on an understanding of the job, each major duty is described in terms of the actions expected. Tasks and activities are identified. Performance is emphasized. Even responsibilities are implied or stated within the job duties. If employees are in a union, the union may want to narrow the duties associated with specific jobs to prevent real or imagined abuses by supervisors.

Management flexibility

Before the union organized, the employee job descriptions contained the phrase "or other work as assigned." The union believed that supervisors abused this clause by assigning idle workers to do unrelated jobs. After the threat of a strike, management removed the phrase, and supervisors lost much of their flexibility in assigning work.

Working conditions.   A job description also explains working conditions that may go beyond descriptions of the physical environment. Hours of work, safety and health hazards, travel requirements, and other features of the job expand the meaning of this section.

Approvals.   Since job descriptions affect most HR decisions, their accuracy should be reviewed by selected jobholders and their supervisors. Once it is acceptable, supervisors are asked to approve a description. This approval serves as a further test of the job description and a further check on the collection of job analysis information. Neither HR specialists nor managers should give their approval lightly. If the description is erroneous, the HR department will become a source of problems rather than assistance.

Job description
errors

In explaining the job of foundry attendant to new employees, recruiters relied on an inaccurate job description. Many new employees quit during the first two weeks. When asked why, most said the duties were less challenging than they had been led to believe. When analysts checked, they found that the job description had never been verified by the supervisors. A more proactive approach of reviewing and revising this information would have prevented this turnover problem before it occurred.

Job Specifications

Human
specifications

The difference between a job description and a job specification is a matter of perspective. A job description defines what a job is; it is a profile of the job. A *job specification* describes the job demands on the employees who do it and the human skills that are required. It is a profile of the human characteristics needed by the person performing the job. These requirements include experience, training, education, and the ability to meet physical and mental demands. When positions cross national boundaries, linguistic, legal, and cultural familiarity may become an important addition to the specifications.

Since job descriptions and job specifications both focus on the job, they are often combined into one document, commonly called a job description. Whether part of a job description or a separate document, job specifications include the information illustrated in Figure 5-7. The information needed to compile job specifications also comes from the job analysis collection process.

Job specifications may include specific tools, actions, experience, education, and training requirements that help clarify individual requirements for successful job performance. They also describe the physical effort in terms of the actions demanded by the job. Again, specifics are preferred to generalizations. For example, "lifts 100-pound bags" is better than "lifts heavy weights."[16] Specifications of mental effort help HR experts determine the intellectual abilities that are needed. Some experts argue for behavioral specifications, particularly for managers, suggesting job descriptions that focus on the varied behaviors needed.[17] Figure 5-7 contains several examples of the physical and mental demands required for jobs in a hospital.

Working conditions

The working conditions found in job descriptions may be translated by job specifications into demands faced by workers. Figure 5-8 provides examples for the job of hospital orderly. It shows that a simple statement of working

Figure 5-7	A Job Specifications Sheet

BREVARD GENERAL HOSPITAL
Job Description

Job Title:	Job Analyst	**Job Code:**	166.088
Date:	January 3, 1996	**Author:**	John Doakes
Job Location:	Personnel Department	**Job Grade:**	
Supervisor:	Harold Grantinni	**Status:**	Exempt

Skill Factors

Education: College degree required.

Experience: At least one year as job analyst trainee, recruiter, or other professional assignment in personnel area.

Communication: Oral and written skills should evidence ability to capsulize job data succinctly. Must be able to communicate effectively with diverse workforce, including foreign-born employees.

Effort Factors

Physical demands: Limited to those normally associated with clerical jobs: sitting, standing, and walking.

Mental demands: Extended visual attention is needed to observe jobs. Initiative and ingenuity are mandatory since job receives only general supervision. Judgment must be exercised on job features to be emphasized, jobs to be studied, and methods used to collect job data. Decision-making discretion is frequent. Analyzes and synthesizes large amounts of abstract information into job descriptions, job specifications, and job standards.

Working Conditions

Travels to hospital clinics in county from one to three days per month. Travels around each work site collecting job information. Works mostly in an office setting.

Figure 5-8	Translation of Working Conditions from Job Description to Job Specifications

HOSPITAL ORDERLY

JOB DESCRIPTION STATEMENT ON WORKING CONDITIONS	JOB SPECIFICATIONS INTERPRETATION OF WORKING CONDITIONS
1. Works in physically comfortable surroundings.	1. Must be willing to work inside.
2. Deals with physically ill and diseased patients.	2. Exposed to unpleasant situations and communicable diseases.
3. Deals with mentally ill patients.	3. Exposed to verbal and physical abuse.

conditions found in the job description can have significant implications for jobholders. For example, compare points 2 and 3 in the job description column with points 2 and 3 of the job specifications.

Job Performance Standards

Job standards

Job analysis has a third application: *job performance standards.* These standards serve two functions. First, they become targets for employee efforts. The challenge of or pride in meeting objectives may motivate employees. Once standards are met, workers may feel a sense of accomplishment and achievement. This outcome contributes to employee satisfaction. Without standards, employee performance may suffer.

Second, standards are criteria against which job success is measured. They are indispensable to managers and HR specialists who attempt to control work performance. Without standards, no control system can evaluate job performance. All control systems have four features: standards, measures, correction, and feedback. The relationship between these factors is illustrated in Figure 5-9. Job performance standards are developed from job analysis information, and then actual employee performance is measured. When measured performance strays from the job standard, HR experts or line managers intervene and corrective action is taken. The action serves as feedback about the standards and actual performance. The feedback leads to changes in either the standards (if they were inappropriate) or job performance.

Veterans Administration

At a regional Veterans Administration (VA) office, each loan supervisor was expected to review a standard of sixteen VA mortgage applications per day. Actual output averaged twelve. After new job analysis information was collected, analysts discovered that Congress, the VA, and area banks had added new duties since the standard was first set. Corrective action involved new job designs, revised job descriptions, and lower standards.

| Figure 5-9 | Diagram of a Job Control System |

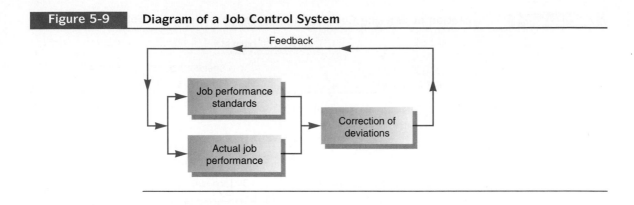

Job standards are a key part of any control system. When the standards are wrong, as in the VA example, they alert managers and HR specialists to problems that need correction. The VA example also underscores the need for keeping job analysis information current. When management seeks to redirect attention to improved quality or customer service efforts, changes in job standards underscore its serious, long-term commitment to these new approaches.

▶ The Human Resource Information System

Job descriptions, job specifications, and performance standards are important additions to the human resource information system (HRIS). As will become apparent in subsequent chapters, this storehouse of information is supplemented by human resource plans, applicant information, performance results, compensation figures, and many other types of data. The result often is an overload of data, with little of it in the form of usable information.

HRIS at TRW

TRW, an aerospace and automotive conglomerate based in Ohio with operations in twenty-seven countries around the world, faced the problem of data overload in its HRIS. Besides job analysis information, the HR department manages other employee-related databases, such as applicant, employee, and benefit information. Valdis Krebs, a manager at TRW's Electronics and Defense Sector in Redondo Beach, California, developed an interactive network of Apple Macintoshes that allows human resource specialists to access these databases in both text and graphic formats. It includes in one information system plant locations, organization charts, photos, benefits information, and other data that can be quickly accessed through menu-driven choices.[18]

The HRIS at TRW is more sophisticated than most HRISs currently in use, which do not allow this wide range of text and graphic information integration. However, the trend toward computer-based support systems for decision makers, combined with the growing use of computers and the need to reduce staff costs, is leading more departments to create on-line systems. Although initially many of these systems may support only one function—such as job analysis information or applicant tracking[19]—the trend in the 1990s is to interconnect various HRIS subsystems, leading to a truly integrated HRIS through which HR professionals and line managers can access HR information. As a result of this trend toward an integrated HRIS, "Human resources systems professionals . . . ask, 'If I was a manager, what would I want from the human resources information system?' The answers often lead to increased functionality and payback from the HRIS."[20]

Of course there will remain a need to document the acquisition and preparation of data,[21] but more and more of the department's information needs will be computerized into an integrated system, such as TRW's. Perhaps the biggest current barrier to creating and maintaining a sophisticated HRIS is gaining support from top management for the transition and maintenance costs associated with a fully interconnected real-time system.[22] Another barrier is getting far-flung operations to standardize and collect information about local personnel practices, according to one survey: "After interviewing the chief executives or financial officers of 153 large European companies, KPMG found that only 8% of them had established common information systems across their European subsidiaries."[23] As one Danish executive observed, "It is not the technical aspects that we find daunting; it's the time and energy we have to spend explaining it to people and persuading them to accept it."[24]

Two concerns about HRIS remain: legal considerations and organization.

Survey results

Legal Considerations

As HR specialists rely on job analysis information to pursue other activities, legal considerations arise, particularly in the area of equal employment opportunity. As was discussed in Chapter 4, *Griggs v. Duke Power Company* provides a classic example of how unneeded job requirements can lead to a violation of equal employment laws.

Court decision

In *Griggs v. Duke Power Company* (1971) the employer required a high school degree for nearly all jobs within the company, except those in the labor pool. When the need for a high school diploma was challenged in court, the employer could not show that this job specification was absolutely necessary to perform many of the jobs for which it was required. Although this requirement was applied equally to all applicants, it had an *unequal impact* on job applicants from minority groups. As a result, many African-Americans were offered jobs only in the labor pool.

As this case illustrates, it is important for HR specialists to include in job descriptions and specifications only items that are job-related. Otherwise, charges of discrimination may result from the adverse impact of a needless job requirement.[25] Even if legal considerations are ignored, needless job requirements exclude potentially qualified individuals from consideration.

Organization of the Database

Job families

Whether job information is kept on written forms or in computer memory, it is organized around individual jobs.[26] In addition, HR departments need job analysis information that is organized around job families. *Job families* are groups of jobs that are closely related in terms of duties, responsibilities, skills, or job elements. For example, the jobs of clerk, typist, clerk-typist, word processor operator, and secretary constitute a job family. Job families allow HR departments to facilitate permanent job transfers, training, career counseling, compensation, and other HR decisions.

Job families can be constructed in several ways. One way is to carefully study job analysis information. When the data in job descriptions are matched, jobs with similar requirements can be identified. A second method is to use the codes in the *Dictionary of Occupational Titles,* where similarities in job codes indicate similarities in jobs. A third approach uses a *position analysis questionnaire* (PAQ). This is a standardized preprinted form used to collect specific information about job tasks and worker traits. Through statistical analysis of the PAQ responses, related jobs can be grouped into job families.[27]

▶ Overview of Job Design

A job is more than a collection of tasks recorded on a job analysis schedule and summarized in a job description. Jobs are the foundation of organizational productivity and employee satisfaction. How well jobs are designed will play an increasingly important role in the success and even survival of many organizations. As the number of new workers coming into the labor market slows and international competition increases, well-designed jobs will become even more important in attracting and retaining a motivated workforce capable of producing quality products and services.

Saturn and GM

Realizing the Japanese superiority at producing small, high-quality cars, General Motors created the Saturn Corporation as a wholly owned subsidiary. Saturn was created on the premise of using the best manufacturing approaches in the world to produce a small car that could match world-class standards. Although new designs and technologies are employed to make the Saturn, perhaps the most radical change has been in the composition of jobs. In a traditional North American automobile factory, workers are placed into a variety of narrowly defined jobs, often doing the same tasks over and over, with little voice in work practices, inventory procedures, or scheduling activities.

"At Saturn, there is only one production classification for unskilled workers and three for specific skilled employees. While there is still an assembly line, employees do not perform repetitive, mundane tasks.

"Instead, groups of 6 to 15 workers decide how to do all necessary tasks, what inventory needs are, how to manage leave and vacation schedules of fellow team members, and other functions usually associated with front-line supervision."[28]

Although the initial reports of car quality from the plant are favorable, it may be years before an accurate assessment of GM's approach at the Saturn plant can be made. Nevertheless, how well people perform is shaped at least in part by the characteristics designed into their jobs.[29] Not only is productivity affected, the quality of work life is tied to job design. If managers and HR departments are to help the organization obtain and maintain a desired workforce, they must have a thorough understanding of job designs.

Figure 5-10 illustrates a systems view of job design. The design of a job reflects the organizational, environmental, and behavioral demands placed on it. Job designers take these elements into consideration and try to create jobs that are both productive and satisfying. However, trade-offs among these elements of job design mean that some jobs are more or less satisfying than are others. Employee productivity and satisfaction provide feedback on how well a job is designed. Poorly designed jobs may lead to lower productivity, employee

Job design trade-offs

Figure 5-10 | **The Job-Design Input-Output Framework**

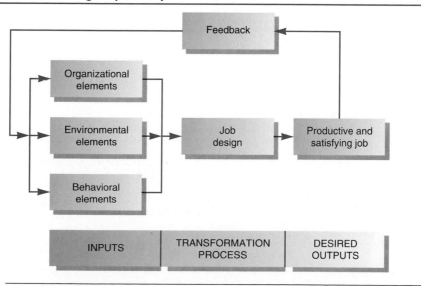

turnover, absenteeism, complaints, sabotage, unionization, resignations, and other problems. Return to the Shenandoah example, consider the impact job redesign had.

Shenandoah Life

> Before the redesign of the jobs at Shenandoah Life, each clerk had narrowly defined responsibilities, performing a specific function before moving the "paperwork" on to someone else. The result was that no one clerk had the responsibility for handling a policy application. In fact, no single department had this responsibility since activities were spread over three departments.
>
> The job redesign grouped the clerks into teams of five to seven employees. Each team was trained to do the functions of all three departments. Members learned new skills, job satisfaction went up, and pay improved since each team member now had new skills and responsibilities.[30]

As suggested by Figure 5-10, organizational, environmental, and behavioral elements were all considered. Customers in Shenandoah's sales environment received better service, the organization achieved better productivity, and the behavioral elements in Figure 5-11 were injected into the jobs.

Repetitive tasks remain

Job redesign does have some trade-offs, and this helps explain why for "75 percent of the labor force, work is still largely divided into simple, repetitive tasks."[31] To explain these trade-offs more fully, a review of the organizational, environmental, and behavioral elements of job design follows. Then the chapter will conclude with a discussion of job-redesign techniques.

Organizational Elements

Organizational elements of job design are concerned with efficiency, as was first formalized by Fredrick Taylor and other management scientists around the turn of the century. They devoted much of their research to finding the best

Figure 5-11	Elements of Job Design

ORGANIZATIONAL ELEMENTS	ENVIRONMENTAL ELEMENTS	BEHAVIORAL ELEMENTS
▪ Mechanistic approach	▪ Employee abilities and availability	▪ Autonomy
▪ Work flow	▪ Social and cultural expectations	▪ Variety
▪ Work practices		▪ Task identity
▪ Ergonomics		▪ Task significance
		▪ Feedback

ways to design efficient jobs. Their success with stopwatches and motion pictures gave rise to the new discipline of industrial engineering and contributed to the formal study of management. From their efforts, we have learned that specialization is a key element in the design of jobs. When workers are limited to a few repetitive tasks, output is usually higher. The findings of these early researchers are still applicable today. They can be summarized under the heading of the mechanistic approach.

Mechanistic approach.   The mechanistic approach involves identifying *every* task in a job so that tasks can be arranged to minimize the time and effort expended by workers. Once task identification is complete, a limited number of tasks are grouped into a job. The result is *specialization*. Specialized jobs lead to short *job cycles*, the time to complete every task in a job. For example:

Job cycles

An assembly-line worker in Detroit might pick up a headlight, plug it in, twist the adjustment screws, and picks up the next headlight within thirty seconds. Completing these tasks in thirty seconds means this worker's job cycle takes half a minute. The job cycle begins when the next headlight is picked up.

Headlight installation is so specialized that training takes only a few minutes. And the short job cycle means that the assembler gains much experience in a short time. Put another way, short job cycles require small investments in training and allow a worker to learn the job quickly.

This mechanistic approach stresses efficiency in effort, time, labor costs, training, and employee learning time. This technique is still widely used in assembly operations. It is especially effective in dealing with poorly educated workers or workers who have little industrial experience, such as those in a developing nation. But the efficient design of jobs also considers such organizational elements as work flow, ergonomics, and work practices.

Work flow.   The product or service usually suggests the sequence of and balance between jobs if the work is to be done efficiently. For example, the frame of a car must be built before the fenders and doors can be added. Once the sequence of jobs is determined, the balance between jobs is established.

Balancing
work flow

Suppose it takes one person thirty seconds to install each headlight. In two minutes an assembler can put on four headlights. If, however, it takes four minutes to install each of the two sets of headlight receptacles, the job designer must balance these two interrelated jobs by assigning two people to install the receptacles. Otherwise, a production bottleneck results. Since the work flow demands two receptacle installers for each headlight installer, one worker specializes in the right-side receptacles and another specializes in the left-side receptacles.

Ergonomics.   Optimal productivity requires that the physical relationship between the worker and the work be considered in designing jobs. *Ergonomics* is the study of how human beings physically interface with their equipment. Although the nature of job tasks may not vary because of ergonomics, the location of tools, swtiches, and the work product itself is evaluated and modified for ease of use. On Mercedes-Benz assembly lines, for example, a car frame is elevated at some workstations so that the worker does not become fatigued from stooping. Similarly, the locations of dashboard instruments in a car are ergonomically engineered to make driving easier.[32]

Ergonomics

Work practices.   Work practices are set ways of performing work. These methods may arise from tradition or the collective wishes of employees. Either way, the flexibility of managers and the HR department in designing jobs is limited, especially when such practices are part of a union-management relationship. Failure to consider work practices can have undesired outcomes.

General Motors decided to increase productivity at its Lordstown, Ohio, plant by eliminating some jobs and adding new tasks to others. These design changes caused workers to stage a strike for several weeks because traditional practices at the plant had required a slower rate of production and less work by the employees. The additional demands on their jobs made by management were seen as an attempt by the company to disregard past work practices.[33]

General Motors

Environmental Elements

A second aspect of job design concerns environmental elements such as the ability and availability of potential employees and their social expectations.

Employee abilities and availability.   Efficiency considerations must be balanced against the abilities and availability of the people who are to do the work. When Henry Ford made use of the assembly line, for example, he was aware that most potential workers lacked any automobile-making experience, and so jobs were designed to be simple and require little training. An extreme example underlines this point.

Governments of less developed countries often think they can "buy" progress. To be "up to date," they seek the most advanced equipment they can find. The leaders of one country ordered a computerized oil refinery. This decision dictated a level of technology that exceeded the abilities of the country's available workforce. As a result, these government leaders have hired Europeans to operate the refinery.

Developing
countries

Social and cultural expectations. The acceptability of a job's design is also influenced by social and cultural expectations. And with the growing diversity of the North American workforce, these expectations will play an increasingly important role in designing jobs. For example, many uneducated immigrants who moved to North America during the early days of the railroad and automobile industries readily accepted highly specialized jobs that demanded long hours and hard physical labor. Often they had left countries where jobs were unavailable; this made a job—any job—acceptable to them.

Social expectations

Today's industrial workers are much better educated and have higher expectations about the quality of work life. Although work flow or work practices may suggest a particular job design, the job must also meet the expectations of workers. When one is designing jobs for international operations, uniform designs are almost certain to overlook national and cultural differences. Hours of work, holidays, vacations, rest breaks, religious beliefs, management styles, and worker sophistication and attitudes are just some of the likely differences that affect the design of jobs across international borders. Failure to consider these social expectations can create dissatisfaction, low motivation, hard-to-fill job openings, and a low quality of work life—especially when foreign nationals are involved in the home country or overseas.

Behavioral Elements

Jobs cannot be designed by using only the elements that aid efficiency. Instead, jobs designers draw heavily on behavioral research to provide a work environment that helps satisfy individual needs. Higher-level needs are of particular importance. One pair of researchers provided a useful framework when they suggested:

> People with a strong desire to satisfy higher-order needs performed their best when placed on jobs that were high on certain dimensions. These were:

Key behavioral elements

> *Autonomy:* responsibility for work
> *Variety:* use of different skills and abilities
> *Task identity:* doing the whole piece of work
> *Feedback:* information on performance.[34]

Task significance should be added to the list because people like to feel that their work has meaning to others inside and outside the organization.

Autonomy. *Autonomy* is having responsibility for what one does. It is freedom to control one's response to the environment. Jobs that give workers authority to make decisions provide added responsibilities that tend to increase an employee's sense of recognition and self-esteem. The absence of autonomy, by contrast, can cause employee apathy or poor performance.[35]

"I don't care"

A common problem in many production operations is that employees develop an "I don't care" attitude because they believe they have no control over their jobs. On the bottling line of a small brewery teams of workers were allowed to speed up or slow down the rate of the bottling line as long as they met daily production goals. Although total output per shift did not change, there were fewer cases of capping machines jamming or breaking down for other reasons. When asked about this unexpected development, the supervisor concluded, "Employees pride themselves on meeting the shift quota. So they are more careful to check for defective bottle caps before they load the machine."

Research summary

Variety. A lack of variety may cause boredom. Boredom leads to fatigue, and fatigue causes errors. By injecting variety into jobs, job designers can reduce fatigue-caused errors. The ability to control the speed of the bottling line in the brewery example added variety to the pace of work and probably reduced both boredom and fatique. One research study found that diversity of work is partially responsible for effective performance.[36] Another study found that autonomy and variety are major contributors to employee satisfaction.[37]

Task identity. One problem with some jobs is that they lack *task identity*. Workers cannot point to a complete piece of work. They have little sense of responsibility and may lack pride in the results. After completing their jobs, they may have little sense of accomplishment. When tasks are grouped so that employees feel they are making an identifiable contribution, job satisfaction can increase significantly.[38] Again, returning to the Shenandoah Life example, productivity and satisfaction increased when employees became responsible for an identifiable group of tasks.

Meaningful work

Task significance. Closely related to task identity is *task significance*. Doing an identifiable piece of work makes a job more satisfying. Task significance—knowing that the work is important to others in the organization or outside it—makes the job more meaningful for incumbents. Their personal sense of self-importance is enhanced because they know that others are depending on what they do. Pride, commitment, motivation, satisfaction, and better performance are likely to result.

Closing the loop

Feedback. When jobs do not give the workers any feedback on how well they are doing, there is little guidance or motivation to perform better. For example, by letting employees know how they are doing relative to the daily production quota, the brewery described above gives workers feedback that allows them to adjust their efforts. Overseas work may require managers to show great sensitivity to the way feedback is provided. In some countries, such as Japan, care must be exercised in providing negative feedback so that those responsible can "save face" and not be unduly embarrassed. Feedback leads to improved motivation.[39]

▶ Behavioral and Efficiency Trade-offs

Trade-offs

The behavioral elements of job design tell managers and job design specialists to add more autonomy, variety, task identity, task significance, and feedback. But efficiency elements stress greater specialization, less variety, and minimum autonomy. Thus, making jobs more efficient may cause them to be less satisfying. Conversely, satisfying jobs may prove to be inefficient. What should specialists do? There is no simple solution. Instead, experts often make trade-offs between efficiency and behavioral elements. Figure 5-12 depicts the most significant trade-offs faced by job designers.

Graph A: Productivity versus Specialization

As jobs are made more specialized, productivity climbs until behavioral elements such as boredom offset the advantages of further specialization. In Figure 5-12A, additional specialization beyond point *b* causes productivity to

| Figure 5-12 | Efficiency versus Behavioral Trade-offs In Job Design |

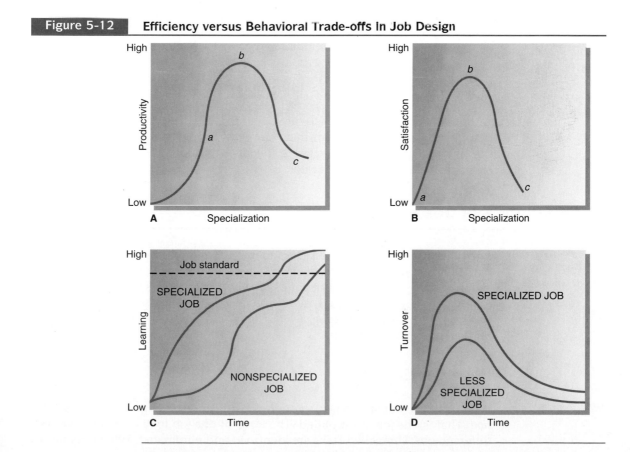

drop. In fact, jobs between b and c can have their productivity *increased* by reducing the degree of specialization.

Graph B: Satisfaction versus Specialization

Satisfaction first goes up with specialization, and then additional specialization causes satisfaction to drop quickly. Jobs without any specialization take too long to learn; frustration is decreased and feedback is increased when some specialization is added. However, when specialization is carried past point b in Figure 5-12B, satisfaction drops because of a lack of autonomy, variety, and task identification. Note that even while satisfaction is falling in graph B, productivity may still increase in graph A from a to b. Productivity continues to go up as long as the advantages of specialization outweigh the disadvantages of dissatisfaction.

Graph C: Learning versus Specialization

It takes less time to learn a specialized job than to learn a nonspecialized one. Graphically, this means that the rate of learning reaches an acceptable standard (shown as a dashed line) more quickly with specialized jobs.

Graph D: Turnover versus Specialization

Although highly specialized jobs are easier to learn, the lower levels of satisfaction generally associated with them can lead to higher turnover rates. When turnover rates are high, redesigning the job with more attention to behavioral elements may reduce the quit rate.

▶ Techniques of Job Redesign

The central question that often faces managers and job designers is whether a particular job should have more or less specialization. As can be seen in graph A in Figure 5-12, the answer depends on whether the job is near point a, b, or c. Jobs near point a may need more specialization to become more effective. Analysis and experimentation are the only sure ways to determine where a particular job is on the graph.

Underspecialization

Work simplification

When jobs are not specialized enough, job designers engage in *work simplification*. That is, the job is simplified. The tasks of one job may be assigned to two different jobs. Unneeded tasks are identified and eliminated. What remains are jobs that contain fewer tasks.

When the *Allyndale Weekly Newspaper* operated with its old press, Guy Parsons could catch the newspapers as they came off the press, stack them, and wrap them. But when a new high-speed press was added, he could not keep up with the output. The circulation manager simplified Guy's job by making him responsible for stacking the newspapers. Two part-time workers took turns catching and wrapping.

The risk with work simplification is that jobs may become so specialized that boredom causes errors or resignations. This potential problem is more common in advanced industrial countries that have a highly educated workforce. In less developed countries, highly specialized factory jobs may be acceptable and even appealing because they provide jobs for workers with limited skills or opportunities.

Reengineering

Another view is called *reengineering,* which identifies the desired outcome of a system or subsystem (such as fast policy conversions at Shenandoah Life) and restructures jobs and even departments to radically increase performance. Often this is done by eliminating unneeded steps and clustering related responsibilities into one job or team organized around the process.

Overspecialization

In advanced industrial societies routine jobs that are very specialized, such as assembly-line positions, have limited appeal. These jobs seldom offer opportunities for accomplishment, recognition, psychological growth, or other sources of satisfaction. To increase the quality of work life for those who hold such jobs, managers and job designers can use a variety of methods to improve jobs. The most widely practiced techniques are job rotation, job enlargement, and job enrichment.

Improving quality of work life

Job rotation.   With *job rotation,* employees are moved from job to job. The jobs themselves are not actually changed; the workers are rotated. Rotation breaks the monotony of highly specialized work by calling on different skills and abilities—even different muscles. The organization benefits because workers become competent in several jobs rather than only one. Knowing a variety of jobs helps the worker's self-image, provides personal growth, and makes the worker more valuable to the organization.

HR experts should caution those who desire to use job rotation. It does not improve the jobs themselves; the relationships between tasks, activities, and objectives remain unchanged. Implementation should occur only after other techniques have been considered.

Horizontal loading

Job enlargement.   *Job enlargement,* also known as *horizontal loading,* expands the number of related tasks in a job. It adds similar duties to provide greater variety. Enlargement reduces monotony by expanding the job cycle and drawing on a wider range of employee skills. According to a summary of job-design research:

IBM and Maytag

IBM reported that job enlargement led to higher wages and more inspection equipment, but improved quality and worker satisfaction offset these costs.

Maytag Company claimed that production quality was improved, labor costs declined, worker satisfaction and overall efficiency were increased, and production schedules became more flexible.[40]

Job enrichment.   *Job enrichment* adds new sources of satisfaction to jobs. It increases responsibility, autonomy, and control. Adding these elements to jobs is sometimes called *vertical loading.* Job enrichment sees jobs as consisting of three elements: plan, do, and control.[41] Job enlargement (horizontal loading) adds more things to *do.* Job enrichment (vertical loading) attempts to add more *planning* and *control* responsibilities. These additions to the job, coupled with rethinking the job, can lead to increased motivation and other improvements, as was seen in the Shenandoah Life example. A similar example comes from one of the former members of AT&T's Bell System.

Vertical loading

Ohio Bell

The Ohio Bell Telephone Company reported that the workforce needed to compile directories in one office declined from 120 to 74 as the result of job enrichment and other changes.[42]

Improvements in directory compilation resulted from allowing individual clerks to have broad responsibility for entire rural (small) directories or identifiable sections of large metropolitan directories. Before the change each clerk's activities were narrowly defined with close controls, little task identity, and limited autonomy. Vertical and horizontal loading lengthened job cycles, added task identity and autonomy, reduced turnover, increased productivity, and lowered labor costs.

No cure-all

Job enrichment, however, is not a cure-all. If it were, this book could end here. Instead, job enrichment techniques are merely tools. They are not applied universally. When the diagnosis indicates that jobs are unrewarding and unchallenging and limit the motivation and satisfaction of employees, managers and HR departments *may* find job enrichment to be the most appropriate strategy. Even then, job enrichment can create problems. One author listed twenty-two arguments against job enrichment.[43] The most compelling points are union resistance, cost of design and implementation, and limited research on the long-term effects of enrichment. Another criticism is that job enrichment does not go far enough. Enriching the job while ignoring other variables that contribute to the quality of work life may simply increase dissatisfaction with the unimproved aspects of the job environment.[44]

Autonomous work teams.   Autonomous work teams (also called "self-directed work teams" and "leaderless work teams") are groups of workers with such widely defined jobs that their responsibilities often include duties normally reserved for supervisors or managers. Work teams usually involve three to fifteen members who are extensively cross-trained to do each other's jobs. Group members are given objectives in production or service to be attained by the team. Then they collectively decide among themselves how they will

Leaderless
work groups

achieve the needed performance. Assignments are made within the group, often with members informally trading off among themselves to relieve boredom and fatique. Peer pressure is often successful in ensuring that everyone contributes to the objectives, especially since group members often vote on new hires, probationary employees, and even pay raises and vacation schedules. The Saturn Corporation facilities discussed earlier in this chapter are an example. Other examples can be found in companies such as TRW, Texas Instruments, Procter & Gamble, Digital Equipment, General Mills, and Federal Express.[45]

Benefits

Self-directed work teams have been created for many reasons.[46] Some companies see these approaches as the best way to achieve high productivity and quality while improving the quality of work life for employees. Other organizations appreciate the reduction in supervisory overhead, although this alone is seldom a motivating force behind the creation of these teams. General Electric's Columbia, Maryland, facility reports that its self-directed workforce has saved $1.5 million in workers' compensation claims over three years.[47]

Sweden and northwestern Europe

In Sweden and other advanced industrial countries with extensive government-provided benefits, companies such as Volvo have used various forms of leaderless work teams to improve the quality of work life. Workers in Sweden and other northwestern European countries receive such extensive unemployment, health, and other social services from their governments that employers with unattractive jobs find it extremely difficult to find and retain workers.[48] As a result, job design among European firms has proved particularly important to their competitive position. With the declining growth rate of the North American workforce, job design is likely to grow in importance on this side of the Atlantic too.

Ultimately, however, managers and HR departments must balance the needs of a good quality of work life with the "bottom-line," or economic, results. The goal is not to produce "happy workers." The firm's managers and HR department must enhance the strategic success of the organization in a socially responsible way while improving the quality of work life within the constraints of competition, technology, cultural diversity, ethics, and economic efficiency.

▶ Summary

Job analysis information provides the foundation for an organization's human resource information system. Analysts seek to gain a general understanding of the organization and the work it performs. Then they design job analysis questionnaires to collect specific data about jobs, jobholder characteristics, and job performance standards. The job analysis information can be collected through interviews, juries of experts, mail questionnaires, employee logs, direct observation, or a combination of these techniques. Once collected, the data are converted into such useful applications as job descriptions, job specifications, and job standards.

Job analysis information is important because it tells HR specialists which duties and responsibilities are associated with each job. This information is used when HR specialists undertake HR management activities such as job design, recruiting, and selection. Jobs are the link between organizations and their human resources. The combined accomplishment of every job allows the organization to meet its objectives. Similarly, jobs represent not only a source of income to workers but also a means for fulfilling their needs. However, for the organization and its employees to receive these mutual benefits, jobs must provide a high quality of work life.

Achieving a high quality of work life requires jobs that are well designed. Effective job design requires a trade-off between efficiency and behavioral elements. Efficiency elements stress productivity; behavioral elements focus on employee needs. The role of managers and HR specialists is to achieve a balance between these trade-offs. When jobs are underspecialized, job designers may simplify a job by reducing the number of tasks. If jobs are overspecialized, they must be expanded or enriched.

▶ Terms for Review

Job analysis	Ergonomics
Job description	Autonomy
Job code	Task identity
Dictionary of Occupational Titles (DOT)	Task significance
Job specification	Work simplification
Job performance standards	Reengineering
Job families	Job rotation
Position analysis questionnaire	Job enlargement
Specialization	Job enrichment
Job cycles	

▶ Review and Discussion Questions

1. What types of raw data are the questions on a job analysis checklist designed to obtain? Are there other data you should seek for management jobs?

2. What are the different methods of collecting job analysis information, and what are the advantages and disadvantages of each technique?

3. In collecting job analysis information for jobs in different countries, what additional factors should analysts and managers consider?

4. Suppose you were assigned to write the job descriptions in a paint factory in El Paso, Texas, that employed mostly Mexican immigrants who spoke little English. What methods would you use to collect job analysis data?

5. If a manager in the paint factory refused to complete a job analysis questionnaire, what reasons would you use to persuade this reluctant manager?

6. What are some of the problems you would expect to arise in an organization that had carefully designed its jobs for maximum efficiency without careful consideration of employee needs?

7. How would your answers to question 6 change if the jobs were located in a developing nation with low educational levels and a workforce that had no prior industrial experience?

8. Suppose you have been assigned to design the job of ticket clerk for an intrastate airline. How would you handle the following trade-offs?

a. Would you recommend highly specialized job designs to minimize training or very broad jobs with all clerks cross-trained to handle multiple tasks? Why?

b. Would you change your answer if you knew that employees tended to quit the job of ticket clerk within the first six months? Why or why not?

9. Assume you are told to evaluate a group of jobs in a boat-building business. After studying each job for a considerable amount of time, you identify the following activities associated with each job. What job-redesign techniques would you recommend for these jobs, if any?

a. *Sailmaker.* Cuts and sews material with very little variety in the type of work from day to day. Job is highly skilled and takes years to learn.

b. *Sander.* Sands rough wood and fiberglass edges almost continuously. Little skill is required.

c. *Sales representative.* Talks to customers, answers phone inquiries, suggests customized additions to special-order boats.

d. *Boat preparer.* Cleans up completed boats, waxes fittings, and generally makes the boat ready for customer delivery. Few skills are required.

▶ Incident 5-1

The Brazilian Subsidiary

A large, well-known Canadian company had fully depreciated the equipment used to make specialized automobile components for North American automobile producers. Although the equipment had been well maintained and worked well, it required considerable hands-on labor to use. The result was high labor costs that made the company's brake assemblies, axle mounts, and related products unprofitable. A decision was made to replace the equipment with more highly automated, numerically controlled machine tools. Since the economic value of the old equipment exceeded its value as scrap, the equipment was shipped to the company's Brazilian operations, where labor costs were considerably lower.

Upon arrival and setup in a new facility, the company received numerous profitable orders from Brazil's rapidly growing automobile industry. Though the labor hours per product remained about the same, the lower Brazilian labor rates allowed the new facility to be profitable. Soon a second shift was added, and problems began. The equipment experienced a growing "downtime" because of machine failures. Quality—particularly on part dimensions—declined dramatically.

At a staff meeting the Brazilian plant manager met with his staff, including several industrial engineers who had been trained in Canada and the United States. The engineers argued that the problems were almost certainly caused by maintenance since the machinery had worked well in Canada and initially in Brazil. The HR director agreed that maintenance on the old machinery was probably involved but also noted that many of the "on-machine" instructions and maintenance manuals had not been translated into Portuguese. He also observed that the problems began after the second shift was hired.

1. From the discussion of job analysis information and job design in this chapter, what actions would you recommend to the HR department?

2. Given the problems associated with the second shift, what differences would you look for between first- and second-shift workers?

3. Since the Canadian workers had considerable experience with the equipment and the workers (particularly on the second shift) in Brazil had little, what implications do you see for job design?

▶ Exercise 5-1

Preparation of a Job Description

As was discussed in this chapter, there are several ways to collect job analysis information. One way is through observation. Using the form in Figure 5-3, complete parts C through J for the job of professor. After you have completed those sections of the job analysis questionnaire, use the format in Figure 5-5 and write a job description for the job of professor. When you are finished, look up the definition of professor in the *Dictionary of Occupational Titles*.

1. How does the description in the *Dictionary of Occupational Titles* vary in format and content from the one you wrote?

2. What parts of the professor's job are the most important in your opinion?

▶ References

1. Robert J. Sahl, "Pressing New Reasons for Accurate Job Descriptions," *The Human Resource Professional,* Fall 1992, p. 20.

2. Margaret Magnus and Morton E. Grossman, "Using Computers Is Catching On," *Recruitment Today,* Summer 1990, p. 17.

3. Valdis E. Krebs, "Planning for Information Effectiveness," *Personnel Administrator,* September 1988, pp. 34–42.

4. William Bridges, "The End of the Job," *Fortune,* Sept. 19, 1994, pp. 62–74.

5. John Hoerr, Michael A. Pollock, and David E. Whiteside, "Management Discovers the Human Side of Automation," *Business Week,* Sept. 29, 1986, pp. 70–75. See also Tody D. Wall, Nigel Kemp, Paul R. Jackson, and Chris W. Clegg, "Outcomes of Autonomous Workgroups: A Long-Term Field Experiment," *Academy of Management Journal,* vol. 29, no. 2, pp. 280–304.

6. Nancy Howe, "Documentation Takes Form," *Personnel Journal,* December 1988, pp. 66–73.

7. Addressing employee concerns before gathering the job analysis information was suggested in personal correspondence from George G. Power, Jr., of the University of Virginia, Falls Church campus.

8. Patrick R. Conley and Paul R. Sackett, "Effects of Using High- Versus Low-Performing Job Incumbents as Sources of Job-Analysis Information," *Journal of Applied Psychology,* vol. 72, no. 83, 1987, pp. 434–437. See also Yitzhak Fried and Gerald R. Ferris, "The Validity of the Job Characteristics Model: A Review and Meta-Analysis," *Personnel Psychology,* vol. 40, 1987, pp. 287–322; Wayman C. Mullins and Wilson W. Kimbrough, "Group Composition as a Determinant of Job Analysis Outcomes," *Journal of Applied Psychology,* vol. 73, no. 4, 1988, pp. 657–664.

9. Ronald Henkoff, "Companies That Train Best," *Fortune,* Mar. 22, 1993, pp. 62–75.

10. P. R. Jeanneret, *A Study of the Job Dimensions of "Worker-Oriented" Job Variables and of Their Attribute Profiles,* West Lafayette, Ind.: Purdue University, 1969 (doctoral dissertation). See also E. J. McCormick, P. R. Jeanneret, and R. C. Mecham, "A Study of Job Characteristics and Job Dimensions as Based on the Position Analysis Questionnaire (PAQ)," *Journal of Applied Psychology,* vol. 56, no. 2, pp. 347–368.

11. Robert J. Harvey, Lee Friedman, Milton D. Hakel, and Edwin T. Cornelius III, "Dimensionality of the Job Element Inventory, a Simplified Worker-Oriented Job Analysis Questionnaire," *Journal of Applied Psychology,* vol. 73, no. 4, pp. 639–646.

12. Ibid., p. 643.

13. Judith A. DeLapa, "Job Descriptions That Work," *Personnel Journal,* June 1989, pp. 156–158, 160. See also Michael A. Campion and Paul W. Thayer, "How Do You Design a Job?" *Personnel Journal,* January 1989, pp. 43–44, 46.

14. Philip C. Grant, "What Use Is a Job Description?" *Personnel Journal,* February 1988, p. 50. See also Mark A. Jones, "Job Descriptions Made Easy," *Personnel Journal,* May 1984, pp. 31–34.

15. Michael A. Campion, "Ability Requirement Implications of Job Design: An Interdisciplinary Perspective," *Personnel Psychology,* vol. 42, no. 1, 1989, pp. 1–24. See also U.S. Department of Labor, *Dictionary of Occupational Titles,* Washington, D.C.: U.S. Superintendent of Publications, 1965, vol. I, p. xvi.

16. Paul Sheibar, "A Simple Selection System Called 'Job Match,' " *Personnel Journal,* January 1979, p. 26.

17. Nanette Fondas, "A Behavioral Description for Managers," *Organizational Dynamics,* Summer 1992, pp. 47–58.

18. Valdis E. Krebs, "TRW Makes the Move to Macintoshes," *Personnel Journal,* December 1989, pp. 58–63.

19. Magnus and Grossman, op. cit.

20. Elliott Witkin, "Emphasize the Human in HRIS," *Personnel Journal,* September 1989, p. 75. See also Joe Pasqualetto, "New Competencies Define the HRIS Manager's Future Role," *Personnel Journal,* January 1993, pp. 91–99.

21. Maureen MacAdam, "HRIS: Document What You're Doing," *Personnel Journal,* February 1990, pp. 57–63.

22. John E. Sprig, "Selling the HRIS to Top Management," *Personnel,* October 1988, pp. 26–32, 34.

23. "The Flowering of Feudalism," *The Economist,* Feb. 27, 1993, p. 70.

24. Ibid.

25. Sahl, op. cit., pp. 18–20.

26. Michael N. Wolfe, "Computerization: It Can Bring Sophistication into Personnel," *Personnel Journal,* June 1978, pp. 325ff. See also Patricia Teets, "Information Access Comes of Age with Online Data Bases," *Personnel Journal,* January 1987, pp. 112–113.

27. Edwin T. Cornelius III, Angelo S. Denisi, and Allyn G. Blencoe, "Expert and Naive Raters Using the PAQ: Does It Matter?" *Personnel Psychology,* 1984, pp. 453–467.

28. Hank Guzda, "Saturn: The Sky's the Limit," *Labor Relations Today,* March–April 1990, p. 2; Alex Taylor III, "GM's $11,000,000,000 Turnaround," *Fortune,* Oct. 17, 1994, pp. 54–74. John Morrell & Co. received a $1.25 million fine because "it exposed workers to 'serious and sometimes disabling" injuries caused by repetitive job motions." Christopher Drew, "Morrell to Pay $1.25 Million in Safety Case," *Chicago Tribune,* Mar. 21, 1990, sect. 3, p. 3.

29. Loretta D. Foxman and Walter L. Polsky, "Job Design v. Job Evaluation," *Personnel Journal,* March 1988, pp. 35–36. See also William H. Glick, G. Douglas Jenkins, Jr., and Nina Gupta, "Method versus Substance: How Strong Are Underlying Relationships between Job Characteristics and Attitudinal Outcomes?" *Academy of Management Journal,* vol. 29, no. 3, 1985, pp. 441–464. See also Daniel A. Ondrack and Martin Evans, "Job Enrichment and Job Satisfaction in Quality of Working Life and Nonquality of Working Life Work Sites," *Human Relations,* vol. 39, no. 9, 1986, pp. 871–889.

30. Hoerr, Pollock, and Whiteside, op. cit.

31. Louis Uchitelle, "Stanching the Loss of Good Jobs," *The New York Times,* National ed., Sept. 12, 1993, p. 3–6.

32. "Dole Announces That Ford Motor Has Agreed to Corporate-wide Ergonomic Improvements in Historic Settlement," *U.S. Department of Labor News Release,* July 23, 1990, pp. 1–3.

33. Barbara Garson, "Luddites in Lordstown," *Harpers,* June 1972, pp. 68–73.

34. J. R. Hackman and E. E. Lawler III, "Employee Reactions to Job Characteristics," in W. E. Scott and L. L. Cummings (eds.), *Readings in Organizational Behavior and Human Performance,* Homewood, Ill.: Richard D. Irwin, 1973, p. 231. For a detailed summary of research on job design, see C. L. Hulin and M. R. Blood, "Job Enlargement, Individual Differences, and Worker Responses," *Psychological Bulletin,* 1968, pp. 41–55. For a more recent summarization, see Jon L. Pierce and Randall B. Dunham, "Task Design: A Literature Review," *The Academy of Management Review,* October 1976, pp. 83–97. See also Ricky W. Griffin, Ann Welsh, and Gregory Moorhead, "Perceived Task Characteristics and Employee Performance: A Literature Review," *Academy of Management Review,* October 1981, pp. 644–664.

35. Frederick Herzberg, Bernard Mausner, and Barbara Snyderman, *The Motivation to Work,* New York: Wiley, 1959. See also E. F. Stone and L. W. Porter, "Job Characteristics and Job Attitudes: A Multivariate Study," *Journal of Applied Psychology,* 1975, pp. 57–64.

36. G. E. Farris, "Organizational Factors and Individual Performance: A Longitudinal Study," *Journal of Applied Psychology,* 1969, pp. 87–92.

37. Stone and Porter, op. cit.

38. Hackman and Lawler, op. cit.

39. Edward E. Lawler III, "Job Attitudes and Employee Motivation: Theory, Research, and Practice," *Personnel Psychology,* Summer 1970, p. 234.

40. Adapted from Richard W. Woodman and John J. Sherwood, "A Comprehensive Look at Job Design," *Personnel Journal,* August 1977, p. 386.

41. J. Barton Cunningham and Ted Eberle, "A Guide to Job Enrichment and Redesign," *Personnel,* February 1990, pp. 56–61. See also M. Scott Myers, *Every Employee and Manager,* New York: McGraw-Hill, 1970.

42. Robert N. Ford, "Job Enrichment Lessons from AT&T," *Harvard Business Review,* January–February 1973, p. 105.

43. Robert H. Schappe, "Twenty-Two Arguments against Job Enrichment," *Personnel Journal,* February 1974, pp. 116–123.

44. William B. Werther, Jr., "Beyond Job Enrichment to Employment Enrichment," *Personnel Journal,* August 1975, pp. 438–442.

45. Brian Dumaine, "Who Needs a Boss?" *Fortune,* May 7, 1990, pp. 52–60.

46. Ibid.

47. John Jenkins, "Self-directed Work Force Promotes Safety," *HRMagazine,* February 1990, pp. 54–56.

48. Larry Eichel, "Model Welfare State Succumbs to Chill of Economics," *The Miami Herald,* Nov. 2, 1990, p. 19A.

6

In the increasingly competitive, globalized economy, managers are more seriously looking for practices, procedures, and policies . . . to gain a competitive advantage.
GERALD R. FERRIS, GAIL S. RUSS, ROBERT ALBANESE, and JOSEPH J. MARTOCCHIO[1]

Merging strategic and human resource planning activities has become a critical source of competitiveness for all organizations.
DAVE ULRICH[2]

Human Resource Planning

CHAPTER OBJECTIVES

After studying this chapter, you should be able to:

1. DISCUSS the relationship between strategic planning and human resource planning.

2. EXPLAIN why large organizations use human resource planning more than small ones do.

3. IDENTIFY the factors that shape an organization's demand for human resources.

4. DESCRIBE the shortcomings of methods used to forecast the demand for human resources.

5. EXPLAIN the role of skills inventories in developing succession plans.

6. RECOMMEND solutions to staffing shortages or surpluses.

HR planning

Armed with information about jobs and their design, *human resource planning* (HR planning) systematically forecasts an organization's future demand for and supply of employees.[3] HR planning—or employment planning, as it is also called—enables managers and HR departments to develop staffing plans that support the organization's strategy by allowing it to fill job openings proactively.

If the organization is not staffed with the right number and types of people, strategic, operational, and functional goals may go unmet. More and more executives now realize, however, that well-conceived HR plans are essential to achieving strategic success.[4] For example, the strategic decision by high-technology firms such as Motorola and IBM to develop new products and enter new markets often depends on the availability of qualified technical and support people. Without sufficient engineering talent, strategy-driven opportunities can be lost to better staffed competitors.[5]

IBM

At IBM, strategic business planning begins with "top-down" revenue and profit targets established by the company's policy committee. Then executives in the different business areas develop the strategies, product thrusts, and sales volumes needed to reach the policy committee's goals. National and international divisions of IBM then create functional strategies for development, manufacturing, marketing, and service. Line managers are responsible for folding the functional plans into divisional ones.

The HR department's role is to review all divisional plans before they are sent to the corporate division. Concerns about human resources are injected into the business plans by HR specialists who work closely with divisional managers, even when the corporate strategy is to downsize. These managers are encouraged to involve the HR department because the business plan will be reviewed for HR considerations before it is finalized.[6] In addition, IBM improves the effectiveness of its planning by holding planners responsible for their estimates.

International HR planning

Through their involvement in the strategic planning process, IBM's managers and HR planners are better able to develop plans that fit with the company's strategic and operational intentions, whether that involves downsizing the organization or growing overseas.[7] For example, international expansion strategies depend on the department's ability to fill key jobs with foreign nationals and the reassignment of home-country employees across national borders. As more and more corporate strategies involve global operations, the need for HR planning will grow in importance because of the increased complexity of staffing needs across foreign borders when international relocation, cultural, linguistic, and development needs are considered.[8] Without effective HR plans, the growing competition for international executives may lead to expensive and strategically disruptive turnover among key decision makers.

Although there is no single right approach to HR planning, all organizations should identify their short-run and long-run employee needs by examining their corporate strategies. Short-range plans point out job openings that must be filled in the coming year; long-range plans estimate HR needs for the next two, five, or more years. Each organization must find a blend of practices that work within the company culture and the realities of business necessity.[9] This view is summarized by John W. Boroski of the Eastman Kodak Company, a worldwide producer of film, cameras, and imaging systems.

Kodak

Like many large companies, Eastman Kodak has experimented with various approaches to human resource (HR) planning over the years. At the corporate level, HR planning was thought of as a means for ensuring that the right number and the right kinds of people were at the right places at the right times.

". . . HR planning has no universally-accepted definition. Our evolving thinking has been . . . influenced by . . . academics, consultants, and practitioners. In effect, we have borrowed, adapted, discovered, and created our way to an approach to HR planning that is congruent with our current business circumstances and responsive to change."[10]

Large company benefits

HR planning is more common in large organizations such as Eastman Kodak because it allows them to:

■ Integrate strategic demands with appropriate staffing levels.

■ Improve the utilization of human resources.

■ Match HR activities and future organizational objectives efficiently.

■ Achieve economies in hiring new workers.

■ Expand the HR information base to assist other HR activities and other organizational units.

■ Make major demands on local labor markets successfully.

■ Coordinate different HR programs such as affirmative action plans and hiring needs.

Small companies

Small organizations can expect similar advantages, but their gains are often considerably less. In fact, the benefits of HR planning for small organizations may not justify the time and costs. Consider the different situations faced by small- and large-city governments.

Rural City employs twenty workers and is growing 10 percent a year. For Rural City, that means adding two new employees each year. Metropolis has 8000 employees and is growing by 5 percent. For Metropolis, that means 400 new employees plus replacements for those who leave. If it costs $4000 to find and hire a typical employee, Rural City will spend $8000 to hire two more workers. Metropolis will spend $1.6 million just to add new employees. If employment planning saves 25 percent, Rural City's manager cannot justify detailed planning efforts that cost $2000. But for $400,000 Metropolis can afford a specialist and still save hundreds of thousands of dollars after planning expenses are deducted.

Nevertheless, HR planning is useful to HR specialists in *both* small and large organizations. It shows small employers the HR considerations they face if their strategy changes to one of rapid expansion. (For example, if Rural City attracted several large factories to its area, expansion of city services would depend partly on the city's HR planning.) Large organizations can benefit from planning because it reveals ways to make the HR function more effective.

This chapter examines how managers and HR departments use HR planning to support their organizations' strategic plans and initiatives. It begins with an explanation of how HR departments and managers estimate future job openings. It ends by showing the methods used to isolate potential sources of employees to fill those vacancies.

▶ The Demand for Human Resources

Research summary | To support the execution of their current strategies, most firms predict their future employment needs (at least informally) even if they do not estimate their sources of supply.[11] For example, a classic study found that employers are two times more likely to estimate HR demand than to estimate supply.[12] The challenges that determine this demand and the methods of forecasting it merit a brief review.

Causes of Demand

Although many challenges influence the demand for human talent, changes in the environment, organization, and workforce that have an impact on the corporate strategy are of primary concern.[13] These factors are common to short-range and long-range employment plans. Some of these causes are within the organization's control, and others are not, as Figure 6-1 summarizes.

External challenges. Developments in the organization's environment that affect the organization's strategies are difficult to predict in the short run and sometimes impossible to estimate in the long run. Reconsider the example of small-city government. City planners seldom know about major factory relocations until shortly before construction begins. Other *economic* developments

| Figure 6-1 | **Cause of Demand for Human Resources in the Future** |

EXTERNAL	ORGANIZATIONAL	WORKFORCE
■ Economics	■ Strategic plans	■ Retirement
■ Social-political-legal	■ Budgets	■ Resignations
■ Technology	■ Sales and production forecasts	■ Terminations
■ Competitors	■ New ventures	■ Deaths
	■ Organization and job designs	■ Leaves of absence

have a noticeable effect but are difficult to estimate. Examples include inflation, unemployment, and changing workforce patterns. For example:

Changing workforce

Nearly 45 million people, more than one-third of the American work force, are either self-employed or working as temps, part-timers, or consultants, calculates Richard Belous, chief economist of the National Planning Association. This so-called contingent work force has grown 57% since 1980, three times faster than the labor force as a whole.[14]

Social, political, and *legal* challenges are easier to predict, but their implications are seldom clear. The impact on HR planning of the civil rights laws passed in the 1960s was uncertain until the 1970s. Now most large firms have affirmative action programs and compliance officers, as was discussed in Chapter 4, and a greater diversity in the workforce, as was discussed in Chapter 2. Likewise, the implications of abolishing the mandatory retirement age in 1986 may not be known until a generation has lived without the "65 and out" tradition.[15] As a result, assumptions about worker demographics made by managers and the HR department may be less reliable. The *Worker Adjustment and Retraining Notification Act* of 1988 restricted employers' ability to make adjustments in the size of their workforces through layoffs by requiring sixty-day advance notification under some circumstances.[16] The Gulf war with Iraq in 1991 upset many HR plans as thousands of military reservists were called to active duty.

WARN Act

Technology changes are difficult to predict and assess but may radically alter strategic and therefore HR plans. Many thought the computer would cause mass unemployment, for example. Today the computer field is a large one, employing millions of people directly or indirectly. Technology complicates HR planning because it tends to reduce employment in one department (bookkeeping, for example) while increasing it in another (such as computer operations). The growing use of computers—especially networks of interconnected personal computers—even allows companies to reorganize and "downsize," further complicating the HR planning process. The use of robots and other forms of computerized automation will undoubtedly complicate future employment planning even more.

Competitors have forced many firms in North America and around the world to reduce their workforces in order to regain the strategic initiative. Corporate strategies that attempt to achieve lower costs have led to facilities being moved "offshore," generally to consolidate operations and find lower labor costs in industries such as automobiles, electronics, data processing, and research and development.

Organizational decisions.   As organizations respond to these changes in their environment, decisions are made to modify the strategic plan.[17] The strategic plan commits the firm to long-range objectives such as growth rates and new products, markets, or services. These objectives dictate the number and types of employees needed in the future. To achieve long-term objectives, senior managers and HR specialists must develop long-range HR plans that accommodate the strategic plan. In the short run, planners find that strategic plans become operational in the form of *budgets*. Budget increases or cuts are the most significant short-run influence on HR needs.

Budgets

Sales and production forecasts are less exact than budgets but may provide even quicker notice of short-run changes in the demand for human resources.

Manager overrides
HR plans

The HR manager for a nationwide chain of furniture outlets observed a sharp decline in sales that was brought on by a recession. The manager quickly discarded the short-run HR plan and imposed an employment freeze on all outlets' hiring plans.

Failure to adjust to changed employment demand may require a reduction in forces or a layoff.

HRP and
corporate planning

New ventures mean changing HR demands. When a new venture is begun internally from scratch, the lead time may allow planners to develop short-run and long-run employment plans. But new ventures begun through acquisitions and mergers cause an immediate revision of HR demands and can lead to new organization and job designs. A reorganization, especially after a merger or acquisition, can radically alter HR needs. Likewise, the redesign of jobs changes the required skill levels of future workers. At a time when companies are constantly acquiring, merging, and spinning off divisions; entering new businesses; and getting out of old ones, management must base strategic decisions more than ever on HR considerations—matching skills with jobs, keeping key personnel after a merger, and solving the human problems that arise from introducing new technology or closing a plant.[18] To ensure that the "people" side of mergers and acquisitions was given full consideration, CSX, a major U.S. railroad, merged its HR group with its corporate planning staff.[19]

Workforce factors.   Demand is modified by employee actions such as retirements, resignations, terminations, deaths, and leaves of absence. When large numbers of employees are involved, past experience usually serves as a reasonably accurate guide. However, reliance on past experience means that managers and HR specialists must be sensitive to changes that alter past trends.

Jim Santino used to keep close track of employees nearing retirement so that his HR plan remained accurate. However, in 1986 Congress prohibited employers from requiring mandatory retirement at any age. This meant that all employees of Universal Book Publishers could continue to work as long as they desired. As a result, Jim can no longer use past experience as a guide to when older workers will retire. This change has caused Jim to seek other ways to forecast his short-run HR needs.

AIDS

Although heart disease and cancer take more lives each year than does AIDS (acquired immune deficiency syndrome), the impact of AIDS on the demand for HR is not as well understood. The limited experience of planners in dealing with a growing epidemic makes the impact of AIDS on the demand for future employees difficult to predict. The incidence of the disease is uneven, affecting the poor and unemployed disproportionately, particularly in large cities. Some industries, especially the fashion industry, have been affected more forcefully than others. However, the Centers for Disease Control in Atlanta estimate that more Americans have died from AIDS than died in World War II and the Vietnam conflict combined. Clearly, the spreading epidemic will significantly affect more organizations and their HR plans as we approach the twenty-first century.[20]

Forecasting Techniques

Human resource forecasts are attempts to predict an organization's future demand for employees. As Figure 6-2 shows, forecasting techniques range from the informal to the sophisticated. Even the most sophisticated methods are not perfectly accurate; they are best viewed as approximations. Most firms make only casual estimates about the immediate future. As they gain experience in

Figure 6-2	Forecasting Techniques for Estimating Future Human Resource Needs

EXPERT	TREND	OTHER
■ Informal and instant decisions	■ Extrapolation	■ Budget and planning analysis
■ Formal expert survey	■ Indexation	■ New-venture analysis
■ Nominal group technique	■ Statistical analysis	■ Computer models
■ Delphi technique		

forecasting HR needs, they may use more sophisticated techniques. Each of the forecasting methods listed in Figure 6-2 is explained below.

Expert forecasts.   *Expert forecasts* are based on the judgments of those who are knowledgeable about future HR needs. Since most employment decisions are made by line managers, HR planners must devise methods to learn about these managers' staffing needs. In small organizations, the director of operations or the HR manager may have all the needed knowledge. In larger organizations, the simplest method is to *survey* those managers who are the ultimate experts in the future staffing needs of their departments.

NGT approach   The survey may be an informal poll, a written questionnaire, or a focused discussion using the *nominal group technique* (NGT). The NGT presents a group of managers with a problem statement such as, What will cause our staffing needs to change over the next year? Then each of the five to fifteen participants writes down as many answers as he or she can imagine. After about five to ten minutes, these ideas are shared in round-robin fashion until all written ideas and any new ideas they have stimulated have been recorded. The group's ideas are then discussed and ranked by having each member vote for the three to five most important ones.[21]

Delphi technique   If the experts cannot be brought together with the nominal group technique, a survey approach can be used in the *Delphi technique*. Estimates are solicited from a group of experts, usually managers. Then HR planners act as an intermediary, summarize the various responses, and report the findings back to the experts. The experts are surveyed again after they get this feedback. Summaries and surveys are repeated until the experts begin to agree on future developments. (Usually four or five surveys are enough.) For example, the HR department may survey all production surpervisors and managers until an agreement is reached on the number of replacements needed for the next year.

Trend projection forecasts.   Perhaps the quickest forecasting technique is to project past trends. The two simplest methods are extrapolation and indexation. *Extrapolation* involves extending past rates of change into the future. For
Extrapolation   example, if an average of 20 production workers was hired each month for the past two years, extrapolating that trend into the future means that 240 production workers will be added during the upcoming year.

Indexation is a method of estimating future employment needs by matching employment growth with an index, such as the ratio of production employees to sales. For example, planners may discover that for each million-dollar increase in sales, the production department requires ten new assemblers.

Extrapolation and indexation are crude approximations in the short run because they assume that the causes of demand—external, organizational, and workforce factors—remain constant, which is seldom the case. These methods are very inaccurate for long-range HR projections. More sophisticated *statistical analyses* make allowances for changes in the underlying causes of demand.

Other forecasting methods.   There are several other ways for planners to estimate the future demand for human resources. One approach is *budget and planning analysis.* Organizations that need HR planning generally have detailed budgets and long-range plans. A study of department budgets reveals financial authorizations for more employees. These data plus extrapolations of work-force changes (resignations, terminations, and the like) can provide short-run estimates of HR needs. Long-term estimates can be made from each department or division's long-range plans.

New ventures

When new ventures complicate employment planning, planners can use new-venture analysis. *New-venture analysis* requires planners to estimate human resource needs through comparisons with firms that perform similar operations. For example, a petroleum company that plans to open a coal mine can estimate its future employment needs by examining the employment levels of other coal mines of similar size.

Computer models

The most sophisticated forecasting approaches involve *computer models,* which are series of mathematical formulas that simultaneously use extrapolation, indexation, survey results, and estimates of workforce changes to compute future staffing needs. Over time, actual changes in HR demand are used to refine the computer's formulas.

There are four levels of complexity in HR forecasting.[22] These stages of forecasting sophistication are summarized in Figure 6-3. As can be seen, they range from informal discussions to highly complex computerized forecasting systems. The more sophisticated techniques are found in large organizations that have had years of experience in HR planning. Small firms and those just beginning to forecast HR needs are more likely to start with stage 1 and progress to other stages as planners seek greater accuracy.

Women overseas

These forecasting techniques must be applied with great sensitivity in the foreign arena. Differences in culture may lead to radically different constraints. For example, in some Arabic nations women are excluded from some jobs and work settings because they are women. In countries such as India, caste systems limit the type of work a person may do. Although country-specific constraints may seem inappropriate, they are often deeply embedded in a nation's culture and religion. HR plans that do not incorporate these variations are likely to be useless or even disruptive.

Human Resource Requirements

Figure 6-4 gives an overview of the key considerations involved in estimating the demand for human resources. It shows that forecasts translate the causes of demand into short-range and long-range statements of needs. The resulting long-range plans are of necessity general statements of *probable* needs. Specific numbers are estimated or omitted entirely because initially they have a low level of accuracy. But as planners become more familiar with the causes of demand and the forecasting techniques, their estimates of HR demand become more accurate.

· Figure 6-3	**Stages of Complexity and Sophistication in Human Resource Forecasting**

STAGE 1	STAGE 2	STAGE 3	STAGE 4
■ Managers discuss goals, plans, and thus types and numbers of people needed in the short term. ■ Highly informal and subjective.	■ Annual planning and budgeting process includes human resource needs. ■ Specify quantity and quality of talent needs as far as possible. ■ Identify problems requiring action: individual or general.	■ Using computer-generated analyses, examine causes of problems and future trends regarding the flow of talent. ■ Use computer to relieve managers of routine forecasting tasks (such as vacancies or turnover).	■ On-line modeling and computer simulation of talent needs, flows, and costs to aid in a continuing process of updating and projecting needs, staffing plans, career opportunities, and thus program plans. ■ Provide best possible current information for managerial decisions. ■ Exchange data (such as economic, employment, and social data) with other companies and with government.

Source: James W. Walker, "Evaluating the Practical Effectiveness of Human Resource Planning Applications," *Human Resource Management,* Spring 1974, p. 21.

Staffing table

Short-range plans are more specific and may be reported in the form of a staffing table (Figure 6-5). A *staffing table* lists the future employment needs for each type of job. The listing may be a specific number or an approximate range of needs, depending on the accuracy of the underlying forecast. Staffing tables (also called "manning" tables) are neither complete nor wholly accurate; they are only approximations. But these estimates allow HR specialists to match short-range demand and supply. They help operating departments run more smoothly and can enhance the image of the HR department.

When they have specific estimates of future HR needs, specialists can become more proactive and systematic. For example, a review of Figure 6-5 shows that the city's HR department must hire thirty-two police academy recruits every three months. This knowledge allows the HR department to plan its recruiting campaign so that it peaks about six weeks before the beginning of the next police academy class. Advanced planning allows the HR department to screen applicants and notify them at least three weeks before the class begins. Recruiters can then inform applicants who cannot be ready that quickly

Figure 6-4	Components of the Future Demand for Human Resources

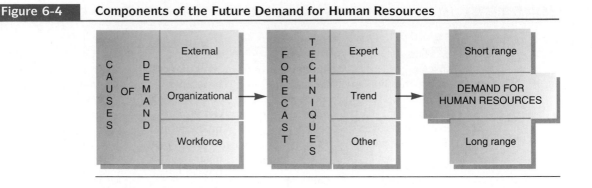

about when the next class will begin. If the recruiters waited for the police department to notify them, notification might come too late to allow a systematic recruiting and screening process. Staffing tables enable recruiters to be proactive and plan their activities better.

Figure 6-5	A Partial Staffing Table for a City Government

METROPOLIS
CITY GOVERNMENT
STAFFING TABLE   Date Compiled _____

Budget Code Number	Job Title	Using Department(s)	Anticipated Openings by Month of the Year												
			Total	1	2	3	4	5	6	7	8	9	10	11	12
100-32	Police Academy Recruit	Police	128	32			32			32			32		
100-33	Police Dispatcher	Police	3	2					1						
100-84	Meter Reader	Police	24	2	2	2	2	2	2	2	2	2	2	2	2
100-85	Traffic Supervisor	Police	5	2			1			1			1		
100-86	Team Supervisor- Police (Sergeant)	Police	5	2			1			1			1		
100-97	Duty Supervisor- Police (Lieut.)	Police	2	1					1						
100-99	Shift Officer- Police (Captain)	Police	1	1											
200-01	Car Washer	Motor Pool	4	1			1			1			1		
200-12	Mechanic's Asst.	Motor Pool	3				1			1			1		
200-13	Mechanic III	Motor Pool	2	1									1		
200-14	Mechanic II	Motor Pool	1						1						
200-15	Mechanic I (Working Supervisor)	Motor Pool	1	1											
300-01	Clerk IV	Administration	27	10			5			6			6		

▶ The Supply of Human Resources

Internal supply
of workers

Once the future demand for human resources is projected, the next major concern is filling projected openings. There are two sources of supply: internal and external. The internal supply consists of present employees who can be promoted, transferred, or demoted to fill expected openings. For example, openings at the police academy might be filled by other city employees who want to transfer from their present jobs into police work. Those people represent the internal supply. The external supply consists of people who do not work for the city.

Estimates of Internal Supply

Estimates of the internal supply of human resources involve more than merely counting the number of employees. As Figure 6-6 implies, planners audit the present workforce to learn about worker capabilities. This information allows these planners to estimate tentatively which openings can be filled by present employees. These tentative assignments usually are recorded on a replacement chart. Considering present employees for future job openings is important if workers are to have lifelong careers rather than dead-end jobs with the employer.

Audits and replacement charts also are important additions to the information base of the human resources department. With greater knowledge of employees, the department can plan recruiting, training, and career planning activities more effectively. This knowledge can even help the HR department meet its affirmative action plan by identifying internal minority candidates for job openings. Since audits and replacement charts are important in proactive human resources work, they are explained more fully in the text below.

| Figure 6-6 | Factors That Determine the Future Supply of Human Resources |

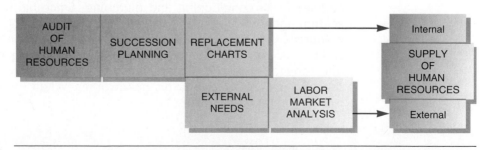

Skills and
management
inventories

Human resource audits. *Human resource audits* summarize each employee's skills, knowledge, and abilities. Audits of nonmanagers are called *skills inventories;* audits of managers are known as *management inventories.* Whatever name is used, an inventory represents a catalog of each employee's skills and abilities. A summary of this sort gives planners a comprehensive understanding of the capabilities that are to be found in the organization's workforce.

A skills inventory form is shown in Figure 6-7. It is divided into four parts. Part I can be completed by the HR department from employee records; it identifies the employee's job title, experience, age, and previous jobs. Part II seeks information about the skills, duties, responsibilities, and education of the worker. From these questions, planners learn about the mix of employee abilities. The HR department may collect these data through telephone or face-to-face interviews, or the questions may be sent periodically to the employee through the company mail. In addition, most firms encourage employees to update their information when significant changes occur. The employee's future potential is briefly summarized by the immediate superior in Part III. Performance, readiness for promotion, and any deficiencies are noted here. The supervisor's signature helps ensure that the accuracy of the form is reviewed by someone who knows the employee better than the HR specialists do. Part IV is added as a final check for completeness and for the addition of recent employee evaluations, which can provide more insight into past performance.

Inventory updates

Inventories of human resources are often computerized to match talent with openings and are updated periodically.[23] Large organizations, such as General Electric and the U.S. Air Force, use computer-based systems to quickly match jobs with personnel. Computerized records also facilitate updating, which should be done at least every two years if employees typically report major changes to the HR department when they occur. Major changes include new skills, degree completions, and changed job duties. Failure to update skills inventories can lead to present employees being overlooked for job openings within the organizations.

 After his regular working hours, Rafael Corda "moonlighted" by helping his brother attend to the maintenance work at a large paint factory. Rafael became interested in maintenance work and completed several courses in air-conditioning and plumbing. Since his full-time employer seldom updated the skills inventory for company employees, the human resources manager at the First National Bank was unaware of Rafael's diverse skills. After several weeks of searching, the manager hired a maintenance worker from outside the bank's present workforce. The bank spent $2000 to find this new worker. When Rafael found out, he was understandably upset.

Figure 6-7 **A Skills Inventory Form**

METROPOLIS
CITY GOVERNMENT
SKILLS INVENTORY   Date: _____

PART I (To be completed by human resource department)
1. Name _____   2. **Employee Number** _____
3. **Job Title** _____   4. **Experience** _____ **Years**
5. **Age** _____   6. **Years with City** _____
7. **Other Jobs Held:**
    With City: Title _____   From _____ to _____
                 Title _____   From _____ to _____
    Elsewhere: Title _____   From _____ to _____
                 Title _____   From _____ to _____

PART II (To be completed by employee)
8. Special Skills. List below any skills you possess even if not used on your present job. Include types and names of machines or tools with which you are experienced.
        Skills: _____
    Languages: _____   Fluency: Speak   Read   Write
    Machines: _____
        Tools: _____

9. Duties. Briefly describe your present duties. _____
_____

10. Responsibilities. Briefly describe your responsibilities for:
            City Equipment: _____
                City Funds: _____
            Employee Safety: _____
    Employee Supervision: _____

11. Education. Briefly describe your education and training background:
            Academic: (Circle highest grade) 6 7 8 9 10 11 12 Fr So Jr Sr Gr
        Job Training: _____
    Special Courses: _____
    Military Training: _____

PART III (To be completed by human resource department with supervisory inputs)
12. Overall Evaluation of Performance _____
_____

13. Overall Readiness for Promotion _____
        To What Job(s): _____
        Comments: _____

14. Current Deficiencies _____
_____

15. Supervisor's Signature _____   **Date:** _____

PART IV (To be completed by human resource department respresentative)
16. Are the two most recent performance evaluations attached? _____Yes   No
17. Prepared by _____   **Date:** _____

Management
inventories

Management inventories should be updated periodically since they are also used for key personnel decisions. In fact, some employers use the same form for managers and nonmanagers. When the forms differ, the management inventory requests information about management activities. Common topics include:

- Number of employees supervised
- Types of employees supervised
- Management training received

- Total budget managed
- Duties of subordinates
- Previous management duties

The growing workforce diversity discussed in Chapter 2 must be considered by many firms as they conduct HR audits. Even in a city government, skills and management audits should solicit information about language abilities. Supervisors and employees who have customer contact may be ideally suited for some job openings if they are bilingual. Of course, such skills should be bona fide occupational qualifications or they form the basis for charges of employment discrimination. Global companies also seek information about language skills, and many ask about international travel as an input for international placement.

Global companies'
needs

Succession planning.   HR audit information is used by planners to make judgments about possible promotions and transfers. *Succession planning* is the process HR planners and operating managers use to convert information about current employees into decisions about future internal job placements. With sophisticated HR information systems, much of the identification and tracking of key employees can be automated.[24] Since potential promotions and other placement decisions are usually the responsibility of operating managers, the HR department plays a confidential advisory role. Given the complexities and time demands involved in developing these plans, succession planning (or continuity planning, as it is also known) is usually limited to key employees and those identified as having long-term potential.

Continuity
planning

Exxon

Exxon is so far ahead in the succession planning game that it has already hired its CEO for the year 2010. Although it is not public knowledge who that person is, he or she is already being challenged, assessed, and groomed for the top spot. The primary purpose of Exxon's succession planning program . . . is to provide a systematic succession of first-rate managers throughout the company. To date, virtually the entire senior management staff . . . is a product of the . . . system.[25]

By identifying successors to key jobs and high-potential employees, corporations, such as Exxon, IBM, and Eastman Kodak help assure a steady flow of internal talent to fill important openings. Not only does succession planning encourage "hiring from within" and create an environment in which employees have careers and not merely jobs, it identifies human resource shortages

Hiring from within

and skill deficiencies before openings occur. Then, through special assign-ments, job rotation, training, and other forms of HR development, candidates can be prepared to accept the greater responsibilities of future job openings.[26] The result for the organization is greater continuity of operations and better qualified incumbents.

Another result of effective continuity planning can be a more unified corpo-rate culture. State Farm Insurance Companies use succession planning to iden-tify potential candidates to fill openings in the regional offices and headquarters. When top managers are moved through regional and headquarter offices, a more uniform company culture results, along with greater dedication to the company rather than to individual operations. In a similar manner, Sara Lee Corporation uses succession planning to better integrate its subsidiaries. Since it has acquired more than forty companies in recent years, its succession planning process man-dates that two of every five candidates come from another subsidiary.[27]

International succession planning

Global companies use succession planning for the same purposes. In addi-tion, international succession planning and the resulting transfers help develop managers and executives with a more global perspective. Assignments in dif-ferent countries and exposure to different cultures challenge an international executive's assumptions about business practices and ways of dealing with people.[28] Of course, international succession planning allows the organization to draw on a larger pool of talent, increasing the possibility of having the best people in the right jobs. However, the job of planning career moves across in-ternational boundaries is more complex than are domestic efforts. The need to consider language, family, cultural differences, relocation complexities, return travel, and related issues makes this newly emerging area of HR management particularly important and difficult.[29]

Replacement charts and summaries.   To consolidate the results of HR au-dits and succession planning, the HR department works with senior managers to develop replacement charts (Figure 6-8) or more detailed replacement sum-maries (Figure 6-9).

Replacement charts are a visual representation of who will replace whom if there is a job opening. The information for constructing the chart comes from the HR audit. Figure 6-8 illustrates a typical replacement chart. It shows the re-placement status of only a few jobs in the administration of a large city.

Replacement status

The figure indicates the minimum information usually included, although different firms may summarize different information in their replacement charts. The chart, much like an organization chart, depicts the various jobs in the organization and shows the status of likely candidates. Replacement status consists of two variables: present performance and promotability. Present per-formance is determined largely from supervisory evaluations. The opinions of other managers, peers, and subordinates may contribute to the appraisal of present performance. Future promotability is based primarily on present per-formance and estimates by immediate superiors of future success in a new job. The HR department may contribute to these estimates through the use of psy-

| Figure 6-8 | A Partial Replacement Chart for City Government |

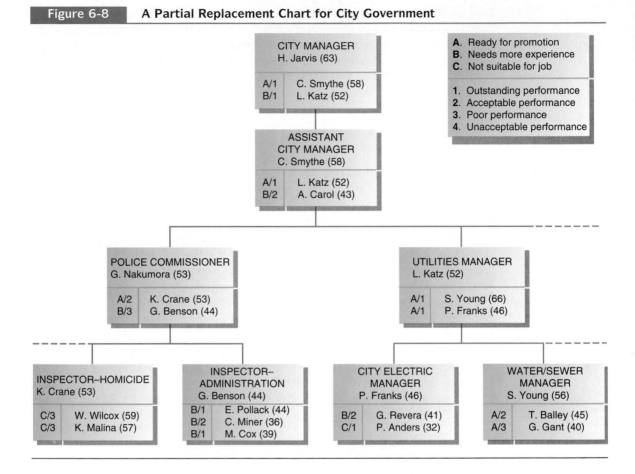

chological tests, interviews, and other methods of assessment. Replacement charts showing candidates' ages could lead to allegations of age discrimination. As a result, this information is often deleted.

Decision makers find that these charts provide a quick reference. Their shortcoming is that they contain very limited information. To supplement the chart and, increasingly, to supplant it, senior managers and HR specialists develop replacement summaries. *Replacement summaries* list likely replacements for each job and indicate their relative strengths and weaknesses. As Figure 6-9 shows, replacement summaries provide considerably more data than do replacement charts. This additional information allows decision makers to make more informed choices.

Most companies that are sophisticated enough to engage in detailed HR planning typically computerize their personnel records, including HR inventories. Then planners can update and compile replacement summaries when needed. These summaries also indicate which positions lack backups.

Replacement summaries

Figure 6-9	**A Replacement Summary for the Position of City Manager**

Replacement Summary for the Position of City Manager

Present Office Holder Harold Jarvis   **Age** 63

Probable Opening In two years   **Reason** Retirement

Salary Grade 99 ($78,500 yearly)   **Experience** 8 years

Candidate 1 Clyde Smythe   **Age** 58

Current Position Assistant City Manager   **Experience** 4 years

Current Performance Outstanding   **Explanation** Clyde's performance

evaluations by the City Manager are always the highest possible.

Promotability Ready now for promotion.   **Explanation** During an extended illness

of the City Manager, Clyde assumed all duties successfully, including major policy

decisions and negotiations with city unions.

Training Needs None

Candidate 2 Larry Katz   **Age** 52

Current Position Utilities Manager   **Experience** 5 years

Current Performance Outstanding   **Explanation** Larry's performance has

kept costs of utilities to citizens 10 to 15 percent below that of comparable city

utilities through careful planning.

Promotability Needs more experience.   **Explanation** Larry's experience is

limited to utilities management. Although successful, he needs more broad

administrative experience in other areas. (He is ready for promotion to Assistant

City Manager at this time.)

Training Needs Training in budget preparation and public relations would be desirable

before promotion to City Manager.

7-Eleven

For example, Southland Corp., the Dallas-based parent of the 7-Eleven convenience-store chain, has computerized its search for fast-trackers—those who are making exceptionally quick career progress. Twice yearly, Southland managers file reports about the promotability of their subordinates. By consolidating the reports on a computer, "we find out whether there will be a deficit of people coming up through the ranks," says Blake Frank, Southland's manager of personnel research. A separate program helps produce career-development plans, pinpointing weaknesses and suggesting solutions—university courses, in-house training, a different job, or a special assignment.[30]

In the long run, managers and HR departments can encourage employees to upgrade their capabilities and prepare for future vacancies. In the short run, an opening without a suitable replacement requires that someone be hired from the external labor market. Whether replacement charts or summaries are used, this information is normally kept confidential. Confidentiality not only guards the privacy of employees but also prevents dissatisfaction among those who are not immediately promotable.[31]

Estimates of External Supply

Externally filled jobs

Not every future opening can be met with present employees. Some jobs lack replacements to fill an opening when it occurs. Other jobs are entry-level positions; that is, they are beginning jobs that are filled with people who do not currently work for the organization. Without internal candidates, there is a need for external supplies of human resources.

External needs.   Employer growth and the effectiveness of the HR department largely determine the need to bring people in from outside the organization. Growth is primarily responsible for the number of entry-level openings, especially if the company promotes from within to fill job vacancies. The number of non-entry-level openings also depends on how well managers and the HR department assist employees in developing their capabilities. If workers are not encouraged to expand their capabilities, they may not be ready to fill future vacancies. A lack of promotable replacements creates job openings that must be filled externally.

Relevant labor markets

Labor market analysis.   Success in finding new employees depends on the labor market and the skills of managers and the employment specialists in the HR department. The relevant labor market is the market from which the organization recruits; its size depends on the skill levels being sought. For highly skilled jobs, the relevant labor market may be the entire country. The labor market for unskilled jobs is generally the local community. Whether employment rates are high or low, many needed skills are difficult to find. During a severe recession, for example, a look at classified advertisements shows that many job openings go unfilled week after week. In the short run, the national unemployment rate serves as an approximate measure of how difficult it is to acquire new employees; however, experienced managers and HR specialists realize that this rate varies among different groups and from region to region and city to city. These regional differences parallel international imbalances in human resource availability, causing some countries, such as Germany, to import *guest workers* from developing countries such as Turkey and Portugal during periods of extremely low unemployment.

Guest workers

Some researchers suggest that there may be a shortage of managerial talent, which is partly related to attitudes held by those in the workforce. If potential managers are not oriented toward work in hierarchical organizational structures, shortages of managerial talent may result whether overall unemployment is high or low.[32]

Regardless of the unemployment rate, external needs may be met by attracting employees who work for others. In the long run, local developments and demographic trends have the most significant impact on labor markets.[33] Local developments include community growth rates and attitudes. For example, many midwestern farm towns have a declining population. When they attempt to attract new business, employers fear that the declining population may mean future shortages in the local labor market and, as a result, often locate elsewhere. The lack of jobs causes still more people to leave the local labor market, and thus the cycle is continued. Conversely, sun belt cities are attractive to employers because their growth promises larger labor markets in the future.

Rural towns versus sun belt cities

Community attitudes.   Community attitudes also affect the nature of the labor market. Antibusiness or no-growth attitudes may cause employers to locate elsewhere. Fewer jobs mean a loss of middle-class workers. The shrinking workforce discourages new businesses, and the cycle is complete.

The people of Santa Barbara, California, limited growth in their community by restricting the number of permits available for connections to the city water system. Construction slowed. In time, housing prices increased dramatically. Young families that could not afford housing left the Santa Barbara labor market. New employers found the situation discouraging. Established employers found it difficult to attract new workers, especially the low-paid workers required for one of the town's major industries, tourism. Regardless of the unemployment rate, HR departments in Santa Barbara faced a difficult task when they had to rely on external supplies of workers.

Demographics.   Demographic trends are another long-term development that affects the availability of external supply. Fortunately for planners, these trends are known years in advance of their impact.[34]

**Birthrates
and HRP**

The low birthrates of the 1930s and early 1940s were followed by a baby boom during the late 1940s and 1950s. When the post–World War II babies started to go to college in the 1960s, the low birthrates of the 1930s led to a shortage of college teachers. These demographic trends were already in motion by 1950. Long-range HR planning, which was sensitive to demographic developments, could have predicted the shortage soon enough for proactive colleges to take corrective action. Today there are fewer 18- to 24-year-olds than a decade ago, affecting military and college enrollments.

Trends in jobs

In regard to the specific shortages that affect a particular industry or occupation in the long run, ample information is readily available. The U.S. Department of Labor publishes the *Occupational Outlook Handbook* and makes quarterly reports in the *Occupational Outlook Quarterly*. These publications discuss the expected developments in various occupational groupings. Similarly, the department publishes the population estimates of the Census Bureau, projections of the total labor force, the percentage of the population that will be in the workforce, and changes in the workforce by sex, age, race, marital status, and other criteria.[35]

Immigration

Although exceptions exist, many postindustrial nations are experiencing a slowing of population growth, especially among the more educated classes. In the United States, Canada, and Australia immigration policies may offset slower growth rates. How European Union countries will be affected by immigration is uncertain, given the increased unification of member nations and the reindustrialization of eastern Europe.

▶ Implementation of Human Resource Plans

Figure 6-10 summarizes the key concepts discussed throughout this chapter. The left side of the figure identifies the major causes of human resource demand: external, organizational, and workforce factors. These causes of demand are forecast by experts, trend data, and other methods to determine the short- and long-range demand for human resources. This demand is fulfilled either internally by present employees or externally by newcomers. The internal supply is shown in replacement charts, which are based on audits of the organization's human resources. External sources are identified through an analysis of the relevant labor market. The results include short- and long-range HR plans that are fulfilled through internal and external staffing processes.

Once the supply and demand of human resources have been estimated, adjustments may be needed. When the internal supply of workers exceeds the firm's demand, an *HR surplus* exists. Most employers respond to a surplus with a hiring freeze. This freeze stops the HR department from filling openings with external supplies. Instead, present employees are reassigned. Voluntary departures, called *attrition,* slowly reduce the surplus. If the surplus persists, leaves of absence are encouraged.

Attrition

Figure 6-10	Supply and Demand Considerations in Human Resource Planning

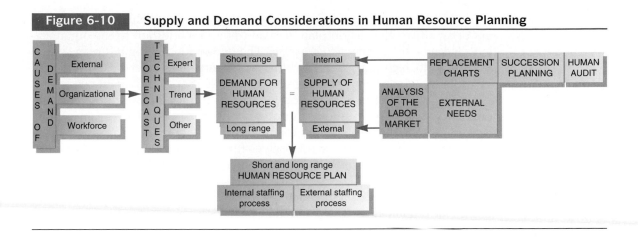

After the summer tourist peak, TWA and other airlines often grant leaves of absence to employees who request them. These leaves help reduce the total workforce during the slack fall and winter months.

Layoffs are a temporary loss of employment to workers and are used in cases of short-range surplus. If the surplus is expected to persist into the foreseeable future, employers often encourage early retirement on a *voluntary* basis. (Forced early retirement could violate the Age Discrimination in Employment Act.) If the surplus persists, employees are discharged. The blow of discharge may be softened through formal *outplacement* procedures, which help present employees find new jobs with other firms. These efforts may include use of office space, secretarial services, use of photocopying machines, long-distance phone calls, counseling, instructions on how to look for work, and even company mailings that encourage competitors to meet with employees.

Outplacement

HR shortages

If the internal supply cannot fulfill the organization's needs, an *HR shortage* exists. Planners have little flexibility in the short run and must rely on the external staffing process to find new employees. In the long run, responses can be more flexible. Planners can use the internal staffing process; that is, they can redouble their efforts to have employees develop the knowledge, skills, and attitudes needed to fill these jobs.

Whether staffing needs are met internally or externally, planners must consider the employer's affirmative action plan. That plan, as was discussed in Chapter 4, contains the company's strategy for undoing past discrimination and ensuring that future discrimination does not occur. As internal and external candidates are selected to fill job openings, these decisions must match the goals and timetables in the affirmative action plan. The HR plan also indicates whether the employer's affirmative action goals will be met. For example, even the modest goal of increasing minority representation in a company is unlikely to be met if the HR plan indicates that no new hires are planned and the company intends to reduce overall employment through attrition.

HRIS

The HR plan does more than serve as a check on the likelihood of the success of an affirmative action plan. It is an important addition to the organization's *human resource information system.* The information in the HR plan serves as a guide to recruiters, trainers, career planners, and other HR specialists. With this knowledge of the firm's internal and external employment needs, HR specialists, operating managers, and individual employees can direct their efforts toward the organization's future staffing needs. Managers can groom their employees through specific training and development efforts, and individual employees can prepare themselves for future openings through education and other self-help efforts. From the perspective of the HR department, however, the HR plan is only one part of the department's information system. Another important part is information about the people who are hired from outside the organization. The external hiring process is discussed in Chapters 7 and 8.

▶ Summary

HR planning requires considerable time, personnel, and financial resources. The return on this investment may not justify the expenditure for small firms. Increasingly, however, large organizations use HR planning as a means of achieving greater effectiveness. This planning represents an attempt by the HR department to estimate its future needs and supplies of staff—data that are increasingly necessary as companies go global.

Given an anticipated level of demand, planners try to estimate the availability of current workers to meet that demand. Such estimates begin with an audit of present employees. Then possible replacements are identified. Internal shortages are resolved by seeking new employees in the external labor market. Surpluses are reduced through normal attrition, leaves of absence, layoffs, or terminations.

As Figure 6-10 illustrates, both external and internal staffing processes are used to fulfill HR plans. The result is short- and long-range plans that outline future demands and likely sources of supply. This information becomes an important addition to the department's human resource information system.

▶ Terms for Review

Strategic plan	Skills inventories
Human resource forecasts	Replacement charts
Delphi technique	Replacement summaries
Extrapolation	Labor market analysis
Indexation	Attrition
Staffing table	Outplacement

▶ Review and Discussion Questions

1. What is the relationship between human resource planning and corporate strategy?

2. Why is HR planning more common among large organizations than among small ones? What are the advantages of HR planning for large organizations?

3. As the workforce in postindustrial societies becomes more diverse, what impact will this have on HR planning?

4. What is the purpose of an HR audit? Specifically, what information acquired from an HR audit is needed to construct a replacement chart or replacement summary?

5. Suppose senior managers and HR planners estimated that because of several technological innovations, your firm will need 25 percent fewer employees in three years. What actions should you take today?

6. Suppose you manage a restaurant in a winter resort area. During the summer it is profitable to keep the business open, but you need only one-half the cooks, table servers, and bartenders. What actions would you take in October for the beginning of the peak tourist season?

7. Explain why replacement charts and replacement summaries must be kept confidential.

8. As organizations become more global, HR planning becomes more important and complex. Explain.

▶ Incident 6-1

Church College's Human Resource Needs

For years Church College had operated at a deficit. Since it was supported by a national religious organization, this loss was made up from the general fund of the national organization. The drain on the general budget had tripled to $21 million by 1995.

Several members of the board of directors had heard that college enrollments had effectively stopped growing, meaning that the budget deficit would probably persist. The president of the college hired Bill Barker to develop a long-range HR plan for the college. An excerpt from his report stated:

> The increase in birthrates beginning in the late 1970s means that there will be a slow growth in the number of college-age students starting in 1996. To cut the ongoing deficit, the college must be sure to add more students without adding more faculty or staff. Furthermore, a committee should be formed to develop new curricula that appeal to the segments of the workforce that are going to experience rapid growth between now and the year 2010, the 45- to 60-year-olds.

The president of the college argued, "Recruiting more students without hiring more faculty will mean larger and larger class sizes, hurting the quality of instruction for which we have become known."

1. Assuming you are a member of the board of directors and feel uncomfortable making a decision on the basis of the knowledge you now have, what additional information would you request from the college's HR department?

2. If Bill Barker used national birthrate information, what other population information would you want to gather?

3. Are there any strategies that you could recommend that would allow the college to hire newly trained faculty members and avoid serious budget deficits in the 1990s if enrollments do not grow?

▶ References

1. Gerald R. Ferris, Gail S. Russ, Robert Albanese, and Joseph J. Martocchio, "Personnel/Human Resource Management, Unionization, and Strategy Determinants of Organizational Performance," *Human Resource Planning,* vol. 13, no. 3, 1990, p. 215.

2. Dave Ulrich, "Strategic and Human Resource Planning: Linking Customers and Employees," *Human Resource Planning,* vol. 15, no. 2, 1992, p. 47.

3. George T. Milkovich and Thomas A. Mahoney, "Human Resource Planning Models: A Perspective," in James W. Walker (ed.), *The Challenge of Human Resource Planning: Selected Readings,* New York: Human Resource Planning Society, 1979, pp. 73–84.

4. Randall S. Schuler and James W. Walker, "Human Resources Strategy: Focusing on Issues and Actions," *Organizational Dynamics,* Spring 1990, pp. 5–19.

5. Ulrich, op. cit.

6. Lee Dyer, "Human Resource Planning at IBM," *Human Resource Planning,* Spring 1984, pp. 111–125.

7. Gerald L. McManis and Michael S. Leibman, "Integrating Human Resource and Business Planning," *Personnel Administrator,* February 1989, pp. 32, 34, 36, 38.

8. Faneuil Adams, Jr., "Developing an International Workforce," *Columbia Journal of World Business,* January 1989, pp. 23–25. See also Rosalie L. Tung, "Human Resource Planning in Japanese Multinationals: A Model for U.S. Firms?" *Journal of International Business Studies,* Fall 1984, pp. 139–149.

9. John W. Boroski, "Putting It Together: HR Planning in '3D' at Eastman Kodak," *Human Resource Planning,* January 1990, pp. 45–57.

10. Ibid.

11. Robert H. Meehan and S. Basheer Ahmed, "Forecasting Human Resource Requirements: A Demand Model," *Human Resource Planning,* vol. 13, no. 4, 1990, pp. 297–307.

12. Herbert Heneman and G. Seltzer, *Employer Manpower Planning and Forecasting* (Manpower Research Monograph No. 19), Washington, D.C.: Department of Labor, 1970, p. 42.

13. Raymond E. Miles and Charles C. Snow, "Designing Strategic Human Resources Systems," *Organizational Dynamics,* Summer 1984, pp. 36–52.

14. Ronald Henkoff, "Winning the New Career Game," *Fortune,* July 12, 1993, p. 46.

15. Eugene H. Seibert and Joanne Seibert, "Retirement: Crisis or Opportunity?" *Personnel Administrator,* August 1986, pp. 43–49.

16. Mark A. de Bernardo, "The New Federal 'Plant Closings' Law: What Employers Should Know," *Congressional Action* (Special Reports 2–4), Aug. 30, 1988, pp. 1–4.

17. Harold L. Angle, Charles C. Manz, and Andres H. Van de Ven, "Integrating Human Resource Management and Corporate Strategy: A Preview of the 3M Story," *Human Resource Management,* Spring 1985, pp. 51–68.

18. Philip H. Mirvis and Mitchell Lee Marks, "The Human Side of Merger Planning: Assessing and Analyzing 'Fit,' " *Human Resource Planning,* vol. 15, no. 3, 1992, pp. 69–92. See also Anthony F. Buono and Aaron J. Nurick, "Intervening in the Middle: Coping Strategies in Mergers and Acquisitions," *Human Resource Planning,* vol. 15, no. 2, 1992, pp. 19–33.

19. Phil Farish, "Novel Link," *Personnel Administrator,* February 1989, p. 22. See also Gary Szakmary, "How HRD Can Contribute to Company Expansion," *Personnel Journal,* August 1988, pp. 39–40.

20. Jeff Miller and William B. Werther, Jr., "AIDS: The Second Decade and Its Implications for EAPs," *EAP Digest,* December 1993, pp. 20–27; "U.S. Death Toll from AIDS Passes 100,000," *The Miami Herald,* Jan. 25, 1991, p. 12A.

21. A. L. Delbecq, A. H. Van de Ven, and D. H. Gustafson, *Group Techniques for Progress Planning: A Guide to Nominal and Delphi Processes,* Glenview, Ill.: Scott, Foresman, 1975; J. M. Bartunek and J. K. Muringhan, "The Nominal Group Technique: Expanding the Basic Procedure and Underlying Assumptions," *Group and Organization\Studies,* vol. 9, 1984, pp. 417–432.

22. James W. Walker, "Evaluating the Practical Effectiveness of Human Resource Planning Applications," *Human Resource Management,* Spring 1974, p. 21; Paul Pakchan, "Effective Manpower Planning," *Personnel Journal,* October 1983, pp. 826–830.

23. Ren Nardoni, "Automating Succession Planning Is a Hands-on Task," *The Human Resource Professional,* July 1992, pp. 54–58.

24. Ibid.

25. Gerald L. McManis and Michael S. Leibman, "Succession Planners," *Personnel Administrator,* March 1989, p. 24.

26. William B. Werther, Jr., "A University/Corporate Solution to Closing the Executive Development Gap," *Journal of Management Development,* vol. 12, no. 4, 1993, pp. 29–36.

27. McManis and Leibman, op. cit.

28. Geert Hofstede, "Cultural Constraints in Management Theories," *Academy of Management Executive,* vol. 7, no. 1, 1993, pp. 81–93.

29. Peter Bamberger, Lee Dyer, and Samuel B. Bacarach, "Human Resource Planning in High Technology Entrepreneurial Startups," *Human Resource Planning*, January 1990, p. 37.

30. William M. Bulkeley, "The Fast Track: Computers Help Firms Decide Whom to Promote," *The Wall Street Journal*, Eastern ed., Sept. 18, 1985, p. 33.

31. Joe Pasqualetto, "Staffing, Privacy and Security Measures," *Personnel Journal*, September 1988, pp. 84, 86–89.

32. John N. Pearson and Jeffrey S. Bracker, "The Coming Shortage of Managerial Talent," *Management Education and Development*, vol. 17, no. 3, 1986, pp. 243–251.

33. George S. Odiorne, "The Crystal Ball of HR Strategy," *Personnel Administrator*, December 1986, pp. 103–106.

34. Alan L. Otten, "Decision Makers Often Fail to Spot Key Changes behind the Statistics," *The Wall Street Journal*, Dec. 6, 1986, p. 33.

35. See the annual *Employment and Training Report of the President*, Washington, D.C.: U.S. Government Printing Office.

7

Labor shortages, which are predicted to last into the next century, are expected to increase the importance of applicant attraction for organizations.
SARA L. RYNES **and** ALISON E. BARBER[1]

Recruitment

CHAPTER OBJECTIVES

After studying this chapter, you should be able to:

1. DESCRIBE how recruitment strategies rely on job analysis information and human resource plans.

2. EXPLAIN the crucial role recruiters play in meeting an organization's affirmative action goals.

3. DISCUSS the constraints under which the recruitment process takes place.

4. MATCH appropriate recruiting methods with different types of jobs.

5. DISCUSS the role of placement firms, state unemployment offices, and other outside organizations that assist recruiters.

6. DESCRIBE the role application blanks play in recruitment and selection.

Recruitment
defined

The quality of an organization's human resources depends on the quality of its recruits. *Recruitment* is the process of finding and attracting capable applicants for employment. The process begins when new recruits are sought and ends when their applications are submitted. The result is a pool of applicants from which new employees are selected. (The process of selecting applicants to become employees is the topic of Chapter 8.)

Recruiters

Managers become involved because they want the best people they can get, and they often know about places where appropriate applicants can be found. However, in large organizations, specialists in the recruiting process, called *recruiters*, are often used to find and attract capable applicants. As Figure 7-1 illustrates, recruiters identify job openings through HR planning or requests by managers. The HR plan can be especially helpful because it shows the recruiter both present openings and those expected in the future. As was mentioned in Chapter 6, advanced knowledge of job openings allows a recruiter to be proactive. Once openings have been identified, the recruiter learns what each job requires by reviewing the job analysis information, particularly the job descriptions and job specifications, as discussed in Chapter 5. Recruiters also may supplement their knowledge about a job's requirements with talks with the appropriate manager. John Hancock Financial Services provides an example.

John Hancock

John Hancock Financial Services is the eighth largest life insurance company in the United States. Headquartered in Boston, Massachusetts, it faces many of the recruiting issues that confront employers throughout North America, Europe, and Japan, including a diverse workforce, tight labor markets, insufficiently educated workers, and a realization that traditional approaches to recruiting are not always successful. Simply put, Hancock was unable to fill the approximately 1000 full-time, part-time, and temporary jobs that became open each year in its headquarters operations.

Adopting a "customer service" orientation to meet the needs of operating managers who faced staffing shortages, Lyn Rosenstein began a variety of efforts to expand the pool of recruits available to her company. As HR director, she expanded community outreach programs to attract more applicants. Recruiters became public relations representatives of the company and were sent out to recruit at local schools and community training agencies for the disadvantaged. Besides these proactive measures, she joined with other Boston-area companies to lobby for increased aid to that city's schools to enhance business education. Rosenstein also hired "qualifiable" candidates—that is, people who were not able to do the jobs for which they were hired without extensive training—relying on her company's extensive in-house training programs to turn "qualifiable" into "qualified."[2]

This example illustrates several challenges related to recruitment. First, recruiters face growing constraints in attracting applicants.[3] Second, traditional sources or channels of recruits are unlikely to be sufficient as the growth in the

| Figure 7-1 | An Overview of the Recruitment Process |

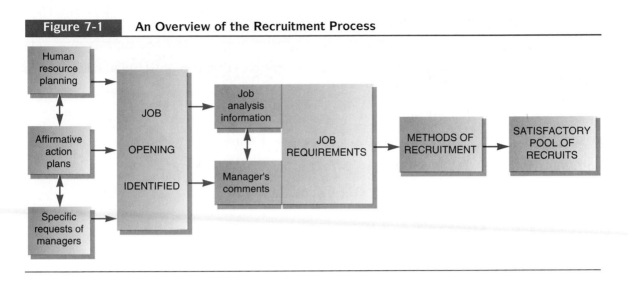

labor force slows during the 1990s.[4] Third, HR departments must continue to meet the needs of their "customers," operating managers who have jobs that need to be filled. Fourth, competition for scarce human resources sometimes causes managers to hire qualifiable candidates who need more extensive posthire training and development.

Qualifiable candidates

The complexity of international recruitment compounds an already difficult recruitment environment. As more firms become international, attracting foreign managers to work for domestic firms and finding domestic workers to join foreign organizations complicate recruitment.[5]

Global managers

"The hunt for the global manager is on. From Amsterdam to Yokohama, recruiters are looking for a new breed of multilingual, multifaceted executive who can map strategy for the whole world. The action is especially heavy in Europe."[6] Even in Japan, where lifetime employment has focused recruiters' attention on hiring recent school graduates almost exclusively, recruiters are facing the need to attract candidates from other employers, especially as non-Japanese firms set up operations in Japan and begin looking for qualified, experienced talent.[7] For example, "managers of Japan's Kentucky Fried Chicken franchises developed a unique strategy for attracting qualified help, offering new hires a trip to Hawaii."[8]

It is against this backdrop of tightening labor markets, both domestic and international, that recruitment takes place. Even when unemployment numbers soar during recessions, qualified applicants can be difficult to find and retain. To understand the recruitment process one must examine the constraints, challenges, and channels of recruitment that result in prospective employees completing an application for employment.

▶ Recruitment: Constraints and Challenges

Recruitment
limitations

Although the emphasis may vary, the most common constraints and challenges faced by recruiters include:

- Strategic and human resource plans
- EEO legislation and affirmative action plans
- Environmental conditions
- Organizational policies

- Recruiter habits
- Job requirements
- Costs
- Incentives

Strategic and Human Resource Plans

Strategic plans point out the direction of the firm and suggest the types of tasks and jobs that need to be undertaken. The HR plan outlines which jobs should be filled by recruiting outside the firm and which are to be filled internally. Internal placements are much less costly and time-consuming than external recruitment, although the available pool of recruits is limited. When external recruiting must take place, bunching up similar jobs for college recruitment trips or advertisements can be a cost-effective move. In short, the strategic and HR plans enable recruiters to place the organization's overall hiring needs in perspective.

EEO Legislation and Affirmative Action Plans

*United States
v. Georgia Power*

Equal employment opportunity legislation prohibits discrimination in all phases of employment, including recruitment. In *United States v. Georgia Power Company*, the Fifth Circuit Court of Appeals ruled that recruitment only at particular scholastic institutions can exclude members of protected classes. Although recruiting at any one school is not wrong, the effect of a limited recruitment policy can be to exclude members of protected classes. When that result occurs, the employer may be guilty of discrimination because its recruiting policies have a disparate impact on protected classes.[9] If an imbalance already exists among protected classes, such as underutilization or concentration of one type of worker, most employers respond with an affirmative action plan. Recruitment is then used to achieve the goals of the affirmative action plan, constraining the options available to recruiters.

Recruiter Habits

A recruiter's past success can lead to certain habits. Admittedly, habits can eliminate time-consuming decisions that yield the same answers, but habits may also continue past mistakes or avoid more effective alternatives.[10] Re-

Research summary cruiters must guard against self-imposed constraints in the form of habits, especially since more than 40 percent of recruiters never receive training from their companies.[11]

Environmental Conditions

External conditions strongly influence recruitment.

Demographic
changes

The number of new entrants in the workforce between the ages of 18 and 24 has actually been lower in the 1990s than it was in the 1980s. Not until the year 2000 will the number of people in this age group be at the same level as it was in 1988. The impact will be a scarcity of entry-level workers, military recruits, and college applicants.

The unemployment rate, spot shortages in specific skills, projections of the labor force by the Department of Labor, labor laws, and the recruiting activities of other employers all affect recruiters' efforts. Although these factors are considered in HR planning, the economic environment can change quickly after a plan is finalized. To be sure that the plan's economic assumptions remain valid, recruiters can check three fast-changing measures:

■ *Leading economic indicators.* Each month the U.S. Department of Commerce announces the direction of the leading indicators. These economic indexes suggest the future course of the national economy. If these indexes signal a sudden downturn in the economy, recruiting plans may have to be modified.

Workforce
predictors

■ *Predicted versus actual volume of business.* Since HR plans are partially based on the firm's predicted volume of business, usually in terms of sales, variations between actual and predicted sales may indicate that these plans need to be changed.

■ *Want-ads index.* The Conference Board monitors the volume of want ads in major metropolitan newspapers. An upward trend in this index indicates increased competition for engineers and managers, who are recruited on a nationwide basis. For clerical and production workers, who are usually recruited on a local basis, the HR department may want to create its own index to monitor changes in want ads.

As the economy, sales, and want ads change, recruiters must adjust their efforts accordingly. Tighter competition for applicants may require more vigorous recruiting efforts. When business conditions decline, the opposite approach is called for, as the following example illustrates.

As a major amusement park was opening in central Florida, the leading economic indicators dropped. Although the HR plan called for recruiting 100 workers a week for the first month, the employment manager set a revised target of 75. Lower recruiting and employment levels helped establish a profitable operation even though first-year admissions fell below the projections used in the HR plan.

Laws are another environmental constraint that cannot be overlooked. Besides equal opportunity prohibitions, other limitations exist. The *Fair Labor Standards Act* prescribes minimum wage and child labor requirements, and the *National Labor Relations Act* prohibits discrimination against those active in labor organizations. A more recent legal constraint comes from the *Immigration Reform and Control Act of 1986*, which may impose fines ranging from $250 to $10,000 for *each* illegal alien hired by an employer. Employers in seasonal agriculture work and those in south Florida, New York, Chicago, California, Arizona, New Mexico, and Texas are affected the most, since those areas have high concentrations of U.S. citizens who are legal immigrants. A major challenge, especially in those areas, is to comply with the act without discriminating against U.S. citizens because of their national origin.[12]

Even the courts have imposed legal constraints. Promises made in recruiting can be enforceable in court.

Immigration laws

Exxon Corporation lost a $10.1 million breach-of-contract judgment when "a jury upheld Ian Dowie's claim that Exxon never intended to keep promises made to him when he was hired as marketing Vice President of Qyx, Inc., Exxon's ill-fated office-systems venture."[13]

Exxon

Another legal constraint concerns recruiting the handicapped. Under the 1990 *Americans with Disabilities Act* (ADA), recruiters cannot discriminate against those with disabilities unless the disability would prevent a person from doing the job after reasonable accommodations by the employer.[14]

Pizza Hut began innovative recruitment programs among the disabled even before the ADA became law. Pizza Hut realized that 8 million disabled Americans want to work but are without jobs. Viewing its need for entry-level workers and seeing a large pool of potential recruits, Pizza Hut began a successful program in Orange County, California, to hire the handicapped, including the mentally retarded.[15]

Pizza Hut

With more than 58 percent of disabled men and 80 percent of handicapped women unemployed before the ADA was passed, the disabled represent an untapped pool of qualified recruits.[16] But as Figure 7-2 suggests, recruiting the disabled requires the HR department to adjust.

Job Requirements

What does the job require? A study by the Committee for Economic Development surveyed 438 large businesses and 6000 small ones and found that specific vocational skills are less crucial than is a high level of literacy. In addition,

| Figure 7-2 | **Recruiting the Disabled under the Americans with Disabilities Act** |

Disabled workers represent a large and often untapped pool of qualified and qualifiable talent. Proactive HR departments are not interested only in complying with the *Americans with Disabilities Act* but seek to improve their effectiveness in recruiting among the differently abled. Some HR departments consider:

■ Providing telecommunications devices for the deaf (TDD) at work and numbers for these devices in company publications and want ads as a means of creating a less hostile environment for the deaf.

■ Making the application area for unsolicited applicants wheelchair-accessible and advocating for the disabled when building renovations are undertaken.

■ Developing alternative application and testing devices for disabled applicants.

■ Recruiting through community organizations that assist the disabled and developing relationships with disabled student coordinators at public and vocational schools, colleges, and universities.

■ Publicizing the employer's commitment to equal opportunity and including in that publicity mention of the disabled.

■ Accommodating the disabled so that they can be productively employed.

■ Maintaining an organizational atmosphere of respect for all employees without regard to disabilities.

■ Asking disabled employees for referrals of disabled and nondisabled applicants.

a responsible attitude toward work, the ability to communicate in English, and the capacity to learn were all found to be important.[17]

Best applicants

"Find the best and most experienced applicant you can" is a constraint that is often imposed on recruiters. At first, this demand seems reasonable; managers want to hire the best and most experienced people. However, this seemingly innocent request has several potential problems. One problem is the recruiter's ability to locate good candidates, especially since the average recruiter maintains thirty-six open requisitions at any given time.[18] If a high level of experience is not necessary, the recruit may become bored with the job. Moreover, if extensive experience is unneeded, experience may be an artificial job requirement that discriminates unfairly. Another problem is cost. People with greater experience usually require a higher salary than do less experienced people. Besides, for some people in some jobs, ten years of experience is another way of saying one year of experience repeated ten times.

Costs

The cost of identifying and attracting recruits is an ever-present limitation. Consider the observations of an analyst who has studied the issue of recruiting costs:

Recruitment costs

The cost-of-employment figures I have seen suggest that the average is over $7,000 per new hire. Even college recruiting can cost as much as $6,000 per hire. . . . At the higher levels of management, the numbers become staggering. Fees plus expenses paid to recruiting firms undertaking a search to fill a $100,000-a-year position can easily top $30,000. These fees are large in and of themselves; if the recruiting process takes several months or if the final candidate fails to remain with the organization, the costs accumulate to a truly respectable total.[19]

Careful HR planning and forethought by recruiters can minimize these expenses. Of course, the best solution is to use proactive HR practices to reduce employee turnover, minimizing the need for recruiting. Evaluating the quantity, quality, and costs of applicants helps ensure that recruiting is efficient and cost-effective.

Incentives

Inducements may be a constraint, as occurs when other employers use them, or they may be a response to other limitations faced by the recruiter. Some examples follow:

Hiring and retention incentives

▪ Fast-food chains usually have a high turnover. To induce recruits and retain present employees longer, Burger King introduced an educational assistance program that allows employees to accrue up to $2000 worth of tuition credits over two years. Turnover among participants is 22 percent versus 97 percent for nonparticipants.[20]

▪ American Bankers Insurance Group uses on-premises day care to attract and retain working mothers.

▪ State Mutual Life Assurance Company of America offers employees and their children a training program to help families adjust to having a mother work outside the home.[21]

▪ As with Burger King, the U.S. military services offer tuition assistance. Preenlistment training options are another inducement.

▪ Northrup's Defense Systems Division used an emotional appeal by compiling a pamphlet that highlights the advantages of living in the Chicago area and directing it to those who once lived there. The brochure was designed around the theme "Northrup DSD has one great reason to come home."[22]

Despite the creative approaches taken by Burger King, American Bankers, and others, the basics still apply. For example, one study found that among college seniors the most sought-after benefits are health and life insurance.[23] Common sense suggests that employers will have to become more proactive, as the John Hancock example earlier in the chapter discussed. Recruiters also will

Customer-service view

have to develop more of a customer-service attitude in dealing with recruits. They will have to keep applicants better informed, schedule interviews at the applicant's convenience, and minimize the number of return interviews.[24] Higher pay and benefits will be important too.

TRW

TRW's Space and Defense Sector faces a particularly difficult recruiting challenge: hiring highly trained technical employees and managers. The company's estimates put the cost of recruiting and bringing a new engineer up the learning curve to be $180,000. The figure jumps to $320,000 for managers. To meet this challenge, TRW strives to become the preferred employer among applicants. It seeks to create a work environment that is compatible with personal and family needs. Benefits programs are customized to individual needs, and ongoing career counseling is also provided.[25]

Organizational Policies

Organizational policies are used to achieve uniformity, economies, public relations benefits, and other objectives that may be unrelated to recruiting. At times, policies can be a source of constraints. Policies that may affect recruitment are highlighted below.

Pay and hiring

Compensation policies. Pay policies are a common constraint faced by recruiters. Organizations with HR departments usually establish pay ranges for different jobs to ensure equitable wages and salaries. Recruiters seldom have the authority to exceed the stated pay ranges. Of course, pay ranges must be adjusted for special cases such as international openings. Applying domestic compensation rates overseas often entails overpaying or underpaying foreign nationals compared with what they would normally earn. At the same time, employees who are reassigned overseas often need and expect an increase to handle extra living expenses.

Employment status policies. Some companies have policies on hiring part-time and temporary employees. Although there is growing interest in hiring these types of workers, policies can cause recruiters to reject all but those seeking full-time work. Limitations on part-time and temporary employees reduce the pool of potential applicants, especially since this segment of the workforce is a fast-growing one. In fact, a study of 484 firms found a one-third increase in the use of part-timers.[26] Policies that discriminate against any identifiable group should be reviewed. When those groups are protected under employment laws, such policies violate the equal employment laws that target those groups.

International hiring policies. Policies also may require that foreign jobs be staffed with local citizens. The use of host-country foreign nationals reduces relocation expenses, lessens the likelihood of nationalization, and, if top jobs are

Foreign viewpoints

held by local citizens, minimizes charges of economic exploitation. Unlike relocated employees, foreign nationals are apt to be involved in the local community and understand local customs and business practices. For example, recruiters for western firms in Japan find it difficult to attract Japanese managers because "most are unwilling to give up the stability and job security they receive in Japan. Most large Japanese companies, after all, offer cradle-to-grave employment."[27] Similarly, many western men and women are reluctant to move to Saudi Arabia because of the societal restraints placed on women there; these restraints often prevent women from working or enjoying a western lifestyle.

Promote-from-within policies.   Promote-from-within policies give present employees the first opportunity for job openings. These policies may limit the recruiter in several ways. They may require the recruiter to search within the company before looking elsewhere for recruits. If an internal search must be completed before recruiting outside the firm can begin, filling job openings will be delayed when internal candidates are unsuitable. Even if internal candidates are acceptable, the pool of potential applicants is likely to be smaller than is the case when internal and external channels are used. Hard choices often must be made when internal recruitment involves the eventual selection of one coworker in preference to another; attendant morale and motivation issues may surround such decisions.

Civil Rights Act

If these policies have an unequal impact on protected groups, the result can be violations of the 1964 *Civil Rights Act,* as amended. Although promote-from-within policies reduce the flow of new people and ideas into different levels of the organization, the alternative is to pass over employees in favor of outsiders. Bypassing current employees can lead to employee dissatisfaction and turnover, whereas the use of present employees underscores the organization's commitment to ensuring that each employee has a career, not just a job.

▶ Internal Recruitment Channels

Current employees are a major source of recruits for all but entry-level positions. Whether for promotions or for "lateral" job transfers, internal candidates already know the informal organization and have detailed information about its formal policies and procedures. Promotions and transfers are typically decided by operating managers with little involvement by the HR department.

Job-Posting Programs

HR departments become involved when internal job openings are publicized to employees through *job-posting programs,* which inform employees about openings and required qualifications and invite qualified employees to apply.

The notices usually are posted on company bulletin boards or electronic bulletin boards or are placed in the company newspaper. Qualifications and other facts typically are drawn from the job analysis information (discussed in Chapter 5). Then, through *self-nominations* or the recommendation of a supervisor, employees who are interested in the posted opening report to the HR department and apply.

Self-nominations

The purpose of job posting is to encourage employees to seek promotions and transfers that help the HR department fill internal openings and meet employees' personal objectives. Not all job openings are posted. Besides entry-level positions, senior management and top staff positions may be filled by merit or with external recruiting. Job posting is most common for lower-level clerical, technical, and supervisory positions, although affirmative action plans suggest a trend toward posting even higher-level management jobs.

Most job bidders seek promotions. However, some self-nominations come from those who seek a transfer to broaden their skills or for personal reasons. Even self-nominated demotions are possible if the person is frustrated in his or her present job or sees the demotion as a means to get a job with better promotion possibilities. For example, a typesetter at a newspaper may seek a demotion to junior reporter because the long-term career options may be more favorable.

Self-nominations may even apply to management trainees. Many organizations hire recent college graduates for management training programs, and this may be little more than an extended job rotation through several departments. After this rotation is completed, some companies allow trainees to nominate themselves to fill posted job openings.

Departing Employees

An often overlooked source of recruits consists of departing employees. Many employees leave because they can no longer work the traditional forty-hour workweek. School, child-care needs, and other commitments are the common reasons. Some might gladly stay if they could rearrange their hours of work or their responsibilities. Instead, they quit when a transfer to a part-time job may retain their valuable skills and training. Even if part-time work is not a solution, a temporary leave of absence may satisfy the employee and some future recruiting need of the employer.

Buyback

Buybacks are a channel worthy of mention, although HR specialists and workers tend to avoid them. A *buyback* occurs when an employee resigns to take another job and the original employer outbids the new job offer. Even when the authority to enter into a bidding war exists, the manager may discover that other workers expect similar raises. Employees may reject a buyback attempt because of the ethical issue raised by not reporting to a job that has already been accepted. Or they may be seen as disloyal and become the first people fired, laid off, or passed over for promotions.

▶ External Recruitment Channels

When job openings cannot be filled internally, the HR department must look outside the organization for applicants. The remainder of the chapter discusses the external recruitment channels most commonly used by employers and applicants.

Walk-ins and Write-ins

Walk-ins are job seekers who arrive at the HR department in search of a job; *write-ins* are those who send a written inquiry. Both groups normally are asked to complete an application blank to determine their interests and abilities. Usable applications are kept in an active file until a suitable opening occurs or until an application is too old to be considered valid, usually six months.

Employee Referrals

Employees may refer job seekers to the HR department. Employee referrals have several advantages. First, employees with hard-to-find job skills may know others who do the same work. For example, a shortage of welders on the Alaskan pipeline was partially solved by having welders ask their friends in the "lower forty-eight states" to apply for the many unfilled openings. TRW and McDonald's pay employees a referral bonus when qualified candidates are recommended at some locations.[28] Second, new recruits already know something about the organization from the employees who referred them. Thus, referred applicants may be more strongly attracted to the organization than are casual walk-ins. Third, employees tend to refer their friends, who are likely to have similar work habits and attitudes. Even if their work values are different, these candidates may have a strong desire to work hard so that they do not embarrass the person who recommended them.

Employee referrals are an excellent and legal recruitment technique, but they tend to maintain the status quo of the workforce in terms of race, religion, sex, and other characteristics, possibly leading to charges of discrimination. For example, in the Georgia Power Company case, the company not only limited its recruitment to a few scholastic institutions but also made extensive use of employee referrals. One civil rights expert noted:

> In *United States v. Georgia Power Company,* the Fifth Circuit Court of Appeals ruled that the respondents' form of recruitment by referrals from present workers had the effect of excluding blacks because it perpetuated the generally all-white makeup of its employees. The court stated: "Word-of-mouth hiring and interviewing for recruitment only at particular scholastic institutions are practices that are neutral on their face. However, under the facts of the instant case, each operates as a 'built-in-head-wind' to blacks and neither is justified by business necessity."[29]

Alaskan pipeline

Employee referrals

Limited recruitment sources

Advertising

Want ads describe the job and the benefits, identify the employer, and tell those who are interested how to apply. They are the most familiar form of employment advertising. For highly specialized recruits, ads may be placed in professional journals or out-of-town newspapers in areas with high concentrations of the desired skills. For example, recruiters in the aerospace industry often advertise in Los Angeles, St. Louis, Dallas–Fort Worth, and Seattle newspapers because those cities are major aerospace centers.

Want ads have severe limitations. They may attract thousands of job seekers for one popular job opening, or few may apply for less attractive jobs. For example, few people apply for door-to-door sales jobs if they know the product is vacuum cleaners or encyclopedias. Likewise, the ideal recruits are probably already employed and not reading want ads. Finally, secret advertising for a recruit to replace an incumbent cannot be done with traditional want ads. These

Blind ads

limitations are avoided through the use of blind ads. A *blind ad* is a want ad that does not identify the employer. Interested applicants are told to send their résumés to a mailbox number at the post office or to the newspaper. A *résumé*, which is a brief summary of an applicant's background, is then forwarded to the employer. These ads allow the opening to remain confidential, prevent countless telephone inquiries, and avoid the public relations problem of disappointed recruits.

Writing ads

An advertisement that is written too narrowly may limit the pool of applicants; one written too broadly may attract too many applicants for the firm to be able to evaluate them effectively. As one writer observed, "Recruitment advertising should be written from the viewpoint of the applicant and his or her motivations rather than exclusively from the point of view of the company."[30] Since the cost of classified advertising is determined by the size of the advertisement, short blurbs are the norm. These ads usually describe the job duties, outline minimum job qualifications, and tell interested readers how to apply. Short telegraphic phrases and sentences, sometimes written in the second person, are the usual format. Figure 7-3 provides an example. However, some ex-

---

Figure 7-3 | **A Sample Want Ad**

ENGINEERING GRADUATES

Blakely Electronics seeks junior mechanical and electrical engineering trainees for our growing team of engineering professionals. You will work with senior engineers in designing state-of-the-art electronic equipment for home and industry. Qualified applicants will be engineers graduating by the end of this term and wanting immediate employment. Send your résumé and transcripts to: Chuck Norris, Employment Office, Blakely Electronics, P.O. Box 473, Salt Lake City, Utah 84199. Do it today for an exciting career tomorrow.

Blakely Electronics is an equal opportunity employer of minority, female, and handicapped workers.

---

perts doubt that traditional approaches will remain sufficient, particularly in recruiting people with hard-to-find skills or when labor markets are tight. As one researcher suggested, employment ads:

> . . . must contain not only information about the job but also information presented in a way that effectively portrays a message about the job and the company. This can't be done if the ad contains information that explains only what responsibilities the job includes, who can be qualified, where it is located, and how and when to apply.[31]
>
> More important, in today's labor market, where increasing demands are being made for job relevance, quality of work life, and other job satisfaction factors . . . the need for more descriptive job information and information concerning working environment, supervisory style and organizational climate are necessary.[32]

Another authority suggests:

Ad design

> Ad layout, design and copy should reflect an accurate image of the company and department represented:
>
> ■ Conservative vs. progressive   ■ Expanding vs. stabilizing
>
> ■ Small, medium or large   ■ Centralized vs. decentralized
>
> ■ Dynamic vs. static
>
> When evaluating the image and layout of an ad, ask yourself whether it commands attention—both by itself and in comparison with other recruitment advertisements.
>
> Remember, you're trying to convince qualified applicants to apply. . . . Be sure to emphasize the benefits of the package while being specific enough about requirements and job responsibilities to screen out candidates who are not right.[33]

Placement of advertisements depends on whether you expect potential recruits to be searching for a job or whether you have to search for applicants. Recruitment efforts must parallel the job search process used by desired applicants. If those applicants are likely to look for work in the want ads or at professional meetings, recruiters must change their ad placement accordingly. Advanced Technology Management, a maker of semiconductors, posts help-wanted ads in the global computer network Internet.[34]

Ads follow
applicants

For many jobs, such as clerical jobs, want ads are an effective choice. For unusual jobs or positions that are hard to fill, advertisements have to go where the likely applicants are. For engineers, for example, advertisements in professional and trade journals may be appropriate. Advertisements for recruits through other media—billboards, television, and radio, for example—are seldom used because the results seldom justify the expense. However, these approaches may be useful when unemployment is low and the target recruits are not likely to read want ads.[35]

Ad design and media selection can be evaluated by monitoring the quality and quantity of responses, using the insights gained to upgrade future employment ads.

State Employment Security Agencies

U.S. Employment
Service

Every state government has a *state employment security agency*. Often called the unemployment office or the employment service, this agency matches job seekers with job openings. The agencies result from a federal and state partnership that was established in 1933. At the federal level, the U.S. Employment Service sets national guidelines. Within these uniform regulations, state agencies operate more than 2400 local offices that help more than one-fifth of all unemployed workers find jobs.

Job bank

To match candidates with job openings, the employment services in virtually every state use a statewide *job bank* that works as follows: When an employer has a job opening, the HR department voluntarily notifies the employment service of the job and its requirements. Then job openings are computerized and reduced to a printout each workday morning. This updated infomation helps employment service counselors identify appropriate openings. Increasingly, data about job seekers are also computerized so that the matching process can be done electronically.

For many years state employment service offices suffered from a poor image. Recruiters often viewed these agencies as a source of unskilled or poorly qualified workers. Such self-fulfilling attitudes encouraged many skilled workers to use other channels to find employment. But government-run employment services remain a source of recruits for HR departments, especially since they are free to both employers and applicants and since a listing with the state unemployment office helps assure wide exposure for affirmative action efforts.[36] However, Cornell labor economist John Bishop does not see this channel as very effective. As *Fortune* reported:

> The least useful hiring channel proved to be the U.S. Department of Labor's Employment Service. . . . Since the mid-1960s, says Bishop, the service has focused on placing workers with real or perceived disadvantages. "It has became an advocacy weapon for affirmative action on behalf of targeted populations," he says. As a result, the Service has steadily lost credibility with employers.[37]

Private Placement Agencies

Private placement agencies, which exist in every major metropolitan area, arose to help employers find capable applicants. They take an employer's request for recruits and then solicit job seekers, usually through advertising or among walk-ins. Candidates are prescreened, matched with employer requests, and then told to report to the employer's HR department for an interview. The matching process conducted by private agencies varies widely. Some placement services carefully prescreen applicants; others simply provide a stream of applicants and let the HR department do most of the screening.

Wide variance
in service

Users of private placement agencies should realize that payment is handled in one of two ways: either the employer or the applicant pays the placement firm a fee, which commonly equals 10 percent of the first year's salary or one month's wages. *Fee-paid* positions are openings for which the employer agrees to pay. Other positions require the recruits to pay once they are offered a job or begin employment.

Users of private placement agencies should be advised to carefully review any contracts the agency asks them to sign. Some agencies will provide minimum assistance, being more interested in the placement and less interested in an appropriate match between the applicant and the employer. Signed contracts may mean that even an unsatisfactory placement leads to a financial obligation on the part of the recruit if the position is not a fee-paid one.[38]

Professional Search Firms

Professional search firms are much more specialized than placement agencies. *Search firms* usually recruit only specific types of human resources for a fee paid by the employer. For example, some search firms specialize in executive talent, while others find technical and scientific personnel. Perhaps the most significant difference between search firms and placement agencies is the approach taken. Placement agencies hope to attract applicants through advertising, but search firms actively seek out recruits among the employees of other companies. Although they may advertise, search firms use the telephone as their primary tool to locate and attract prospective recruits.[39]

The Nelson Radar Company needed a quality control manager for its amplifier assembly line. After several weeks of unsuccessful recruiting efforts, the HR manager hired a search firm, which reviewed the in-house phone directories of Nelson's competitors and telephoned the assistant quality control manager at one of them. The phone call was used to encourage this assistant manager to apply for the position at Nelson.

This brief example illustrates several important points. First, search firms may have in-depth experience with specific types of applicants. Second, search firms are often willing to undertake actions that an employer would not perform, such as calling a competitor. Third, some HR professionals consider

Headhunters

search firms unethical because these firms engage in "stealing," "raiding," or "pirating" among their clients' competitors. This last point suggests why search firms sometimes are called headhunters.[40]

Educational Institutions

School graduates

Many educational institutions offer current students and alumni placement assistance.[41] Although some applicants sought through educational institutions are experienced, many are not. And new entrants are more likely to be swayed by the recruiter's manner and behavior during the interview than by the attributes of the job, which appears to be the deciding factor for experienced workers.[42]

Educational institutions also are an excellent source for hiring foreign nationals. Foreign students in domestic schools have the advantage of being bilingual and bicultural. Some foreign students desire jobs with domestic firms to gain experience or secure citizenship.

Professional Associations

Professional groups of engineers, accountants, trainers, and others often maintain placement rosters and hold job fairs, especially at annual conventions. Some have publications that accept classified ads that reach their membership, and a growing number of associations are willing to sell mailing lists classified by geographic areas and ZIP codes that make direct-mail appeals possible. What makes this channel particularly attractive to recruiters is the fact that members of professional associations are more likely to remain informed of the latest developments in their fields, possibly leading to higher-quality applicants from these sources. Another advantage of these sources is that recruiters can zero in on specific specialties, especially in hard-to-fill technical areas.[43]

Labor Organizations

Many people with trade skills, such as carpenters, plumbers, electricians, and others in the construction trades, use the local union as a source of job referrals. In the construction industry, for example, the union hiring hall often represents the most efficient way to find qualified tradespeople.

Military Operations

Military downsizing

Many communities are located near military bases, which have trained people leaving every day. Mechanics, welders, pilots, heavy equipment operators, and a wide range of other skilled workers can be found through this recruitment channel.[44]

Government-Funded and Community Training Programs

Many people lack the skills to compete for meaningful jobs. Some are the victims of a poor education; others have been displaced by the downsizing, mergers, and bankruptcies that have resulted from domestic and international competition. In an attempt to reduce unemployment among these groups and provide employers with better qualified workers, government and community organizations have created a variety of training and retraining programs. Some are aimed at specific groups, such as the hard-core unemployed, who have experienced long-term underemployment or unemployment. Other programs seek to ease the transition of displaced workers as businesses or entire industries have undergone major reductions in employment.[45]

Structural unemployment

Government concern stems from the belief that some unemployment is structural in nature. *Structural unemployment* occurs when people are ready, willing, and able to work but their skills do not match the jobs available. For example, an unemployed coal miner in the Appalachian region of the United States is of little use to an electronics firm that seeks trained assemblers and technicians. Through government-sponsored training and retraining programs, unemployed workers learn skills that make them employable in today's labor markets.

HR departments that have an ongoing demand for skilled or semiskilled entry-level employees should work closely with their local training centers, which may prove to be a low-cost source of recruits. Since many of these centers are operated by minority groups and often seek trainees from protected classes, their graduates may help a firm meet its affirmative action plans. At the same time, the HR department can help fulfill the societal goal of turning the unemployed into productive, taxpaying citizens.

Temporary Help Agencies

Temporary help agencies do not provide recruits. Instead, they are a source of supplemental workers. The temporary workers actually work for the agency and are "on loan" to the requesting employer. For temporary jobs—during vacations, flu epidemics, or peak seasons—these agencies can be a better alternative than recruiting new workers for short periods of employment. Some companies, such as Motorola, TRW, Merrill Lynch, Control Data, and IBM, rely on temporary workers to fill part of the company's staffing needs. They use

Temps as a buffer

"temps" as a buffer of people who can be put on layoff status quickly without cutting the company's full-time, career-oriented employees. Besides handling the recruiting and bookkeeping tasks associated with hiring new employees, these agencies often provide clerical and secretarial talent on short notice, sometimes less than a day.[46] When the temporary shortage is over, there is no need to lay off surplus workers because the temporaries work for the agency, not for the company. Of course, for jobs that require a detailed understanding of company procedures, temps may not be appropriate. Organizations such as Travelers, Grumman, Wells Fargo, and Hewlett-Packard find that retirees have knowledge of company procedures and often a strong work ethic, and so they have established job banks of retirees to meet their temporary staffing needs.

Occasionally temporary workers are recruited to become permanent employees. However, many of the people who work for temporary help agencies do so because they do not want long-term, full-time careers. College students, retirees, homemakers, and others who do not want a long-term job make up the bulk of the temporary workforce.[47]

Leased Employees

Similar to for-profit temporary agencies, some agencies lease employees to employers as long-term employees. Instead of the employer having to recruit, hire, pay, train, and perform other traditional HR functions, some companies simply lease a workforce from another organization. Often small businesses find the complexities of modern HR management, with its detailed laws, mandated payroll taxes, and other requirements, worth avoiding.

No employees

When Dale Voss bought Noel Ice Co. . . . the first thing he did was fire all the employees.

But the cube-making didn't melt down for a minute. Those same employees were back at the freezers of the Nashville-based company the next day, although another company was signing the paychecks.

Noel joined the growing number of businesses leasing some or all of their employees, a strategy that can cut costs and eliminate management headaches ranging from payroll deductions to employer-sponsored health insurance.[48]

Open House

A relatively unusual technique of recruiting involves holding an open house. People in the adjacent community are invited to see the company facilities, have refreshments, and maybe view a film about the company. This method has proved successful in recruiting clerical workers when people with office skills are in tight supply. As one writer observed, "Low-budget, single-employer job fairs are in."[49]

G.D. Searle & Co.

G. D. Searle & Co., in Skokie, Illinois, used this method when it had problems recruiting enough clerical help. From the seventy-five people who attended the open house, the company expected to hire twenty secretaries and clerks.[50]

International Recruiting

International considerations

Recruitment in foreign countries presents special challenges. In advanced industrial nations, recruiters find many of the same channels that exist in North America. Additional help can sometimes be obtained from embassy or consular offices. Recruitment help from consultants or other professionals may be necessary for higher-level positions. These positions may require social acceptance, school ties, and other appropriate hallmarks of success, which may be considered more important than past experience or the other, more traditional criteria used in the home country.

In developing nations, recruiters often find that they have to develop their own network of contacts, ranging from newspaper reporters to government officials in the host country. Of particular importance are cultural conflicts. Historical animosities may exist between different factions within the country, whether different native tribes, elements of a formal caste system, or enmity by virtue of long-standing traditions.

International differences

Recruitment of employees to move internationally has many similarities with domestic efforts; unfortunately, the problems encountered by recruiters are often more difficult to resolve. Members of two-career families may be reluctant to apply for overseas jobs. Immigration barriers, employment laws, and other roadblocks may prevent a promising recruit from a becoming a bona fide

---

Figure 7-4 **A Summary of the Recruiting Process**

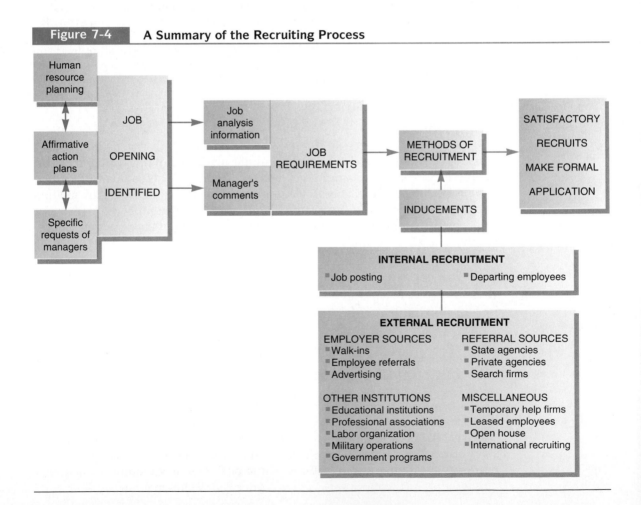

applicant because of concerns about the spouse's employment possibilities. Costs are another problem. Cost-of-living differentials, moving expenses, education for children, income tax requirements of the home and foreign locations, and housing costs are common issues. These complexities apply whether the recruiter is trying to fill an overseas position with a domestic employee or trying to recruit a foreign national into the home country.[51]

Japanese and Mexican differences

When recruiting internationally, recruiters should become familiar with the employment practices in the foreign country. Not only are employment contracts different, but cultural expectations may lead to unforeseen problems. For example, some Japanese view working for foreign firms as less prestigious than staying with a Japanese-owned company. In Mexico, recruiting from competitors is seldom done, and so the common practice of hiring from competitors as a way to ensure a fast start-up may have to be rethought by recruiters interested in staffing jobs there.[52]

Figure 7-4 summarizes the recruiting process and identifies each of the commonly used channels of recruitment. As the figure indicates, the recruitment process ends when a recruit makes a formal application, usually by completing an application blank.

▶ Job Application Blanks

The *job application blank* collects information about recruits in a uniform manner. Even when recruits volunteer detailed information about themselves in the form of a résumé, applications are often required so that the information gathered is comparable. Figure 7-5 provides an example of an application blank and its major divisions. Although the application blank is a fairly typical one, it may contain questions that are illegal under some state jurisdictions. As one writer observed:

State laws

> While the majority of employers may be aware of . . . relevant federal regulations, many aren't aware that equal opportunity laws in some states are more stringent than federal requirements. For example, while federal regulations require the employer to be able to justify pre-employment inquiries as bone fide occupational qualifications (BFOQs) upon request, Ohio law says inquiries into inappropriate areas (i.e., sex, race, etc.) must be certified by the Ohio Civil Rights Commission prior to their use.
>
> In states where local laws are more stringent than federal law, job application forms are an even more critical concern.[53]

Research summaries

When the two levels of law conflict, usually the most stringent one must be followed, and ignorance of state laws is no defense in court. In a study of application blanks, two researchers reported that 73 percent of the forms had one or more inappropriate preemployment inquiries.[54] The remainder of this chapter discusses the various parts of the application blank shown in Figure 7-5.

Figure 7-5	A Typical Application Blank

BLAKELY ELECTRONICS, INC.

"An Equal Opportunity Employer"

Application for Employment

Personal Data

1. Name _____

2. Address _____ 3. Phone number _____

   _____

Employment Status

4. Type of employment sought _____ Full-time _____ Part-time
   _____ Permanent _____ Temporary

5. Job or position sought _____

6. Date of availability, if hired _____

7. Are you willing to accept other employment if the position you seek is unavailable?
   _____ Yes _____ No

8. Approximate wages/salary desired $_____ per month.

Education and Skills

9. Circle the highest grade completed:

   8 9 10 11 12   13 14 15 16   **Graduate School**
      High School   **College**

10. Please provide the following information about your education. (Include high
    school, trade or vocational schools, and colleges.)

    a. School name _____ Degree(s) or diploma _____

    School address _____

    b. School name _____ Degree(s) or diploma _____

    School address _____

11. Please describe your work skills. (Include machines, tools, equipment, and other
    abilities you possess.) _____

    _____

    _____

    _____

Work History

Beginning with your most recent or current employer, please provide the following
information about each employer. (If additional space is needed, please use an
additional sheet.)

12. **a.** Employer _____ Dates of employment _____

    Employer's address _____

    Job title _____ Supervisor's name _____

    Job duties _____

    Starting pay _____ Ending pay _____

b. Employer _____ Dates of employment _____

Employer's address _____

Job title _____ Supervisor's name _____

Job duties _____

Starting pay _____ Ending pay _____

Military Background

If you were ever a member of the Armed Services, please complete the following:

13. Branch of service _____ Rank at discharge _____

Dates of service _____ to _____

Responsibilities _____

Memberships, Awards, and Hobbies

14. What are your hobbies? _____

15. List civic/professional organizations to which you have belonged. _____

_____

16. List any awards you have received. _____

_____

References

In the space provided, list three references who are not members of your family:

17. a. Name _____ Address _____

b. Name _____ Address _____

c. Name _____ Address _____

18. Please feel free to add any other information you think should be considered in evaluating your application.

_____

_____

By my signature on this application, I:

a. Authorize the verification of the above information and any other necessary inquiries that may be needed to determine my suitability for employment.

b. Affirm that the above information is true to the best of my knowledge.

c. Realize that falsification may be grounds for dismissal.

Date _____

_____

Applicant's Signature

_____

Personal Data

Most application blanks begin with a request for personal data. Requests for name, address, and telephone number are nearly universal. But requests for some personal data, such as place of birth, sex, race, religion, or national origin, may lead to charges of discrimination. The HR department must be able to show that these questions are job-related or collect this information after the applicant is hired.

Applications may solicit information about health, height, weight, handicaps that relate to the job, major illnesses, and previous claims for injuries. Here again there may be legal problems, since employers may not discriminate against the handicapped under the *Americans with Disabilities Act*.[55] The burden of proof in showing the job-relatedness of such questions falls on the employer. Information about marital status and dependents and about whom to contact in a medical emergency is also commonly sought. This information cannot be used to discriminate against the members of a protected class.

ADA

Employment Status

Included here are questions about the position sought, willingness to accept other positions, date available for work, salary or wages desired, and acceptability of part-time and full-time work schedules. This information helps a recruiter match the applicant's objective and the organization's needs.

Education and Skills

Traditionally, education has been a major criterion in evaluating job seekers, but its importance has been diminished by the requirement that HR departments show how education is job-related. Questions about specific skills are also used to judge prospective employees. More than any other part of the application blank, the skills section reveals the suitability of a candidate for a particular job.

Work History

Job seekers must frequently list their past jobs. From this information, a recruiter can tell whether the applicant is one who hops from job to job or is likely to be a long-service employee. A quick review of the stated job title, duties, and responsibilities also shows whether the candidate is a potentially capable applicant. If this information does not coincide with what an experienced recruiter expects to see, it may be that the candidate exaggerated his or her job title, duties, or responsibilities.

Military Background

Many applications request information about military experience. The questions usually include date of discharge, branch of service, and rank at discharge. This information helps explain the applicant's background and ability to function in a structured environment, and it suggests specialized training. Increasingly, applications omit this information to avoid questions of discrimination against veterans.

Memberships, Awards, and Hobbies

For managerial and professional positions, off-the-job activities may make one candidate preferable to another. Memberships in civic, social, and professional organizations that are related to the job indicate the recruit's concern about community and career. Awards show recognition for noteworthy achievements. Hobbies may reinforce important job skills and indicate outlets for stress and frustration or opportunities for further service to the company. Some companies have dropped questions in this area since such activities often are not clearly related to the job requirements.

Golf as a criterion

> When handed a pile of completed applications for manager of the car- and truck-leasing department, Frank Simmons, the HR manager for a New Orleans Ford dealership, sorted the completed applications into two piles. When asked what criteria were being used to sort the applicants, he said, "I'm looking for golfers. Many of our largest car and truck accounts are sold on Saturday afternoons at the golf course."

References

Besides traditional references from friends and previous employers, applications may ask for other "referencelike" information. Questions may explore the job seeker's criminal record, credit history, friends and relatives who work for the employer, or previous employment with the organization. Criminal record, credit history, and friends or relatives who work for the company may be important considerations if the job involves sensitive information, work with children, or work with cash or other valuables. Job-relatedness must be substantiated if these criteria disproportionately discriminate against a protected group. Previous employment with the organization means that there are records of the applicant's performance.

Signature Line

Candidates usually are required to sign and date applications. Adjacent to the signature line, a blanket authorization commonly appears. This authorization allows the employer to check with references; verify medical, criminal, or financial records; and undertake any other necessary investigations. Some employers include an "at will" statement in which the employee acknowledges that his or her employment is at the will of the employer—only for as long as

"At will" statements

the employer wishes to retain the employee. Another common provision of the signature line is a statement that the applicant affirms the information in the application to be true and accurate as far as is known. Although many people give this clause little thought, falsification of an application blank is grounds for discharge in most organizations.

Truth in applications

Jim LaVera lied about his age to get into the police officers training program. As he neared retirement age, Jim was notified that he would have to retire in six months, instead of thirty months as he had planned. When Jim protested, the lie he had told years before came to the surface. Jim was given the option of being terminated or taking early retirement with substantially reduced benefits.

When the application is completed and signed, the recruitment process is finished. Its unanswered questions and implications continue to affect HR management and the employment process, as the Jim LaVera example illustrates. In fact, the end of the recruitment process marks the beginning of the selection process, which is discussed in Chapter 8.

▶ Summary

Recruitment is the process of finding and attracting capable applicants to apply for employment. Although operating managers are often involved, much of the recruitment process is the responsibility of professionals in the HR department; these professionals are called recruiters. Recruiters should be aware of the constraints and challenges surrounding the recruitment process before they attempt to find suitable applicants.

Recruiters pursue applicants through a variety of channels. Although walk-ins and write-ins are a common source, the growing diversity in the workforce and changing demographics often require recruiters to be more proactive. Employee referrals and advertisements are other sources. To help recruiters, a variety of public and private organizations exist, such as state unemployment offices, private placement agencies, and search firms. Many institutions—schools, labor organizations, professional associations, military facilities, government and community training programs—also provide placement assistance that recruiters can access. Temporary, leased, and departing employees are other sources of potential recruits.

International recruitment faces many of the same issues as domestic staffing, except that the issues are often far more complex regardless of whether the recruiter seeks to bring someone to the home country or send that person overseas. Of particular importance, recruiters must be aware of national differences in recruitment practices and employee expectations.

Completed application blanks from ready, willing, and able applicants mark the end of the recruitment process and the beginning of the selection process.

▶ **Terms for Review**

Recruitment	Résumé
Buyback	State employment security agency
Walk-ins	Search firms
Write-ins	Structural unemployment
Blind ads	

▶ **Review and Discussion Questions**

1. What background information should a recruiter have before beginning to recruit job seekers?

2. Under what circumstances would a blind ad be a useful recruiting technique?

3. After months of insufficient recognition and two years without a raise, you accept an offer from another firm for $4500 a year more than your present salary. When you inform your boss that you are resigning, you are told how crucial you are to the business and are offered a raise of $6250 a year. What do you do? Why? What problems may exist if you accept the buyback?

4. Suppose you are a manager who just accepted the resignation of a crucial employee. After you send your request for a replacement to the HR department, how could you help the recruiter do a more effective job?

5. If your company's regular college recruiter became ill and you were assigned to recruit at six universities in two weeks, what information would you need before leaving on the trip?

6. In small businesses, managers usually handle their own recruiting. What methods would you use for the following situations? Why?

   a. The regular janitor is going on vacation for three weeks.
   b. Your secretary has the flu.
   c. Two more salespeople are needed: one to help local customers and one to open a sales office in Puerto Rico.
   d. Your only chemist is retiring and must be replaced with a highly skilled individual.

7. "If a job application omits important questions, needed information about recruits will not be available. But if a needless question is asked, the information can be ignored by the recruiter without any other complications." Do you agree or disagree? Why?

8. In recruiting a worker to fill a job in another country, what issues are likely to arise that complicate the international move but probably would not be present in a domestic opening?

▶ **Exercise 7-1**

Two Perspectives on Filling the Job

Although recruiters and applicants use similar channels as part of the employment process, recruiters and applicants often seek different outcomes from "filling a job."

Create two columns on a sheet of paper, one labeled "Recruiter" and the other labeled "Applicant." In the column labeled "Recruiter," list the general characteristics a recruiter seeks in applicants. Then, under "Applicant," list what you believe most job seekers are looking for in a job. Now rank-order each list, putting the items in each column in order from most to least important.

1. What differences do you see?

2. How would you characterize those differences?

Incident 7-1

The International Nurse Connection

Several hospitals and large nursing homes in New York faced an ongoing shortage of nurses. Although the problem was not a new one, high occupancy (called a high census in the health-care field) of the hospitals forced them to use an excessive amount of overtime to cover all shifts and weekends. The nurses were complaining, and many resigned. Many other nurses were specializing to achieve higher pay levels or were looking for positions in administration, away from hands-on nursing. Although the shortage of nurses affected all nursing classifications, it appeared to be most acute among general-duty nurses who attended to patients while they recovered in the hospital or were assigned to nursing homes.

The shortage became so critical that even the temporary nursing services were unable to fill all the requests, prompting still more nurses to leave the area's hospitals and nursing homes in favor of the higher-paying jobs offered through the various visiting nurses services.

Several HR directors at New York–area hospitals met to explore the possibility of recruiting degreed nurses from overseas. Given the high proportion of Spanish-speaking patients, it was decided to recruit nurses from the Philippines, Spain, and Latin American countries. A Spanish-speaking recruiter from one of the hospitals was selected by the group to explore the possibility of recruiting nurses overseas into New York–area hospitals.

Assume that you were given the responsibility for developing a recruitment strategy for this consortium of health-care organizations.

1. Identify the major roadblocks you might encounter in recruiting these nurses.

2. What recruitment channels would you use to find and attract qualified applicants? Why?

▶ References

1. Sara L. Rynes and Alison E. Barber, "Applicant Application Strategies: An Organizational Perspective," *Academy of Management Review,* vol. 15, no. 2, 1990, p. 286.

2. Jill Andresky Fraser, "The Making of a Work Force," *Business Month,* September 1989, pp. 58–62.

3. Joshua Hyatt, "Hire Employees," *Inc.,* March 1990, pp. 106–108.

4. Brian Bremmer, "Among Restaurateurs, It's Dog Eat Dog," *Business Week,* Jan. 9, 1989, p. 86.

5. Tom Casey, "How Corporate Culture Influences the Recruitment Process," *The Human Resource Professional,* Fall 1992, pp. 21–23.

6. Shawn Tully, "The Hunt for the Global Manager," *Fortune,* May 21, 1990, p. 140.

7. Ibid, p. 144.

8. C. S. Manegold, Bill Powell, and Yuriko Hoshiai, "Hang Up the Help-Wanted Sign," *Newsweek,* July 16, 1990, p. 39.

9. Jeane C. Poole and E. Theodore Kantz, "An EEO/AA Program That Exceeds Quotas—It Targets Biases," *Personnel Journal,* January 1987, p. 104.

10. Laura M. Graves and Gary N. Powell, "An Investigation of Sex Discrimination in Recruiters' Evaluations of Actual Applicants," *Journal of Applied Psychology,* vol. 73, no. 1, 1988, pp. 20–29. See also Jean Powell Kirnan, John A. Farley, and Kurt F. Geisinger, "The Relationship between Recruiting Source, Applicant Quality, and Hire Performance: An Analysis by Sex, Ethnicity, and Age," *Personnel Psychology,* vol. 42, 1989, pp. 293–308.

11. B. Posner, "Comparing Recruiter, Student, and Faculty Perceptions of Important Applicant and Job Characteristics," *Personnel Psychology,* vol. 33, 1980, pp. 329–339.

12. Bruno Lopez, "Mexican Leaders, Scholars Differ on Effects of U.S. Immigration Bill," *The Miami Herald,* Nov. 2, 1986, pp. A10–A11.

13. Selwyn Feinstein, "Recruiting Promises Take on New Substance with Court Decision," *The Wall Street Journal,* Midwest ed., Sept. 30, 1986, p. 1.

14. Bernard S. Hodes, "Recruiting within the Disabled Market and within ADA Boundaries," *The Human Resource Professional,* Fall 1992, pp. 9–11. "What the ADA Means to You," *Recruitment Today,* Summer 1990, pp. 6, 8, 10. See also Susan R. Meisinger, *Legal Report—The Americans with Disabilities Act of 1990: A New Challenge for Human Resource Managers,* Alexandria, Va.: Society for Human Resource Management, 1990, pp. 1–16.

15. "Disabled Win at Pizza Hut," *Business Month,* September 1989, p. 16.

16. Lee Smith, "What the Boss Knows about You," *Fortune,* Aug. 9, 1993, p. 91.

17. Owen B. Butler, "Why Johnny Can't Get a Job," *Fortune,* Oct. 28, 1985, pp. 163–168.

18. "HRM Update: Recruiter Work Loads," *Personnel Administrator,* September 1986, p. 16.

19. Jeffrey J. Hallett, "Why Does Recruitment Cost So Much?" *Personnel Administrator,* November 1986, p. 22.

20. Sal D. Rinella and Robert J. Kopecky, "Burger King Hooks Employees with Educational Incentives," *Personnel Journal,* October 1989, pp. 90–99; Rynes and Barber, op. cit., pp. 286–310. See also Liz Amante, "Help Wanted: Creative Recruitment Tactics," *Personnel,* October 1989, pp. 32–36.

21. Allan Halcrow, "Child Care: The Latchkey Option," *Personnel Journal,* July 1986, p. 12.

22. "HRM Update: Magnetic Appeal," *Personnel Administrator,* October 1986, p. 14.

23. "Benefits Preferences of New Hires," *Small Business Reports,* January 1989, p. 78.

24. Linda B. Robin, "Troubleshoot Recruitment Problems," *Personnel Journal,* September 1988, pp. 94–96.

25. Chris Chen, "TRW S&D Strives to Be the Preferred Employer," *Personnel Journal,* July 1990, pp. 70–73.

26. "More Firms Offer Benefits to Part-Timers, Survey Shows," *Resource,* November 1985, p. 105.

27. Stephanie Strom, "The Art of Luring Japanese Executives to American Firms," *The New York Times,* National ed., March 25, 1990, p. 12.

28. Allan Halcrow, "Employees Are Your Best Recruiters," *Personnel Journal,* November 1988, pp. 42–48. See also Jennifer J. Laabs, "The Pizza Party Incentive: New Life for TJ Maxx's Referral Program," *Recruitment Today,* Summer 1990, pp. 48–49.

29. Richard Peres, *Dealing with Employment Discrimination,* New York: McGraw-Hill, 1978, p. 20.

30. Van M. Evans, "Recruitment Advertising in the '80's," *Personnel Administrator,* March 1978, p. 20. See also Jennifer Koch, "Ads with Flair," *Personnel Journal,* October 1989, pp. 46–55.

31. James W. Schreier, "Deciphering Messages in Recruitment Ads," *Personnel Administrator,* March 1983, p. 35. See also Nancy A. Mason and John A. Belt, "Effectiveness of Specificity in Recruitment Advertising," *Journal of Management,* vol. 12, no. 3, Fall 1986, pp. 425–432.

32. Schreier, op. cit., p. 39.

33. Cathy Edwards, "Aggressive Recruitment: The Lessons of High-Tech Hiring," *Personnel Journal*, January 1986, pp. 41–48. See also Margaret Magnus, "Is Your Recruitment All It Can Be?" *Personnel Journal*, February 1987, pp. 54–63.

34. Marc Levinson, "Help Wanted—Reluctantly," *Newsweek*, Mar. 14, 1994, p. 36.

35. Margaret Magnus, "TV Channels Recruitment Effort," *Recruitment Today*, August 1988, pp. 86–88. See also Jennifer Koch, "Applicants Tune in Radio," *Recruitment Today*, Fall 1989, pp. 7–8, 10–12.

36. "Cooperation Called Key in Recruitment," *Resource*, August 1988, pp. 1, 6–7.

37. Louis S. Richman, "The Dark Side of Job Churn," *Fortune*, Aug. 9, 1993, p. 24.

38. Clyde J. Scott, "Employing a Private Employment Firm," *Personnel Journal*, September 1989, pp. 78–83.

39. Kenneth J. Cole, *The Headhunter Stratregy: How to Make it Work for You*, New York: Wiley, 1985. See also John Byrne, "The New Headhunters," *Business Week*, Feb. 6, 1990, pp. 63–71.

40. Claudia H. Deutsch, "Inviting the Headhunters Inside," *The New York Times*, National ed., Aug. 5, 1990, sect. 3, part 2, p. 25; Mark S. Van Clieaf, "Strategy and Structure Follow People: Improving Organizational Performance through Effective Search," *Human Resource Planning*, March 1992, pp. 33–46.

41. Alan Farnham, "Out of College, What's Next?" *Fortune*, July 12, 1993, pp. 58–64; Patrick C. Ross, "How to Find the Perfect Intern," *Recruitment Today*, Spring 1990, pp. 40–42.

42. Dawn Gunsch, "Comprehensive College Strategy Strengthens NCR's Recruitment," *Personnel Journal*, September 1993, pp. 58–62. See also Daniel B. Turban and Thomas W. Dougherty, "Influences of Campus Recruiting on Applicant Attraction to Firms," *Academy of Management Journal*, October 1992, pp. 739–765.

43. Gloria Glickstein and Donald C. Z. Ramer, "The Alternative Employment Marketplace," *Personnel Administrator*, February 1988, pp. 100–104.

44. Stephen L. Mangum and David E. Ball, "The Transferability of Military-Provided Occupational Training in the Post-Draft Era," *Industrial and Labor Relations Review*, January 1989, pp. 230–245.

45. "Cooperation Called Key in Recruitment," op. cit.

46. William Smith, "They Serve Two Masters," *Personnel Administrator*, April 1988, pp. 112–114, 116.

47. Harold E. Johnson, "Older Workers Help Meet Employment Needs," *Personnel Journal*, May 1988, pp. 100–105.

48. Mariann Caprino, "Leased Employees Save Money for Most Firms," *The Miami Herald*, Apr. 16, 1989, p. C-1. See also Suzanne Woolley, "Give Your Employees a Break—By Leasing Them," *Business Week*, Aug. 14, 1989, p. 135.

49. Levinson, op. cit.

50. "Open House: It's a New Technique for Employers to Find the Workers They Want," *The Wall Street Journal,* Western ed., May 23, 1978, p. 1. See also Roberta M. Kenney, "The Open House Complements Recruiting Strategies," *Personnel Administrator,* March 1982, pp. 27–32.

51. Carole Gould, "A Checklist for Accepting a Job Abroad," *The New York Times,* National ed., July 17, 1988, p. 33. See also Faye Rice, "Should You Work for a Foreigner?" *Fortune,* Aug. 1, 1988, pp. 123, 126, 130, 134.

52. Brian O'Reilly, "Doing Business on Mexico's Volcano," *Fortune,* Aug. 29, 1988, pp. 72–74.

53. Carl Camden and Bill Wallace, "Job Application Forms: A Hazardous Employment Practice," *Personnel Administrator,* March 1983, p. 31.

54. Ibid.

55. Hodes, op. cit.

8

Before they hire, employers want to be sure applicants can handle the demands.
MARC LEVINSON[1]

Considering the ample storehouse of procedures now available, it is ironic that organizations still rely on one of the least sophisticated methods—the interview.
ROBERT L. DIPBOYE[2]

Selection

CHAPTER OBJECTIVES

After studying this chapter, you should be able to:

1. DISCUSS the central importance of the selection process to human resource activities.

2. EXPLAIN how the EEOC's Uniform Guidelines on Employee Selection affect selection activities.

3. DISCUSS the importance of using a differential approach with multiple measures in selecting a diverse workforce.

4. DESCRIBE the importance of validity and reliability in employee selection.

5. PLAN an employment interview that avoids the major pitfalls.

6. DETAIL the supervisor's role in the selection process and in realistic job previews.

By way of introduction, consider an overview of the hiring process at Merrill Lynch, Pierce, Fenner & Smith Inc., the largest securities firm in the United States.

Merrill Lynch

Applicants for the position of account executive (stockbroker) at Merrill Lynch complete an application, take a written test, and undergo an interview. But none of these steps prepare them for the account-executive simulation test. As described by a reporter for *The Wall Street Journal,* the test can be unnerving.

"Welcome to the Merrill Lynch account-executive simulation exercise, or, as dubbed by some, the Merrill Lynch stress test. It's a nail-biting three hours . . . that leaves many longing for the good old days of calculus finals.

"The stakes are high, too. Those taking part in the simulaton, except me, are applicants for the job of account executive, or stockbroker. . . . The simulation exercise is designed to gauge how they will perform under conditions similar to those that a real stockbroker faces."[3]

The test works by telling each applicant that he or she is replacing a stockbroker who has gone to another office. The stockbroker has left the client book, which describes the accounts of each client. In addition, the applicants are given a variety of unanswered memos, letters, and telephone messages that they must sort through and take action on. In the background, recorded sounds of a brokerage office are played to add an air of confusing noises, shouts, telephone rings, and other unexpected distractions. During the three hours, fictitious clients call and other messages and reports are dropped on the applicant's "desk." As one applicant commented an hour after the simulation was over, "I just can't calm down. It was a real high."[4]

The simulation exercise is only one part of Merrill Lynch's selection process. Other steps precede and follow it.

Selection defined

Although most employers do not use such an elaborate screening device, all employers put applicants through a selection process. The *selection process* is a series of specific steps used to decide which recruits should be hired. The process begins when recruits apply for employment and ends with the hiring decision. Though the final hiring decision is made by the immediate supervisor or manager in many cases, the HR department evaluates applicants in regard to their potential suitability through the use of valid procedures.

Employment function

Recruiting and selection are combined and called the *employment function* in many HR departments. In a large HR department, the employment function is the responsibility of the employment manager. In a smaller department, the HR manager handles these duties. Employment is often the primary reason for the department's existence, since the selection process is central to the HR function. Improper selection causes the department to fail at the objectives set forth in Chapter 1 and the challenges discussed in Chapter 2. Therefore, it is not an exaggeration to say that selection is central to the success of the department and the organization; an organization cannot be better than the people it hires.

When the selection process discussed in this chapter does not weed out poor performers or dangerous applicants, poor productivity or legal risks may result. For example, employers may be held liable for the criminal acts of those they hire.[5] When employers are negligent in hiring or retaining employees who are likely to be harmful to others, those injured may sue and win, as suggested by the following examples:

Fort Worth Cab and Baggage

A judgment was rendered against the Fort Worth Cab and Baggage Company for nearly $5 million after one of its drivers raped a passenger in his cab. An illinois court ordered the Apollo Detective Agency to pay $25,000 to the victim of a sexual assault by one of its security guards in the building the guard was assigned to protect. A Maryland landlord reportedly settled a similar suit for $375,000[6]

▶ Inputs and Challenges to Selection

The selection process relies on three helpful inputs, as Figure 8-1 shows. Job analysis information, discussed in Chapter 5, yields the description of the jobs, the human specifications, and the performance standards each job requires. HR plans, explained in Chapter 6, identify likely job openings and allow selection to proceed in a logical and proactive manner. Chapter 7 described how recruits form a pool of applicants form which employees are selected. Other challenges to the selection process limit the actions of HR specialists and line managers. As Chapter 4 outlined, laws against discrimination reinforce external prohibitions, and the international challenges discussed in Chapter 3 complicate nearly every HR activity. At the same time, workforce diversity and other internal challenges further complicate, and thus slow, the HR department's selection activities.

Computerized applicant tracking

Although computerized applicant tracking within the HR information system can speed up the department's processing,[7] line managers may see days

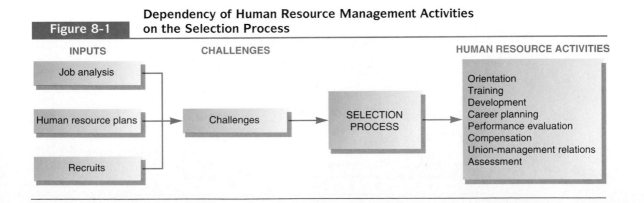

| Figure 8-1 | Dependency of Human Resource Management Activities on the Selection Process |

slip into weeks or months and then pressure employment managers for action. But quick action may mean that qualified applicants are few or nonexistent. Whichever side of the trade-off—quickness versus quality—employment specialists choose, criticisms from operating managers are likely.

▶ ## Selection: An Overview

The selection process is a series of steps through which applicants pass. A typical set of steps is shown in Figure 8-2. Although the sequence of steps may vary from firm to firm, with some steps taking place simultaneously, the process seeks candidates who are likely to be successful and strives to elminate those who are likely to fail.[8] Within each step, multiple approaches help distinguish between performance and nonperformance issues, which may arise from the cultural and ethnic diversity of those in the applicant pool. Ultimately, the selection decision must focus on performance-related issues if it is to contribute to the firm's success. At the same time, selection is strongly influenced by whether candidates are being picked from within or outside the firm, the availability of applicants, and equal employment opportunity challenges. These issues will be discussed before an examination of each step in the selection process.

Internal Selection

Succession planning (discussed in Chapter 6) identifies potential internal candidates. When this information is stored in the HRIS, internal selection can be accelerated.

Figure 8-2	**Steps in the Selection Process**

Hiring decision	Step 8
Reallstic job previews	Step 7
Supervisory interview	Step 6
Medical evaluation	Step 5
References and background checks	Step 4
Selection interview	Step 3
Employment tests	Step 2
Preliminary reception of applications	Step 1

Citibank

At Citibank in New York City, the selection process has been simplified and computerized to match present employees with internal openings. The "Job Match" selection system rests on matching a profile of candidates for a nonprofessional job with the task requirements of the job. The specific tasks required of the job are programmed into the computer, along with the specific abilities of employees. The employees with the highest match with a given opening are then considered for the job. One shortcoming of the Job Match system is that it does not consider nontask factors, such as whether the employee actually wants the job.[9]

With internal applicants, some of the steps in Figure 8-2 can be scaled down or eliminated. For example, there is seldom a need to provide a preliminary reception of applicants, verify references, or do medical evaluations. But when external applicants are being considered, the steps in Figure 8-2 are common.

Selection Ratio

Selection quality

Some jobs are so hard to fill that there are few applicants. Low-paying jobs and openings for extremely specialized work are examples of positions with small selection ratios. A *selection ratio* is the relationship between the number of applicants hired and the total number of applicants available. A ratio of one hiree to twenty-five applicants, or 1:25, is an example of a high ratio; a low selection ratio is 1:2. Attractive jobs with attractive employers can have very large selection ratios, as Toyota experienced when it had 120,000 applicants for 1700 jobs in its Kentucky plant,[10] or a selection ratio of about 1:70. A low selection ratio means that there are few applicants from which to select. In many instances a low selection ratio also means a low quality of recruits. The ratio is computed as follows:

$$\frac{\text{Number of applicants hired}}{\text{Total number of applicants}} = \text{Selection ratio}$$

Uniform Guidelines on Employee Selection

Uniform guidelines

Equal employment opportunity is an ongoing challenge to all phases of HR work and demands that the selection process be free of even unintentional discrimination. To reduce discrimination in selection, the Equal Employment Opportunity Commission (EEOC) has created the *Uniform Guidelines on Employee Selection*. These guidelines establish standards that employers must meet to prevent a disparate or unequal impact. As was described in Chapter 4, an adverse impact results when an employer's actions have a disproportionate effect on members of protected groups.

Four-fifths rule

A quick test for disparate impact suggested by the guidelines is the *four-fifths rule*. Generally, a disparate impact is assumed when the *proportion* of protected-class applicants who are actually hired is less than 80 percent (four-fifths) of the *proportion* for the majority group applicants selected. The four-fifths rule addresses the proportions of people hired, *not* the total numbers. For example, assume an employer has 100 white male applicants for an entry-level job and hires one-half of them, for a selection ratio of 1:2, or 50 percent (50/100). The four-fifths rule *does not* mean that the employer must hire four-fifths, or 40 protected-class members. Instead, the rule means that the employer's selection ratio of protected-class applicants should be at least four-fifths of that of the majority group. Assume that during the same time period during which the employer had 100 majority applicants and hired 50 of them, the employer has 50 protected-class applicants but hires only 10 of them. Thus, the selection ratio is 1:2 (50/100, or 50 percent) for majority applicants and 1:5 (10/50, or 20 percent) for protected-class members. The *proportion* of protected-class new hires to the *proportion* of majority-class hires is only 40 percent (20 percent divided by 50 percent equals 40 percent). This ratio can be calculated as follows:[11]

$$\frac{S(PCM)}{A(PCM)} \text{ divided by } \frac{S(MAJ)}{A(MAJ)} \text{ or } \frac{10}{50} \text{ divided by } \frac{50}{100} \text{ or } \frac{2}{5} \text{ or } 40\%$$

where A(PCM) = total number of applicants from protected class
       S(PCM) = number of applicants selected from protected-class members
       A(MAJ) = total number of applicants from the majority group
       S(MAJ) = number of selected applicants who are members of the majority group

Since the ratio of protected-class members hired (10/50) to the ratio of the majority group hired (50/100) is 2/5, protected-class members are hired at a rate less than four-fifths of that of the majority applicants (40 percent in this example). As a result, it would be reasonable to assume that the employer's selection procedures have a disparate impact on members of the protected class.

Bottom-line test

Historically, when an employer's overall selection process met the four-fifths rule (or *bottom-line test*, as it is called in the guidelines), the EEOC allowed some steps within a firm's selection process to have an adverse impact as long as the overall selection process did not. However, the U.S. Supreme Court ruled in *Connecticut v. Teal* that the courts would ignore the four-fifths rule if an adverse impact occurred in any step of the selection process. The implication is obvious: When one step in the selection process has an adverse impact, it should be reviewed and improved.

Types of errors

The remainder of this chapter explains the selection process by examining the challenges and different approaches associated with each step in Figure 8-2. It should be noted, however, that even following each of these steps does not guarantee perfect hiring decisions. In some cases, the process eliminates people who would have performed well (called false-negative errors); at other times, people will be hired who fail (called false-positive errors). Selection is not an exact science.

▶ Preliminary Reception: Step 1

Slowing workforce growth

Courtesy interview

The organization selects employees, and *applicants select employers*. Simply put, the selection process is a two-way street. It usually begins with a visit to the HR office or a written request for an application. The applicant begins to form an opinion of the employer with this early step. Some researchers suggest that applicants' perceptions of an organization influence their intention to sign up for interviews and request further information.[12] As the growth rate of the workforce slows in the 1990s and beyond, applicants' intentions become increasingly important in ensuring an acceptable pool of applicants.

A preliminary interview may be granted as a courtesy, and then the applicant appears in person. This "courtesy interview," as it is often called, is a matter of good public relations. It also helps the department screen out obvious misfits and get information on these "drop-in" applicants. Later steps in the selection process verify this application information if the courtesy interview suggests a fit between the applicant and the employer's needs.

▶ Employment Tests: Step 2

Research summary

Employment tests are devices that assess the match between applicants and job requirements. Some are paper-and-pencil tests; others are exercises that simulate work conditions. A math test for a bookkeeper is an example of a paper-and-pencil test, and the account-executive test at Merrill Lynch is an example of a simulation. Tests are used more frequently for candidates for jobs that are paid by the hour than for management openings because hourly jobs usually have a limited number of skills that are more easily tested.[13] A survey by the Society for Human Resource Management found that 84 percent of employers "include testing in their employment decision-making procedures."[14] Management and staff jobs are often too complex to be tested fairly and economically. When tests are used for these positions, however, they often simulate real-life situations and are evaluated by several raters, as is the case at Merrill Lynch.

Besides testing for specific skills and abilities, tests may have other screening goals. In a study of 390 firms by the Society for Human Resource Management (SHRM), for example, 17 percent of the firms used drug screening tests on applicants and 12 percent applied those tests to current workers; only 13 percent of applicants and 9 percent of employees were screened for alcoholism. What is even more telling is that over two-thirds (68 percent) of these companies had increased the use of testing or were considering increases.[15]

Foreign nationals

Considerable care must be taken in testing foreign nationals whether they are applying for a job in the home country or elsewhere. First and most obvious, the test may have cultural biases, including slang terms that are unfamiliar. Second, laws in other countries may prevent some types of testing. Third, because of cultural differences, social standing, or political connections, taking a test may be seen as an insult.[16]

Test Validation

Testing became popular on a large scale during World War I, when intelligence tests were given to army recruits. During the following years tests were developed for a wide range of employment uses, but many of those tests were assumed to be valid without sufficient proof. *Validity* means that test scores relate significantly to job performance or to another job-relevant criterion. The stronger the relationship is between test results and performance, the more effective the test is as a selection tool. When scores and performance are unrelated, the test is invalid and should not be used for selection.

Validity

A Miami, Florida, trucking company gave all applicants an extensive reading test. One-third of the applicants were Cuban immigrants, but there were no Cuban drivers. Since the drivers received their instructions orally and were shown on a map where to go, the reading test had no relationship to job performance. It thus was invalid. The test did not distinguish good drivers from bad ones. It only distinguished among those who could and could not read English well.[17]

Tests and the Civil Rights Act

When an invalid test rejects people of a particular race, sex, religion, or national origin, it violates the 1964 Civil Rights Act, as amended. The U.S. Supreme Court has ruled that a test (or any other selection method) that has a disparate impact on a protected class and is not job-related violates the act.[18] This ruling in *Griggs v. Duke Power* means that testing specialists should be especially cautious when a test disproportionately excludes an identifiable group. In *Griggs* and later in *Albemarle Paper Co v. Moody,* the U.S. Supreme Court gave recognition to the EEOC Uniform Guidelines on Employee Selection, which outline how tests should be evaluated to determine if they are valid.[19]

Ensuring that tests are valid requires validation studies. These studies compare test results with performance or the traits needed to perform the job. Figure 8-3 summarizes the most common approaches to validation, which often demand a statistical analysis of test scores and performance.

Empirical validation approaches rely on predictive or concurrent validity. Both methods attempt to relate test scores to a criterion, usually performance. Courts and the EEOC guidelines generally prefer empirical approaches because they are less subjective than rational methods.[20]

Rational validation approaches include content and construct validity. These techniques are used when empirical validation is not feasible because the small number of subjects does not permit a reasonable sample on which to conduct the validation study, for example.

Regardless of which approach is used, testing experts advise the use of separate validation studies for different subgroups, such as women and minority group members. The use of separate studies for different subgroups is called *differential validity.* Without differential validity, a test may be valid for a large group (white male applicants) but not for subgroups of minorities or women.

Differential validity

| Figure 8-3 | **An Explanation of Common Approaches to Test Validation** |

EMPIRICAL APPROACHES

Empirical approaches to test validation attempt to relate test scores with a job-related criterion, usually performance. If the test actually measures a job-related criterion, the test and the criterion exhibit a positive correlation between 0 and 1.0. The higher the correlation, the better the match.

■ *Predictive validity* is determined by giving a test to a group of applicants. After these applicants have been hired and have mastered the job reasonably well, their performance is measured. This measurement and the test score are then correlated.

■ *Concurrent validity* allows the personnel department to test present employees and correlate these scores with measures of their performance. This approach does not require an interval between hiring and mastery of the job.

RATIONAL APPROACHES

When the number of subjects is too low to have a reasonable sample of people to test, rational approaches are used. These approaches are considered inferior to empirical techniques, but are acceptable validation strategies when empirical approaches are not feasible.

■ *Content validity* is assumed to exist when the test includes reasonable samples of the skills needed to successfully perform the job. A typing test for an applicant who is being hired simply to do typing is an example of a test with content validity.

■ *Construct validity* seeks to establish a relationship between performance and other characteristics that are assumed to be necessary for successful job performance. Tests of intelligence and scientific terms would be considered to have construct validity if they were used to hire researchers for a chemical company.

Even when tests are validated, courts may examine how effective such validation attempts are. Invalid procedures, no matter how well intentioned, cannot be relied on to prove a test's validity.

The Albemarle Paper Company gave several African-American workers a battery of tests that had not been validated. The workers sued Albemarle, and the company then implemented a validation study. However, the study had several weaknesses, and the court ruled the tests invalid and discriminatory.
The problems faced by Albemarle were that:[21]

■ The company used tests that had been validated for advanced jobs, not for the entry-level positions to which the tests were being applied. Validation for advanced jobs does not prove that the tests are valid for entry-level positions. Tests must be validated on those jobs to which they are being applied.

■ The company validated the test on one group (white workers) and then applied it to another group (African-American workers). Tests must be validated for all the groups to which they are applied.

Reliability

To be valid, a test must be reliable. *Reliability* means that the test should yield consistent results each time an individual takes it. For example, a test of manual dexterity for an assembly worker should produce a similar score each time the person takes the test. If the results vary widely with each retest because good scores depend on luck or because the evaluators of the test cannot objectively score the results, the test is not reliable and therefore is not valid.

Validity and reliability are most closely associated with testing. However, other steps in the selection process must be both valid and reliable if the HR department is to do an effective job of selection.

Testing Tools and Cautions

Many employment tests exist, but each type of test has only limited usefulness. The exact purpose of a test, its design, its directions for administration, and its applications are recorded in the test manual, which should be reviewed before a test is used. The manual also reports the test's reliability and the results of validation efforts by the test designer. Many tests have been validated on large populations, but testing specialists should conduct their own studies to make sure a particular test is valid for its planned use. Each type of test has a different purpose.[22] Figure 8-4 lists examples and gives a brief explanation of several different types of tests.

Questionable validity

Psychological tests measure personality or temperament. They are among the least reliable tests. Validity suffers because the relationship between personality and performance is often vague or nonexistent.

Knowledge tests are more reliable because they determine information or knowledge. A math test for an accountant and a weather test for a pilot are examples. But specialists must be able to demonstrate that the knowledge is needed to perform the job. The Miami trucking company example is a case where the tested knowledge (reading at an advanced level) was unneeded.

Performance tests measure the ability of applicants to do some parts of the work for which they are to be hired, for example, a typing test for typists. Validity is often assumed when the test includes a representative sample of the work the applicant is to do upon being hired. However, if the test discriminates against a protected group, it must be backed by detailed validation studies. Merrill Lynch's test is likely to be considered valid (as discussed in connection with content and construct validity under rational validation approaches in Figure 8-3) because it includes samples of the work an account representative would be expected to do.

Lie detectors

Attitude and honesty tests are being used in some circumstances to learn about the attitudes of applicants and employees toward a variety of job-related subjects. Since the passage of the *Employee Polygraph Protection Act* in 1988, poly-

Figure 8-4	**Some Applications of Employment-Related Tests**

NAME	APPLICATION
PSYCHOLOGICAL TESTS	
■ Minnesota Multiphasic Personality Inventory	Measures personality or temperament (executives, nuclear power, security)
■ California Psychological Inventory	Measures personality or temperament (executives, managers, supervisors)
■ Guilford-Zimmerman Temperament Survey	Measures personality or temperament (sales personnel)
■ Watson-Glaser Critical Thinking Appraisal	Measures logic and reasoning ability (executives, managers, supervisors)
■ Owens Creativity Test	Measures creativity and judgment ability (engineers)
■ Myers-Briggs Type Indicator	Measures personality components
KNOWLEDGE TESTS	
■ Leadership opinion questionnaire	Measures knowledge of leadership practices (managers and supervisors)
■ General aptitude test battery	Measures verbal, spatial, numeric, and other aptitudes and dexterity (job seekers at unemployment offices)
PERFORMANCE TESTS	
■ Stromberg Dexterity Test	Measures physical coordination (shop workers)
■ Revised Minnesota Paper Form Board Test	Measures spatial visualization (draftsmen and draftswomen)
■ Minnesota Clerical Test	Measures ability to work with numbers and names (clerks)
■ Job simulation tests	Measure a sample of "on-the-job" demands (managers, professionals)
GRAPHIC RESPONSE TEST	
■ Polygraph (Lie Detector)	Measures physiological responses to questions (police, retail store workers)
ATTITUDE TESTS	
■ Honesty Test	Measures attitudes about theft and related subjects (retail workers, securities employees, banks)
■ Work opinion questionnaire	Measures attitudes about work and values (entry-level, low-income workers)
MEDICAL TESTS	
■ Drug tests	Measure the presence of illegal or performance-affecting drugs (athletes, government employees, equipment operators)
■ Genetic screening	Identifies genetic predispositions to specific medical problems
■ Medical screening	Measures and monitors exposure to hazardous chemicals (miners, factory workers, researchers)

graph (lie detector) tests have been effectively banned in employment situations.[23] In their place, attitude tests are being used to assess attitudes about honesty and, presumably, on-the-job behaviors.[24] Attitude tests also reveal employee attitudes and values about work. The *Work Opinion Questionnaire*, for example, has been effectively used in predicting the job performance of entry-level low-income workers.[25]

Drug tests

Medical tests have grown in popularity in recent years. Through an analysis of urine, hair, or blood samples, laboratories are able to screen for the presence of drugs. Concern about employee drug abuse has spurred IBM, American Airlines, Storer Communications, and many others to require all job applicants to pass a urinalysis for marijuana and cocaine.[26]

AIDS

As technology has improved, testing for genetic defects or predispositions has become technically and financially feasible. Genetic screening may alert employers to those with higher chances of developing specific diseases. Medical monitoring of diseases such as acquired immune deficiency syndrome (AIDS) or of the buildup of toxic chemicals such as lead or mercury among workers may alert employers to high-risk employees or shortcomings in health standards in the workplace. Since the *Americans with Disabilities Act* became effective in 1992, medical or other tests that discriminate against those who are "differently abled" also may constitute an EEO violation.[27] To many applicants and employees these tests represent an invasion of privacy.

Testing is not always feasible. The cost may not be justified for jobs that have low selection ratios or are seldom filled. Examples include technical, professional, and managerial jobs. Even when feasible, the use of tests must be flexible. Tests need not be the first or last step in the selection process. Consider the comments of an experienced manager for a chain of grocery stores.

Tests as a preliminary screen

Too many HR managers use testing only after other steps in the selection process. In the grocery business you must test first. Why waste time interviewing a grocery clerk who doesn't know that three for 88 cents is 30 cents apiece? Besides, when we take applications on Tuesdays, we may have 300 of them. Interviews would take 75 hours a week, and my staff consists of a clerk and myself. But through testing, we can test the entire group in an hour. Then we interview only those who score well.

Employment tests are limited to factors that can be easily tested and validated. Other items, which may not be measurable through testing, may be equally important, such as enthusiasm and motivation.

▶ Selection Interview: Step 3

Interviews defined

The *selection interview* is a formal, in-depth conversation conducted to evaluate an applicant's acceptability. The interviewer seeks to answer three broad questions: Can the applicant do the job? Will the applicant do the job? How does the applicant compare with others who are being considered for the job?

Selection interviews are the most widely used selection technique.[28] Their popularity stems from their flexibility. They can be adapted to unskilled, skilled, managerial, and staff employees. They also allow a two-way exchange of information: Interviewers learn about the applicant, and the applicant learns about the employer.

Interviews have certain shortcomings. Their most noticeable flaws are in the areas of reliability and validity. Good reliability means that the interpretation of the interview results does not vary from interviewer to interviewer, but it is common for different interviewers to form different opinions. Reliability is improved when identical questions are asked, especially if interviewers are trained to record responses systematically.[29]

American Bankers

For example, American Bankers Insurance Group uses a computer-driven interview process in which clerical applicants are asked standardized questions via a computer. The computer measures the time needed to answer individual questions and indicates areas where the applicant hesitated, suggesting follow-up questions in the subsequent face-to-face interview.[30]

Validation interviews

The validity of interviews is often questionable because few departments use standardized questions, as in the case of American Bankers, with which validation studies can be conducted. However, proactive departments are beginning to recognize this problem and are comparing interview results with actual performance or other criteria, such as stability of employment. More validation of interviews is needed because they may relate more to the personal features of candidates than to candidates' potential performance. If these findings are applicable to most employment interviews, the results of interviews may not correlate well with potential performance. Nevertheless, face-to-face interviews continue to be used because of their adaptability and believed effectiveness, whether validated or not.[31]

Types of Interviews

Group interviews

One-to-one interviews between the applicant and the interviewer are the most common; group interviews, however, are sometimes used. Variations of group interviews appear in Figure 8-5. One variation is to have applicants meet with two or more interviewers, allowing all the interviewers to evaluate the individual on the same questions and answers. Another major variation shown in the figure is to have two or more applicants be interviewed together by one or more interviewers. Park workers at Disneyland, for example, meet in groups of three with an interviewer for forty-five minutes to allow the interviewer to observe how potential workers will interact with others.[32] This saves time and permits the answers and interactions of different applicants to be compared immediately.

| Figure 8-5 | Different Combinations of Interviewers and Applicants |

NUMBER OF INTERVIEWERS	NUMBER OF APPLICANTS
INDIVIDUAL INTERVIEW	
1	1
GROUP INTERVIEWS	
2 or more	1
1	2 or more
2 or more	2 or more

Interview formats

Beyond individual and group approaches, there are different interview formats. The questions can appear in structured, unstructured, mixed, problem-solving, or stress-producing formats. Figure 8-6 compares the different formats. The mixed format is the most common in practice, although each of the others has an appropriate role to play.

Unstructured interviews.   As the summary in Figure 8-6 indicates, an unstructured interview allows employment specialists to develop questions as the interview proceeds. The interviewer goes into topic areas as they arise, trying to simulate a friendly conversation. Unfortunately, this method, which also is called nondirective interviewing, lacks the reliability of a structured interview because each applicant is asked a different series of questions. Even worse, this approach may overlook key areas of the applicant's skills or background. In Japan, for example, where EEOC guidelines do not apply, managers prefer wide-ranging unstructured interviews as a means of getting to know applicants and their personal lives better.

Structured interviews.   *Structured,* or directive, *interviews* rely on a predetermined set of questions. The questions are developed before the interview begins and are asked of every applicant, as in the computerized approach used by American Bankers. Structured questions improve the reliability of the interview process but do not allow the interviewer to follow up on interesting or unusual responses. The process seems quite mechanical to all concerned. The rigid format may even convey disinterest to applicants who are used to more flexible interviews.

Typical approach

Mixed interviews.   Interviewers typically use a blend of structured and unstructured questions. The structured questions provide a base of information that allows comparisons between candidates; the unstructured questions make the interview more conversational and permit greater insights into the unique differences between applicants. College recruiters, for example, use mixed interviews most of the time.

Figure 8-6	Different Question Formats in Interviews

INTERVIEW FORMAT	TYPES OF QUESTIONS	USEFUL APPLICATIONS
UNSTRUCTURED	Few if any planned questions. Questions are made up during the interview.	Useful when trying to help interviewees solve personal problems or understand why they are not right for a job.
STRUCTURED	A predetermined checklist of questions, usually asked of all applicants.	Useful for valid results, especially when dealing with large numbers of applicants.
MIXED	A combination of structured and unstructured questions that resemble what is usually done in practice.	Realistic approach that yields comparable answers plus in-depth insights.
BEHAVIORAL	Questions limited to hypothetical situations. Evaluation is on the solution and the approach of the applicant.	Useful to understand applicant's reasoning and analytic abilities under modest stress.
STRESS	A series of harsh, rapid-fire questions intended to upset the applicant.	Useful for stressful jobs, such as handling complaints.

Behavioral interviewing.   Behavioral interviewing focuses on a problem or a hypothetical situation that the applicant is asked to solve. Often these are hypothetical situations, and the applicant is asked what should be done. Both the answer and the approach are evaluated. This interview technique has a very narrow scope. It primarily reveals the applicant's ability to solve the types of problems presented.[33] Validity is more likely if the hypothetical situations match those found on the job. The interview might consist of situations similar to the following:

Behavioral interview situation

Suppose you had to decide between two candidates for a promotion. Candidate A is loyal, cooperative, punctual, and hardworking. Candidate B is a complainer and is tardy and discourteous but is the best producer in your department. Whom would you recommend for promotion to supervisor? Why?

The way the applicant reacts to the questions is noted. That also produces modest amounts of stress and suggests how the applicant may function under moderately stressful situations.

Stress interviews.   *Stress interviews* attempt to learn how the applicant will respond to job pressures. Originally developed during World War II to see how selected recruits might react under stress behind enemy lines, these interviews have useful applications in civilian employment. For example, applicants for police work are sometimes put through a stress interview to see how they might react to problems encountered in the street. The interview consists of a series of harsh questions asked in rapid-fire succession and in an unfriendly manner. Since stressful situations are usually only part of the job, this technique should be used in connection with other interview formats. Even then, negative reactions are likely among those who are not hired. Reliability and validity are hard to demonstrate, since job stress may differ from the stress posed in the interview.

The Interview Process

Regardless of the type of interview, the interview process has sequential steps, as shown in Figure 8-7. Stages include interviewer preparation, creation of rapport, information exchange, termination, and evaluation. They are discussed below to illustrate how the actual interview process occurs.

Interviewer preparation.   The interviewer should review the application and job description information to prepare specific questions before beginning the interview. Answers to these questions determine the applicant's suitability. Since interviews help persuade top applicants to accept subsequent job offers, interviewers need to be able to explain job duties, performance standards, pay, benefits, and other areas of interest.

Typical questions

Typical questions asked by college recruiters and other interviewers appear in Figure 8-8. These questions are intended to give the interviewer insights into the applicant's interests, attitudes, and background. Specific or technical questions are added to the list in accordance with the job opening. A review of the job description and position specifications helps the interviewer prepare specific questions. In preparing those questions, the interviewers must be espe-

| Figure 8-7 | Stages in the Typical Employment Interview |

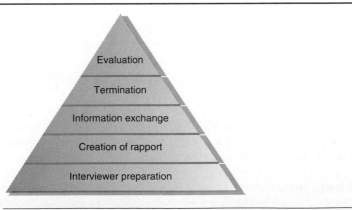

| Figure 8-8 | **Sample Questions in Employment Interviews** |

1. How do you spend your spare time? What are your hobbies?
2. What community or school activities have you been involved in?
3. Describe your ideal job. In what type of work are you interested?
4. Why do you want to work for our company?
5. What were your favorite classes? Why?
6. Do you have any geographic preferences?
7. Why did you select your college major?
8. What do you know about our company's products or services?
9. Describe the ideal boss.
10. How often do you expect to be promoted?
11. What is your major weakness? Strength?
12. Why do you think your friends like you?
13. Do you plan to take additional college courses? Which ones?
14. What jobs have you had that you liked most? Least?
15. Describe your favorite boss or teacher.
16. What are your career goals?
17. If you could go back five years, what would you do the same? Differently?
18. Why should you be hired by our company?
19. Describe your last job.
20. How many hours do you think you will have to work at your job?
21. What job skills do you have?

cially careful not to ask any that could be interpreted as discriminatory. Questions asked of a protected group but not of members of the majority group are usually the ones that cause violations. An example is asking women about child-care arrangements but not asking men the same question. Questions about sex, age, national origin, handicaps, or religion are likely to be considered discriminatorily motivated unless they are related to a bona fide occupational qualification. (See Chapter 4 for a discussion of BFOQs.)

Creation of rapport.   The burden of establishing rapport falls on the interviewer, although applicants can improve their prospects by sharing this responsibility. One writer addressed the interviewer's role as follows:

Interviewer's role

Comes the appointed hour, you will act the perfect host or hostess, greeting the candidate with a warm smile, showing him into your office, making small talk in the hope of putting him at ease. Of course he's nervous, acting stiff, withdrawn, or cocky as a result. Your challenge—it being your show, and you so self-assured from all the preparation you have done—is to reduce that nervousness; the closer the interview comes to a friendly conversation, the more you will learn about the real him or her.[34]

Rapport is aided by beginning the interview on time and starting with non-threatening questions such as: Did you have any parking problems? At the same time, the interviewer may use body language to help relax the applicant. A smile, a handshake, a relaxed posture, and the moving aside of paperwork—all communicate without words. This rapport is maintained through such non-verbal communications as nodding one's head, smiling, and relaxing one's posture during the session.

Information exchange.   The interview process is a conversation in which information is exchanged. To help establish rapport while learning about the candidate, some interviewers begin by asking the interviewee if he or she has any questions. This establishes two-way communication and allows the interviewer to begin judging the recruit by the types of questions asked. Consider these responses to the interviewer's opening statement: "Let's start with any questions you may have." Which gives the most favorable impression?

Applicant's questions

APPLICANT 1:   I don't have any questions.

APPLICANT 2:   I have several questions. How much does the job pay? Will I get a two-week vacation at the end of the first year?

APPLICANT 3:   What will my responsibilities be? I am hoping to find a job that offers me challenges now and career potential down the road.

Each response makes a different impression on the interviewer. Only the third applicant appears to be concerned about the job. The other two are unconcerned or interested only in the benefits they will receive.

Open-ended questions

In general, an interviewer will ask questions in a way that elicits as much information as possible. Questions that begin with "how," "what," "why," "compare," "describe," "expand," or "could you tell me more about" are more likely to elicit an open response. Questions that can be answered with a simple yes or no do not give the interviewer much insight. For example, an interviewer is likely to get narrow, limited answers by asking questions that begin "Are you" or "Did you." Specific questions and areas of interest to an interviewer are suggested in Figure 8-8. Besides getting answers to those questions, the interviewer may want more specific information about the applicant's background, skills, and interests.

Termination.   As the list of questions dwindles or the available time ends, the interviewer must draw the session to a close. Once again, nonverbal communication is useful. Sitting erect, turning toward the door, glancing at a watch or clock—all tell the applicant that the end is near. Some interviewers terminate

Wrapping up

the interview by asking, Do you have any final questions? At this point the interviewer notifies the applicant of the next step in the interview process, which may be to wait for a call or letter. Regardless of the interviewer's opinion, the applicant should not be given an indication of his or her prospects for getting the job. Not only may a subsequent candidate look better, but subsequent steps in the selection process may cause the final selection decision to be much different from the way it might appear at the end of the interview.

Evaluation.   Immediately after the interview ends, the interviewer should record specific answers by and general impressions about the candidate. Figure 8-9 shows a typical checklist used to record the interviewer's impressions. The use of a checklist like this one can improve the reliability of the interview as a selection technique. As the checklist shows, the interviewer is able to obtain a large amount of information even from a short interview.

Figure 8-9   **A Postinterview Checklist**

EMPIRE, INC.

"An Equal Opportunity Employer"

Postinterview Checklist

Applicant's Name _____   **Date** _____

Position under Consideration _____   **Interviewer** _____

Interviewer's Comments
A. Rate the applicant on the following (1 = low; 10 = high):
_____ Appearance   _____ Ability to perform job
_____ Apparent interest   _____ Education / training
_____ Experience / background   _____ Timely availability
_____ Reasonable expectations   _____ Past employment stability

B. List specific comments that reveal the candidate's strengths and weaknesses for the job being considered:
   1. Attitude toward previous job _____
   2. Attitude toward previous boss _____
   3. Expectations about job duties _____
   4. Career or occupational expectations _____
   5. Other specific comments about applicant _____

Follow-up Actions Required
_____ None   _____ Follow-up interview with personnel
_____ Testing   _____ Applicant unacceptable (file)
_____ Supervisory interview _____ Notify applicant of rejection
_____ Applicant unacceptable for job under consideration. Reconsider for job as

_____

Interviewer Errors

Interviewer biases   Mistakes or errors occur regardless of the steps an interviewer follows. To the extent that the cautions in Figure 8-10 are not followed, the effectiveness—particularly the validity and reliability—of the interview is lessened. When the applicant is judged according to the halo effect or personal biases, results are mis-

| Figure 8-10 | A Summary of Typical Interviewer Errors |

HALO EFFECT

Interviewers who allow limited information about an applicant to bias their evaluation of that person's other characteristics are subject to the halo effect.

Examples:

- An applicant who has a pleasant smile and firm handshake is considered a leading candidate before the interview begins.

- An applicant who wears blue jeans to the interview is rejected unconsciously.

LEADING QUESTIONS

Interviewers who "telegraph" the desired answer by the way they frame their questions are using leading questions.

Examples:

- "Do you think you'll like this work?"

- "Do you agree that profits are necessary?"

PERSONAL BIASES

Interviewers who harbor prejudice against specific groups are exhibiting a personal bias.

Examples:

- "I prefer sales personnel who are tall."

- "Some jobs are for men, and others are for women."

INTERVIEWER DOMINATION

Interviewers who use the interview to oversell the applicant, brag about their successes, or carry on a social conversation instead of an interview are guilty of interviewer domination.

Examples:

- Spending the entire interview telling the applicant about company plans or benefits.

- Using the interview to tell the applicant how important the interviewer's job is.

interpreted. Applicants are accepted or rejected for reasons that may bear no relationship to their potential performance, harming the validity of the interview. Similarly, leading questions and domination do not allow the interviewer to learn about the applicant's potential. The evaluation of the applicant is then based on guesswork, with little or no substantiation. No matter which pitfall is involved, it reduces the reliability and validity of the interview. When biases are presented, the interview wastes both organizational resources and the applicant's time.

Foreign nationals present a special case. Interviewers should not expect similar body language, expressions, and behaviors.[35] For example, if an applicant does not look the interviewer directly in the eye, the subtle message sent by this behavior may be interpreted as the candidate lacking self-confidence and perhaps hiding something. However, in some cultures direct eye contact from someone in a subservient position (such as an interviewee) may be seen as highly inappropriate. Similar comments can be made about physical appearance, dress, and even hygiene. Allowing these cultural or behavioral differences to interfere with the interviewer's judgment may cause a good candidate to be excluded from further consideration, again harming the validity of the process.

Foreign nationals

Interviewee Errors

Interviewees make errors too. Some may result from an attempt to cover up job-related weaknesses. Others may emerge from simple nervousness. While interviewers—especially those in the HR department—may conduct hundreds of job interviews in a year, most applicants never experience that many in a lifetime. The National Association of Corporate and Professional Recruiters asked executive headhunters and HR specialists to identify common interviewing mistakes made by job candidates. The top five mistakes were playing games, talking too much, boasting, not listening, and being unprepared.

Research summary

Games such as acting nonchalant are often taken at face value: The interviewer assumes that the candidate is not interested. Although the candidate may be excited or nervous, talking too much, especially about irrelevant topics such as sports or the weather, may entertain the interviewer but is not appropriate. Instead, applicants should stick to the subject at hand. Boasting also is a common mistake. Applicants need to "sell themselves," but distorting credentials—even by just "embellishing"—that relate to responsibilities and accomplishments or simply bragging too much can turn off the interviewer's interest. Failure to listen may result from anxiety about the interview. Unfortunately, it usually means missing the interviewer's questions and failing to maintain rapport. Of course, being unprepared leads to asking poorly thought-out questions and even conveying disinterest, neither of which is likely to help the applicant land the job being sought.

Embellishing

▶ References and Background Checks: Step 4

Is the applicant a good, reliable worker? Are the job accomplishments, titles, educational background, and other facts on the résumé or application true? What type of person is the applicant? Most important, what information is relevant to matching the applicant and the job? To answer these questions, managers and employment specialists use references and background checks. They may even supplement the application form with a biographical information blank that goes beyond the one in the typical application.

Credential distortion by applicants suggests that reference and background checks are important, especially when customers or coworkers may be harmed by poor performance or illegal behavior.[36] Research suggests that credential distortion occurs frequently.

Credential distortion

> Jeremiah McAward, president of a New York City credential verification agency, states, "Of the thousands of resumes we investigate, there are outright lies on 22 percent."[37]
>
> According to the National Credential Verification Service, approximately one-third of the résumés it examines contain mildly embellished or fabricated academic degrees.[38]
>
> In a survey of 501 executives by Ward Howell International Inc., an executive search firm, 17 percent of the executives said that their new hires had misrepresented job qualifications and 9 percent of their employee applicants had inflated their salaries.[39]

Failure to verify credentials can result in public relations, financial, or other problems for the employer.

> Janet Cooke, a journalist for the *Washington Post,* confessed to having fabricated her Pulitzer Prize–winning story about an 8-year-old heroin addict living in the Washington, D.C., slums. Upon closer scrutiny of her credentials, "irregularities" surfaced in her educational background. She had claimed to be a magna cum laude graduate of Vassar and to have earned a master's degree from the University of Toledo; actually, she only *attended* Vassar during her freshman year and held a *bachelor's* degree from the University of Toledo.[40]

Imagine the personal and professional embarrassment of the hiring manager and the HR department at the *Washington Post* when the distorted credentials were uncovered. In this example, the selection processes lacked a thorough evaluation of credentials.

Personal versus employment references

References are viewed in different ways by different professionals. *Personal references*—ones that attest to the applicant's sound character—are usually provided by friends or family members. Their objectivity and candor are certainly questionable. When writing a reference, the author usually includes only positive points. Thus personal references are less commonly used. *Employment references* discuss the applicant's work history. As privacy legislation continues to expand, many supervisors and HR departments are becoming less willing to provide employment references because they fear potential lawsuits for libel and slander. Even though supervisors and HR specialists may be protected under what the law calls "qualified privilege," that protection may end if there are doubts about the truth of the recommendation, about whether the recommendation has been made with malice, or about whether the information involves issues not covered by privilege, such as personal information not related to employment. As a result, many HR departments have policies that limit reference information to little more than verifying that the person actually worked for a company.[41] Some HR departments will not even do that much. As a result, 68 percent of the companies in one survey reported that it is becoming harder to get references.[42]

Telephone inquiries

This lack of candor has caused some employers to omit this step entirely from the selection process.[43] Other companies have substituted telephone inquiries for written references,[44] although these inquiries are also subject to legal complications and restrictive policies. Besides a faster response, often at lower cost, voice inflections or hesitancy to answer blunt questions may reveal underlying problems.

Bonding and Security Checks

Background checks

When an applicant is going to have access to money, valuables, or classified information—as an account executive at Merrill Lynch would—a background search may be conducted that goes far beyond letters of reference. Bonding companies may want far more detail than appears in the application. The HR department may want to check criminal records and credit ratings. If national defense is involved, a detailed background check may be needed before the employee can receive the necessary clearance to work on classified materials. For some highly secret jobs with government contractors, these clearances may take up to six months or longer and may involve checks on family members and the applicant's past.

Immigration and Naturalization Rules

I-9 form

The *Immigration Reform and Control Act* of 1986 has added a complicating twist to background checks. While EEO laws and regulations preclude discrimination on the basis of national origin, the Immigration Reform and Control Act demands that employers not hire undocumented aliens ("illegal aliens"). To comply with the law, employers must complete and retain an Immigration and Naturalization form, I-9, for every employee hired, as shown in Figure 8-11. The list of acceptable documents for verifying eligibility is shown in Figure 8-12.

U.S. Department of Justice
Immigration and Naturalization Service

OMB No. 1115-0136

Employment Eligibility Verification

Please read instructions carefully before completing this form. The instructions must be available during completion of this form. **ANTI-DISCRIMINATION NOTICE.** It is illegal to discriminate against work eligible individuals. Employers **CANNOT** specify which document(s) they will accept from an employee. The refusal to hire an individual because of a future expiration date may also constitute illegal discrimination.

Section 1.   **Employee Information and Verification.** To be completed and signed by employee at the time employment begins

Print Name: Last	First	Middle Initial	Maiden Name

Address (Street Name and Number)	Apt. #	Date of Birth (month/day/year)

City	State	Zip Code	Social Security #

I am aware that federal law provides for imprisonment and/or fines for false statements or use of false documents in connection with the completion of this form.

I attest, under penalty of perjury, that I am (check one of the following):
- ☐ A citizen or national of the United States
- ☐ A Lawful Permanent Resident (Alien # A _____)
- ☐ An alien authorized to work until ____/____/____
  (Alien # or Admission # _____)

Employee's Signature	Date (month/day/year)

Preparer and/or Translator Certification. (To be completed and signed if Section 1 is prepared by a person other than the employee.) I attest, under penalty of perjury, that I have assisted in the completion of this form and that to the best of my knowledge the information is true and correct.

Preparer's/Translator's Signature	Print Name

Address (Street Name and Number, City, State, Zip Code)	Date (month/day/year)

Section 2.   **Employer Review and Verification.** To be completed and signed by employer. Examine one document from List A OR examine one document from List B **and** one from List C as listed on the reverse of this form and record the title, number and expiration date, if any, of the document(s)

List A	OR	List B	AND	List C
Document title: _____		_____		_____
Issuing authority: _____		_____		_____
Document #: _____		_____		_____
Expiration Date (if any): ___/___/___		___/___/___		___/___/___
Document #: _____				
Expiration Date (if any): ___/___/___				

CERTIFICATION - I attest, under penalty of perjury, that I have examined the document(s) presented by the above-named employee, that the above-listed document(s) appear to be genuine and to relate to the employee named, that the employee began employment on (month/day/year) ____/____/____ and that to the best of my knowledge the employee is eligible to work in the United States. (State employment agencies may omit the date the employee began employment).

Signature of Employer or Authorized Representative	Print Name	Title

Business or Organization Name	Address (Street Name and Number, City, State, Zip Code)	Date (month/day/year)

Section 3.   **Updating and Reverification.** To be completed and signed by employer

A. New Name (if applicable)	B. Date of rehire (month/day/year) (if applicable)

C. If employee's previous grant of work authorization has expired, provide the information below for the document that establishes current employment eligibility.

Document Title: _____ Document #: _____ Expiration Date (if any): ___/___/___

I attest, under penalty of perjury, that to the best of my knowledge, this employee is eligible to work in the United States, and if the employee presented document(s), the document(s) I have examined appear to be genuine and to relate to the individual.

Signature of Employer or Authorized Representative	Date (month/day/year)

Form I-9 (Rev. 11-21-91) N

Figure 8-12	List of Acceptable Documents for Completing an I-9 Form

LIST A   OR   **LIST B**   AND   **LIST C**

Documents that Establish Both Identity and Employment Eligibility	**Documents that Establish Identity**	**Documents that Establish Employment Eligibility**
1. U.S. Passport (unexpired or expired)	1. Driver's license or ID card issued by a state or outlying possession of the United States provided it contains a photograph or information such as name, date of birth, sex, height, eye color, and address	1. U.S. social security card issued by the Social Security Administration *(other than a card stating it is not valid for employment)*
2. Certificate of U.S. Citizenship *(INS Form N-560 or N-561)*		
3. Certificate of Naturalization *(INS Form N-550 or N-570)*	2. ID card issued by federal, state, or local government agencies or entities provided it contains a photograph or information such as name, date of birth, sex, height, eye color, and address	2. Certification of Birth Abroad issued by the Department of State *(Form FS-545 or Form DS 1350)*
4. Unexpired foreign passport, with *I-551 stamp or* attached *INS Form I-94* indicating unexpired employment authorization	3. School ID card with a photograph	3. Original or certified copy of a birth certificate issued by a state, county, municipal authority or outlying possession of the United States bearing an official seal
5. Alien Registration Receipt Card with photograph *(INS Form I-151 or I-551)*	4. Voter's registration card	
	5. U.S. Military card or draft record	
6. Unexpired Temporary Resident Card *(INS Form I-688)*	6. Military dependent's ID card	4. Native American tribal document
7. Unexpired Employment Authorization Card *(INS Form I-688A)*	7. U.S. Coast Guard Merchant Mariner Card	5. U.S. Citizen ID Card *(INS Form I-197)*
	8. Native American tribal document	
8. Unexpired Reentry Permit *(INS Form I-327)*	9. Driver's license issued by a Canadian government authority	6. ID Card for use of Resident Citizen in the United States *(INS Form I-179)*
9. Unexpired Refugee Travel Document *(INS Form I-571)*	**For persons under age 18 who are unable to present a document listed above:**	7. Unexpired employment authorization document issued by the INS *(other than those listed under List A)*
10. Unexpired Employment Authorization Document issued by the INS which contains a photograph *(INS Form I-688B)*	10. School record or report card	
	11. Clinic, doctor, or hospital record	
	12. Day-care or nursery school record	

Illustrations of many of these documents appear in Part 8 of the Handbook for Employers (M-274)

Form I-9 (Rev. 11-21-91) N

    Employers who knowingly recruit, hire, or refer foreign aliens for employment are subject to civil and/or criminal penalties. However, HR specialists who vigorously seek to comply with the immigration act may discriminate (or at least appear to discriminate) against applicants of specific national or ethnic origins. The challenge for employment specialists is to verify that applicants are not undocumented aliens without discriminating against U.S. citizens or properly documented aliens.

▶ Medical Evaluation: Step 5

The selection process may include a medical evaluation of the applicant before the hiring decision is made. Normally, the evaluation consists of a health checklist that asks the applicant to indicate health and accident information. The questionnaire is sometimes supplemented with a physical examination by a company nurse or physician. The medical evaluation may:

Medical
evaluations

- Entitle the employer to lower health or life insurance rates for company-paid insurance.

- Be required by state or local health officials, particularly in food-handling operations where communicable diseases are a danger.

- Be useful to evaluate whether the applicant can handle the physical or mental stress of a job.

ADA and medical
evaluations

Many employers have done away with this step because the *Americans with Disabilities Act* makes the qualified disabled a protected class under equal employment opportunity laws. A medical evaluation may uncover disabilities or potential disabilities.[45] Then, if the applicant is not hired, charges of discrimination may be brought under the act. A preexisting health condition may be considered a disability, and failure to hire may be seen as discrimination against the qualified handicapped. When the employer wants a medical evaluation, it is increasingly scheduled *after* the hiring decision. As *Fortune* magazine observed:

> After the employer offers a job to the candidate, he can make it conditional upon passing a physical exam. But the employer may rescind the offer only if the physical turns up a defect that prevents the newcomer from doing the job. A curvature of the spine, for example, might be a handicap on the loading dock, but progressive diabetes won't prevent someone from evaluating loan applications—at least not tomorrow.[46]

Drug testing is a noteworthy exception to the trend toward fewer medical evaluations. A growing number of corporations and governments include drug screening as part of the employment process either before or immediately after the hiring decision is made. These organizations seek to avoid the economic and legal risks associated with drug users. Increases in mortality rates, accidents, theft, and poor performance affect the employer's economic performance. If a drug user's performance carries negative consequences for customers or fellow employees, lawsuits are likely.[47]

▶ Supervisory Interview: Step 6

Research summary

The ultimate responsibility for a newly hired worker's success falls to the worker's immediate supervisor. The supervisor is often able to evaluate the applicant's technical abilities. Likewise, the immediate supervisor can often answer the interviewee's specific job-related questions with precision. As a result, one study reported that in over three-fourths of the organizations surveyed, the supervisor has the authority to make the hiring decision.

When supervisors make the final decision, the employment function provides a supervisor with the best prescreened applicants available. From those two or three applicants, the supervisor decides whom to hire. Some employers leave the final hiring decision to the HR department, especially when applicants are hired for a training program instead of a specific job. If supervisors reject particular groups, such as minorities or women, the department may be given final hiring authority to avoid charges of discrimination.

Supervisory commitment

Regardless of who has the final hiring authority, the commitment of supervisors is generally higher if they participate in the selection process. When a supervisor recommends hiring someone, it creates within the supervisor a psychological commitment to ensure the employee's success. If the candidate turns out to be unsatisfactory, the supervisor is more likely to accept some of the responsibility for failure.

▶ Realistic Job Previews: Step 7

RJPs

Realistic job previews supplement the supervisory interview. A *realistic job preview* (RJP) shows the employee the job and the job setting before the hiring decision is made. Often this involves showing the candidate the type of work, equipment, and working conditions involved. In some cases an RJP is provided as part of the recruiting process to weed out inappropriate candidates. Not all companies use RJPs.

Unmet expectations about a job can contribute to job dissatisfaction. RJPs reduce the initial surprise of a new job—and potential job dissatisfaction—by giving newcomers insight into the job. Recently hired employees who have an RJP are less likely to be shocked by the job or the job setting when they report to work. Two writers concluded that:

> The RJP functions very much like a medical vaccination. The typical medical vaccination infects one with a small, weakened dose of germs, so that one's body can develop a natural resistance to that disease. The RJP functions similarly by presenting job candidates with a small dose of "organizational reality." And, like the medical vaccination, the RJP is probably much less effective after a person has already entered a new organization.[48]

Research summary   Employee turnover is lower when job previews are used, according to research. The average turnover rate in nine of ten studies was 28.8 percent higher when there were no RJPs.[49] Although research findings vary, RJPs may help reduce turnover. RJPs are most appropriate when the applicant is not familiar with the job and least appropriate when expectations about the job are accurate.

▶ Hiring Decision: Step 8

Regardless of whether the supervisor or the HR department makes the final hiring decision, hiring marks the end of the selection process, assuming that the candidate accepts the job offer. The hiring process involves more than just extending an offer. To maintain good public relations, employers should notify applicants who were not selected. Employment specialists may want to consider rejected applicants for other openings since these recruits already have gone through the stages of the selection process. Even if no openings are available, the applications of unsuccessful candidates should be kept on file for future openings. Retaining these applications can be useful in defending the company against charges of employment discrimination.

Employee's HR file   The applications of those hired should also be retained. The application blank begins the employee's HR file. Additional background information should be added to the file concerning who to contact in case of emergency and the results of posthiring medical evaluations and other tests. This is just the beginning of the employment-related paperwork.

> The paperwork does not stop after the initial job application, interview and reference checking. There are recordkeeping responsibilities for pay, Social Security, unemployment insurance, workers' compensation, Consolidated Omnibus Budget Reconciliation Act (COBRA), federal and state income tax, and disability insurance, all mandated by law for each worker. These records must be continued for at least six years regardless of the employee's length of service or date of discharge.[50]

The employee's file is supplemented with information needed for bonding or security clearances, along with decisions about fringe benefits options and other decisions. Even at this point, the employee is often considered probationary and not eligible for all the firm's benefits until thirty, sixty, or ninety days have passed.

Leaving an audit trail   Retaining application information on those hired and those not hired proves useful for studies that the HR department may conduct to learn about the source of its applicants, such as which recruiting channels work best. If some recruits prove to be unsatisfactory after they are hired, for example, the employment managers may be able to reconstruct the selection process beginning with the application and uncover invalid tests, improperly conducted interviews, or other flaws in the selection process.

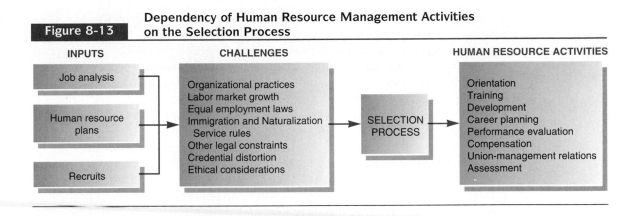

Figure 8-13   Dependency of Human Resource Management Activities on the Selection Process

INPUTS	CHALLENGES		HUMAN RESOURCE ACTIVITIES
Job analysis	Organizational practices Labor market growth Equal employment laws Immigration and Naturalization Service rules Other legal constraints Credential distortion Ethical considerations	SELECTION PROCESS	Orientation Training Development Career planning Performance evaluation Compensation Union-management relations Assessment
Human resource plans			
Recruits			

▶ Challenges, Process, and Feedback

Challenges discussed throughout this chapter and identified in Figure 8-13 include slow growth in labor markets, credential distortion, rules of the Immigration and Naturalization Service, and other legal constraints.

Ethical issues

A particularly important challenge involves the ethics of controlling the selection process. Since employment specialists strongly influence the hiring decision, that decision is shaped by their ethics. The hiring of an unqualified friend, gifts from a placement agency, and bribes (especially overseas) all challenge employment specialists' ethical standards. If those standards are low, new employees may not be properly selected.

Feedback represents another element crucial for an effective selection process. Learning about successful employees is sometimes hard since supervisors usually claim responsibility for them. However, feedback on failures is ample. It can include lawsuits, displeased supervisors, growing employee turnover and absenteeism, poor performance, low employee satisfaction, and union activity.[51]

More constructive feedback is obtained through specific questions. How well does the new employee adapt to the organization? To the job? To the career of which the job is a part? Finally, how well does the employee perform? Answers to each of these questions provide feedback about the employee and the selection process. The chapters in Part III examine each of these questions in depth.

▶ Summary

As suggested by Figure 8-13, the selection process depends heavily on inputs such as job analysis, HR plans, and recruitment. These inputs are used within the context of challenges posed by organizational policies, equal employment laws, Immigration and Naturalization Service rules, a slow-growing supply of labor, credential distortion, and other legal concerns faced by the organization.

The key challenge that underlies the entire selection process is to ensure that the steps in the process are valid. In all phases of the selection process, HR professionals also must be concerned about the potential for an adverse impact during the various steps of the process. Even when the overall selection process does not have an adverse impact on members of protected classes, evidence of a discriminatory impact at any stage of the process should be investigated and the discrimination should be eliminated wherever it is found.

The selection process must take recruits and put them through a series of steps to evaluate their potential. These steps vary from organization to organization and from one job opening to another. In general, the selection procedure relies on testing for many hourly jobs and on interviews for virtually every opening that is to be filled. References and medical evaluations are common aspects of the selection process of many employers.

The supervisor's role should include participation in the selection process, usually through an interview with job candidates. As a result of this participation, the supervisor is more likely to be committed to the new worker's success. Growing research evidence supports the use of realistic job previews.

Once the hiring decision is made, the HRIS should be updated with detailed information about the new hire. If the department uses valid procedures and ethical behaviors, it can make a substantial contribution to the success of the employer and therefore the bottom line.

▶ Terms for Review

Selection process	Differential validity
Employment function	Reliability
Selection ratio	Selection interview
Four-fifths rule	Structured interviews
Bottom-line test	Stress interviews
Validity	Realistic job preview

▶ Review and Discussion Questions

1. Would a high or a low selection ratio be expected for job openings among (*a*) unskilled laborers, (*b*) computer-aided design operators, (*c*) blacksmiths, (*d*) cardiovascular surgeons, (*e*) auto mechanics in northern Alaska or southern Florida?

2. Assume you were asked to streamline the number of steps used in the employment process. What steps would you consider dropping, and why?

3. If the employment manager asked you to develop a selection process for identifying and selecting internal candidates for job openings, how would you change the steps described in this chapter for selecting external candidates?

4. If a friend told you she was going to conduct the interviews of foreign nationals for the company's overseas operations, what cautions would you advise her about?

5. Why should tests be validated?

6. If you were interviewing a promising candidate but he or she seemed nervous, what actions might you undertake to calm the candidate?

7. Some people believe that the HR department should have the authority to decide who is hired because it contains the experts on hiring. Others say that the immediate supervisor is responsible for employee performance and should have the final authority. Support one argument or the other and explain your reasoning.

8. Explain why realistic job previews help reduce turnover among recently hired employees.

▶ **Incident 8-1**

The National Food Brokers Selection Process

National Food Brokers buys carload orders of nonperishable food products for resale to food wholesalers. Phone-sales personnel take orders from major food wholesalers, write up the orders, and send them to the appropriate food producers. Nearly 90 of National's 130 employees work in the phone-sales department. Since the job requires long hours on the phone with different accounts, the work is not very pleasant and turnover is high.

The manager of the phone-sales department, Carol Decinni, made the following observations to the personnel manager, Craig Reems:

Most of the people that work in the department fall into two groups. There are those who have been here for two or more years. They seem reasonably content and are the top sellers we have. The other group consists of people who have been here for less than two years. Most of our turnover comes from this group. In fact, we lose one of every three new employees during the first two months. When I talk with the people who are quitting, most of them tell me that they have no idea how much time they had to spend on the phone. I am generally pleased with the quality of recruits the personnel department provides. But we cannot continue with this high turnover. My supervisors are spending most of their time training new workers. Is there anything the HR department can do to hire more stable workers?

1. Suppose you are asked by the HR manager to suggest some strategies for improving the selection process in order to hire more stable workers. What suggestions do you have for (a) preemployment testing and (b) reference checks?

2. Do you believe that an interview with a supervisor in the department would help applicants understand the work better?

3. What do you think supervisors should do to give applicants a realistic understanding of the job before they are hired?

▶ **Exercise 8-1**

Uniform Guidelines: The Four-Fifths Rule versus the Bottom-Line Test

During the last three years a company had 600 applicants, 400 whites and 200 blacks. Of this group, 100 whites and 20 blacks passed the company's standardized preemployment test. Among the 100 whites who passed the test, 80 were rated by interviewers as usable candidates; of that 80, 60 passed the company's detailed background check. Of the twenty blacks who passed the test, eighteen received acceptable evaluations from the interviewers and nine passed the detailed background check. The end result was that the company hired sixty white workers and nine black workers during the past three years.

1. Would this company pass the bottom-line test specified by the EEOC in its Uniform Guidelines?

2. Which of the selection steps above, if any, fail the four-fifths rule?

3. What recommendations would you make to this company?

▶ **References**

1. Marc Levinson, "Help Wanted—Reluctantly," *Newsweek,* Mar. 14, 1994, p. 37.

2. Robert L. Dipboye, *Selection Interviews: Process Perspectives,* Cincinnati: South-Western, 1992, p. 1.

3. Lawrence Rout, "Going for Broker: Our Man Takes Part in Stock-Selling Test," *The Wall Street Journal,* Eastern ed., Apr. 4, 1979, p. 1.

4. Ibid.

5. Lee Smith, "What the Boss Knows about You," *Fortune,* Aug. 9, 1993, pp. 89–90. See also Tim Chauran, "The Nightmare of Negligent Hiring," *Recruitment Today,* February–March 1989, pp. 33–37.

6. R. Craig Scott, "Negligent Hiring: Guilt by Association," *Personnel Administrator,* July 1987, p. 32.

7. Elliott Witkin, "Information, Not Paperwork," *Recruitment Today,* November–December 1988, pp. 29–41.

8. For a concise review of recent research into employment selection, see Edwin A. Fleishman, "Some New Frontiers in Personnel Selection Research," *Personnel Psychology,* vol. 41, 1988, pp. 679–701. See also Dipboye, op. cit.

9. Paul Sheibar, "A Simple Selection System Called 'Job Match,' " *Personnel Journal,* January 1979, pp. 26–29, 53.

10. Blayne Cutler, "My Old Kentucky Tatami," *American Demographics,* June 1989, p. 46.

11. James Ledvinka, *Federal Regulation of Personnel and Human Resource Management,* Belmont, Calif.: Wadsworth, 1982, pp. 101–110.

12. James W. Smither et al., "Applicant Reactions to Selection Procedures," *Personnel Psychology,* Spring 1993, pp. 49–76. See also Gary Dessler, "Value-Based Hiring Builds Commitment," *Personnel Journal,* November 1993, pp. 98–102.

13. James D. Walls, "Testing Has Survived Time and Trial," *Recruitment Today,* January–February 1990, pp. 14–16. See also Neal Schmitt, Stephen W. Gilliland, Roland S. Landis, and Dennis Devine, "Computer-Based Testing Applied to Selection of Secretarial Applicants," *Personnel Psychology,* 1993, pp. 149–165.

14. "Most Employers Test New Job Candidates, ASPA Survey Shows," *Resource,* June 1988, p. 2.

15. Ibid. See also James P. Guthrie and Judy D. Olian, "Drug and Alcohol Testing Programs: Do Firms Consider Their Operating Environment?" *Human Resource Planning,* vol. 14, no. 3, 1991, pp. 221–232.

16. Shawn Tully, "The Hunt for the Global Manager," *Fortune,* May 21, 1990, pp. 140–144.

17. Fritz Drasgow, "Study of the Measurement Bias of Two Standardized Psychological Tests," *Journal of Applied Psychology,* vol. 72, no. 1, 1987, pp. 19–29. See also Charlene Marmer Solomon, "Testing Is Not at Odds with Diversity Efforts," *Personnel Journal,* March 1993, pp. 100–104.

18. *Willie S. Griggs et al. v. Duke Power Company,* 401 U.S. 424 (1971).

19. In *Griggs v. Duke Power Company* the U.S. Supreme Court said that the EEOC's uniform guidelines were "entitled to great deference." *Albermarle Paper Company v. Moody,* 422 U.S. 405 (1975). See also Douglas D. Baker and David E. Terostra, "Employee Selection: Must Every Job Test Be Validated?" *Personnel Journal,* August 1982, pp. 602–604; James M. Norborg, "A Warning Regarding the Simplified Approach to the Evaluation of Test Fairness in Employee Selection Procedures," *Personnel Psychology,* vol. 37, no. 2, Summer 1984, pp. 483–486.

20. Gerald V. Barrett, Ralph A. Alexander, and Dennis Doverspike, "The Implications for Personnel Selection of Apparent Declines in Predictive Validities over Time: A Critique of Hulin, Henry, and Noon," *Personnel Psychology,* Autumn 1992, pp. 601–617.

21. James Ledvinka and Lyle F. Schoenfeldt, "Legal Developments in Employment Testing: Albemarle and Beyond," *Personnel Psychology,* Spring 1978, pp. 1–3.

22. Garry L. Hughes and Erich P. Prien, "Evaluation of Task and Job Skill Linkage Judgments Used to Develop Test Specifications," *Personnel Psychology,* vol. 42, 1989, pp. 283–342.

23. Michael J. Lotito, "The Employee Polygraph Protection Act: Striking a Balance between Employer and Employee Rights," *Legal Report,* Winter 1988, pp. 1–8. See also John W. Jones and William Terris, "After the Polygraph Ban," *Recruitment Today,* May–June 1989, pp. 25–31.

24. Elizabeth M. Cosin, "Test to Spot the Pinocchios May Fail the Honest Abes," *Insight,* July 30, 1990, pp. 42–43. See also Claudia H. Deutsch, "Pen-and-Pencil Integrity Tests," *The New York Times,* Feb. 11, 1990, sect. 3, part 2, p. 29.

25. Charles D. Johnson, Lawrence A. Messe, and William D. Crano, "Predicting Job Performance of Low Income Workers: The Work Opinion Questionnaire," *Personnel Psychology,* vol. 37, no. 2, Summer 1984, pp. 291–299.

26. "Motorola Drug Testing Invades Privacy, Judge Says," *The Miami Herald,* Nov. 24, 1992, p. 3C.

27. Catherine Yang, "The Disabilities Act Is a Godsend—For Lawyers," *Business Week,* Aug. 17, 1992, p. 29. See also Gopal C. Pati and Guy Stubblefield, "The Disabled Are Able to Work," *Personnel Journal,* December 1990, pp. 30–34.

28. Dipboye, op. cit., p. 1.

29. Ibid.

30. Christopher L. Martin and Dennis H. Nagao, "Some Effects of Computerized Interviewing on Job Applicant Responses," *Journal of Applied Psychology,* vol. 74, no. 1, 1989, pp. 72–80. See also Schmitt, Gilliland, Landis, and Devine, op. cit.

31. Brooks Mitchell, "Face-to-Interface," *Personnel,* January 1990, pp. 23–25. See also Anil K. Gupta, "Executive Selection: A Strategic Perspective," *Human Resource Planning,* March 1992, pp. 47–61.

32. Charlene Marmer Solomon, "How Does Disney Do It?" *Personnel Journal,* December 1989, pp. 50–57.

33. John Byrne, "All the Right Moves for Interviewers," *Business Week,* Sept. 17, 1990, p. 156. See also "How to Conduct a Behavioral Interview," *Impact,* Aug. 9, 1989, p. 4.

34. Walter Kiechel III, "How to Pick Talent," *Fortune,* Dec. 8, 1986, pp. 201, 203.

35. Sondra Thiederman, "Overcoming Cultural and Language Barriers," *Personnel Journal,* December 1988, pp. 34–40.

36. Dianna L. Stone and Eugene F. Stone, "Effects of Missing Application-Blank Information on Personnel Selection Decisons: Do Privacy Protection Strategies Bias the Outcome?" *Journal of Applied Psychology,* vol. 72, no. 3, 1987, pp. 452–456.

37. Richard D. Broussard and Dalton E. Brannen, "Credential Distortions: Personnel Practitioners Give Their Views," *Personnel Administrator,* June 1986, p. 129.

38. Ibid.

39. Winifred Yu, "Firms Tighten Resume Checks of Applicants," *The Wall Street Journal,* Western ed., Aug. 20, 1985, p. 27.

40. Broussard and Brannen, op. cit.

41. David Stier, "Many Ask, but Don't Give References," *HR News,* February 1990, p. A2.

42. Christopher Conte, "Reliable References Are Getting Difficult to Find," *The Wall Street Journal,* Eastern ed., Feb. 23, 1993, p. 1.

43. Amal Kumar Naj, "Companies Remain Wary of Beefing Up Background Checks," *The Wall Street Journal,* Eastern ed., Mar. 12, 1993, p. 32.

44. Erwin S. Stanton, "Fast-and-Easy Reference Checking by Telephone," *Personnel Journal,* November 1988, pp. 123–130.

45. Rosemary M. Collyer, "Pre-Employment Medical Testing: An Overview," *Legal Report,* Summer 1989, pp. 1–8.

46. Smith, "What the Boss Knows about You."

47. Catherine D. Fyock, "Hiring Disabled Workers Is Easier Than You Think," *The Human Resources Professional,* Fall 1992, pp. 12–16.

48. Paula Popovich and John P. Wanous, "The Realistic Job Preview as a Persuasive Communication," *Academy of Management Review,* October 1982, p. 571.

49. Ibid, p. 572. See also Bruce M. Meglino, Angelo S. Denisi, and Elizabeth C. Ravlin, "Effects of Previous Job Exposure and Subsequent Job Status on the Functioning of a Realistic Job Preview," *Personnel Psychology,* 1993, pp. 803–822.

50. Kevin M. Kelly, "Employment by Trial," *Personnel Journal,* March 1989, pp. 40–43.

51. Jean Powell Kirnan, John A. Farley, and Kurt F. Geisinger, "The Relationship between Recruiting Source, Applicant Quality, and Hire Performance: An Analysis by Sex, Ethnicity, and Age," *Personnel Psychology,* vol. 42, 1989, pp. 293–308.

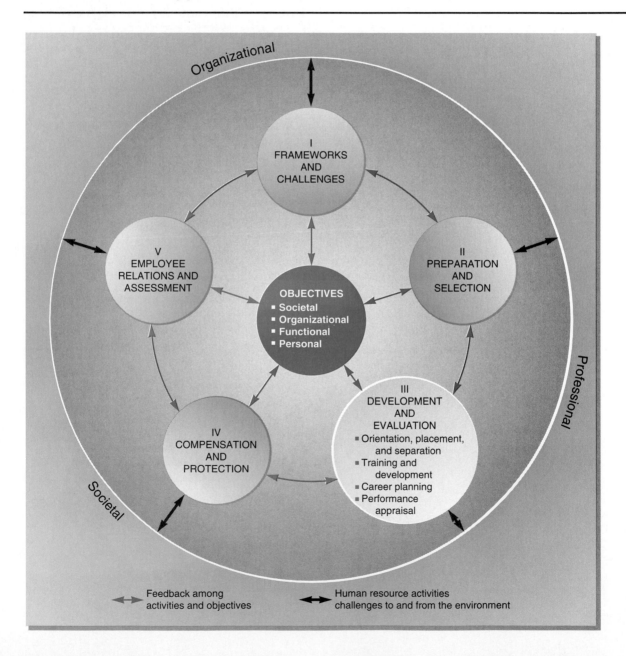

DEVELOPMENT AND EVALUATION

WHEN A new employee is hired or a current employee is reassigned, orientation should follow. Then, as strategies and tactics change in response to the competitive environment, workers need to be placed into new jobs or even separated from the company. New jobholders need to be trained, and experienced workers need to be retrained to do their current jobs and developed to handle future responsibilities. Some employers even offer career planning assistance to further encourage employee development. The success of the individual, the manager, and the HR department depends on receiving feedback about performance. Through performance appraisal, all three learn how successful their efforts have been.

Chapters 9 through 12 are about employee development and evaluation. The role of the HR department in these activities affects you whether you work as a manager, in a human resource department, or elsewhere in an organization. Knowledge of these activities allows you to be a better employee and a more effective manager.

In today's global economy, many corporations are finding that success depends . . . on a company's ability to ensure world-wide employee mobility.
JOHN P. SENKO[1]

Tomorrow's organization certainly must turn a significant part of its work over to a contingent work force that can grow and shrink and reshape itself as its situation demands.
WILLIAM BRIDGES[2]

Orientation, Placement, and Separation

CHAPTER OBJECTIVES

After studying this chapter, you should be able to:

1. OUTLINE the key elements of an orientation program.

2. DESCRIBE how orientation for new employees affects turnover and learning.

3. IDENTIFY the organizational roles and responsibilities for employee orientation.

4. EXPLAIN how the HR department becomes involved in placement decisions.

5. DISCUSS the HR department's role in separations.

6. IDENTIFY strategies the HR department can deploy to ensure greater job security.

When starting a new job, many people wonder: Will I be able to do the job? or Will I fit in around here? or Will the boss like me? These "first-day jitters" may be natural, but they reduce a new employee's satisfaction and ability to learn. Psychologists say that initial impressions are strong and lasting because new-comers have little else by which to judge. To help an employee become a satis-fied and productive member, the manager and the HR department must make those initial impressions favorable.

Once the selection process has taken place, managers and the HR depart-ment help the "new hire" fit in. This help extends to current employees who are reassigned to new jobs. As Chapters 7 and 8 have shown, organizations devote considerable time and resources to hiring people. By the first day, the employer already has an investment in the worker. And there is a job—or at least a poten-tial job—that needs to be done. To help new employees fit in, orientation pro-grams familiarize employees with their roles, the organization, its policies, and other employees. Consider how Metropolitan Life (Met Life) used the new hire orientation to contribute to employee effectiveness.

Met Life

Metropolitan Life (Met Life) is a major life insurance company based in New York City. When the HR department set out to redevelop the com-pany's orientation program, it began by determining who was responsi-ble for employee orientation. The answer was those who stood to gain or lose from the program: new employees and their managers.

Fifty managers from different lines of business were interviewed to determine what was important to include in the orientation and how it should be addressed. Figure 9-1 is a list of what managers wanted the orientation program to achieve.

The training department involved customers to reinforce the impor-tance of customer service while describing this large and complex busi-ness to those being oriented. The content of the orientation is sug-gested by the program's name, "Quality from the Start." It addressed "quality and customer focus" along with "accountability of results" and "teamwork." Emphasis also was placed on Met Life's mission and the importance of individual contributions to the success of the company.

The resulting program was done in modules. It included a core mod-ule covering general company information. Other modules addressed more specific concerns of individual lines of business. These modules also reflected the suggestions of more than 1000 employees who were surveyed about what they thought would be appropriate content to speed the newcomers' integration into the organization. The core mod-ule was designed to have multiple uses for dealing with the general pub-lic, current employees, and prospective employees.

Not only were managers involved in the design of the program, they also received an employee orientation checklist. Surveys were sent to employees and their managers after the orientation to further evaluate the Quality from the Start program. The survey sought to find out which modules were actually used, their effectiveness, and the need for changes.[3]

Figure 9-1	Goals of Metropolitan Life Managers for Company Orientation Program

▪ *Fosters* pride in belonging to a quality company.

▪ *Creates* an awareness of the scope of the company's business and its impact as a major financial institution.

▪ *Emphasizes* that customer focus and service are a competitive advantage.

▪ *Decreases* the concerns associated with a new job.

▪ *Helps* speed the development of a contributing team member.

▪ *Clarifies* the standards of quality by which performance is measured.

▪ *Establishes* that the responsibility for personal growth and development is shared by the employee and management.

Source: Susan Berger and Karen Huchendorf, "Ongoing Orientation at Metropolitan Life," *Personnel Journal,* December 1989, p. 34.

This example illustrates a proactive approach to creating an effective orientation program. The Quality from the Start program illustrates several important dimensions. First, orientation efforts must involve the employee's manager. Not only does supervisory involvement start their relationship, it also gives the employee specific details about his or her job and job setting. Second, requesting the suggestions of other employees ensures that the content of the program is relevant. Third, from a systems viewpoint, the follow-up survey provides the department with a feedback loop with which to refine the program. Fourth, modules enable the relevant parts to be used with employees who change jobs.

▶ Placement Obstacles to Productivity

Quitting early

One obstacle to a productive and satisfied workforce is that employees are more likely to quit during their first few months than at any other time in their employment. This initial turnover is common. It may even be beneficial if it occurs among new hires who sense that the organization or the job is not right for them.[4]

Dissonance Reduction

Dissatisfaction

As was discussed at the end of Chapter 8, realistic job previews close the psychological gap between what newcomers expect and what they find. This difference between what one anticipates and what one encounters is called *cogni-*

tive dissonance.[5] If dissonance is too high, people take action. For new employees, that may mean quitting.

New Employee Turnover

Turnover costs

Turnover is expensive. Besides recruiting and selection expenses, the costs associated with creating new employee records in the HR department, establishing payroll records in accounting, giving new employees training, and providing them with safety equipment are lost when employees leave.[6] These costs never appear on the profit and loss statement as "turnover expenses," although if they did, hiring managers might pay closer attention to turnover. Instead, turnover costs are reflected in the budgets of the HR, accounting, training, and safety departments. The exact cost per employee probably cannot be determined accurately. For entry-level unskilled workers who quit in the first day or so, the expense is likely to be a few hundred to a few thousand dollars. For newly hired salaried managers and professionals—particularly if the employer had to pay a search firm fee—the cost of turnover can be many thousands of dollars.

To a large firm a few thousand dollars may seem inconsequential, but if thousands of employees leave each year, the costs of turnover can quickly escalate into the millions of dollars. When experienced, long-service employees quit, the loss may be incalculable because of the training, knowledge, and skills these workers take with them. In general, the HR department can reduce turnover by using orientation to help meet the personal objectives of employees. When that happens, both the employee and the organization can benefit.

The remainder of this book discusses what HR departments can do to maintain and retain a productive workforce. This chapter shows how the department can ease an employee's transition into a new job. Chapter 10 discusses how organizations seek to make current employees more productive in their current jobs and prepare them for future responsibilities.

▶ Orientation Programs

Consider the situation faced some years ago by Texas Instruments, a worldwide producer of microelectronics and electronic equipment.[7]

Texas Instruments

At Texas Instruments—or TI, as it is called by the employees—the orientation program was superficial at best. New employees went to a large room where they were quickly told about the company and its fringe benefits. They completed forms about benefits and other job-related matters and then were sent to their supervisors to report for work.

Most supervisors took a few minutes to introduce the newcomer to the other assemblers. The supervisor often "assigned" the new employee to a workstation with instructions for nearby workers to show the newcomer what to do. After being put through a superficial orientation program and being quickly introduced to coworkers, the employee found herself or himself (most of the employees were female) sitting between two other employees, trying to learn how to assemble electronic components.

As many groups of workers do, the experienced ones had developed a little ritual for newcomers to endure. It was mild hazing, which is nearly impossible for a manager or an HR department to stop. The trainees were told that Texas Instruments treated employees unfairly and that their current supervisor was one of the worst in the company. The newcomers' anxieties were greatly increased, to say the least. Their ability to learn and do the job suffered, and some would even go on a break or go to lunch and never return—not even to pick up their half-day paychecks.

The HR department reacted by recruiting an even larger number of new employees to offset the high initial turnover. After an internal investigation into the causes of this turnover, the department revamped its entire orientation process. New employees were given an extended orientation that explored the background and HR policies of the company and lasted nearly all morning. Some forms were completed at the session, but the thrust of the orientation was to create a more positive attitude about TI among the recently hired recruits. Newcomers also were told that they had a high probability of success and were warned about the hazing. Shortly before lunch, the new employees were taken to a roped-off section of the cafeteria where they had lunch with their future supervisors.

After lunch, the supervisor would take the new employee back to the department and provide introductions to the other assemblers. Although the hazing went on for some time, the new employees had a more wholesome understanding of the company and were apparently better able to recognize the hazing for what it was, a ritualized introduction to the work group.

Benefits at TI

The newly revised approach to orientation led to some significant changes at TI. The two major developments are illustrated in Figure 9-2. Turnover among recently hired employees dropped, as shown in Figure 9-2A. A higher percentage of employees stayed on the job. The turnover lines merge after a short time because orientation programs have little measurable impact on workers' intention to remain after they have been with the company for a year or more. Other factors, such as supervision, policies, and pay, seem to have more influence on turnover among long-service employees. Both turnover curves in the figure start at the same point because an orientation program cannot have an impact on the "turnover" that occurs before the first day of work. For example, if an HR department hires twenty people and asks them to report for orientation in

| Figure 9-2. | The Impact of Thorough Orientation on Employee Turnover and Employee Learning |

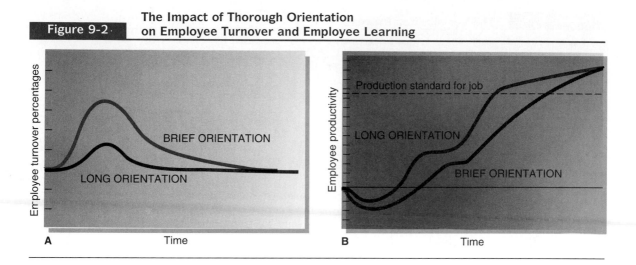

A   Time

B   Time

two weeks, it is likely that some of the twenty will find better jobs in the interim and not show up at all.

Orientation and learning

The orientation program had another interesting impact, which is diagrammed in Figure 9-2B: Recipients of the new program learned their jobs more quickly. That is, the more fully oriented employees mastered their jobs at the acceptable level of productivity more quickly than did employees who had the short orientation. This outcome was unexpected, since the workers in the new program were off the job for four hours while the workers in the shorter program missed only an hour or so of work. It would seem, particularly since this job was not very skilled, that a short orientation would get newcomers on the job quicker so that they might learn their jobs faster. However, the more fully oriented employees probably had fewer anxieties. They probably felt more at ease and more motivated to stay with the organization, and this seems to explain why they mastered their jobs sooner than did those with the shorter and more superficial orientation. Quick mastery of the job also may help lower turnover further because research suggests that good performers are more likely to stay with an organization.[8]

Socialization

"Fitting in"

The HR department's efforts help integrate newcomers into the organization and enable socialization to take place. *Socialization* is the ongoing process through which an employee begins to understand and accept the values, norms, and beliefs held by others in the organization.[9] The socialization process helps the organization meet its need for productive employees while enabling new employees to meet their needs. As was described in Chapter 1, an impor-

Figure 9-3	The Socialization Process

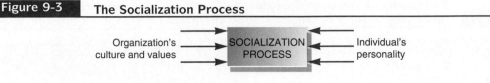

tant objective of HR management is to assist employees in achieving their personal goals, at least insofar as those goals enhance the individual's contribution to the organization.

The TI orientation program succeeded because it accelerated the socialization of new employees. Figure 9-3 depicts the socialization process as the meeting of the organization's culture and the individual's personality. Through formal methods such as orientation programs and informal ones such as hazing, the values of the organization are transmitted to newcomers.

Socialization through orientation

Orientation programs are particularly effective socialization tools because they are used among new employees. Since most newcomers have a strong desire to be accepted, they attempt to internalize "the way things are done in the organization" and make it "their way" too. Training (discussed in Chapter 10) furthers the socialization process by having the employee actually learn and perform the desired behavior.

The organizational values, beliefs, and traditions are slowly absorbed as a person is exposed to orientation, training, and the peer group.[10] Eventually the newcomer becomes more fully integrated into the organization, after which acceptable levels of satisfaction, productivity, and stability of employment are more likely.

Content and Responsibility for Orientation

Formal orientation programs usually rely on the HR department and the supervisor. This *two-tiered orientation program* is used because the issues covered in an orientation fall into two broad categories: general topics of interest to most new employees and specific, job-related issues of concern only to specific jobholders. Figure 9-4 shows the topics commonly included in an orientation program. Those labeled "organizational issues" and "employee benefits" are general concerns for virtually every new employee, and so they are typically explained by representatives from the HR department. The coverage of organizational issues and fringe benefits often is supplemented with an *employee handbook* that describes company policies, rules, regulations, benefits, and other items. Sophisticated orientation programs such as Met Life's and TI's may include films or videotapes about the company's history as well as videotaped greetings from key executives. However, the bulk of the company-related information comes from the HR department's representative.

Employee handbook

Supervisory role

In addition to the HR department's presentation, the orientation is continued by the employee's supervisor, who handles the job-related introductions. This tier of the orientation program should include introducing new employees to their coworkers. Sometimes newcomers also need to meet others who work in different departments. Inspectors, supervisors, accountants, and peers in other departments may be part of the social network to which a new employee becomes attached. Equally important are job duties and related issues. These items are normally explained by the supervisor too. The supervisory-level orientation reviews the job and its objectives. The session covers specific information about tasks, safety requirements, job location, the relationship of the job to other jobs, and other issues shown in Figure 9-4. To be truly effective, employees need a two-tiered orientation using both the HR department and the supervisor. One study reported that 9.8 percent of orientations lasted one hour while 51 percent took a day or longer. More than two-thirds of the firms surveyed conducted the orientation immediately after the employee reported to work.[11]

Figure 9-4	Topics Often Covered in Employee Orientation Programs

ORGANIZATIONAL ISSUES

▪ History of employer	▪ Product line or services provided
▪ Organization of employer	▪ Overview of production process
▪ Names and titles of key executives	▪ Company policies and rules
▪ Employee's title and department	▪ Disciplinary regulations
▪ Layout of physical facilities	▪ Employee handbook
▪ Probationary period	▪ Safety procedures and enforcement

EMPLOYEE BENEFITS

▪ Pay scales and paydays	▪ Insurance benefits
▪ Vacations and holidays	▪ Retirement program
▪ Rest breaks	▪ Employer-provided services for employees
▪ Training and education benefits	▪ Rehabilitation programs
▪ Counseling	

INTRODUCTIONS

▪ To supervisor	▪ To coworkers
▪ To trainers	▪ To employee counselor

JOB DUTIES

▪ Job location	▪ Overview of job
▪ Job tasks	▪ Job objectives
▪ Job safety requirements	▪ Relationship to other jobs

Opportunities and Pitfalls

The weakest part of most orientation programs occurs at the supervisory level. Even when the HR department has designed an effective orientation program and trained supervisors to conduct their part of it, supervisors may have more pressing problems or everything may seem so familiar to them that nothing stands out as important for the newcomer to learn. To help ensure a systematic orientation, the supervisor may be given a checklist of topics to cover, as is done at Met Life. The *supervisor's checklist* focuses on the introductions and job duties shown in Figure 9-4.

Buddy system

A helpful supplement to the newcomer orientation is the assignment of a buddy. Under the third tier, the *buddy system* of orientation, an experienced employee is asked to show the new worker around, conduct the introductions for the supervisor, and answer the newcomer's questions. Moreover, the "buddy" will probably take the new employee to lunch and perhaps to after-work activities. These social interactions can help accelerate the new employee's feelings of acceptance within the work group.

The buddy system is a *supplement* to the supervisor's orientation efforts. If it is *substituted* for the supervisory orientation, the supervisor loses an excellent opportunity to establish open communications with new employees. Supervisors who pass up the opportunity to spend time with new employees miss a chance to create a favorable relationship before the employees are influenced by what other people think.

Both the HR department and the supervisor are responsible to see that the employee is not:

- *Overwhelmed* with too much to absorb in a short time.

- *Overloaded* with forms to complete.

- *Given* only menial tasks that discourage job interest and company loyalty.

- *Asked* to perform tasks with a high chance for failure.

- *Pushed* into the job with a sketchy orientation under the mistaken belief that "trial by fire" is the best orientation.

- *Forced* to fill in the gaps between a broad orientation by the HR department and a narrow one by the supervisor.

Benefits of Orientation Programs

Although research on orientation programs is limited, several benefits are commonly reported.[12] Most of these benefits revolve around reducing employees' anxieties. With less anxiety, newcomers can learn their duties better. Hazing by peers or criticism by supervisors can be kept in perspective since properly oriented workers have more realistic job expectations. As a result, well-oriented newcomers need less attention from coworkers and supervisors, perform better, and are less likely to quit.[13] Reconsider the Texas Instruments example.

Texas Instruments

At Texas Instruments, one group of employees received an extended orientation program. This special program focused on the problems of social adaptation usually encountered by employees at TI. They were told that they had a high probability of success, that other employees might kid or haze them, that their supervisors were helpful people, and that as new employees they should initiate communications with supervisors if there were any questions.

The results showed that in the specially oriented group material waste was reduced by 80 percent, training costs dropped by two-thirds, product costs were 15 percent lower, and training time, absenteeism, and tardiness were cut in half.[14]

Orientation Follow-up

Face-to-face follow-up

Successful orientation programs include built-in follow-up procedures, such as those at Met Life. Follow-up is needed because new employees often are reluctant to admit that they do not recall everything they were told in the initial orientation sessions. The HR department often uses a prescheduled meeting or a simple checklist that asks the employee to critique the weaknesses of the orientation program. Weaknesses presumably are topics about which an employee needs more information. The checklist also serves as feedback to help the HR department identify the parts of the program that are strong. Although the checklist can be effective, face-to-face meetings between the employee and the supervisor are the most important type of orientation follow-up.

Supervisors believe that they follow up with new hires frequently, but many new employees do not perceive a supervisor's actions as true follow-up. One problem may be the supervisor's body language. For example, a supervisor may ask, "Is everything okay? Let me know if you have any questions." But if this is said as the supervisor continues to walk past the employee, the body language received by the employee says, "My supervisor really doesn't want to stop and talk." Instead of raising questions, the employee responds that everything is okay.

Sometimes the supervisor cannot answer an employee's question and must refer it to someone else. Even though a referral may be the best answer, the employee may feel that the supervisor does not care about the problem. An even worse situation occurs when the supervisor offers to "find out" and never gets back to the employee with the correct answer. That *is* indifference. Consider how Exxon attacked this problem of weak follow-up by supervisors at its Research and Engineering Company in Florham Park, New Jersey.

Exxon

At Exxon Research and Engineering Company, 50 to 150 engineers have been hired each year for several years. In recognition of the need for a smooth entry into the organization, Exxon developed an action guide and reference manual to help supervisors do a better job with newcomers. The manual outlines actions the supervisor should take before the employee arrives, such as arranging for work space, telephones, and office supplies. It also describes the actions a supervisor should take after a new employee arrives.

The particularly innovative parts of the program are the follow-up meetings supervisors are supposed to have with their new engineers. These sessions are called "How's It Going" meetings and are intended to open communications between the newcomer and the supervisor. Information is shared, concern is shown, and matters of interest are discussed. To make these sessions as effective as possible, they are held separately from meetings that give work assignments or review performance. Supervisors are trained to conduct these meetings.

Internal company research showed that after the training, supervisors were 40 percent more likely to hold initial orientation discussions with newcomers and 20 percent more likely to hold follow-up sessions at the end of three months.[15]

International Implications

When new hires or employees are moved across international borders, orientation becomes more important and complicated.[16] The traditional use of a company orientation (usually done by the HR department), the supervisory orientation, the buddy system, and the need for follow-up remain valid. What makes orientation of people who have moved across international borders different is the need for additional background.[17]

Foreign Corrupt
Practices Act

Cultural practices, language, and differences in business laws should be included in orientations that involve cross-border moves. For U.S. nationals going overseas or foreign nationals working for United States–based firms, for example, it is particularly important to include a briefing about the *Foreign Corrupt Practices Act*. This U.S. law restricts—with potentially severe penalties—the use of bribes (sometimes thinly disguised as "commissions"). Even though false commissions or "kickbacks" may be a culturally accepted method of conducting business overseas, they may violate this law.

International orientation should include additional follow-up. Even before the employee arrives in the foreign country or returns home, extra assistance may be needed with local customs, housing, shopping, or schooling.[18] The HR department may even be called on to find employment for the employee's spouse. Finding traditional foods of the expected quality can be a source of problems. Otherwise, a good placement may fail when the family-related pressures of a foreign assignment lead to a request to return to the home country or a resignation.[19] These concerns apply whether people are being transferred from or to the headquarter country. Good follow-up by the HR department and the immediate supervisor can be crucial to a successful international placement.

▶ Employee Placement

As was discussed in Chapter 6, staffing needs are met in two ways: new hires from outside the firm and a reassignment of current employees, which may be referred to as *inplacement*.[20] Too often, the reassignment of current employees takes place without an orientation program, under the assumption that these "experienced" employees know all they need to know about the company. Unfortunately, such an assumption may be only half correct. The "experienced" employee may be well informed about company plans, structure, employee benefits, and other items of general interest. However, recently transferred employees often have many of the same interpersonal and job-related concerns: Will they be accepted? Can they do the new job?

Taking over a different job in the same department may require little orientation. Movement between departments demands a progressively more complete orientation, as do promotions and demotions. When current employees are assigned to a new job, for example, they seldom need both tiers of the orientation program. The HR department's part usually can be skipped, although the supervisory orientation still is needed to speed up socialization within the new work group.

Placement is the assignment or reassignment of an employee to a new job. Most placement decisions are made by line managers. Usually the employee's supervisor, in consultation with higher levels of line management, decides on the future placement of each employee. The HR department's role is to advise the line managers about the company's policies and provide counseling to the employees.

Types of placement

Within these constraints, the three major classes of placement decisions are promotions, transfers, and demotions. Each of these decisions should be coupled with an orientation and follow-up whether the placement is caused by downsizing, merger, acquisition, or another change in internal staffing needs. The following sections review these three placement decisions and then discuss separations.

Promotions

A *promotion* occurs when an employee is moved from a job to another position that is higher in pay, responsibility, and/or organizational level. Generally, it is given as a recognition of a person's past performance and future promise. However, with downsizing and the resulting "flatter" organizations, there are fewer levels to which one can be promoted, prompting some to argue that "supervisors have to be more open-minded about job hunting by subordinates."[21] Promotions usually are based on merit and/or seniority.[22]

Merit-based promotions.   *Merit-based promotions* occur when an employee is promoted because of superior performance in the current job. When promotion is mostly a "reward" for past efforts and successes, two problems may be encountered.

One problem is whether decision makers can objectively distinguish strong performers from weak ones. When merit-based promotions are used, the decision should reflect the individual's performance, not selection biases (discussed in Chapter 8). This may occur when the best performer is a member of a protected class and the decision maker is prejudiced. The decision maker should not allow personal prejudices to affect promotions. When promotion decisions result from personal biases, the organization ends up with a less competent person in a higher, more important position, and this leads to poor performance and resentment by other employees.

Peter Principle

A second problem with merit-based promotions is the *Peter Principle*,[23] which states that in a hierarchy people tend to rise to their level of *incompetence*. Although not universally true, the "principle" suggests that good performance in one job is no guarantee of good performance in another. If one of the new engineers hired at Exxon's Research and Engineering Company consistently made major cost-saving design changes in a refinery, that would be an example of superior performance. However, suppose the engineer were promoted to supervisor. The skills needed to be an effective supervisor are very different from those needed to be a top engineer. As a result of such a promotion, Exxon might gain an ineffective supervisor and lose a superior engineer.

Seniority

Seniority-based promotions.   In some situations, the most senior employee gets the promotion. "Senior" in this case means the employee who has the longest length of service with the employer. The advantage of this approach is that it is objective. All one has to do is compare the seniority records of the candidates to determine who should be promoted.

Part of the rationale for this approach is that it eliminates biased promotions and requires management to develop its senior employees since they will be promoted eventually. *Seniority-based promotions* usually are limited to hourly employees. For example, a promotion from mechanic second class to mechanic first class may occur automatically through seniority whenever an opening for a mechanic first class occurs. Labor organizations often seek this type of promotion to prevent employers from discriminating among union members. Most HR experts express concern about the competency of those promoted solely because of seniority since not all workers are equally capable.

Transfers and Demotions

Transfers and demotions are the other two major placement actions available to the organization. *Transfers* occur when an employee is moved from one job to another position that is relatively *equal* in pay, responsibility, and/or organizational level. *Demotions* occur when an employee is moved from one job to another position that is *lower* in pay, responsibility, and/or organizational level.

Flexibility is often a key to an organization's success. Decision makers must be able to reallocate people to meet internal and external challenges. A common tool here is the employee transfer.[24] By moving people into jobs that are neither a promotion nor a demotion, managers may be able to improve the utilization of their human resources. Transfers may even be beneficial to jobholders, since the experience may provide a person with new skills and a different perspective that makes that person a better performer now and a better candidate for promotion in the future. Transfers may improve an individual's motivation and satisfaction, especially when a person finds little challenge in the old job. Even if the challenges remain minimal, the transfer at least offers some variety, which may enhance feelings of job satisfaction.

Dual-career families

Transfers that involve geographic moves increasingly affect *dual-career families,* or families in which the husband and the wife are pursuing separate careers. Whether by a promotion, a demotion, or a lateral move, a placement decision that transfers the employee out of the local community involves more than the employee; the spouse is affected too. HR departments ease the transition in several ways. HR professionals often join a network of other professionals through the Society for Human Resource Management's local chapters. These contacts can be used to find job leads for spouses. Some departments may recommend using and even paying local placement professionals to help the spouse. In extreme cases, especially in international transfers, the company may recommend a higher salary to offset the loss of income.[25]

Demotions seldom hold positive outcomes for the individual. Usually they are associated with discipline; the individual is demoted for poor job performance or for inappropriate behavior such as excessive absenteeism. One problem with demotions is that the demoted employee may become "demotivated" or, worse, openly antagonistic toward those responsible for the demotion decision. Besides being a negative influence on the morale of others, this person is likely to be a poor producer, and lawsuits over demotions will be more likely.[26]

Sometimes demotions are intended to be a kindly alternative to firing an employee who cannot do his or her current job. Rather than sever the employment relationship, the company decides to retain the employee at a lower level of responsibility. If the reasons for the demotion are beyond the employee's control, such as poor health, the wage or salary may be left unchanged, although future raises are unlikely.

Bumping

When employees are members of a union, they may be "bumped" into a lower job. Bumping occurs when a worker with seniority is told that his or her job is being eliminated. That worker can either become unemployed or take a lower-level job for which he or she is qualified. In other words, the more senior employee can "bump" another employee out of a job. In turn, the newly bumped employee may displace a still less senior worker in a similar or lower-level job, which sets off another round of bumpings and demotions. These bumping rights give senior workers greater job security.

Job-Posting Programs

Job-posting programs inform employees about unfilled job openings and qualifications. The announcement of an opening invites qualified employees to apply. The notices usually are posted on company bulletin boards, in the company newspaper, or in the firm's electronic bulletin boards via E-mail. The posted qualifications and other facts typically are drawn from the job analysis information (discussed in Chapter 5). Then, through *self-nominations* or the recommendation of a supervisor, employees who are interested in the posted opening report to the HR department and apply.

Self-nominations

The purpose of job posting is to encourage employees to seek promotions and transfers that help the HR department fill internal openings and meet employees' personal objectives. Not all job openings are posted. Besides entry-level positions, senior management and top staff positions may be filled by merit or by external recruiting. Job posting is most common among lower-level clerical, technical, and supervisory positions. However, more higher-level jobs are being posted to help the organization comply with affirmative action plans and become an equal opportunity employer. When lower-level jobs are filled without being posted, employees may believe that they should have been allowed to apply through the posting program. Therefore, it is important for the HR department to make the rules of the job-posting program known and follow them consistently.

Although most job bidders seek promotions, some self-nominations come from those who seek a transfer to broaden their skills or for personal reasons. Even self-nominated demotions are possible if a person is frustrated in his or her current job or sees the demotion as a means to get a job with more favorable promotion possibilities. For example, a typesetter at a newspaper may seek a "demotion" to a junior reporter because the long-term career options as a reporter are more favorable.

Self-nominations may also be used by management trainees. Many organizations hire recent college graduates for management training programs. Many of these programs are little more than an extended job rotation throughout each of several departments. After the rotation is completed, the company may allow the trainees to nominate themselves to fill posted job openings.

▶ Separations

A *separation* is a decision that the individual and the organization should part. It may be initiated by the employer or the employee. Additionally, it may be motivated by disciplinary, economic, business, or personal reasons. The HR department's role is to find the most satisfactory method of conducting the separation in a way that minimizes the harm to the organization and the individual.

Separations can take several forms, such as temporary leaves of absence, attrition, layoffs, and termination.

Temporary Leaves of Absence

Employees sometimes need to leave their jobs temporarily. The reasons may include medical, family, educational, recreational, and other motives. When the reasons are birth or adoption; caring for an ill spouse, child, or parent; or a serious health condition that makes the employee unable to perform his or her job, the employee is entitled to twelve weeks' leave in a twelve-month period under the *Family and Medical Leave Act of 1993.*

Beyond legal requirements, most HR departments have policies that allow employees to obtain a leave of absence. Leave policies have the advantage of preventing an employee from quitting, potentially saving recruiting and other costs when the employee returns. Except those covered by the Family and Medical Leave Act, employers are not obligated to extend leaves of absence.[27]

Attrition

Attrition is the normal separation of people from an organization as a result of resignation, retirement, or death. It is initiated by the individual worker, not by the company. In most organizations, the key component of attrition is resignation, which is a voluntary separation.

Although attrition is a slow way to reduce the employment base in an organization, it presents the fewest problems. A voluntary departure simply creates a vacancy that is not filled, and the staffing level declines without anyone being forced out of a job. HR planning enables organizations to rely more heavily on attrition rather than layoffs because this planning process attempts to project future employment needs, as was explained in Chapter 6. When the projections indicate that a surplus of employees is likely, the HR department can recommend an *employment freeze,* which curtails future hiring. Then the employment level begins to decline as people voluntarily leave the organization. When there is sufficient lead time, attrition can reduce or even eliminate the projected surplus.

Age discrimination caution

A special form of attrition that the HR department can actively control is *early retirement.* Early retirement plans encourage long-service workers to retire before the traditional age of 65. Of course, an employer must take care not to discriminate against those who wish to stay past age 65, since they are protected under the *Age Discrimination in Employment Act,* as amended. If the employer is eager to reduce the number of senior workers, the early retirement provisions may be supplemented to encourage departures. One advantage is that early retirements can start a chain reaction of promotions for several layers of junior workers. Moreover, senior workers tend to be the highest paid employees; when they resign, the employer's labor costs may decline.[28]

Layoffs

Layoffs entail the separation of employees from the organization for economic or business reasons. The separation may last only a few weeks if its purpose is to adjust inventory levels or allow a factory to retool for a new product. When caused by a business cycle, layoffs may last many months or years. However, if it occurs because of restructuring, such as downsizing or mergers and acquisitions, a "temporary" layoff may become permanent.

Permanent layoffs

A startling number of recent layoffs appear to be permanent. Only 15% of workers recently laid off expect to return to the same job, says the Bureau of Labor Statistics. During the previous four recessions, an average of 44% laid-off workers expected to be recalled.[29]

When placement decisions are driven by a need to reduce costs or absorb a recent merger or acquisition, the HR department's role is much more involved.[30] Consider the HR activities undertaken to restructure IBM's costs and make the company more responsive to its markets.

Shortly after John F. Akers assumed the chairmanship of IBM, the computer industry went into a severe slump, fueled in part by the growing use of PCs to replace the much more profitable IBM mainframes.[31] Sales and profits stalled. Compounding IBM's situation, the company initially honored its "no-layoff" policy. Within these constraints, a variety of HR actions were taken.

IBM

Domestic employment was frozen at 242,000. Overtime was cut from 5 percent of total hours to 1 percent, the equivalent of cutting 1000 jobs. Summer student help was reduced, and 4000 temporary workers were not reemployed when their contracts ended. Even some of the $10 billion of work normally done by IBM's 35,000 subcontractors was done in-house. At a cost of $550 million, employees were trained or retrained, with 10,000 being trained for new jobs. Although some employees joke that IBM (International Business Machines) stands for "*I've Been Moved,*" 7300 employees changed locations at a cost of $60,000 *each* to rebalance staffing needs.[32] The hiring of college students was cut from 6100 to only 1000. Further rebalancing was achieved by merging five marketing staffs into one, freeing 2500 people to join 4000 coming from laboratories and plants to boost IBMs sales force to 28,000.[33] A typical trimmed-down division, says IBM's director of organization and planning, Keith Austin, has shrunk from eight layers of management to six. "Historically," Austin explains almost casually, "managers would provide technical support." Now the worker, with his or her personal computer, can generally find what he or she is looking for without help. And the pruning is not finished. "We will continue to move in the direction of fewer layers," Austin says.[34]

Since these extensive actions were not sufficient to restore IBM to profitability, layoffs were undertaken for tens of thousands of workers. Two-thirds of the top sixty managers listed in IBM's 1985 annual report are gone,[35] and the board of directors replaced John Akers.

Downsizing, or reducing the levels of an organization, has been a feature of the 1980s and 1990s. IBM and many others have been forced to downsize to reduce costs. Although downsizing can leave emotional scars on those who remain,[36] a side benefit is greater responsibility and greater organizational responsiveness since changes must go through fewer levels of approval. Of course, fewer people and the continuing pressures of competition usually mean more work too, along with morale and other problems.

> Bill Flint, an electrician who has worked for 27 years for Florida Power & Light, has the layoff survivor blues.
>
> He was upset when 2,300 employees were cut in a restructuring two years ago. He resents the chairman's $2 million annual pay. He doesn't believe it when he's told FPL needs another $100 million.
>
> "They're losing right now because no one is giving 100 percent," Flint says. "Everyone is worried about losing their job. I just hate to come to work."[37]

The impact of downsizing on HR departments at companies such as IBM has meant many more placement decisions, separations, orientations, and revised succession and HR plans (first discussed in Chapter 6). "Flatter" organizations also have meant fewer career opportunities. Although some people get new responsibilities and challenges, many HR departments use lateral transfers, overseas assignments, and other placement approaches to motivate, stimulate, and retain employees who in the past would have received promotions.

Mergers and acquisitions require different but equally extensive orientation and placement activities. In fact, many merger and acquisition specialists are coming to realize that blending different organizational cultures may be their most important challenge. Sophisticated orientation efforts, like Metropolitan Life's and Exxon's, and intelligent placement decisions, like IBM's, can reduce the emotional impact and help unify the company culture during downsizing or mergers and acquisitions.

WARN

The *Worker Adjustment and Retraining Notification Act* (WARN) of 1988 requires employers to give affected workers or their union representative written notice 60 days in advance of layoffs. It applies to employers with 100 or more workers when a closed or discontinued facility affects 50 employees. Layoffs of more than 50 people that constitute a third of the workforce at one site and layoffs of 500 or more require notification even if the facility is not to be closed or discontinued. The WARN Act further underscores the importance of HR planning.[38]

In international operations layoffs are often more complicated. For U.S. firms, the *Civil Rights Act of 1991* extended civil rights protection to American workers working for U.S. companies overseas. In Japan, especially among very large, well-known firms, employment for men is considered to be for life or at least until the company's retirement age. Severe morale and public relations pressures have virtually eliminated layoffs as an option in these firms, although the severe recession in the early 1990s caused some firms, such as Nissan, to close a plant and forced Mazda to shift 500 white-collar workers to assembly lines. Other firms have elminated their "no-layoff" tradition.[39] In western Europe, legislation severely restricts the use of layoffs, perhaps making European managers more reluctant to hire new workers; this helps explain why U.S. workers stay unemployed for a far shorter time than do Europeans.[40] At the same time, these restrictive approaches force European employers to carefully plan workforce growth and utilization, leading many firms to become export-oriented to offset domestic economic cycles. Nevertheless, layoffs may be required when attrition is insufficient. Though this is harsh for the affected employees, the company's alternative may be bankruptcy, which would affect an even larger number of employees. Most developed nations cushion the blow of layoffs and terminations with unemployment insurance, which may be supplemented by vacation pay, continued health insurance, or other supplemental unemployment benefits.

Termination

Of course, employees may be separated by termination of the employment relationship. *Termination* is a broad term that encompasses permanent separation from the organization for any reason. Usually this term implies that the person was fired as a form of discipline. When people are discharged for business or economic reasons, it is commonly, although not always, called a layoff. Sometimes, however, the employer needs to separate some employees for business reasons and has no plans to rehire them. Rather than being laid off, those people are simply terminated.

Severance pay is money—often equal to one week's salary or more—that is given to employees who are being permanently separated. Many organizations give severance pay only for involuntary separations and only to employees who have performed satisfactorily. For example, if a factory is going to close and move its operations to another state, employees who are terminated may be given an extra week's salary for each year they have worked for the company. It is unlikely that someone who is being fired for poor performance or for disciplinary reasons will receive severance pay or outplacement assistance, though severance pay in Europe is more liberal.

> A study by the William M. Mercer Company finds that the costs of layoffs in most EC countries greatly exceeds that in the United States.
>
> Italy, Spain, and Belgium were found to have the most generous statutory protection for workers, and laying off a manager with 20 years of service and a $50,000 annual salary in these countries would cost $94,000 to $130,000. In the U.S., by comparison, the layoff would cost $19,000, according to Mercer.[41]

Outplacement

Outplacement assistance includes efforts made by the employer directly or indirectly through a private firm to help a recently separated worker find a job. Not only do such efforts help the former employee, they also assure the remaining employees of management's commitment to their welfare if a further reduction in the workforce is necessary. Outplacement may even reduce the negative consequences for those who remain, since "employees who are spared layoffs suffer low morale, declining productivity, anxiety and distrust."[42] Although outplacement is a relatively new benefit, it has gained widespread support and is offered by 73.6 percent of the employers interviewed for one study.[43] Assistance typically includes professional help with résumé preparation, counseling, and the use of an office with telephone answering assistance. For executives, outplacement assistance may mean more liberal packages, including the purchase of an executive's home at the fair market value.[44]

▶ Issues in Placement

Three placement decisions that are overriding concerns to HR departments are effectiveness, legal compliance, and prevention of separations.

Effectiveness

The effectiveness of a placement decision depends on minimizing disruption to the employee and the organization. To reduce disruption, promotions and transfer decisions should be made in accordance with the selection steps given in Chapter 8. Similarly, demotions should be well documented and follow the rules of effective discipline discussed in Chapter 18. Once the placement has been made, the new employee should get an orientation to reduce personal anxieties and speed up the socialization and learning processes.

Legal Compliance

For many years employment relationships that were not based on a formal written contract were considered to be *employment-at-will* relationships—employment at the will (or discretion) of either party and continued by mutual agreement. All either party had to do to end the relationship was notify the other. The employer's historical right to terminate an employee at any time without cause became known as the *employment-at-will doctrine*. This doctrine argues that owners (or their agents, management) have property rights that supersede an employee's right to his or her job. Simply stated, an employee can be fired for any reason, including "no reason." Over the years, however, government and the courts have limited these rights. Courts have looked to employee handbooks, management promises, and other sources to find implied employment contracts. Additionally, dismissal is restricted by:

▪ Conditions controlled by equal opportunity laws, such as race, religion, national origin, sex, pregnancy, and age (more than forty)[45]

▪ Union activities, as determined by law

▪ Refusal to ignore Occupational Safety and Health Act violations

▪ The right to refuse to perform an unusual work assignment that the employee believes is hazardous or even life-threatening

▪ The right to refuse to perform an act that is clearly in violation of law, such as cooperating in a price-fixing scheme

Other employment restrictions also may apply, depending on circumstances and local laws. In general, a dismissal may be challenged if it is arbitrary and unjust. It also cannot be contrary to clear public policy, as occurs when an employee is fired for serving on a jury.

As a matter of public policy, adverse placement decisions (primarily transfers, demotions, and separations) are restricted in their application to employees who are exercising their rights under other laws, such as the *Fair Labor Standards Act*, which specifies minimim wage and overtime pay, and the *National Labor Relations Act*, which gives some employees the right to form unions and collectively bargain with management. Employment-related laws, courts, and government agencies often protect *"whistle-blowers,"* employees who report employer violations of occupational safety and health laws, insider trading violations of Securities Exchange Commission regulations, or similar violations of public policy. Simply put, the courts are likely to reverse and penalize an employer that makes placement decisions that thwart employees' efforts to force the employer's compliance with laws or public policy.

Whistle-blowers

Courts have further limited the employment-at-will doctrine by finding that an employment contract has been created by past actions. For example, promises made during recruitment or commitments in new employee orientation programs or handbooks have been considered as forming the basis for an implied employment contract. Courts have even forced employers to reverse their placement decisions because company procedures were not followed carefully.[46] All these limitations are not without consequences:

> The threat of wrongful-termination suits seems to be changing companies' human-resource practices in ways that boost business costs and increase incentives to curb payrolls.
> . . . The new doctrines and the possible size of damage awards have held down long-run hiring by local businesses. Particularly in large companies and in finance and service industries, the threat of litigation has reduced employment levels by 2% to 5% from where they otherwise would be.[47]

When a placement decision is mutually supported or favorable to the employee (a promotion, for example), legal entanglements are unlikely, assuming that the decision did not have negative consequences for others. However, unfavorable transfers, demotions, and involuntary separations should be arranged in accordance with the law and with company procedure and only for justifiable business reasons. Even then, the *Comprehensive Omnibus Budget Reconciliation Act* (COBRA) of 1986 requires employers to grant health-care coverage at the employer's cost to former employees who, having been separated from the employer, wish to continue coverage and are willing to pay for it. This coverage extends to all employees who are separated, regardless of the reason. Failure to comply with employment-related laws may lead to costly suits, as one Japanese subsidiary discovered.

COBRA

Quasar

> In what is believed to be the first such verdict, a federal judge . . . found Quasar, a unit of Matsushita Electric, guilty of racial discrimination against American employees. Quasar was ordered to pay nearly $2.5 million in damages to three former Quasar executives, all in their 50s, who brought charges of age and racial discrimination against the consumer-electronics company after they and 63 other American managers—but no Japanese executives—were fired.[48]

Prevention of Separations

One of the more creative areas of HR management involves the prevention of separations. When HR departments can prevent their organizations from losing valuable human resources, the money invested in recruitment, selection, orientation, and training is not lost. Money is saved by reducing the need to redeploy remaining employees.

> Chevron, which has slimmed down by 6,500 employees . . . has redeployed over 1,000 people to different areas of the company. Says CEO Kenneth Derr: "That's not as easy as it sounds. Relocation and retraining expenses can run around $75,000 a person."[49]

> General Motors' contract with the United Auto Workers has caused GM to increase its relocation allowance to a maximum of $20,000 and allows GM to force some workers to take jobs up to 110 miles or more from home. Although done largely to increase job security of UAW workers, these changes allow GM to reduce separations of key employees.[50]

Although a minimum amount of attrition ensures a flow of new people into the organization and promotional opportunities for those already there, each departing employee represents a lost investment. Through proactive programs, losses of employees through voluntary resignations, death, layoffs, and terminations can be reduced.

Voluntary resignations.   Voluntary resignations can be reduced by a satisfying work environment, a challenging job, high-quality supervision, and opportunities for personal growth. Managers and HR departments are involved with these issues through supervisor training, career planning, and other activities. As was described in Chapter 5, the HR department can play an especially powerful role as an adviser to line managers who seek better ways to redesign the jobs they supervise. Realistic job previews and orientation programs are two other ways for the HR department to reduce voluntary turnover. In a survey that asked HR directors and top executives why good employees quit, it was found that:

> Forty-seven percent of valued employees who quit their jobs do so because advancement opportunities are not available. Additional reasons why good employees resign include:
>
> - Lack of recognition, 26%
>
> - Dissatisfaction with management, 15%
>
> - Inadequate salaries or benefits, 6%
>
> - Boredom with job responsibilities, 6%[51]

Retirement is another type of separation. Some companies offer part-time work to retiring employees to help them move from work to retirement while retaining access to their valued skills and knowledge.

Equitable Life

Equitable Life Assurance Society's part-time program for retirees is called the "Retiree Talent Bank." Equitable uses salaried employees who have retired to staff temporary openings instead of hiring workers from temporary help providers or consultants. Retirees may work up to 780 hours per year while drawing full-time retirement benefits.

Death.   Even death as a source of separation is a target for progressive HR departments through safety, preventive health care, and wellness programs designed to keep employees healthy. As far back as the 1970s, Sentry Insurance Company installed a multi-million-dollar recreational complex in its western regional office in Scottsdale, Arizona. Part of the reason for this combination of weight rooms, jogging tracks, tennis courts, and other athletic facilities is to encourage employees to maintain better physical health in order to continue working longer. Today, many companies are following Sentry's example.

Layoffs.   Layoffs are minimized in some companies by careful HR planning. By projecting employment needs several years into the future, employers such as State Farm Insurance Company have avoided layoffs even during the worst recessions. Then, as the needed skill mixes of their businesses change, training and transfers help these organizations adjust to economic challenges while providing secure employment for their employees. Companies such as Control

Data, Motorola, and IBM take another step to protect their full-time workers. As Figure 9-5 illustrates, Control Data Corporation uses a "rings of defense" approach. At the center ring are the prized full-time employees. At the next level are permanent part-time employees who would be put on layoff before the full-timers.[52] Before permanent part-timers are laid off, temporary employees would be given notices to leave. Suppliers and vendors become the first line of defense because Control Data (along with Motorola, IBM, and other companies) contracts out some jobs that its own people could do. Before Control Data employees would be separated, janitorial, maintenance, and other jobs that are now done by contractors would be done by Control Data employees.

Part-time layoffs   Layoffs also can be reduced through other approaches. One method that has gained popularity is the use of reduced workweeks or *"part-time layoffs,"* which allow employers to lay off workers for part of each week. In such cases, the employees can collect a pro rata share of their weekly unemployment benefits. A person usually must be out of work for an entire week to collect unemployment compensation. However, new laws in some states allow employees to collect unemployment insurance if they are put on a short-time or reduced

Figure 9-5 | **"Rings of Defense" at Control Data Corporation**

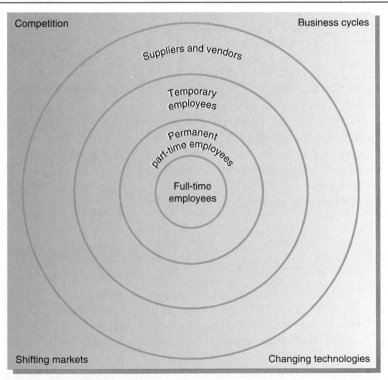

workweek. For example, employees who have their workweek reduced from five to four days can collect unemployment compensation for the day they are "unemployed." This approach spreads the available work among employees while allowing the employer to retain the workforce without imposing traditional layoffs.

Job sharing allows two or more workers to do the same job because each one works part-time. Although most workers who want full-time work may find a part-time job unacceptable, job sharing may be preferable to a layoff, especially if it is of short duration or if both employees want part-time work. It also may be a preferred work arrangement for those who seek less than full-time employment. The combination of both viewpoints may help explain why 74 percent of American firms offer some form of job sharing.[53]

Terminations.   In a nationwide study of why people were fired,

Why people
are fired

The reasons include: incompetence (39%); inability to get along with co-workers (17%); dishonesty or lying (12%); negative attitude (10%); lack of motivation (7%); and failure or refusal to follow instructions (7%).

   "An employer's perception of incompetence may arise from a mismatch of a candidate's professional skills and personality with the actual requirements of the job," notes Max Messmer, chairman of Robert Half International.

   He suggests that thorough reviews of corporate interviewing, reference checking and job specification procedures would "significantly reduce the high percentage of hiring mistakes and the unfortunate consequences for employees and employer alike."[54]

By contrast, only 55 percent of employees surveyed by Wyatt Co., a human resources consulting firm, believe their companies provide security to workers who perform well.[55]

Training and employee development are another means of reducing terminations for poor performance. Through effective training, new and long-service employees can be taught how to do their jobs successfully. The training and development of human resources are so important to the success of most firms that Chapter 10 will discuss the distinction between training and development and review different approaches.

▶ Summary

Once the selection process has been completed, new employees must be oriented in order to become productive contributors. Orientation not only improves the rate at which employees are able to perform their jobs but also helps employees satisfy their personal desire to feel they are part of the organization's social fabric. The HR department generally orients newcomers to broad organizational issues and fringe benefits. Supervisors complete the orientation by introducing new employees to coworkers and others involved in the job. A "buddy" may be assigned to continue the process.

Proactive HR departments follow up after the orientation to ensure that the employees do not have any remaining questions and check on the quality of the orientation.

When job openings are filled internally, the placement process also should include an orientation, especially placement decisions that involve moving people across international borders. The process of placing current employees in different jobs or separating them from the organization often involves a decision made by line managers in consultation with the HR department. Included here are promotions, transfers, and demotions. Although promotions come about in a variety of ways, they usually result from merit, seniority, self-nomination, or a combination of those approaches. Transfers and demotions also call for the advice of the HR department.

Separations from the organization may result from disciplinary, economic, or business reasons. The HR department's job is to minimize the harm done to the organization and the individual. Separations may be caused by attrition, layoffs, and terminations.

▶ Terms for Review

Cognitive dissonance	Demotions
Orientation program	Job-posting programs
Socialization	Attrition
Employee handbook	Employment freeze
Buddy system	Early retirement
Placement	Layoffs
Promotions	Severance pay
Merit-based promotions	Employment-at-will
Peter Principle	Whistle-blowers
Seniority-based promotions	Part-time layoffs
Transfers	

▶ Review and Discussion Questions

1. Orientation programs are needed only if the selection process is defective. Otherwise, properly selected employees do not need to be oriented. Do you agree or disagree with this statement? Why?

2. If you were asked to audit the effectiveness of an orientation program, what shortcoming might you expect to find?

3. Assume you were asked to design an orientation program for freshmen arriving at your school next fall. Describe how you might apply the three levels of orientation discussed in this chapter. What follow-up would you suggest at the end of the first term?

4. When employees are being moved across international borders to fill internal openings, what unique considerations arise? What elements might be added to an orientation program?

5. Describe a job-posting program. What benefits and problems might arise under such a program?

6. In what ways are job analysis information and human resource planning helpful in orientation and placement decisions?

7. Layoffs outside North America are handled differently because of differences in laws and social expectations. Describe how layoffs differ in Japan, the United States, and western Europe.

8. Assume your company is dedicated to giving employees careers, not just jobs. What actions would you recommend to minimize layoffs resulting from the ups and downs of economic cycles?

▶ Incident 9-1

Reductions in Force at IBM

During the 1980s, personal computers went from specialized products used primarily by authors of computer software to widespread business tools. When connected into networks of workstations with parallel processing capabilities, these collections of PCs would rival the largest supercomputers of earlier years. Yet IBM was slow to enter the PC market and failed to use its technological and marketing strengths to dominate that market, preferring instead to "push" the vastly more profitable mainframes.

As competitors, technology, and the economy converged to slow the growth rate of mainframe sales, IBM found itself about to be a $100 billion corporation with barely $60 billion in sales. Losses in the billions of dollars were recorded before the board of directors replaced the CEO. As one IBM employee observed about rosy but unrealistic projections, "We were so good at dressing up the corpse, you couldn't even tell the mainframe business was dead."

1. Assuming that the HR department sensed the end of IBM's growth soon enough, what actions might it have taken to enable the company to avoid the need for layoffs?

2. What impact do you imagine the "firing" of the CEO had on employees at IBM during this turbulent period in the company's history?

▶ Incident 9-2

Orientation at International Warehousing, Inc.

International Warehousing owns and leases a variety of warehouse facilities at major seaports and airports around the world. Most of its facilities are concentrated in North America, Japan, Korea, Hong Kong, and throughout the European Union. Employees are usually hired locally to work as stockers, loaders, and equipment operators. Likewise, many staff professionals—such as accountants, systems analysts, and human resource professionals—are local hires too.

However, the warehouse and sales managers in each location are considered executives within the company. Although many have worked their way up from the loading docks, most have received extensive education through the company's training department and outside universities and institutes. As new facilities are planned in different regions of the world, teams of executives from adjoining areas serve as project leaders and advisers in designing, building, and leasing warehouse space. Most executives even claim to enjoy the occasional trips to nearby countries or cities to work on these projects. But when a new facility is about to open, the HR department often faces great difficulty in convincing an experienced executive to move to the new operation to help ensure a smooth start-up. Even those who move typically request a transfer to their "home country" after the start-up period is over.

1. If you were advising the HR department, what explanations could you give for the reluctance of these executives to move to new locations?

2. What recommendations do you have that the HR department could implement to ensure a better supply of internal talent for international openings?

▶ References

1. John P. Senko, "Is the Foreign Service Premium Becoming Obsolete?" *HR News,* January 1993, p. C12.

2. William Bridges, "The End of the Job," *Fortune,* Sept. 19, 1994, p. 64.

3. Susan Berger and Karen Huchendorf, "Ongoing Orientation at Metropolitan Life," *Personnel Journal,* December 1989, pp. 28–35.

4. Dan R. Dalton and William D. Todor, "Turnover: A Lucrative Hard Dollar Phenomenon," *Academy of Management Review,* April 1982, pp. 212–218.

5. L. Festinger, *A Theory of Cognitive Dissonance,* Evanston, Ill.: Row, Peterson, 1957.

6. Kenneth Oldfield, "Survival of the Newest," *Personnel Journal,* March 1989, pp. 53–59.

7. Earl G. Gomersall and M. Scott Myers, "Breakthrough in On-the-Job Training," *Harvard Business Review,* July–August 1966, pp. 66–72.

8. George F. Dreher, "The Role of Performance in the Turnover Process," *Academy of Management Journal,* March 1982, pp. 137–147. See also Gareth R. Jones, "Socialization Tactics, Self-Efficacy and Newcomers' Adjustments to Organizations," *Academy of Management Journal,* June 1986, pp. 262–279.

9. Oldfield, op. cit.

10. Cheri Ostroff and Steve W. J. Kozlowski, "Organizational Socialization as a Learning Process: The Role of Information Acquisition," *Personnel Psychology,* vol. 45, Winter 1992, pp. 849–873. See also Milan Moravec and Kevin Wheeler, "Speed New Hires into Success," *Personnel Journal,* March 1989, pp. 74–75.

11. Steven L. McShane and Trudy Baal, *Employee Socialization Practices of Canada's West Coast: A Management Report,* Vancouver, Canada: Simon Fraser University, 1984.

12. Richard Pascale, "Fitting New Employees into the Company Culture," *Fortune,* May 1984, pp. 28, 30, 34, 38–40.

13. Gomersall and Myers, op. cit.

14. Ibid.

15. Thomas K. Meier and Susan Hough, "Beyond Orientation: Assimilating New Employees," *Human Resource Management,* Spring 1982, pp. 27–29.

16. Anne V. Corey, "Ensuring Strength in Each Country: A Challenge for Corporate Headquarters Global Human Resource Executives," *Human Resource Planning,* March 1991, pp. 1–8.

17. Carole Gould, "A Checklist for Accepting a Job Abroad," *The New York Times,* July 17, 1988, p. C2.

18. Nancy K. Napier and Richard B. Peterson, "Expatriate Re-Entry: What Do Repatriates Have to Say?" *Human Resource Planning,* March 1991, pp. 19–28. See also Raymond J. Stone, "Expatriate Selection and Failure," *Human Resource Planning,* March 1991, pp. 9–18.

19. Rosalie L. Tung, "Career Issues in International Assignments," *The Academy of Management Executives,* August 1988, pp. 241–244.

20. "Pass the Dictionary," *The Economist,* May 7, 1994, p. 78.

21. Joann S. Lublin, "Decisions to Search for a Greener Pasture Might Be Something Worth Telling the Boss," *The Wall Street Journal,* European ed., July 30–31, 1993, p. 4. See also John A. Byrne, "Why Downsizing Looks Different These Days," *Business Week,* Oct. 10, 1994, p. 63.

22. Gerald R. Ferris, M. Ronald Buckly, and Gillian M. Allen, "Promotion Systems in Organizations," *Human Resource Planning,* vol. 15, no. 3, 1992, pp. 47–68.

23. Laurence J. Peter and Raymond Hull, *The Peter Principle,* New York: William Morrow, 1969.

24. Amy Saltzman, "Sidestepping Your Way to the Top," *U.S. News & World Report,* Sept. 17, 1990, pp. 60–61. See also Nancy J. Carter, "Moving Managers Internationally: The Need for Flexibility," *Human Resource Planning,* February 1989, pp. 43–46, and James E. Harris, "Moving Managers Internationally: The Care and Feeding of Expatriates," *Human Resource Planning,* February 1989, pp. 49–53.

25. Alice H. Cook, "Public Policies to Help Dual-Earner Families Meet the Demands of the Work World," *Industrial and Labor Relations Review,* January 1989, pp. 201–215.

26. David B. Stephens and John P. Kohl, "Demotion as a Human Resource Management Practice: An Analysis of the Oil and Gas Industry," *Journal of Managerial Issues,* Fall 1989, pp. 35–43. The demotion of a 52-year-old employee was ruled to be the equivalent of a discharge because of the physical demands of the new job. A suit brought against the employer, Caterpillar Tractor Company, under the Age Discrimination in Employment Act was successful. See "Employment Update: Demotion of Employee Constitutes Constructive Discharge," *Resources,* November 1985, p. 3.

27. Barbara Presley Noble, "The Family Leave Bargain," *The New York Times,* Feb. 7, 1993, p. F25.

28. Richard A. Ippolito, "Toward Explaining Earlier Retirement after 1970," *Industrial and Labor Relations Review,* July 1990, pp. 556–569.

29. Kenneth Laboch, "The New Unemployment," *Fortune,* Mar. 8, 1993, p. 41.

30. Leonard Greenhalgh, Anne T. Lawrence, and Robert I. Sutton, "Determinants of Work Force Reduction Strategies in Declining Organizations," *Academy of Management Review,* vol. 13, no. 2, 1988, pp. 241–254.

31. Craig Mellow, "A Delayered Big Blue," *Business Month,* January 1990, p. 13.

32. Marilyn A. Harris, "A Lifetime at IBM Gets a Little Shorter for Some," *Business Week,* Sept. 29, 1986, p. 40.

33. Ibid.

34. Mellow, op. cit.

35. Leah Nathans Spiro, John A. Burne, Bart Ziegle, and Maria Mallory, "The Flight of the Managers," *Business Week,* Feb. 22, 1993, p. 79.

36. Wayne F. Cascio, "Downsizing: What Do We Know? What Have We Learned?" *Academy of Management Executive,* vol. 7, no. 1, 1993, pp. 95–104. See also Elizabeth Lesly and Larry Light, "When Layoffs Alone Don't Turn the Tide," *Business Week,* Dec. 7, 1992, pp. 100–101.

37. Susana Barciela, "New Rules for a Layoff-Weary Workplace," *The Miami Herald,* Sept. 29, 1993, p. C3. See also David M. Noer, *Healing the Wounds: Overcoming the Trauma of Layoffs and Revitalizing the Downsized Organizations,* San Francisco: Jossey-Bass, 1993, and Samuel Greengard, "Don't Rush Downsizing: Plan, Plan, Plan," *Personnel Journal,* November 1993, pp. 64–76.

38. Paul D. Staudohar, "New Plant Closing Law Aids Workers in Transition," *Personnel Journal,* January 1989, pp. 87–90; Barbara Presley Noble, "60-Day Notice on Layoffs Undercut, G.A.O. Says," *The New York Times,* National ed., Feb. 25, 1993, p. C8.

39. Karen Lowry Miller, "Stress and Uncertainty: The Price of Restructuring," *Business Week,* Mar. 29, 1993, p. 74. See also Andrew Pollack, "Japan Finds Ways to Save Tradition of Lifetime Jobs," *The New York Times,* National ed., Nov. 28, 1993, p. 1.

40. Christopher Conte, "U.S. Workers," *The Wall Street Journal,* Eastern ed., Oct. 5, 1993, p. 1.

41. Christine D. Keen, "Breaking Up Is Hard to Do in the EC," *HR Update,* June–July 1992, p. 4.

42. Christopher Conte, "Layoff Survivors Get Some Attention from Their Restructured Firms," *The Wall Street Journal,* Eastern ed., Oct. 5, 1993, p. 1.

43. Elaine M. Duffy, Richard M. O'Brien, William P. Brittain, and Stephen Cuthrell, "Behavioral Outplacement: A Shorter, Sweeter Approach," *Personnel,* March 1988, pp. 28–33. See also Loretta D. Foxman and Walter Polsky, "Outplacement Results in Success," *Personnel Journal,* February 1990, pp. 30, 32, 36–37.

44. Walter Kiechel III, "Preparing for Your Outplacement," *Fortune,* Nov. 30, 1992, pp. 153–154.

45. Janis Klotchman and Linda L. Neider, "EEO Alert: Watch Out for Discrimination in Discharge," *Personnel,* January–February 1983, pp. 60–66.

46. Alan B. Krueger, "The Evolution of Unjust-Dismissal Legislation in the United States," *Industrial and Labor Relations Review,* July 1991, pp. 644–660. See also Julie Amparano Lopez, "Many New Executives Are Being Discharged with Stunning Speed," *The Wall Street Journal,* Eastern ed., Mar. 4, 1994, p. 1.

47. Gene Koretz, "Do Stronger Legal Rights for Workers Depress Hiring?" *Business Week,* Sept. 21, 1992, p. 22.

48. "Ex-Quasar Execs Win a Bias Suit," *Business Week,* Dec. 24, 1990, pp. 51–52.

49. Jaclyn Fierman, "Beating the Middle Career Crisis," *Fortune,* Sept. 6, 1993, p. 58.

50. David Woodruff, "Home Is Where the Work Is," *Business Week,* Nov. 15, 1993, p. 40.

51. "Lack of Opportunity Causes Key Workers to Quit," *Small Business Reports,* December 1988, p. 12.

52. "More Companies Use Part-Time Employees—And Give Them Reasonably Good Grades," *William M. Mercer News Release,* Apr. 7, 1993, pp. 1–2.

53. "Job Sharing: Box and Cox," *The Economist,* Aug. 6, 1994, p. 56.

54. "Why Are Workers Fired?" *Personnel Journal,* June 1989, p. 14.

55. Ronald Henkoff, "Winning the New Career Game," *Fortune,* July 12, 1993, p. 46.

10

Training and Development

CHAPTER OBJECTIVES

After studying this chapter, you should be able to:

1. EXPLAIN how training and development differ.

2. JUSTIFY employee and organizational motives for training and development.

3. DISCUSS the reasons for including needs analysis in the design of training and development programs.

4. EXPLAIN the impact of trends in global business and workforce diversity on training and development.

5. MATCH different approaches to training with key learning principles.

6. EVALUATE the effectiveness of training and development programs.

Placing employees in jobs does not ensure their success. New employees are often uncertain about their roles and responsibilities. As Figure 10-1 shows, job demands and employees' capabilities must be balanced through orientation and training programs: Both are needed. Once employees have been trained and have mastered their jobs, they may need further development to prepare for their future responsibilities. And with ongoing trends toward greater workforce diversity, flatter organizations, and increased global competition, training and development efforts enable employees to assume expanded duties and greater responsibilities.

Training versus development

Although *training* helps employees do their current jobs, the benefits of training may extend throughout a person's career and help *develop* that person for future responsibilities. *Development,* by contrast, helps the individual handle future responsibilities, with little concern for current job duties. Since the distinction between training (now) and development (future) is often blurred and is primarily one of intent, both are discussed together throughout the chapter, with significant differences noted.

Looked at from the overall corporate perspective, the distinction between training for a current job and development for a future one blurs even further. What most firms seek to create is an organization where people engage in continuous learning. Consider the training program at one Corning operation.

"At the Corning Glass Works plant in Harrodsburg, Kentucky, we adopted a systematic approach in the development of a plant-wide training program. Our concept of training focuses on the individual. We at the Harrodsburg plant believe all employees, regardless of salary grade, position or department assignment, can benefit from quality training."[3]

Corning Glass

The training program at Corning has four phases. The first phase is called individual training. This phase includes an extensive orientation program for new employees and on-the-job training for those who have transferred to a new job. The second phase is departmental training. Hourly and management employees receive specialized courses that are intended to increase departmental productivity. These courses focus

| **Figure 10-1** | **The Balance between New Employee Capabilities and Job Demands** |

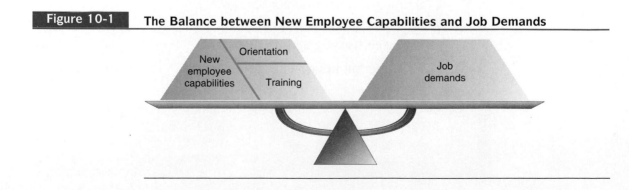

primarily on the standard operating procedures used to run specific operations in the department. The third phase, plant or facilities training, conveys information of general interest to those at the plant. Safety training and courses for personal or professional development are included in this category. The final phase is corporate and outside training and development. It includes training and development efforts made by corporate offices, private consultants, and universities. These courses tend to be more general and developmental in nature, forming the backbone of employees' efforts at continuous learning.

To support these various levels of training, the plant training coordinator develops a master training schedule that is published monthly on a department-by-department basis. It shows the name, type, and appropriate audience for each training session to be held that month. This calendar is supplemented by a catalog that shows whether the training subject is an operational, safety, departmental, or plantwide session.[4]

At Corning, learning opportunities range from skills-oriented training to seminars that deal with broad developmental issues that upwardly mobile managers can expect to face during their careers. Neither the training coordinator nor the students care much whether a class is intended to be "training" or "development." The more appropriate concern is whether the seminars help the employees and the organization.

 As an HR assistant and plant training coordinator at Corning asked: "So, where have over two hundred various courses for our employees taken us? First, we have increased productivity."[5] In one department, record production runs were achieved after the formalized on-the-job training of some of the employees. Workplace practices also have become more standardized, and employees have an in-plant means of self-improvement.[6]

Training also played an important role when Corning opened a new facility in Blacksburg, Virginia, to make automobile filters.

After sorting through 8000 job applicants to identify potential workers with the best problem-solving skills and a willingness to work in teams, Corning hired 150 employees. Even though most had at least one year of college, they were put through extensive training in both technical and interpersonal subjects. In the first year of operation, 25 percent of all hours worked were devoted to training, at a cost of $750,000.[7]

Corning's Virginia operations

The training provided by Corning was directed at employees at all levels in both the Kentucky and the Virginia operations. However, at many companies these activities are concentrated among managers and professionals,[8] unlike in Japan and Europe, where greater attention is given to the skills training of workers. "For example, in America, only 10% of young recruits had any formal training from their company, compared with around 70% in Japan and Germany."[9]

> Says Labor Secretary Robert Reich: "American companies have got to be urged to treat their workers as assets to be developed, rather than as costs to be cut."
> The Bureau of Labor Statistics estimates that nearly two-thirds of the workers who will be in the labor force in the year 2005 are already on the job.
> But most companies don't offer them any training at all. Just 15,000 employers—a mere 0.5% of the total—account for 90% of the $30 billion spent on training annually, according to the American Society for Training and Development (ASTD).[10]

The result, according to one researcher, is that only 35 percent of Americans receive upgrading on the job.[11] At the same time, many organizations provide remedial education, teaching reading, writing, and arithmetic skills to workers. These workers may be part of the nearly 14 percent of 18- to 21-year-olds who lack high school degrees,[12] compared with 6 percent in Japan.[13] Restated, one in seven American adults, or about 25 million people, are functionally illiterate.[14]

As businesses become more global, competition demands a more competent workforce. When a nation's educational system does not provide sufficiently educated workers, the burden falls on businesses. It has been estimated that U.S. businesses spend more than $30 billion annually on training and development.[15] A survey by the American Society for Training and Development found that firms should invest at least 2 percent of payroll in training and development.[16] In France, by comparison, employers with ten or more employees are required to spend 1.4 percent of payroll on training or pay what is not spent to the government as a tax.[17] Some leading U.S. companies, such as General Electric, Texas Instruments, and Motorola, spend even more than the French mandate or the U.S. average of 1.2 percent of payroll.[18] IBM, Motorola, Xerox, McDonald's, Ford, and others have built education centers to meet their commitment to the training and development of their workforces. These and other companies have been called "learning organizations" because they treat training and development as an "investment" in their future, not an "expense."[19]

> As Paul Banas, Ford's manager of human resource strategies and planning, explains, "If education and training are seen as a cost, then in tough times when costs are cut, education and training budgets disappear. However, if a corporation has developed a set of values and principles that view employees as an important asset, then the education and training remain even during corporate downswings."[20]

Training and development pay dividends to the employee and the organization, as suggested in Figure 10-2. Though no single program yields all the benefits in the figure, the personal and career goals of the employee are furthered, adding to his or her abilities and value to the employer, which furthers the objectives of managers and the HR department. However, training and development are not universal solutions to every need. Effective job designs, selection, placement, and other activities are necessary too. Nevertheless, training can make a substantial contribution when done properly.

Estimation of training costs

Ford

| Figure 10-2 | **The Benefits of Employee Training** |

HOW TRAINING BENEFITS THE ORGANIZATION

- Leads to improved profitability and/or more positive attitudes toward profit orientation.
- Improves the job knowledge and skills at all levels of the organization.
- Improves the morale of the workforce.
- Helps people identify with organizational goals.
- Helps create a better corporate image.
- Fosters authenticity, openness and trust.
- Improves the relationship between boss and subordinate.
- Aids in organizational development.
- Learns from the trainee.
- Helps prepare guidelines for work.
- Aids in understanding and carrying out organizational policies.
- Provides information for future needs in all areas of the organization.
- Organization gets more effective decision making and problem solving.
- Aids in development for promotion from within.
- Aids in developing leadership skill, motivation, loyalty, better attitudes, and other aspects that successful workers and managers usually display.
- Aids in increasing productivity and/or quality of work.
- Helps keep costs down in many areas, e.g., production, personnel, administration, etc.
- Develops a sense of responsibility to the organization for being competent and knowledgeable.
- Improves labor-management relations.
- Reduces outside consulting costs by utilizing competent internal consulting.
- Stimulates preventive management as opposed to putting out fires.
- Eliminates suboptimal behavior (such as hiding tools).
- Creates an appropriate climate for growth, communication.
- Aids in improving organizational communication.
- Helps employees adjust to change.
- Aids in handling conflict, thereby helping to prevent stress and tension.

BENEFITS TO THE INDIVIDUAL WHICH IN TURN ULTIMATELY SHOULD BENEFIT THE ORGANIZATION

- Helps the individual in making better decisions and effective problem solving.
- Through training and development, motivational variables of recognition, achievement, growth, responsibility and advancement are internalized and operationalized.
- Aids in encouraging and achieving self-development and self-confidence.
- Helps a person handle stress, tension, frustration and conflict.
- Provides information for improving leadership knowledge, communication skills and attitudes.
- Increases job satisfaction and recognition.
- Moves a person toward personal goals while improving interaction skills.
- Satisfies personal needs of the trainer (and trainee!).
- Provides trainee an avenue for growth and a say in his/her own future.
- Develops a sense of growth in learning.
- Helps a person develop speaking and listening skills; also writing skills when exercises are required.
- Helps eliminate fear in attempting new tasks.

BENEFITS IN PERSONNEL AND HUMAN RELATIONS, INTRA- AND INTERGROUP RELATIONS AND POLICY IMPLEMENTATION

- Improves communication between groups and individuals.
- Aids in orientation for new employees and those taking new jobs through transfer or promotion.
- Provides information on equal opportunity and affirmative action.
- Provides information on other governmental laws and administrative policies.
- Improves interpersonal skills.
- Makes organization policies, rules and regulations viable.
- Improves morale.
- Builds cohesiveness in groups.
- Provides a good climate for learning, growth, and coordination.
- Makes the organization a better place to work and live.

Source: From M. J. Tessin, "Once Again, Why Training?" *Training,* February 1978, p. 7. Reprinted by permission.

In Boynton Beach, Florida, Motorola can make 200% more pagers than it could four years ago with just 22% more manufacturing employees. Says general manager Hector Ruiz: "The factory doesn't look much different. The improvement came about through training. Our return on training is on the order of 30 to 1."[21]

▶ Steps to Training and Development

To receive the benefits listed in Figure 10-2, HR specialists and managers must assess the needs, objectives, content, and learning principles associated with training. Figure 10-3 diagrams the sequence that should be followed before training and development begin. As implied by the figure, the person who is responsible for training or development (usually a trainer) must assess the needs of the employee and the organization to learn which objectives should be sought. Once objectives are set, the specific content and learning principles are considered.

Needs Assessment

Needs assessment diagnoses current problems and future challenges to be met through training and development. For example, competitive pressure or a change in the organization's strategy may lead to downsizing and the restructuring that accompanies it. As a result, the remaining employees may need to be more broadly trained. The comments of one training director illustrate how the external environment affects training.

ADA

After the *Americans with Disabilities Act of 1990* changed the *Civil Rights Act of 1964*, we had to train every interviewer in the personnel department. This training was needed to ensure that our interviewers would not ask questions that might violate federal laws. When managers in other departments heard of the training, they too wanted to sign up. We decided that since they interviewed recruits, they should also be trained. What was to be a one-time seminar became a monthly session for nearly three years.

Although training is not an organizational cure-all, undesirable trends may provide evidence of a poorly prepared workforce. Thus, needs assessment must consider each person. The individual employee's needs may be determined by the HR department, by supervisors, or by self-nomination.

To pinpoint the range of training needs and define their content, the HR department uses different approaches to needs assessment. It may survey potential trainees to identify specific topics about which they want to learn more; this suggests that trainees are more likely to be receptive to the resulting programs when they are viewed as relevant. Of course, this approach presumes that those surveyed know what training they need. For new employees at Corning, for example, this method is not likely to be successful, but for the

| Figure 10-3 | **Preliminary Steps in Preparing a Training and Development Program** |

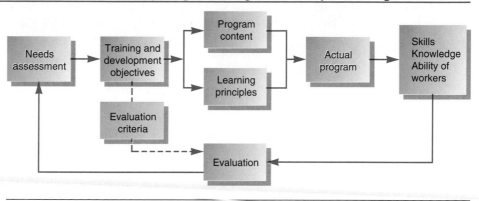

more general needs that are found at Corning's facilities, group recommendations may be the best way to identify training needs. The group's expertise may be tapped through a group discussion, a questionnaire, the Delphi procedure, or a nominal group meeting (see Chapter 6).

Another HR-led approach is task identification. Trainers begin by evaluating the job description to identify the salient tasks the job requires. Then, once they have an understanding of those tasks, specific plans are developed to provide the necessary training so that job incumbents can perform the tasks. The individual and departmental training phases of the training program at the Corning Glass Works are an example of a task identification approach.

The HR department may find weaknesses among HR trends in the company that can be traced to other HR activities. Inappropriate placement, orientation, selection, or recruiting may lead to workers with deficiencies. Errors in these activities may stem from weaknesses in HR planning, job design, or the department's HR information system. Although training and development may be needed to bolster workers' performance, proactive HR departments treat assessment information as feedback on other HR activities. By uncovering repeated shortcomings, the department can modify other activities to ensure a better fit between people and performance.

Trainers are also alert to other sources of information that may indicate a need for training. Production records, quality control reports, grievances, safety reports, absenteeism and turnover statistics, and exit interviews of departing employees may reveal problems that should be addressed through training and development efforts. Training needs also may become apparent from career planning discussions or performance appraisal reviews (see Chapters 11 and 12).

Supervisors see employees on a daily basis and thus are another source of recommendations for training. However, supervisors may use training sessions as a means to banish troublemakers, "hide" surplus employees who are temporarily not needed, or reward good employees, especially when the training involves travel to another city. Since these are not valid reasons, the HR department often reviews supervisory recommendations to verify the need for training.

The HR department also reviews self-nominations to learn whether the training actually is needed. In one research study, more training attendees were chosen through supervisor recommendation than through self-nomination.[22] Self-nomination appears to be less common for training situations but more common for developmental activities such as getting an M.B.A. degree under the employer's tuition reimbursement program.

Needs assessment also considers diversity and international issues. Training may be wasted if poor performance stems from language or cultural barriers.[23] For example, employees in developing nations may have different views about time ranging from problems with punctuality and attendance to attitudes in which interpersonal relationships are valued more highly than is timely performance. A common reaction is to provide more training in how to do the job, but when cultural imperatives dictate that performance is secondary to customs, skills training may be inappropriate or even wasteful.[24] (However, it should be noted that training is one of the major tools used to increase awareness of diversity issues and build cooperation among diverse groups within organizations.)

The success of the remaining steps in Figure 10-3 depends on the accuracy of the needs assessment process and the resulting training and development objectives.

Training and Development Objectives

Goals of training

Needs result in training and development objectives, which should state the desired behavior and the conditions under which it is to occur.[25] These stated objectives then become standards against which individual performance and the program can be measured. For example, the objectives for an airline reservationist might be stated as follows:

1. Provide flight information to call-in customers within thirty seconds.

2. Complete a one-city round-trip reservation in two minutes after all information has been obtained from the customer.

Specific, measurable, time-targeted objectives like those listed above for a reservationist give the trainer and the trainee specific goals that can be used to evaluate their success. If the objectives are not met, failure gives the HR department feedback on the program and the participants.

Program Content

The program's content is shaped by the needs assessment and the learning objectives. The objective here may be to teach specific skills, provide needed knowledge, or try to influence attitudes. Whatever its content, the program must meet the needs of the organization and the participants. If the company's goals are not furthered, resources are wasted. Participants must view the content as relevant to their needs or their motivation to learn may be low.

When a training program is a prerequisite to selection, retention, or placement, the training content must be valid. As was discussed in Chapter 4, the Equal Employment Opportunity Commission's Uniform Guidelines on Employee Selection Procedures require job-relatedness of selection criteria.[26] This requirement applies in cases where the training program is a criterion for initial hiring, retention, internal placement, or other conditions of employment.

Learning Principles

Learning
guidelines

Learning curve

Ideally, training and development are more effective when the training methods match the learning styles of the participants and the types of jobs needed by the organization. Unfortunately, learning cannot be observed; only its results can be measured. From studies of learning, however, researchers have sketched a broad picture of the learning process and have developed some tentative learning principles. Perhaps the best way to illustrate learning is through the use of the *learning curve* shown in Figure 10-4. As the curve indicates, learning takes place in bursts (from points *A* to *B*) and on plateaus (from points *B* to *C*). Trainers have two goals related to the shape of each employee's learning curve. First, they want the learning curve to reach a satisfactory level of performance, shown as a dashed line in the figure. Second, they want the learning curve to get to the satisfactory level as quickly as possible. Although the rate at which people learn depends on the individual, learning principles help speed up the learning process.

| Figure 10-4 | A Typical Learning Curve |

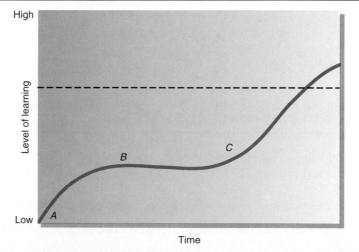

Learning principles are guidelines to the ways in which people learn most effectively. The more these principles are reflected in training, the more effective training is likely to be. These principles are participation, repetition, relevance, transference, and feedback. Research suggests that they apply equally to domestic and international training situations.

Participation.   Learning usually is quicker and longer-lasting when the learner participates actively. Participation improves motivation and apparently engages more senses that reinforce the learning process. As a result of participation, people learn more quickly and retain that learning longer. For example, most people never forget how to ride a bicycle because they actively participated in the learning process.

Repetition.   Although seldom fun, *repetition* apparently etches a pattern into one's memory. Studying for an examination, for example, involves the repetition of key ideas so that they can be recalled during a test. Similarly, most people learn the alphabet and the multiplication tables by means of repetition.

Relevance.   Learning is helped when the material to be learned is meaningful. For example, trainers usually explain the overall purpose of a job to trainees before explaining specific tasks. This allows the worker to see the relevance of each task and of following the correct procedures.

Transference.   The more closely the demands of the training program match the demands of the job, the faster a person learns to master the job. For example, pilots usually are trained in flight simulators because the simulators very closely resemble the cockpit and flight characteristics of the plane. The close match between the simulator and the plane allows the trainee to quickly *transfer* the learning in the simulator to actual flight conditions.

Feedback.   *Feedback* gives learners information on their progress. With feedback, motivated learners can adjust their behavior to achieve the quickest possible learning curve; without it, they cannot gauge their progress and may become discouraged. Test grades are feedback on the study habits of test takers, for example. Feedback is so important that Chapter 12 is devoted to performance appraisals.

▶ Training and Development Approaches

Trade-offs

In selecting training and development techniques, trade-offs exist. That is, no single technique is always best; the best method depends on:

- Cost-effectiveness
- Desired program content
- Learning principles

- Appropriateness of the facilities
- Trainee preferences and capabilities
- Trainer preferences and capabilities

The importance of these six trade-offs depends on the situation. For example, cost-effectiveness may be a minor factor in training an airline pilot in emergency maneuvers. But whatever method is selected, it has certain learning principles associated with it. Figure 10-5 lists the most common training and development techniques and the learning principles each one includes. As the figure reveals, some techniques make more effective use of learning principles than others do. Even approaches that use few learning principles, such as the lecture, are valuable tools because they may satisfy one of the other six trade-offs listed above. For example, a lecture may be the best way to communicate academic content in the most cost-effective manner, especially if the classroom is large and the room does not lend itself to other approaches. Although these trade-offs affect the methods used, HR specialists must be familiar with all the techniques and learning principles in Figure 10-5.

Job Instruction Training

On-the-job training

Job instruction training is received directly on the job, and so it is often called "on-the-job" training. It is used primarily to teach workers how to do their current jobs. A trainer, supervisor, or coworker serves as the instructor. When it is properly planned and executed, this method includes each of the learning principles shown in Figure 10-5.

Figure 10-5	**Learning Principles in Different Training and Development Techniques**				
	PARTICIPATION	**REPETITION**	**RELEVANCE**	**TRANSFERENCE**	**FEEDBACK**
ON-THE-JOB TECHNIQUES					
Job instruction training	Yes	Yes	Yes	Yes	Sometimes
Job rotation	Yes	Sometimes	Yes	Sometimes	No
Apprenticeships	Yes	Sometimes	Yes	Sometimes	Sometimes
Coaching	Yes	Sometimes	Yes	Sometimes	Yes
OFF-THE-JOB TECHNIQUES					
Lecture	No	No	No	Sometimes	No
Video presentation	No	No	No	Yes	No
Vestibule training	Yes	Yes	Sometimes	Yes	Sometimes
Role playing	Yes	Sometimes	Sometimes	No	Sometimes
Case study	Yes	Sometimes	Sometimes	Sometimes	Sometimes
Simulation	Yes	Sometimes	Sometimes	Sometimes	Sometimes
Self-study	Yes	Yes	Sometimes	Sometimes	No
Programmed learning	Yes	Yes	No	Yes	Yes
Laboratory training	Yes	Yes	Sometimes	No	Yes

Source: From *Training in Industry: The Management of Learning*, by B. M. Bass and J. A. Vaughn. Copyright © 1966 by Wadsworth Publishing Company, Inc. Reprinted by permission of the publisher, Brooks/Cole Publishing Company, Monterey, Calif.

On-the-job training (OJT) includes several steps. First, the trainee receives an overview of the job, its purpose, and its desired outcomes, with an emphasis on the relevance of the training. Then the trainer demonstrates the job to give the employee a model to copy. Since the employee is shown the actions that the job requires, the training is transferable to the job. Next the employee is allowed to mimic the trainer's example. Demonstrations by the trainer and practice by the trainee are repeated until the job is mastered. Repeated demonstrations and practice provide repetition and feedback. Finally, the employee performs the job without supervision, although the trainer may visit the employee to see if there are any lingering questions.

Job Rotation

To cross-train employees in a variety of jobs, some trainers move a trainee from job to job. Each move normally is preceded by job instruction training. Besides giving workers variety in their jobs, cross-training helps the organization when vacations, absences, downsizing, or resignations occur. Learner participation and high job transferability are the learning advantages of job rotation. Though rotation is most often associated with hourly employees, it can be used for jobs on many levels within the organization.

McDonnell Douglas Corporation is a major defense contractor that employs over 100,000 people. As a company, it is committed to being a learning organization that devotes an average of forty hours of training per year for each employee. To ensure the development of key employees, the company created a "High Potential" program as part of its management succession planning. The program sought to identify and develop employees who were assessed as having high potential. The centerpiece of the program is job rotation.

McDonnell Douglas

McDonnell's rotation program has three parts. The "Corporate Rotation" program attempts to develop top executives with a breadth of experience. The "Functional Rotation" program seeks to give people with a background in accounting, human resources, or other functions broad exposure within the function. The "Intracompany Rotation" program targets those below middle management for two-year rotational assignments within the organization.[27]

Each of these programs seeks to give employees exposure to a variety of assignments. Among hourly employees, job rotation is an effective way to train workers and give management greater flexibility in making job assignments. Among managerial, technical, and professional employees, job rotation can provide a broader perspective, often developing these employees for potential career advancement.

Apprenticeships and Coaching

Apprenticeships involve learning from a more experienced employee or employees, though it may be supplemented with off-the-job classroom training.[28] Most craft workers, such as plumbers and carpenters, are trained through formal apprenticeship programs. Assistantships and internships are similar to apprenticeships because they use high levels of participation by the trainee and have high transferability to the job.

Coaching is similar to apprenticeships because the coach attempts to provide a model for the trainee to copy. Most companies use coaching. It tends to be less formal than an apprenticeship program because there are few formal classroom sessions and because it is provided when needed rather than being part of a carefully planned program. Coaching is almost always handled by the supervisor or manager, not by the HR department. Sometimes a manager or another professional takes an interest and plays the role of mentor, giving both skills and career advice. Participation, feedback, and job transference are likely to be high in this form of learning.

Assignments to task forces or committees may help develop people in much the same way that apprenticeships and coaching do. Through periodic staff meetings or work with task forces and committees, a manager develops interpersonal skills, learns to evaluate information, and gains experience in observing other potential models.

Coaching is common

Lecture and Video Presentations

Lecture and other off-the-job techniques tend to rely more heavily on communications than on modeling. These methods are applied in both training and development. Lecturing is a popular approach because it offers relative economy and a meaningful organization of materials. However, participation, feedback, transference, and repetition are often low. Feedback and participation can be improved when discussion is permitted along with the lecture process.

Television, films, slides, and filmstrip presentations are similar to lectures. A meaningful organization of materials is a potential strength, along with initial audience interest. The growth of video presentations has been encouraged by the use of satellite communications to bring courses into the work site, particularly in engineering and other technical fields.[29]

TV and training

Vestibule Training

To keep instruction from disrupting normal operations, some organizations use *vestibule training*. Separate areas or vestibules are set up with equipment similar to that used on the job. This arrangement allows transference, repetition, and participation. Meaningful organization of materials and feedback are also possible.

Best Western motels

At the corporate training facilities of Best Western motels and hotels, vestibules duplicate a typical motel room, a typical front desk, and a typical restaurant kitchen. This allows trainees to practice housekeeping, front counter, and kitchen skills without disrupting the operations of any property.

Role Playing and Behavior Modeling

Role playing is a device that forces trainees to assume different identities. For example, a male worker may assume the role of a female supervisor and a female supervisor may assume the role of a male worker. Then both may be given a typical work situation and told to respond as they would expect the other to do. The result? Usually participants exaggerate each other's behavior. Ideally, they get to see themselves as others see them. The experience may create greater empathy and tolerance of individual differences and is therefore well suited to *diversity training,* which aims to create a work environment conducive to a diverse workforce. This technique is used to change attitudes, for example, to improve racial understanding. It also helps develop interpersonal skills. Although participation and feedback are present, the inclusion of other learning principles depends on the situation.

U.S. Navy

The U.S. Navy has used role playing to reduce racial tensions. Friction among sailors of different races—within the limited confines of ships on extended patrol duty—not only harmed morale and crew efficiency but also caused low rates of reenlistment among highly trained personnel. This high turnover impaired the Navy's ability to function.

The role-playing exercises required small groups of black sailors and white sailors to assume the role of the opposite race. The role-playing leader gave the members of each group an assignment and then directed them to carry it out as they thought members of the other race would. With the other group watching, each group in turn acted out the behavior of the others. Through these exercises and the subsequent discussions, members of the different races were able to learn how their behavior and attitudes affected one another.

Behavior modeling

Closely related to role playing and apprenticeships is *behavior modeling,* which has been described by two writers as follows:

> Modeling is one of the fundamental psychological processes by which new patterns of behavior can be acquired, and existing patterns can be altered. The fundamental characteristic of modeling is that learning takes place, *not* through actual experience, but through observation or imagination of another individual's experience. Modeling is a "vicarious process," which implies sharing in the experience of another person through imagination or sympathetic participation.[30]

Whether behavior modeling is referred to as "matching" or "copying" or as "observational learning" or "imitation," "all of these terms imply that a behavior is learned or modified through the observation of some other individual."[31] Employees may learn a new behavior through modeling by observing a new behavior and then imitating it. The re-creation of the behavior may be videotaped so that the trainer and the trainee can review and critique it. When watching the ideal behavior, the trainee also gets to see the negative consequences that befall someone who does not use it as recommended. By observing the positive and negative consequences, the employee receives vicarious reinforcement that encourages the correct behavior. An area where this approach has been used successfully is in teaching supervisors how to discipline employees, and it is particularly common in athletics.[32]

Positive and negative consequences

In the supervisory training program of a large unionized steel company, supervisors were put through a half-day disciplinary training session that used videotape-based behavior modeling. After a short lecture on the principles of discipline, the trainees were shown a brief tape of a supervisor conducting a disciplinary interview incorrectly and another tape in which the discipline was handled properly. Then the supervisors were paired into groups of two. Each supervisor was told to "discipline" his or her partner by using the correct method they had just observed. These mock discipline sessions were filmed and played back—often to the horror of the participants. Each saw how others saw him or her during a disciplinary interview. After a brief and largely positive critique from the trainer, each supervisor conducted a second and a third discipline session that was followed by a critique. By the end of the morning each supervisor was capable of conducting a disciplinary interview in the correct manner. Whether this training was actually transferred to their day-to-day behavior on the job was not evaluated by the training department or the shop manager.

Case Study

By studying a case situation, trainees learn about real or hypothetical circumstances and the actions others take under those circumstances. Besides learning from the content of the case, a person can develop decision-making skills. When cases are meaningful and similar to work-related situations, there is some transference. There also is the advantage of participation through discussion of the case. At Ogilvy & Mather International, a major advertising agency, new recruits are assigned to a specific account, which becomes a "live" case and is discussed at three lunchtime seminars each week.[33] Feedback and repetition, though, are usually lacking. Research indicates that this technique is most effective for developing problem-solving skills.[34]

Cases in advertising

Simulation

Simulation exercises come in two forms. One involves a mechanical simulator that replicates the major features of the work situation. Driving simulators used in driver's education programs are an example. This training method is similar to vestibule training, except that the simulator more often provides instantaneous feedback on performance.

Computer simulations are the other form. For training and development purposes, this method often comes in the form of games. Players make a decision, and the computer determines the outcome in the context of the conditions under which it was programmed. This technique is used most commonly to train managers, who otherwise might have to use trial and error to learn decision making.

Self-Study and Progammed Learning

Carefully planned instructional materials can be used to train and develop employees. These materials are particularly helpful when employees are dispersed geographically or when learning requires little interaction. Self-study techniques range from manuals to prerecorded cassettes or videotapes. Several learning principles are included in this type of training.

Pepsi-Cola

The Pepsi-Cola Management Institute is responsible for training bottlers all over the world. To contend with this dispersion, it created a network of videotape recorders and supplied bottlers with videotaped materials. The institute also uses other techniques.

Programmed learning materials are another form of self-study. Usually these are computer programs or printed booklets that contain a series of questions and answers. After reading and answering a question, the reader gets immediate feedback. If right, the learner proceeds; if wrong, the reader is directed to review the accompanying materials. Of course, computer programs with visual displays may be used instead of printed booklets. For example, Federal Express requires the following:

> At least once a year, every one of the company's 40,000 couriers and customer service agents plugs into an interactive, PC-based program that tests their job knowledge.
>
> The computer-based exams, which contain 90 questions and take about two hours, pinpoint areas where workers need help and then prescribe remedial action. The computer keeps an electronic record of every employee's job skills, which managers review when they recommend promotions.[35]

The U.S. Army uses interactive videodiscs that show maintenance personnel how to repair complicated military hardware. The Army's approach is likely to have high transference, though other forms of programmed learning often do not. Programmed materials provide learner participation, repetition, relevance, and feedback, however. Illiteracy, whether in industrialized or developing nations, limits the feasibility of this approach, especially among entry-level employees.

Laboratory Training

Laboratory training is designed to enhance interpersonal skills. It too can be used to develop desired behaviors for future job responsibilities. Participants seek to improve their human relations skills by better understanding themselves and others. This involves sharing experiences and examining the feelings, behaviors, perceptions, and reactions that result. Usually a trained professional serves as a facilitator. The process relies on participation, feedback, and repetition. A popular form of laboratory training is sensitivity training, which seeks to increase a person's sensitivity to the feelings of others.

Action Learning

Action learning takes place in small groups that seek a solution to a real problem confronting the organization, aided by a facilitator who is either an outside consultant or a member of the firm's in-house staff. The group's focus on the problem becomes a learning vehicle as the members explore solutions, drawing on the facilitator to provide guidance in group, problem-solving, and other problem-related matters. Training and development needs emerge and are often self-evident when the group is stumped technically or procedurally. At GE, one of the pioneers of action learning, senior executives work in teams on business problems identified by top management. Then, at the end of the training, they make a presentation to the CEO or other senior executives.[36] Action learning focuses on learning new behaviors, while lectures and video presentations target knowledge and role playing and sensitivity training addresses feelings.

▶ Evaluation of Training and Development

To verify a program's success, HR managers increasingly demand that training and development activities be evaluated systematically. A lack of evaluation may be the most serious flaw in most training and development efforts. Simply stated, HR professionals too seldom ask, Did the program achieve the objectives established for it? They often assume it had value because the content seemed important. Trainers may rely on the evaluations of the trainees, who reported how enjoyable the experience was for them, rather than evaluate the content themselves.

In the early 1990s, R. R. Donnelly & Sons spent $125,000 on training senior sales representatives. But executives wondered if the expenditure was worth the money. Trainers developed a series of measures that centered on improving the commissions of the trained salespeople in comparison with those who were not trained. When adjustments were made to these figures for the marketing efforts of the company, sales personnel maturity, and the cost of the program, the $125,000 expenditure resulted in more than a $12 million increase in revenues.[37]

Effective criteria used to evaluate training focus on outcomes. Trainers are particularly concerned about:

Training outcomes

1. The *reactions* by trainees to the training content and process.

2. The *knowledge* or learning acquired through the training experience.

3. Changes in *behavior* that result from the training.

4. Measurable *results or improvements* in the individuals or the organization, such as lower turnover, fewer accidents, or less absenteeism.[38]

Evaluation of training and development should follow the steps in Figure 10-6. First, evaluation criteria should be established before training begins, closely matching the training and development objectives in Figure 10-3. Then participants should be given a pretest; that is, they should be tested to establish their level of knowledge before the program begins. Ideally, this test should be given to both the group to be trained and a control group that will not receive the training. After training or development has been completed, a posttest or posttraining evaluation should reveal the improvement that resulted from the program.[39] If the improvement in the trained group is statistically significant— that is, if it did not result from chance—it can be assumed that the program actually made a difference, as was the case of R. R. Donnelley & Sons.

Posttests are useful ways to determine whether information was communicated. However, the program is a success only if the improvement meets the evaluation criteria and is transferred to the job, resulting in behavioral change that is best measured by improved job performance. Follow-up studies may be conducted months later to see how well learning was retained.

▶ Development of Human Resources

The long-term development of human resources—as distinct from training for a specific job—is of growing concern to HR departments. Through the development of current employees, the department reduces the company's dependence on hiring new workers. If employees are developed properly, the job openings found through HR planning are more likely to be filled internally.

Figure 10-6	**Steps in the Evaluation of Training and Development**

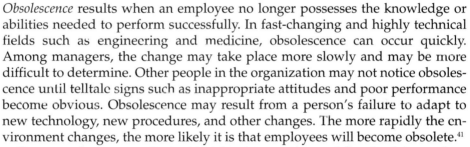

Promotions and transfers also show employees that they have a career, not just a job. The employer benefits from increased continuity in operations and from employees who feel a greater commitment to the firm.

HR development is also an effective way to meet several challenges, including employee obsolescence, international and domestic workforce diversity, technical changes, affirmative action, and employee turnover. By meeting these challenges, the department can maintain an effective workforce.[40]

Employee Obsolescence

Obsolescence

Obsolescence results when an employee no longer possesses the knowledge or abilities needed to perform successfully. In fast-changing and highly technical fields such as engineering and medicine, obsolescence can occur quickly. Among managers, the change may take place more slowly and may be more difficult to determine. Other people in the organization may not notice obsolescence until telltale signs such as inappropriate attitudes and poor performance become obvious. Obsolescence may result from a person's failure to adapt to new technology, new procedures, and other changes. The more rapidly the environment changes, the more likely it is that employees will become obsolete.[41]

Some employers are reluctant to take strong action and fire obsolete employees, particularly employees who have been with the company a long time. Instead, such workers may be given jobs where their obsolescence does not matter as much or their skills are not as obsolete. For example, when top executives do not perform satisfactorily, they sometimes are "promoted" to vice chairperson of the board, where they may play an advisory role or attend ceremonial functions such as banquets for retiring employees. For lower-level workers, the solution is often additional development programs.

Avoiding obsolescence

Avoiding obsolescence before it occurs is a major challenge for the HR department. By assessing the needs of employees and giving them programs to develop new skills, the department is using development programs proactively. If programs are designed reactively, after obsolescence occurs, they are likely to be less effective and more costly. Consider the situation faced by a regional airline.

Sam Oliver had been a ground crew chief in the Air Force for many of his twenty years in the service. After retirement, he joined a regional airline as a mechanic. Since he had extensive supervisory experience, he was promoted to ground crew chief. Sam had been successful in the Air Force by giving direct orders with little explanation, and he used the same leadership style in his civilian job.

The HR department realized something was wrong when an unusually large number of grievances were filed with the union by Sam's ground crew. To correct the problems, Sam was enrolled in an intensive sixteen-week supervisory training program at the local community college. Although he changed his approach after the program, Sam now showed resentment.

If the department had been proactive before Sam was promoted rather than reacting to his obsolescence, his resentment might have been avoided.

Career plateau

When an employee reaches a career plateau, obsolescence may be more likely. A *career plateau* occurs when an employee does well enough not to be demoted or fired but not so well that he or she is likely to be promoted. When the employee realizes that he or she is at this plateau, the motivation to stay current may be reduced.

Many companies use continuing education for middle- and upper-level management to combat obsolescence. Western Electric conducts "Corporate Symposiums on Emerging Issues" at its corporate education center in Hopewell, New Jersey. General Electric operates the GE Management Institute outside New York City. IBM runs the IBM Country Club and Management Institute on Long Island, and the federal government operates the Federal Executive Institute in Virginia. These opportunities are supplemented by educational leaves at companies such as IBM and Xerox and by university-based programs that typically last four to fourteen weeks.[42]

International and Domestic Workforce Diversity

Adjusting to diversity

The trends toward global businesses and the diversity of the workforce also challenge the HR department. For example, cultural attitudes about women in the workforce caused many companies to redesign their development programs and put women in jobs that had been largely held by men. The diversity of educational attainment among workers has led companies to provide increasing amounts of remedial education in reading, writing, arithmetic, and English as a foreign language. With the large number of non-English-speaking workers in some firms, training materials are sometimes adapted to a second or third language.

Proactive HR departments are expanding their programs to include diversity training. Here the concern is less with techniques—such as role playing or behavior modeling, as discussed earlier—and more with creating sensitivity to diversity in the workplace. For example, a survey by a major U.S. based consulting firm found:

Employers in one survey reported providing:

1. Cultural Diversity Sensitivity Training in 53% of firms;
2. Communication-Across-Cultures Training in 32% of firms;
3. Gender Issues Training in 42% of firms;
4. Harassment-free Workplace Training in 71% of firms;
5. Sexual Awareness Training in 15% of firms;
6. Disability Awareness Training in 56% of firms; and,
7. Elder Issues Awareness Training in 225 firms.

> "Today's workforce is a melting pot of human differences," says Mercer consultant Richard F. Federico. . . . "But companies that capitalize on this human mosaic can gain an edge, particularly after corporate right-sizing, restructuring and reengineering have run their course. . . . being sensitive to a diverse workforce isn't just the right thing to do—it's the good business thing to do." As global workforces and empowered teams become more prevalent, he says, "employees will need to work closely together—despite differences—to satisfy equally diverse customers."[43]

When a firm is providing training for foreign nationals, the content and delivery must take into account local customs and expectations, down to seating arrangements, duration and ending times, meals, and accommodations.[44] When an international move is involved, some companies facilitate the process with in-house mentoring programs. At Colgate-Palmolive, the mentor is usually at or above the level of vice president. Dow assigns a high-level person to conduct training in that individual's specialty.[45] The assignment of mentors can be crucial because the development of international managers generally involves job rotation across borders. As one commentator observed:

> To complicate matters, many executives steer clear of overseas assignments because they feel that their absence from their company's headquarters will hurt their chances for career advancement and that good jobs will not be waiting for them at home when they do repatriate.[46]

Mentors reduce these fears and facilitate the move by providing both guidance and contacts.

Technological Change

Rapid changes in technology require technically based firms to engage in nearly continuous development. Twenty years ago IBM was in the computer and office equipment business and AT&T was in the telephone business. Today technological changes have made AT&T and IBM major competitors in the information industry. Improvements in information handling and transmission technology have opened new markets for these two huge organizations. These changes are having a profound impact on training and development, increasing the need to assess the developmental requirements of current and future managers, professionals, and technical people.

Development, EEO, and Affirmative Action

The Civil Rights Act prohibits discrimination with respect to the terms, conditions, or privileges of employment. As a result, training and development activities must be conducted in such a way that they do not discriminate against protected classes. When being admitted to or passing a training program is a condition of employment or promotion, for example, the HR department must be able to show that the training requirements are related to job success. If the training or development activities are not validated, the employer may be charged with violating the act.

The training or development program itself may have a discriminatory impact if barriers to training are not related to subsequent job success. For example, women had significant difficulty passing the training for outside craft positions at AT&T subsidiaries. Part of the problem was that some of the training equipment had been designed for the larger feet of men, thus causing a disproportionate number of women and smaller men to fail the course. Another problem may occur when scores on parts of the training program are used for future placement decisions. Under these circumstances, the burden falls on the HR department to show that the scores are valid.

Key case

In *Weber v. Kaiser Aluminum and Chemical Corporation*, the U.S. Supreme Court recognized that affirmative action may require a disproportionately high number of minorities to be admitted to training programs. If this form of "reverse discrimination" is meant to achieve the goals of an affirmative action plan, the courts consider it legal.

Employee Turnover

Turnover—the willingness of employees to leave one organization for another—creates a special challenge for HR development. Because departures are largely unpredictable, development activities must prepare employees to succeed those who leave. Although research has shown that the leaders of very large industrial companies spend nearly all of their careers with one firm, the same research found that mobility is widespread among other managers.[47]

Sometimes an employer with excellent development programs finds that those programs *contribute* to employee turnover. Some companies "are reluctant to invest time and money in workers who may then take their new skills to a new job at a higher-paying competitor. Training works best when all the companies in a particular industry, or all the employees in a particular community, cooperate—a common practice in Japan but not exactly standard operating procedure in the U.S."[48]

Ironically, the widely recognized development programs of companies such as General Electric, Procter & Gamble, General Motors, and IBM cause some employee mobility. These programs produce such high-quality results that recruiters from other companies are attracted to the employees.

Of course, these companies realize that it is better to have some trained employees who leave than to have an untrained workforce that stays.

Ultimately, the effectiveness of training and development depends on their integration with the other HR activities discussed so far in this book and with the topics to be described in the following chapters. Incentive compensation such as stock options and fringe benefits such as pension plans are other powerful ways to reduce turnover, especially among executives.[49] These HR tools are examined more thoroughly in Part IV of this book.

▶ Summary

After workers have been selected and oriented, they may still lack the skills, knowledge, and abilities needed to perform successfully. Most workers require some training to do their current jobs properly. If the organization wishes to place these employees in more responsible positions in the future, developmental activities also have to take place. For most workers and trainers, individual learning sessions are a blend of training and development.

Most large organizations make available a broad array of educational opportunities. However, trainers should conduct a needs assessment to determine if the training is truly needed and, if it is needed, what it should cover. Training and development, or learning, objectives result from the needs assessment. Trainers can plan the content of the course from these objectives and incorporate as many learning principles as is feasible.

Merely conducting training—even when a careful needs assessment has been undertaken—is insufficient. Experienced trainers try to evaluate the impact of training and development activities. Often this involves a pretest and a posttest and even follow-up studies to see if the learning was transferred to the job.

HR development prepares individuals for future job responsibilities. At the same time, it attempts to contend with employee obsolescence, international and domestic workforce diversity, technological changes, affirmative action, and employee turnover.

▶ Terms for Review

Needs assessment
Learning principles
Repetition
Transference
Feedback
Learning curve
Job instruction training

Vestibule training
Role playing
Behavior modeling
Laboratory training
Obsolescence
Career plateau

▶ Review and Discussion Questions

1. How are external changes in the environment of business affecting the training and development function in human resource departments?

2. Suppose you are a department manager with twenty-four employees and have been asked to determine the training needs of your group by the training specialists in the human resource department. What approaches would you use to make this assessment?

3. What connection do you see between learning objectives and evaluating the effectiveness of a training program?

4. Assume that an HR manager told you: "My formula for preventing obsolescence and burnout is simple: As soon as someone has mastered his or her job—whether they be hourly or salaried—move that person to another job. Sure you have to invest in training, but burnout and obsolescence are not a problem." What benefits and problems do you see with this approach?

5. Specify the training techniques you recommend for each of the following occupations: (*a*) a clerk in an office setting, (*b*) a plumber, (*c*) an unskilled assembly-line worker, (*d*) an inexperienced manager. Why?

6. Why should operating managers be concerned about learning principles since they are not professional trainers?

7. Suppose you were a supervisor in an accounting department and the training manager wanted to implement a new training program to teach bookkeepers how to complete new accounting forms. What steps would you recommend to evaluate the effectiveness of the training program?

8. Assume you were hired to manage a law firm. After a few weeks you noticed that some lawyers were more effective than others and that the less effective ones received little recognition from their more productive counterparts. What forms of development would you consider for both groups?

▶ Incident 10-1

Executive Development at General Electric

Stanley Gault (Goodyear), Lawrence Bossidy (Allied-Signal), and William Anders (General Dynamics) are all CEOs and chairmen of their companies' boards of directors. Another thing they have in common with many other CEOs is that all three are alumni of General Electric. As *Investor's Business Daily* observed:

General Electric, which traces its roots back to 1878 and founder Thomas Edison, has developed a reputation as the premier supplier of management talent to corporate America.

A rigorous management training program, early responsibility and diverse business experience are some of the hallmarks of management development at GE. Those who make it to positions of responsibility at the company have unimpeachable credentials, experts say.[50]

GE is good not only in general management; *Investor's Business Daily* ranked it second best in finance and accounting and third in research and development management.[51] By nearly any financial or other business measure, the company is among the most successful in the United States, if not the world. Yet for all its attention to management development, it loses top talent to others, as the CEOs of Goodyear, Allied-Signal, and General Dynamics indicate.

Assume you are Jack Welch, CEO of GE, and have to defend to the board of directors the company's large outlays to support its "GE University" in Crotonville, New York, and other training and development activities that come to about 2 percent of GE's payroll.[52]

1. What justifications would you use to maintain the board's support for training and development?

2. Besides their increased attractiveness to executive search firms and other employers, what advantages do GE employees gain from the obvious success of GE's training and development activities?

▶ References

1. Ronald Henkoff, "Where Will the Jobs Come From?" *Fortune,* Oct. 19, 1992, p. 58.

2. Anthony Patrick Carnevale, *America and the New Economy*, Alexandria, Va.: American Society for Training and Development, 1991, p. 95.

3. John D. Dickey, "Training with a Focus on the Individual," *Personnel Administrator,* June 1982, p. 35.

4. Ibid., pp. 35, 37.

5. Ibid., p. 38.

6. Ibid., p. 37.

7. John Hoerr, "Sharpening Minds for a Competitive Advantage," *Business Week*, Dec. 17, 1990, p. 72.

8. Ronald Henkoff, "Companies That Train Best," *Fortune,* Mar. 22, 1993, pp. 62–71; John Hoerr, "With Job Training, A Little Dab Won't Do Ya," *Business Week*, Sept. 24, 1990, p. 95.

9. "Musical Chairs," *The Economist,* July 17, 1993, p. 67.

10. Henkoff, op. cit., p. 62.

11. Diane E. Kirrane, "Training: HR's Number One Priority," *Personnel Administrator,* December 1988, pp. 70–74.

12. Sar A. Levitan and Frank Gallo, "Uncle Sam's Helping Hand: Educating, Training, and Employing the Disadvantaged," in Louis A. Ferman, Michele Hoyman, Joel Cutcher-Gershenfeld, and Ernest J. Savoie (eds.), *New Developments in Worker Training: A Legacy for the 1990s,* Madison, Wis.: Industrial Relations Research Association, 1990, p. 226.

13. Gary S. Becker, "Why Don't We Value Schooling as Much as the Asians Do?" *Business Week,* Dec. 12, 1988, p. 22.

14. "Fight Workplace Illiteracy," *Personnel Journal,* August 1988, p. 18.

15. Dominic J. DiMattia and Raymond J. Yeager, "Emotional Barriers to Learning," *Personnel Journal,* November 1989, pp. 86–89.

16. "Training as an Investment," *Small Business Reports,* December 1988, p. 11.

17. John H. Bishop, "The French Mandate to Spend on Training: A Model for the United States?" in John F. Burton (ed.), *The Industrial Relations and Research Association 45th Annual Proceedings,* Madison, Wis.: Industrial Relations Research Association, 1993, pp. 285–295.

18. Kevin Kelly and Peter Burrows, "Motorola: Training for the Millennium, *Business Week,* Mar. 28, 1994, p. 159. See also Anthony Patrick Carnevale, *Put Quality to Work: Train America's Workforce,* Alexandria, Va.: American Society for Training and Development, 1990, p. 10.

19. Peter M. Senge, "The Leader's New Work: Building Learning Organizations," *Sloan Management Review,* Fall 1990, pp. 7–23.

20. Gerald L. McManis and Michael S. Leibman, "Management Development: A Lifetime Commitment," *Personnel Administrator,* September 1988, pp. 53–58.

21. Thomas A Stewart, "U.S. Productivity: First but Fading," *Fortune,* Oct. 19, 1992, p. 57. See also Aaron Bernstein and Paul Magnusson, "How Much Good Will Training Do?" *Business Week,* Feb. 22, 1993, pp. 76–77.

22. J. Kevin Ford and Raymond Noe, "Self-Assessed Training Needs: The Effects of Attitudes toward Training, Managerial Level, and Function," *Personnel Psychology,* vol. 40, 1987, pp. 39–53.

23. Geert Hofstede, "Cultural Constraints in Management Theories," *Academy of Management Executive,* vol. 7, no. 1, 1993, pp. 81–93.

24. Irene Chew Keng Howe, Anthony Tsai-pen Tseng, and Adrian Teo Kim Hong, "The Role of Culture in Training in a Multinational Context," *The Journal of Management Development* (Special Issue: Management Development in Asia), vol. 9, no. 5, 1990, pp. 51–57.

25. Lori Bongiorno, "Corporate America's New Lesson Plan," *Business Week,* Oct. 25, 1993, pp. 102–104.

26. Equal Employment Opportunity Commission, Department of Labor, "Uniform Guidelines on Employee Selection Procedures," *Federal Register,* vol. 43, no. 166, 1978, pp. 38290–38315.

27. Mary Settle, "Up Through the Ranks at McDonnell Douglas," *Personnel,* December 1989, pp. 17–22.

28. Dan Jacoby, "Legal Foundations of Human Capital Markets," *Industrial Relations,* vol. 30, no. 2, Spring 1991, pp. 229–249.

29. David Green, "Business Television: A Dynamic New Training Channel," *Personnel,* October 1988, pp. 62–66. See also Robert Neff, "Videos Are Starring in More and More Training Programs," *Business Week,* Sept. 7, 1987, pp. 108–110.

30. Henry P. Sims, Jr., and Charles C. Manz, "Modeling Influence on Employee Behavior," *Personnel Journal,* January 1982, p. 58.

31. Ibid.

32. William M. Fox, "Getting the Most from Behavior Modeling Training," *National Productivity Review,* Summer 1988, pp. 238–245.

33. Marian L. Salzman, "The 10 Best Company Training Programs," *Business Week's Guide to Careers,* Spring–Summer 1985, p. 26.

34. John W. Newstrom, "Evaluating the Effectiveness of Training Methods," *Personnel Administrator,* January 1980, pp. 55–60.

35. Henkoff, op. cit., p. 64.

36. Brian O'Reilly, "How Execs Learn," *Fortune,* Apr. 5, 1993, pp. 52–58.

37. Anthony R. Montebello and Maureen Haga, "To Justify Training, Test, Test Again," *Personnel Journal,* January 1994, pp. 83–87.

38. George M. Alliger and Elizabeth A. Janak, "Kirkpatrick's Levels of Training Criteria: Thirty Years Later," *Personnel Psychology,* vol. 42, 1989, pp. 331–343. See also D. L. Kirkpatrick, "Evaluation of Training," in R. L. Craig and L. R. Bittel (eds.), *Training and Development Handbook,* New York: McGraw-Hill, 1967, pp. 87–112.

39. Mary D. Carolan, "Just-in-Time Training Yields Long-Term Training Benefits," *The Human Resource Profession,* Fall 1992, pp. 41–43. See also Paul R. Sackett and Ellen J. Mullen, "Beyond Formal Experimental Design: Towards an Expanded View of the Training Evaluation Process," *Personnel Psychology,* vol. 46, 1993, pp. 613–627.

40. Gail S. Robinson and Calhoun W. Wick, "Executive Development That Makes a Business Difference," *Human Resource Planning,* vol. 15, no. 1, 1992, pp. 63–76.

41. Lee Smith, "Burned-Out Bosses," *Fortune,* July 25, 1994, pp. 44–52; Bernard M. Kessler, "How to Prevent Executive Derailment," *The Human Resources Professional,* Fall 1992, pp. 44–47. See also Jeffrey S. Bracker and John N. Pearson, "Worker Obsolescence: The Human Resource Dilemma of the '80s," *Personnel Administrator,* December 1986, pp. 109–117.

42. Beverly McQuigg-Martinetz and Edward E. Sutton, "New York Telephone Connects to Training and Development," *Personnel Journal,* January 1990, pp. 64–71.

43. Richard R. Federico, "More Employers Launch Diversity-Related Training Programs," *William M. Mercer News Release,* July 30, 1993, pp. 1–2.

44. Bob Hagerty, "Trainers Help Expatriate Employees Build Bridges to Different Cultures," *The Wall Street Journal,* Western ed., June 14, 1993, p. B1. See also a monthly newsletter published by the Jamestown Area Labor Management Committee, Inc., entitled *Managing Diversity* for more extensive examples of how training is used to address workplace diversity.

45. Paul L. Blocklyn, "Developing the International Executive," *Personnel,* March 1989, pp. 44–47.

46. Ibid.

47. William B. Werther, Jr., "Management Turnover Implications of Career Mobility," *Personnel Administrator,* February 1977, pp. 63–66.

48. Henkoff, op. cit., p. 62. See also Farrell Kramer, "GE's School of Business: Why Grads Are Coveted," *Investor's Business Daily,* Nov. 6, 1992, p. 4.

49. "Hanging on to Know-Alls," *The Economist,* Aug. 21, 1993, p. 55.

50. Kramer, op. cit.

51. Ibid.

52. Carnevale, op. cit.

11

Job security is an oxymoron.
VIVIAN BROWNSTEIN[1]

Career Planning

CHAPTER OBJECTIVES

After studying this chapter, you should be able to:

1. ADVISE someone about the major points in career planning.

2. DESCRIBE how HR departments encourage and assist career planning.

3. DISCUSS career planning issues related to workforce diversity and international employees.

4. IDENTIFY the major advantages of career planning.

5. EXPLAIN the relationship between career planning and career development.

6. LIST the major actions that aid career development.

Common concerns

▪ Do company training programs help my chances for a promotion?

▪ How do I advance my career?

▪ Why hasn't my boss given me career counseling?

▪ Aren't most promotions based on luck and knowing the right people?

▪ Do I need a degree for that job?

▪ With all the talk of downsizing, how secure is my job?

Career defined

Nearly everyone asks these questions at some point during his or her working life, and the answers help identify the actions needed to further one's career. A *career* consists of all the jobs held during one's working life. For some people, these jobs are part of a careful plan. For others, a career is simply a matter of luck. Merely planning a career does not guarantee success. Superior performance, experience, education, and occasional luck play an important role. When people rely largely on luck, however, they seldom are prepared for the career opportunities that arise. Successful people identify their career goals, plan, and then take action. For them, "luck" occurs when opportunity meets preparation.

With modern employers continuously restructuring in response to their competitive environment, traditional lifelong employment relationships with a single employer are becoming less likely. As the managing editor of *Fortune* observed:

> Work will persist and be done by individuals hired for a particular project and assigned to that project's team. When the task is complete and the team disbands, the individual will go on to the next project, maybe with the same organization, like the people who design a new chip for Intel, or perhaps back in the freelance swim, as with the artists and artisans who come together to make a movie.[2]

This turbulent job environment argues for increased individual responsibility and effort in managing one's career. Yet some people argue, Who can look ten, twenty, or thirty years into the future and predict where a career will lead? True, an accurate prediction that far into the future is impossible. Other people ignore career planning because they mistakenly assume that the HR department or their boss will assume that responsibility. Some people are simply unaware of the basic career planning concepts described in Figure 11-1. Without an understanding of career goals and career paths,[3] planning is unlikely. However, when one asks, What are my career goals? and What is my first step? a career plan can be started.[4]

Key questions

Although the immediate manager and the HR department can facilitate the career planning process and help answer questions about appropriate career paths, the employee remains ultimately responsible for his or her career progress.[5] In fact, some departments offer no formal career planning assistance because they lack the sophistication to do so (as is the case in many small organizations). Even in some large businesses, senior managers may see career planning as the responsibility of the employee, not the company.[6] Nevertheless,

Figure 11-1	Selected Career Planning Terms

■ *Career.* A career is all the jobs that are held during one's working life.

■ *Career path.* A career path is the sequential pattern of jobs that forms one's career.

■ *Career goals.* Career goals are the future positions one strives to reach as part of a career. These goals serve as benchmarks along one's career path.

■ *Career planning.* Career planning is the process by which one selects career goals and the path to those goals.

■ *Career development.* Career development consists of the personal improvements one undertakes to achieve a personal career plan.

more and more sophisticated organizations see career planning assistance as a means to help ensure an adequate supply of internal talent. As one writer observed:

> During the past 30 years, career development programs have become an important and vital activity in business and industry. Career development is now an accepted human resource strategy among training and development administrators, personnel officers, and organizational consultants. The principal aim of such programs has been to help employees analyze their abilities and interests to better match personnel needs for growth and development with the needs of the organization. In addition, career development is a critical tool through which management can increase productivity, improve employee attitudes toward work, and develop greater worker satisfaction.[7]

Effective career planning programs also may reduce turnover, especially among those who have the greatest career mobility—the best employees.[8]

Dow Jones

Dow Jones & Company, Inc., is the publisher of the *Wall Street Journal, Barron's,* and other business information sources. During the 1980s, the vice president for staff development created a task force that designed the "Druthers Program" for the company. Endorsed by top management and the union that represents most of the company's clerical and professional employees, this program puts responsibility for career development where it belongs: on the employees.

An employee initiates the Druthers Program by writing a letter to his or her manager. The letter identifies a specific career objective and, if known, the next job being sought. Then the letter describes relevant education and experience and may discuss willingness to travel or relocate. The style and content of the letter give an indication of the writer's logic and writing skills. These letters are kept on file for twelve months by the manager. If a job is sought outside the department, a copy of the letter goes to the national coordinator of the program, the director of employment and career planning.

When a job opening occurs, the letters are reviewed. If suitable candidates are not on file, referrals are sought from the program coordinator. Although managers may recruit outside the firm, they are encouraged to review internal candidates first.

The Druthers Program is supported by the department in several ways. Seminars give employees insight into career planning and self-assessment. Briefings about career options and job requirements are given by people from key departments. Seminars even show employees how to present their qualifications in writing and in person.

Employees receive *The Dow Jones Job Information Handbook,* which describes the various departments and jobs within the company, including summaries of job responsibilities, locations, and qualifications. Dow Jones members also can get a booklet entitled *Writing Your Own Success Story: A Guide to Using the Druthers System.* It answers questions about the Dow Jones career development and placement service and gives sample Druthers letters along with the biographies of those who wrote them.[9]

The Dow Jones program gives employees a way to express their "druthers" about the work they want to do. The role of the HR department includes creating, publicizing, and maintaining the program through training and information. However, the responsibility for career planning and development stays with the employee because he or she is the person most keenly interested. Since each person's career is unique, only the employee can decide if a career path is appropriate.

Although each person's career is unique, consider the insights contained in one executive's career path over forty-one years in the banking industry that were almost certainly less turbulent than the next four decades will be. This executive's name and the names of his employers have been changed to protect his privacy, and so we will call him "Joe."[10] His career progress is summarized in Figure 11-2 and explained below:

After graduation from college and three years in the Marine Corps, Joe joined the First National Bank as a teller trainee. At that point in his career his *goal* was to become a banking executive. He had no idea of the *career path* he would follow, but Joe realized that his first step was to become a supervisor. This *career planning* caused him to enroll in the bank's supervisory management training program. After being promoted to teller, he enrolled in other training programs and took some noncredit courses from the American Banking Institute. These programs were the first of many *career development* actions he undertook. Two promotions later, he became head teller.

After four years Joe felt that his career plan was stalled, and so he accepted a transfer into the bank's new account department. Although the transfer was not a promotion and did not include a raise, Joe needed some diversification in his background to increase his chances

Figure 11-2	The Career Path for a Retired Executive Vice President in the Banking Industry

JOB NUMBER	JOB LEVEL	JOB TITLE	TYPE OF JOB CHANGE	YEARS IN JOB	ENDING AGE
1	Worker	Teller Trainee	———	$\frac{1}{2}$	24
2	Worker	Teller	Promotion	$3\frac{1}{2}$	28
3	Worker	Asst. Head Teller	Promotion	2	30
4	Supervisory	Head Teller	Promotion	4	34
5	Supervisory	New Account Supervisor	Transfer	3	37
6	Management	Asst. Branch Manager for Loans	Promotion	3	40
7			Educational leave (finish M.B.A.)	1	41
8	Management	Asst. Branch Manager	Transfer	1	42
9	Management	Branch Manager	Promotion	3	45
10	Management	Branch Manager	Transfer	4	49
11	Management	Loan Officer	Transfer	5	54
12	Management	Chief Loan Officer	Promotion	3	57
13	Executive	Vice President, Operations Center	Resignation/Promotion (joins another bank)	3	60
14	Executive	Senior Vice President for Operations	Promotion	1	61
15	Executive	Executive Vice President	Promotion	4	65
16			Retired		

of becoming an assistant branch manager. Three years later he became assistant branch manager for loans.

After three years as an assistant branch manager for loans, Joe again felt that his career progress was too slow, and so he took an educational leave and finished his master of business administration degree (M.B.A.). With the M.B.A., he returned to the bank as an assistant manager in a new branch. A year later he was promoted to branch manager. To gain a wider array of skills, Joe transferred to another branch as manager and then to the home office as a loan officer. In five years he became chief loan officer, and three years later he achieved his goal by accepting a job as vice president in a competing bank. His success as an executive led to two more promotions before he retired as an executive vice president at age 65.

As a review of Figure 11-2 indicates, Joe's career plan involved well-timed transfers and an educational leave. Figure 11-3 superimposes Joe's career changes on the organization charts of the two banks for which he worked. As the organization charts show, a career seldom progresses straight up in an or-

Career progression

| Figure 11-3 | A Career Path for an Executive Vice President in the Banking Industry |

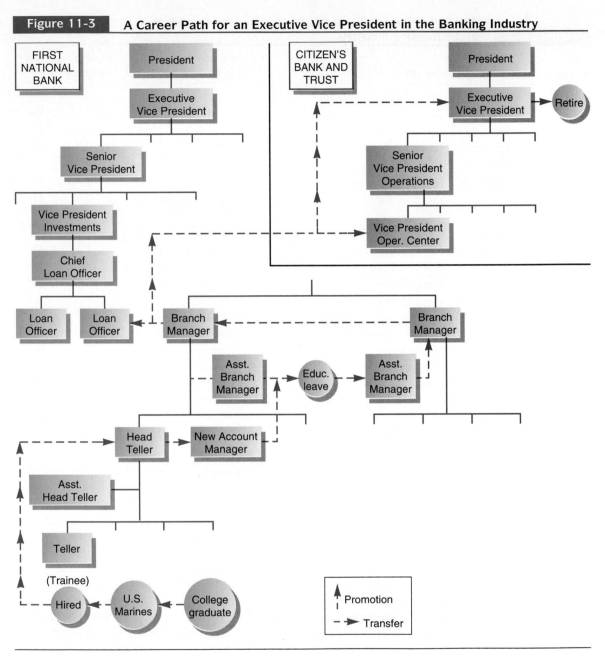

ganization. Lateral transfers, leaves, and even resignations are used. When Joe started as a teller trainee at age 24, he could not have predicted the career path he would follow. But through career planning, he reassessed his career progress and then undertook development activities to achieve intermediate career goals such as becoming a supervisor. As a result of career planning and development, Joe's career path led him to his goal of becoming an executive in the banking industry.

▶ Career Planning and Employee Needs

During the forty years of Joe's career, HR departments in banks and other organizations gave little support to career planning. When promotable talent was scarce, employers usually reacted with crash training programs or additional recruitment. HR planning and career planning seldom occurred. Instead of seeking proactive solutions, organizations and employees reacted to new developments.[11] Historically, this limited role for the HR department is understandable because career plans were seen as an individual matter.[12] Even when HR managers wanted their departments to provide assistance, they often lacked the resources to become involved. As a result, only a few (mostly large) organizations encouraged career planning by employees.[13]

Internal staffing help

Today an increasing number of HR experts see career planning as a way to meet their internal staffing needs.[14] Although career planning assistance is generally reserved for managerial, professional, and technical employees because of limited funds, ideally all workers would have access to this advice, as they do at Dow Jones. When employers encourage career planning, employees are more likely to set career goals and work toward them. In turn, these goals may motivate employees to pursue further education, training, and other developmental activities; this gives the department a larger internal pool of qualified applicants. Consider the comments of Harold Burlingame, a senior vice president for human resources at AT&T: "We used to say, 'Come here for a job for life.' Today we say, 'Invest in us, we'll invest in you.' As we proceed in the market together, out of that comes a career."[15]

But what do employees want? A study of one group of employees revealed five factors of concern.[16] Those factors were:

What employees want

■ *Career equity.* Employees want equity in the promotion system with respect to opportunities for career advancement.

■ *Supervisory concern.* Employees want their supervisors to play an active role in career development and provide timely feedback on performance.

■ *Awareness of opportunities.* Employees want knowledge of opportunities for career advancement.

■ *Employment interest.* Employees need different amounts of information and have different degrees of interest in career advancement, depending on a variety of factors.

■ *Career satisfaction.* Employees, depending on their age and occupation, have different levels of career satisfaction.

Effective career programs must consider these different perceptions and desires of employees.[17] What workers expect from the career programs developed by the HR department varies with age, sex, occupation, education, and other factors. In short, whatever approach the HR department adopts, it must be flexible and proactive. An HR manager associated with the Hanes Group in Winston-Salem, North Carolina, came to this conclusion:

> Flexibility in career development programs is paramount if the goals of improved productivity, increased personal satisfaction, growth and ultimately increased organizational effectiveness are to be achieved. In many cases, this will require the modification of basic existing programs to address the specific needs of a particular group of employees.[18]

▶ Human Resource Departments and Career Planning

Corporate strategies require an appropriate mix of human talents. Effective HR plans translate corporate strategy into employment needs.[19] To meet those staffing needs with internal candidates, the HR department uses placement decisions, training and development, and career planning assistance to fulfill the organization's future employment requirements domestically and globally.

HR becomes involved in career planning for other reasons too. Departmental experts are more likely to be aware of training and other developmental opportunities. Of course, individual managers also should assist employees with career planning. However, if specialists leave career planning to operating managers, it may not get done. Not all managers take a strong interest in their employees' careers, although 68 percent of the firms in one study have formal succession plans.[20]

Downsizing and careers

As organizations downsize, career opportunities shrink. The HR department can help employees identify career building opportunities ranging from lateral transfers to special task forces. If successful, these efforts can convince the employees who remain that they have a future with the company. Since those remaining are usually viewed as the "best" employees, it is essential that they be retained and motivated.

The primary risk for the HR department and the company is the creation of career expectations that cannot be met. Career guidance suggests that if employees follow the advice, career opportunities will follow. However, company growth, downsizing, and changes in business strategies may prevent opportunities from materializing. Disappointment may lower morale and performance and lead to resignations. Nevertheless, the involvement of the HR department in career planning has grown in recent years because of its benefits. Here is a partial list of those benefits:

Career planning benefits

■ *Aligns strategy and internal staffing requirements.* By assisting employees with career planning, the HR department can better prepare them for anticipated job openings identified in the HR plan, resulting in a better mix of the talents needed to support company strategies.

■ *Develops promotable employees.* Career planning helps develop internal supplies of promotable talent to meet openings caused by retirement, resignations, and growth.

■ *Facilitates international placement.* Global organizations use career planning to help identify and prepare for placement across international borders.

■ *Assists with workforce diversity.* When they are given career planning assistance, workers with diverse backgrounds can learn about the organization's expectations for self-growth and development.

■ *Lowers turnover.* Increased attention and concern for individual careers may generate more organizational loyalty and lower employee turnover.

■ *Taps employee potential.* Career planning encourages employees to tap more of their potential abilities because they have specific career goals. Not only does this prepare employees for future openings, it can lead to better performance among incumbents in their current jobs.

■ *Furthers personal growth.* Career plans and goals motivate employees to grow and develop.

■ *Reduces hoarding.* Career planning causes employees, managers, and the HR department to become aware of employee qualifications, preventing selfish managers from hoarding key subordinates.

■ *Satisfies employee needs.* With less hoarding and improved growth opportunities, an individual's esteem needs, such as recognition and accomplishment, are more readily satisfied.

■ *Assist affirmative action plans.* Career planning can help members of protected groups prepare for more important jobs. This preparation can contribute to meeting affirmative action timetables.

To realize these benefits, companies are supporting career planning through career education, information, and counseling.

Career Education

Surprisingly, many employees are unaware of the need for and advantages of career planning. Once they are made aware, they often lack the necessary information to plan their careers successfully. HR departments are suited to solve both shortcomings and can increase employee awareness through a variety of educational techniques. For example, speeches, memorandums, and position papers from top executives stimulate employee interest at low cost to the employer. If executives communicate their belief in career planning, other managers are likely to do the same.

Workshops and seminars increase employee interest by pointing out the key concepts associated with career planning. Workshops also help employees set career goals, identify career paths, and uncover specific career development activities. These educational efforts may be supplemented by printed or taped information. The John Deere Company offers an example of these varied approaches to career education.

John Deere

The John Deere Harvester Works has been in East Moline, Illinois, since the company moved into the "new" technology of combine harvesting around the turn of this century. Although many employees have decades of service, the company has hired many newcomers. Not all of the new employees have the loyalty of their long-service coworkers and are more prone to ask, What is the company doing for my career?

At the East Moline operation, members of the HR department have taken the view that career planning and development are the responsibility of the employee. With that philosophy, a four-hour career planning workshop was developed. Attendance is voluntary. Employees go to the workshop on their own time and are not paid for attending. This "on-your-own-time" approach is intended to reinforce the point that career development rests with the individual. Instructors from the HR department are not paid either; the fact that they volunteer to do the sessions helps convey the idea that the department is interested in the participants as people, not just as employees.

Figure 11-4 lists the goals of these career information seminars. As the seminars begin, participants are assigned to teams. Introductions and a discussion about the confidentiality of the sessions follow. Then the groups discuss career planning and list enjoyable and not so enjoyable activities as a step toward creating a personal inventory and identifying alternatives. Discussions also center on an internal staffing decision where the teams are asked to fill a hypothetical opening immediately. As two members of the HR department observed: "The arguments which are created in this exercise are highly beneficial for promoting acceptance of the management perspective on internal selection and promotion, a perspective which many have not previously considered. Many participants realize for the first time that being passed over only means someone else was slightly better qualified—not that they're in disfavor with the company."[21]

When the HR department lacks the necessary staff to design and conduct educational programs, public programs conducted by local colleges or consultants may help.

| Figure 11-4 | Goals of the Career Information Seminar at John Deere |

JOHN DEERE HARVESTER WORKS

Career Information Seminar

Goals

1. To help employees better understand how their jobs and careers at John Deere can contribute to their goals.

2. To provide employees with an approach to individualized career planning.

3. To define the roles of employees, their supervisors, and the personnel department in career planning and personal development

4. To provide realistic job and career information upon which to build career plans.

Source: Reprinted, with permission, from Karl A. Hickerson and Richard C. Anderson, "Career Development: Whose Responsibility?" *Personnel Administrator,* June 1982, p. 45. Copyright © 1982, the American Society for Personnel Administration, 30 Park Drive, Berea, Ohio 44017.

TPF&C consultants

One worldwide consulting firm—Towers, Perrin, Forster & Crosby—provides its clients with a four-step package. The packaged program includes (1) a strategy for the organization to solve its unique needs, (2) support systems based on the current HRIS to give employees the data they need to plan their careers, (3) workbooks that allow employees to perform career planning, and (4) a career resource center that offers employees assistance with career planning.

Pressures on HR

Competition and downsizing have put cost pressures on many HR departments. To keep career planning information flowing, some departments have enlisted the support of line managers instead of staff in the department:

> At Anheuser-Busch, certain employees receive five days of training, which equips them to run two-day career management workshops for fellow employees.
>   B. F. Goodrich's Career Growth System includes a twelve-hour training program . . . to enhance managers' ability to handle career-related discussions with employees.[22]

Many companies still rely on staff-run centers and staff-provided information on career planning:

3M

> 3M has a company-funded Career Information Center that provides continuing education and training, job vacancy information, individual assessments, and counseling, along with . . . career-growth workshops that are attended on company time.[23]

Information about Career Planning

Regardless of the educational strategy the HR department selects, it should provide employees with other information they need to plan their careers. Much of the needed career information is already part of the department's HRIS.[24] For instance, job descriptions and specifications can be valuable to someone who is trying to estimate reasonable career goals at a firm such as Dow Jones. HR specialists can also share their knowledge of potential career paths. For example, they are often keenly aware of the similarities between seemingly unrelated jobs.

 Consider the possible career paths faced by a clerk-typist at the *Wall Street Journal.* In this type of work, the jobs of typist, word processor, and Teletype and Linotype operator require a similar characteristic: finger dexterity. But clerk-typists in the advertising department may not realize that similar skills applied to a Linotype machine may earn them three times as much as the other jobs.

Job progression ladder

When different jobs require similar skills, they form *job families.* Career paths within a job family demand little additional training since the skills of each job are closely related. If information about job families is made available, employees can find feasible career paths. They then can assess the career paths by talking to persons who already hold those jobs. One problem with job families is that employees may want to skip less pleasant or lower-paying jobs. To prevent this, the HR department may establish a sequential progression of jobs. A *job progression ladder* is a partial career path where some jobs have prerequisites, as shown in Figure 11-5. The ladder shown in the figure requires a clerk-typist to become a word processor and then a Teletype operator before moving to the better-paying job of Linotype operator. This requirement assures the HR department of an ample internal supply of Teletype operators because this job is a prerequisite to a better-paying one.

| Figure 11-5 | **Four Jobs with Similar Requirements Grouped into a Job Family** |

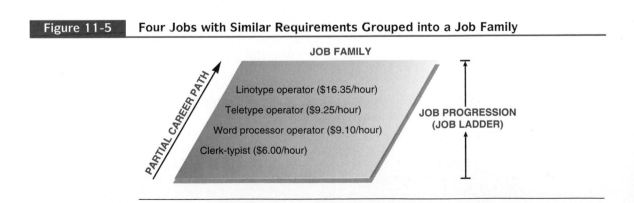

The department also can encourage career planning by providing information about alternative career paths.

At the John Deere Harvester Works, the HR department provides an extensive brochure that describes every factory job below the level of management. However, the brochure is available only through the career information seminar.[25]

Figure 11-5 shows that clerk-typists face multiple career paths. If a particular clerk-typist does not want to become a Linotype operator, the HR department can provide information about alternatives. In the newspaper example, a clerk-typist might prefer a career in editorial, secretarial, or advertising work because these careers offer more long-term potential, especially since most organizations are phasing out Linotype machines in favor of newer technologies.

Career Counseling

Vocational interest tests

To help employees establish career goals and find appropriate career paths, some departments offer *career counseling*. The career counselor may simply be someone who listens to an employee's interests and provides the specific job-related information.[26] Or the counselor may help employees uncover their interests by administering and interpreting aptitude, skills, psychological, and other tests. Two tests in particular—the *Kuder Preference Record* and the *Strong Vocational Interest Blank*—are useful for guiding people into occupations that are likely to be of interest to them. Other tests are available to measure individual abilities and interests in specific types of work. But to be truly successful, career counselors must get employees to assess themselves and their environment.

Employee self-assessment. Career counselors realize that a career is only a part of one's life plan. It may be a large part or even a central part, but it is only a part. A *life plan* is the often ill-defined series of hopes, dreams, and personal goals that each person carries through life. For example, broad objectives to be happy, healthy, and successful combine with specific goals to be a good spouse, parent, student, citizen, neighbor, and manager. Together these roles form one's life plan. Ideally, a career plan is an integral part of one's life plan. Otherwise, career goals become ends (sometimes dead ends!) rather than means toward fulfilling a life plan.[27] An example can be drawn from an overworked movie plot:

The husband struggles for decades to achieve a degree of career success. When that success is within reach, he realizes that his personal life—friendships, marriage, and paternal relationships—is in shambles. It is in shambles because career plans were pursued to the exclusion of an integrated life plan.

Besides a life plan, self-assessment includes a self-inventory. The components of a self-inventory are listed in Figure 11-6. With a detailed and honest self-evaluation, employees can match their interests and abilities with the career information available to them from the HR department.[28] They also can match their aptitudes and career goals with their life plans.

Environmental assessment.   A career plan that matches employee interests with likely career paths actually may do a disservice to the employee if environmental factors are overlooked. A return to the choices faced by clerk-typists at the newspaper provides an example.

Figure 11-6	A Self-Inventory for Career Planning

	LOW				HIGH
WORK INTERESTS AND APTITUDES	1	2	3	4	5
Physical work (fixing, building, using hands)	—	—	—	—	—
Written work (writing, reading, using words)	—	—	—	—	—
Oral work (talking, giving speeches, using words)	—	—	—	—	—
Quantitative work (calculating, doing accounting, using numbers)	—	—	—	—	—
Visual work (watching, inspecting, using eyes)	—	—	—	—	—
Interpersonal work (counseling, interviewing)	—	—	—	—	—
Creative work (inventing, designing, ideas)	—	—	—	—	—
Analytic work (doing research, solving problems)	—	—	—	—	—
Managerial work (initiating, directing, coordinating)	—	—	—	—	—
Clerical work (keeping records)	—	—	—	—	—
Outdoor work (farming, traveling, doing athletics)	—	—	—	—	—
Mechanical work (repairing, fixing, tinkering)	—	—	—	—	—

WORK SKILLS AND ABILITIES
List below specialized skills, unique personal assets, enjoyable experiences, and major accomplishments. Then evaluate.

	PHYSICAL	WRITTEN	ORAL	QUANTITATIVE	VISUAL	INTERPERSONAL	CREATIVE	ANALYTIC	MANAGERIAL	CLERICAL	OUTDOOR	MECHANICAL
_____	—	—	—	—	—	—	—	—	—	—	—	—
_____	—	—	—	—	—	—	—	—	—	—	—	—
_____	—	—	—	—	—	—	—	—	—	—	—	—
_____	—	—	—	—	—	—	—	—	—	—	—	—
_____	—	—	—	—	—	—	—	—	—	—	—	—
_____	—	—	—	—	—	—	—	—	—	—	—	—
_____	—	—	—	—	—	—	—	—	—	—	—	—
_____	—	—	—	—	—	—	—	—	—	—	—	—

The job family of clerk-typist, word processor, Teletype operator, and Linotype operator may appear to be a reasonable career path since clerk-typists possess the basic typing skills needed for all four jobs, but techological changes in the newspaper industry have reduced the need for Linotype operators. Photographic and computer developments are quickly making the use of Linotype machines in newspaper printing obsolete. If career counselors do not point out this development, clerk-typists may find their careers stalled in the job of Teletype operator.

Regardless of the match between one's skills and the organization's career paths, counselors need to inform employees of likely changes that will affect their occupational choices. Occupational information is readily available from the U.S. Department of Labor's Bureau of Labor Statistics.

Career counseling process.   Counseling about careers is a very sensitive and potentially explosive issue. Employees may see only parts of some jobs that pay much better and think that they are qualified. When the counselor tries to explain the need for additional skills that are not apparent, employees may feel that they are not being treated fairly. A typical reaction is, If old Mary can do that job, certainly I can do it. Even if that reaction is true, others who are even more qualified may be better choices. Or when the counselor points out the steps needed to become qualified for a job, the employee may resist additional training or schooling. Finally, the mere presence of career counselors may be a trap. Employees may think that someone else is taking responsibility for their career planning and development. Returning to the observations of two HR specialists at the John Deere Harvester Works:

John Deere

> We find, for example, there is a great unspoken lesson about the nature of competition for "career" advancement at the moment people gather on their own time at the workplace on a Saturday morning. All they have to do is look around.
> "Looking around" emphasizes that there are other people who are interested in advancing, too. Although a counselor can point this out, seeing thirty or forty people at the plant on a Saturday morning probably makes a deeper impression. The group training sessions also can illustrate some issues that counseling may not be able to do as well. When HR specialists state during the seminar that people who are flexible, energetic, and willing to improve their skills have an advantage, there is less defensive behavior than when those comments are made in a private counseling session.[29]

Stalled Careers

Research summary

A particularly difficult issue in career planning assistance is addressing stalled careers. As two researchers observed, retaining employees with critical skills, creating career paths to help senior employees break out of career plateaus, and retraining senior employees whose skills have become outdated will pose special challenges to human resource managers.[30]

Slow growth and restructuring through downsizing have eliminated many career opportunities for otherwise good, hardworking employees.[31] Simply put, many people have found their careers stalled through no fault of their own. Since many companies have scaled back their levels of middle management and staff, finding career advancement opportunities outside the firm entails considerable competition from others.[32] At the same time, the HR department needs to keep the remaining employees motivated and developing.[33] With fewer levels of jobs between entry-level positions and senior management in many firms, HR departments have focused on planning that includes lateral job transfers, or job rotation, among staff members and middle managers. Greater responsibility also has helped develop those who remain on the payroll. Even the trend toward connecting pay to performance has helped serve as a motivator.

When stalled careers result from limited skills, knowledge, abilities, or personal attributes among employees, the HR department faces a different set of challenges. If the problem is a simple deficiency of knowledge, skills, or abilities, retraining may be the solution.[34] Often, however, shortcomings are intertwined with issues of motivation or personal attributes that preclude advancement even with training. And as organizations attempt to accommodate workforce diversity, affirmative action plans may stall otherwise promotable employees.

Some people reach a career plateau beyond which they are not capable of advancing even with training and development. Yet these same employees may be good performers in their current jobs and may be important to the smooth operation of the organization.[35]

Burnout

Other employees may experience burnout. *Burnout* is a condition of mental, emotional, and sometimes physical exhaustion that results from substantial and prolonged stress. For example, managers who have had to deal repeatedly with downsizing and the agony of personally laying off workers may experience burnout.[36] Stress-reduction training can eliminate or reduce the problem before or after it occurs. However, people who experience burnout are not likely candidates for advancement to jobs with greater responsibility and perhaps greater stress. Even after the feelings of burnout pass, personal motivation or the reputation of having gone through a period of burnout may eliminate a person from consideration for advancement.

As a result of personal burnout or downsizing, "companies have an interest in reinvigorating diminished and demoralized rank, so they are trying to spur productivity by offering employees a host of ways to juice up their jobs. Among them: additional training, lateral moves, short sabbaticals, and compensation based on a person's contribution, not title."[37] As a result, employer-facilitated career development efforts are likely to become more important in the future.

▶ Career Development

Career development consists of the personal actions one undertakes to achieve a career plan. These actions may be sponsored by the HR department or the manager, or they may be undertaken independently of the HR department. This section reviews the tactics employees use to achieve their career plans and then discusses the HR department's role in career development.

Individual Career Development

Personal responsibility

Each person must accept his or her responsibility for career development or career progress is likely to suffer. Once this personal commitment is made, several career development actions may prove useful. These actions involve:

- Job performance
- Exposure
- Networking
- Resignations
- Organizational loyalty
- Mentors and sponsors
- Key subordinates
- Growth opportunities
- International experience

Job performance.   The most important action an individual can take to further his or her career is good, ethical job performance. The assumption of good performance underlies all career development activities. When performance is substandard, regardless of other career development efforts, even modest career goals are usually unattainable. *Career progress rests largely on performance.*

Exposure.   Career progress also is furthered by exposure.[38] Exposure means becoming known (and, it is hoped, held in high regard) by those who decide on promotions, transfers, and other career opportunities. Without exposure, good performers may not get the opportunities needed to achieve their career goals. Managers gain exposure primarily through their performance, written reports, oral presentations, committee work, and hours worked. Exposure also comes from enhancing the organization's social responsibility through involvement in professional associations and nonprofit community groups such as the United Way, chambers of commerce, and other civic-minded groups. Simply put, exposure makes an individual stand out from the crowd—a necessary ingredient in career success, especially in large organizations.[39] Consider how one management trainee gained some vital exposure early in her career:

Being known

Paula Dorsey noticed that two executives worked on Saturday mornings. As one of twelve new management trainess, she decided that coming to work on Saturday mornings would give her additional exposure to those key decision makers. Soon the two executives began greeting her by name whenever they passed in the hall. While still in the training program, she was assigned to the product introduction committee, which planned the strategy for new products. At the end of the training program Paula was made an assistant product manager for a new line of phones. The other eleven trainees received less important jobs.

In small organizations, exposure to decision makers occurs more frequently and is less dependent on reports, presentations, and the like. In some situations, especially in other nations, social status, school ties, and seniority can be more important than exposure.

Networking.   Networking means gaining exposure outside the firm. Personal and professional contacts—particularly through professional associations—give one contacts that can be useful in identifying better jobs. Then, when a career track reaches a dead end or a layoff forces one to swim in the freelance pool, these contacts can help aim one toward job possibilities. Among the sad paradoxes of the 1980s and 1990s have been loyal, well-intentioned, hardworking employees who have dedicated themselves to a company only to find themselves on the layoff list. For some, dedication to the company, not to their careers, found them forgoing the opportunity to socialize outside the firm in conventions, trade associations, and professional groups. Then, when they were laid off, they lacked a network of associates outside the company who could assist them in finding work.

Resignations.   When greater career opportunities exist outside the organization, a resignation may be the only way to meet one's career goals. Some employees—professionals and managers in particular—change employers as part of a conscious career strategy. If done effectively, these resignations usually result in a promotion, a pay increase, and a new learning experience. Resigning to further one's career with another employer has been called *leveraging*.[40] Astute managers and professionals use this technique sparingly because too many moves can lead to the label of "job hopper." Those who leave seldom benefit the previous organization because they almost never return with their new experiences.

Leveraging

In a study of 268 mobile executives, only 3 percent (7 of the executives) ever returned to an organization that they had left during their careers.[41] This means that organizations seldom benefit from the return of managers who quit and go elsewhere. Thus, HR departments must work to develop the loyalty of their employees to reduce turnover and retain valuable human resources.

Organizational loyalty.   In some organizations people put loyalty to career above loyalty to the organization. Low levels of organizational loyalty are common among recent college graduates (whose high expectations often lead to disappointment with their first few employers) and professionals (whose first loyalty is often to the profession). Career-long dedication to the same organization complements the HR department's objective of reducing employee turnover. Sometimes employers try to "buy" this loyalty with high pay or benefits. Other organizations may limit mobility by requiring employees to sign noncompete contracts to prohibit them from working for competitors, usually for one or more years. Still other organizations try to build employee loyalty through effective HR practices, including career planning and development.

Dedication

By offering careers, not just jobs, many organizations nurture a pool of talent that allows them to staff senior management positions internally. Many employees use their dedication and loyalty to the company as a career tactic. For example, one study showed that in the 100 largest industrial companies in the United States, 51 percent of the chief executive officers spent their entire careers with the same organization.[42] In Japan, employees tend to be very loyal to the employer because many firms will hire only entry-level workers; also, in many large firms, men are given lifetime employment. Thus, changing jobs to another firm to further one's career is seldom done.

Lifetime employment

Mentors and sponsors.   Many employees quickly learn that a *mentor* can aid their career development. A mentor is someone who offers informal career advice. Neither the mentor nor the employee always recognizes that the relationship exists. Instead, a junior worker simply knows someone who gives good advice.[43]

If the mentor can nominate the employee for career development activities such as training programs, transfers, and promotions, the mentor becomes a sponsor. A *sponsor* is someone in the organization who can create career development opportunities. Often an employee's sponsor is the immediate supervisor, although others may serve as nominators.[44]

Many Japanese firms rely on senior managers to use their storehouse of insight and wisdom to help junior managers with career development. In a relationship based on school ties or another non-work-related factor, the senior manager serves as a career counselor, mentor, and sponsor for the junior employee, who often works in a different department. In return, the senior manager's actions are reinforced by the respect received from other managers.

Japanese approach

Key subordinates.   Successful managers rely on subordinates who aid their performance. The subordinates may possess highly specialized knowledge or skills that the manager may learn from them, or they may perform a crucial role in helping a manager achieve good performance. In either case, employees of this type are *key subordinates*. They exhibit loyalty to their bosses and a high

Crucial subordinates

ethical standard. They gather and interpret information, offer skills that supplement those of their managers, and work unselfishly to further their managers' careers. They benefit by also moving up the career ladder when the manager is promoted and by receiving important assignments that serve to develop their careers. These people complement HR objectives through their teamwork, motivation, and dedication. But when a manager resigns and takes a string of key subordinates along, the results can be devastating.[45]

 A small West Coast research firm had a ten-month lead in developing a new type of memory component for computers. A major electronics company hired away the project manager, the chief engineer, and their key subordinates. After this loss, the small firm was forced to recruit replacements at a higher salary and at a cost of several months' delay.

Shelf-sitters

As a career strategy, perceptive subordinates are careful not to become attached to an immobile manager. One researcher calls such immobiles "shelf-sitters."[46] Not only do shelf-sitters block promotion channels, their key subordinates can be unfairly labeled as shelf-sitters too. Although working for a shelf-sitter may prove to be a development opportunity, such a label can arrest one's career progress.

Growth opportunities.   When employees expand their abilities, they complement the organization's objectives. For example, enrolling in a training program, taking noncredit courses, pursuing an additional degree, or seeking a new work assignment can contribute to employee growth. These growth opportunities aid both the HR department's objective of developing internal replacements and the individual's personal career plan.

Rachel Holmes was the chief recruiter in the employment department of Brem Paper Products. Her department manager was 60 years old and had indicated that he planned to retire at age 65. At 37, with three years' experience as a recruiter, Rachel felt she was in a dead-end job and obtained a transfer to the wage and salary department. Two years later the company planned a new facility and made Rachel the plant's HR manager. She was selected because of her broad experience in recruiting and compensation—two major concerns in starting the new operation.

Rachel initiated the transfer through self-nomination because she wanted to further her career development. But the real opportunity she obtained from the transfer was a chance to grow—a chance to develop new skills and knowledge.

Besides self-nomination, groups outside the organization may help one's career. For years, men have used private clubs and professional associations to form "old-boy networks," which afford growth opportunities and often a fair amount of exposure among organizational decision makers.[47] Women who are excluded from the informal networks in an organization can miss the exposure and visibility needed to gain career advancement. The result may be a "glass ceiling" where women can see the higher rungs on the corporate ladder but are blocked from reaching them.[48] However, a short piece in the *Wall Street Journal* noted:

Women's groups

> Women's groups spring up in a variety of occupations to aid members. These groups tend to push career advancement rather than general women's issues. Women in Information Processing, Washington, D.C., helps its 4,000 members achieve industry visibility in part by lining up speaking engagements.
>
> The National Association of Professional Saleswomen, Sacramento, stresses education for members. Its chapters in 35 cities hold monthly meetings to discuss sales training. Formed in 1980 with 900 members, it now has 5,000 saleswomen. The National Association of Black Women Entrepreneurs, Detroit . . . helps its 3,000 members get information about business opportunities for minorities.[49]

Community service activities provide opportunities for both growth and recognition. United Way campaigns, chamber of commerce committees, arts organizations, and other community groups offer even junior managers opportunities to use their leadership skills. Learning to work with other volunteers uncovers different management skills and exposes one to different styles of leadership. Accounting, law, consulting, and other professional service firms often expect their members to be active as a means of developing new business. In large organizations, community involvement may be an effective way to gain visibility within the company. And the network of contacts outside the company may be useful in looking for another job or beginning an entrepreneurial venture.

International experience.   For those who aspire to senior operating or staff positions, international experience is becoming an increasingly important growth opportunity. Among major domestic corporations, a growing percentage of sales is often derived from international operations, particularly in industries such as automobiles, pharmaceuticals, computers, electronics, and aerospace. As the proportion of international sales and operations grows, the importance of international experience increases, becoming a virtual prerequisite in global corporations such as Coca Cola, Eli Lily, Procter & Gamble, Ford, and General Dynamics. Being overseas, however, does not mean losing touch with the home office or home-country managers. Consider this quote about a vice president at General Dynamics, a major military defense contractor.

> William L. Godsey had headed the General Dynamics Corporation's European operations in Brussels for three years when he got a call from Frederick S. Wood, a vice president at St. Louis headquarters. Mr. Wood thought Mr. Godsey should apply for the newly opened job of vice president for international programs at the company's Pomona, Calif., division.

Mr. Godsey did just that. He got the job. . . . "If Fred hadn't called," Mr. Godsey said, "I would never have known the job existed."[50]

Whether international experience is gained by working internationally for a company based in one's home country or working for a foreign company, a variety of considerations affect the HR department and the individual. Figure 11-7 suggests some of those issues.[51]

Human Resource–Supported Career Development

Career development should not rely solely on individual efforts. As the discussion about accepting an international job suggests, career development often involves the assistance of managers and the HR department. Perhaps even more important than assistance is guidance. Without coaching from operating managers or the HR department, employees may take actions that are not in the best interest of the company or themselves. For example, employees may move to another employer, as in the West Coast research example, or may be unaware of opportunities to further their careers.

John Deere

The John Deere career information seminar is a good example. It helps employees with education and information. The brochure handed out to attendees describes the range of jobs available at the job site. HR representatives also are available. But since the meetings are voluntary and on the employees' own time, the HR department is able to emphasize that career development is the employee's responsibility.

There can be little doubt that employees want such company-based programs if the results from the Harvester Works are representative. In the first two weeks after the program was announced, 50 percent of the eligible salaried employees enrolled in the program. For employees who attended the seminar, there was a 50 percent improvement in their understanding of career planning compared with a control group that did not participate. And comments from the participants have been favorable.[52]

The HR department does more to help employees' careers than just conduct career information seminars. For example, the training and development programs discussed in Chapter 10 are a big stepping-stone in most people's careers.

HR goals

In addition to helping employees, the HR department seeks many goals through its career planning activities. A key goal is to develop an internal pool of talent. Career planning can help trainers identify training needs among employees. It also can be used to help guide members of protected classes into jobs where the employer has an underutilization of women and minority group members. Improvements in performance, loyalty to the company, and motivation also may be outcomes of career planning. Simply put, career plan-

Figure 11-7   **Accepting an Overseas Job**

Career development increasingly means gaining international experience, especially for those working in large global corporations. Unlike Europeans, who are frequently exposed to different cultures and languages, North Americans (particularly U.S. citizens) often have little contact with foreign nationals, foreign culture, and different languages. Europeans are typically educated in more than just their native tongue; it is not uncommon for educated Europeans to know two or three languages and to have been exposed to other cultures within Europe. Although the language of business and science is dominated by the worldwide use of English, understanding a foreign language offers insights into a culture and its people. When one is seeking international job experience, language skills are an important career development consideration, leading many HR departments to arrange intensive language and cultural education courses.

Although the acceptance of an international job often includes additional compensation for living costs, many HR departments also assist transferees with moving, housing, banking, language training, child education, job location assistance for spouses, and other needs peculiar to overseas assignments. An international move also requires considering the impact such a move can have on family members, ranging from finding suitable housing to finding traditional foods of expected quality, which is a particular concern in developing countries. Even the availability of common household appliances such as refrigerators and washers may be different, requiring more frequent shopping or different approaches to household chores.

Legal conditions change too. Tax laws can be considerably different, for example. In many developed countries, taxes are much higher. This often includes higher income taxes and much higher sales taxes that are sometimes called value-added taxes, which can substantially increase the cost of major consumer purchases such as automobiles. Living in another country does not always eliminate home-country taxes, leading some transferees to face considerable tax increases. For example, selling a home in the United States before moving overseas can lead to capital gains taxes on the profit. Some relocation plans by HR departments include "tax equalization" adjustments so that the extra taxes associated with foreign work do not burden the employee. Even relatively simple matters of reviewing wills and leaving a power of attorney should be considered.

The HR department also must adjust benefits to comply with national laws and appropriate coverages, especially with respect to health care. Travel benefits, such as return trips to the home country for vacations, business, and emergencies, should be reviewed.

In accepting a job for a foreign employer, whether in the home country or overseas, many of these considerations apply. Although work with a foreign company can be a developmental experience, some unique issues may arise. For example, working for a foreign company in the home country helps one sidestep many legal and tax concerns. However, learning the employer's home-country language often becomes crucial for advancement to senior positions. Otherwise, informal acceptance—and therefore career progress—is almost certain to be limited. In many foreign companies, the seniormost positions are reserved for home-country nationals, creating a "glass ceiling" on career progress. Informal rules and formal assistance from the HR department also may be different. For example, salaries in foreign companies are often considered highly confidential; discussing one's salary among peers can be seen as highly inappropriate even though such conversations are common in North American–based firms.

For both the HR department and the transferee, an international assignment or work with a foreign employer may be a powerful career development experience. However, such opportunities involve complex considerations.

ning makes good business sense; it can enhance profits, productivity, and employees' quality of work life, as the following example underscores:

One bank's career counseling program saved $1.95 million in a year. This estimate, based on tabulations by an industrial engineer, reflected a 65 percent reduction in turnover, a 25 percent increase in productivity, and a 75 percent increase in promotability.[53]

However, for the benefits of career planning and development to accrue to the organization and its people, the HR department must enlist the support of management, particularly top management.

Management support. The HR department's efforts to encourage career development have little impact unless they are supported by managers. Commitment by top management is crucial. Without it, middle-level managers may show much less support of their subordinates' careers. This commitment must go beyond mere permission; top management must lead through example by taking an active interest in the career plans of middle-level managers. When executives show an active concern, other managers emulate that behavior. Without broad-based support among all levels of management, others in the organization are likely to ignore career development and place their attention elsewhere. Many North American and European managers do not have a tradition of giving meaningful peer recognition to those who voluntarily support employee development, for example, even though such recognition is common among managers in Japan.

One way North American firms are showing support for career development activities is by monitoring the progress of *fast-trackers,* those who seem destined to make rapid career progress. The act of identifying, tracking, and evaluating those likely to be on the way up the organizational hierarchy sends a message to those involved that they have more than just a job; they have career potential.

Southland Corp., parent company to the 7-Eleven convenience-store chain, has managers file reports twice a year about the promotability of their subordinates. Reports are consolidated on a computer to identify future shortages of talent. These deficits are then addressed through career development activities.

Gulf & Western Industries tracks 125 high-potential executives, and John Deere & Company uses a computer program to track more than 1000 managers.[54]

7-Eleven

Support for the career development of employees varies widely from company to company. However, among the leading companies, the development of successful employees is considered a hallmark of the organization. These successes could not exist without long-term support from generation after generation of top management. McGraw-Hill, the publisher of this book, is one of several examples. At McGraw-Hill:

> The corporate point of view . . . is that management's involvement in career planning helps to ensure that the individual career plans of the employees mesh with the . . . goals of the corporation. In essence, the organization tries to ensure that "the grass is greener at home than across the street."[55]

> In a 10-year period, General Electric produced a highly admirable earnings growth record while 61 of its 360 vice presidents became presidents of other companies. This means GE is producing talent for other companies.
> Donald Burnham was not the first chief engineer at GM to become the head of another company. He left . . . to lead Westinghouse.
> And finally . . . IBM. They give their employees such good training and experience that after five years these individuals can go to almost any company and name their price.[56]

Feedback.   Without feedback about their career development efforts, it is difficult for employees to sustain the years of preparation sometimes needed to reach career goals. The HR department can provide feedback in several ways. One way is to give employees information about job placement decisions. An employee who pursues career development activities and is passed over for promotion may conclude that career development is not worth the effort. Unsuccessful candidates for internal job openings should be told why they did not get the career opportunities they sought. This feedback has three objectives:

1. *To assure* bypassed employees that they are still valued and will be considered for future promotions if they are qualified.

2. *To explain* why they were not selected.

3. *To indicate* what specific career development actions they should undertake.

Care should be exercised not to imply that these actions automatically mean a promotion. Instead, the individual's *candidacy* for selection is influenced by appropriate career development actions.

Feedback about job performance is perhaps the most important feedback an employee gets. As was stated earlier in this chapter, career success rests largely on performance. In the long run, there can be no substitute for doing the job well. Although objective measures of performance are sometimes absent and some promotions are based on "whom you know," most managers are rational and want to promote people who can do the job. If their subordinates are successful, they look good too. To give employees feedback about their job performance, many HR departments develop formal performance evaluation procedures. The resulting feedback allows the employee to adjust his or her performance and career plans. Then job placement actions, developmental opportunities, and compensation decisions can be made that best meet the organization's future needs and the employees' desires. Chapter 12 discusses the importance of performance feedback and the HR department's role.

▶ Summary

Career planning and development are relatively new concepts in many HR departments. In recent years, these departments have begun to recognize the need for more proactive career-related efforts. As a result, some departments provide career education, information, and counseling. However, the primary responsibility for career planning and development rests with the individual employee.

Figure 11-8 gives an overview of career planning and development. The planning process enables employees to identify career goals and the paths to those goals. Then, through developmental activities, the workers seek ways to improve themselves and further their career goals. Even today, most developmental activities are individual and voluntary. Individual efforts include good job performance, favorable exposure, leveraging, and the building of alliances. The HR department becomes involved by providing information and obtaining management support to help make career planning a success for both the employees and the organization.

Career planning does not guarantee success, but without it, employees are seldom ready for the career opportunities that arise. As a result, their career progress may be slowed and the HR department may be unable to fill openings internally.

| Figure 11-8 | A Systems View of Career Planning and Development |

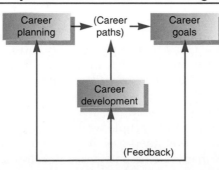

▶ Terms for Review

Career	Life plan
Career path	Exposure
Career planning	Networking
Career development	Mentor
Job families	Sponsor
Job progression ladder	Key subordinates
Career counseling	

▶ Review and Discussion Questions

1. Why should the HR department be concerned about career planning, especially since employees' plans may conflict with the organization's objectives? What advantages does the department expect to receive from assisting in career planning?

2. Explain the reasoning behind the following statement: HR departments should not be involved with career planning since the company's future may change so much that the advice HR gives today may not be the right advice in the future.

3. If you were interested in making a career out of your ability to play a musical instrument, what types of career goals would you set for yourself? How would you find out about the career prospects for musicians before you took your first job?

4. What types of information would you seek from the HR department to help you develop your career plan if you were just starting with a large multinational corporation?

5. Why is international job experience growing in importance to employees and the HR department?

6. Suppose you are assigned to develop a career planning and development program in a large organization with a diverse workforce. What unique concerns might you have because of this diversity?

7. Given the slow growth and downsizing that have occurred in many companies, what challenges does this present for the HR department? How and why should the department help?

8. Suppose a hardworking and loyal employee is passed over for promotion. What would you tell this person?

▶ **Incident 11-1**

The Turnaround at Allied-Signal

When Lawrence A. Bossidy was appointed chief executive officer of Allied-Signal, he was told that the company faced a negative cash flow of more than $870 million over the next two years. Within a year and a half the company produced a $255 million positive cash flow. Bossidy cut the dividend, chopped capital spending, put eight small divisions up for sale, and lopped off 6200 salaried jobs. But rather than just cut costs, he was concerned about building the company for the future. As *Fortune* reported:

> Bossidy then told his three executive vice presidents and President Alan Belzer to lead teams to prepare detailed plans to improve college recruiting, career development, and training and education. They benchmarked the best—companies like Corning, Bechtel, Hewlett-Packard, Johnson & Johnson—and held focus groups to learn how employees felt human resources could help their careers more. Says aerospace head Daniel Burnham: "Can you imagine this much senior management attention? . . . But it is the heart of what we do."[57]

1. Given that Allied-Signal is an aerospace, automotive, chemical conglomerate, explain Mr. Burnham's closing comment: "But it is the heart of what we do."

2. Assuming you were in Bossidy's role as CEO, what reasons might you give to the board of directors for assembling such high-level talent to focus on career development and related HR issues?

▶ **References**

1. Vivian Brownstein, "The Job Engine Begins to Rev," *Fortune,* Nov. 15, 1993, p. 25.

2. Walter Kiechel III, "A Manager's Career in the New Economy," *Fortune,* Apr. 4, 1994, p. 68.

3. Lewis Newman, "Career Management: Start with Goals," *Personnel Journal,* April 1989, pp. 91–92. See also William J. Kuchta, "Options in Career Paths," *Personnel Journal,* December 1989, pp. 28, 31–32.

4. Lorraine M. Carulli, Cheryl L. Noroian, and Cindy Levine, "Employee-Driven Career Development," *Personnel Administrator,* March 1989, pp. 67–68, 70.

5. Stratford Sherman, "A Brave New Darwinian Workplace," *Fortune,* Jan. 25, 1993, pp. 50–56.

6. Jack Keller and Chris Piotrowski, "Career Development Programs in *Fortune* 500 Firms," *Psychological Reports,* vol. 61, 1987, pp. 920–922.

7. Jerry W. Gilley, "Career Development as a Partnership," *Personnel Administrator,* April 1988, pp. 62–68.

8. Phil Farish, "Why People Leave," *Personnel Administrator,* August 1988, p. 18.

9. Richard K. Broszeit, "If I Had My Druthers . . . ," *Personnel Journal,* October 1986, pp. 84–90.

10. Two interesting articles offer added richness to the example of "Joe." The first is a conversation with Bob Beck, the senior human resource executive at Bank of America; the second offers a thirty-year perspective on "making it to the top." Martha I. Finney, "A Matter of Balance," *Personnel Administrator,* October 1988, pp. 66–70; Joel E. Ross and Darab Unwalla, "Making It to the Top: A Thirty Year Perspective," *Personnel,* April 1988, pp. 71–78.

11. Joseph A. Raelin, "An Examination of Deviant/Adaptive Behaviors in the Organizational Careers of Professionals," *Academy of Management Review,* vol. 9, no. 3, 1984, pp. 413–427; William L. Mihal, Patricia A. Sorce, and Thomas E. Conte, "A Process Model of Individual Career Decision Making," *Academy of Management Review,* vol. 9, no. 1, 1984, pp. 95–103.

12. This individual-organization dichotomy is useful for distinguishing between the role of the individual and the role of the personnel department. For a more detailed discussion of this distinction, see Dorothy Heider and Elliot N. Kushell, "I Can Develop My Management Skills By: _____" *Personnel Journal,* June 1984, pp. 52–54.

13. Martin G. Friedman, "Ten Steps to Objective Appraisals," *Personnel Journal,* June 1986, pp. 66–72.

14. Ellryn Mirides and Andre Cote, "Women in Management: Strategies for Removing the Barriers," *Personnel Administrator,* April 1980, pp. 25–28, 48; Friedman, op. cit., pp. 191–213.

15. David Kirkpatrick, "Could AT&T Rule the World?" *Fortune,* May 17, 1993, p. 66.

16. William F. Rothenbach, "Career Development: Ask Your Employees for Their Opinions," *Personnel Administrator,* November 1982, pp. 43–46, 51.

17. Loretta D. Foxman and Walter L. Polsky, "Aid in Employee Career Development," *Personnel Journal,* January 1990, pp. 22, 24.

18. Ibid., p. 51.

19. Bernadette Steele, Jerold R. Bratkovich, and Thomas Rollins, "Implementing Strategic Redirection through the Career Management System," *Human Resource Planning,* December 1990, pp. 241–263.

20. Friedman, op. cit., p. 200.

21. Karl A. Hickerson and Richard C. Anderson, "Career Development: Whose Responsibility?" *Personnel Administrator,* June 1982, p. 46.

22. "HRM Update," *Personnel Administrator,* March 1987, p. 26.

23. Ibid., p. 28.

24. Amiel T. Sharon, "Skills Bank Tracks Talent, Not Training," *Personnel Journal,* June 1988, pp. 44–49.

25. Hickerson and Anderson, op. cit.

26. Edward G. Verlander, "Incorporating Career Counseling into Management Development," *Journal of Management Development,* vol. 5, no. 3, 1986, pp. 36–45; Peter C. Cairo, "Counseling in Industry: A Selected Review of the Literature," *Personnel Psychology,* vol. 36, 1983, pp. 1–18.

27. Charles R. Stoner and Richard I. Hartman, "Family Responsibilities and Career Progress: The God, the Bad, and the Ugly," *Business Horizons,* May–June, 1990, pp. 7–14; Douglas T. Hall and Judith Richter, "Balancing Work Life and Home Life: What Can Organizations Do to Help?" *Academy of Management Executive,* August 1988, pp. 213–223.

28. Cairo, op. cit.

29. Hickerson and Anderson, op. cit.

30. Benson Rosen and Thomas H. Jerdee, "Middle and Late Career Problems: Causes, Consequences, and Research Needs," *Human Resource Planning,* December 1990, pp. 59–70.

31. Joseph Weber, Lisa Driscoll, and Richard Brandt, "Farewell Fast Track," *Business Week,* Dec. 10, 1990, pp. 192–200.

32. Jaclyn Fierman, "Beating the Middle Midlife Career Crisis," *Fortune,* Sept. 6, 1993, pp. 52–62.

33. Ronald E. Gerevas, "Keeping Good Managers Happy on a Slower Track," *Business Month,* May 1989, p. 79.

34. Paul L. Blocklyn, "Employee Retraining Programs," *Personnel,* November 1988, pp. 64–66.

35. Benson Rosen and Thomas H. Jerdee, "Middle and Late Career Problems: Causes, Consequences, and Research Needs," *Human Resource Planning,* December 1990, pp. 59–70; Amy Saltzman, "Sidestepping Your Way to the Top," *U.S. News & World Report,* Sept. 17, 1990, p. 61.

36. Lee Smith, "Burned-Out Bosses," *Fortune,* July 25, 1994, pp. 44–51.

37. Fierman, op. cit., pp. 52–53.

38. Eugene E. Jennings, *The Mobile Manager,* New York: McGraw-Hill, 1976.

39. Justin Martin, "Employees Are Fighting Back," *Fortune,* Aug. 8, 1994, p. 12. See also Eugene E. Jennings, "How to Develop Your Management Talent Internally," *Personnel Administrator,* July 1981, pp. 20–23; Teresa Carson and John A. Byrne, "Fast-Track Kids," *Business Week,* Nov. 10, 1986, pp. 90–92.

40. Jennings, *The Mobile Manager*; Walter L. Polsky and Loretta D. Foxman, "Career Counselors," *Personnel Journal,* December 1986, pp. 35–38.

41. William B. Werther, Jr., "Management Turnover Implications of Career Mobility," *Personnel Administrator,* February 1977, pp. 63–66. See also Ellen F. Jacofsky and Lawrence H. Peters, "The Hypothesized Effects of Ability in the Turnover Process," *Academy of Management Review,* January 1983, pp. 46–49.

42. Werther, op. cit.

43. Robert G. Wright and William B. Werther, Jr., "Mentors at Work," *Journal of Management Development,* vol. 10, no. 3, 1991, pp. 25–32. See also Terri A. Scandura, "Mentorship and Career Mobility: An Empirical Investigation," *Journal of Organizational Behavior,* vol. 13, 1992, pp. 169–174; Kathy E. Kram and Lynn A. Isabella, "Mentoring Alternatives: The Role of Peer Relationships in Career Development," *Academy of Management Journal,* vol. 28, no. 1, 1985, pp. 110–132.

44. James A. Wilson and Nancy S. Elman, "Organizational Benefits of Mentoring," *Academy of Management Executive,* vol. 4, no. 4, 1990, pp. 88–94. See also Jennings, "How to Develop Your Management Talent Internally."

45. John F. Veiga, "Plateaued versus Nonplateaued Managers: Career Patterns, Attitudes, and Path Potential," *Academy of Management Journal,* September 1981, pp. 566–578.

46. Jennings, *The Mobile Manager.*

47. Kathleen Cannings and Claude Montmarquette, "Managerial Momentum: A Simultaneous Model of the Career Progress of Male and Female Managers," *Industrial and Labor Relations Review,* January 1991, pp. 212–228.

48. Ibid. See also Bernice R. Sandler, "Women as Mentors: Myths and Commandments," *The Chronicle of Higher Education,* Mar. 10, 1993, p. B3; Jaclyn Fierman, "Why Women Still Don't Hit the Top," *Fortune,* July 30, 1990, pp. 40–62.

49. Robert S. Greenberger, "Women's Groups Spring Up in a Variety of Occupations to Aid Members," *The Wall Street Journal,* Western ed., Jan. 11, 1983, p. 1.

50. Claudia H. Deutsch, "Getting the Brightest to Go Abroad," *The New York Times,* National ed., June 17, 1990, sec. 3, part 2, p. 25.

51. Rita Bennet, "Solving the Dual International Career Dilemma," *HR News,* January 1993, p. C5. See also Helen Benjamin, "Expatriate Banking: The Forgotten Detail," *HR News,* January 1993, pp. C2, C4; John P. Senko, "Is the Foreign Service Premium Becoming Obsolete?" *HR News,* January 1993, p. C12.

52. Hickerson and Anderson, op. cit.

53. Milan Moravec, "A Cost-Effective Career Planning Program Requires a Strategy," *Personnel Administrator,* June 1982, p. 28.

54. William M. Bulkeley, "The Fast Track: Computers Help Firms Decide Whom to Promote," *The Wall Street Journal,* Eastern ed., Sept. 18, 1985, p. 25.

55. "Is Career Development the Answer?" *Training and Development Journal,* March 1981, pp. 81–82.

56. Jennings, "How to Develop Your Management Talent Internally," p. 20.

57. Thomas A. Stewart, "Allied-Signal's Turnaround Blitz," *Fortune,* Nov. 30, 1992, pp. 72–76.

12

To embed our values, we give our people 360-degree evaluations, with input from superiors, peers, and subordinates. These are the roughest evaluations you can get, because people hear things about themselves they've never heard before.

JOHN F. WELCH[1]

Performance appraisal continues to be a perennial irritant to a substantial number of organizational members.

WILLIAM M. FOX[2]

Performance Appraisal

CHAPTER OBJECTIVES

After studying this chapter, you should be able to:

1. DISCUSS the manager's and HR department's role in performance appraisals.

2. EXPLAIN the uses of performance appraisals.

3. IDENTIFY the strengths and common shortfalls of most performance appraisal systems.

4. DESCRIBE commonly used appraisal methods.

5. OUTLINE the major considerations in providing employees with performance feedback through an evaluation interview.

6. PLACE performance appraisals in the perspective of other HR tools.

Performance appraisal is the process by which organizations evaluate individual job performance. When it is done correctly, employees, their supervisors, the HR department, and ultimately the organization benefit by ensuring that individual efforts contribute to the strategic focus of the organization. However, performance appraisals are influenced by other activities in the organization and in turn affect the organization's success. Often they can be a part of the way a company executes its strategy.

> When IBM spun off its PC-printer and typewriter business . . . "We concluded that we had to change nearly everything in our business . . ." says Marvin Mann, CEO of the new company, Lexmark International. It parted ways with roughly half its workers, reorganized the rest into new, customer focused units, gave every employee stock options, and created a strict system of performance measurements that forced accountability. The Mann revolution at $1.8 billion-a-year Lexmark has produced . . . a five percentage-point increase in gross profit margins and a huge reduction in debt ahead of schedule.[3]

Appraisals and feedback

Performance appraisals are about employee performance and accountability. In a globally competitive world, companies need high performance. At the same time, employees need feedback on their performance as a guide to future behavior. This need is most evident among newcomers who are trying to understand their jobs and the work setting. Longer-service workers also want positive feedback on the good things they do, although they may resent corrective feedback that feels like criticism.[4] Supervisors and managers must evaluate performance in order to know what actions to take. Specific feedback enables them to help with career planning, training and development, pay increases, promotions, and other placement decisions.

Allied-Signal

> Upon arrival as the CEO of Allied-Signal, Lawrence A. Bossidy assigned his three executive vice presidents to improve key HR activities, which led the HR department to redo its employee appraisal process. "Starting in January, a boss must offer subordinates help such as special training or outside courses to improve weaknesses he or she identifies. Salaried workers will fill out a form listing their skills, describing their career goals, and naming other divisions they would like to work for. This information will create a database of people who might fill various openings through the company and will become an agenda for an annual, informal, but mandatory 'How'm I doing?' chat with the boss separate from appraisals."[5]

HR departments use the information gathered through performance appraisals to evaluate the success of recruitment, selection, orientation, placement, training, and other activities. Although informal and ongoing appraisals on a day-to-day basis are necessary to a smooth operation, these methods are insufficient for the HR department's needs. Formal appraisals are needed to help managers with placement, pay, and other HR decisions. In a study of 324 organizations in southern California, for example, 94 percent had a formal appraisal system. This survey research revealed that the major uses of appraisals were for compensation (74.9 percent), performance improvement (48.4 percent), feedback (40.4 percent), placement-related decisions (40.1 percent), and documentation (30.2 percent).[6] Figure 12-1 describes these and other uses.

Yet even in otherwise well-managed organizations, appraisals are associated with problems. Supervisors and managers often view formal appraisals as unneeded. They already know how their employees are performing, so why

Why do a performance appraisal?

Figure 12-1	**Uses of Performance Appraisals**

■ *Performance improvement.* Performance feedback allows the employee, the manager, and personnel specialists to intervene with appropriate actions to improve performance.

■ *Compensation adjustments.* Performance evaluations help decision makers determine who should receive pay raises. Many firms grant part or all of their pay increases and bonuses on the basis of merit, which is determined mostly through performance appraisals.

■ *Placement decisions.* Promotions, transfers, and demotions are usually based on past or anticipated performance. Often promotions are a reward for past performance.

■ *Training and development needs.* Poor performance may indicate a need for retraining. Likewise, good performance may indicate untapped potential that should be developed.

■ *Career planning and development.* Performance feedback guides career decisions about specific career paths one should investigate.

■ *Staffing process deficiencies.* Good or bad performance implies strengths or weaknesses in the personnel department's staffing procedures.

■ *Informational inaccuracies.* Poor performance may indicate errors in job analysis information, human resource plans, or other parts of the personnel management information system. Reliance on inaccurate information may have led to inappropriate hiring, training, or counseling decisions.

■ *Job-design errors.* Poor performance may be a symptom of ill-conceived job designs. Appraisals help diagnose these errors.

■ *Equal employment opportunity.* Accurate performance appraisals that actually measure job-related performance ensure that internal placement decisions are not discriminatory.

■ *External challenges.* Sometimes performance is influenced by factors outside the work environment, such as family, financial, health, or other personal matters. If these factors are uncovered through appraisals, the human resource department may be able to provide assistance.

■ *Feedback to human resources.* Good or bad performance throughout the organization indicates how well the human resource function is performing.

spend precious time going through some form developed by the HR department? In addition, the design of the system may encourage unintended actions by employees and supervisors, as happened in one part of Xerox.

Xerox

Xerox's main copier organization, the Reprographic Business Group, was getting few benefits from its performance appraisal approach, which had been in place for more than twenty years. The old system provided annual performance reviews that were based on employees' documentation of their accomplishments during the previous year. The manager developed a written appraisal and a numerical rating, ranging from 1 (unsatisfactory performance) to 5 (exceptional performance). The higher the rating, the higher an employee's raise.

Under the old system, more than 95 percent of all ratings were a 3 ("meets and sometimes exceeds expected performance") or a 4 ("consistently exceeds expected performance"), with the majority being a 4. In fact, so many people received a rating of 4 that a rating of 3 was seen as substandard. Contributing to the ratings problem was the lack of objectives among managers and subordinates at the beginning of the evaluation year. Since ratings were tied to compensation, the inflated numerical rating meant that a higher raise was more likely.

To overcome these problems, a new process called "Performance Feedback and Development" was created by a task force of senior HR personnel and middle managers. The new system requires employee objectives to be set at the outset of the year and approved by a second-level manager. An interim review is conducted after six months to discuss good and bad performance, update objectives, and review progress.

Discussion of pay increases is no longer coupled to the performance review; raises are discussed one or two months later. The numerical rating has been dropped altogether, although a written summary is included with the evaluation.

When Xerox is setting out the next year's targets, financial and people-related goals are discussed, but so are development objectives that relate to one's specialty and to general skills such as time management, human relations, and communications.[7]

As this example emphasizes, an organization cannot have just *any* appraisal system; the system must be effective, accepted, and properly used. With those conditions met, performance appraisal systems can identify needed improvements in HR information related to job analysis and design (Chapter 5), human resource planning (Chapter 6), staffing (Chapters 7 and 8), orientation and placement (Chapter 9), training and development (Chapter 10), and career planning (Chapter 11). Besides the uses suggested in Figure 12-1, performance appraisals are crucial for focusing employees on strategic goals and objectives and for developing replacement summaries for succession planning and learning objectives for training and development.

▶ Elements of Performance Appraisal Systems

Figure 12-2 shows the elements of an effective appraisal system. Appraisal approaches must identify performance-related standards, measure those criteria, and then give feedback to employees and the HR department. If performance standards or measures are not job-related, the evaluation can lead to inaccurate or biased results, harming the managers' relationship with their employees and violating equal employment opportunity rulings. Without feedback, improvement in human behavior is not likely and the department will not have accurate records in its HR information system on which to base decisions ranging from job design to compensation.

The HR department usually designs and administers the company's performance appraisal system. Centralization ensures uniformity. Although the HR department may develop different approaches for managers, professionals, workers, and other groups, uniformity within each group is needed to ensure comparability of results. The department itself seldom evaluates actual performance, however. According to one study, the employee's immediate supervisor performs the evaluation 92 percent of the time[8] because the immediate supervisor is often in the best position to make the appraisal. However, multiple raters—including peers and even subordinates, sometimes called "360-degree" evaluations because the person is being evaluated from all directions—offer additional perspectives at progressive companies such as General Electric, General Motors, and AT&T. At AT&T, for example, 800 high-level executives have rated their superiors and have been rated in return.[9] As jobs and teams become more fluid, some companies use electronic mail (E-mail) to track who people interact with and who should be the evaluators:

"360-degree" evaluations

| Figure 12-2 | **Key Elements of Performance Appraisal Systems** |

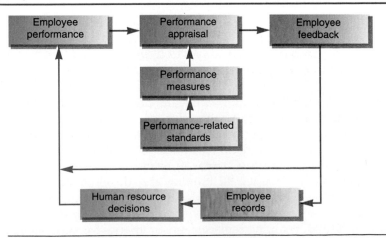

On Wall Street they watch your E-mail. The bosses at one big investment bank aren't snooping on what you say—but whom you say it to. Those very recipients are later asked to evaluate you. The theory: New teams form constantly and a staffer can have many superiors, so the E-mail check helps keep reviews fair.[10]

The appraisal should create an accurate picture of an individual's *typical* job performance. Appraisals are not done just to uncover poor performance; acceptable and good results also must be identified so that they can be reinforced. To achieve this goal, appraisal systems should be job-related and practical, include standards, and use dependable measures.[11] *Job-related* means that the system evaluates critical behaviors that constitute job success, as identified in the job analysis process discussed in Chapter 5. If the evaluation is not job-related, it is invalid. Without validity and reliability, the system may discriminate in violation of equal opportunity laws.

Practicality

A *practical* system is understood by evaluators and employees. A complicated, impractical approach may cause resentment, confusion, and nonuse.

Standardization

A *standardized* system within the organization is helpful because it allows the establishment of uniform practices. A standardized system often has well-thought-out performance standards and measures.

Performance Standards

Standards

Appraisal systems require *performance standards,* which serve as benchmarks against which performance is measured. To be effective, standards should relate to the desired results of each job.[12] As was discussed in Chapter 5, job analysis uncovers specific performance criteria by analyzing the performance of current employees. Perhaps no better example of detailed work standards exists than at United Parcel Service (UPS), where more than 1000 industrial engineers study and time every aspect of worker performance. Consider this quote from the *Wall Street Journal:*

UPS

> Joseph Polise . . . bounds from his brown delivery truck and towards an office building. . . . A few paces behind him, Marjorie Cusack, a UPS industrial engineer, clutches a digital timer.
>
> She counts his steps and times his contact with customers, traffic, detours, doorbells, walkways, stairways, and coffee breaks.
>
> "We don't use the standards as hammers, but they do give accountability," says Larry P. Breakiron, the company's senior vice president for engineering. "Our ability to manage labor and hold it accountable is the key to our success."[13]

To hold employees accountable, a written record of the standards should exist and employees should be advised of those standards before the evaluation occurs. Ideally, the appraisal of each employee's performance should be based on actual performance of the critical elements identified through job analysis.[14] The Xerox example earlier in this chapter meets these standards.

Performance Measures

Performance evaluation also requires dependable *performance measures,* the ratings used to evaluate performance. To be helpful, they must be easy to use, be reliable, and report on the critical behaviors that determine performance. Dependable *measures* also allow others—using the same measures applied against the same standards—to reach the same conclusions about performance, adding to the reliability of the appraisal system. For example, a telephone company supervisor must observe each operator's:

Telephone operators

- *Use of company procedures:* staying calm, applying tariff rates for phone calls, and following company rules and regulations

- *Pleasant phone manners:* speaking clearly and courteously

- *Call-placement accuracy:* placing operator-assisted calls accurately

These observations can be made directly or indirectly. *Direct* observation occurs when the rater actually sees the performance. *Indirect* observation, which is less accurate, occurs when the rater can evaluate only substitutes for actual performance; these substitutes are called constructs. For example, a supervisor's monitoring of an operator's calls is direct observation; a written test for telephone operators about company procedures for handling emergency calls is a construct and thus only an indirect observation of actual on-line performance.

Constructs

To test how well operators might respond to emergency calls, an independent telephone company developed a paper-and-pencil test. The test was intended to determine whether each operator knew exactly how to proceed with emergency calls. After several hundred operators were tested, it was noticed that fast readers scored better. The HR department decided to scrap the test and use false emergency calls to evaluate the operators.

Objective measures

Performance measures also may be objective or subjective. *Objective performance measures* are indications of job performance that are verifiable by others and are usually quantitative. For example, if two supervisors monitor an operator's calls, they can count the number of misdialings. The results are objective and verifiable, since each supervisor gets the same percentage of call-placement accuracy.

With millions of workers using video-display terminals, new ways of objectively measuring employee performance are emerging. About one-third of these workers are in jobs that can be scrutinized automatically by computer. With program modifications, most master computers can "not only process information from each employee's terminal but also

Computer measures

| Figure 12-3 | Types and Accuracy of Performance Measures | | |

TYPES OF PERFORMANCE MEASURE	RELATIVE DEGREE OF ACCURACY	
	DIRECT	INDIRECT
OBJECTIVE	Very high	High
SUBJECTIVE	Low	Very low

measure, record and tabulate dozens of details about how efficiently the worker is putting information into the machine."[15]

"Airline-reservation computers, for example, closely measure how long individual clerks take to handle each customer and the amount of time . . . between calls."[16]

Of course, having "Big Brother" constantly monitor performance can be psychologically oppressive. HR specialists need to consider the impact on morale. Otherwise, legislation or union efforts may force changes.

Subjective measures

Subjective performance measures are ratings that are based on the personal standards or opinions of those doing the evaluation and are not verifiable by others. Figure 12-3 compares the accuracy of objective and subjective measures. When subjective measures are also indirect, accuracy becomes even lower. For example, measurement of an operator's phone manners is done subjectively; supervisors must use their personal opinions of good or bad manners. Since the evaluation is subjective, accuracy is usually low even if the supervisor observes the operator directly. Accuracy is likely to be even lower when the rater uses an indirect measure, or construct, such as an essay test of phone manners. HR specialists always prefer objective and direct measures of performance.[17]

▶ Performance Appraisal Challenges

The design of the performance appraisal system often contributes to the challenges facing HR professionals. Important challenges include legal constraints, rater biases, and appraisal acceptance.

Legal Constraints

Performance appraisals must be free of illegal discrimination. Whatever form of evaluation the HR department uses, it should be both reliable and valid, as was explained in Chapter 4. Otherwise, placement decisions may be challenged because they violate equal employment laws or other laws. Nowhere are such suits more likely than in cases of "wrongful discharge," which occur when someone is improperly fired. They also arise when decisions involve lay-offs, demotions, or failure to promote.[18]

Key case

General Motors, for example, was found guilty of discrimination in *Rowe v. General Motors* because a supervisor used an appraisal method that relied almost entirely on subjective evaluations of initiative and attitude. The courts ruled that a company could not rely solely on the recommendations of supervisors in selecting employees for promotion where standards used by the foremen were vague and subjective.[19]

Rater Biases

The problem with subjective measures is the opportunity they provide for bias. *Bias* is the inaccurate distortion of a measurement. Although training in how to conduct performance appraisals can reduce bias,[20] bias often occurs when raters do not remain emotionally unattached while they evaluate employee performance. The most common rater biases include:[21]

Biases

- The halo effect
- The error of central tendency
- Leniency and strictness bias
- Cross-cultural biases
- Personal prejudice
- The recency effect

The halo effect.   The *halo effect* occurs when the rater's personal opinion of the employee influences the measurement of performance. For example, if a supervisor likes an employee, that opinion may distort estimates of the employee's performance. This problem is most severe when raters must evaluate personality traits (instead of behaviors), their friends, or people they strongly dislike.[22]

The error of central tendency.   Some raters do not like to rate employees as effective or ineffective, and so they distort the ratings to make each employee appear average. On rating forms, this distortion causes evaluators to avoid checking extremes, such as very poor or excellent. Instead, they place their marks near the center of the rating sheet. Thus the term *error of central tendency* has been applied to this bias. HR departments sometimes unintentionally encourage this behavior by requiring raters to provide written justification of extremely high or low ratings.

Leniency and strictness bias.   The *leniency bias* results when raters tend to be easy in evaluating the performance of employees. Such raters see all employee performance as good and rate it favorably. The *strictness bias* is the opposite; it results from raters being too harsh in their evaluations. Sometimes the strictness bias results because the rater wants others to think he or she is a "tough judge" of people's performance. Both leniency and strictness errors more commonly occur when performance standards are vague.[23]

Cross-cultural biases.   Every rater holds expectations about human behavior that are based on his or her culture. When people are expected to evaluate others from different cultures, they may apply their cultural expectations to someone who has a different set of beliefs or behaviors. In Denmark, for example, many employees and organizations resisted the use of formal performance appraisals for many years on the grounds that they were inappropriate for Danes. In many Asian cultures the elderly are treated with greater respect and are held in higher esteem than they are in many western cultures. If a young worker is asked to rate an older subordinate, this cultural value of "respect and esteem" may bias the rating. Similarly, in some Arabic cultures women are expected to play a very subservient role, especially in public. Assertive women may receive biased ratings because of these cross-cultural differences. With greater cultural diversity and the movement of employees across international borders, this potential source of bias becomes more likely.

International issues

Personal prejudice.   A rater's dislike for a group or class of people may distort the ratings those people receive. For example, some HR departments have noticed that male supervisors give undeserved low ratings to women who hold "traditionally male jobs." Sometimes raters are unaware of their prejudice, and this makes such biases more difficult to overcome. Nevertheless, specialists should pay close attention to patterns in appraisals that suggest prejudice. Such prejudice prevents effective evaluations and may violate antidiscrimination laws. Whereas the halo bias affects one's judgment of an individual, prejudice affects one's judgment of entire groups. When prejudice affects the ratings of protected class members, this form of discrimination can lead to equal employment violations.

The recency effect.   When one uses subjective performance measures, ratings are affected strongly by the employee's most recent actions. Recent actions—either good or bad—are more likely to be remembered by the rater.

Reducing rater bias.   When subjective performance measures must be used, biases can be reduced through training, feedback, and the proper selection of performance appraisal techniques. Training for raters should involve three steps. First, biases and their causes should be explained. Second, the role of performance appraisals in employee decisions should be explained to stress the need for impartiality and objectivity. Third, if subjective measures are to be used, raters should apply them as part of their training. For example, classroom exercises may require evaluation of the trainer or of videotapes showing workers and working situations. Mistakes uncovered during simulated evaluations then can be corrected through additional training or counseling.

Merck

Merck & Company, a worldwide pharmaceutical company, developed a new performance appraisal system and pilot tested it in three divisions. Before it was made a companywide program, a formal training program was developed for all salaried employees. The training explained the new forms, the rating criteria, and how the approach would relate to the company's compensation program. Higher-level employees were trained in reviewing the ratings of others and administering the program.[24]

Once subjective performance measures move out of the classroom and into practice, raters should get feedback about their previous ratings.[25] Whether ratings prove relatively accurate or inaccurate, feedback helps raters adjust their behavior accordingly. HR departments also can reduce distortion through the careful selection of performance appraisal techniques. For ease of discussion, these techniques are grouped into those which focus on past performance and those which focus on future performance.

▶ Past-Oriented Appraisal Methods

The importance of performance evaluations has led academicians and practitioners to create many methods to appraise past performance. Most of these techniques represent a direct attempt to minimize particular problems found in other approaches. No single technique is perfect; each has advantages and disadvantages.[26]

Pros and cons of past-oriented appraisals

Past-oriented approaches have the advantage of dealing with performance that has already occurred and to some degree can be measured. The obvious disadvantage is that past performance cannot be changed. But when their past performance is evaluated, employees can get feedback that may lead to renewed efforts at improved performance. The most widely used appraisal techniques that have an orientation to the past include:

Past-oriented approaches

- Rating scales
- Checklists
- Forced choice method
- Critical incident method
- Accomplishment records

- Behaviorally anchored rating scales
- Field review method
- Performance tests and observations
- Comparative evaluation approaches

Rating Scales

Perhaps the oldest and most widely used form of performance appraisal is the *rating scale,* which requires the rater to provide a subjective evaluation of an individual's performance along a scale from low to high. An example appears in

Figure 12-4. As the figure indicates, the evaluation is based solely on the opinions of the rater, and in many cases the criteria are not directly related to job performance. Although subordinates or peers may use it, the form is usually completed by the supervisor, who checks the most appropriate response for each performance dimension. Responses may be given numerical values to allow an average score to be computed and compared. The number of points attained may be linked to salary increases—so many points equal a raise of some percentage. Other advantages of this method are that it is inexpensive to develop and administer, raters need little training or time to complete the form, and it can be applied to a large number of employees.

Reflections of bias

The disadvantages are numerous. A rater's biases are likely to be reflected in a subjective instrument of this type. Specific criteria may be omitted to make the form applicable to a variety of jobs. For example, "maintenance of equipment" may be left out because it applies to only a few workers, although for some employees it may be the most important part of the job. This omission and others tend to limit specific feedback. These descriptive evaluations also are subject to individual biases and interpretations. When specific performance criteria are hard to identify, the form may rely on irrelevant personality traits that dilute the

---

Figure 12-4   **A Sample Rating Scale for Performance Evaluation**

Instructions: For the following performance factors, please indicate on the rating scale your evaluation of the named employee.

Employee's Name _____   **Department**_____

Rater's Name _____   **Date** _____

	Excellent 5	Good 4	Acceptable 3	Fair 2	Poor 1
1. Dependability	____	____	____	____	____
2. Initiative	____	____	____	____	____
3. Overall output	____	____	____	____	____
4. Attendance	____	____	____	____	____
5. Attitude	____	____	____	____	____
6. Cooperation	____	____	____	____	____
▪ ▪	·	·	·	·	·
▪ ▪	·	·	·	·	·
▪ ▪	·	·	·	·	·
20. Quality of work					
Results	____	____	____	____	____
Totals	____ +	____ +	____ +	____ +	____ = ____

Total Score

meaning of the evaluation. Like the subjective evaluations in the General Motors case discussed earlier, rating scales may prove to be discriminatory.

Checklists

The *checklist* method requires the rater to select words or statements that describe the employee's performance and characteristics. Again, the rater is usually the immediate superior. However, with or without the rater's knowledge, the HR department may assign weights to different items on the checklist depending on each item's importance. The result is called a *weighted checklist*. The weights allow the rating to be quantified so that total scores can be determined. Figure 12-5 shows a portion of a checklist. The weights for each item are in parentheses but usually are omitted from the form the rater sees. If the list contains enough items, it may provide an accurate picture of employee performance. Although this method is practical and standardized, the use of general statements reduces its job-relatedness.[27]

Weighted checklist

The advantages of a checklist are economy, ease of administration, the limited training required of raters, and standardization. The disadvantages include susceptibility to rater biases (especially the halo effect), use of personality criteria instead of performance criteria, misinterpretation of checklist items, and the use of improper weights by the HR department. Another disadvantage is that this approach does not allow the rater to give relative ratings. For exam-

---

Figure 12-5   **An Example of a Weighted-Performance Checklist**

Instructions: Check each of the following items that apply to the named employee's performance.

Employee's Name _____   Department _____

Rater's Name _____   Date _____

Weights		Check Here
(6.5)	**1.** Employee works overtime when asked.	_____
(4.0)	**2.** Employee keeps workstation or desk well organized.	_____
(3.9)	**3.** Employee cooperatively assists others who need help.	_____
(4.3)	**4.** Employee plans actions before beginning job.	_____
•	• •	•
•	• •	•
•	• •	•
(0.2)	**30.** Employee listens to others' advice but seldom follows it.	_____
100.0	Total of all weights.	

ple, on item 1 in the figure, employees who gladly work overtime get the same score as do those who put in overtime unwillingly.

Forced Choice Method

The *forced choice method* requires the rater to choose the most descriptive statement in each pair of statements about the employee being rated. Often both statements in the pair are positive or negative. For example:

1. Learns quickly........................... Works hard.

2. Work is reliable........................Performance is a good example for others.

3. Absent too often.......................Usually tardy.

Sometimes the rater must select the best statement (or even pair of statements) from four choices. However the form is constructed, HR specialists usually code the items on the form into predetermined categories such as learning ability, performance, and interpersonal relations. Then effectiveness can be computed for each category by adding up the number of times each category is selected by the rater. The results then show which areas need further improvement. Again, the supervisor is usually the rater, although subordinates or peers may provide evaluations.

The forced choice method has the advantage of reducing rater bias because some employees must be rated as superior to others. This approach also is easy to administer and fits a wide variety of jobs. Although practical and easily standardized, the general statements may not be specifically job-related. Thus this method may have limited usefulness in helping employees improve their performance. Even worse, an employee may feel slighted when one statement is checked in preference to another. For example, if the rater checks "learns quickly" in number 1 above, the worker may feel that his or her hard work is being overlooked. This method is seldom liked by either the evaluator or the employee because it provides little useful feedback.[28]

Critical Incident Method

The *critical incident method* requires the rater to record statements that describe extremely good or bad behavior related to job performance. The statements are called critical incidents and are usually recorded by the supervisor during the evaluation period for each subordinate. Recorded incidents include a brief explanation of what happened. Several typical entries for a laboratory assistant appear in Figure 12-6. As shown in the figure, both positive and negative incidents are recorded and classified (either as they occur or later by the HR department) into categories such as control of safety hazards, control of scrap material, and employee development.[29]

Figure 12-6	A Critical Incidents Record for a Lab Assistant

Instructions: In each category below, record specific incidents of employee behavior that were either extremely good or extremely poor.

Employee's Name Kay Watts   **Department** Chemistry Lab

Rater's Name Nat Cordoba   **Rating Period of** 10/1   to   12/31

Control of Safety Hazards

Date	Positive Employee Behavior	Date	Negative Employee Behavior
10/12	Reported broken rung on utility ladder and flagged ladder as unsafe.	11/3	Left hose across storeroom aisle.
10/15	Put out small trash fire promptly.	11/27	Smoked in chemical storeroom.

Control of Material Scrap

Date	Positive Employee Behavior	Date	Negative Employee Behavior
10/3	Sorted through damaged shipment of glassware to salvage usable beakers.	11/7	Used glass containers for strong bases, ruining glass.
		11/19	Repeatedly used glass for storage of lye and other bases.
			Poured acid into plastic container, ruining countertop.

Specific feedback

The critical incident method is extremely useful for giving employees job-related feedback. It also reduces the recency bias if raters record incidents throughout the rating period. Of course, the main drawback is that supervisors often do not record incidents as they occur. Many start out recording incidents faithfully but then lose interest. Then, just before the evaluation period ends, they add new entries. When this happens, the recency bias is exaggerated and employees may feel that their supervisors are building a case to support their subjective opinions. Even when the form is filled out over the entire rating period, employees may feel that the supervisor is unwilling to forget negative incidents that occurred months earlier.[30]

Accomplishment Records

Closely related to the critical incident method are *accomplishment records*, which are used primarily by professionals. These are employee-produced listings of accomplishments such as publications, speeches, leadership roles, and other professionally related activities. This information is typically used to generate an annual report detailing the professional's contributions during the year. The report is used by supervisors in determining raises and promotions and in counseling the person about his or her future performance. The interpretation of the listed items may be subjective, and the items are likely to be biased because they include only the "good" things the person did.

Behaviorally Anchored Rating Scales

Behaviorally anchored rating scales are a family of evaluation approaches that identify and evaluate relevant job-related behaviors. Specific named behaviors are used to give the rater reference points in making the evaluation. Since job-related behaviors are used, validity is more likely than with bipolar rating scales or the forced choice method.[31] The most popular approaches are called behavioral expectation scales and behavioral observation scales.[32]

Keying on behaviors

Behavioral expectation scales (BES) use specific named behaviors as benchmarks to help the rater. This method attempts to reduce some of the subjectivity and biases of other approaches to performance measurement. From descriptions of good and bad performance provided by incumbents, peers, and supervisors, job analysts or knowledgeable employees classify behaviors into major categories of job performance. For example, a listing of job-related behaviors for a bartender in the category of customer relations appears in Figure 12-7. Other rating sheets would be assembled for other aspects of the bartender's job, such as the ability to maintain equipment, keep the bar area clean, and mix drinks. Specific behaviors are ranked along a scale—from 1 to 7 in Figure 12-7—by the analyst or by a group of knowledgeable workers.

Behavioral expectation scales are expressed in terms with which the rater and the employee are familiar. The rater, usually the supervisor, can review the identified behavioral anchors and indicate the items the bartender needs to improve. Since these scales are "anchored" by specific behaviors within each category, the supervisor is better able to provide specific feedback to each bartender. If the rater also collects specific incidents during the rating period, the evaluation is apt to be more accurate and more legally defensible and is likely to be a more effective counseling tool.[33] A serious limitation is that raters look only at a limited number of performance categories, such as, in the case of a bartender, customer relations or drink mixing. And each of these categories includes only a limited number of specific behaviors. As in the critical incident method, most supervisors are reluctant to maintain records of specific incidents, and this reduces the effectiveness of this approach when it is time to counsel the employee.

Behavioral observation scales (BOS) use specific named behaviors as benchmarks and require the rater to report the frequency of those behaviors. The behavioral expectation scales discussed above are concerned primarily with defining poor to superior performance; BOS ask the rater to indicate the *fre-*

Figure 12-7	A Behavioral Expectation Scale for a Bartender's Customer Relations

Behavioral Expectation Rating Scale for <u>Hotel Bartender</u>

Performance Category: Customer Relations

Extremely Outstanding Performance	7	You can expect this bartender to help customers in need.
Good Performance	6	You can expect this bartender to calm down arguments before they erupt into fights.
Fairly Good Performance	5	You can expect this bartender to use discretion about whether to continue serving intoxicated customers who are with the other patrons.
Acceptable Performance	4	You can expect this bartender to stop serving drinks to those who are intoxicated and alone.
Fairly Poor Performance	3	You can expect this bartender to make idle conversation with customers who are alone.
Poor Performance	2	You can expect this bartender to check identification of young customers on their first time in the bar.
Extremely Poor Performance	1	You can expect this bartender to pick up customers' drinks, finished or not, with little or no warning at closing time.

quency of the identified behavioral anchors, usually along a five-point scale from "almost never" to "almost always." These differences between behavioral expectation scales and behavioral observation scales can best be seen by contrasting Figures 12-7 and 12-8. In Figure 12-8, the anchors used in Figure 12-7 have been converted into frequency ranges.[34]

Research summary   A pair of researchers found that a year after BOS were installed in a company, senior management reported satisfaction with this method. They believed that this minimized personality disputes, enabled raters to explain low ratings, led to comprehensive reviews, and improved feedback between raters and workers.[35]

Behaviorally anchored rating scales are complex to develop and administer. Their development considers specific job-related behaviors, which appear to make their validity more defensible than is the case with ratings based on sub-

Figure 12-8	Behavioral Observation Scales for a Bartender's Customer Relations

1. You can expect this bartender to help customers in need:

Almost				**Almost**
Never				**Always**
1	2	3	4	5

2. You can expect this bartender to calm down arguments before they erupt into fights:

Almost				**Almost**
Never				**Always**
1	2	3	4	5

.
.
.

7. You can expect this bartender to pick up customers' drinks, finished or not, with little or no warning at closing time.

Almost				**Almost**
Never				**Always**
1	2	3	4	5

jective personality traits. However, this job-specific feature makes them costly and time-consuming to develop since they must be developed for each job.

Field Review Method

Whenever subjective performance measures are used, differences in rater perceptions cause bias. To provide greater standardization in reviews, some employers use the *field review method.* In this method, a skilled representative of the HR department goes into the "field" and assists supervisors with their ratings. The HR specialist solicits from the immediate supervisor specific information about the employee's performance. Then the expert prepares an evaluation that is based on this information. The evaluation is sent to the supervisor for review, changes, approval, and discussion with the employee who was rated. The expert records the rating on whatever specific type of rating form the employer uses. Since a skilled professional is completing the form, reliability and comparability are more likely and rater biases are less common. But the use of skilled professionals makes this approach costly and impractical for many firms. Also, since the supervisor is the primary source of information, bias may still exist.

Costly approach

Performance Tests and Observations

With a limited number of jobs, performance appraisals may be based on a test of knowledge or skills. These tests are particularly appropriate when a company relies on a pay-for-knowledge or pay-for-skills approach to compensation, rewarding employees primarily on the basis of the skills or job knowledge they have mastered. The test may be of the paper-and-pencil variety or may require an actual demonstration of skills. The test must be reliable and validated to be useful. Even then, it is more apt to measure potential than performance. For the method to be job-related, observations should be made under circumstances that are likely to be encountered. Practicality may suffer if the costs of test development or administration are high.

Flight simulators

Pilots at all major airlines are subject to evaluation by airline raters and the Federal Aviation Administration. Evaluations of flying ability are usually made in a flight simulator and in actual flight. The evaluation is based on how well the pilot follows prescribed flight procedures and safety rules. Although testing is expensive, public safety makes this approach practical in addition to being job-related and standardized.

Comparative Evaluation Approaches

Comparative evaluation approaches are a collection of different methods that compare one person's performance with that of coworkers. Usually comparative appraisals are conducted by the supervisor. They are useful for deciding about merit pay increases, promotions, and organizational rewards because they can result in a ranking of employees from best to worst. The most common forms of comparative evaluations are the ranking method, forced distributions, the point allocation method, and paired comparisons. Although these methods are practical and easily standardized, they are subject to bias and offer little job-related feedback. Usually, they are based on the rater's overall subjective evaluation of the employee's performance.

FP&L   Companies can lessen these disadvantages. Florida Power and Light, which uses an eleborate group evaluation method, is a case in point. Biases are reduced at this utility because multiple raters are used, and some feedback results when managers and professionals learn how they compared with others on each critical factor.[36] However, many of the comparative approaches described in this section offer employees little if any feedback. Often the comparative results are not shared with the employee because the supervisor and the HR department want to create an atmosphere of cooperation among employees. Sharing comparative rankings may lead to internal competition instead of cooperation. However, two simple and powerful arguments in favor of comparative approaches merit mention before specific methods are discussed.

The simple part is that organizations do it anyway, all the time. Whenever HR decisions are made, the performance of those being considered is ranked, even if only subjectively. People are not promoted because they achieve their objectives but because they achieve their objectives *better* than others do.

The second reason for using comparative as opposed to noncomparative methods is that they are more reliable because reliability is controlled by the rating process itself, not by rules, policies, and other external constraints.[37]

Ranking method.   The *ranking method* requires the rater to place each employee in order from best to worst. The HR department knows that certain employees are better than others, but it does not know by how much. The employee ranked second may be almost as good as the one ranked first or may be considerably worse. This method is subject to the halo and recency effects, although rankings by two or more raters can be averaged to help reduce biases. Its advantages include ease of administration and explanation.

Forced distributions.   *Forced distributions* require raters to sort employees into different classifications, usually with specified proportions in each category. Figure 12-9 shows how a rater might classify ten subordinates. The criterion shown in the figure is overall performance, but this method can be used for other performance criteria, such as reliability and control of costs. As with the ranking method, relative differences among employees are not known, but this method does overcome the biases of central tendency, leniency, and strictness errors. Some workers and supervisors at American Express's Western Regional Operations Center strongly dislike this method because some employees received lower ratings than they or their supervisor-raters thought were correct. However, forced distributions required that some employees be rated low.

 Merck & Company uses a forced distribution system that is based on a bell-shaped curve where employee evaluations are distributed as follows:

Merck

Exceptional within Merck	5%
Merck standard with distinction	15%
High Merck standard	70%
Merck standard with room for improvement	8%
Not adequate for Merck	2%

Adjustments are made through "roll-up" meetings, which allow supervisors to meet with their common manager to explain why their evaluations should be allowed to deviate from the expected distribution. These meetings allow supervisors with an exceptionally high-performing team to receive evaluations skewed toward the upper end. The manager can then permit adjustments among the groups so that the resulting distribution follows the company's norms.[38]

| Figure 12-9 | The Forced Distribution Method of Appraisal of Ten Subordinates |

CLASSIFICATION: OVERALL PERFORMANCE

BEST 10% OF SUBORDINATES	NEXT 20% OF SUBORDINATES	MIDDLE 40% OF SUBORDINATES	NEXT 20% OF SUBORDINATES	LOWEST 10% OF SUBORDINATES
A. Wilson	G. Carrs	B. Johnson	K. McDougal	W. Symthe
	M. Lopez	E. Wilson	L. Ray	
		C. Grant		
		T. Valley		

Point allocation method. The *point allocation method* requires the rater to allocate a fixed number of points among employees in the group, as shown in Figure 12-10. Good performers are given more points than are poor performers. The advantage of this method is that the rater can recognize the relative differences between employees, although the halo effect and the recency bias remain.

Paired comparisons. *Paired comparisons* force raters to compare each employee with all the other employees in the same group who are being rated. An example of paired comparisons appears in Figure 12-11. The basis for comparison is usually overall performance. The number of times each employee is rated superior to another can be summed to develop an index. The employee

| Figure 12-10 | The Point Allocation Method of Appraisal |

Instructions: Allocate all 100 points to all employees according to their relative worth. The employee with the maximum points is the best employee.

POINTS	EMPLOYEE
17	A. Wilson
14	G. Carrs
13	M. Lopez
11	B. Johnson
10	E. Wilson
10	C. Grant
9	T. Valley
6	K. McDougal
5	L. Ray
5	W. Smythe
100	

Figure 12-11	The Paired Comparison Method of Evaluating Employees

Instructions: Compare each employee on overall performance with every other employee. For each comparison, write the number of the employee who is best in the intersecting box. Each time an employee is found superior to another employee, the better employee receives one point. Employees then can be ranked according to the number of times each is selected as best by the rater.

Employee	2	3	4	5	6	7	8	9	10
1. G. Carrs	1	1	4	1	1	1	1	9	1
2. C. Grant		3	4	2	2	2	2	9	2
3. B. Johnson			4	3	3	3	3	9	3
4. M. Lopez				4	4	4	4	9	4
5. K. McDougal					6	5	8	9	10
6. L. Ray						6	8	9	10
7. W. Symthe							8	9	10
8. T. Valley								9	10
9. A. Wilson									9
10. E. Wilson									

who is preferred the most is the best employee on the criterion selected. In the figure, A. Wilson is selected nine times and is the top-ranking worker. Although subject to halo and recency effects, this method overcomes the leniency, strictness, and central errors because some employees must be rated higher than others.

▶ Future-Oriented Appraisals

Using past-oriented approaches is like driving a car by looking through the rearview mirror; you know only where you have been, not where you are going. Future-oriented appraisals focus on future performance by evaluating an employee's potential or setting future performance goals. In practice, many past-oriented approaches include a section for the supervisor and employee to record future plans. Four common approaches to evaluating future performance are:

- Self-appraisals
- Management by objectives
- Psychological appraisals
- Assessment centers

Self-Appraisals

Getting employees to conduct a self-appraisal can be a useful evaluation technique if the goal of evaluation is to further self-development. When employees evaluate themselves, defensive behavior is less likely to occur and self-improvement is thus more likely. When self-appraisals are used to determine areas of needed improvement, they can help users set personal goals for the future. The risk is that the employee will be too lenient or too critical of his or her performance. If self-appraisals are used among a diverse or international workforce, home-office HR specialists must be aware of cultural differences that may lead to evaluations that over- or understate performance and future plans. Obviously, self-appraisals can be used with any evaluation approach, past- or future-oriented. The important dimension of self-appraisals is the employee's involvement in and commitment to the improvement process.[39]

Bechtel

At the Bechtel Company, the largest privately held construction and engineering firm in the world, the performance planning system involves the employees in a process of self-appraisal. The process starts with the supervisors telling the employees what is expected. Then the employees get a work sheet on which they write down their understanding of the job. About ten to fifteen days before a performance evaluation is to be done, the employees complete the work sheet by filling in the portions that relate to job accomplishments, performance difficulties, and suggestions for improvement. Not only does the work sheet get the employees involved in forming a self-appraisal of improvement areas, it also indicates to the supervisors what they need to do in the future to "eliminate roadblocks to meeting or exceeding job standards."[40]

Management by Objectives

The heart of the *management by objectives* (MBO) approach consists of goals that are objectively measurable and mutually agreed on by the employee and the manager.[41] Since an employee gets to participate in setting his or her goals, the expectation is that employees will be motivated to achieve those goals. Moreover, since they can measure their progress, employees can adjust their behavior to ensure attainment of the objectives. However, to adjust their efforts, employees must receive performance feedback on a timely basis.

Objectives also help the employee and supervisor discuss the specific development needs of the employee, which can make future training and development efforts appear more relevant to the employee. When done correctly, performance discussions focus on the job's objectives, not on personality variables. Biases are reduced to the extent that goal attainment can be measured objectively.

In practice, MBO programs have encountered difficulties. The objectives are sometimes too ambitious or too narrow or are not set participatively but imposed by the superior. The result is frustrated employees or overlooked areas of performance. For example, employees may set objectives that are quantitatively measurable to the exclusion of subjectively measurable ones that may be equally important. The classic illustration is quantity versus quality of work. When employees and managers focus on subjectively measured objectives, special care is needed to ensure that biases do not distort the manager's evaluation.

Xerox

At Xerox's Reprographic Business Group, objectives are set between the manager and the employee annually. A second-level manager reviews and approves those objectives. They are then subjected to an interim review after six months by the manager and the employee. Adjustments, if any, are made. At the end of the year a written appraisal evaluates performance against the objectives. The appraisal then serves as a basis for setting the next year's performance and developmental objectives.[42]

Psychological Appraisals

Some organizations employ industrial psychologists on a full-time or retainer basis. When psychologists are used for evaluations, they assess an individual's future potential, not that individual's past performance. The appraisal normally consists of in-depth interviews, psychological tests, discussions with supervisors, and a review of other evaluations. The psychologist then writes an evaluation of the employee's intellectual, emotional, motivational, and other work-related characteristics that involve individual potential and may predict future performance. The estimate by the psychologist may relate to a specific job opening for which the person is being considered, or it may be a global assessment of the person's future potential. From these evaluations, placement and development decisions may be made to shape the person's career.

Because this approach is slow and costly, it is usually reserved for executive-level decisions or for bright young managers who others think have considerable potential within the organization. Since the quality of these appraisals depends largely on the skills of the psychologist, some employees object to this type of evaluation, especially if cross-cultural differences exist.

Assessment Centers

Assessment centers are another method of evaluating future potential, but they do not rely on the conclusions of one psychologist. *Assessment centers* are a form of standardized employee appraisal that relies on multiple types of evaluation and multiple raters.[43] They are usually applied to managers who appear to have the potential to perform more responsible jobs. Often the members in the group first meet at a hotel or training facility. During their stay, they are individually evaluated.

The process puts selected employees through in-depth interviews, psychological tests, personal background histories, peer ratings by other attendees, leaderless group discussions, ratings by psychologists and managers, and simulated work exercises to evaluate their future potential. The simulated work experiences usually include in-basket exercises, decision-making exercises, computer-based business games, and other joblike opportunities that test the employee in realistic ways. These activities usually are performed during a few days at a location physically removed from the jobsite. During this time, the psychologists and managers who do the rating attempt to estimate the strengths, weaknesses, and potential of each attendee. They then pool their estimates to arrive at a conclusion about each member of the group.[44]

Assessment centers are both time-consuming and costly. Not only are the candidates away from their jobs, with the company paying for travel and lodging, the evaluators are often company managers who are assigned to the assessment center for short periods. These managers are often supplemented by the psychologists and HR professionals who run the center and also make evaluations. Some critics question whether the procedures used are objective and job-related, especially since rater biases may affect the subjective opinions of attendees.[45] Nevertheless, assessment centers have widespread use, and researchers are finding ways to validate the process.

The results assist management development and placement decisions. From the composite ratings, a report is prepared on each attendee. This information goes into the HR information system to assist HR planning (particularly the development of replacement charts) and other HR decisions. Interestingly, research indicates that the results of assessment centers constitute a good prediction of on-the-job performance.[46] Unfortunately, this method is expensive since it usually requires both a separate facility and the time of multiple raters. Consider how the process works at Johnson Wax:

Johnson Wax

For years the Consumer Products Division of S. C. Johnson & Son, Inc., ran a traditional assessment center. Twice a year selected managers from each division in the company attended the assessment center for five days and were evaluated on a variety of skills. On the fourth day, the candidates attended a debriefing and career development session while the raters wrote their final evaluations. On the fifth day, attendees received a report of their performance and some counseling. The assessment process was successful in helping select employees for promotion. However, the results of the center tended to be overemphasized; people were seen as having "passed" or "failed" the process. Those who "failed" became dissatisfied because they believed their career potential had been severely limited. Many people who attended the center "failed" because field management had few guidelines about who should be sent and at what stage of their career development. Likewise, few programs existed to prepare people for the assessment center process.

To overcome these shortcomings, a project group was formed that included people from the HR department, field sales management, and a consultant. It changed the thrust of the assessment center by recommending that the results be given less emphasis and instead be used to identify strengths and weaknesses in regard to individual skills. The group also recommended that field management become more involved with career and development activities. The project group made sure that management knew what the purpose of the center was and gave them guidelines for recommending people to attend the center. A voluntary program for skill development was also undertaken. Even the name of the center was changed to the Management Skill Identification Center.[47]

"Today, the MSI Center results are but one element in the 'management promotion equation.' This equation consists of four weighted elements which are used by management to make a promotion determination: (1) the individual's record of performance on the job; (2) the individual's sales experience level; (3) the individual's previous job-related experience (i.e., previous employment experience, education experience, etc.); and (4) the individual's MSI Center results."[48]

As this example illustrates, assessment center results must be kept in perspective. If they are the sole determinant of future career progress in the organization, people will see the assessment process as threatening. However, if it is used to appraise an individual's strengths and weaknesses and the person has a way of improving areas of deficiency, the center can be a positive force in developing future talent.

To reduce the expense but still capture some of the benefits associated with assessment centers, some companies use "mail-in" assessments. A package of tests, exercises, and required reports is mailed to the individual, who mails it to the raters for subsequent evaluation. Not only does it cost less, but raters and employers do not spend time away at a centralized location. Training and career development benefits are another justification of the high costs associated with assessment centers. As a result of the process, the future training needs of candidates are often clearly identified.

▶ Implications of the Appraisal Process

A successful performance appraisal system requires more than good technique. It depends on a consistent approach for comparability of results, clear standards and measures, and bias-free ratings. Using multiple raters, even peers,[49] suggests multiple viewpoints, which may reduce biases and offer a better evaluation. If nothing else, employees may feel the process is fair, though being graded may still be uncomfortable.[50] AT&T, General Motors, General Electric, Monsanto, Massachusetts Mutual Life Insurance, and other companies are experimenting with having employees evaluate their bosses. As the chief operating officer of the Waldorf Corporation observed, "Who better to tell you what kind of manager you are than your subordinates?"[51]

Mail-in assessments

Regardless of the method used, it must be implemented, usually among operating and staff managers who have other priorities. Since these managers already believe they know who their good and poor performers are, formal appraisals may seem neither important nor urgent. Nevertheless, successful appraisal almost always depends on management involvement and support. Building involvement through a task force at Xerox or using multiple raters in an assessment center at Johnson Wax, for example, reaches only a few people in those large organizations. For widespread understanding and support, training may be needed.

Training Raters and Evaluators

Whether a simple comparative method or a sophisticated assessment center is used, the evaluators need knowledge of the system and its purpose. Just knowing whether the appraisal is to be used for compensation or for placement may change the rater's evaluation because different criteria may be weighted for different uses.

HR support

Two major problems are evaluator understanding and consistency of evaluations. HR departments provided raters with written instructions in 82 percent of the organizations in one study, and 60 percent provided training.[52] Guidelines for conducting the evaluation or for providing raters with feedback often are included, along with definitions for key terms such as "shows initiative" and "provides leadership."

Companies such as Bechtel and Glendale Federal Savings and Loan Association are part of the 60 percent of firms that solve this knowledge gap through training. Training workshops are usually intended to explain to raters the purpose of the procedure, the mechanics of "how to do it," pitfalls or biases they may encounter, and answers to their questions. The training may include trial runs evaluating other classmates to gain some supervised experience. Bechtel and Glendale even use videotapes and role-playing evaluation sessions to give raters both experience with and insight into the evaluation process. During the training, the timing and scheduling of evaluations are discussed. Typically, most companies do formal evaluations annually near the individual's employment anniversary. For new employees and those with performance problems, evaluations may be done more frequently as part of the HR department's formal program or as the supervisor sees fit. Consider how the vice president and manager of human resources at Glendale Federal Savings and Loan viewed the implementation of his firm's program:

Glendale Federal

With the new appraisal process and related forms in place, the next major step was educating managers and supervisors in the use of the program. Mandatory one-day training workshops were set up, giving each manager an opportunity to review, discuss, and understand the objectives of the program. The appraisal forms were reviewed in detail, with an explanation of how to use the various sections in each form. A videotaped appraisal discussion was presented to demonstrate how performance appraisal worked. Finally, during the workshops, managers were given role-playing situations using the new appraisal forms.[53]

Then, on the biweekly payroll sheets that included everyone in the department or branch, the manager received a notification of who was due to be evaluated during the next month. If the review date had passed, a reminder would appear on the payroll sheets showing that the review date for the indicated employee was past due. As a result, managers knew how to complete the forms, and few delinquencies occurred. The HR department at Glendale Federal also has valuable data that allow it to anticipate and respond to training needs and employees' concerns.[54]

Once evaluators are trained, the appraisal process can begin. But the results of the appraisal do little to improve performance unless the employees receive feedback. This feedback process is called the evaluation interview.

Evaluation Interviews

Giving feedback

Evaluation interviews are performance review sessions that give employees essential feedback about their past performance or future potential. Their importance demands preparation.[55] Normally this includes a review of previous appraisals, identification of specific behaviors to be reinforced during the evaluation interview, and a plan or approach to be used in providing the feedback.

The evaluator may provide this feedback through several approaches: tell and sell, tell and listen, and problem solving.[56] The *tell-and-sell approach* reviews the employee's performance and tries to persuade the employee to perform better. It works best with new employees. The *tell-and-listen method* allows the employee to explain reasons, give excuses, and describe defensive feelings about performance. It attempts to overcome these reactions by counseling the employeee on how to perform better. The *problem-solving approach* identifies problems that are interfering with employee performance. Then, through training, coaching, or counseling, goals for future performance are set to remove those deficiencies.

Regardless of which approach is used to give employees feedback, the guidelines listed in Figure 12-12 can help make the performance review session more effective.[57] The intent of these suggestions is to make the interview a positive, performance-improving dialogue. By stressing desirable aspects of employee performance, the evaluator can give the employee renewed confidence in her or his ability to perform satisfactorily. This positive approach also enables the employee to keep desirable and undesirable performance in perspective because it prevents the employee from feeling that performance review sessions are entirely negative. When negative comments are made, they focus

| Figure 12-12 | Guidelines for Effective Performance Evaluation Interviews |

1. *Emphasize* positive aspects of employee performance.

2. *Tell* each employee that the evaluation session is to improve performance, not to discipline.

3. *Conduct* the performance review session in private with minimum interruptions.

4. *Review* performance formally at least annually and more frequently for new employees or those who are performing poorly.

5. *Make* criticisms specific, not general and vague.

6. *Focus* criticisms on performance, not personality characteristics.

7. *Stay* calm and do not argue with the person being evaluated.

8. *Identify* specific actions the employee can take to improve performance.

9. *Emphasize* the evaluator's willingness to assist the employee's efforts and to improve performance.

10. *End* the evaluation sessions by stressing the positive aspects of the employee's performance.

on work performance, not on the individual's personality. Specific, not general and vague, examples of the employee's shortcomings are used so that the individual knows exactly which behaviors need to be changed.

The review session concludes by focusing on actions that the employee may take to improve areas of poor performance. In that concluding discussion, the evaluator usually offers to provide whatever assistance the employee needs to overcome those deficiencies.

After the review session, the manager must monitor employee performance. Of course, deviations need to be corrected. However, the emphasis during the postperformance evaluation should be on helping the employee attain his or her performance improvement goals. Behaviorally, the manager wants to find opportunities to positively reinforce improvements in the employee's performance. Additional training or other agreed on support should be arranged by the manager. Tracking the manager's commitments, the employee's performance targets, and multiple projects—especially for the increasing numbers of people some managers find in their span of control after downsizing—can be a formidable task. Some managers rely on sophisticated calendar and tracking systems, and others use PC-based software. Managepro tracks project schedules and personnel files so that:

Managepro

... goals are listed on a scoreboard, similar to a spreadsheet, showing ... a description, the deadline, the person or teams responsible for achieving the goal, and an indicator for how the project is going—whether it is on track, behind schedule.
But ... the manager can then shift to the people dimension. ...

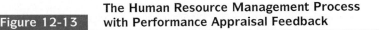

| Figure 12-13 | The Human Resource Management Process with Performance Appraisal Feedback |

A series of buttons on screen can be clicked to summon information for each employee: goals, progress, feedback, review, recognition, development, commitment, calendar, details and notes. The information is kept confidential with a simple password protection scheme.[58]

▶ Feedback for the Human Resource Function

The performance appraisal process also provides insight into the effectiveness of the HR function. Figure 12-13 summarizes the major concepts discussed so far in this book. As can be seen, performance appraisal serves as a "quality control check." If the appraisal process indicates that poor performance is widespread, many employees are excluded from internal placement decisions. They will not be promoted or transferred; in fact, they may be excluded through termination.

Unacceptably high numbers of poor performers may indicate errors elsewhere among HR management functions. For example, development may be failing to fulfill career plans because the people who are hired during the selection process are poorly screened. Or the HR plan may be in error because the job analysis information is wrong or the affirmative action plan seeks the wrong objectives. Sometimes the HR function is pursuing the wrong objectives. The appraisal system itself may be faulty because of management resistance, incorrect performance standards or measures, or a lack of constructive feedback.

Wherever the problem lies, HR specialists need to monitor carefully the results of the organization's performance appraisal process. These results can serve as a barometer of the entire HR function. Furthermore, performance appraisals serve as a foundation for compensation and other activities discussed in subsequent chapters.

▶ Summary

Performance appraisal is a critical activity of HR management. Its goal is to provide an accurate picture of past and/or future employee performance. To achieve this, performance standards are established. The standards are based on the job-related criteria that best determine successful job performance. Where possible, actual performance is measured directly and objectively. From a wide variety of appraisal techniques, specialists select the methods that most effectively measure employee performance against the previously set standards. Techniques can be selected both to review past performance and to anticipate performance in the future.

The appraisal process is usually designed by the HR department, often with little input from other parts of the organization. When it is time to implement a new appraisal approach, those who do the rating may have little idea about the appraisal process or its objectives. To overcome this shortcoming, the HR department may design and conduct appraisal workshops to train managers.

A necessary requirement of the appraisal process is employee feedback through an evaluation interview. The interviewer tries to balance positive areas of good performance with areas where performance is deficient so that the employee receives a realistic view. Perhaps the most significant challenge raised by performance appraisals is the feedback they provide about the HR department's performance. HR specialists need to be keenly aware that poor performance, especially when it is widespread, may reflect problems with previous HR management activities.

▶ Terms for Review

Performance standards	Critical incident method
Performance measures	Behaviorally anchored ratings scales
Constructs	Field review method
Halo effect	Comparative evaluation approaches
Error of central tendency	Management by objectives
Recency effect	Assessment centers
Rating scale	Evaluation interviews
Forced choice method	

▶ Review and Discussion Questions

1. How do performance appraisals affect the execution of corporate strategy?

2. What criticisms do you have of the critical incident method? When it is done correctly, what are its strengths?

3. If you were dean of your college, explain why accomplishment records might be an appropriate tool in evaluating the faculty.

4. If the dean of your college asked you to serve on a committee to develop a performance appraisal system for evaluating the faculty, what performance criteria would you identify? Of those criteria, which ones do you think are most likely to determine a faculty member's success at your school? What standards would you recommend to the dean regardless of the specific evaluation instrument selected?

5. If you were designing a performance appraisal system for use in multiple overseas locations, what factors would you consider in preparing to implement the new system?

6. Suppose you were asked to design a training program to ensure that supervisors performed more accurate performance appraisals. What key topics would you include?

7. Describe how you would conduct a typical performance evaluation interview.

8. How do the results of performance appraisals affect other human resource management activities?

▶ **Incident 12-1**

International Electronics, Inc.'s, Performance Appraisal

International Electronics, Inc., is a major worldwide manufacturer of electronic equipment used in manufacturing, scientific, and business applications. It designs its products mosty in North America, Japan, and the European Union, with manufacturing done in those areas and in a variety of developing countries, mostly in southeast Asia. Spanning twenty-seven countries, the HR department is concerned about developing a single performance appraisal instrument that can be used in all countries among all types of professional, managerial, technical, clerical, and assembly workers. Though the HR department realizes that it must translate the instrument into different languages, it seeks uniformity in its performance appraisal instrument to ensure comparability of results. For these reasons and for simplicity of administration, a decision was made to use a weighted rating scale translated into the twenty-three languages used in the company's twenty-seven countries.

1. What criticisms do you have of the company's decision?

2. Although you failed to persuade the senior HR executive to use another approach, you have been assigned to draft the directions for implementing the new procedure. What recommendations would you give to managers and supervisors throughout the company?

▶ References

1. John F. Welch, "A Master Class in Radical Change," *Fortune*, Dec. 13, 1993, p. 83.

2. William M. Fox, "Improving Performance Appraisal Systems," *National Productivity Review,* Winter 1987–1988, p. 20.

3. Stratford Sherman, "How Will We Live with the Tumult?" *Fortune*, Dec. 13, 1993, p. 123.

4. Kenneth Blanchard and Spencer Johnson, *The One Minute Manager,* New York: William Morrow, 1982, p. 100.

5. Thomas A. Stewart, "Allied-Signal's Turnaround Blitz," *Fortune,* Nov. 20, 1992, p. 75.

6. Alan H. Locher and Kenneth S. Teel, "Appraisal Trends," *Personnel Journal,* September 1988, pp. 139–145. See also Jeanette N. Cleveland, Kevin R. Murphy, and Richard E. Williams, "Multiple Uses of Performance Appraisal: Prevalence and Correlates," *Journal of Applied Psychology,* vol. 74, no. 1, 1989, pp. 130–135.

7. Norman R. Deets and D. Timothy Tyler, "How Xerox Improved Its Performance Appraisal," *Personnel Journal,* April 1986, pp. 50–52.

8. Locher and Teel, op. cit.

9. Brian O'Reilly, "360 Feedback Can Change Your Life," *Fortune*, Oct. 17, 1994, pp. 93–100. See also David Kirkpatrick, "Could AT&T Rule the World?" *Fortune*, May 17, 1993, p. 64.

10. Alison Rogers, "The Insider," *Fortune*, Dec. 13, 1993, p. 11.

11. Christina G. Banks and Kevin R. Murphy, "Toward Narrowing the Research-Practice Gap in Performance Appraisal," *Personnel Psychology,* vol. 39, 1985, pp. 335–345.

12. James A. Buford, Jr., Bettye B. Burkhalter, and Grover T. Jacobs, "Link Job Descriptions to Performance Appraisals," *Personnel Journal,* June 1988, pp. 132–140.

13. Daniel Machalaba, "Up to Speed: United Parcel Service Gets Deliveries Done by Driving Its Workers," *The Wall Street Journal,* Eastern ed., Apr. 22, 1986, pp. 1, 26.

14. Gary P. Latham and Kenneth N. Wexley, *Increasing Productivity through Performance Appraisal,* Menlo Park, Calif.: Addison-Wesley, 1981, pp. 28–29. See also H. John Bernardin, "Subordinate Appraisal: A Valuable Source of Information about Managers," *Human Resource Management,* Fall 1986, pp. 421–439.

15. Stephen Koepp, "The Boss That Never Blinks," *Time,* July 28, 1986, p. 38.

16. Ibid., pp. 38–39.

17. H. John Bernardin, "Increasing the Accuracy of Performance Measurement: A Proposed Solution to Erroneous Attributions," *Human Resource Planning,* September 1989, pp. 239–250.

18. Patricia S. Eyres, "Legally Defensible Performance Appraisal Systems," *Personnel Journal,* July 1989, pp. 58–62. See also Robert W. Goddard, "Is Your Appraisal System Headed for Court?" *Personnel Journal,* January 1989, pp. 114–118; Gerald V. Barrett and

Mary C. Kernan, "Performance Appraisal and Terminations: A Review of Court Decisions since *Brito v. Zia* with Implications for Personnel Practices," *Personnel Psychology,* vol. 40, 1987, pp. 489–503.

19. Mary Green Miner and John B. Miner, *Employee Selection within the Law,* Washington, D.C.: Bureau of National Affairs, 1978, p. 27. See also Ronald G. Wells, "Guidelines for Effective and Defensible Performance Systems," *Personnel Journal,* October 1982, pp. 776–782.

20. Jerry W. Hedge and Michael J. Kavanagh, "Improving the Accuracy of Performance Evaluations: Comparison of Three Methods of Performance Appraiser Training," *Journal of Applied Psychology,* vol. 73, 1988, pp. 68–73. See also Stephen B. Wehrenberg, "Train Supervisors to Measure and Evaluate Performance," *Personnel Journal,* February 1988, pp. 77–79.

21. Robert J. Wherry, Sr., and C. J. Bartlett, "The Control of Bias in Ratings: A Theory of Rating," *Personnel Psychology,* 1982, pp. 521–551. See also Robert Dipboye, "Some Neglected Variables in Research Discrimination in Appraisals," *Academy of Management Review,* vol. 10, no. 1, 1985, pp. 116–127.

22. Barry R. Nathan and Mancy Tippins, "The Consequences of Halo 'Error' in Performance Ratings: A Field Study of the Moderating Effect of Halo on Test Validation Results," *Journal of Applied Psychology,* vol. 75, no. 3, 1990, pp. 290–296. See also "Sebastiano A. Fisicaro, "A Reexamination of the Relation between Halo Error and Accuracy," *Journal of Applied Psychology,* vol. 73, 1988, pp. 239–244.

23. Jiing-Lih Farh and Gregory H. Dobbins, "Effects of Self-Esteem on Leniency Bias in Self-Reports of Performance: A Structural Equation Model Analysis," *Personnel Psychology,* vol. 42, 1989, pp. 835–848.

24. "Merck's New Performance Appraisal/Merit Pay System Is Based on a Bell-Shaped Distribution, E. Jeffrey Stoll, Director, Corporate Personnel Relations, Says," *Ideas & Trends in Personnel Management,* no. 195, May 17, 1989, pp. 88–92.

25. Kevin R. Murphy and William K. Balzer, "Rater Errors and Rating Accuracy," *Journal of Applied Psychology,* vol. 74, 1989, pp. 619–624.

26. Martin Levy, "Almost-Perfect Performance Appraisals," *Personnel Journal,* April 1989, pp. 76–83.

27. Wherry and Bartlett, op. cit.

28. Ibid.

29. John C. Flanagan, "The Critical Incident Technique," *Psychological Bulletin,* vol. 51, 1954, pp. 327–358.

30. Fox, op. cit.

31. Toni S. Locklear, Barbara B. Granger, and John G. Veres III, "Evaluation of a Behaviorally-Based Appraisal System," *Journal of Managerial Issues,* Fall 1989, pp. 66–75. See also Kevin R. Murphy and Joseph I. Constans, "Behavioral Anchors as a Source of Bias in Rating," *Journal of Applied Psychology,* vol. 72, 1987, pp. 573–577; Kevin R. Murphy and Virginia A. Pardaffy, "Bias in Behaviorally Anchored Rating Scales: Global or Scale-Specific," *Journal of Applied Psychology,* vol. 74, 1989, pp. 343–346.

32. George Rosinger et al., "Development of a Behaviorally Based Performance Appraisal System," *Personnel Psychology,* vol. 36, 1982, pp. 75–88.

33. Angelo J. Kinicki, Brendan D. Bannister, Peter Hom, and Angelo S. Denisi, "Behaviorally Anchored Rating Scales vs. Summated Rating Scales: Psychometric Properties and Susceptibility to Rating Bias," *Educational and Psychological Measurement,* vol. 12, 1985, pp. 535–549.

34. Uco Wiersma and Gary Latham, "The Practicality of Behavioral Observation Scales, Behavioral Expectation Scales, and Trait Scales," *Personnel Psychology,* vol. 40, 1986, pp. 619–628.

35. Ibid., p. 627.

36. "Tapping Managerial and Professional Talent at FPL," *The Career Development Bulletin,* vol. 3, no. 3, 1982, pp. 4–6.

37. J. Peter Graves, "Let's Put Appraisal Back in Performance Appraisal: II," *Personnel Journal,* December 1982, p. 918.

38. "Merck's New Performance Appraisal," op. cit.

39. Jiayuan Yu and Kevin R. Murphy, "Modesty Bias in Self-Ratings of Performance: A Test of the Cultural Relativity Hypothesis," *Personnel Psychology,* vol. 46, 1993, pp. 357–363. See also Manuel London and Arthur J. Wohlers, "Agreement between Subordinate and Self-Ratings in Upward Feedback," *Personnel Psychology,* vol. 44, 1991, pp. 375–390; Donald J. Campbell and Cynthia Lee, "Self-Appraisal in Performance Evaluation: Development versus Evaluation," *Academy of Management Review,* vol. 13, 1988, pp. 302–314; and Bernardin, "Subordinate Appraisal."

40. Milan Moravec, "How Performance Appraisal Can Tie Communication to Productivity," *Personnel Administrator,* January 1981, pp. 51–52.

41. William B. Werther, Jr., and Heinz Weihrich, "Refining MBO through Negotiations," *MSU Business Topics,* Summer 1975, pp. 53–58. See also Deets and Tyler, op. cit.

42. Deets and Tyler, op. cit.

43. Michael M. Harris and John Schaubroeck, "A Meta-Analysis of Self-Supervisor, Self-Peer, and Peer-Supervisor Ratings," *Personnel Psychology,* vol. 41, 1988, pp. 43–62.

44. Douglas W. Bray, "Fifty Years of Assessment Centres: A Retrospective and Prospective View," *Journal of Management Development,* vol. 4, no. 4, 1985, pp. 4–11. See also Paul R. Sackett and Ann Marie Ryan, "A Review of Recent Assessment Centre Research," *Journal of Management Development,* vol. 4, no. 4, 1985, pp. 13–25.

45. Peter Rea, Julie Rea, and Charles Moomaw, "Use Assessment Centers in Skill Development," *Personnel Journal,* April 1990, pp. 126–131.

46. Glenn M. McEvoy and Richard W. Beatty, "Assessment Centers and Subordinate Appraisals of Managers: A Seven-Year Examination of Predictive Validity," *Personnel Psychology,* vol. 42, 1989, pp. 37–52.

47. Leland C. Nichols and Joseph Hudson, "Dual-Role Assessment Center: Selection and Development," *Personnel Journal,* May 1981, pp. 380–386.

48. Ibid., p. 382.

49. Glenn M. McEvoy, Paul F. Buller, and Steven R. Roghaar, "A Jury of One's Peers," *Personnel Administrator,* May 1988, pp. 94–101.

50. Jim Laumeyer and Tim Beebe, "Employees and Their Appraisal," *Personnel Administrator,* December 1988, pp. 76–80.

51. Walter Kiechell III, "When Subordinates Evaluate the Boss," *Fortune,* June 19, 1989, p. 102. See also Glenn M. McEvoy, "Evaluating the Boss," *Personnel Administrator,* September 1988, pp. 115–120.

52. Locher and Teel, op. cit., p. 145.

53. William J. Birch, "Performance Appraisal: One Company's Experience," *Personnel Journal,* June 1981, pp. 456–460. For another view, see Virginia Bianco, "In Praise of Performance," *Personnel Journal,* June 1984, pp. 40–45, 47–48, 50.

54. Birch, op. cit. See also Timothy R. Athey and Robert M. McIntyre, "Effect of Rater Training on Rater Accuracy: Levels-of-Processing Theory and Social Facilitation Theory Perspectives," *Journal of Applied Psychology,* vol. 72, 1987, pp. 567–572.

55. John Lawrie, "Prepare for a Performance Appraisal," *Personnel Journal,* April 1990, pp. 132–136.

56. Norman R. F. Maier, *The Appraisal Interview: Three Basic Approaches,* La Jolla, Calif.: University Associates, 1976. See also Stratford Sherman, "Leaders Learn to Heed the Voice Within," *Fortune,* Aug. 22, 1994, pp. 92–100.

57. Ibid.

58. Peter H. Lewis, "Pairing People Management with Project Management," *The New York Times,* National ed., Apr. 11, 1993, p. F12. See also Edward C. Baig, "So You Hate Rating Your Workers," *Business Week,* Aug. 22, 1994, p. 14.

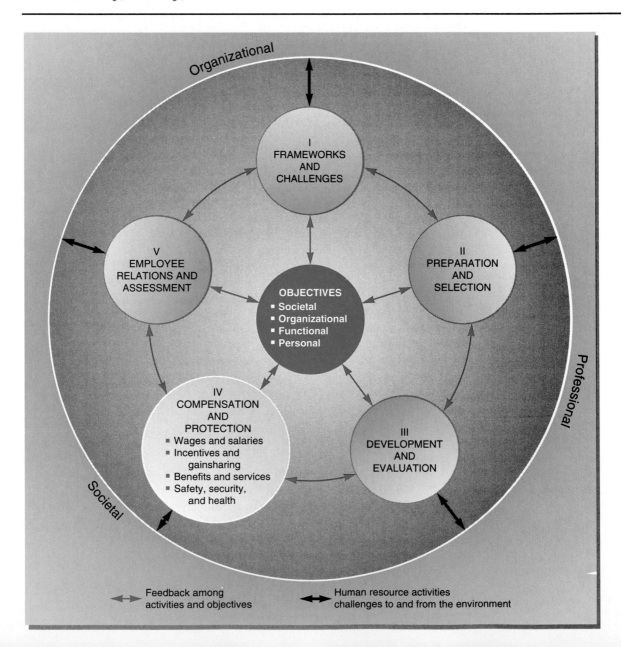

COMPENSATION AND PROTECTION

Employees exchange their physical and mental efforts for compensation, but compensation means more than wages and salaries. It may include incentives that motivate employees and relate labor costs to productivity. Almost always, a wide range of benefits and services are part of the total compensation package each worker receives in developed nations. Financial and physical security also are provided to employees because of laws that impose social responsibilities on employers in a variety of areas.

These concerns play an important role in any manager's or HR department's efforts to obtain, maintain, and retain an effective workforce. Understanding the role of compensation and protection is important for your well-being as an employee and for the well-being of your current and future employees.

13

Results from a representative sample of the labor force in seven countries . . . showed that the two most dominant work goals are "interesting work" and "good pay."
ITZHAK HARPAZ[1]

Comparable worth pressure is just the tip of a quiet revolution occurring in pay practice.
ROSABETH MOSS KANTER[2]

Wages and Salaries

CHAPTER OBJECTIVES

After studying this chapter, you should be able to:

1. DEFINE the conditions needed for a well-managed compensation system.

2. DISCUSS the objectives of effective compensation management.

3. EXPLAIN the major laws and other challenges that affect pay plans.

4. DESCRIBE how wages and salaries are determined.

5. DEBATE both sides of the comparable worth issue.

6. IDENTIFY key concerns in international compensation.

Compensation is what employees receive in exchange for their contribution to the organization. When managed correctly, it helps the organization achieve its objectives and obtain, maintain, and retain a productive workforce. Without adequate compensation, current employees are likely to leave and replacements will be difficult to recruit. Other implications of pay dissatisfaction are diagrammed in Figure 13-1.

Pay dissatisfaction

The outcomes of pay dissatisfaction shown in Figure 13-1 harm productivity and affect the quality of work life. In severe cases, pay dissatisfaction may lower performance, cause strikes, increase grievances, and lead to forms of physical or psychological withdrawal ranging from absenteeism and turnover to increased visits to the dispensary and poor mental health. Overpayment also can harm the organization and its people, reducing the firm's competitiveness and causing anxiety, guilt, and discomfort among the employees.[3]

| Figure 13-1 | A Model of the Consequences of Pay Dissatisfaction |

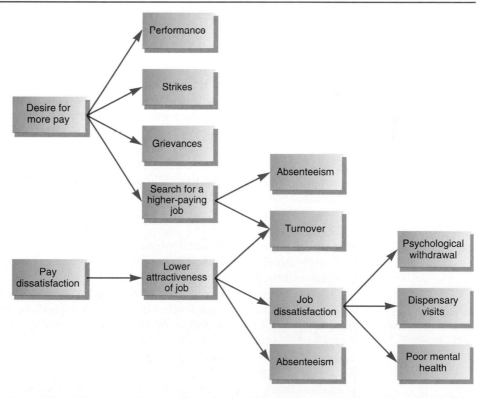

Source: Edward E. Lawler III, *Pay and Organizational Effectiveness: A Psychological View,* New York: McGraw-Hill, 1971, p. 233. Used with permission of McGraw-Hill, Inc.

An HR department can contribute to the organization's strategic objectives through the firm's compensation program. An example comes from a General Electric facility in Puerto Rico.

General Electric

In the early 1990s General Electric (GE) built a new factory in Bayamon, Puerto Rico, to produce surge protectors. Besides the plant manager, the facility has two broad job categories: about 200 associate producers and 15 salaried associate advisers. Twice a year associates switch to different job tasks and are required to sign up for the appropriate vocational courses.

"As they gain proficiency and knowledge in their new tasks, they are paid commensurately for their acquired skills. Subsequently, the workforce evolves into a team capable of performing all operative job tasks in the business. Skill and knowledge level, not seniority, determine promotions and layoffs.

"The aggregate of the two job classifications, the compensation plan and the educational program have elevated the Bayamon employees to one of the most productive workforces in the world. In the first year, the workforce was 20 percent more productive than its nearest company equivalent on the mainland. . . ."[4]

GE's avowed strategy is to be number one or two in every industry or get out of that industry. In products such as surge arresters, which are devices that protect equipment against electrical surges, being a low-cost producer is essential to industry leadership. When wages and salaries are linked to "pay for knowledge" and "pay for skills," employees have an incentive to pursue vocational training. At the same time, GE benefits from having better trained workers who are more productive, allowing GE to maintain cost leadership for surge arresters. The result of linking compensation to continuous learning is a perpetual learning machine that furthers corporate strategy.

Compensation is not the only way to align performance with strategy. Human resource planning, recruiting, selection, placement, development, performance appraisals, and career planning also align individual efforts and company strategy. But unlike staffing and developing activities, compensation programs can be quickly modified and linked with new strategies.

Direct and indirect compensation

The flexibility and responsiveness of compensation management[5] come from its broad scope. It embraces *direct* compensation, which includes wages and salaries and, increasingly, incentives and gainsharing, and *indirect* compensation, which includes fringe benefits. This chapter examines direct compensation: wages and salaries. Chapter 14 discusses other forms of direct compensation, such as incentives and gainsharing. Chapters 15 and 16 describe indirect compensation, primarily employer-provided benefits and services in Chapter 15 and legally mandated benefits and services in Chapter 16. Underlying direct and indirect compensation are a variety of objectives.

▶ Objectives of Compensation Management

Equity

Broadly defined, the objectives of compensation management are to help the organization achieve strategic success while ensuring internal and external equity. *Internal equity* ensures that more demanding positions or better qualified people within the organization are paid more. *External equity* assures that jobs are fairly compensated in comparison with similar jobs in the labor market.[6] Sometimes these objectives, which are listed in Figure 13-2, conflict with one another, and trade-offs must be made. For example, to retain employees and ensure equity, wage and salary analysts recommend paying similar amounts for similar jobs. But a recruiter may want to offer an unusually high salary to attract a qualified recruit. At this point, compensation strategy must make a trade-off between the recruiting objectives and the consistency objectives. Other objectives of compensation are to reward desired behavior and control costs. These objectives may conflict too. For example, GE's approach to perpet-

Figure 13-2	Objectives Sought through Effective Compensation Management

- *Acquire qualified personnel.* Compensation needs to be high enough to attract applicants. Pay levels must respond to the supply and demand of workers in the labor market since employers compete for workers. Premium wages are sometimes needed to attract applicants already working for others.

- *Retain current employees.* Employees may quit when compensation levels are not competitive, resulting in higher turnover.

- *Ensure equity.* Compensation management strives for internal and external equity. *Internal equity* requires that pay be related to the relative worth of a job so that similar jobs get similar pay. *External equity* means paying workers what comparable workers are paid by other firms in the labor market.

- *Reward desired behavior.* Pay should reinforce desired behaviors and act as an incentive for those behaviors to occur in the future. Effective compensation plans reward performance, loyalty, experience, responsibility, and other behaviors.

- *Control costs.* A rational compensation system helps the organization obtain and retain workers at a reasonable cost. Without effective compensation management, workers could be overpaid or underpaid.

- *Comply with legal regulations.* A sound wage and salary system considers the legal challenges imposed by the government and ensures the employer's compliance.

- *Facilitate understanding.* The compensation management system should be easily understood by human resource specialists, operating managers, and employees.

- *Further administrative efficiency.* Wage and salary programs should be designed to be managed efficiently, making optimal use of the HRIS, although this objective should be a secondary consideration compared with other objectives.

ual learning at its Bayamon facility might lead to all workers being paid the highest wage rates once they are all cross-trained. The result may be that GE's wages are above those paid by competitors. If superior productivity does not result, GE's internal equity based on skill levels may be above what external equity would dictate, making GE a high-cost producer.

Legal compliance

Regardless of the trade-offs, an overriding objective is to maintain legal compliance. For example, the Fair Labor Standards Act of 1938 requires employers to pay the minimum wage and time and a half for overtime. Periodically, Congress raises the minimum wage, and employers must comply regardless of their other objectives. Likewise, the Equal Pay Act requires employers to provide equal pay for equal work without regard to a person's sex. Discrimination in pay among workers 40 years of age and older is outlawed by the Age Discrimination in Employment Act, and Title VII of the 1964 Civil Rights Act prohibits discrimination in pay because of race, sex, religion, or national origin.[7] (Each of these nondiscrimination laws is discussed in Chapter 4.)

Compensation objectives are not rules; they are guidelines. But the more the objectives in Figure 13-2 are followed, the more effective wage and salary administration will be. To meet these objectives, the major phases of compensation management include the following:

Phase 1. Evaluate every job, using job analysis information to ensure internal equity based on each job's relative worth.

Phase 2. Conduct wage and salary surveys to determine external equity based on the rates paid in the labor market.

Phase 3. Price each job to determine the rate of pay based on internal and external equity.

Figure 13-3 depicts these three major phases of compensation management, which are discussed in the following sections.

▶ Job Analysis and Evaluations

Job analysis and the HRIS

As was discussed in Chapter 5, job analysis collects information about jobs (through surveys, observation, and discussions among workers and supervisors) to produce job and position descriptions. With job analysis information as part of the department's HR information system, compensation analysts have the minimum information needed to undertake job evaluations.

Job evaluations are systematic procedures to determine the relative worth of jobs. Although different approaches exist, each one considers the responsibilities, skills, efforts, and working conditions inherent in the job. It determines which jobs are worth more to the organization than others.[8] Without job evalu-

| Figure 13-3 | Major Phases of Compensation Management |

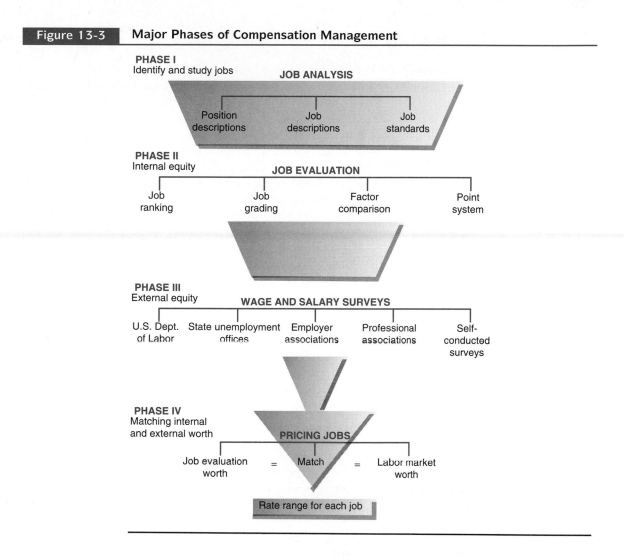

ations, the HR department would be unable to develop a rational approach to pay.

Since evaluation is subjective, it is conducted by specially trained personnel called job analysts or compensation specialists. When a group of managers or specialists is used for this purpose, the group is called a *job evaluation committee*.[9] The committee reviews job analysis information to learn about duties, responsibilities, and working conditions. With this knowledge, jobs are put in a hierarchy according to their relative worth through the use of a job evaluation method. The most common methods are job ranking, job grading, factor comparison, and the point system.

Job Ranking

The simplest and least precise method of job evaluation is *job ranking.* Specialists review the job analysis information and then rank each job subjectively according to its relative importance in comparison with other jobs in the firm. These are overall rankings, although raters may consider individual factors such as the responsibility, skill, effort, and working conditions involved in each job. Subjectively determined global rankings mean that important elements of some jobs may be overlooked while unimportant items are weighted too heavily. Even more damaging, these rankings do not differentiate between jobs in terms of their *relative* importance. For example, the job of janitor may be ranked as 1, the secretary's job may get a 2, and the office manager is ranked 3. But the secretarial position may be three times as important as the janitorial job and half as important as the job of office manager. Pay scales based on these broad rankings ensure that more important jobs are paid more, but this does not capture the relative differences between jobs. As a result, pay levels may be inaccurate.

Job Grading

Job grading, or job classification, is slightly more sophisticated than job ranking but still not very precise. It works by having each job assigned to a grade by matching standard descriptions with each job's description, as illustrated in Figure 13-4. The standard description in the figure that most nearly matches the job's description determines its relative value, which is expressed as a job grade. More important jobs are paid more, but the lack of precision can lead to inaccurate pay levels. The largest user of this approach has been the U.S. Civil Service Commission, which gradually is replacing it with more sophisticated approaches.

Factor Comparison

With the *factor comparison method,* the job evaluation committee compares critical or compensable job factors. These compensable factors are the job elements common to all the jobs being evaluated, such as responsibility, skill, mental effort, physical effort, and working conditions. Each factor is compared, one at a time, with the same factor for other key jobs, and then the separate evaluations are combined by the committee to determine the relative importance of each job. This method involves the following five steps:

Step 1: Determine the critical factors.   Analysts must first decide which factors are common and important in a broad range of jobs. The critical factors shown in Figure 13-5 are the ones most commonly used. Some organizations use different factors for managerial, professional, sales, and other types of jobs.

Figure 13-4	A Job Classification Schedule for Use with the Job Grading Method

Directions: To determine appropriate job grade, match standard description with job description.

JOB GRADE	STANDARD DESCRIPTION
I	Work is simple and highly repetitive, done under close supervision, requiring minimal training and little responsibility or initiative. *Examples:* Janitor, file clerk
II	Work is simple and repetitive, done under close supervision, requiring some training or skill. Employee is expected to assume responsibility or exhibit initiative only rarely. *Examples:* Clerk-typist I, machine cleaner
III	Work is simple, with little variation, done under general supervision. Training or skill required. Employee has minimum responsibilities and must take some initiative to perform satisfactorily. *Examples:* Parts expediter, machine oiler, clerk-typist II
IV	Work is moderately complex, with some variation, done under general supervision. High level of skill required. Employee is responsible for equipment or safety; regularly exhibits initiative. *Examples:* Machine operator I, tool and die apprentice
V	Work is complex, varied, done under general supervision. Advanced skill level required. Employee is responsible for equipment and safety; shows high degree of initiative. *Examples:* Machine operator II, tool and die specialist

Step 2: Determine key jobs.   *Key jobs* are jobs that are commonly found throughout the organization and in the employer's labor market. Common jobs are selected because it is easier to discover the market rate for them. Ideally, these benchmark jobs should be widely held and accepted by employees as key jobs and should encompass a wide variety of critical factors.

Step 3: Apportion current wages for key jobs.   The job evaluation committee then allocates a part of each key job's current wage rate to each critical factor, as shown in Figure 13-5. The proportion of each wage assigned to the different compensable factors depends on the importance of the individual factor.

For example, a janitor receives $6.70 an hour. This amount is apportioned in Figure 13-5 as follows: 80 cents for responsibility, 80 cents for skill, 50 cents for

| Figure 13-5 · | The Apportionment of Wages for Key Jobs |

COMPENSABLE OR CRITICAL FACTORS	KEY JOBS				
	MACHINIST	FORKLIFT DRIVER	SECRETARY	JANITOR	FILE CLERK
Responsibility	$ 3.20	$1.80	$2.40	$ .80	$1.40
Skill	4.00	1.80	2.00	.80	1.30
Mental effort	3.00	1.20	1.80	.50	1.40
Physical effort	2.00	1.80	.70	2.70	.90
Working conditions	.70	.60	.60	1.90	.60
Total	$12.90	$7.20	$7.50	$6.70	$5.60
Wage rate	$12.90	$7.20	$7.50	$6.70	$5.60

mental effort, $2.70 for physical effort, and $1.90 for working conditions. In apportioning these wage rates, the evaluation committee must make two comparisons. First, the amount assigned to each factor should reflect its importance compared with other factors of the job. For example, if $4 is assigned to skill and $2 is assigned to physical effort for a machinist, this implies that skill is twice as important as physical effort. Second, the amount allocated to a factor should reflect the relative importance of that factor among the different jobs. For example, if the responsibility of a secretary is three times that of a janitor, the money allocated to a secretary for responsibility ($2.40) should be three times that allocated to a janitor (80 cents).

Step 4: Place key jobs on a factor comparison chart.   Once the compensable factors of each key job have been assigned a proportion of the wage rate, this information is transferred to a factor comparison chart such as the one shown in Figure 13-6. Key jobs are placed in the columns according to the amount of wages assigned to each critical factor. In the responsibility column, for example, the title of secretary is placed next to the $2.40 rate to reflect how much the secretary's responsibility is worth to the organization. This job also appears under the other critical factors according to the relative worth of those factors in the job of secretary. The same assignment process takes place for every other key job.

Step 5: Evaluate other jobs.   The titles of key jobs in each column in Figure 13-6 serve as benchmarks. Other, *nonkey* jobs are then evaluated by being fitted on the scale in each column.

Nonkey jobs

For the nonkey job of maintenance mechanic, the evaluation committee compares the responsibility of the mechanic with the responsibility of other key jobs already on the chart. It is decided subjectively that the mechanic's responsibility is between that of the forklift driver and that of the secretary. Since the mechanic's job requires about three-fourths

Figure 13-6	A Factor Comparison Chart

RATE	RESPONSIBILITY	SKILL	MENTAL EFFORT	PHYSICAL EFFORT	WORKING CONDITIONS
4.00 —		— Machinist	—	—	—
—		—	—	—	—
—		—	—	—	—
—		—	—	—	—
—		—	—	—	—
—		—	—	—	—
—		—	—	—	—
—		—	—	—	—
—	Machinist	—	—	—	—
—		—	—	—	—
3.00 —		— MECHANIC	— Machinist	—	—
—		—	—	—	—
—		—	—	—	—
—		—	— MECHANIC	— Janitor	—
—		—	—	—	—
2.50 —		—	—	—	—
—	Secretary	—	—	—	—
—		—	—	—	—
—		—	—	—	—
—	MECHANIC	—	—	—	—
2.00 —		— Secretary	—	— Machinist	—
—		—	—	— MECHANIC	— Janitor
—	Forklift driver	— Forklift driver	— Secretary	— Forklift driver	—
—		—	—	—	—
—		—	—	—	—
1.50 —		—	—	—	—
—	File clerk	—	— File clerk	—	—
—		— File clerk	—	—	— MECHANIC
—		—	— Forklift driver	—	—
—		—	—	—	—
1.00 —		—	—	—	—
—		—	—	— File clerk	—
—	Janitor	— Janitor	—	—	—
—		—	—	— Secretary	— Machinist
—		—	—	—	— { Forklift driver
.50 —		—	— Janitor	—	— { Secretary
—		—	—	—	File clerk
—		—	—	—	—
—		—	—	—	—
.00 —		—	—	—	—

of the machinist's skills, the skill component of this job is placed below that of the machinist in the skill column. This procedure is repeated for each compensable factor. When the task is completed, the committee can determine the worth of the mechanic's job, which is:

Responsibility	$ 2.10
Skill	3.00
Mental effort	2.70
Physical effort	1.90
Working conditions	1.30
TOTAL WAGE	$11.00

By using this procedure, the committee can rank every other job according to its relative worth as indicated by its wage rate. These rankings should be reviewed by department managers to verify their appropriateness.

Point System

The most common approach

Research shows that the *point system* is used more than is any other method.[10] This system evaluates the compensable factors of each job, but instead of using wages as the factor comparison method does, it uses points. Although more difficult to develop initially, the point system is more precise than the factor comparison method because it can handle critical, compensable factors in more detail.[11] This system requires six steps and is usually implemented by a job evaluation committee or an individual analyst.

Step 1: Determine critical factors. The point system can use the same factors used in the factor comparison method, but it generally adds more detail by breaking down those factors into subfactors. For example, Figure 13-7 shows how the factor of responsibility can be broken down into (*a*) safety of others, (*b*) equipment and materials, (*c*) assisting trainees, and (*d*) product and service quality.

Step 2: Determine the levels of factors. Since the amount of responsibility or other factors may vary from job to job, the point system creates several levels associated with each factor. Figure 13-7 shows four levels, although more or fewer may be used. These levels help analysts reward different degrees of responsibility, skills, and other critical factors.

Step 3: Allocate points to subfactors. With the factors listed down one side of Figure 13-7 and the levels placed across the top, the result is a point system matrix. Starting with level IV, the job evaluation committee subjectively as-

Figure 13-7	A Point System Matrix

COMPENSABLE OR CRITICAL FACTORS	LEVELS			
	MINIMUM I	LOW II	MODERATE III	HIGH IV
1. Responsibility				
a. Safety of others	25	50	75	100
b. Equipment and materials	20	40	60	80
c. Assisting trainees	5	20	35	50
d. Product/service quality	20	40	60	80
2. Skill				
a. Experience	45	90	135	180
b. Education/training	25	50	75	100
3. Effort				
a. Physical	25	50	75	100
b. Mental	35	70	105	150
4. Working conditions				
a. Unpleasant conditions	20	40	60	80
b. Hazards	20	40	60	80
Total points				1000

signs the maximum possible points to each subfactor. For example, if safety (100) is twice as important as assisting trainees (50), it gets twice as many points.

Step 4: Allocate points to levels. Once the maximum total points for each job element are assigned under level IV, analysts allocate points across each row to reflect the importance of the different levels. For simplicity, equal point differences usually are assigned between levels, as was done for "safety of others" in Figure 13-7. Alternatively, point differences between levels can be variable, as shown for "assisting trainees." Both approaches are used, depending on the importance of each level of each subfactor.

Step 5: Develop the point manual. Analysts then develop a point manual that contains a written explanation of each job element, as shown in Figure 13-8 for responsibility for equipment and materials. It also defines what is expected for the four levels of each subfactor. This information is needed to assign jobs to the appropriate level.

Step 6: Apply the point system. When the point matrix and manual are ready, the relative value of each job can be determined. This process is subjec-

| **Figure 13-8** | **A Point Manual Description of "Responsibility: Equipment and Materials"** |

1. RESPONSIBILITY

  b. *Equipment and materials.* Each employee is responsible for conserving the company's equipment and materials. This includes reporting malfunctioning equipment or defective materials, keeping equipment and materials cleaned or in proper order, and maintaining, repairing, or modifying equipment and materials according to individual job duties. The company recognizes that the degree of responsibility for equipment and material varies widely throughout the organization.

  Level I.   Employee reports malfunctioning equipment or defective materials to immediate superior.

  Level II.   Employee maintains the appearance of equipment or order of materials and has responsibility for the security of such equipment or materials.

  Level III. Employee performs preventive maintenance and minor repairs on equipment or corrects minor defects in materials.

  Level IV.   Employee performs major maintenance or overhauls of equipment or is responsible for deciding type, quantity, and quality of materials to be used.

tive, requiring specialists to compare job descriptions with the standard point manual description for each subfactor. The match between the job description and the point manual statement reveals the level and points for each subfactor of every job. The points for each subfactor are added to find the total number of points for the job. Here, for example, is the matching process for a machine operator I:

The role of job descriptions

The job description of a machine operator I states that the "operator is responsible for performing preventive maintenance (such as, cleaning, oiling, and adjusting belts) and minor repairs." The sample point manual excerpt in Figure 13-8 states, "Level III: . . . performs preventive maintenance and minor repairs." Since the job description and the point manual match at level III, the points for the equipment subfactor equal 60. Repeating this matching process for every subfactor yields the total points for the job of machine operator I.

After the total points for each job are known, the jobs are ranked. As with the job ranking, job grading, and factor comparison systems, this relative ranking should be reviewed by department managers to ensure that it is appropriate.

Variations in job evaluations

Beyond the job evaluation methods discussed in this section, many other variations exist. Large organizations often modify standard approaches to create unique in-house variations. The Salt River Project, a large quasi-government utility in Arizona, for example, has been working to make its job evaluation methods more objective than a traditional point system. The "Hay Plan" is another variation widely used by U.S. and Canadian firms. This proprietary method is marketed by a large consulting firm, Hay and Associates, and relies on a committee's evaluation of critical job factors to determine each job's relative worth. Although other job evaluation approaches exist, all effective job evaluation schemes attempt to determine a job's relative worth to ensure internal equity.[12]

▶ Wage and Salary Surveys

Equity

All job evaluation techniques result in a ranking of jobs based on their relative worth within the firm to ensure *internal* equity. What constitutes *external equity*? To determine a fair rate of compensation, most firms rely on *wage and salary surveys.* These surveys discover what other employers in the *same* labor market are paying for specific key jobs. Generally, the *labor market* is the surrounding area within commuting distance from which the employer recruits. However, firms may have to compete for workers in a labor market that extends beyond the community. Consider how the president of a large university viewed the labor market:

> Our labor market depends on the type of position we are trying to fill. For the hourly paid jobs such as janitor, clerk, typist, and secretary, the labor market is the surrounding metropolitan community. When we hire professors, our labor market is the entire country. We have to compete with universities in other parts of the country to get the type of faculty member we seek. When we have the funds to hire a distinguished professor, our market is the world.

Sources of Compensation Data

Market surveys

Wage and salary survey data are benchmarks against which analysts compare compensation levels. One source of these data is the U.S. Department of Labor, which periodically conducts surveys in major metropolitan labor markets. Sometimes these surveys go out of date in a fast-changing labor market, and so other sources may be needed. Many state unemployment offices also compile this information for employers. If compiled frequently, this information may be current enough for use by compensation analysts. A third source of compensation data may be an employer association that surveys member firms. Employer associations or a fourth source—professional associations—may be the only source of compensation data for highly specialized jobs.

The major probem with all these published surveys is comparability. Analysts cannot always be sure that their jobs match the jobs reported in a survey. Matching job titles may be misleading. Federal, state, and association job de-

Equal Pay Act   In 1963, the FLSA was amended by the *Equal Pay Act*, as discussed in Chapter 4. This amendment was passed to eliminate sex-based discrimination in pay. It requires employers to pay men and women equal wages when their jobs are equal in skill, effort, and responsibility and are performed under similar conditions. Exceptions are allowed when a valid seniority or merit system exists. In that case employers can pay more to senior workers or workers who perform better. Exceptions also are allowed when pay is determined by the employee's productivity, as in the case of sales commissions. As explained more fully in Chapter 4, the federal government enforces these provisions by requiring wrongdoers to equalize pay and make up for past discrepancies.

Comparable Worth and Equal Pay

Beyond "equal pay for equal work" is the idea of "comparable pay for comparable work," called *comparable worth*. It requires employers to pay equal wages for jobs of *comparable* value. Under the Equal Pay Act, for example, male and female nurses would have to be paid the same if their seniority and merit matched but a female nurse and a male electrician could be paid different rates. Under comparable worth, however, if a nurse and an electrician both receive approximately the same number of points under a job evaluation point system, they have to be paid the same, subject presumably to merit and seniority differences.[26]

Comparable worth is used to eliminate the historical gap between the incomes of men and women. (In the United States women earn on average 71 percent as much as men do.[27]) This gap exists in part because women have traditionally found work in lower-paying occupations such as teaching, retailing, and nursing. Part of the difference in earnings results from women leaving the workforce to have and care for children or parents,[28] and part probably results from discrimination. Although comparable worth approaches may reduce the gap, this compensation theory ignores the marketplace. If in the previous example nurses were paid $34,000 a year and electricians were paid $42,000, comparable worth would require paying the nurses $42,000 even though salary surveys showed the market rate to be $34,000. If legislative bodies or the courts mandate comparable worth, analysts will face a major challenge in restructuring their compensation plans to comply while trying to obtain, maintain, and retain a cost-effective workforce.[29]

State and local governments   Limited experience with comparable worth doctrines comes almost exclusively from the public sector. More than 100 state and local government initiatives in support of comparable worth have been launched. Minnesota, for example, has a statute that mandates the implementation of comparable worth in each political subdivision in the state.[30] Since they are not subject to the direct marketplace pressures faced by for-profit organizations, political subdivisions may have greater latitude to experiment.

Research into comparable worth shows that different job evaluation approaches can widen or narrow the gap in pay for comparable jobs. For example, interpersonal or communication skills are important in female-dominated occupations such as bank tellers, public school teachers, and nurses. But a review of a traditional factor comparison chart (Figure 13-6) or point system matrix (Figure 13-7) does not directly acknowledge those skills, presumably lumping them under "responsibility" and "mental effort." As a pair of researchers concluded:

> In short, analyses of equity in pay structures are highly sensitive to differences in job evaluation methods. . . . comparable worth initiatives tend to ignore the fact that there is no definitive test of the fairness of a pay structure. Equity in a pay structure is like beauty—in the eye of the beholder.[31]

Compensation Strategies and Adjustments

Most organizations have compensation strategies and policies that cause wages and salaries to be adjusted.[32] A common strategy is to give nonunion workers the same raises that are given to unionized employees; this often is done to prevent further unionization. Premiums or bonuses for international assignments are another adjustment. Some companies, particularly large ones, pay a premium above the prevailing wages to attract and retain the best employees.[33] Also, some employers, such as State Farm Insurance Companies, have cost-of-living clauses that give employees automatic raises when the U.S. Department of Labor's cost-of-living index increases.[34] Strategies or policies that increase employee compensation move the wage-trend line upward. Compensation strategies are further complicated by international challenges.

International Compensation Challenges

The globalization of business affects compensation management. Compensation analysts must focus not only on equity but on competitiveness too. Firms that compete globally may find that using local area salary surveys in the home country—even for compensating home-country employees—may ensure equity in the home labor market, but benchmarking wages and salaries among home-country competitors—especially if they are all in a developed nation—may lead to labor costs that are too high to compete with foreign operations that have lower compensation costs. Jobs may have to be restructured to use less expensive labor, be automated, or be moved to lower-cost countries for the organization to survive.

Globalization   The growing globalization of business also means greater movement of employees among countries. As employees are relocated, compensation specialists are challenged to make adjustments that are fair to the employee and the company while keeping competitiveness in mind. Figure 13-12 lists the top six

Figure 13-12	The Top Six Issues Facing HR Managers of Global Firms

In a brief survey conducted by the Institute for International Human Resources, the following items were identified in order of priority:

1. Managing expatriate expectations
2. Adding "appropriate" value to expatriate compensation packages
3. "Localization" of expatriate compensation
4. Cost containment
5. Global pension schemes
6. Integration of HR planning with expatriate compensation

Source: International HR Update, January–February 1993, p. 1.

compensation issues facing HR managers in global firms. Most commonly, these challenges affect executive compensation, although professional, managerial, and technical workers are increasingly affected. As two researchers observed:

> A crucial question that arises . . . is the degree to which reward systems must be customized to cope with diverse cultural contingencies, or the extent to which the effectiveness of particular compensation strategies vary from one country to another. The old days, when lower labor costs were a primary reason for a firm relocating overseas, are gone. Closeness to markets, competitive advantages, and strategic flexibility now are at the fore. The emerging challenge from a compensation perspective . . . is not to take advantage of low-wage opportunities, but to design compensation strategies that are most appropriate for specific cultural conditions.[35]

Relocation

When international assignments are temporary, usually under a year, the employee is paid his or her regular salary plus adjustments. These additional amounts typically cover transportation, temporary living quarters, and cost-of-living differentials. Educational supplements may be added if children join the employee. Bonuses may be used to compensate for hardships, particularly if the employee is sent to a less than desirable location. For extended stays, relocation expenses may also include the purchase of the employee's residence at the appraised value, company-paid trips back to the home country, legal expenses for adjusting wills, supplements to offset higher taxes in the new country, and other adjustments to income.

Additional compensation costs may include benefits not common in the home country but usually provided to employees overseas. For example, the high taxes in many developed nations have led to a long list of nonpay (and therefore nontaxed) benefits—such as company cars (with drivers), servants, and club memberships—being provided instead of the high salaries drawn by U.S. executives.

Productivity and Costs

Regardless of company or social policies, employers must make a profit to survive. Without profits, they cannot attract enough investors to remain competitive. Therefore, a company cannot pay its workers more than the workers give back to the firm through their productivity. However, if this should happen (because of labor scarcity or union power), the company must redesign those jobs, train new workers to increase the supply, automate, innovate, or go out of business.

Two-tiered wages

Two-tiered wages and bonuses are innovations that became widespread during the 1980s. As the name implies, employers created two wage structures, usually one for current employees and one for future recruits. Current employees often retain their current wages and rate ranges; future employees, however, are paid a lower rate to start. The lower starting rate—often combined with a lower midpoint and maximum in the rate range—assures the employer lower labor costs as current employees leave and are replaced by lower-cost recruits.[36] These two tiers are most commonly found in unionized companies, especially those which have faced extreme cost cutting within the industry. Meatpacking, automobiles, trucking, and airlines are a few of the more widely publicized industries with two-tiered wage structures.[37] This approach allows union leaders to maintain the wages of their current (and voting) members while enabling employers to reduce their labor costs. Since some two-tiered systems allow recruits to catch up to the first-tier rates over two, five, or ten years, these savings may be temporary.[38] In recent years, the use of two-tiered wage approaches has declined because workers and researchers have raised questions about the equity of different rates of pay for the same work.[39]

Compensation innovations

Other innovations help employer productivity and costs. Instead of wage increases that permanently raise workers' pay levels, about one-fifth of employers give lump-sum bonuses.[40] These bonuses are not part of the employees' base pay. If sales, productivity, or profits falter the following year, bonuses are not given, providing a cushion of lower labor costs in years of poor performance.[41] And since lump-sum bonuses do not raise the base wage, future merit or across-the-board raises start from a lower base pay. Likewise, overtime, pensions, disability insurance, and other benefits are usually linked to base pay. By using lump-sum bonuses instead of increasing the hourly rate, General Motors might save as much as $86 million in one year.[42]

Of course, productivity and cost innovations are not limited to wages. Outdated work rules have been changed by union-management negotiators in return for pay increases (or no pay cuts). Narrow job classifications, for example, may be expanded, giving operating managers more flexibility in job assignments and giving compensation specialists broader job groupings, with the savings allowing the employer to maintain and even improve compensation.[43] GE's use of two job classifications in its Puerto Rican operation and the corporate office's decision to compress the number of salary grades are two examples of greater flexibility.

Fringe benefits
and productivity

Two other productivity and cost-related areas merit mention. First, fringe benefits—especially medical costs—have been a major target of cost-reducing efforts. These areas of cost improvement are addressed more fully in Chapter 15. Second, more employers are trying to increase productivity and relate pay increases to gains in productivity through incentives and gainsharing, the topics of Chapter 14.

▶ Summary

Employee compensation, when properly administered, can further corporate strategy and be an effective tool to obtain, maintain, and retain a productive workforce. Since compensation can signal which behaviors are most valued, it has the potential to influence individual productivity strongly. If it is mismanaged, the results may be high turnover, increased absenteeism, more grievances, increased job dissatisfaction, poor productivity, and unfulfilled strategic plans.

For the pay component of compensation programs to be appropriate, wages and salaries must be internally and externally equitable. The relative worth of jobs is determined through job evaluation techniques. This ensures internal equity. Wage and salary surveys then determine external equity. Once internal and external equity have been determined, jobs are priced to determine their specific pay levels, which may be grouped into rate ranges for easier administration.

The actual amount paid may be further influenced by challenges such as strategic objectives, prevailing wage rates, union power, compensation policies, government constraints, globalization of business, and worker productivity. The Fair Labor Standards Act is the major federal law affecting compensation management. It regulates minimum wages, overtime, and child labor. The Equal Pay Act seeks to eliminate sex-based pay differentials.

▶ Terms for Review

Job evaluations	Rate ranges
Job ranking	Prevailing wage rates
Job grading	Red-circle rate
Factor comparison method	Fair Labor Standards Act
Key jobs	Wage compression
Point system	Equal Pay Act
Wage and salary surveys	Comparable worth
Merit increase	Two-tiered wages

▶ **Review and Discussion Questions**

1. Research suggests that interesting jobs and good pay are the two factors in jobs that are most important to people. Briefly describe what is meant by "good pay."

2. How does effective compensation management help an organization achieve its strategic objectives?

3. Assume your company has a properly conducted compensation program. If several employees ask you why they receive different hourly pay rates even though they perform the same job, how will you respond?

4. What role does job analysis information (discussed in Chapter 5) play in the job evaluation process?

5. If you wanted to learn what different jobs in your community pay, what sources of information would you turn to?

6. Explain how jobs that are internally and externally equitable in pay may harm an organization's ability to compete globally.

7. Explain why equal pay does not mean comparable worth.

8. Provide examples of changes in compensation that might have to be made for someone assigned to an international job.

▶ **Incident 13-1**

The Mexican Connection at TexaSlacks

TexaSlacks is a small Texas-based contractor specializing primarily in men's slacks. With facilities in several south Texas cities, the company historically relied on first- and second-generation Mexican Americans to staff its cutting and sewing operations. Pay was usually set at the federal minimum wage or slightly higher for high-performing, long-service workers. The company did not discriminate in its hiring or wage practices, paying men and women equally on the basis of their job classifications.

Yet each year the management of the company found it increasingly difficult to contract with U.S.-based retailers, TexaSlacks' primary customers. Low-cost imports from Asia, the Caribbean, and increasingly Mexico kept competition keen and profit margins razor thin. After the North American Free Trade Act was passed in late 1993, a decision was made by senior management to move some of the company's operations to northern Mexico. Although the lower wage rates were an attractive inducement to move and the declining tariffs under NAFTA made such a move feasible, the primary motive was to avoid the growing list of government regulations that greatly complicated the company's hiring and employment policies.

In late 1995, the HR director reported that yet another plant manager had quit as head of one of the Mexican plants. This was the third manager to leave in less than two years. The inability to keep U.S. citizens as plant managers in the Mexican facilities was perplexing and frustrating. The owner urged the HR director to reevaluate the compensation package for Mexican plant managers before more quit.

1. Assuming you were the corporate HR director for TexaSlacks, what factors would you consider in evaluating the compensation package for U.S. managers assigned to run Mexican plants?

2. Although TexaSlacks moved some of its operations to Mexico to avoid U.S. regulations, the result was that it had operations in both countries and had to comply with two different sets of employment laws. Besides lower hourly wages, what other gains might accrue to an employer that moves some of its operations to a developing country?

▶ References

1. Itzhak Harpaz, "The Importance of Work Goals: An International Perspective," *Journal of International Business Studies,* First Quarter, 1990, p. 75.

2. Rosabeth Moss Kanter, "From Status to Contribution: Some Organizational Implications of the Changing Basis for Pay," *Personnel,* January 1987, p. 12.

3. Edward E. Lawler III, *Pay and Organizational Effectiveness: A Psychological View,* New York: McGraw-Hill, 1971, p. 71.

4. "General Electric's Perpetual Learning Machine," *Positive Employee Practices Institute Update,* June–July 1993, pp. 1–2.

5. Shari Cuadron, "Master the Compensation Maze," *Personnel Journal,* June 1993, pp. 64b–64o.

6. Eddie C. Smith, "Support Objectives Using Base Compensation," *Personnel Journal,* February 1990, pp. 86–90.

7. George W. Bohlander, "A Statistical Approach to Assessing Minority/White Pay Equity," *Compensation Review,* Fourth Quarter 1980, pp. 15–24.

8. Maeve Quaid, *Job Evaluation: The Myth of Equitable Assessment,* Buffalo, N.Y.: University of Toronto Press, 1993.

9. Robert M. Madigan and David H. Hoover, "Effects of Alternative Job Evaluation Methods on Decisions Involving Pay Equity," *Academy of Management Journal,* March 1986, pp. 84–100.

10. Edward E. Lawler, "What's Wrong with Point-Factor Job Evaluation?" *Personnel,* January 1987, p. 41.

11. Robert J. Sahl, "How to Install a Point-Factor Job-Evaluation System," *Personnel,* March 1989, pp. 38–42.

12. Jaclyn Fierman, "The Perilous New World of Fair Pay," *Fortune,* June 13, 1994, pp. 57–64.

13. Michael A. Conway, "Salary Surveys: Avoid the Pitfalls," *Personnel Journal,* June 1984, pp. 62–65.

14. The least squares method is explained in most introductory statistics books.

15. Frederick S. Hills, Robert M. Madigan, K. Dow Scott, and Steven E. Markham, "Tracking the Merit of Merit Pay," *Personnel Administrator,* March 1987, pp. 50–57. See also Lawrence B. Chonko and Ricky W. Griffin, "Trade-Off Analysis Finds the Best Reward Combination," *Personnel Administrator,* May 1983, pp. 45, 47, 99.

16. Jane Bryant Quinn, "A Generation Topped Out," *Newsweek,* Sept. 20, 1993, p. 42.

17. Joseph Weber, Lisa Driscoll, and Richard Brandt, "Farewell Fast Track," *Business Week,* December 1990, p. 200.

18. Carol A. Braddick, Michael B. Jones, and Paul M. Shafer, "A Look at Broadbanding in Practice," *Journal of Compensation and Benefits,* July–August 1992, pp. 28–32. See also Jaclyn Fierman, "Beating the Midlife Career Crisis," *Fortune,* Sept. 6, 1993, pp. 52–62; Caroline Weber and Sara L. Rynes, "Effects of Compensation Strategy on Job Pay Decisions," *Academy of Management Journal,* March 1991, pp. 86–109.

19. Timothy Haigh, "Aligning Executive Total Compensation with Business Strategy," *Human Resource Planning,* September 1989, pp. 221–227.

20. Peter Eyes, "Realignment Ties Pay to Performance," *Personnel Journal,* January 1993, pp. 74–77. See also Mary Rowland, "For Each New Skill, More Money," *The New York Times,* National ed., June 13, 1993, p. 16.

21. "Rich Man, Poor Man," *The Economist,* July 24, 1993, p. 71.

22. Brian Dumaine, "Illegal Child Labor Comes Back," *Fortune,* Apr. 5, 1993, p. 86.

23. In the public sector, workers can be compensated by receiving 1.5 hours off for each hour of overtime under the 1985 amendments to the Fair Labor Standards Act (FLSA). These amendments were passed to reduce the impact of the U.S. Supreme Court decision in *Garcia v. San Antonio Transit Authority,* 1985, which forced state and local governments to comply with the FLSA. See "Garcia Bill Seen as Relief for Government HRM," *Resource,* January 1986, p. 3.

24. John A. Dantico, "Wage-Hour Law Clarifies Exempt/Non-Exempt," *HR News,* January 1990, pp. 3, 12.

25. David Gold and Beth Madigan, "More than One-Third Pay Overtime to Exempt," *Resource,* July 1989, p. 5.

26. Carl C. Hoffman and Kathleen P. Hoffman, "Does Comparable Worth Obscure the Real Issues?" *Personnel Journal,* January 1987, pp. 83–95. See also Kanter, op. cit.

27. "Low Paid, with Children," *The Economist,* July 31, 1993, p. 26.

28. Ibid.

29. Judy B. Flughum, "The Employer's Liabilities under Comparable Worth," *Personnel Journal,* May 1983, pp. 400–404, 406, 408, 410, 412. See also Thomas A. Mahoney, "Approaches to the Definition of Comparable Worth," *The Academy of Management Review,* January 1983, pp. 14–22; John R. Schnebly, "Comparable Worth: A Legal Overview," *Personnel Administrator,* April 1982, pp. 43–48, 90; George L. Whaley, "Controversy Swirls over Comparable Worth Issue," *Personnel Administrator,* April 1982, pp. 51–61, 92; and Gary R. Siniscalo and Cynthia L. Remmers, "A Special Update: Comparable Worth," *Employee Relations Law Journal,* Winter 1983–1984, pp. 496–499.

30. Madigan and Hoover, op. cit., p. 84.

31. Ibid., pp. 96–97.

32. Ronald G. Ehrenberg, "Introduction: Do Compensation Policies Matter?" *Industrial and Labor Relations Review,* vol. 43 (Special Issue), February 1990, pp. 3-S–10-S.

33. Richard A. Ippolito, "Encouraging Long-Term Tenure: Wage Tilt or Pensions?" *Industrial and Labor Relations Review,* April 1991, pp. 520–535.

34. During the rapid deflation in early 1983, COLA caused some wages to drop. See "The Wage Spiral Has Lost Its Bounce," *Business Week,* Apr. 11, 1983, p. 28.

35. Luis R. Gomez-Mejia and Theresa Welbourne, "Compensation Strategies in a Global Context," *Human Resource Planning,* March 1991, p. 29.

36. James E. Martin and Melanie M. Peterson, "Two-Tier Wage Structures: Implications for Equity Theory," *Academy of Management Journal,* June 1987, pp. 297–315. See also Mollie H. Bowers and Roger D. Roderick, "Two Tier Pay Systems: The Good, the Bad and the Debatable," *Personnel Administrator,* June 1987, pp. 101, 102, 104, 106, 108, 110, 112.

37. Daniel J. B. Mitchell, "Why Are Wage Concessions So Prevalent?" *Personnel Journal,* August 1986, p. 131.

38. Ibid., pp. 131–133.

39. Martin and Peterson, op. cit.

40. Linda Ison and Edward L. Hansen, "Bonuses, Not Raises, for More Employees," *William M. Mercer News Release,* Aug. 19, 1993, pp. 1–3. See also Suzanne L. Minken, "Does Lump-Sum Pay Merit Attention?" *Personnel Journal,* June 1988, pp. 77–83.

41. Mitchell, op. cit. See also Donald P. Schwab and Craig A. Olson, "Merit Pay Practices: Implications for Pay-Performance Relationships," *Industrial and Labor Relations Review,* February 1990, pp. 237-S–255-S.

42. Susan Gelfond, "A Pile of Cash That Doesn't Stack Up to a Raise," *Business Week,* Dec. 23, 1985, p. 33. The issue of paying overtime related to bonuses may require rethinking overtime pay. See, for example, Gina Ameci, "Bonuses and Commissions: Is Your Overtime Pay Legal?" *Personnel Journal,* January 1987, pp. 107–110.

43. Clemens P. Work, Jack A. Seamonds, and Robert F. Black, "Making It Clear Who's Boss," *U.S. News & World Report,* Sept. 8, 1986, p. 45. See also Richard W. Walton, "From Control to Commitment in the Workplace," *Harvard Business Review,* March–April 1985, p. 82.

A lot of managers say that the best results come when you combine profit sharing with greater worker involvement and give employees information about the company's financial performance.

JOHN LABATE[1]

Incentives and Gainsharing

CHAPTER OBJECTIVES

After studying this chapter, you should be able to:

1. DISTINGUISH between incentives and gainsharing.

2. EXPLAIN why incentives and gainsharing are growing in popularity.

3. DISCUSS the major challenges in developing incentives and gainsharing for international operations.

4. IDENTIFY nonmonetary incentives.

5. EXPLAIN what the key factors are in executive incentives.

6. DISTINGUISH between gainsharing approaches employees can control and those controlled by the external government.

Definitions

An organization's success requires an effective strategy that is attained by achieving the underlying goals and objectives. Managers and HR departments can use incentives and gainsharing as tools to motivate employees to attain organizational goals and objectives because these are compensation approaches that reward specified outcomes. *Incentive systems* link compensation and performance by rewarding performance instead of seniority or hours worked. Although incentives may be given to a group, they often reward individual behavior. Many farm workers are paid for each pound or bag of fruit they pick, for example. *Gainsharing* matches an improvement (*gain*) in performance with a distribution (*sharing*) of the benefits with employees. Usually, gainsharing applies to a group of employees rather than an individual.

Fast-growing trends

Both incentives and gainsharing supplement the more traditional wage and salary approaches, which account for the majority of compensation costs. However, as discussed in Chapter 13, incentives and gainsharing are the fastest-growing trends in compensation management. Though companies still give traditional annual merit increases for good overall performance, rewards increasingly are being tied directly to performance in the form of one-time bonuses.[2] In fact, a survey of 2000 firms found that "these companies now pay out far more in incentive compensation than in salary increases."[3] And 20,000 DuPont "workers and managers agreed to accept 2% average raises for three years, in exchange for bonuses if the division posted strong growth in earnings. In the third year the maximum bonus could reach 18% of base salary."[4]

Although performance-based compensation has a long history, it often is considered a nontraditional compensation approach, since most people receive wages and salaries. However, with inflation-adjusted pay per employee in the United States stuck under $24,000 a year since the early 1970s, incentives and gainsharing offer employees a way to take charge of their pay.[5] Employer interest in performance-based compensation is motivated by increased competition.[6]

Creating a sense of common fate or destiny makes people feel they have a shared destiny and need to cooperate to prosper. The result can be a greater commitment to improve performance, productivity, and quality through teamwork. Even though individual compensation may rise, overall labor costs may actually drop as the same number of workers (inputs) produce more goods and services (outputs). Consider a classic example, the Lincoln Electric Company.

Lincoln Electric

The Lincoln Electric Company is a manufacturer of arc-welding and electric motor products. Its equipment is considered to be among the best in the world because productivity and quality are so good. Lincoln's employees are $2^1/_2$ to 3 times as productive as their counterparts in similar settings,[7] and much of this advantage is attributed to the company's use of incentives and gainsharing.

Each year the gainsharing process begins with a commitment to employees, "guaranteeing" each worker a minimum of thirty hours of work per week during the next year. (The company aims for forty-two to forty-three hours per week, adjusting that number up or down to match sales.) The company honors its pledge by using extensive overtime rather than hiring new workers who might have to be laid off during a recession. Applicants are screened so that they fit Lincoln's strong "promote-from-within" policy. Even then, they are considered probationary for two years before they receive "guaranteed" employment.

Lincoln's compensation program has four parts: traditional wages and salaries, incentives, gainsharing, and fringe benefits. Wages are comparable to those in the Cleveland area. Managers' salaries, however, are fixed at about 80 percent of what similar jobs pay. About 90 percent of the workers are on an incentive system. Salespeople, interestingly, are salaried, not on commission. All employees—whether receiving salaries, wages, or piece rates—are part of the merit and bonus system. This system has resulted in bonuses averaging 97.6 percent of regular earnings since 1934, which is almost like a second paycheck. Fringe benefits are also provided.

The bonus amount equals total profits minus taxes, reinvestment reserves, and the stockholders' dividend. Individual bonuses, however, are determined by merit. In twice-a-year reviews, workers are evaluated on the quality and quantity of their output, their dependability, and their ideas and cooperation. With input from other departments, the supervisor allocates a predetermined pool of points among workers to determine each person's bonus.[8]

Although Lincoln Electric is a unique example, research shows that nontraditional pay plans are gaining in popularity. A study of 1600 companies found that 75 percent had implemented reward and incentive systems during the preceding five years.[9] Another study found that:

Research summary

Directors of top firms favor a stronger pay/performance link, according to a national survey of directors, CEOs, and human resource executives. More than 70 percent of all directors, and 74 percent of HR managers rated "more effectively relating pay to performance" as the most important issue facing large companies. . . .

One out of five respondents to the survey conducted by Gibson & Co. said "pay without performance" is the most worrisome abuse of a company's payroll.[10]

Chapter 13 discussed how analysts ensure internal pay equity among employees and external pay equity between employees and the labor market. This chapter addresses how incentives and gainsharing link pay and performance; the following chapters cover benefits.

▶ **Incentive and Gainsharing Issues**

Faced with a slump in demand . . . companies often . . . can't cut wages; instead, they lay off workers.

Lincoln Electric

Lincoln Electric . . . hasn't laid off a worker in more than three decades, according to Richard Sabo, assistant to the chief executive officer. Even during the severe recession of 1982, when the company's sales plummeted 40%, employment stayed steady. Workers reduced their hours, and bonus payments fell from a total of $59 million in 1981 to $26.5 million in 1983. The combined result: the average production worker's pay fell from $44,000 in 1981 to $22,500 in 1983.[11]

Besides providing greater flexibility in matching labor costs to organizational success, incentives and gainsharing raise issues that should be considered *before* a particular approach is selected. Managers and HR specialists should understand the purpose, eligibility and coverage, payout standard, and administration of pay-for-performance plans. These issues are summarized in Figure 14-1 and discussed below.

The Purpose of Nontraditional Compensation

Employees who work under a financial incentive system find that their performance determines their pay in whole or in part. As a result, incentives reinforce performance on a regular basis. Unlike raises and promotions, the reinforcement is generally quick and frequent—usually with each paycheck. Since the worker sees the results of the desired behavior quickly, that behavior is more likely to continue. Employers benefit because payouts are in proportion to productivity. And if the system motivates employees to expand their output, recruiting expenses for additional employees and capital outlays for new workstations are minimized. As one economist observed:

Incentives and cooperation

> With fixed wages individual workers also have little incentive to cooperate with management or to take the initiative in suggesting new ideas for raising productivity. At the level of the individual worker, higher productivity has no immediate payoff—wages are fixed for the length of the contract. The immediate effect of higher productivity is, in fact, negative. Less labor is needed, and the probability of layoffs rises.

Figure 14-1	**Key Considerations in Designing Incentives and Gainsharing Approaches**
ISSUES	**KEY CONSIDERATIONS**
Purpose of nontraditional compensation	■ Why is nontraditional compensation under consideration? ■ What are the key goals of this nontraditional compensation program?
Eligibility	■ Who will be covered under the nontraditional compensation program?
Coverage	■ Where will nontraditional compensation be applied? All facilities?
Payout standard	■ What will trigger an incentive or gainsharing bonus? When will it be paid?
Administration	■ How will the program be administered? By personnel? By line management? Both?

The higher productivity growth rates of the Japanese may also be due to their bonus system that encourages labor to take a direct interest in raising productivity.[12]

Many experts believe that bonuses contribute to Japan's success. More than one-fourth of an industrial worker's pay may arrive as an annual bonus, tied to company profits. Some economists think that this form of payment helps explain why Japan's savings rate is triple that of the United States. And since companies can adjust labor costs by adjusting their bonuses, layoffs may not be necessary; this may help explain why unemployment levels in Japan seldom rise above 3 percent.[13]

Eligibility and Coverage

Who gets incentives?

Who is eligible for incentives, gainsharing, and other forms of nontraditional compensation? The extent of coverage is crucial because it affects motivation, teamwork, and perceptions of equity. Eligibility may differ for different programs even within the same firm. As is the case at Lincoln Electric, workers paid by the hour get individual incentives (piece rates) while managers and workers share in the profits. Individual incentives such as sales commissions work best when cooperation and teamwork are less important to success. When success requires cooperation and coordination among those doing the work, group incentives and gainsharing work best. Coverage must be defined broadly enough to facilitate equity and teamwork but narrowly enough to include only those who affect the results. Deciding *who* is eligible largely determines *where* coverage will be found in the company. But as two compensation consultants caution:

> Our experience has been that most organizations can identify several groups whose needs can only be met through separate plans. Across-the-board profit-sharing plans may be appreciated, but a program tailored to the results of a small team or group tends to be the most effective in modifying behavior and getting results. The tendency to include various goups for "equity" should be avoided.[14]

Payout Standards

Standards for paying

Besides answering why, who, and where, nontraditional compensation plans also must answer *what* and *when:* What triggers the payout? When? With individual and even group incentives, the trigger is usually one or two clearly stated standards. For example, under piece rates, workers are paid for each unit produced. With gainsharing, the standard is usually a percentage of the cost savings or increased profits.

Payout rates

When should the payout occur? In agriculture, pickers are often paid daily. In production or sales, the payout is added to the weekly or biweekly paycheck. Gainsharing may delay the payout until quarterly or even annual payments are given. The delay in gainsharing helps smooth out seasonal and even monthly variations caused by sales and production. Although longer delays separate the reward from the performance, the resulting bonuses may be larger and thus more significant.

Administration

The administration of an incentive system can be complex. As with any control system, standards have to be established and results must be measured. For many jobs, the standards and measures are too imprecise or costly to develop. This means that the incentive system may result in inequities. For example, sometimes workers make more money than do their supervisors, who are on salary. Or employees may not achieve the standard because of uncontrollable forces such as machine breakdowns and other work delays.

Union reactions

Unions often resist incentive systems because they prefer seniority-based rewards and fear that increased productivity may mean layoffs among their members. They also worry that management will later raise the standard, and employees will have to work harder in the future for the same pay. This fear of a speedup often leads to peer pressure against anyone who exceeds the group's output norms. The advantages of the incentive system are essentially lost when peer pressure restricts output.

Who should compute the payout? Should the payout be included with the regular paycheck, or should it be a separate payment? Should payments be made frequently to quickly relate performance to pay, or should payouts be larger and less frequent? These and other questions must be answered in designing nontraditional plans. The answers depend on the purpose, eligibility, coverage, and payout standards for each form of nonstandard compensation. When employees can estimate the additional income from their work effort or results—for example, when a real estate agent can estimate a sales commission—greater confidence exists that the payout is correct. Including the extra income in the regular paycheck may dilute its impact because it is not separated from regular wages or salaries and is diminished by payroll deduc-

Payout speed versus size

tions such as taxes. Payouts should follow performance as quickly as is administratively feasible. Here the goal is quick reinforcement. However, daily or weekly payouts may be so small that they provide little incentive for extra effort.

The development of performance standards and measures, the tracking of performance measures, and the related administrative and clerical support often add to the costs and complexity of compensation management. If competitive, technological, or other changes lead to a redesign of the firm's nontraditional compensation, additional expenses are incurred. And if employees see these changes as cutting their payouts, trust, morale, and productivity can suffer. The remainder of this chapter will examine different approaches to incentives and gainsharing, beginning with incentives.

▶ Incentive Systems

Incentive systems exist for almost every type of job from manual labor to professional, managerial, and executive work. The more common incentives are discussed in the following pages.

Piecework

Per-unit payments

Piecework is an incentive system that compensates the worker for each unit of output. Daily or weekly pay is determined by multiplying the output in units times the rate per unit. For example, in agricultural labor, workers are often paid a specific amount per bushel of produce picked. Piecework does not always mean higher productivity, however. As the Hawthorne studies showed, group norms may have a more significant impact if peer pressure works against higher productivity. And it may be difficult to measure a person's contribution (for example, a receptionist), or an employee may not be able to control the output (as with an assembly-line worker).

Production Bonuses

Pay and bonuses

Production bonuses are incentives paid to workers for exceeding output goals. Often employees receive a base pay rate. Then, through extra effort that results in output above the standard, they get a supplemental bonus, which is usually figured at a given rate for each unit of production over the standard. One variation rewards the employee for saving time. For example, if the standard time for replacing an automobile transmission is four hours and the mechanic does it in three, the mechanic may be paid for four hours. A third method combines production bonuses with piecework by compensating workers on an hourly basis, plus an incentive payment for each unit produced. For example, the employee may be paid $9 an hour plus 25 cents per unit. A stepped or tiered bonus might pay 35 cents for each unit over thirty per day.

Commissions

In sales jobs, the seller may be paid a percentage of the selling price or a flat amount for each unit sold. When no base compensation is paid, total earnings come from commissions. Real estate agents and automobile sellers are often on this form of "straight commission," as are a growing number of retail clerks.[15] Even though 50 percent of all sales jobs are now held by women, "Employers offer sales incentives to men on their payrolls nearly twice as often as to women," 72 to 37 percent.[16]

Maturity Curves

What happens when technical or scientific employees reach the top of their rate range?[17] As discussed in Chapter 13, one answer is "broadbanding," which widens the rate range to accommodate senior or top performers.[18] Another approach is *maturity curves,* which are adjustments to the top of the rate range for selected jobs. Employees are rated on productivity and experience. Outstanding contributors are assigned to the top curve, as shown in Figure 14-2. Good but less outstanding performers are placed on the curve next to the top. Through this technique, high-performing professionals continue to be rewarded for their efforts above the top of their jobs' rate ranges without being required to seek a management position or switch jobs to increase their earnings.

Merit Raises

Merit pay and standards

As discussed in Chapter 13, *merit raises* are pay increases given after an evaluation of performance. These raises are usually decided by the employee's immediate supervisor, often in conjunction with superiors. Although merit raises reward above-average performance, they are seldom tied to any specific payout standard. This lack of clear standards causes some companies to rely on a management by objectives (MBO) approach that sets standards against which merit

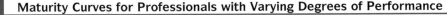

| **Figure 14-2** | **Maturity Curves for Professionals with Varying Degrees of Performance** |

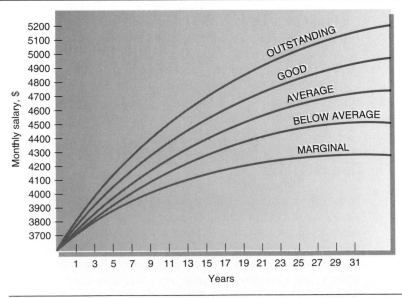

raises can be given. MBO is particularly common among administrative and managerial employees because their productivity is not objectively measurable.

As a result, merit raises are subject to many of the biases discussed in Chapter 12. When raises are distorted by biases, meritorious performance goes unrewarded. Furthermore, employees are sent incorrect messages about what is expected of them. For example, if a company values quality but gives merit raises to managers who exceed their production goals regardless of quality, other managers soon realize that quality is not valued as highly as quantity is. When merit raises are severely limited, some managers give an equal raise to everyone, which really does not reward merit. However, if a manager gives meaningful raises to only a few of the best performers, dissatisfaction among those who received no raises may become a serious morale problem.[19]

Pay-for-Knowledge/Pay-for-Skills Compensation

As mentioned in Chapter 13, *pay-for-knowledge* and *pay-for-skill* compensation systems reward employees with higher pay as an incentive for the increased knowledge or skills they acquire.

An emerging innovation

> Most organizations have traditionally designed their compensation systems around specific jobs. The wage and salary structure of these systems has typically been based on job analyses and evaluations; this process determines a job's worth and salary range. In recent years, however, a new alternative to this job-based approach has been developed; this new system pays employees for the skills and knowledge they possess, rather than for the job they do or a particular job category.[20]

Whether the compensation system is called knowledge-based pay, skill-based pay, or pay for knowledge, pay levels are based not on what an employee *does* but on the range of jobs the employee *can* do. Employees are rewarded for each new job or skill. These learning-based pay systems evaluate the employee's worth to the employer. Increased skills and job mastery give management greater staffing flexibility. The increased employee knowledge also may reduce the total number of workers needed and may lead to higher-quality results. The higher pay and greater diversity of work may mean higher levels of satisfaction and therefore lower absenteeism and turnover. At the same time, the HR department creates a continuous learning organization where continued growth is valued by employees and the company. In short, employees are paid more because they are worth more.[21]

To the extent that operations like those of Westinghouse in College Station, Texas, benefit from this nontraditional approach, the idea is likely to spread.

Westinghouse

Westinghouse's College Station facility makes electronic assemblies for military radar. Each worker averages 12 assemblies a day, compared with a more traditional operation in Baltimore, where employees average $1\frac{1}{2}$ assemblies per day. Although part of the difference stems from the College Station plant's investment in automated equipment and use of teamwork, some of it can be attributed to the plant's pay-for-knowledge compensation system. Under this pay-for-knowledge approach, employees can increase their annual salaries by 60 percent in three years, depending on how many jobs they master. As each new job is mastered, the employee receives a pay increase.[22]

Nonmonetary Incentives

Noncash rewards

Incentives usually mean money, but performance incentives also come in other forms. For example, many companies have recognition programs in which employees receive plaques, novelty items (from key chains to baseball caps), certificates, time off, vacations, and other noncash incentives for job performance, suggestions, and even community service. In fact, a survey of 3200 companies found that 60 percent used noncash rewards, with Federal Express sending employees more than 50,000 "thank you" notes in one year.[23] These *nonmonetary incentives* are particularly common among salespeople, who may already be eligible for commissions or other financial incentives. Here nonmonetary incentives encourage extra or more narrowly focused efforts.

Beyond specific rewards connected to specific behaviors, changes in the job or the work setting may serve as an incentive to improve one's performance. As discussed more fully in subsequent chapters, people may be motivated to apply for employment or work diligently to retain the current job because of fringe benefits. For example, health insurance for those with sickly family members and tuition waivers for university employees with college-age children may be a powerful incentive.[24]

Efforts at job redesign (see Chapter 5) such as job rotation, enlargement, and enrichment also may be viewed as incentives to induce improved performance. Other incentives include increased responsibility, greater autonomy, and other efforts to empower workers and enhance the quality of work life.

Executive Incentives

Incentives—especially executive incentives—need to achieve a balance between short-term results and long-term performance.[25] Although incentives that relate to long-term improvements were found in 45 percent of 112 firms researched in one study,[26] most companies still tie executive bonuses to annual profits, which are considered short-term. In some companies, this short-term orientation may lead to reductions in product quality and cuts in research and development, advertising, new capital equipment, employee development, and other long-term investments. As a report from the management consulting firm of Towers, Perrin, Forster & Crosby concluded:

> The point is simple: If you're intent on maximizing current earnings, there are myriad ways to do it. And some of them, to use the Surgeon General's words, are dangerous to your health.
>
> Faced with the results of this short-term thinking, most companies began to take action:

Short- versus long-term compensation

> ■ They either cut down on the size of their short-term incentives or they cut down on the degree to which incentive payments would respond to changes in short-term profits.
>
> ■ They beefed up their long-term incentive programs; in some cases, designing entirely new programs.[27]

At the same time, incentives must be matched to the needs of executives. Young and middle-aged executives are likely to desire *cash bonuses* to meet the needs of a growing or maturing family. Older executives often seek to defer incentive compensation to build retirement savings. In Europe, where tax rates on income tend to be higher than they are in the United States, executives frequently receive nontaxable benefits as rewards for good performance. A chauffeured limousine paid for by the company is a common reward for a senior executive. In Japan, expensive club memberships and liberal expense accounts are common perks of the executive life.

Stock options

Sometimes executives are granted *stock options*—the right to purchase the company's stock at a predetermined price. This price may be set at, below, or above the market value. The intent is to give executives an incentive to improve the company's performance, with some companies actually requiring executives to buy stock in the firm.[28] (In recent years, stock options and other incentives have been pushed further down the organization. In PepsiCo, for example, stock options equal to 10 percent of compensation are now available to all employees.[29])

Other forms of incentives exist, including some that allow executives to design their own compensation packages. The common element in most executive plans, however, is their relation to the performance of the organization. When these systems do not relate the incentive to performance, no matter what they are called, they are not incentive plans. And many plans have been criticized when executive incentives have been paid while company performance or stock prices declined. In fact, criticisms of executive pay have led to the *Omnibus Budget Reconciliation Act* of 1993, which contains a provision that limits the tax deductibility of executive compensation to $1 million per year in the United States.

To overcome these criticisms, companies are trying to tie executive incentives to gains for shareholders. As two writers observed:

> The new reward systems are being built around performance measures that will constantly propel managers to obtain long-term benefits for the companies.

According to compensation experts, a top manager's salary should be based on:

- Company size
- Return to shareholders of the company
- Profitability
- The complexity and importance of the job[30]

Given the volatility of the stock market, incentives might be more effective if tied to improvements in key organizationwide measures that executives control. For example, *weighted incentive systems* reward executives on the basis of improvements in multiple areas of business performance. Depending on the weights used, part of the incentive bonus can be tied to combinations of improvements in market share, profit margins, return on assets, cash flow, and other indexes.[31] Some companies even weight their bonuses by executive contributions to social goals such as cutting accidents or pollution.

Deferred stock incentive systems award stock to executives gradually over several years. Not only is there an incentive for the executive to stay until the stock is owned, its value depends on what the executive team has done to improve the company's performance during this period. Corning Glass Works, for example, uses stock incentives that take four years for complete ownership by executives.[32]

International Incentives

To attract, retain, and motivate international executives and key employees, many global companies are setting up *foreign allowances* that are incentives for international employees. Some companies find it advantageous to pay foreign housing and transportation costs and taxes directly rather than give allowances and incentives to work overseas.[33] Other companies prefer to use pay-for-performance plans. In one study, thirty-two of forty U.S. multinational corporations had created long-term plans to reward improvements in performance.[34] One expert recommends that international incentives be based on financial and strategic goals within the control of the country manager. Payouts and eligibility should be flexible to accommodate individual and national differences. Some companies even give equity ownership in foreign subsidiaries. As a consultant observed:

> Designing and implementing long-term incentive and direct ownership programs is a complex task. The companies that are putting them in place, however, are realizing significant benefits. They've found that the program development process has itself been valuable as an "audit" of their international executive compensation programs. They've also taken advantage of the opportunity to improve the linkages between the human resources function and the management of the international business. Finally, they're confident that programs tailored to local needs will help ensure that long-term incentives are an integral part of the management process worldwide.[35]

▶ Gainsharing Approaches

Sharing the gains

Gainsharing matches an improvement in company performance with some distribution of the benefits for employees. This approach has experienced explosive growth, with nearly three of every four plans installed during the 1980s using it. This rapid growth appears to be a response to competitive pressures and the resulting need for higher productivity. To create a greater sense of teamwork, 80 percent of the firms with gainsharing in one study included managers and workers, similar to what happens at Lincoln Electric. Employers with gainsharing are likely to share financial and nonfinancial information with employees much more frequently (65 percent) than are companies without gainsharing (37 percent).[36] And 84 percent of the firms in one study report that employees view gainsharing favorably,[37] while another study found productivity gains of 25 to 35 percent.[38]

Although gainsharing should be customized for individual plants or specific groups, most gainsharing falls into four broad categories: employee ownership, production-sharing, profit-sharing, and cost reduction plans.

Employee Ownership

Perhaps the ultimate gainsharing approach is for employees to own the company. Many companies have stock purchase plans that allow workers to buy shares in the company, thus "owning" a fractional part of the firm and sharing in its success.

ESOPs

A revolutionary approach by which employees may own their company is called an employee stock ownership plan (ESOP). Although it may be created in a variety of ways, an ESOP is a means for employees to buy stock in the company. Stock is "sold" to employees, who often "pay" for it by accepting stock shares instead of pay or pay raises. Or employees may simply pledge to buy stock as a way of helping a company pay off a debt.

ESOPs can be used in other ways that can be called "creative financing." The ESOP as a separate legal entity may:

▪ Buy the stock with borrowed money secured by the stock and employee pledges.

▪ Buy the stock with the funds from a tax-deductible contribution made by the company. (An owner who wants to sell may authorize a tax-deductible contribution to the ESOP so it can buy the stock, leaving the owner with cash and a tax deduction.)

▪ Create a new employeee benefit when a company contributes new stock issues to the plan.

▪ Make public companies private, spin off or divest subsidiaries, or save failing companies.[39]

Perhaps the most widely publicized ESOP involved National Steel Corporation's creation of Weirton Steel Corporation.

The National Steel Corporation created an ESOP to divest its steelworks in Weirton, West Virginia. National assumed $5 million in unfunded pension liabilities and lent money to Weirton. Employees took a 20 percent cut in wages and benefits and agreed to a six-year freeze in their wage levels. As employees bought stock, National was repaid. The following year Weirton posted a profit, which was the largest profit per ton of steel among the six major steel companies.

When the final distribution of shares is made, employees will have control of 80 percent of the stock. The company will be substantially owned and controlled by its employees.[40]

With employee ownership, workers may accept lower wages since they share in the company's profits. After the spin-off from National, for example, employee participation teams were created to enhance communications and tap employees' ideas. Such employee-oriented actions may yield high productivity even at the reduced wages.

Not all ESOPs result in such a positive outcome. Often stock sales to ESOPs are only partial ones, leaving control of the operation in the hands of others. The ESOP may be used to shelter the company from corporate raiders, since employees may be reluctant to support a corporate raider and an uncertain fate. Or, as was the case at National, the ESOP may be a way to divest an unprofitable operation with dim prospects. Yet even under the worst conditions, turnarounds were achieved at Weirton, Bridgeport Brass, a division of the Great Atlantic & Pacific Tea Company, and others.[41] According to the National Center of Employee Ownership in Oakland, California, ESOP employers grow about 10 percent faster than they did before the buyout. And "about 9,500 American companies—accounting for almost 10% of the country's workforce—have employee share-ownership plans, or ESOPs."[42]

Production-Sharing Plans

Production-sharing plans allow groups of workers to receive bonuses for exceeding predetermined levels of output. The plans tend to be short-range and related to very specific production goals. For example, a team may get a bonus for a specific goal. One well-publicized example comes from Nucor Corporation.

Nucor's management transformed the company into a steel producer in the late 1960s, a time when the North American steel industry was beginning to face strong competition from European and Japanese producers. Nucor's strategy was to be a low-cost steel producer.

Nucor

Nucor's nonunion production workers earn a base wage below that received by employees in the United Steelworkers Union. But if they reach progressively higher production targets, they are able to supplement their weekly pay with bonuses ranging from 100 to 200 percent of their base wage. If production does not reach the target, no bonuses are paid.

The results? Workers are motivated as a team to find ways to improve productivity. Employees who do not do their share receive considerable peer pressure. Workers earn about 20 percent more than do their unionized counterparts and about 250 percent more than does the average production worker in South Carolina, the home of Nucor's flagship steel mill. The company has been able to add mills in Texas, Nebraska, and Utah while producing steel at prices equal to or below those charged by foreign producers.[43]

Profit-Sharing Plans

Profit-sharing plans share profits with the employees. When these plans work well, they create trust and a feeling of a common fate among workers and management. Usually profit plans reserve a percentage of the firm's overall profits or a percentage above a threshold and distribute those monies to employees. The distribution formulas vary, though many give a flat bonus to each employee based on the employee's job category or tenure. Some plans give employees a percentage of their annual pay. AT&T, for example, uses economic value added (EVA)—which is net profits after a deduction for the capital used—paying bonuses of 15 percent for middle managers and up to 30 percent for executives who reach their EVA targets.[44] Research by Rutgers economist Douglas Kruse suggests that:

EVA-based profit sharing

> An estimated 16% of employees in medium-size and large companies share in the gains, and some 25% of small firms offer profit sharing.
>
> His initial findings: Productivity increases 3.5% to 5% on average after companies adopt profit-sharing programs. Cash plans have more than twice the impact of deferred-payments plans, and those that tie contributions to a percentage of employee pay rather than profits are the least effective.[45]

The effectiveness of these plans may suffer because profitability is not always related to the employee's performance, as is the case when a recession or new competitors affect the results. Or employees may not perceive their efforts as making much difference because of the way profits are distributed. Some plans, for example, divert the payouts into retirement plans, reducing the immediate reinforcement value.[46] Since each individual worker has little impact on overall profits, profit sharing is more common among senior managers.

Nucor

Nucor, the Charlotte, North Carolina, steel producer . . . rewards 14 of its plant managers based on the company's overall performance. Plant managers earn between $80,000 and $150,000 a year, which is about 25% less than managers at competing plants get. But the managers can also earn huge bonuses if Nucor achieves a 10% return on equity, high for the steel industry.

John A. Doherty, boss of Nucor's mill in Norfolk, Nebraska, pocketed an extra $80,000 in cash and $40,000 in stock. "These bonuses aren't entitlements," he says. "We're running our own businesses, and we'd better perform."[47]

Cost Reduction Plans

Some critics of group incentive plans argue that profit-sharing schemes such as those found at Nucor and Lincoln Electric do not always reward employees' efforts. For example, the pay received by workers at Lincoln Electric fell from $44,000 in one year to $22,500 two years later because of a slowdown in the economy. The reasons for the drop were largely beyond the employees' control.

Cutting costs by sharing savings

Another approach is to reward workers for something they can control: labor costs. To reduce costs, some companies form an employee committee to facilitate the communication of new ideas and employee involvement in the firm's day-to-day operations, usually through periodic meetings. Perhaps the

Scanlon Plan

best known of these approaches is the *Scanlon Plan,* which bases bonuses on improvements in labor costs compared with historical norms. See the first column of Figure 14-3.

Under a Scanlon Plan, employees aim to reduce costs and then share in the savings that result. If, for example, productivity increases at a company that has a Scanlon Plan, such as the American Valve and Hydrant Manufacturing Company, labor costs drop as a percentage of net sales revenue. These savings are shared with employees in the form of a bonus.

Rucker and *Improshare plans* are similar to the Scanlon approach, but they differ in how bonuses are calculated and in other administrative matters. All three differ from profit sharing in that they focus on something the employee can influence (costs), not on something the employee can control only indirectly (profits). A summary of these differences appears in Figure 14-3 and is discussed in the following paragraphs.

Cost cutting and commitment building

Scanlon, Rucker, and Improshare plans primarily aim to reduce costs and create improved commitment from workers through various approaches. The Scanlon Plan focuses primarily on labor costs and quality. Employees usually get to vote for a one-year trial of the plan. A vote at the end of the trial period makes it a permanent form of compensation. The Scanlon Plan normally covers production areas, making production employees eligible. Rucker and Improshare plans typically extend to an entire facility or firm, excluding senior management. A Rucker Plan seeks reductions in labor and materials costs by including those reductions in the calculation of gainsharing bonuses. A Rucker Plan is sometimes instituted as a result of an employee vote, but it and Improshare are commonly initiated by management. Improshare differs in that it

Figure 14-3	A Comparison of Scanlon, Rucker, and Improshare Gainsharing Approaches		
	SCANLON	**RUCKER**	**IMPROSHARE**
PURPOSE	Improve labor costs and/or quality	Improve labor and/or material costs	Reduce labor hours
CREATION	By vote of employees	By management or optional vote	By management
TYPE OF EMPLOYER	Usually goods producers	Usually goods producers	Usually goods producers
COVERAGE	Production areas	Company- or facilitywide or smaller groups	Usually entire firm or facility
ELIGIBILITY	Production workers	Usually all employees excluding senior management	Usually all employees excluding senior management
PAYOUT STANDARD	Reductions in historical labor costs as a percentage of sales revenue, adjusted for inventory	Reductions in labor costs as a percentage of sales, adjusted for inventory, materials, and supplies	Reduction in labor hours for unit of output
FREQUENCY OF PAYOUT	Monthly bonus as a percentage of wages with a reserve for year-end bonus and seasonality	Monthly bonus as a percentage of wages with reserves for seasonality	Usually weekly (or payroll period) or a four-week moving average
EMPLOYEE INVOLVEMENT IN PROCESS	Extensive through formal suggestion system; also weekly department production committee and a monthly screening committee composed of production committee representatives, both of which review suggestions	Extensive through formal suggestion system and Rucker committees composed of employees and managers to improve communications about suggestions and problems	Limited primarily to employees figuring out how to reduce the number of hours needed to produce a standard of output

focuses on reducing labor hours as a means of reducing costs. Although these plans can work in service industries, they are more common in goods-producing ones.

Scanlon and Rucker plans are perhaps more accurately seen as management philosophies that stress employees' suggestions and a review of those suggestions by employee committees. The involvement helps build employee interest and commitment. Although Improshare features less involvement of employees, it rewards gains in performance by sharing the benefits, as do Scanlon and Rucker plans. The success of these plans often hinges on managers allowing employees to influence the job and job setting. As two economists observed:

Redistribution
of power

The real problem with establishing meaningful worker participation programs that contribute to greater productivity is that they require a redistribution of power within the workplace. The traditional management perspective is that the retention of control and final decision making authority is essential to profit maximization. Although some employers may seek the advice of their employees in order to solve production problems, management in general is more likely to want workers to "feel" involved rather than actually to help make policy.[48]

Ways for the HR department to help build employee involvement and commitment are examined in Part V. Before those approaches are discussed, however, Chapters 15 and 16 examine indirect and legally mandated benefits and services because compensation consists of more than wages, salaries, and bonuses. Remuneration includes an ever-growing list of fringe benefits and services. Although these benefits are referred to as noncash compensation, they represent a significant part of most employers' total labor costs. Chapter 15 describes the fringe benefits and services offered by employers.

Incentive Matrix Summary

Figure 14-4 summarizes the various incentive and gainsharing approaches discussed in this chapter according to whether the employee receives cash. As can be seen from the figure, some incentives do not put cash into the employee's

Figure 14-4	**Incentive Summary Matrix**

WORKERS RECEIVE CASH	WORKERS RECEIVE NO CASH
INDIVIDUAL INCENTIVES	
Piecework	Recognition programs
Production bonuses	Job redesign
Commissions	
Maturity curves	
Merit raises	
Pay for knowledge/pay for skill	
Cash bonuses	
Stock options	
Weighted incentives	
Foreign allowances	
GROUP INCENTIVES	
Profit sharing	Fringe benefits
Production sharing	Job redesign
Cost reduction plans:	Employee ownership
Scanlon	
Rucker	
Improshare	

hands, substituting benefits, redesigned jobs, or even fractional ownership of the organization.

Besides the distinction between cash and noncash approaches, another important distinction is whether the incentive is for individual or group effort. Individual incentives may actually work against teamwork by putting employees into competition with each other. When cooperation is relatively unimportant, individual incentives are probably best. But when teamwork is required, group incentives are preferred.

▶ Summary

Incentives and gainsharing are compensation approaches that reward specified outcomes. Incentives usually link individual performance and rewards, while gainsharing usually embraces groups of employees. These nontraditional compensation approaches have gained in popularity in recent years as a means of stimulating increased productivity in the face of growing international competition. They also help employers relate pay to performance while improving employee commitment.

Nontraditional compensation approaches must consider the purpose, eligibility, coverage, payout standard, and administrative issues.

Many different incentive systems exist, including merit raises, piecework, production bonuses, commissions, maturity curves, pay-for-knowledge compensation, and nonmonetary and executive incentives.

Gainsharing approaches share the benefits of an improvement in company performance with employees. These approaches include production- and profit-sharing plans. Also popular are cost reduction methods such as Scanlon, Rucker, and Improshare plans.

▶ Terms for Review

Incentive systems	Nonmonetary incentives
Gainsharing	Weighted incentive systems
Payout standards	Deferred stock incentive systems
Piecework	Production-sharing plans
Production bonuses	Profit-sharing plans
Broadbanding	Scanlon Plan
Maturity curves	Rucker Plan
Pay-for-knowledge compensation systems	Improshare Plan
Merit raises	

▶ Review and Discussion Questions

1. Describe the advantages of incentive and gainsharing approaches for employees and for employers.

2. If you were hired as a consultant by Lincoln Electric, what suggestions could you offer that might improve on the company's successful approach?

3. If you were to design an international compensation program for senior executives, how might it differ from one for executives in the home country?

4. How do production-sharing and cost reduction plans differ? List the major differences between Scanlon, Rucker, and Improshare plans.

5. What are employee stock ownership programs (ESOPs)? What advantages and risks do they hold for employees?

6. In what fundamental ways do pay-for-knowledge compensation systems differ from traditional compensation approaches?

7. If you become a manager of an assembly-line operation and wanted to improve performance, what type of incentives or gainsharing would you select? Why? What would you do if your boss said you could not give monetary incentives or gainsharing bonuses?

8. Critics of the American business scene argue that companies focus too much on the short run. If you were designing a company compensation program, what ideas would you deploy to avoid a short-run orientation among executives?

▶ Incident 14-1

Incentives at Brothers-Two Hotel

Bill and Bob Kronolski owned and operated the Brothers-Two Hotel since it opened in 1993. Bob was in charge of human resources and finance, preferring office work; Bob ran hotel operations, including housekeeping, the grounds, and foods and beverages. Bill was often heard to say, "I believe in paying people for what they do, not for how many hours they work." And his brother, Bob, agreed with him wholeheartedly. Their management philosophy was expressed through a variety of incentive plans that Bob designed himself. Although he was firmly committed to the use of incentives, Bob hired a management consulting team to make recommendations about his compensation program.

To help the consultants, the owners wrote down the major features of each incentive program. Their notes were as follows:

■ Executives have no equity in the partnership but get 1 percent of the profits each quarter.

■ Every time occupancy reaches 95 percent, hourly employees get a complimentary lunch in the hotel coffee shop.

■ Housekeepers are paid the minimum wage plus $3 for each cleaned room that meets the hotel's "20-point checklist."

■ Reservationists are also paid the minimum wage but get 50 cents for each reservation they book.

1. What problems do you see with incentives for (*a*) executives, (*b*) hourly workers, (*c*) housekeepers, (*d*) reservationists?

2. If you were a member of the consulting team, what incentives would you recommend for each group?

▶ References

1. John Labate, "Deal Those Workers In," *Fortune,* Apr. 19, 1993, p. 26.

2. Donald P. Schwab and Craig A. Olson, "Merit Pay Practices: Implications for Pay-Performance Relationships," *Industrial and Labor Relations Review,* Special Issue, February 1990, pp. 237-S–255-S.

3. Shawn Tully, "Your Paycheck Gets Exciting," *Fortune,* Nov. 1, 1993, p. 83.

4. Ibid., p. 84.

5. Jaclyn Fierman, "When Will You Get a Raise?" *Fortune,* July 12, 1993, p. 35.

6. Ira Sager et al., "IBM Leans on Its Sales Force," *Business Week,* Feb. 7, 1994, p. 110. See also Carla O'Dell and Jerry McAdams, *Major Findings from People, Performance and Pay,* Houston, Tex.: American Productivity Center, 1986, pp. 10–12. See also Victoria A. Hoevemeyer, "Performance-Based Compensation: Miracle or Waste?" *Personnel Journal,* July 1989, pp. 64–68.

7. Barnaby J. Feder, "Recasting a Model Incentive System," *The New York Times,* National ed., Sept. 5, 1994, pp. Y1, Y20. See also "The Lincoln Electric Company" (Case Study 48), Houston: American Productivity Center, 1985, p. 5.

8. "The Lincoln Electric Company," op. cit., pp. 1–8. See also Feder, op. cit.

9. "Non-Traditional Pay Plans Gaining Popularity, Study Shows," *Resource,* December 1986, pp. 1, 6.

10. "Directors of Top Firms Favor a Stronger Pay/Performance Link," *Resource,* November 1986, p. 10.

11. Alan Murray, "Democrats Latch onto Bonus Pay System in Search of New Ideas," *The Wall Street Journal,* Eastern ed., Apr. 28, 1987, p. 1. See also James Chelius and Robert S. Smith, "Profit Sharing and Employment Stability," *Industrial and Labor Relations Review,* Special Ed., February 1990, pp. 256-S–272-S.

12. Lester Thurow, "Productivity Pay," *Newsweek,* May 3, 1982, p. 69. See also Denis Collins, Larry Hatcher, and Timothy L. Ross, "The Decision to Implement Gainsharing: The Role of Work, Climate, Expected Outcomes, and Union Status," *Personnel Psychology,* vol. 46, 1993, pp. 77–104.

13. Thurow, op. cit.

14. Hoyt Doyel and Thomas Riles, "Considerations in Developing Incentive Plans," *Management Review,* March 1987, pp. 34–37.

15. Beth J. Asch, "Do Incentives Matter? The Case of Navy Recruiters," *Industrial and Labor Relations Review,* Special Issue, February 1990, pp. 89-S–106-S.

16. Stephanie Losee, "Gender Gap in Incentive Pay," *Fortune,* Nov. 2, 1992, pp. 14–15.

17. Luis R. Gomez-Mejia, David B. Balkin, and George T. Milkovich, "Rethinking Rewards for Technical Employees," *Organizational Dynamics,* Spring 1990, pp. 62–75.

18. Carol A. Braddick, Michael B. Jones, and Paul M. Shafer, "A Look at Broadbanding in Practice," *Journal of Compensation and Benefits,* July–August 1992, pp. 28–32.

19. Lawrence M. Kahn and Peter D. Sherer, "Contingent Pay and Managerial Performance," *Industrial and Labor Relations Review,* Special Ed., February 1990, pp. 107-S–120-S.

20. Jaclyn Fierman, "The Perilous New World of Fair Pay," *Fortune,* June 13, 1994, pp. 57–64. See also Fred Luthans and Marilyn L. Fox, "Update on Skill-Based Pay," *Personnel,* March 1989, pp. 26–31.

21. Earl Ingram II, "The Advantages of Knowledge-Based Pay," *Personnel Journal,* April 1990, pp. 138–140.

22. "Yesterday's Despair Can Be Tomorrow's Triumph," *Behavioral Science Newsletter,* Sept. 8, 1986, p. 1.

23. Fierman, "When Will You Get a Raise?" pp. 34, 36.

24. Peter W. Stonebraker, "Flexible and Incentive Benefits: A Guide to Program Development," *Compensation Review,* Second Quarter 1985, pp. 40–53.

25. Sumer C. Aggarwal and Sudhir Aggarwal, "A Management Rewards System for the Long and Short Terms," *Personnel Journal,* December 1986, pp. 115–126.

27. *Paying for Divisional Executive Performance,* New York: Towers, Perrin, Forster & Crosby, 1985, p. 1.

28. Susan Scherreik, "Putting Stock Options to Their Best Use," *The New York Times,* National ed., Apr. 30, 1994, p. 30Y. See also Alan Farnham, "Buy Stock—or Die," *Fortune,* Aug. 23, 1993, p. 14; John A. Byrne, " 'Hands Off My Stock Pile,' " *Business Week,* Apr. 12, 1993, pp. 28–30.

29. "How You'll Be Paid in the 1990's," *Fortune,* Apr. 9, 1990, p. 11.

30. Aggarwal and Aggarwal, op. cit., p. 115.

31. Ibid., p. 118.

32. Ibid.

33. Lin P. Crandall and Mark I. Phelps, "Pay for a Global Work Force," *Personnel Journal,* February 1991, pp. 28, 30–33.

34. Brian J. Brooks, "Long-Term Incentives: International Executives," *Personnel,* August 1988, pp. 40–42.

35. Ibid.

36. Carla O'Dell and Jerry McAdams, "The Revolution in Employee Rewards," *Management Review,* March 1987, p. 32.

37. "Does Your Pay Plan Demotivate?" *Personnel Journal,* June 1988, p. 10.

38. Thomas Owens, "Gainsharing," *Small Business Reports,* December 1988, pp. 19–28.

39. *NCEO Membership Services and Publications,* Arlington, Va.: The National Center for Employee Ownership, 1986, p. 1. See also Keith Bradley, Saul Estrin, and Simon Taylor, "Employee Ownership and Company Performance," *Industrial Relations,* Fall 1990, pp. 385–402.

40. "Making Money—and History—at Weirton," *Business Week,* Nov. 12, 1984, pp. 136, 138, 140.

41. Robert Kuttner, "Worker Ownership: A Commitment That's More Often a Con," *Business Week,* July 6, 1987, p. 16.

42. "A Firm of Their Own," *The Economist,* June 11, 1994, pp. 59–60. See also *NCEO Membership Services and Publications* and other publications of the National Center for Employee Ownership.

43. Richard I. Kirkland, Jr., "Pilgrims' Profits at Nucor," *Fortune,* Apr. 6, 1981, p. 44.

44. Tully, op. cit., pp. 88–89.

45. Labate, op. cit.

46. Ronald Henkof, "The Payoff from Peer Pressure," *Fortune,* Dec. 14, 1992, p. 94.

47. Tully, op. cit., p. 88.

48. Sar A. Levitan and Diane Wernke, "Worker Participation and Productivity Change," *Monthly Labor Review,* September 1984, p. 32.

15

We know we can't afford everything for everyone; but neither do we want to deny anything to anyone.
ROBERT J. SAMUELSON[1]

Benefits and Services

CHAPTER OBJECTIVES

After studying this chapter, you should be able to:

1. EXPLAIN the multiple objectives of benefits management.

2. DESCRIBE policies that minimize health benefit costs.

3. DISCUSS the differences in pensions between defined benefits and defined contributions.

4. IDENTIFY unique concerns in managing the benefits of international workers.

5. EXPLAIN the pros and cons of flexible benefits and services.

6. ELABORATE the likely trends in benefits and services.

Most people think of "compensation" as "money," received in the form of wages, salaries, and incentives. These "cash" outlays make up the majority of an employer's compensation costs. However, benefits and services—sometimes called "indirect compensation"—account for nearly 40 percent of the average firm's compensation costs in the United States and an even higher percentage in most countries in the European Union.[2]

Figure 15-1 summarizes these relationships, showing that total compensation consists of direct and indirect compensation. Chapters 13 and 14 addressed direct compensation in the forms of base wages and salaries (Chapter 13) and incentives and gainsharing (Chapter 14). This chapter and Chapter 16 describe indirect compensation in the forms of "fringe" benefits and services (Chapter 15) and legally mandated security, safety, and health requirements (Chapter 16).

Decades ago, benefits and services were labeled "fringe" benefits because they were relatively insignificant, or fringe, components of compensation. During the early 1940s, World War II led to government-mandated controls on wage and salary increases. To obtain and retain scarce workers during the war, many organizations added or improved fringe benefits. During the half century after World War II, the use of employment-related benefits and services continued to expand. To see how comprehensive benefits and services have become, consider *some* of the fringe benefits one electronics firm gives its employees.

Intel

The Intel Corporation is a multi-billion-dollar company that produces sophisticated microelectronics for the computer, communications, automotive, and other industries. Most IBM-compatible computers rely on "Intel Inside" chips, for example. This fast-growing profitable company is responsible for some of the significant breakthroughs in computer-on-a-chip technology. Along the way, however, Intel has encouraged innovation by giving employees rewards and security through its benefits program.

Some of its fringe benefits include group life insurance, supplemental life insurance, business travel accident insurance, dependent life insur-

Figure 15-1	**The Elements of Total Compensation**	
INDIRECT COMPENSATION	SECURITY, SAFETY, AND HEALTH (Legally Mandated Benefits)	Chapter 16
	BENEFITS AND SERVICES ("Fringe" Benefits)	Chapter 15
DIRECT COMPENSATION	INCENTIVES AND GAINSHARING (Pay-for-Performance)	Chapter 14
	COMPENSATION MANAGEMENT (Base Wages and Salaries)	Chapter 13

ance, accidental death and dismemberment insurance, a voluntary short-term disability plan, a long-term disability plan, medical insurance, dental insurance, a stock purchase plan, tuition reimbursement, vacation and personal absence time, holidays, a profit-sharing retirement plan, sabbaticals, subsidized cafeterias, free parking, rest breaks, and legally required services (social security, unemployment insurance, workers' compensation, and a safe work environment). Moreover, most of these benefits and services are fully paid for by the company. With the exception of sabbaticals, most large employers would be able to produce a similar list.

The point of this illustration is that "fringes" embrace a broad range of benefits and services that employees receive as part of the total compensation package. In fact, benefits administration has become so administratively and legally complex that some large employers, such as the pharmaceutical giant Merck, contract out some or all of their benefits administration. Others, such as IBM, have spun off benefits administration into a separate for-profit company.

As with most employers, pay—or *direct compensation*—at Intel is based on critical job factors and performance. Benefits and services, however, are *indirect compensation* because they are usually extended as a condition of employment and are not directly related to performance.

This chapter describes the role of indirect compensation in an organization's overall compensation program. Then the discussion turns to common benefits and services, including insurance, security, time off, and scheduling benefits, in addition to educational, financial, and social services. The chapter ends with an explanation of benefits administration. Legally required benefits and services are covered in Chapter 16.

▶ The Role of Indirect Compensation

Societal, organizational, and employee objectives are sought through the use of indirect compensation.

Societal Objectives

Nonbusiness objectives

Within the last century, Europe, Japan, and North America have changed from rural nations of independent farmers and ranchers to urban nations of interdependent wage earners. This interdependence was illustrated forcefully by massive unemployment during the Great Depression of the 1930s and the recession of the early 1990s. To help provide security, governments rely on the support of employers.[3] Through favorable tax treatment, employees can receive most benefits tax-free, while employers can deduct the cost of benefits as a business expense. Although tax breaks reduce government receipts, health-care, disability, life insurance, and retirement benefits lower the burden on society when ill health, retirement, or death occurs. Even if these tax breaks are eliminated, benefits are so widely used that they are almost certain to continue.

The great struggle for the American society during the 1990s will be the continued assault on rising medical costs. As *Fortune* noted, "An aging population with nearly unlimited access to high-priced doctors and technology is pushing medical costs skyward."[4]

Organizational Objectives

What do employers gain from their huge outlays for fringe benefits? Besides the desires of many companies to be socially responsible, employers such as Intel offer benefits to recruit and retain workers. If Intel did not offer health insurance and paid vacations, for example, recruits and current employees might favor Motorola, Texas Instruments, National Semiconductor, or other competitors who did offer those "fringes." Similarly, many employees will stay with a company because they do not want to give up a benefit, and so employee turnover is lowered. For example, an employee who has been at Intel for $6^1/_2$ years might stay through the seventh year to earn his or her eleven-week sabbatical. Likewise, employees at other companies may stay to save pension credits or their rights to the extended vacations that typically come with greater seniority.

Time-off benefits such as vacations, holidays, and rest breaks help employees reduce fatigue, enhancing productivity during the hours when the employees do work. Similarly, retirement, health-care, and disability benefits may allow workers to be more productive by freeing them of concern about medical and retirement costs. If these benefits were not available, employees might elect to form a union and collectively bargain with the employer. (Although collective action is legal, employers such as Intel prefer to remain nonunion.) Thus indirect compensation may:

- Reduce fatigue
- Discourage labor unrest
- Satisfy employee objectives
- Aid recruitment
- Reduce turnover
- Minimize overtime costs

Employee Objectives

The real advantages to employees of employer-provided benefits are lower costs and availability. For example, insurance benefits are usually less expensive because the employer may pay some or all of the costs, as Intel does. Group plans save the cost of administering and selling many individual policies. The insurer also can reduce the risk of *adverse selection*, which occurs when individuals sign up for insurance because they are heavy users. Actuaries—the specialists who compute insurance rates—can pass on these savings in the form of smaller premiums even if workers pay the entire premium.

Lower taxes is another employee objective. For example, an employee in a 28 percent tax bracket has to earn $1000 to buy a $720 policy. But for $1000 the company can buy the same policy and give the worker a $280 raise. The employee has a policy and a $280 raise, while the employer is no worse off. And in many cases the company's purchasing power that derives from buying many policies may actually lower the cost for each policy so that the policy may cost only $600 instead of $720. Whether the tax advantages of company-provided benefits will continue is uncertain because government deficits may lead to the taxation of these fringes in the future.

Inflation protection

"Inflation protection" also results when the employer pays for a benefit. For example, a two-week paid vacation is not reduced in value by inflation.

"Preexisting conditions" often prevent people from obtaining insurance because it is unavailable or unaffordable, although health-care reform in the United States is likely to reduce the incidence of unavailability. In the European Union, Canada, Sweden, and other developed nations, health-care insurance may be of less importance because of government-provided health insurance or care.

Coverage for "domestic partners"

"Domestic partnership" coverage is emerging as a new benefit for employees, especially with the growing diversity of workers and their relationships. Usually benefit coverage is extended to the employee, spouse, and children, depriving nonfamily members of coverage regardless of their relationship with the employee. Some employers—such as Ben and Jerry's Homemade Ice Cream, Inc., Levi Strauss, the University of Iowa, Stanford, Harvard, and the city of Seattle—extend benefit coverage to "domestic partners" regardless of whether they are married.[5]

The objectives of society, organizations, and employees have encouraged the rapid growth of benefits and services. This growth has affected all areas of fringe benefits and services, including insurance, security, time-off, and work scheduling benefits.

▶ Insurance Benefits

The financial risks encountered by employees and their families can be spread by insurance. These risks are shared when funds are pooled in the form of insurance premiums. Then, when insured risks occur, the covered employees or their families are compensated.

Health-Related Insurance

Among large employers, 99 percent report making payments for health insurance.[6] Contrast this finding in the United States with Europe, where many firms face no direct medical insurance costs since health care is provided by the government.

Medical insurance.   Medical insurance pays for sickness, accident, and hospitalization expenses up to the dollar limits (or "policy ceiling") of the policy. In addition, most policies contain a schedule of benefits. This schedule sets forth which sickness, accident, or hospitalization costs are covered and how much of those expenses will be paid. Otherwise, the insurer agrees to pay "reasonable and customary" expenses.

Cost savers

   If the company pays part or all of the premiums, HR managers should require a deductible or coinsurance clause in addition to a ceiling on the policy's benefits. A *deductible clause* requires the covered employee to pay a specified amount (usually $100, $200, or more) before the insurer is obligated to pay. Xerox, for example, pays 100 percent of medical costs after a deductible equal to 4 percent of the employee's annual wages or salary. The deductible clause has two significant cost advantages. First, if each minor illness resulted in a claim, premium costs would soar because of the added administrative burden. Second, a deductible discourages employees from abusing the benefit through overuse. A *coinsurance clause* requires the employee to pay a percentage of the medical expenses, typically a copayment equal to 20 percent of the expenses. These clauses often specify a maximum liability for the employee but require cost sharing to discourage malingering and give employees a reason to hold down these costs.

   Even when deductibles, coinsurance, and policy ceilings are used, premiums continue to increase rapidly. As a health-care adviser to the White House observed, "The cost of health care has risen so high for employers, it's undermining industrial efficiency and international competitiveness."[7] For example, the National Association of Manufacturers reported that health-care costs amounted to 37.2 percent of net profits.[8] As a result, HR managers find that holding down medical insurance costs is a major concern. And the growing AIDS epidemic means even more attention paid to health-care costs.

Cutting health-care costs

   The trade-off faced by benefit administrators is to meet the basic health-care needs of employees in ways that minimize the cost to the employer. Some of the more innovative efforts include requirements for second opinions in nonemergency surgery, more extensive outpatient surgery, preadmission testing to reduce the time spent as a hospital inpatient, and a greater analysis of medical claims costs. Through analysis of claims costs, employers try to identify the most cost-effective doctors and hospitals in the area.

   Companies such as Mobil, Chemical Bank, and Quaker Oats pay employees *not* to get sick. These companies set aside a cash amount that employees can keep if they do not use those moneys for health care.

Quaker Oats

   The Quaker Oats plan is a combination of a flexible spending account and a group plan. Each of the 6000 Quaker Oats employees gets $300 that can be applied to medical-related expenses. If an employee does not need the $300 for such expenses, he or she keeps what is left. If employees reduce their medical expenses and Quaker Oats does not spend the planned $1535 per employee, the unspent balance is shared among the employees. The director of employee benefits at Quaker estimates that each employee could receive as much as $200 while reducing the company's total outlays for medical care and insurance premiums.[9]

Southern California Edison

Many other approaches besides Quaker's incentive-based method have been tried. Southern California Edison operates ten clinics with its own doctors and buys pharmaceuticals in bulk, saving 40 percent on its drug purchases alone. Caterpillar negotiates lower hospital and doctor costs for its employees.[10] Preventive, or "wellness," care seeks to keep employees healthy through "quit-smoking," weight-reduction, exercise, and other programs.

General Electric, for example, reports saving a million dollars annually at its aircraft engine headquarters in Cincinnati since installing voluntary fitness programs. "In a study, GE tracked the health-care costs of 800 fitness center members of similar age, gender and work classification. . . . In the six months before the members-to-be joined the health

General Electric

club, their medical costs averaged 35% higher than those of nonmembers.

"But in the year after they joined . . . their annual health costs plunged 38% to $757. For nonmembers, costs jumped 21% to $841."[11]

For every dollar spent on wellness, savings average $3.44, according to the Health Research Institute.[12]

Managed care. The *Health Maintenance Act* of 1973 required firms with twenty-five or more employees to offer their employees *health maintenance organization* (HMO) coverage if it is available in their area and the employer offers

HMOs

other forms of health benefits. HMOs are organizations that provide their own doctors and facilities. Usually a company's covered employees and their dependents can use the HMO's services for any health-related problem. Most large employers in metropolitan areas (where HMOs are located) offer this alternative to encourage preventive rather than remedial health care. The hope here is that through better management, preventive care, and fewer unneeded tests, exams, and other medical procedures, rising medical costs will be slowed. The attraction of HMOs for employees is that they offer "well care"

"Well care"

such as free or "low-cost" physical examinations and usually have a small ($5 to $15) charge for office visits, called a copayment. Most large employers offer both HMOs and indemnity plans. Indemnity plans reimburse the employee for medical expenses according to the company's medical insurance plan, often giving the employee greater freedom in selecting health-care providers but making the employee pay a larger share of each health-care bill. Employers are split, however, on whether HMOs really provide lower costs. One study found that 75 percent of employers offer HMOs.[13]

PPOs

Closely related to HMOs are preferred-provider organizations (PPOs), which were offered by 60 percent of the employers in one study.[14] HMOs generally operate hospital or cliniclike facilities where members receive services from those employed by the HMO. PPOs allow subscribers to select doctors and hospitals from an approved list, helping to assure cost containment because those on the list usually agree to discount their services. If the member uses another health-care provider, the cost may not be fully reimbursable. HMOs and PPOs encourage affiliated health-care providers to minimize tests, hospital admissions, and other sources of rising medical-care costs. Simply put, these alternative delivery systems provide *managed care* intended to reduce medical-care costs. One survey found that:

Research summary

> . . . employees tend to have the highest satisfaction levels (86%) with the quality of care they receive through traditional indemnity plans; the lowest satisfaction levels (75%) with PPOs; and a nominal satisfaction level (80%) with HMOs.[15]

Other types of health-related benefits have gained in popularity during recent years, including vision, dental, and mental health insurance.

Vision insurance.   Representing less than 1 percent of benefit outlays, vision care—often including examinations and eyeglasses—is a developing benefit. As with other insurance, deductibles and copayments usually apply, along with policy limits. Some plans limit benefits to twelve- to twenty-four-month intervals for services such as new glasses. The availability and cost of this benefit are likely to grow since the need for eye correction grows with age and the age of the workforce is increasing. Since more than two-thirds of the workforce needs vision correction, vision insurance is likely to be an increasingly popular benefit.

Dental insurance.   Dental policies tend to be narrow in scope. Besides deductibles and coinsurance clauses, most plans have benefit ceilings of $1000 per year or less. On the average, dental insurance costs employers less than one-half of 1 percent of payroll.[16]

Intel

Intel's dental plan pays for 90 percent of all routine care for employees who have been with the company for three years or more. It pays 70 percent in the first year and 80 percent in the second. The plan has a one-time deductible of $25 and an annual maximum benefit of $1000 per person. Orthodontia is not covered, and other major costs are covered 50 percent by the company and 50 percent by the employee.

Mental health insurance.   Mental health coverage pays for psychiatric care and counseling. Although most policies have special limits, there appears to be a trend toward comprehensive employer-provided mental health insurance. At Intel, for example, the coverage for outpatient psychiatric care is 50 percent of usual, customary, and reasonable charges up to a $25 benefit for each of fifty visits per year.

Life Insurance

"Burial policies" helped cover funeral expenses and were the first form of insurance offered to workers by employers. Today life insurance often goes beyond merely helping with funeral expenses. Although some firms provide a flat amount for all workers, the majority pay a multiple of the employee's salary. For example, the multiple at Intel is 2, and so a $30,000-a-year worker has $60,000 of coverage. Unlike health insurance, employer-provided life insurance is not typically extended to the worker's family members. Most HR managers and benefits experts reason that life insurance is meant to protect the family from the loss of the worker's income. Since group life insurance is considerably cheaper than most private policies, supplemental life policies also may be available. These policies allow employees to increase their coverage or include dependents, but the employees must pay the premiums.

Disability Insurance

When an employee is disabled and unable to work, what happens? Often short-term disabilities are handled through the company's time-off benefits and *accident and sickness* policies, providing a partial replacement of wages or salaries for up to six months or a year. When a worker is unable to work for a prolonged period, most companies provide some form of *long-term disability* (LTD) *insurance.* LTD policies generally have an extended waiting period, usually six months. They pay the employee only a fraction (usually 50 to 60 percent) of his or her wages or salaries and usually end within a few years unless the insured is unable to perform any type of work. All these features protect the worker and hold down employer costs without encouraging malingerers. In a study of 366 firms, 90 percent offered LTD coverage and three-quarters offered short-term disability plans.[17] In Canada, Great Britain, and Scandinavian countries, long-term disability is largely provided by local or national governments.[18] At Intel, there is a 180-day wait, after which the employee receives 65 percent of his or her base monthly earnings up to a maximum of $4000 a month. The payment is reduced by any social security or workers' compensation payments.

LTD insurance

Foreign approaches

    Cost-saving measures may not discriminate against protected classes under equal employment laws. For example, disability payments must be extended to pregnant women if such payments are made to other workers for non-job-related disabilities. Human resource departments that discriminate against pregnant women in their disability policies (or in medical benefits) may be in violation of equal employment laws.

Other Insurance Benefits

The economies of group plans have led a few companies to provide a variety of other insurance programs. *Legal insurance* gives employees access to low-cost legal aid. It is like group medical programs, which pool prepaid amounts, allowing members to obtain legal assistance that might not be readily available to individuals. HR departments usually control costs by means of maximum dollar limits on total services received per year or a dollar limit on each type of legal service, such as selling a house, handling a divorce, or drawing up a will. At present, unions are encouraging these plans through their negotiations with employers.[19]

Some employers even offer group home owners' and group automobile insurance. Since individual rates vary widely and not all employees have houses or cars, employers seldom contribute to the cost of these premiums. However, Procter & Gamble, Honeywell, Control Data, and others provide financial assistance to employees who adopt children.

▶ Employee Security Benefits

In addition to insurance, there are noninsurance benefits that enhance employees' security. These benefits seek to ensure an income before and after retirement.

Employment Income Security

Severance pay

The loss of a job holds potentially severe economic consequences for an employee, but this can be cushioned by employer-provided benefits. *Severance pay* benefits entitle the worker to a lump-sum payment at the time of separation from the company. The payment is either a flat amount equal to a few weeks' pay or a graduated amount based on salary and length of service with the employer. For top executives, the figure can reach six months' or a year's pay. HR policies may limit severance pay to situations where the employee leaves involuntarily and has done nothing wrong, as in the case of a layoff, a plant closing, or job elimination caused by a merger.

International Harvester

When International Harvester restructured itself to become Navistar, several managers were asked to sell or liquidate parts of the firm that included their jobs. They were compensated with employment contracts guaranteeing them up to two years' salary and benefits.[20]

"Golden parachutes"

Golden parachutes are agreements by a company to compensate executives with bonuses and benefits if they are displaced by a merger or acquisition. Many boards of directors have approved "golden parachutes" out of fear that a hostile takeover attempt might cause valued executives to leave rather than fight the takeover. The agreements allow the executive to focus on his or her duties with little concern about financial security or the need to search for a new job as soon as merger talks begin. These "parachutes" often bestow significant cash bonuses on senior managers, but they seldom make provisions for others in the organization. An exception to this trend (and an attempt to make the company less attractive to raiders) comes from the second largest producer of office furniture, Herman Miller, Inc.

Herman Miller, Inc.

On the basis of the employees' years of continuous, full-time employment with the company, each worker (regardless of title or position) would be compensated if harmed within two years of a takeover. If a worker's job is eliminated, the compensation package (salary and benefits) is reduced, or working conditions are changed, the worker is eligible for a "silver parachute."

Compensation must be paid within ten days of termination and in amounts equal to 2.5 times the total compensation during the previous twelve months for employees who have been employed for more than five years. Employees with shorter service receive a smaller compensation package.[21]

Of the 325 firms surveyed in one study, 84.6 percent have severance pay policies for some or all of their employees. Almost half of these firms (47.9 percent) provide employees with help in finding other jobs, called *outplacement assistance*. The provision of severance pay and outplacement help was found to be more common among larger firms.[22]

Layoffs overseas

Layoffs are less common in Europe because of legislation and severance requirements that make getting rid of workers legally complex and expensive. By contrast, Japan's largest firms typically offer lifetime employment (usually for adult males only) and historically steady growth to avoid layoffs.

Layoffs also may be eased by accrued vacation pay. A few companies go so far as to provide a *guaranteed annual wage* (GAW). These plans ensure that the worker receives a minimum amount of work or pay. For example, employees may be promised a minimum of 1500 hours of work or pay a year (compared with the "normal" fifty-two forty-hour weeks for a total of 2080 hours). Some employers guarantee thirty hours per week. Even on layoff, the employees draw some income. Lincoln Electric has such a plan, for example.

SUB

The auto industry is a leader in another benefit: *supplemental unemployment benefits* (SUB). When employees are out of work, their state unemployment benefits are supplemented by the employer from moneys previously paid to the SUB fund. This ensures covered employees of an income almost equal to their previous earnings for as long as the SUB fund remains solvent.[23] Take the case of Alfredo Sedona:

Alfredo Sedona was put on indefinite layoff. Under the SUB plan, he received 95 percent of his previous take-home pay, minus $12.50 that would otherwise have gone for commuting, lunches, and other work-related expenses. He typically took home $380 a week; therefore, he is entitled to get $348.50 [($380 × .95) − $12.50]. Since the state unemployment benefits will pay Alfredo $98.50 a week, the SUB plan makes up the difference, paying him $250 a week ($348.50 − 98.50 = $250). Alfredo continues to get $348.50 until the SUB fund is depleted, or he finds another job, or he is called back to work.

Although SUB plans are expensive, costing General Motors nearly a billion dollars a year during the early 1990s, a very high percentage of workers are available for work when recalled. This high return rate occurs because few employees find jobs that pay as much as they receive while on layoff. One societal drawback is that these unemployed workers have little incentive to find other work, and so they may draw public unemployment funds for a longer period than do unemployed workers who have no access to a SUB plan.

Retirement Security

Retirement plans originally were designed to reward long-service employees. Through employer generosity and union pressures, retirement plans have generally grown in scope and coverage. However, with the rapidly growing health-care costs of the 1980s and early 1990s, many companies have cut back or eliminated health-care benefits for retirees.[24]

Key questions

Developing a retirement plan.   When an HR department develops a retirement plan, several critical questions must be answered, such as: Who will pay for it? In a *noncontributory plan,* the employer pays the entire amount; *contributory plans* require both the employee and the employer to contribute. Another question is: When will the pension rights vest? *Vesting* gives a worker the right to pension benefits even if he or she leaves the company. Pension rights usually vest after several years of service. If an employee leaves before pension benefits are vested, that worker has no rights except the right to regain his or her contributions to the plan. Some pensions have *portability clauses* that allow accumulated pension rights to be transferred to another employer.

A third question is: How will the firm meet its financial obligations? Some companies pay pensions out of current income when employees retire. This is called an *unfunded plan. Funded plans* require the employer to accumulate moneys in advance so that the employer's contribution plus interest will cover the pension obligation.

How much money should be put aside by the employer depends on whether the pension is a *defined contribution* or a *defined benefit* plan. Defined contribution plans occur when the employer agrees to contribute a specific amount into an account. Often this amount is a percentage of the employee's pay. A defined benefit plan obligates the employer to pay the retiree a specific amount at retirement. For example, the employer may agree to calculate an employee's average salary for the last five years. Then the employee is paid 2 percent of that amount for each year he or she worked for the firm. Thus, the retirement income for employees who had been employed for twenty years would be 40 percent (twenty years times 2 percent) of their average pay during their last five years of work. When retirement plans are integrated with social security, the calculation assumes that the actual amount paid by the company each month is reduced by the amount of social security payments the

The decline of
defined benefit
plans

retiree will receive. Since retirement may be many years away for some employees, the retirement income obligations of the firm are difficult to calculate accurately. As a result, overfunding or underfunding of the company's pension obligations is more likely under a defined benefit program, leading companies such as General Motors and Chrysler to face unfunded multi-billion-dollar pension liabilities. As a result, many firms have canceled defined benefit plans.[25] Instead, many employers offer 401(k) plans that enable employees to invest part of their earnings in tax-deferred savings accounts. Employees' contributions to these plans are often partially matched by the employer.[26]

Another important question is: Will the plan be *trusted* or *insured*? A trusted plan calls for all moneys to be deposited into a trust fund, usually in a bank. The bank manages and protects the funds; it does not guarantee that the employer's pension liabilities will be met. With an insured plan, the pension moneys are used to buy employee annuities from an insurer. Each annuity represents an insurance company's pledge to pay the worker a given amount per month upon retirement.

Pension problems

Two significant problems have developed in the administration of pension plans. First, some employers go out of business, leaving the pension plan unfunded or only partially funded. Second, some companies minimize their pension costs by having very long vesting periods or firing employees before they are vested. An employee who quits or is fired before becoming vested often has no pension rights. Since both of these problems may impose hardships on employees and increase the nation's welfare burden, Congress passed the *Employee Retirement Income Security Act* of 1974 (ERISA).

ERISA

ERISA.   ERISA and the Tax Reform Act of 1986 impose restrictions on the operation of pension plans. As can be seen in Figure 15-2, this pension reform law sets forth participation, vesting, and funding requirements. To protect workers in the event of employer insolvency, employers are required to participate in a federal insurance program.

The insurance aspect of ERISA provides employees with a guarantee of a pension even if the employer goes out of business before the pension plan is fully funded. But ERISA is more than just an insurance plan. It requires employers to have their plans funded and vested. However, the Pension Benefit Guarantee Corporation created under the act must still oversee plans that are still not fully funded more than two decades after the law was enacted. General Motors, for example, has an unfinanced pension liability of more than $20 billion.[27]

The "prudent man"
rule

ERISA requires trustees to apply the "prudent man" rule when investing pension funds and to report annually on the plan's operations.[28] For example, the fiduciary standards set by ERISA prohibit the pension plan from investing in stock or real estate above a fixed level. When the Grumman Corporation put more than 10 percent of its pension fund assets into its own stock to avoid a takeover by the LTV Corporation, for example, the U.S. Department of Labor successfully sued Grumman for violating ERISA.

Figure 15-2	Highlights of the Pension Reform Act, as Amended

MAJOR PROVISIONS

PARTICIPATION	Prohibits plans from requiring service eligibility over 1 year; 2 years of eligibility is permitted if plan vests 100 percent immediately.
VESTING	Plan vesting provision must be: 1. 100 percent vested after 5 years of service 2. 20 percent vested after 3 years of service, increasing yearly by 20 percent until fully vested in a total of 7 years
FUNDING	The plan must fund current year's benefit accruals and must amortize any unfunded costs over 30 years (40 years for existing plans and multiemployer plans).
FIDUCIARY STANDARDS	Establishes the "prudent man" rule as the basic standard of conduct, outlaws various transactions between parties-in-interest, and prohibits investment of more than 10 percent of fund assets in employer securities or real estate.
REPORTING AND DISCLOSURE	Requires the plan to provide participants with a comprehensive booklet describing pension plan provisions and to report annually to the Secretary of Labor on numerous operating and financial details of the plan.
PLAN TERMINATION INSURANCE	Creates a federal insurance organization to protect beneficiaries against loss of vested pension on plan termination where assets are inadequate.
PORTABILITY	Encourages some voluntary portability by allowing a worker, if the employer agrees to it, to transfer his or her pension rights tax-free from one employer pension fund to another by establishing a tax-free individual retirement account.
JOINT AND SURVIVORSHIP OPTION	Unless a married worker specifically requests the plan's normal retirement benefit, the worker is required to receive a pension payable for his or her lifetime and continuing in 50 percent of that amount to the spouse if the spouse survives the employee. The worker's normal retirement benefit may be actuarially reduced to pay for the cost of this provision.

Source: Adapted from *The American Federationist*, October 1975, p. 19 (used by permission); Employee Retirement Income Security Act of 1974; and the 1986 Tax Reform Act.

Continental Can

Some companies, such as Continental Can, committed more substantive violations. According to *Time* magazine:

> . . . the company employed a secret computer program called BELL, a reverse acronym for Let's Limit Employee Benefits. Managers used the program to . . . lay off employees just weeks or months before they were vested in the company pension plan. In that way the company aimed to avoid millions of dollars in pension payments.

It was a costly mistake. The United Steel Workers of America filed a class-action suit in 1982 under the Employee Retirement Income Security Act. Continental finally reached an agreement under which it will pay $415 million to 3,000 people, the largest settlement in the 17-year history of ERISA.[29]

Portability

Portability was also encouraged by the act. *Portability* allows the pension credits earned in one employer's retirement plan to be transferred into another retirement plan when the worker changes companies. About 10 million mostly unionized employees have portability in their pension plans.

In the defense contracting industry, for example, engineers change employers when the government contracts they are working on expire. As a result, many of them never stay with an employer long enough to earn a vested pension. Lockheed Engineering & Management Services Company recognized this problem and modified its pension plan to make it a more attractive recruiting tool. Its retirement program now offers immediate vesting once an employee joins the plan and allows portability when the employee leaves.[30]

Early retirement.   As retirement plans mature, companies tend to liberalize them. Increasingly, this has meant early retirement provisions, which allow workers to retire before the traditional retirement age of 65.[31] Benefits are normally reduced for early retirement because the employee draws benefits longer and the employer has less time to fund its contribution. Some pensions—those used by the military, for example—pay the retiree an amount based on years of service regardless of age. When economic conditions require a layoff, the company may encourage senior employees to retire early by reducing or eliminating the penalty for early retirement.[32] This lowers the employer's staffing costs in a voluntary manner and helps explain why the average retirement age has declined to 62. Since this benefit is often based on the employee's age, age discrimination suits may result if these early retirement programs are not properly designed and implemented.[33]

Du Pont

Du Pont, in an attempt to reduce its employment levels, used an early retirement option as part of its first companywide employee-reduction program. The result was that 11,200 employees, or about 8 percent of its workforce, departed.[34]

As the number of new entrants into the workforce slows and retirees increase in number after the turn of the century, early retirement policies may fade away. As two researchers observed:

Currently, human resource policies in many organizations encourage early retirement. Senior employees have been offered early retirement as an alternative to layoffs . . . as an alternative to possible termination . . . and . . . as a way to unclog career channels and create affirmative action promotion opportunities.

Looking toward the future, however, the policy emphasis on early retirement may prove quite shortsighted. With changing workforce demographics, organizations are likely to encounter critical shortages among technical, professional, and managerial personnel.[35]

Retirement counseling.   As part of the retirement program, 44 percent of employers in one study offer retirement counseling.[36] The primary purpose of *preretirement counseling* is to encourage an employee to plan for retirement emotionally and financially. These sessions also explain the nature of the employee's retirement program to indicate the likely financial and emotional adjustments a retiree may face. Ultimately, preretirement counseling causes people to grapple with questions such as: How much money do I need to retire? How will I arrange to have a sufficient retirement income? and What will I do in retirement?

An important part of preretirement planning is to consider the spouse. ERISA allows survivorship options, enabling the surviving spouse to receive 50 percent of the worker's pension. The prevalence of divorce left some spouses without any pension rights until Congress passed the *Retirement Equity Act* (REA) of 1984. This act allows divorce settlements to include court orders called *qualified domestic relations orders* (QDRO). These court orders require the pension plan administrator to reduce an employee's retirement benefits by a specified amount. These amounts then go to the divorced spouse when the worker retires. This assures that long-married spouses can receive some share of pension benefits as part of the divorce settlement.

Postretirement counseling is designed to ease the transition from worker to retiree. The retiree is made aware of community and company programs for retired people. Retired employees of Mountain Bell Telephone Company, for example, can join an organization of other retired telephone workers. This type of association provides social contacts, community projects, and recreational opportunities.

REA

▶ Time-Off Benefits

Time-off benefits include breaks, sick days, holidays and vacations, and leaves of absence.

On-the-Job Breaks

Some of the most common forms of time-off benefits are those found during working hours. Examples include rest breaks, meal breaks, and wash-up time. A rest from the physical and mental effort of a job may renew employees' energy and increase productivity. The major problem for HR and line managers is the tendency of employees to stretch these periods.

When one manager was confronted by a supervisor with the problem of stretched breaks, she suggested a simple solution. Each employee was assigned a specific break time—9:15 to 9:30 A.M. or 9:30 to 9:45 A.M., for example—but could not leave for the break until the preceding employee returned. Since each clerk was anxious to go on break, the peer group policed the length of breaks and the stretched breaks ended.

Sick Days and Well Pay

Some absences from work are unavoidable. Today most companies pay workers when they are absent for medical reasons by granting a limited number of sick days per year. Unfortunately, this fringe benefit is often abused when workers take the attitude that these are simply extra days off with pay. If HR policies prohibit employees from crediting unused sick leave to the next year's account, absences increase near the end of the year. To minimize abuses, some companies require medical verification of illness or pay employees for unused sick leave. Payment for unused sick leave is sometimes called *well pay,* which may serve as an incentive for attendance. In Sweden, for example, sick pay gives employees 90 percent of their salary and is paid by the government directly to the worker, providing employers with less of a cost reduction incentive to reduce absenteeism than would be the case if the firm made the payment directly to employees with high absenteeism. This may explain why the average Swedish worker takes twenty-seven sick days a year.[37]

Some firms, such as Intel, avoid the abuse question by granting *personal leave days.* This approach allows an employee to skip work for any reason and get paid up to a specified number of days per year. *Sick leave banks* allow employees to "borrow" extra days above the specified number when they use up their individual allocation. Then, when they earn additional days, the borrowed days are repaid to the sick leave bank.

Holidays and Vacations

Ten paid holidays are typical among U.S. firms.[38] Like sick days, however, this benefit is subject to abuse. Employees sometimes try to stretch the holiday by missing the workday before or after it. HR policies that require attendance the day before and the day after the holiday as a condition of holiday pay lessen this problem. Other firms ignore this issue of "stretched holidays" by using the personal leave days concept instead of holidays or sick days. Paterson Food in the United Kingdom grants "working holidays" that pay employees to visit vendors as a bonus for long service. Other companies provide *contingent time off* in the form of paid "holidays" to workers who meet productivity or other goals.

Stretched holidays

Contingent time off

Vacations usually are based on the employee's length of service: one week for one year of service, two weeks for two years of service, three weeks for five or ten years of employment, and so on. Policies for vacations vary widely. Some companies allow employees to use vacation days a few at a time; others insist that workers take the vacation all at once. A few employers actually close down during designated periods and require that vacations be taken during that time. (This "plant shutdown" approach is sometimes required to perform major maintenance on equipment, and it is more common in the European Union, where vacations are generally longer than those enjoyed in Japan and North America.) Still other companies negate the reason for vacations completely by allowing employees to work and receive vacation pay as a bonus.

 Intel created a sabbatical leave policy that is one of the more unusual industrial time-off benefits. It gives permanent U.S. and Canadian employees eight weeks off with full pay after seven years of service. And with executive staff management approval, employees can get up to six months of leave with pay for public service, teaching, or exceptional educational opportunities.

Leaves of Absence

Pregnancy leaves

Leaves of absence are often granted for pregnancy, extended illness, accidents, summer military camps, military reserve call-ups, jury duty, funeral services, and other reasons specified in a company's HR policies. Extended leaves are normally given without pay. Shorter absences, especially for jury duty or funerals of close relatives, often come with pay. Under the *Pregnancy Discrimination Act of 1978*, employers may not discriminate against pregnant women by treating pregnancy leave differently from other leaves of absence. AT&T, for example, grants one-year unpaid leaves to employees for the care of infants or ill dependents.[39] A growing number of companies are creating "Mommy" and "Daddy" career tracks that grant leaves or reductions in the workweek to accommodate new mothers and fathers who want to participate actively in child rearing.[40] In Sweden and other countries, maternity and paternity leaves are mandated by law.

Family and Medical Leave Act of 1993

For the rest of the 1990s, some studies project, two out of three new workers will be female. By 2000, half the work force will be women, mostly of childbearing age. And four out of five women in the work force will probably have children during their working lives.[41]

In the United States, the *Family and Medical Leave Act of 1993* states that eligible employees are entitled to twelve weeks of unpaid leave during any twelve-month period under certain circumstances. Employees are entitled to a leave to take care of a baby, including birth, adoption, and the placement of a child in foster care. Employees are also eligible when a serious health condition results in the employee being unable to work or when there is a need for the employee to care for a spouse, parent, or child with a serious health condition. The law applies only to employers who have at least fifty employees within seventy-five miles of the worksite.[42]

▶ Work Scheduling Benefits

The nature of the typical workweek has changed significantly since the early days of the industrial revolution, as illustrated in Figure 15-3. The norm of a five-day forty-hour workweek remained relatively unchanged from the 1930s to the early 1970s. Today:

> . . . an estimated 14.5 million employees work nonstandard hours—evenings, overnight, rotating shifts and split shifts—and in an economy gone global and a culture hungry for 24-hour *everything*, the numbers are growing. Already one out of five full-timers works a non-traditional shift, according to the Bureau of Labor Statistics.[43]

As a result, several new approaches to scheduling work have gained popularity: shorter work times, flextime, and job sharing.

Shorter Work Times

Shorter workdays and workweeks are not new ideas when it comes to raising employee productivity.

Kellogg

> When the Kellogg Company adopted a 6-hour day in the 1930's, workers packed more cereal than they had in an 8-hour shift. The Kellogg experience is hardly unique. Late 19th-century estimates showed that, for three-fourths of all companies, reducing daily hours not only raised productivity per hour, but also each worker's total daily production.
> Aside from productivity, shorter hours can soothe the growing problems of stress, burnout and disrupted personal lives that long hours incur.[44]

A *shorter workweek* compresses forty hours of work into less than five full days. Some plans even shorten the workweek to less than 40 hours, with a growing number of companies moving to 37.5 or even 35 hours per five-day week. One version has been forty hours of work compressed into four days. It presents child-care problems for some working mothers and causes fatigue in physically demanding jobs but has the advantage of only four instead of five commutes each week.

| Figure 15-3 | A Typical Work Schedule before the Civil War |

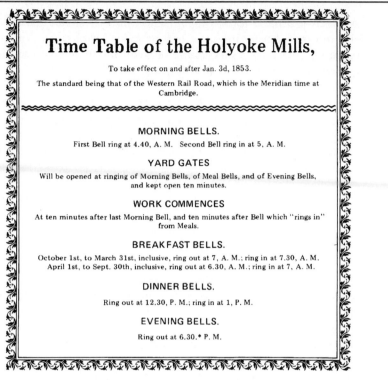

Time Table of the Holyoke Mills,

To take effect on and after Jan. 3d, 1853.

The standard being that of the Western Rail Road, which is the Meridian time at Cambridge.

MORNING BELLS.

First Bell ring at 4.40, A. M.   Second Bell ring in at 5, A. M.

YARD GATES

Will be opened at ringing of Morning Bells, of Meal Bells, and of Evening Bells, and kept open ten minutes.

WORK COMMENCES

At ten minutes after last Morning Bell, and ten minutes after Bell which "rings in" from Meals.

BREAKFAST BELLS.

October 1st, to March 31st, inclusive, ring out at 7, A. M.; ring in at 7.30, A. M.
April 1st, to Sept. 30th, inclusive, ring out at 6.30, A. M.; ring in at 7, A. M.

DINNER BELLS.

Ring out at 12.30, P. M.; ring in at 1, P. M.

EVENING BELLS.

Ring out at 6.30.* P. M.

Source: Labor's Long Hard Road, Air Line Employees Association, International, p. 4. Used by permission.

Flextime

The introduction of *flextime* from Europe apparently resulted in slower growth of four-day workweeks.[45] Flextime eliminates rigid starting and ending times for the workday. Instead, employees are allowed to report to work at any time during a range of hours. For example, starting time may be from 7 A.M. to 9 A.M. with all employees expected to work the *core hours* of 9 A.M. to 3 P.M.

Core hours

The outcome of a flextime program, however, depends on the nature of the firm's operations. For example, the major disadvantage of flextime is difficulty meeting minimum staffing needs early and late in the day. Assembly-line and customer service operations find this problem especially significant. But in most clerical operations, some users have reported noteworthy successes. With Manpower, Inc., a temporary help agency, becoming the largest private employer in the United States, part-time work probably offers the greatest flexibility, even if most part-timers in the United States are excluded from receiving benefits.

Job Sharing

A third approach to employee scheduling that has gained popularity is job sharing. *Job sharing* involves one or more employees doing the same job but working different hours, days, or even weeks. Most commonly, two people handle the duties of one full-time job.

Karen and Bob Rosen both taught English at Lincoln High School. After Karen had her first child one summer, Karen, Bob, and their principal agreed to a job-sharing arrangement. Bob taught three classes of English literature and composition in the morning. He then drove home and gave Karen the car, and she returned to school and taught three English classes in the afternoon. The school benefited because teachers normally had five classes and a planning period; with job sharing, the school received six classes of English instruction. Bob and Karen also were able to share in raising their child, with neither of them completely giving up his or her career.

The major advantage claimed for job sharing is increased productivity. Problems arise from the increased administrative burden associated with two employees doing the job of one. Another problem is benefits. HR specialists are forced to decide whether job sharers should be given benefits equal to those of other employees or whether the benefits should be scaled down in proportion to an employee's hours. Most state unemployment offices will not scale down unemployment benefits when job sharers are put on layoff status. Instead, job sharers simply are considered ineligible for unemployment compensation. In Europe, unions are lobbying for full benefits for part-timers as part of the current effort to standardize employment practices in the European Union.[46]

▶ Employee Services

Some companies go beyond pay and traditional benefits and provide services for their employees. Which services and at what costs are policy decisions that should be part of the organization's HR management strategy. The most common ones are educational, financial, and social programs.

Educational Assistance

Tuition refunds

Tuition refund programs are among the more common employer services, with 97 percent of the 617 companies in one survey offering this assistance.[47] These programs partially or completely reimburse employees for furthering their education but may be limited to courses that are related to an employee's job. Some companies make the amount of reimbursement contingent on grades.

Beckman Instruments, Inc., for example, refunds 100 percent of the college tuition for an A or a B, 50 percent for a C, and nothing for a D or F. In the future, more companies may follow the lead of FelPro, an Illinois gasket maker. If you work for the company:

> . . . here are some of the perks each of your children can expect: a $1,000 savings bond at birth, free summer camp, private tutoring if he or she is a slow learner, a $100 check at high school graduation and $3,000 a year for four years toward college tuition.[48]

Financial Services

Probably the oldest service is the employee discount plan. These programs, which are common among retail stores and consumer goods manufacturers, allow workers to buy products from the company at a discount. For example, employees of Broadway Department Stores may buy clothes from the store at a 10 percent discount.

Credit unions

Credit unions are another well-established employee service. The interest collected on loans and investments is distributed to members in the form of dividends. The dividends (interest payments) are allocated in proportion to the amount employees have in their share (savings) accounts. The lower interest rate on loans, the higher interest on deposits, and the payroll deductions are the major employee advantages.

Stock purchase programs enable employees to buy company stock, usually through payroll deductions. In some programs employee outlays may be matched by company contributions, or the stock may be purchased by employees at a discount from its market value. At Intel, employees in the purchase plan can buy company stock at 85 percent of its market price.

ESOPs

An *employee stock option plan* (ESOP) enables the employer to raise money and also encourages employee ownership of stock. The employer sells a block of stock to an employee group, which uses it as collateral for a loan. The proceeds from the loan then repay the company for the stock. The dividends and purchases of stock by employees from the ESOP retire the loan. Employees end up with stock in the company and share in its prosperity. Of course, if the company faces hard times, the employees may find that their jobs *and* their investments are at risk.

Social Services

A wide range of social services are provided by employers as they adapt to a changing and diverse workforce.[49] At one extreme are simple interest groups such as bowling leagues and baseball teams. At the other extreme are comprehensive *employee assistance programs* (EAPs) designed to help employees with personal problems ranging from drug and alcohol issues to family problems to dealing with employees who are among the World Health Organization's estimated 40 million people who will be HIV-positive by the year 2000.[50] As the introduction in Xerox's booklet about its employee assistance program states:

Xerox

The Xerox Employee Assistance Program (XEAP) is a benefit for employees, retirees and their families. Its purpose is to help people suffering from alcohol or drug misuse, as well as other emotional or family problems.

In the home, these problems surface as marital discord, parent/child conflict and financial troubles. If left unchecked, they can devastate a family.

On the job, these problems can also be serious and costly. They impair work relationships, erode individual job performance and result in the loss of valuable work time.[51]

The program is available to employees, retirees, and their families. It entitles users to two free diagnostic visits for any problem. The company pays 80 percent of the first eight outpatient therapy sessions related to drug or alcohol problems. Other medical or therapy needs are covered through Xerox's medical plan.

Like most EAPs, the XEAP is not limited to drug and alcohol problems. Individual emotional problems and problems related to marriage, children, and finances also are covered.

Access to the program is provided through referral by the HR department or by calling a toll-free number given to all employees. To assure confidentiality, the use of the XEAP and the nature of the employee's problem do not become part of the employee's records. In fact, Xerox contracts with another organization, Family Service America, to provide counseling and referral.[52]

Even though EAPs are not a universal benefit, 79 percent of the firms in a 409-company survey report providing them.[53] They exist because HR managers and executives realize that workers' problems affect their performance. Xerox's program is typical of those found in major corporations, although many early EAPs began as alcohol (and then drug) rehabilitation programs.

General Motors

General Motors Corporation evaluated the job performance of seventy-one alcoholic employees who had been treated in an alcohol rehabilitation program. The results of a several-month-long experiment showed over an 85 percent decline in employee lost time and a 72 percent reduction in claims for accident and sickness benefits.[54] Whether these savings repaid the company's outlays was not reported. However, this limited study indicates that positive benefits accrue to employers who sponsor such programs either separately or as part of a comprehensive employee assistance plan.

Child care. Child care is fast becoming an important benefit. During the 1990s, 18 million working mothers will be in the workforce. More than 50 percent of women who have children during their careers return to work within one year. The need is obvious. Some employers, such as the American Bankers Insurance Company, provide on-site child care. Other companies subsidize off-site providers, hoping to avoid liability and ill feelings if an accident on company property harms an employee's child (as well as avoiding the cost of providing facilities that meet state and local standards). Du Pont, for example, spent half a million dollars renovating a building and gave it to the local YMCA to use as a child-care center for its employees and the public.[55] Tenneco and Amoco reimburse child-care expenses when employees have to be out of town and their spouses aren't around.[56] Since child-care expenses average 10 percent of a family's gross income, employer-provided child care appears to offer strong recruiting and retention value.

American Bankers Insurance

Child care at Du Pont

Intermedics, Inc., a Texas manufacturer of heart pacemakers, reported a 23 percent drop in turnover and approximately a 2 percent decline in absenteeism since offering its heavily subsidized child-care benefit.[57]

Elder care

Elder care.   Elderly parents present a special problem because of the limited day-care options available to their working children. As *Fortune* magazine concluded, "elder care could soon replace child care as the hottest employee benefit."[58] Researchers at the University of Bridgeport's Center for the Studying of Aging found that almost a fourth of employees age 40 and over provided some form of elder care, and half of them were the chief providers.[59] Although EAPs may provide referrals to locate sources of day care, a growing number of employees are part of a "sandwich" generation, having responsibility for both children and aging parents. As a result, the distinction between child care and elder care is blurring, with a growing number of HR departments developing "dependent care" policies. At the same time, employees often seek more than referrals, looking for temporary and permanent subsidized care at or near work.[60]

Relocation payments

Relocation programs.   Relocation programs consist of the support in dollars or services that a company provides to transferred or new employees. At a minimum, this benefit includes payment for moving expenses. Some employees receive fully paid house-hunting trips with their spouses to the new location before the move, temporary living expenses, subsidized home mortgages, placement assistance for working spouses, and even family counseling to reduce the stress of the move. A transferred employee also may be able to sell his or her home to the employer for the appraised value. As a result, the half million relocated employees cost employers an average of $37,000 per home-owning family.[61]

Of particular difficulty to HR professionals are dual-career families, which contribute to the three of eight employees who reject transfer offers.[62] Not only are married employees with career-oriented spouses less likely to move, when they do move, the HR department is often called on to help the spouse find a job. As a growing proportion of women reach key positions, more employers find that this involves finding jobs for trailing husbands.[63]

With international transfers, relocation expenses increase, fueled by language training, bonuses, cost-of-living and tax-equalization adjustments, educational allowances, reimbursements for annual or semiannual return trips to the home country, and other outlays.[64] When the career track leads overseas,[65] companies such as Amoco provide special benefits, including paying for extra baggage allowances, arranging access to government or military stores, and expediting personal mail through courier services.

Social service leave programs. *Social service leave programs* are not widespread, but leading organizations such as Intel, Xerox, American Express, and IBM give fully paid leaves to employees who wish to work full-time in a community program.

At Xerox, employees are loaned out at full salary and benefits to non-profit organizations. Employees initiate proposals to the community and the Employee Programs manager. The proposal outlines the employee's project, relevant skills, a description of the organization, and a letter of support from the sponsoring organization. Leaves may last from one to twelve months. In one year, the review committee received about sixty applications to which it allocated a total of 264 months of leave. This program costs Xerox $300,000 to $350,000 each year.[66]

Xerox

▶ Administration of Benefits and Services

A serious shortcoming of HR management has been poor administration of indirect compensation. Even in otherwise well-managed departments, benefits and services have grown in a haphazard manner. Many costly supplements were added in response to social trends, union demands, employee pressures, and management wishes, and so HR departments seldom established objectives, systematic plans, and standards to determine the appropriateness of the programs. This patchwork of benefits and services has caused several problems.

Problems in Administration

The central problem in indirect compensation is a lack of employee participation. Once a fringe benefit program is designed by the company (and the labor union if there is one), employees have little discretion. For example, the same pension and maternity benefits usually are granted to all workers. Younger employees see pensions as distant and largely irrelevant; older workers feel that maternity benefits are unneeded. This uniformity fails to recognize workforce diversity. Admittedly, uniformity leads to administrative and actuarial economies, but when employees receive benefits they neither want nor need, these economies are questionable.

Since employees have little choice in their benefit packages, most workers are unaware of all the benefits to which they are entitled. As three researchers at the University of Arizona concluded after studying employees' valuation of medical insurance:

> One hundred eighty-two University of Arizona employees each participated in one of two field studies of the valuation of fringe benefits. Findings include: (*a*) a lack of employee knowledge regarding employer cost and market value of the studied benefit, and (*b*) significant undervaluation of the benefit by employees. These findings are consistent with the hypothesis that employee benefit valuations anchor on employee contributions [not employer costs].[67]

This lack of knowledge often causes employees to request more benefits to meet their needs. For example, older workers may want improved retirement plans while younger workers seek improved insurance coverage for dependents. Often the result is a proliferation of benefits and increased employer costs. Perhaps even worse, employee confusion can lead to complaints about and dissatisfaction with the fringe benefit package, particularly, as the University of Arizona researchers observed, when employees do not have to contribute financially.

Traditional Remedies

The traditional remedy for benefit problems has been to increase employee awareness, usually by publicizing employee benefits.[68] This publicity starts with orientation sessions and employee handbooks. Company newspapers, special mailings, employee meetings, and bulletin-board announcements are also used to publicize the benefit package.

Mass Mutual

The Massachusetts Mutual Life Insurance Company has developed an interesting variation on these traditional approaches. With the consent of the employer, this insurer evaluates the benefits each employee receives and provides a booklet that summarizes this information. A representative of the insurer explains the booklet and indicates gaps in the employee's coverage (with the object of selling the worker any needed insurance).

Publicizing the benefits and services only attacks the symptoms of the problem: employee disinterest and growing costs. Moreover, this reactive approach adds to the costs of administration through increased "advertising" expenses. As a result, some employers have reduced their contributions or reduced the benefits, especially in the area of health care. Cuts in benefits do little to further employee participation and understanding and can harm employee morale. In fact, during recent years, many strikes by unions have been attempts to reduce these cuts. A more proactive approach has been the growing use of flexible benefits.

Cafeteria Benefits: A Proactive Solution

Flex benefits

Cafeteria benefit, or flexible benefit, programs allow employees to select benefits and services that match their needs. Workers are provided a benefit and services account with a specified number of dollars in it. With the money from this account, employees choose and "purchase" specific benefits from among those offered by the employer, although some flexible plans require all employees to take a set of "core benefits" such as life or health insurance to ensure minimum coverage. If they want more benefits than their account holds, they can arrange for a pretax deduction from their pay to be put into a *flexible spending account* (FSA) so that benefits can be paid for with "pretax" monies. (Many employers that do not have cafeteria benefits also use flexible spending accounts so that employees can pay for their benefits with pretax dollars.)

The types and prices of benefits are provided to each worker in the form of a computer printout. This cost sheet also describes each benefit. Then, as illustrated in Figure 15-4, employees elect their package of benefits and services for the coming year.

Figure 15-4 indicates how two different workers might spend the $8600 the company grants each employee. Workers A and B elect two different sets of benefits because their personal situations differ dramatically. Worker A is a young parent who is supporting a family and her husband. If they were to have another child or if they had some other health-related expense, it might seriously affect their plans, and so they have elected to be well insured for pregnancy and health costs. Worker B can more easily afford unexpected medical expenses, and so he bought health insurance with a larger deductible and

| Figure 15-4 | Hypothetical Benefit Selection by Two Different Workers |

WORKER A		WORKER B	
Age 27, female, married with one child. Husband in graduate school.		Age 56, male, married with two grown and married children. Wife does not work.	
	Health insurance:		
$ 345	Maternity	0	
2435	$100 deductible	0	
0	$1000 deductible	$2025	
	Life insurance:		
100	$20,000 for worker	100	
150	$10,000 for spouse	0	
1600	Vacations	1900	
700	Holidays	900	
1200	Pension plan	2270	
0	Jury duty pay	0	
200	Disability insurance	200	
1870	Sick pay	1205	
$8600	Total	$8600	

allocated fewer dollars for sick pay. Instead, he put a large portion of his benefit moneys into the company pension plan, reflecting his greater age.

Although this approach creates additional administrative costs and an obligation for the HR department to advise employees, there are advantages. The main advantage is employee participation. Through participation, workers understand exactly what benefits the employer is offering and can better match their benefits with their needs.[69]

Beyond the wide range of benefits and services described in this chapter, employers are required to provide social security, workers' compensation, and a workplace free from recognizable safety and health hazards. These legally imposed benefits and services are described in Chapter 16, which concludes this section of the book.

▶ Summary

Employee benefits and services are the fastest-growing component of compensation. Employers have sought to expand them to discourage labor unrest, respond to employee pressures, and remain competitive in the labor market. Employees have wanted to obtain benefits and services through the employer because of the low costs, tax advantages, and inflation protection that provides.

Benefits are classified into four major types: insurance, security, time-off, and scheduling benefits. Services include educational, financial, and social programs. This diversity contributes to several serious administrative problems, especially the orientation of managers and HR specialists toward cost savings. In pursuit of administrative and actuarial economies, most companies and unions do not allow individualized benefit packages in indirect compensation programs, although flexible benefits are gaining in popularity.

▶ Terms for Review

Adverse selection	Vesting
Coinsurance clause	Portability clauses
Health maintenance organizations (HMOs)	Employee Retirement Income Security Act (ERISA)
Long-term disability insurance	Well pay
Legal insurance	Personal leave days
Severance pay	Family and Medical Leave Act
Golden parachutes	Shorter workweek
Guaranteed annual wage	Flextime
Supplemental unemployment benefits (SUB)	Cafeteria benefit programs
	Flexible spending account
Contributory plans	

▶ Review and Discussion Questions

1. For many years the costs of benefits have increased faster than have wages and salaries. How do you explain that trend?

2. What can employers do to reduce the rise in insurance costs?

3. How would you explain to a group of new workers in a company orientation program why a package of pay and benefits is almost certainly superior to pay with no benefits?

4. Briefly describe the benefits an organization might give employees to provide them with greater financial security.

5. What is the Employee Retirement Income Security Act, and why was it needed?

6. When a company makes the transition from a five-day, forty-hour workweek to a four-day, forty-hour one, what benefits and problems might the HR department experience among (*a*) working mothers, (*b*) laborers, and (*c*) assembly-line workers?

7. To remain flexible, large companies often need to redeploy their human resources, including domestic and international moves. In what ways does an HR department become involved?

8. Explain the advantages and disadvantages of flexible, or "cafeteria," benefits.

▶ Incident 15-1

Kimberly-Clark's Educational Assistance

Kimberly-Clark created an educational savings account for employees and their dependents. The company gives employees credits for each year of service. Then, when an employee or dependent wants to go to college, he or she can be reimbursed partially from the educational savings account established by the company.

1. In an era of increased international competition, why would Kimberly-Clark spend considerable amounts of money to fund an educational savings account for its employees?

2. What impact would cancellation of the program have on the current employees?

▶ **Incident 15-2**

Flexibility at Steelcase, Inc.

Steelcase, Inc., is a Grand Rapids–based manufacturer of office furniture. During the 1980s Steelcase rethought its approach to employee compensation and benefits. While paying modest wages, the company offers extensive bonus opportunities, ranging from piecework to profit sharing.

Perhaps the most radical changes were in its approaches to being flexible with employees. About 20 percent of the office employees are on flexible schedules, and forty employees share twenty jobs. Fringe benefits are "cafeteria style," with eight medical and three dental options. Long- and short-term disability plans and life insurance are also offered. The moneys left over can be put into tax-free accounts to cover out-of-pocket health care of off-site day care.

Company officials like to stress those advantages to workers. "People are becoming good at choosing what they need, as opposed to us playing God," says James Soule, vice president for human resources. But the cafeteria plan will also save Steelcase a good deal of money. It stipulates that as health-care costs go up, benefit dollars will increase only 80 percent as quickly, leaving employees to fill the 20 percent gap.[70]

1. Since employees can change their benefit selection each year, what type of abuses might occur?

2. Even though the flexibility shown to employees appears desirable, what problems might result from having 20 percent of the office workers on flexible work schedules?

3. If Steelcase opened operations in a foreign country, what parts of the benefit program would be likely to need rethinking?

▶ **Incident 15-3**

Outsourcing Benefits Administration at Merck

"Merck & Company is an international research-intensive health products company, focusing on the discovery, development, and marketing of important human and animal health products. Merck has approximately 34,000 employees worldwide and a lot of experience outsourcing."[71]

Merck outsources its "flexible benefits enrollment and data maintenance, medical and dental claims processing, flexible spending account administration, pension calculations and projections, and their HMO negotiations."[72]

1. Since Merck has a large and sophisticated HR department, why would it outsource much of its benefits administration other than to save money?

2. What problems might outsourcing create for Merck?

▶ **References**

1. Robert J. Samuelson, "Will Reform Bankrupt Us?" *Newsweek,* Aug. 15, 1994, p. 54.

2. "Delorsism or Darwinism?" *The Economist,* July 3, 1993, p. 9.

3. Daniel J. B. Mitchell, "Employee Benefits and the New Economy: A Proposal for Reform," *California Management Review,* Fall 1990, pp. 113–130.

4. Lee Smith, "The Right Cure for Health Care," *Fortune,* Oct. 19, 1992, p. 88.

5. Katrine Amers et al., "Domesticated Bliss," *Newsweek,* Mar. 23, 1992. See also Jennifer Haupt, "Employee Action Prompts Management to Respond to Work-and-Family Needs," *Personnel Journal,* January 1993, pp. 96–107.

6. *Employee Benefits 1985,* Washington, D.C.: Chamber of Commerce of the United States, 1986, p. 5.

7. Susan J. Duncan, "What's Next on Health Cost Control?" *Nation's Business,* November 1982, p. 24. See also "Shifting Health Costs to Employees 'More Expensive,' " *Resource,* June 1984, p. 12.

8. "Perspectives," *Personnel Journal,* July 1989, p. 8. See also Edmund Faltermayer, "Why Health Costs Can Keep Slowing," *Fortune,* Jan. 24, 1994, pp. 76–81.

9. "Paying Employees Not to Go to the Doctor," *Business Week,* Mar. 21, 1983, p. 150. See also Thomas N. Fannin and Teresa Ann Fannin, "Coordination of Benefits: Uncovering a Buried Treasure," *Personnel Journal,* May 1983, pp. 386–391.

10. Glenn Kramon, "Four Health Care Vigilantes," *The New York Times,* National ed., Sept. 24, 1989, pp. 1, 6.

11. Hilary Stout, "Fitness Center Gets Couch Potatoes Moving," *The Wall Street Journal,* Eastern ed., Apr. 12, 1991, p. B1.

12. Leonard Abramson, "Boost to the Bottom Line," *Personnel Administrator,* July 1988, pp. 36–39.

13. Edward L. Hansen, "Mercer Publishes 1993 Human Resource Management Compensation Survey," *Mercer News Release,* July 14, 1993, p. 1.

14. Ibid.

15. Douglas C. Harper, "Control Health Care Costs," *Personnel Journal,* October 1988, pp. 65–70. See also Thomas P. Burke and Rita S. Jain, "Trends in Employer-Provided Health Care Benefits," *Monthly Labor Review,* February 1991, pp. 24–29.

16. *Employee Benefits 1985,* p. 11. See also Carroll Roarty, "Biting Dental Insurance Costs," *Personnel Administrator,* November 1988, pp. 68–71.

17. "Most Employers Offer Disability Leaves," *Resource,* December 1988, p. 4.

18. Martin Tolchin, "Other Countries Do Much More for Disabled," *The New York Times,* National ed., Mar. 29, 1990, p. 9.

19. Kevin J. O'Donnell and Kathy A. Lawler, "Group Legal Services Plans," *Personnel Administrator,* March 1987, pp. 92–97.

20. Nancy Russell, "Compensation Key in Navistar Restructuring," *Resource,* December 1986, p. 7.

21. " 'Silver Parachute' Protects Work Force," *Resource,* January 1987, p. 3.

22. "Most Firms Have Severance Pay Programs," *Resource,* October 1986, p. 2.

23. Calvin Sims, "After the Layoffs, Checks in the Mail," *The New York Times,* National ed., Nov. 18, 1993, pp. C1, C2.

24. Amy Dunkin, "Retirees, Your Health Plans Look a Bit Peaked," *Business Week,* Nov. 30, 1992, pp. 114–115. See also Faltermayer, op. cit.

25. Alan L. Gustman and Thomas L. Steinmeier, "The Stampede toward Defined Contribution Pension Plans: Fact or Fiction?" *Industrial Relations,* Spring 1992, pp. 361–369.

26. Tim Smart and Karen Thurston, "Putting a Shine on the Golden Years," *Business Week,* Dec. 21, 1992, p. 38.

27. Leslie Wayne, "Pension Arithmetic with Low Rates," *The New York Times,* National ed., Nov. 29, 1993, p. C1.

28. Stephanie Overman, "Regulating Retirement Fund Plans," *Personnel Administrator,* November 1989, pp. 43–44, 96.

29. "Too Slick with the Pink Slip," *Time,* Jan. 14, 1991, p. 45.

30. "Pension Plans Get More Flexible," *Business Week,* Nov. 8, 1982, pp. 82, 87.

31. The elimination of the age 70 cap in the Age Discrimination in Employment Act (which became effective January 1, 1987) is estimated to have kept 200,000 additional workers on the job who otherwise would have retired. See "Retirement Age Law to Keep 200,000 on Job," *Resource,* November 1986, p. 3. Benefit calculations and pension accruals were also affected. See "Changes in Mandatory Retirement and Benefit Accounts Take Effect," *Personnel Journal,* January 1987, pp. 24–25.

32. Eric Schine et al., "Take the Money and Run—Or Take Your Chances," *Business Week,* Aug. 16, 1993, pp. 28–29.

33. "Median Age of Retirement Drops to 62," *Resource,* January 1987, p. 15. See also David R. Godofsky, "Early Retirement Pensions: Penalty or Perk," *Personnel Journal,* August 1988, pp. 69–73.

34. Alix M. Freedman, "DuPont Trims Costs, Bureaucracy to Bolster Competitive Position," *The Wall Street Journal,* Eastern ed., Sept. 25, 1985, p. 1.

35. Benson Rosen and Thomas H. Jerdee, "Retirement Policies for the 21st Century," *Human Resource Management,* Fall 1986, p. 405.

36. Robert B. Aglira and Edward L. Hansen, "Employees Often on Their Own in Planning Retirement Finances," *Mercer News Release,* Aug. 2, 1993, p. 1.

37. Larry Eichel, "Model Welfare State Succumbs to Chill of Economics," *The Miami Herald,* Nov. 2, 1990, p. 19A.

38. "How Many Annual Paid Holidays Do Companies Normally Grant to Employees?" *Resource,* April 1988, p. 3.

39. "AT&T: All in the Family," *Newsweek,* June 12, 1989, p. 4.

40. Arlene A. Johnson, "Parental Leave—Is It the Business of Business?" *Human Resource Planning,* June 1990, pp. 119–131. See also Helene Paris, "Balancing Work and Family Responsibilities: Canadian Employer and Employee Viewpoints," *Human Resource Planning,* June 1990, pp. 147–157.

41. Barbara Presley Noble, "The Family Leave Bargain," *The New York Times,* National ed., Feb. 7, 1993, p. F25.

42. Michele Galen, "Sure, 'Unpaid Leave' Sounds Simple, But . . ." *Business Week,* Aug. 9, 1993, pp. 32–33.

43. Michele Ingrassia and Karen Springen, "Living on Dracula Time," *Newsweek,* July 12, 1993, p. 68.

44. Juliet B. Schor, "All Work and No Play: It Doesn't Pay," *The New York Times,* National ed., Aug. 29, 1993, p. F9.

45. Mary C. Mattis, "New Forms of Flexible Work Arrangements for Managers and Professionals: Myths and Realities," *Human Resource Planning,* June 1990, pp. 133–146.

46. Jonathan Kapstein, Blanca Riemer, and Richard A. Melcher, "Workers Want Their Piece of Europe Inc." *Business Week,* Oct. 29, 1990, pp. 46–47.

47. "Most Companies Offer Tuition Aid," *Resource,* August 1988, p. 3.

48. David Lamb, "Firms Find That Employee Perks Return Big Bonuses," *The Los Angeles Times,* Oct. 25, 1993, p. A1.

49. Frances J. Milliken, Jane E. Dutton, and Janice M. Beyer, "Understanding Organizational Adaptation to Change: The Case of Work-Family Issues," *Human Resource Planning,* June 1990, pp. 91–107.

50. Jennifer J. Koch, "Wells Fargo's and IBM's HIV Policies Help Protect Employees' Rights," *Personnel Journal,* April 1990, pp. 40–49. See also Christine D. Keen, "Issues in HR," *HR News,* May–June 1993, p. 10; Jeff Miller and William B. Werther, Jr., "An American Perspective on AIDS: Executive and HR Implications for the Next Decade," *EAP International,* vol. 1, no. 3, 1993, pp. 29–36.

51. "You, Your Family, and XEAP: The Xerox Employee Assistance Program" (an internal company brochure), no date, p. 1.

52. Ibid.

53. "79% of Companies Have EAPs; Most Use Community Sources," *Resource,* April 1989, p. 2. See also Diane Kirrane, "EAPS: Dawning of a New Age," *HRMagazine,* January 1990, pp. 30–34. See also Peggy Stuart, "Investments in EAPs Pay Off," *Personnel Journal,* February 1993, pp. 43–54.

54. "More Help for Emotionally Troubled Employees," *Business Week,* Mar. 12, 1979, p. 102. See also Robert Witte and Marsha Cannon, "Employee Assistance Programs: Getting Top Management's Support," *Personnel Administrator,* June 1979, pp. 23–28.

55. "Day Care, Inc." *American Demographics,* May 1989, p. 19.

56. Lucinda Harper, "Business Travel Can Be Rough on an Employee's Personal Life," *The Wall Street Journal,* Eastern ed., Oct. 5, 1993, p. 1.

57. "Child Care Grows as a Benefit," *Business Week,* Dec. 21, 1981, pp. 60, 63. See also Sandra E. LaMarre and Kate Thompson, "Industry-Sponsored Day Care," *Personnel Administrator,* February 1984, pp. 53–55, 58, 60, 62, 64–65.

58. "Your Next Employee Benefits," *Fortune,* Mar. 30, 1987, pp. 8–9.

59. Cathy Trost, "Aiding Aging Relatives Is a Task Companies Seek to Ease for Employees," *The Wall Street Journal,* Aug. 12, 1986, p. 1. See also William B. Werther, Jr., "Childcare and Eldercare Benefits," *Personnel,* September 1989, pp. 42–46.

60. Troy Segal, Eric Schine, and Chandrika Narayan, "Family Care: Tips for Companies That Are Trying to Help," *Business Week,* Sept. 28, 1992, pp. 36–37.

61. Carol Hymowitz, "Lures for Relocation Come in New Shapes," *The Wall Street Journal,* Eastern ed., Mar. 1, 1990, p. B1.

62. Ibid. See also Shari Caudron, "Options Alleviate Employee Qualms about Relocating," *Personnel Journal,* March 1993, pp. 35–40.

63. Joann S. Lublin, "Husbands in Limbo," *The Wall Street Journal,* Western ed., Apr. 13, 1993, pp. A1, A8.

64. Linda K. Strob, Anne H. Reilly, and Jeanne M. Brett, "New Trends in Relocation," *HRMagazine,* February 1990, pp. 42–44.

65. Patrick Oster et al., "The Fast Track Leads Overseas," *Business Week,* Nov. 1, 1993, pp. 64–68.

66. Marie Wilson, Gregory B. Northcraft, and Margaret A. Neale, "The Perceived Value of Fringe Benefits," *Personnel Psychology,* vol. 38, 1985, p. 309.

67. Catherine Murino, "What Benefit Is Communication?" *Personnel Journal,* February 1990, pp. 64–69.

68. Albert Cole, Jr., "Flexible Benefits Are a Key to Better Employee Relations," *Personnel Journal,* January 1983, pp. 49–53. See also William B. Werther, Jr., "A New Direction in Rethinking Employee Benefits," *MSU Business Topics,* Winter 1974, pp. 36–37.

69. Cole, op. cit.; Werther, op. cit.

70. Bob Cohn, "A Glimpse of the 'Flex' Future," *Newsweek,* Aug. 1, 1988, pp. 38–39.

71. Susan Pedigo, "The Power of Outsourcing," *The Wyatt Communicator,* Fall 1993, p. 6.

72. Ibid.

16

Business groups already say the costs of government-dictated benefits will destroy jobs.
ROBERT J. SAMUELSON[1]

Security, Safety, and Health

CHAPTER OBJECTIVES

After studying this chapter, you should be able to:

1. **IDENTIFY** government-mandated approaches to employee security.

2. **EXPLAIN** why managers and HR departments need to take a proactive approach to employee security, safety, and health.

3. **DESCRIBE** how managers can slow the rise in workers' compensation costs.

4. **DISCUSS** the typical objectives of safety and health programs.

5. **OUTLINE** OSHA record-keeping requirements.

6. **SUMMARIZE** the safety and health responsibilities of employers and employees.

In wealthy democratic nations most people earn a livelihood by working for others, and so governments mandate security, safety, and health requirements for employers. While Chapter 15 described the benefits and services employers voluntarily give their employees, this chapter examines legally required benefits and services, including social security, unemployment compensation, workers' compensation, and occupational safety and health.

Unregulated employment

Industrial nations decided long ago that the consequences of unregulated employment relationships imposed burdens on society. For example, before workers' compensation laws required payment for job-related injuries, the burden of job injuries fell on society through government or charitable organizations. Today, employers must compensate workers for on-the-job injuries and comply with laws aimed at furthering societal objectives or face legal sanctions. The intent of these laws is to help employees deal with hardships and protect them from future workplace hazards. Although these mandate coverages are expensive, they are common in developed nations.

The challenge for HR specialists becomes how to comply proactively with the least cost to the employer and the greatest benefit for the employees. In the area of employee safety and health, for example, Du Pont has been a proactive leader.

Du Pont

Du Pont's nylon fiber plant in Seaford, Delaware, provides an example of the company's safety efforts. The last accident at the plant that was serious enough to cause an employee to miss a day of work happened when an employee tripped in the parking lot and fractured her wrist. "Like any other accident serious enough to keep one of Du Pont's 140,000 employees off the job for a day or more, this one was reported to Du Pont's chairman within 24 hours."[2] Since that accident, the plant has operated for more than two years without a lost-time case.

This commitment to safety by top management is shared by other managers at Du Pont. The plant manager at the Seaford plant, for example, has his staff conduct regular one-hour safety tours that look for deviations from sound safety practices. On one tour the safety defects that were found included a worker without hearing protectors, a ladder leaning against a wall without anyone attending to it, and an open desk drawer that could trip someone. Although these items are seemingly minor in a large nylon plant, attention to such minor "safety defects" prevents them from leading to accidents.

This level of attention to safety does not happen just because top management is notified of accidents. Employee safety and health must be part of an ongoing concern by top management that is built into the firm's culture. Du Pont has been fortunate to have had that concern from its beginning: Pierre Samuel Du Pont founded the American branch of the family and set an early example of top-managment involvement. In 1817 he left his sickbed at age 77 to help put out a fire at a gunpowder mill. Today that aspect of Du Pont's organizational character is reflected in the regular Friday meetings of the company's top management in Wilmington, Delaware; safety is the first item on the agenda at each meeting. This pattern occurs at lower-level management meetings too. People inside the company realize that to do a job right, it must be done safely. Supervisors and managers also realize that promotions are hindered by poor safety records.

Has all this attention to safety paid off? "Du Pont, which probably has the lowest accident rate of any major manufacturer, counts savings in the tens of millions a year from its safety programs."[3] For example, in one year it had 129 lost-time accidents at all of its operations, for an annual rate of 0.12 accident per 100 workers. This accident rate was one twenty-third of the National Safety Council's average for all manufacturers. If Du Pont's rate had been average, its workers' compensation and related costs would have been $26 million higher. That $26 million is equivalent to 3.6 percent of Du Pont's profits. Put another way, Du Pont would have had to sell another $500 million worth of products to make as much money as its safety program saved the company.[4]

Du Pont's successful safety record results from top management's active commitment. That commitment cascades down the organization to all levels of management and employees, relying on a variety of employee safety committees.[5] But not all organizations exhibit the commitment Du Pont does. The result has been government-imposed measures that provide a base level of security that goes beyond safe and healthy working conditions, as suggested by Figure 16-1.

Legally mandated benefits

The legally required benefits and services outlined in Figure 16-1 are impor-

---

Figure 16-1   **Sources of Financial and Physical Protection for Workers**

PROTECTION FOR WORKERS	SOURCES OF PROTECTION
FINANCIAL SECURITY	
Retirement	Social Security Act, 1935
Survivors and dependents	1939 amendments to Social Security
Total disability	1956 amendments to Social Security
Involuntary unemployment	Title IX of the 1935 Social Security Act
Industrial accidents	State workers' compensation acts
Postemployment medical coverage	Consolidated Omnibus Budget Reconciliation Act, 1985
PHYSICAL SECURITY	
Unsafe situations and unhealthful work environments	Occupational Safety and Health Act, 1970, and its enforcement agency, the Occupational Safety and Health Administration

tant to managers because they too are employees. Moreover, these protections help ensure a more stable, experienced, and productive workforce. These required benefits and services are also important to the HR department for a variety of reasons. First, top management holds the department responsible for keeping the firm in compliance. Second, the HR department's failure to comply can lead to severe hardship for employees, along with fines, higher taxes, or higher insurance premiums for the company. Third, for the HR department to contribute to the organization's objectives, it must at a minimum assure legal compliance. Fourth, for international companies such as Du Pont, good treatment of employees creates a favorable impression of the company, ensuring greater acceptance of its plans at home and abroad.

The safety and other protections listed in Figure 16-1 are not intended to fully meet the needs of workers. Instead, employees are provided a floor of protection that is supplemented by individual efforts and voluntarily provided company benefits and services. As the figure suggests, these protections can be divided into financial and physical security.

▶ Financial Security

Workers in developed nations are financially dependent on a paycheck. Anything that keeps them from earning a paycheck threatens their financial security. Because retirement, disability, layoffs, and injuries limit the earning power of many citizens, government has intervened with social security, unemployment compensation, and workers' compensation acts.

Social Security

Social security is more than a compulsory retirement plan, although it does provide an income for life upon retirement. Figure 16-2 shows other aspects of social security. These provisions give covered workers and their families disability, death, survivor, and health insurance benefits.

Since social security results in payroll deductions, questions and complaints often end up in the HR department, confronting it with widely differing views, such as the following:

 CHUCK LYONS: With five children and a wife to support, I can't afford social security, even if it is a good deal. More money is taken out of my paycheck every week for social security than for income taxes. My grandfather gets a check every month that amounts to around $628. If he didn't live with my parents, how would he survive? I pay in nearly $200 a month. If I put $200 in a bank every month until I'm 65, I would get a lot more than $628 a month when I retire. I'm against social security.

Figure 16-2	Nonretirement Provisions of the Social Security Act, as Amended

- *Disability benefits.* After a six-month waiting period, disabled workers can collect social security checks. To qualify, the disability must prevent the individual from working and be expected to last twelve months or result in death.

- *Death benefits.* The surviving spouse or other family member may receive a lump-sum payment upon the death of a worker. This nominal amount is designed to assist with burial expenses.

- *Survivors benefits.* Dependents of a retired, disabled, or deceased worker may also receive monthly social security checks. Such payments generally are limited to dependent children, parents, or spouses.

- *Health insurance benefits.* Medicare is the portion of social security that helps those over 65 (or under 65 if disabled) meet the costs of health care. Medicare coverage includes hospital insurance (to pay hospital costs), medical insurance (to pay physicians and other nonhospital costs), and payment for kidney transplants or dialysis.

MARTHA KEARNY: Social security is a great bargain. My parents, who retired last year, receive $890 every month, and that goes up with inflation! Even their medical bills are paid by the medicare provisions of social security. I even know one 29-year-old man who gets social security checks because he is disabled.

HR departments could do much to reduce the resentment of people like Chuck Lyons by explaining the other benefits in Figure 16-2 that Chuck and his family are eligible to receive from the Social Security Administration.

Coverage and administration.   The Social Security Act covers virtually all workers in the United States. Benefits are determined by the amount and duration of a worker's earnings. The more an employee earns (up to a limit that changes annually), the more the payroll department is required to deduct from each paycheck. This figure is matched by the employer and paid to the federal government.

Employees who have made contributions for forty quarters (ten years) are *fully insured workers,* eligible for a pension at retirement and for all the benefits in Figure 16-2. Those who are fully insured and have paid in at the highest rate receive the largest benefits. The total benefits received may be more or less than the amount credited to the individual's social security account. There also are eligibility requirements. For example, if a retired employee takes a part-time job, that employee may lose social security income or have it reduced. This federal program is administered by the Social Security Board in the Department of Health and Human Services.

Fully insured workers

Implications for the HR department.   The implicatons of social security for the HR department are multiple. First, specialists need to explain social security to workers. Some employees do not realize that the employer must make these deductions by law. Other employees—especially those with large families and low incomes, like Chuck Lyons in the previous example—do not understand why social security is a bigger deduction than income tax. Like many people, Lyons also appears to be unaware of the nonretirement benefits in Figure 16-2. Specialists can reduce employee confusion and morale-lowering resentment by explaining how social security works. This explanation is an especially important part of any preretirement counseling program, as discussed in Chapter 15. The local Social Security Administration office can often provide informative booklets for use in orientation and preretirement counseling sessions.

Social security offsets

A second implication is to consider social security in designing other benefits and services. For example, one hospital discovered an unintended outcome of its pension plan:

EXIT INTERVIEWER: Why are you taking early retirement at age 62?

HOUSEKEEPER: I cannot afford to stay here. I can make more money if I retire.

EXIT INTERVIEWER: How can that be? According to our retirement plan, you are eligible for only 80 percent of your average salary based on the last three years. That's still 20 percent less than you earn now.

HOUSEKEEPER: Not if you consider social security. Even with the lower social security rates of early retirement at age 62, I figure I will make $7 more a week by not working. If I stay and work, the government will reduce my social security benefits.

The hospital's retirement plan probably was not intended to encourage retirement in this way. A less expensive program might have freed resources for other employee benefits and services. Likewise, thought should be given to social security when one is designing health insurance. Kidney dialysis and transplants should be excluded from the company's major medical policy since both types of treatment are covered under social security.

The wave of post–World War II "baby boomers" will start to retire shortly after the turn of the century and will severely strain the system. Then the proportion of workers to retirees will drop dramatically. And since the current surplus of social security revenues above current outlays is used to offset ongoing budget deficits, reserves are not being accumulated. If surpluses are not created before the baby boomers retire or if the funds are used to expand other social security benefits, such as medicare, the high taxes that concerned Chuck Lyons in the earlier example will rise sharply in the future.[6] To minimize the need to raise taxes, the federal government has sought to reduce the payout to social security recipients by raising the age at which one becomes eligible for full benefits and then taxing previously untaxed payouts to middle- and high-income recipients.

Holding down social security costs

Social security is one of the most comprehensive and least understood social programs ever enacted in the United States. Although it is a cornerstone of financial security, to some people it is a high-priced pension. Others see it as a wide-ranging program of social insurance. In the future, it is likely to be little more than another welfare program, with the poor, the chronically unemployed, and the unskilled more likely to receive a good return on their contributions than are highly paid workers who contribute more and are more heavily taxed on their subsequent benefits.[7] As *Business Week* observed:

> Millions of Americans have got back far more in benefits than they paid in Social Security taxes.
>
> But that era has come to an end. For the first time, some Americans who are retiring will be getting less in benefits than the accumulated value of what they and their employers paid in taxes, and it's only going to get worse. While everyone knows that the program transfers money from young to old, few realize that its biggest impact these days is to redistribute income from rich and middle-class retirees to poor ones.[8]

By the time the average undergraduate readers of this text reach age 67 (or 70 or 75) and become eligible for full benefits, they will probably be excluded from receiving those benefits if their college degrees have led to typical middle-class affluence.[9]

Though some form of social security is common in developed nations, northern European countries provide benefits more liberal than those found in the United States, while Japan's benefits are lower. At the same time, Japan, Germany, and Italy, for example, will actually have fewer people in the prime working ages of 16 to 64 in the future, losing millions to retirement by 2025. As a result, while the United States will have about 3.3 workers for each retiree, Germany (2.5) and Japan (2.3) will have a smaller base of workers to support their social security programs.[10] In less socialistic countries such as Chile, the moneys deducted for social security do not go to fund government deficits but are dedicated to individually controlled retirement accounts regardless of income, age, or government deficits.[11]

Unemployment Compensation

Unemployment compensation represents payments to those who lose their jobs. It began as a voluntary fringe benefit in companies such as General Electric and Eastman Kodak.[12] But with the massive unemployment of the 1930s, Congress decided that unemployment compensation should become more widely available.

Following Great Britain's example

Legally required unemployment compensation began in 1935 as part of the Social Security Act and was modeled after similar legislation in Great Britain. The federal government allowed the states to create their own unemployment services, which prompted *every* state to create an unemployment compensation program and its tax benefits. The moneys collected by each state created the funds from which unemployment compensation claims are paid. The federal share finances the U.S. Employment Service and maintains emergency funds against which states can borrow during severe economic downturns. This state-federal partnership still works the same way. However, the tax rate and the tax base have changed. The U.S. Employment Service determines the federal tax rate and tax base and allows each state to set its own tax rate and tax base.

Coverage and administration.   Employers with four or more employees must participate in their state's unemployment program. Their employees are

Unemployment criteria

eligible for compensation if they meet two tests. First, an employee must be *involuntarily separated;* that is, the employee's actions did not cause the unemployment. For example, if a drop in sales causes an employee to be laid off, that employee is considered involuntarily separated. Applicants for unemployment compensation who quit or are fired for just cause may be denied payments.

The second test requires that the applicant make a *good-faith attempt* to secure *suitable employment.* A "good-faith attempt" means that the individual is *willing and able* to accept employment. Willingness is usually evidenced by actively looking for another job. This means at least pursuing job interviews arranged by a counselor at the state unemployment office. Being "able" means being available, and this explains why full-time college students are often denied unemployment compensation.

The phrase "willing and able" does not require acceptance of any job. Only "suitable employment" must be accepted. An unemployed engineer cannot be told to take the job of a janitor, for example, because that job is not suited to the engineer's training and experience. If an unemployed individual rejects a suitable job, that person is considered unavailable for employment and therefore ineligible for unemployment compensation. However, some states have amended their laws to permit unemployment compensation for striking workers.[13]

Limited benefits

When a claim is received by a state unemployment office, the employer is allowed to challenge it. The employer certainly should challenge the claim if the termination was the employee's fault. If the claim appears proper, the worker receives weekly compensation until another job is found or for the maximum duration of benefits. Weekly payments typically amount to half or two-thirds of a worker's previous pay, except for highly paid workers, who receive up to the state's maximum benefit, which is likely to be far below one-half of their previous income. If the employer can show that the unemployment was caused by the employee's actions, the claim may be denied or, if paid, not charged to the employer. Benefits do not continue indefinitely. An unemployed worker receives benefits only for a specified period or until a new job is found. During periods of severe unemployment, Congress often extends the duration of benefits for states with high levels of unemployment. As a result, benefits vary from state to state.

Implications for HR management.   The unemployment tax is controllable. Employers pay the maximum tax rate in their state *minus* credits for favorable

Experience rating

experience. The use of *experience rating* encourages employers to stabilize employment so that they will pay a lower payroll tax. By stabilizing employment, the HR department can lower the unemployment tax. Simply put, fewer layoffs mean lower taxes because the employer has a more favorable experience.

There are six major ways an HR department can lower the unemployment tax rate.[14] First, as explained in Chapter 6, HR planning minimizes overhiring and subsequent layoffs; shortages and surpluses of employees are anticipated. Then retraining or attrition can lead to proper staffing levels without layoffs. Second, the department can educate decision makers—particularly production planners and schedulers—who may not realize that "hire-then-lay-off" policies increase payroll taxes. Third, the department can review all discharges to make sure they are justified. Unjustified dismissal decisions by supervisors can be reversed or changed to intracompany transfers to prevent higher payroll taxes.

A fourth approach is to challenge all unjustified claims for unemployment compensation made against the employer. Claims that are successfully challenged may reduce the employer's costs in the future.

Kevin Hirtsman was fired for stealing from the company. (The employee manual stated that stealing was grounds for immediate dismissal.) When his claim for unemployment insurance was sent to the company for comment, the HR manager replied that Kevin was terminated for cause. Keven's claim for unemployment compensation was denied. If there had been no objection to Kevin's claim, the company's unemployment tax rate might have increased.

A fifth way to reduce the tax is to use workweek reductions instead of layoffs. When a company must lower its labor costs, a reduction in everyone's hours rather than a partial layoff does not create claims for unemployment compensation in most states. And even the smaller paycheck for a short workweek usually exceeds unemployment compensation. In some states, such as California, employees are allowed to collect unemployment compensation for a reduced workweek. For example, if an employer needs to reduce labor expenses by 20 percent, workers may be put on layoff one day a week, collecting four-fifths of their regular earnings. Employees in states that allow unemployment compensation for reduced workweeks can then collect unemployment compensation for the day they are on layoff.

A final means of reducing the unemployment tax is to adopt the "rings of defense" strategy used by Control Data and other companies. As described at the end of Chapter 9, the company contracts some tasks to outside firms. When the amount of work for permanent full-time employees is insufficient, they are assigned jobs previously handled by outside contractors.

Extended Medical Insurance under COBRA

Changes in employment, marital, or dependency status affect insurance coverage. To prevent these changes from causing an involuntary lapse in protection, Title 10 of the *Consolidated Omnibus Budget Reconciliation Act* (COBRA) of 1986

Lowering unemployment taxes *(margin note)*

COBRA *(margin note)*

offers employees and their families a temporary extension of health coverage at group rates in situations that otherwise cause insurance to end. COBRA requires an employer to continue offering health insurance to employees and their dependents *after* a covered worker's employment status changes, although the employee must pay the full premium.[15]

Coverage and administration.   COBRA applies to employers who provide health insurance and have twenty or more employees. Employees and their dependents (spouses and children) are eligible for COBRA coverage if they notify the employer within sixty days of a qualifying event. A qualifying event includes the following:

- Employee's employment is terminated (other than for gross misconduct).
- Employee's hours are reduced.
- Employee dies (making dependents eligible).
- Employee is divorced or legally separated (making dependents eligible).
- Employee becomes eligible for medicare.
- Employee's dependent child loses dependency status (making the son or daughter eligible).

After being notified of a qualifying event, the plan administrator has fourteen days in which to inform qualified beneficiaries that they are eligible for coverage. Once notified, the person has sixty days in which to elect coverage and another forty-five days from that decision to pay the premium. A continuation of prior coverage must be extended to qualified beneficiaries for eighteen months when employees are terminated or their hours are reduced. All other qualifying events (death, marital change, medicare eligibility, and loss of dependency status) require that coverage be extended for thirty-six months.

Exemptions
from COBRA

Not covered under this act are small employers (those with fewer than twenty employees), church employers (such as church-sponsored hospitals, universities, and other operations), and certain government employers (such as the federal government, U.S. territories, and Washington, D.C.).

Implications for HR management.   More than 12 percent of eligible employees elect COBRA coverage. The most common problems for the HR department are record keeping and collecting the premiums, since the department must set up a collection system to take in payments from those who elect coverage.[16] Whether done by the department or by an outside vendor, record keeping for notices, payments, reimbursements, and policy changes confronts HR managers with a new burden.

Workers' Compensation

Another threat to the financial security of employees consists of work-related accidents and illnesses. In the nineteenth century a worker could get compensation for an industrial accident or illness only by suing the employer. With the cost of medical treatment, the loss of income, and the loss of a wage earner, many workers and their families found it financially impossible to bring such suits. The result was a severe burden on society in general and on the affected workers and their families in particular.

Once again, the problem became widespread and government acted, this time by requiring *workers' compensation.* Starting in 1908, states began passing *workers' compensation laws.* Today every state has these laws, which are designed to compensate employees at least partially under a wide range of situations. The following are covered under these laws:

Purpose of workers' compensation

- Medical expenses.

- Lost income due to total disabilities that prevent working. Such disabilities may be temporary (sprains, burns, broken limbs) or permanent (loss of limbs, blindness).

- Death benefits, including funeral allowances and survivor benefits.

All states, for example, require at least partial payment of the medical bill that results from a work-related accident or illness, and most states require that the entire bill be paid. Every state pays disabled employees between 55 and 75 percent of their average weekly earnings up to a specified limit, and all states pay benefits to survivors in the event of death. The operation of the law is straightforward. A covered employee with a compensable injury or illness files the proper documentation with the state agency, insurer, or employer. After a waiting period of three to seven days, the employee is compensated at the rate determined by the state.

Coverage and administration.   Most employees in the United States are covered under workers' compensation laws. The major exceptions are farm workers, domestics, casual laborers, athletes, and businesses with fewer than five full-time workers. Since these laws vary from state to state, there are significant differences in how the laws are administered. Most states have compulsory laws, although a few have elective laws. Regardless of which approach is followed, the employer ultimately pays.

State variations

Compulsory laws require employers to comply fully with the decision of the state agency that administers the law. Some states administer their own insurance funds and compel the employer to contribute. Other states permit employers to buy policies from insurance companies or allow an employer to be self-insuring by paying compensation claims out of reserves or company income. Regardless of how the fund is financed, the employer must compensate affected employees in accordance with the decision of the state agency.

Elective laws allow an employer to refuse coverage under the state's workers' compensation law. In these states, the decision of the state agency that administers these laws is *not* binding on the employer. If the employer rejects the state agency's decision on the amount of compensation for an affected worker, the worker can sue.[17]

Skyrocketing costs **Implications for HR management.** Along with rising health-care costs (discussed in Chapter 15), workers' compensation claims are expensive and are rising rapidly. The Workers' Compensation Research Institute estimates, for example, that workers' compensation costs tripled from the early 1980s to the early 1990s, reaching $70 billion a year.[18] If the employer carries a policy for its employees, the funds devoted to workers' compensation increase with each injured or disabled employee. Before the state government reformed workers' compensation, rates became so high in California during the early 1990s that firms began relocating to neighboring states to avoid California's high workers' compensation costs,[19] which a Rutgers industrial relations professor, John Burton, estimated as being 50 percent above the national average.[20]

Company efforts, such as Du Pont's, to restrain these costs are an ongoing concern to those in HR management in small and large organizations alike because these outlays are some of the fastest-growing costs employers face. Figure 16-3 outlines specific recommendations for minimizing workers' compensation costs. Additionally, specialists must stay alert to suspicious situations that suggest malingering. The examples suggested by one expert include:

Suspicious situations
- A high frequency of work-related back strains at 10 A.M. on Monday morning during weekend softball season

- The rash of tendinitis on one assembly line on one shift of one plant in a company with three shifts in three plants doing identical work under the same conditions

- A sudden surge in medical disabilities just before a major layoff

- The employee who never wanted to work, gets into a minor auto accident and then files a permanent total disability claim for chronic pain arising from a soft tissue injury unsubstantiated by observable medical evidence.

All of these cases smack of malingering.[21]

Malingering
Malingering is more likely to occur after workers' compensation reinbursement increases; one study found that a 10 percent increase in benefits meant a 3 to 4 percent increase in recovery time.[22] Even company sports teams can be a source of workers' compensation claims:

> Edward Carr, a lawyer at insurance broker Alexander & Alexander, Inc., says companies that organize or benefit from athletic programs may be liable under workers' compensation laws for any injuries. And the risk can be significant, he says. At a large division of a major corporation that he declines to identify, more than half the workers' compensation costs stemmed from company athletic team injuries, he contends.
>
> Many corporations, pooh-poohing the risk, say there's more to be gained through improved employee health and morale than is lost. . . . "There are very, very few injuries," says Burlington Industries.[23]

| Figure 16-3 | **Ten Ways to Protect Employers under Workers' Compensation Laws** |

1. *Know your state law:*
   - Posting requirements
   - Time limits
   - Application
   - Coverage
   - Insurance requirements
   - Related laws

2. *Have clear rules on the scope of employees' duties:*
   - On/off the clock
   - Use of company vehicle
   - More than one employee
   - Personal business in the workplace
   - No horseplay
   - "Outside" staff
   - Injuries during breaks

3. *Develop a communication program.* It is important to maintain a consistent and effective communication program with employees on workers' compensation problems.

4. *Investigate accidents early.* Investigate accidents promptly and thoroughly. Always get affidavits from witnesses. Promptly contest a claim if the employee is at fault.

5. *Pay valid claims without delay.* Employers have a legal and moral obligation to do so. This practice ensures good employee relations.

6. *Keep accurate records.* Maintain a file on all claims. Keep on file all witness affidavits obtained.

7. *Coordinate claims with your labor attorney.* Consider all other labor cases that are pending with the same employee, such as wage and hour, unemployment insurance, wrongful discharge and discrimination claims, and so on. One case can affect another.

8. *Do not reemploy the worker without a doctor's letter.* Any injury serious enough for workers' compensation payments is serious enough for a doctor's letter vouching for the employee's ability to return to work.

9. *Do not change the employee's position on staff without a doctor's letter.* Take nothing for granted. Protect yourself from future claims before reassigning an employee.

10. *Fight frivolous claims.* The best way to discourage frivolous claims is to fight each one. Employees must know that you investigate all claims, promptly pay valid claims, and dispute frivolous and questionable cases.

Source: From "The Preventive Program," copyrighted by the law firm of Stokes, Lazarus & Carmichael, Atlanta, Ga. Used by permission.

Many courts view stress-related disabilities with growing sympathy. Disabilities caused by stress appear to be the fastest-growing source of workers' compensation claims, and a growing number of these claims are coming from workers who use video display terminals.[24] Given the relative youth of some claimants, the costs to the employer may be significant. For example:

> . . . when a new boss arrived . . . Wilson saw his star begin to fade. After refusing for months to heed hints to quit, he was transferred—at full salary—to a janitor's job, pushing a broom in the warehouse and mopping the employee cafeteria. Wilson soon suffered a nervous breakdown and left the company.

Eventually, he struck back. Wilson had no previous psychological problems, and he believed his boss's brutal management tactics led to his collapse. So did a jury. Wilson won $3.5 million in damages, most of it for emotional abuse.[25]

Besides providing a safe and healthy work environment, HR professionals can help restrain workers' compensation costs by promptly reporting injuries and getting employees to receive appropriate medical care: "Early reports reduce payouts by 33%."[26] Not only does getting injured employees back on the job as quickly as possible reduce costly benefit payments, the sooner the employee returns to the workplace, the less likely it is that the injury will become a permanent disability. In other words, the sooner the injured employee returns—even if it is not to his or her "old job"—the less likely it is that the employee will become used to receiving compensation without working.

IAM and Boeing

The International Association of Machinists Union and Boeing used some federal funds to retrain 200 disabled ex-Boeing workers. The union provides job counseling information about rehabilitation programs and then works with Boeing to find jobs for those people. The injury may mean that the employee cannot do the job he or she had done previously. But if other jobs that require different physical attributes are available and if those who are disabled are reached soon enough with retraining, the company may be able to reduce the number of short-term disabilities that become long-term ones. As one union counselor said, "We try to get them within six months of their accident, before they learn to live on compensation payments and lose their work habits."[27]

A "return-to-work" program at Steelcase had successful results too.

Steelcase, Inc., a major office furniture manufacturer, saved four million dollars in the six years since it began its "return-to-work" program. Through the use of staff doctors and greater involvement by supervisors, the company has cut its average claim cost in half, to $2500.[28]

This aim of getting workers back on the job—any job—after a disabling injury has led some companies to hire outside firms to monitor and track workers' compensation costs and the workers who receive benefits. As the *Wall Street Journal* reported:

Workers' Compensation costs are rising mostly because of deficiencies in the handling of claims, not because of increased claims or higher benefits, says the Workers Compensation Research Institute. It cites growing duration of disability, more attorney involvement, and increasing lump-sum settlements. Higher medical costs are a factor, too.[29]

As a result, a variety of firms have emerged to help HR management monitor claims and claimants.

QCS

Quality Care Systems, Inc. (QCS), manages workers' compensation claims from dealing with injury reports through medical care, rehabilitation, and the worker's return to the job. By proactively managing the medical care received through a case management approach to each injury, outside firms, such as QVC, can sometimes reduce overall workers' compensation costs and return workers to productive employment quicker.

Another concern for HR specialists is that employees often are only vaguely aware of these compensation laws and are even less aware of their rights. Consider the comments of one employee:

Limitations of coverage

It really came as a shock to learn that the state would only pay me 60 percent of my wages while I was unable to work. On top of that the state paid nothing for the first seven days I was out. I guess I am lucky that the disability wasn't permanent or my weekly benefit would have been even lower.

As this incident illustrates, employees are sometimes shocked by workers' compensation rules that pay only a fraction of the regular paycheck. For example, every state pays disabled claimants only part of their regular pay to discourage self-inflicted accidents and malingering. To encourage a speedy return to work, payments are lower than wages. Another universal state rule involves a waiting period to limit claims for trivial accidents. Payments eventually are reduced or even discontinued to encourage the permanently disabled to seek rehabilitation.

The inadequacy of workers' compensation coverage holds several implications for HR departments. First, workers need to be informed of the limited financial security provided by these laws. Second, gaps in employees' financial security need to be closed with supplemental disability and life insurance. Third, HR departments must guard against supervisors and managers who have decided that they do not want rehabilitated employees to return to work. Employers must make reasonable accommodations so that injured workers can return to the job. Otherwise, discrimination against workers who are injured on the job, who are less than 100 percent recovered, or who have a history of job-related injuries may lead to violations of the Americans with Disabilities Act, which was discussed in Chapter 4.[30]

A fourth consideration for the human resources department is the need to be concerned about reducing the number of accidents to lower the cost of workers' compensation.

Safety incentives

Oceaneering International, the largest underwater service contractor, offered bonuses to employees for safely conducted dives. The $2000 average bonuses reduced lost-time accidents from 31 to 18, saving between $340,000 to $500,000 compared to the $170,000 paid-out in bonuses.[31]

Beyond cost considerations, many managers feel an obligation to provide a safe working environment, as is the case at Oceaneering and Du Pont. Unfortunately, few employers have achieved such dramatic success, and so government involvement has resulted in safety laws that encourage safer practices and conditions in some workplaces. "The key to success is to prevent the claim in the first place."[32]

▶ Physical Security

The defect in workers' compensation programs is that they are reactive, after-the-fact efforts. These laws attempt to compensate employees for accidents and illnesses that have already occurred. For this reason, the government intervened and passed a comprehensive law: the *Occupational Safety and Health Act* (OSHA) of 1970. The statistical support justifying this safety legislation was overwhelming. In 1970, Congress considered annual figures such as these:

- Job-related accidents accounted for more than 14,000 worker deaths.

- Nearly 2½ million workers were disabled, either temporarily or permanently.

- Ten times more workdays were lost from job-related disabilities than from strikes.

- Estimated new cases of occupational diseases totaled 300,000.[33]

Injury trends

Figure 16-4 tells the story of workplace injuries since OSHA began collecting statistics in 1972. The trend from 1972 to 1993 shows that total injuries per 100 full-time workers have declined from 10.5 to 8.9, up from 1991's low of 8.4. Among the 6.8 million injuries and illnesses reported in 1993, the accidental death rate was 7 per 100,000.[34] The incidence of injuries without lost workdays has declined also, from 7.3 to 4.0. However, injuries that have led to lost workdays have actually increased from 3.2 to 4.6 incidents per 100 full-time workers, which has been attributed to the political philosophy in the White House in regard to OSHA: "Under Presidents Reagan and Bush, it had a hands-off approach—with the result that more work time is now lost to injuries, on a per-employee basis, than 20 years ago."[35] Part of the increase in lost workdays may be due to more accurate recording and reporting of *lost-time accidents.*[36]

Implications of OSHA for the Workplace

Congress's purpose

In passing OSHA, Congress declared that its purpose was "to assure so far as possible every working man and woman in the nation safe and healthful working conditions and to preserve our human resources." Congress imposed on

Figure 16-4	Total Number of Lost-Workday and Non-Lost-Workday Injuries for 1972, 1989, and 1992

	INCIDENCE RATES PER 100 FULL-TIME WORKERS				
			NONFATAL INJURIES		
	TOTAL		WITHOUT		LOST WORKDAY
YEAR	INJURIES		LOST WORKDAYS		INJURIES
1972	10.5	=	7.3	+	3.2
1989	8.6	=	4.6	+	4.0
1992	8.4	=	4.5	+	3.9

Source: "BLS Reports on Survey of Occupational Injuries and Illnesses in 1989," *News,* U.S. Department of Labor, Nov. 14, 1990, p. 5; "BLS Reports on Survey of Occupational Injuries and Illnesses in 1992," *News,* U.S. Department of Labor, Nov. 16, 1992, p. 6.

covered employers a general duty to provide a safe and healthy workplace. Figure 16-5 summarizes the major objectives of this legislation. As the figure indicates, Congress sought improved attention to safety and health by employers *and* employees. It also sought to enforce safety standards and uncover causes of accidents. OSHA has been one of the most far-reaching efforts by government to control the work environment. Since OSHA directly affects employees, the HR department typically is responsible for compliance.

Coverage and administration.   OSHA covers all workers except those who are self-employed, those who are protected under other federal agencies or statutes, and those who work on family-owned and -operated farms. It is administered and enforced by the secretary of labor through the *Occupational Safety and Health Administration* (also called OSHA). This organization conducts safety and health inspections according to its targeting system. Besides cases involving serious accidents, fatalities, or complaints, the agency's inspectors focus their efforts on high-hazard industries. Within these industries, OSHA inspectors concentrate on firms with injury rates above the national average. These inspections help the agency directly meet some of the objectives in Figure 16.5.

Employers want to reduce safety and health hazards through effective programs. However, many line managers and HR professionals have found some aspects of OSHA burdensome, such as the reporting requirements, the on-site inspections, and the fines for violations. To meet these objections, OSHA has eliminated some of the more trivial safety requirements, exempted some low-hazard industries from routine inspection, allowed some industries to drastically reduce their reporting requirements, and even exempted some employers from routine safety inspections and allowed them to begin their own self-policing of worksite safety and health. Mobil Chemical Company provides an example of a voluntary worker protection program called Star.

Figure 16-5	Objectives of OSHA

1. To encourage employers and employees to reduce safety and health hazards

2. To encourage employers and employees to perfect safety and health programs

3. To authorize the Secretary of Labor to establish mandatory occupational health and safety standards

4. To create an Occupational Safety and Health Review Commission to hear appeals under the act

5. To provide health and safety research through the National Institute for Occupational Safety and Health

6. To discover the causal connections between diseases and work, and to establish appropriate standards to eliminate industrial disease

7. To establish medical criteria to assure no employee will suffer diminished health, ability, or life expectancy

8. To implement training programs to improve the quantity and quality of people engaged in the safety and health field

9. To provide an effective program of enforcement of safety and health standards

10. To encourage the states to assume responsibility for administration and enforcement of safety and health regulations

11. To provide appropriate reporting procedures with regard to safety and health

12. To encourage joint labor-management efforts to reduce injuries and disease

Source: The Occupational Safety and Health Act of 1970.

Mobil Chemical

With about one-half of Mobil Chemical's plants covered under OSHA's Star program, it is easy to see why the company seeks 100 percent coverage.

The Star program allows self-policing of qualified companies, permitting OSHA to focus on other employers. The program requires Mobil to adhere to safety and health standards as rigorous as OSHA's. OSHA inspects company records as part of a triennial inspection unless an employee complaint or serious problem causes an inspection to be needed sooner.

So good is Mobil's safety system that OSHA's compliance officers audit Mobil's training program as part of their training.

Employees get recognition for their safety efforts, weaknesses in the company's efforts are uncovered, and the number and severity of injuries have declined along with the number of lost workdays. In one year, workers' compensation costs dropped in half, from $2.4 million to $1.2 million.[37]

Besides the Star program, OSHA also has the Try and Praise programs. The Try program allows employers such as Mobil to implement experimental safety efforts that may differ from traditional approaches. The Praise program attempts to recognize the lowest-hazard firms in low-hazard industries. It is a performance recognition program by OSHA for firms that have an exceptional safety and health program but do not normally receive inspections because they are in a low-hazard industry.

Inspections.   A variety of situations can lead to an OSHA inspection, although only 2 percent of this country's million workplaces are inspected in a given year.[38] When an inspection occurs, an employer *and* an employee representative normally accompany the OSHA compliance officer. Situations of interest to OSHA that lead to inspections are summarized below.

1. *Imminent danger.* This refers to a condition likely to cause death or a serious injury if it is allowed to continue. Included are situations that could cause severe bodily damage, disability, or a life-shortening illness. Improperly shored ditches, machines with open gears, and toxic fumes and dust are examples. Compliance officers must seek an immediate voluntary solution or obtain a court order to correct any imminent dangers. Cases of imminent danger receive OSHA's highest priority for inspection.

2. *Catastrophes and fatal accidents.* Catastrophes, deaths, or accidents resulting in hospitalization of five or more employees merit a high priority from compliance officers. The compliance officer determines if any OSHA standards have been violated and how similar events can be avoided in the future.

3. *Employee complaints.* Employees can complain to OSHA about safety violations or unsafe or unhealthy conditions; these allegations receive OSHA's attention and lead to an inspection. Employees have the right under OSHA to request an inspection when they believe improper safety and health conditions exist. When complaints of imminent danger are made, the employee's name is withheld from the employer if the employee wishes.

4. *Programmed high-hazard inspections.* Occupations, industries, or substances that lead to high levels of accidents or illnesses receive special attention and extra inspections under OSHA. Meat cutting, sheet metal working, logging, and their associated industries are examples of target occupations and industries. Asbestos and lead are examples of hazardous health substances. To encourage all employers to comply with the act, inspections are conducted randomly among firms in hazardous industries, with an emphasis on employers whose safety records are worse than industry norms.

5. *Follow-up inspections.* Employers who have been cited for violations of OSHA are reinspected to ensure that hazards have been corrected and compliance is maintained.[39]

Standards and appeals.   The standards to which employers must adhere are extremely detailed. Although the cowboy in Figure 16-6 is an obvious exaggeration, OSHA does have jurisdiction over every chemical substance, piece of equipment, and work environment that poses even a potential threat to worker health or safety. To conduct research and develop additional safety and health standards, the act also created the *National Institute of Occupational Safety and Health* (NIOSH). Although NIOSH's standards are sometimes viewed by industry as arbitrary, they can form the basis for serious fines or jail sentences.

Safety and health standards

Jail time

Three executives of Film Recovery Systems, Inc., were sentenced to twenty-five years in jail for causing the death of an employee who was exposed to cyanide on the job. Testimony revealed that employees worked without adequate protection and that management took no action even after repeated complaints.[40]

Figure 16-6	The Cowboy after OSHA

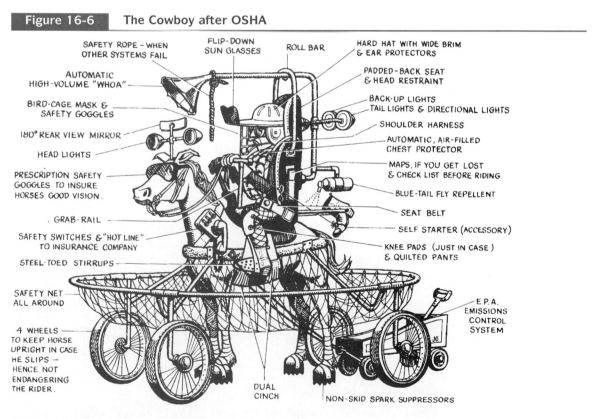

Source: Copyright © 1972 by James N. Devin. Used by Permission.

Hazard
communication

Because of incidents like this, OSHA requires employers to give employees *hazard communications.* More popularly known as "right-to-know" laws, these OSHA regulations require an employer to inform employees of known risks associated with the hazardous materials encountered on the job. Employers must develop a written orientation and training program to communicate those hazards to employees. In addition, hazardous materials must be labeled. OSHA's

Figure 16-7	**Violations and Penalties under OSHA**	
TYPE	**DESCRIPTION**	**PENALTY**
DE MINIMIS	Violation with no direct or immediate relationship to job safety or health.	None
NONSERIOUS VIOLATION	Violation of safety or health standards that probably would not cause serious physical harm or death.	Up to $1000 per day beyond the abatement period allowed by OSHA. Penalty is discretionary and may be reduced because of the employer's size, past actions, and good-faith cooperation.
SERIOUS VIOLATION	Violation likely to cause death or serious injury due to hazard of which the employer was or should have been aware.	A $1000 mandatory penalty that can be reduced by 50 percent because of the employer's size, past actions, and good-faith cooperation.
IMMINENT DANGER	Violation that is expected to cause death or serious physical harm immediately or before usual enforcement procedures can eliminate the danger.	Immediate voluntary abatement or court order closing the operations. Financial penalties same as serious violation, unless a willful or repeated violation.
WILLFUL OR REPEATED	Intentional or continuous violations of safety and health standards.	Up to $70,000 per violation. A willful violation that leads to death of an employee can be fined up to $70,000 and/or six months' imprisonment. These maximums are doubled for second convictions.
FALSIFYING RECORDS	Any improper and willful falsification of records.	Fine of up to $70,000 and six months in jail.
POSTING VIOLATIONS	Failure to post OSHA notices after violations are cited by OSHA.	Civil penalty of up to $1000.
INTERFERING WITH COMPLIANCE	Assaulting a compliance officer or otherwise resisting or obstructing a safety inspection.	Fine of up to $5000 and up to three years' imprisonment.

hazard communication ruling also requires employers to maintain material safety data sheets for each hazard item handled by employees. These sheets specify the maker, characteristics, health risks, and precautions associated with the product. Employees must have access to this information. If these procedures had been in effect and had been followed at Film Recovery Systems, Inc., the employee fatality might have been avoided.

Figure 16-7 summarizes the types and extent of fines imposed on a noncomplying employer. Note that fines are imposed for *each* violation, no matter how many violations are discovered per inspection. If an employer wants to challenge a citation, a "notice of contest" can be filed with the nearest area director of OSHA. This appeal is reviewed by a judge from the *Occupational Safety and Health Review Commission.* The judge's decision can be appealed to the review commission and even to the federal courts.

Federal and state involvement

Participation by other governments. As with unemployment compensation, state involvement was encouraged under the law. Any state that wanted to assume the duties of enforcing safety and health standards could submit a qualified plan to the U.S. Department of Labor. If the state plan was considered "at least as effective as" the federal program, the department allowed the state to have jurisdiction. Fifty percent of the operating costs of a qualified state plan is paid for by the federal government.

In the name of employee safety and health, many local governments have become involved, primarily by passing specific workplace-related ordinances. For example, San Francisco has passed a law to address the hazards of extended work at video display terminals.[41] Although these terminals are generally considered safe, the concern with these workers is repetitive strain injury, which emerges in a wide variety of jobs that require repeated actions over an extended period (such as typing, meatpacking, and textile work). In fact, the Bureau of Labor Statistics has reported that nearly half of all workplace illnesses involve a repetitive strain injury, such as carpal-tunnel syndrome, which is common among typists and word processors. Samsonite Corp., the luggage maker, paid $495,000 in fines and agreed to provide a comprehensive ergonomics management program at its Denver facilities to address a variety of cumulative trauma disorders.[42] Likewise, some state and municipal ordinances restrict smoking in the workplace because of the potential hazards associated with secondary cigarette smoke.

Implications of OSHA for HR Management

The act requires that an employer:

   1. shall furnish to each of his employees . . . a place of employment . . . free from recognized hazards that are . . . likely to cause death or serious physical harm to his employees;

   2. shall comply with occupational safety and health standards promulgated under this Act.[43]

Likewise, the act imposes certain duties on employees:

> Each employee shall comply with occupational safety and health standards and all rules, regulations, and orders issued pursuant to this Act.[44]

These two quotes from the act hold several implications for HR managers: They must obtain organizationwide compliance, maintain records, seek consistent enforcement, and permit workers to exercise their rights without punishment.

Compliance.   Organizationwide compliance requires a detailed safety program. To be effective, the program should have several characteristics. Top-management support is crucial because without it, other managers often fail to make the necessary commitment of time and resources. The Du Pont example earlier in this chapter illustrates how strong top-management commitment can lead to organizationwide compliance.

Top-management support

With this support, the HR or safety department needs to conduct a self-inspection so that health and accident hazards can be eliminated and unsafe practices can be corrected. Then training should include safety awareness programs for both employees and supervisors, whose support is essential. Firm enforcement of safety rules by the supervisor quickly establishes a safety-conscious work environment. Supervisory commitment also requires that rewards (such as pay increases and promotions) depend on a good safety record, as they do at Du Pont. Finally, the HR department must communicate directly with employees about safety. Not only do communications elevate safety awareness, they reinforce supervisory actions as well. Some companies even develop safety slogan contests or offer rewards to employees to increase safety awareness.

Direct communications

In Gainesville, Florida, a city-owned utility conducted a successful safety program managed by a city employee who had been seriously injured on his job as a utility lineman. Once a week he changed a large sign in the office showing how many total hours had been worked since the last departmental accident. When the figure reached 10,000 hours (about three months), every employee and spouse was entitled to a free dinner at any restaurant in the city. This program succeeded because safety was reinforced: weekly by the sign and quarterly by the free dinners.

Records.   The HR department must maintain proper records, as shown in Figure 16-8. Not only are these records required by OSHA, they can be used to identify the causes of accidents. By referring to these records, safety experts can detect patterns of accidents or illnesses and then undertake corrective action. Accurate record keeping is also important because falsification can lead to severe fines and jail sentences.

Figure 16-8	Recordability of Cases under OSHA

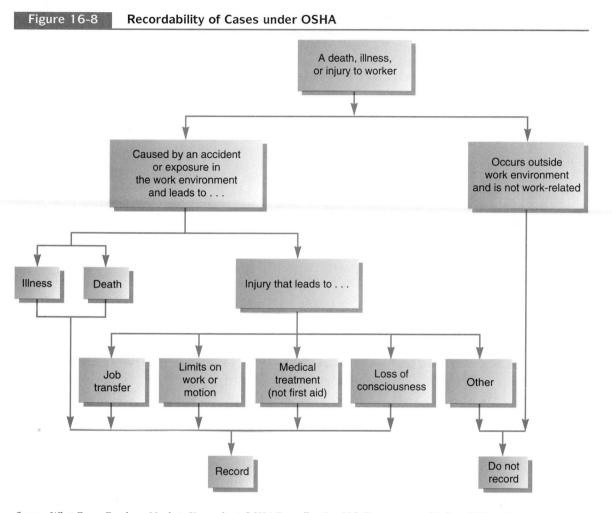

Source: *What Every Employer Needs to Know about OSHA Recordkeeping,* U.S. Department of Labor, 1975, p. 2.

Chrysler
Corporation

The U.S. Department of Labor . . . cited Chrysler Corporation for 182 alleged willful violations of the Occupational Safety and Health Administration's recordkeeping requirements and proposed fines totalling $910,000.

The citations, issued . . . at Chrysler's assembly plant at Belvidere, Ill., follow a thorough review of the plant's injury records. . . . The review began when an OSHA inspector noticed numerous discrepancies in the company's injury records during the course of a fatality investigation. . . .

In announcing the citations, Assistant Secretary of Labor for Occupational Safety and Health John A. Pendergrass said the action "was a necessary response to an apparent pattern of disregard for OSHA's recordkeeping requirements."

"We cannot allow complacency by some employers in maintaining accurate and dependable injury reports," Pendergrass said. "Recordkeeping must be the cornerstone of any successful safety and health program."

Although the Belvidere plant employs an estimated 3,900 people, a review of its records indicated an unusually low number of injuries were reported. The agency found 182 instances of work-related injuries that had not been recorded on the log, as required by federal regulations, including 133 workers' compensation cases.

OSHA proposed penalties of $5,000 for each of the 182 alleged recordkeeping violations.

As a result of the recordkeeping investigation, OSHA . . . started a comprehensive safety inspection of the entire Chrysler facility at the Belvidere plant.[45]

Record-keeping violations are treated with heavy fines because accurate records are necessary for the evaluation and correction of safety and health problems. At the same time, managers may see such reports as taking up too much of their time and diverting them from other responsibilities. Pressure from senior management and the HR department may turn out to be an incentive not to record every incident, especially those which are seen as "minor" by line managers.

Furthermore, the records are needed by employers so that for the entire month of February they can post a summary of the total job-connected accidents and illnesses which happened in the previous year. This information is found on the right-hand side of OSHA Form 200, which is available for employee inspection.

Enforcement. Enforcement of safety and health rules must be consistent. Is management too harsh when it fires a worker who refused to wear safety shoes? Probably not. If safety policies allow one worker to violate the rules, others may do the same. If an accident results, it is the employer that is fined by OSHA. By being firm—even if this means a discharge—management quickly convinces employees that safety is important. Sometimes just the threat of discipline will get employees to comply with safety regulations. And a strong record of enforcing safety rules may persuade OSHA to reduce penalties when citations are received.

Employee rights. Figure 16-9 explains the last major implication of OSHA: employees' rights to safe working conditions. To ensure the effectiveness of OSHA, the law permits employees to refuse to work when working conditions are unsafe. This is not an unqualified right. Employees first are expected to ask the employer to correct the situation if it is reasonable to do so. They may also request an OSHA inspection and have an employee representative accompany the inspector. When employees exercise their rights under the act, they are protected from discrimination by the employer. Management may not retaliate against workers who have sought changes in unsafe or unhealthful working conditions.

| Figure 16-9 | Worker Rights under OSHA |

IT'S AGAINST THE LAW FOR YOUR EMPLOYER TO PUNISH YOU
FOR EXERCISING YOUR OSHA RIGHTS

Section ELEVEN-C of the OSHA law was written to protect you from discrimination or punishment by your employer if you do such things as:

- Complain to your employer about job safety or health conditions.
- Discuss health or safety matters with other workers.
- Participate in union activities concerning health and safety matters.
- Participate in workplace health and safety committee activities.
- File health or safety grievances.
- File a complaint about workplace health or safety hazards with OSHA, state agencies, your local health department or fire department, or any other government agency.
- Participate in OSHA inspections.
- Testify before any panel, agency, or court about job hazards.
- File ELEVEN-C complaints.
- Give evidence in connection with ELEVEN-C complaints.
- Refuse a dangerous task, but only under certain conditions.

Section ELEVEN-C of the OSHA law makes it illegal for your employer to do any of the following as punishment for exercising your OSHA rights:

- Fire you.
- Demote you.
- Assign you to an undesirable job or shift.
- Take away your seniority.
- Deny you a promotion.
- Deny you benefits you've earned, such as sick leave or vacation time.
- Spy on you.
- Harass you.
- Blacklist you with other employers.
- Take away your company housing.
- Try to cut off your credit at banks or credit unions.

OSHA can protect you from these and other punishments only if they result from your exercising OSHA rights. If you want to protest discrimination or punishment which is not related to your OSHA rights, you should contact your union or the appropriate government agency. OSHA cannot protect you if you are disciplined solely for refusing to comply with OSHA regulations or valid health or safety rules established by your employer.

Source: "OSHA: Your Workplace Rights in Action," U.S. Department of Labor, 1980, pp. 2–3.

OSHA and the Future

Budget cuts at OSHA

With OSHA's compliance staff cut by 25 percent to 1120 compliance officers, its antiquated computer system making it difficult to target key violators and high-risk areas, and the courts having overturned 400 exposure standards, OSHA reaches its twenty-fifth anniversary in disarray. As a result, much new legislation has been proposed, ranging from budget increases and stiffer penalties to requirements that employers with as few as eleven workers create joint labor-management safety and health committees with elected employee representatives.[46]

OSHA is unlikely to go away.[47] It is equally unlikely that safety and health regulations and reporting requirements will become less burdensome to employers. Though regulations that assure a safe and healthy worksite are supported by labor and management, cumbersome regulations with detailed training and reporting requirements hurt international competitiveness, undermining individual economic security while helping safety and health.

▶ Summary

To further societal objectives, legally required benefits and services are imposed by government. The government—primarily the federal government—seeks to provide workers with financial and physical security.

Financial security is achieved partially through benefits such as social security, unemployment compensation, extended medical coverage, and workers' compensation. Social security provides income at retirement or upon disability. It also provides the family members of a deceased worker with a death benefit and a survivor's annuity under certain conditions.

Unemployment compensation pays the worker a modest income to reduce the hardships of losing a job. These payments go to employees who are involuntarily separated from their work. Payments last until the worker finds suitable employment or receives the maximum number of payments permitted by the state.

Extended benefits coverage under COBRA ensures that workers or their dependents will continue to receive medical-related insurance coverage after their employment or dependent status changes.

Workers' compensation pays employees who are injured in the course of employment. The payments are made to prevent the employee from having to sue to be compensated for injuries. If an employee dies, benefits are paid to the survivors.

The government has tried to provide physical security through the Occupational Safety and Health Act of 1970. This act imposes a duty on employers to provide a safe and healthy place of employment. Violations of this law, which can lead to serious injuries or industrial diseases, are subject to severe penalties. The success of a department's program depends heavily on top management's support of and commitment to employee safety and health.

▶ **Terms for Review**

Social security

Fully insured workers

Unemployment compensation

Suitable employment

Experience rating

Workers' compensation

Occupational Safety and Health Act (OSHA)

Lost-time accidents

Occupational Safety and Health Administration

Imminent danger

National Institute of Occupational Safety and Health (NIOSH)

Hazard communication

Occupational Safety and Health Review Commission (OSHRC)

Repetitive strain injury

▶ **Review and Discussion Questions**

1. Why has government been interested in providing financial security to workers through laws? What areas do you think are likely to receive federal attention in the future to ensure employees' financial security?

2. Some people feel that social security is greatly overpriced for the benefits it delivers, but many people who are retired or permanently disabled think it is an excellent social program. What do you think of social security? Why?

3. Explain why someone from the human resource department should follow up on employees who are injured on the job and are beginning to receive workers' compensation checks at home.

4. Suppose a friend of yours contracted lead poisoning on the job. What sources of income could this person rely on while recovering during the next two months? What if it took two years to recover? Are other sources of income available? If you worked at the same plant, what actions would you take?

5. If your company began using a new chemical for its photocopier and fax machines, what information would you want from the supplier? What other actions should you take to inform the employees?

6. Indicate whether each of the following people would be eligible for unemployment compensation and why: (*a*) a worker who took voluntary retirement at age 62, (*b*) a disabled employee confined to a hospital bed, (*c*) a soldier on active duty.

7. When must an accident or illness be recorded by an employer?

8. Although most OSHA penalties are in the form of fines, when can criminal penalties apply?

▶ **Incident 16-1**

Mandated Benefits and Overtime: A Connection?

During debate over President Clinton's health-care proposals, the United States set a little-noted record: Average overtime hours among factory workers reached a level not seen since World War II, nearly fifty years earlier. One explanation for this was that the United States was slowly coming out of a severe recession and employers were reluctant to hire new employees until the recovery seemed assured. Another explanation was that employers preferred to work employees overtime rather than hire new employees because new employees added to the current costs of fringe benefits and would become even more costly because of employer-provided and paid-for health insurance. In support of this second argument, many economists pointed to the "double-digit" unemployment rates common throughout most of the European Union at the time, attributing the reluctance of employers to hire more workers to the very high required social benefits imposed by government on European Union employers.

1. Why would uncertainty about the economic recovery in the middle 1990s make employers reluctant to hire new workers?

2. If mandatory benefits (workers compensation, social security, and others) add to the cost of each employee, how does the use of large amounts of overtime at time and a half help hold down labor costs?

▶ **Incident 16-2**

Cutting the K & D Company's Tax Bill

Karen Carrea, an HR specialist, recently was hired by the K & D consulting firm. The president of the firm was concerned about the taxes the company paid for employee benefits such as social security, workers' compensation, and unemployment compensation. The president assigned Karen to uncover ways in which the firm could legally reduce its labor costs by reducing its tax liability.

Karen's report contained several novel solutions. To reduce workers' compensation costs, she suggested that the HR department ask OSHA to inspect the company's printing shop, which produced the firm's reports and most of its accidents. To reduce unemployment compensation costs, Karen suggested that the department change its policy of hiring additional consultants on a project basis. She had found that every time a project ended, the temporary consultants were laid off and filed for unemployment compensation. She suggested that the company subcontract its overload to freelance consultants at the nearby university. Since the consultants would be independent contractors, their loss of consulting business would not affect the firm's unemployment insurance taxes, and the consultants would pay their own social security taxes. Karen was unable to suggest any other way social security taxes could be lowered, since they were a percentage of payroll.

1. What is your evaluation of Karen's suggestions?

2. What other methods might Karen suggest to hold down the cost of these required benefits?

▶ References

1. Robert J. Samuelson, "Will Reform Bankrupt Us?" *Newsweek*, Aug. 15, 1994, p. 50.

2. Jeremy Main, "When Accidents Don't Happen," *Fortune*, Sept. 6, 1982, p. 62.

3. Ibid.

4. Ibid, pp. 62, 64, 68.

5. Barbara Presley Nobel, "Worker-Involvement Program Violates Labor Law, U.S. Rules," *The New York Times*, National ed., June 8, 1993, p. A11.

6. Howard Gleckman, Susan B. Garland, and Paula Dwyer, "Social Security's 'Dirty Little Secret,' " *Business Week*, Jan. 29, 1990, pp. 66–67.

7. Michael J. Mandel, "From New Deal to Raw Deal," *Business Week*, Apr. 5, 1993, pp. 68–69.

8. Ibid., p. 68.

9. Alan L. Gustman and Thomas L. Steinmeier, "Changing the Social Security Rules for Work After 65," *Industrial and Labor Relations Review*, July 1991, pp. 733–745.

10. Gene Korety and Rochelle Shoretz, "The Upside of America's Population Upsurge," *Business Week*, Aug. 9, 1993, p. 20.

11. Robert C. Perez, "Let Social Security Earn More Money," *The New York Times*, National ed., June 13, 1993, p. F13.

12. Russell L. Greenman and Eric J. Schmertz, *Personnel Administration and the Law*, Washington, D.C.: Bureau of National Affairs, 1972, p. 129.

13. Craig S. Weaver, "Should Workers Be Paid to Strike?' *Personnel Administrator*, June 1988, pp. 108–111.

14. Philip Kaplan, "Unemployment Taxes Are Variable, Controllable Expenses Which Employers Must Recognize as Growing Profit Drain," *Personnel Journal*, April 1976, pp. 170–172, 184–185.

15. "Companies Report Administrative Problems with COBRA," *Small Business Reports*, December 1988, p. 7.

16. Gary B. Kushner and Gina Williams, "COBRA: Answers to the Most-Asked Questions," *Legal Report*, Fall 1990, pp. 1–8.

17. Greenman and Schmertz, op. cit., pp. 152–153.

18. Eric Schine and Dori Jones Yang, "Workers' Comp Goes under the Knife," *Business Week,* Oct. 19, 1992, p. 90.

19. Marc Levinson and Andrew Murr, "Getting Back to Business," *Newsweek,* Jan. 31, 1994, p. 35–36. See also Ronald Grover, "How Workers' Comp Could Get Mangled," *Business Week,* Dec. 14, 1992, p. 44.

20. Schine and Yang, op. cit, p. 91.

21. Paul R. Lees-Haley, "How to Detect Malingerers in the Workplace," *Personnel Journal,* July 1986, pp. 106, 108, 110.

22. Gene Koretz, "Does Better Workers' Comp Mean Longer Absences?" *Business Week,* Jan. 28, 1991, p. 22.

23. Selwyn Feinstein, "Labor Letter: Company Sports Teams Often Are Winners, but a Fumble Can Be Expensive," *The Wall Street Journal,* Midwest ed., Sept. 30, 1986, p. 1.

24. "More Workers' Compensation Claims for Stress, Costs Rising," *Resource,* December 1989, p. 19.

25. Elizabeth Lesly, "Good-Bye Mr. Dithers," *Business Week,* Sept. 21, 1992, p. 52.

26. Chris Roush, "Making Workers' Comp Work," *Business Week,* Oct. 25, 1993, p. 114.

27. "Disabled Workers Get Training to Begin New Careers in a Union Program," *The Wall Street Journal,* Western ed., July 7, 1981, p. 1.

28. Schine and Yang, op. cit. See also Jennifer J. Laabs, "Steelcase Slashes Workers' Comp Costs," *Personnel Journal,* February 1993, pp. 72–87.

29. Christopher Conte, "Labor Letter: Workers' Compensation," *The Wall Street Journal,* Eastern ed., Feb. 23, 1993, p. 1.

30. Aaron Bernstein, "A Giant Loophole Called the Disabilities Act," *Business Week,* Oct. 19, 1992, pp. 91–92.

31. Laurel B. Calkins, "No Pain, Some Gain," *Business Month,* October 1989, p. 21.

32. Roush, op. cit.

33. "All about OSHA," Washington, D.C.: U.S. Department of Labor, 1985, p. 1.

34. Bill Saporito, "The Most Dangerous Job in America," *Fortune,* May 31, 1993, p. 131.

35. Dean Foust, "Stepping into the Middle of OSHA's Muddle," *Business Week,* Aug. 2, 1993, p. 53.

36. "BLS Reports on Survey of Occupational Injuries and Illnesses in 1989," *News,* U.S. Department of Labor, Nov. 14, 1990, pp. 1–7.

37. "HRM Update: Safety Stars," *Personnel Administrator,* June 1986, p. 22.

38. Susan B. Garland, "A New Chief Has OSHA Growling Again," *Business Week,* Aug. 20, 1990, p. 57.

39. "All about OSHA," pp. 19–23.

40. Peter A. Susser, "Criminal Prosecution for Workplace Safety Problems," *Personnel Administrator,* July 1986, pp. 34, 36, 38.

41. "San Francisco Has Nation's Sole VDT Law," *The Miami Herald,* Dec. 28, 1990, p. 10A.

42. "Samsonite Corp. Agrees with OSHA to Provide Comprehensive Ergonomics Program in Denver Plant; Pay $495,000 in Fines," U.S. Department of Labor *News Release,* Feb. 2, 1993, p. 1. See also Michele Galen et al., "Repetitive Stress: The Pain Has Just Begun," *Business Week,* July 13, 1992, pp. 142ff; "Office Technology: Key Decisions," *The Economist,* Apr. 3, 1993, pp. 78–79; and Barbara Kantrowitz and Rebecca Crandall, "Casualties of the Keyboard," *Newsweek,* Aug. 20, 1990, p. 57.

43. Occupational Safety and Health Act of 1970.

44. Ibid.

45. "OSHA Cites Chrysler Corporaton for 182 Alleged Willful Violations, Proposes $910,000 in Penalties," *News,* U.S. Department of Labor, Nov. 5, 1986, pp. 1–2.

46. Foust, op. cit.

47. "17 American Workers a Day Died on the Job During the 80's," *The New York Times,* National ed., Apr. 15, 1994, p. 15.

17. Employee Relations Challenges
18. Union-Management Relations
19. Assessment and Prospects

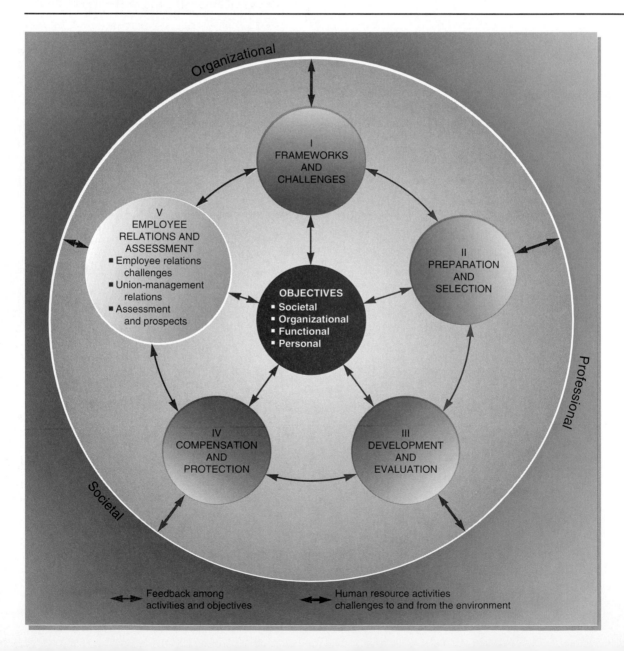

EMPLOYEE RELATIONS AND ASSESSMENT

B Y CREATING a productive and satisfying work environment through effective employee relations, a proactive HR department contributes to its organization's success. Employee relations practices that meet organizational objectives and employee needs result in a high quality of work life. When unions are present, employee relations efforts face new challenges from laws, labor agreements, and past practices. The HR department also must search for new ways to help the firm and its people. One way is through an audit of its activities; another way is to help the firm and its people anticipate future challenges. By doing this in an ethical manner, the HR department helps the firm meet its employee and social responsibilities.

Although HR departments conduct organizationwide activities to facilitate good employee relations, your success as a manager depends on effective employee relations among those you lead. As a manager or HR professional, you will find that audits give feedback on how you perform, affecting the way you manage in the future.

Worker satisfaction and organizational effectiveness are key responsibilities of the human resource function. . . .
CARLA C. CARTER[1]

The move toward a global work force takes many forms and consists of far more than a stampede to backward low-wage countries.
BRIAN O'REILLY[2]

Employee Relations Challenges

CHAPTER OBJECTIVES

After studying this chapter, you should be able to:

1. **JUSTIFY** the efforts to improve the quality of work life (QWL) through better employee relations.

2. **EXPLAIN** how managers and human resource departments affect QWL.

3. **DESCRIBE** the HR department's role in organizational communications.

4. **IDENTIFY** the trade-offs between the production- and QWL-oriented concerns facing operating managers.

5. **EXPLAIN** the reasoning behind progressive discipline.

6. **DISCUSS** the differences between preventive discipline and corrective discipline.

Global competition is relentless, forcing organizations to continually upgrade their strategies and execution. Proactive managers and HR departments contribute by finding new ways to improve productivity. While some strategies rely heavily on new capital and technology, other approaches pursue improvements in employee relations practices.[3] Contrast the General Motors response to increased global competition with Ford's response.

GM versus Ford

F. Alan Smith, chief financial officer at General Motors, estimated that in response to competitive pressures (especially from Japan), GM spent $80 billion on plant and equipment. In an attempt to use capital investment and technology to leapfrog the quality and cost advantages of Japanese car makers, GM spent more money than it would have cost to buy every share of Toyota *and* Nissan. The resulting depreciation charges on all of GM's invested capital exceeded Chrysler's capital assets. Even more telling, GM's market share fell from 48 percent in the late 1970s to 33 percent in the mid-1990s.[4]

Ford, in contrast, made smaller capital investments and created its "Quality is 'Job 1' " program, in which small groups of employees were formed into teams, often led by a coworker. These teams were empowered to find areas of quality or productivity improvement and make changes.[5]

The result? GM needed forty-one worker-hours to assemble a mid-size car, while Ford built Taurus and Sable models in twenty-five worker-hours.[6] The lesson is "that 'brains and wits will beat capital spending ten times out of ten.' "[7]

QWL

HR efforts to improve productivity through changes in employee relations rely on "brains and wit," not capital outlays. Ford's success had come from tapping the ideas and enthusiasm of its employees by providing them with a good *quality of work life* (QWL). *QWL* means having good supervision, good working conditions, good pay and benefits, and an interesting, challenging, and rewarding job. High QWL is sought through an employee relations philosophy that encourages the use of *QWL efforts*, which are systematic attempts by an organization to give workers greater opportunities to affect their jobs and their contributions to the organization's overall effectiveness. That is, proactive managers and HR departments find ways to empower employees so that they draw on their "brains and wits," usually by getting the employees more involved in the decision-making process.

Empowering employees

▶ The Role of the Human Resource Department

The HR department's role in employee relations efforts varies widely. In some organizations, such as TRW, BankAmerica, Control Data, and NASA, top management appoints an executive to ensure that QWL and productivity efforts occur throughout the organization.[8] These executives usually have a small staff and must rely on the HR department and operating managers for employee training, communications, attitude survey feedback, and similar assistance.[9] In most organizations, the HR department is responsible for initiating and directing the firm's employee relations efforts aimed at enhancing QWL and its productivity efforts. The HR department's attempt to improve employee relations means that it must earn management support and address issues of employee motivation and job satisfaction. Without the support of managers throughout the organization, however, these efforts almost always fail. Management support is essential.

Management Support

Management support—particularly top-management support—appears to be an almost universal prerequisite for any employee relations effort that seeks to improve employee QWL or productivity.[10] By substantiating employee satisfaction and bottom-line benefits ranging from lower absenteeism and turnover to higher productivity and fewer accidents, the HR department can help convince doubting managers.[11] Sometimes documentation of performance before and after a QWL effort helps establish the business benefits of a new approach to employee relations. Ohio Bell, for example, achieved better sales from its phone installers, a reduction in lost inventory, fewer strikes, better employee attitudes, and improved productivity as a result of employee relations efforts aimed at improving QWL for its workers. Without documentation of these results, top management might not have continued its strong support.

Ohio Bell

Individual Motivation and Job Satisfaction

The HR department also has both a direct and an indirect influence on employee motivation and satisfaction. As Figure 17-1 illustrates, the HR department makes direct contact with employees and supervisors through orientation, training and development, career planning, and counseling activities. At the same time, these activities may help a supervisor do a better job of motivating employees.

The policies and practices of the HR department also influence motivation and satisfaction indirectly. Rigorously enforced safety and health programs can give employees and supervisors a greater sense of safety from accidents and industrial health hazards. Compensation policies may motivate and satisfy employees through incentive plans or may harm motivation and satisfaction through insufficient raises or salary freezes. The motivation and satisfaction of employees act as feedback on the organization's QWL and the HR department's day-to-day employee relations activities.

Motivation and satisfaction as feedback

Motivation is a complex subject. It involves the unique feelings, thoughts, and past experiences of each of us as we share a variety of relationships within and outside organizations. To expect a single motivational approach to work in

| Figure 17-1 | Influence of the Human Resource Function on Motivation and Satisfaction |

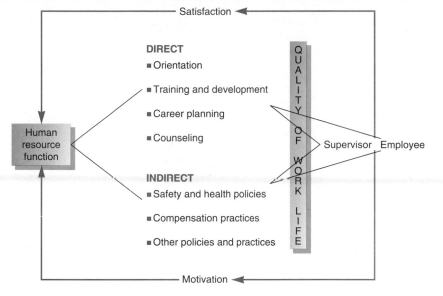

every situation is probably unrealistic. In fact, theorists and researchers take different points of view about motivation. Nevertheless, *motivation* can be defined as a person's drive to take an action because that person wants to do so. People act because they feel that they have to. However, if they are motivated, they make a positive choice to do something because, for example, it may satisfy some of their needs.

Motivation

Job satisfaction is the favorableness or unfavorableness with which employees view their work. As with motivation, it is affected by the environment. The job itself affects satisfaction through its design, as discussed in Chapter 5. Jobs that are rich in behavioral elements such as autonomy, variety, task identity, task insignificance, and feedback contribute to an employee's satisfaction. Orientation was emphasized in Chapter 9 because the employee's acceptance by the work group is important to satisfaction. In short, each element of the environmental system can add to or detract from job satisfaction.

Job satisfaction

A basic issue is whether satisfaction leads to better performance or whether better performance leads to satisfaction. Which comes first? The reason for the apparently uncertain relationship between performance and satisfaction is that rewards intervene, as shown at the top of Figure 17-2. Whether satisfaction is going to be improved depends on whether the rewards match the expectations, needs, and desires of the employee, as shown at the bottom of the figure. If better performance leads to higher rewards and if those rewards are seen as fair and equitable, improved satisfaction results.[12] Conversely, inadequate rewards can lead to dissatisfaction. In either case, satisfaction becomes feedback that af-

Performance and satisfaction

Figure 17-2	A Reward-Performance Model of Motivation

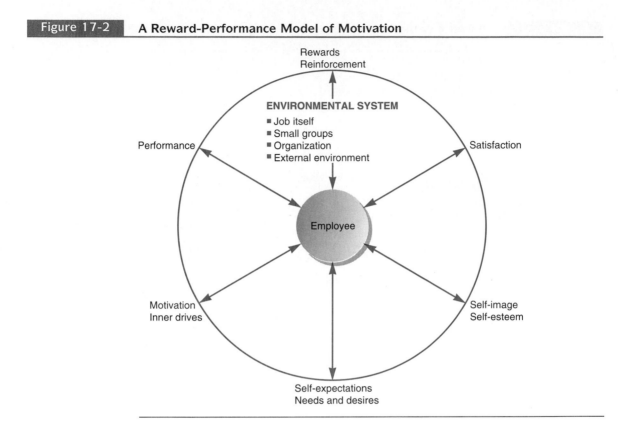

fects one's self-image and motivation to perform. The total performance-satisfaction relationship is a continuous system, making it difficult to assess the impact of satisfaction on motivation or performance and vice versa.

This chapter describes how managers and HR departments meet the challenge of higher productivity and QWL through a variety of efforts to empower employees. Then the discussion focuses on three important practices that help mold the unique character of an organization's employee relations: communications, counseling, and discipline.

▶ QWL through Employee Involvement

EI

Ownership

One of the most common methods used to improve QWL is employee involvement. *Employee involvement* (EI) consists of a variety of systematic methods that empower employees to participate in decisions that affect them and their relationship with their work, job, and organization. Through EI, employees feel a sense of responsibility for and even "ownership" of decisions in which they have participated. To be successful, however, EI must be more than a systematic approach; it must become part of the organization's culture by being part of the firm's philosophy of management.[13] Some companies have had this philosophy ingrained in their corporate structure for decades; Hewlett-Packard is an example. Other companies, such as USX, General Motors, and Ford, are trying to improve employee relations and create a high-QWL corporate culture through employee empowerment approaches. Consider, for example, Ford's Sharonville operation.

Ford

The Sharonville plant was built in 1957. Over the years it developed a "confrontational" form of labor-management relations. Plant management was autocratic, and employment dropped from 5000 in 1979 to 2500 a few years afterward. A new plant manager who was not satisfied with the old autocratic style observed, "Times have changed and we have to take a new approach."[14]

Shortly after his arrival, this manager proposed a joint union-management coordinating committee to be cochaired by the head of the union's bargaining group and a top-ranked management employee. The committee helped create several groups of six or seven hourly employees. To each group was added a representative from quality control and one from process engineering. The groups were formed to find solutions to workplace problems. One of the hourly members was elected leader, and meetings were held for one hour each week.

Soon members of the original committee could no longer keep up with the demand for creating and training more groups. Additional "minicoordinators" were used, and within two years the small problem-solving groups existed throughout the plant. "In effect, a parallel organization overlay the regular hierarchical structure. EI had become a permanent process interlocking at all points with the formal organization."[15]

Efforts like these at Ford—and similar ones at Du Pont, IBM, AT&T, Westinghouse, Motorola, Texas Instruments, Citibank, TRW, NASA, Reynolds Metals, and many others shown in Figure 17-3—indicate that interest in improving QWL is no accident. It parallels, and some might say reflects, growing international competitive forces and growing workforce diversity. In Europe this trend is often labeled *industrial democracy.*

Industrial democracy

Pygmalion effect

The implications for managers and HR specialists are to create an organizational culture that truly treats people as though they were experts at their jobs and empowers them to use that expertise. When management does this, a *Pygmalion effect* may result; this occurs when people live up to the high expectations others have of them.[16] If management further assumes that people want to contribute and seeks ways to tap that contribution, better decisions, improved productivity, and a higher QWL are likely.

A caution is in order: The federal government does not allow the use of employee involvement to undermine or avoid dealing with unions. If it is ruled by the courts or the National Labor Relations Board that EI is being used to control or avoid dealing with unions, the employer can be found guilty of violating the nation's labor relations laws. Moreover, these prohibitions involving employee

| Figure 17-3 | **A Partial List of North American Organizations Concerned with Quality of Work Life and Employee Involvement** |

Allen Bradley Company	General Telephone and Electric Co.
American Express, Inc.	General Tire Company
American Telephone and Telegraph	Honeywell, Inc.
AmHoist, Inc.	Ideal Basic Industries
Arcata Redwood Company	Inland Steel Company
Arizona Public Service	International Business Machine Co.
Atwood Vacuum Machine Company	Lincoln Electric Company
Babcock & Wilcox	Motorola, Inc.
Bank of America	NASA
Beech Aircraft Corporation	Owens-Illinois, Inc.
Bendix Company	Penn Central, Inc.
Boeing, Inc.	Pennzoil, Inc.
Boise Cascade Company	Philadelphia Electric Company
Champion International	Phillips Petroleum Company
Chrysler Corporation	Reynolds Metals Company
Citibank Corporation	Tektronix, Incorporated
City of Phoenix	Texas Instruments, Inc.
Consolidated Foods, Inc.	TRW, Inc.
Control Data Corporation	Union Carbide
Flemming Foods, Inc.	Valley National Bank
Ford Motor Company	Waters Associates Inc.
General Dynamics, Inc.	Western Electric
General Electric Company	Westinghouse, Inc.
General Motors Company	W. R. Grace and Company

groups or teams apply whether the company is unionized (as happened to E. I. Du Pont de Nemours & Company) or nonunionzed (as happened to the Electromation Company). As with many other aspects of HR management, guidance from legal counsel is needed before a firm creates work groups or teams that might appear to be substitutes for unions.[17]

▶ QWL and Empowerment Interventions

The economic dominance of the United States during the post–World War II period created little need for evolutionary changes in the way people were managed. However, in Europe and Japan, national economic survival during the late 1940s and early 1950s meant that new, innovative HR methods were needed. Some of these innovations began in legislative halls, while other developments started on the shop floor. Most of these approaches were based on sound behavioral and sociological research, much of which had been initially conducted in the United States and Canada but was applied first in Japan and northern Europe. During subsequent decades these EI approaches to QWL were modified and in many cases "imported" back into North America.

A wide variety of companies have undertaken interventions to empower employees and improve QWL.[18] Examples include Ford's Sharonville plant and Motorola's Participative Management Program (discussed in Chapter 2). Boeing uses a single-focus task force approach called "tiger teams," which are assembled to solve production-delaying problems that the supervisor and employees cannot overcome. Various approaches to team building share a common underlying philosophy: Groups of people usually are better at solving problems than an individual is. Even though the "purpose" of these approaches may be to find a solution, a by-product is improved QWL.

Tiger teams (margin note)

Quality Circles

Quality circles are small groups of employees who meet regularly with a common leader to identify and solve work-related problems.[19] They are a highly specific form of team building that is common in Japan and that gained popularity in North America in the late 1970s and early 1980s.

Quality circles (margin note)

Several characteristics make this approach unique. First, membership in the circle is voluntary for both the leader (usually the supervisor) and the members (usually hourly workers). Second, the creation of quality circles is usually preceded by in-house training. For supervisors these sessions typically last for two or three days. Most of the time is devoted to discussions of small-group dynamics, leadership skills, and indoctrination in the QWL and quality circle philosophies. About a day is spent on the different approaches to problem solving. Employees are usually given one day of intensive training in problem-solving techniques. The workers also receive an explanation of the supervisor's role as the group's discussion leader and information about the quality circle concept. Third, as is pointed out during the training, the group is permitted to select the problems it wants to tackle. Management may suggest problems of concern, but the group can decide which ones to focus on. Ideally, the selection is not done by democratic vote but arrived at by consensus, in which everyone agrees on the problem to be tackled. (If management has pressing problems that need to be solved, these problems can be handled in the same way they were treated before the introduction of quality circles.)

Unique features (margin note)

At Solar Turbines International (a Caterpillar Tractor Company subsidiary) employees were frustrated by the lack of power hand tools. They studied the lost production time caused by waiting for tools and showed management how to save more than $30,000 a year by making a $2200 investment in additional hand tools.

Solar Turbines (margin note)

The employees did not select this problem to save management money; they did it because of the inconvenience insufficient tools caused them. The fact that the solution saved more than a dozen times what it cost was the type of by-product many companies report from successful quality circle efforts.

When employees are allowed to select the problems they want to work on, they are likely to be more motivated to find a solution. They are also more likely to be motivated to stay on as members of the circle and solve additional problems in the future.

This concept is based squarely on behavioral research conducted in U.S. factories and universities, beginning with Western Electric and the famous Hawthorne experiments of the 1930s. By the 1980s most medium- and large-sized Japanese firms had quality control circles for hourly employees. This effort began as a quality improvement program but has since become a routine procedure for many Japanese managers and a cornerstone of QWL efforts in many Japanese firms.

Sociotechnical Systems

Another intervention to improve QWL is the use of sociotechnical systems. *Sociotechnical systems* are interventions in the work situation that restructure the work, the work groups, and the relationship beween workers and the technologies they use to do their jobs. More than just enlarging or enriching a job, these approaches may result in radical changes in the work environment.

Siemens

At a Siemens plant in Karlsruhe, Germany, workers assembling electronics products used to perform simple tasks over and over, spending less than one minute on each unit as it moved along a conveyor belt. Today many employees work in teams of three to seven at well-designed "work islands," where they can avoid boredom by rotating jobs, socializing, and using job cycles of up to twenty minutes rather than a few seconds.[20]

This rearrangement of social and technical relationships on the job offers workers an opportunity for a better QWL. Efforts to "humanize" the workplace seem to be most advanced in Germany, where the government funds 50 percent of selected work restructuring and retraining efforts in private industry. Shell Canada Ltd. and Procter & Gamble provide North American examples.[21]

Ergonomics

Germany also has done considerable work in the area of ergonomics. *Ergonomics* is the study of the biotechnical relationships between the physical attributes of workers and the physical demands of the job. The objective is to reduce physical and mental strain in order to increase productivity and improve

QWL. The Germans have made considerable strides in reducing the strain of lifting, bending, and reaching through their ergonomic approach to structuring jobs, arranging equipment, and improving lighting.[22]

Raising or lowering work surfaces slightly, shifting handles to more convenient locations, and tilting a parts bin can all reduce worker strain. Those were the initial findings of a four-year, $2.5 million project of Ford Motor Company and the University of Michigan's Center for Ergonomics, which studies the physical relationship between workers and machines. Ford claims that quality and productivity are up at plants where ergonomic changes were made. Workers also report feeling better on the job. The program is "an everybody-wins situation."[23] And with the growing concern about repetitive stress injuries (discussed in Chapter 16), ergonomics offers a productivity- and QWL-enhancing solution.

Codetermination

One of the early attempts at achieving industrial democracy on a broad scale occurred in Germany under the name *codetermination.* Through formal sessions with company management, codetermination allows workers' representatives to discuss and vote on key decisions that affect the workers. This form of industrial democracy has spread throughout most of the European Union. As a result, decisions to close plants or lay off large numbers of employees meet with far more formal resistance in Europe than they do in North America. On the plus side, European firms are forced to plan their HR needs more carefully and seek export markets to offset national economic cycles. Since major North American corporations operate in Europe under codetermination, HR management in multinational corporations is affected. For international HR experts, codetermination is a consideration in the design of overseas jobs. In North America, the first steps toward codetermination may have begun in the 1980s when Chrysler Corporation appointed the president of the United Automobile Workers to its board of directors.[24]

Union-management involvement

Autonomous Work Groups

Leaderless work groups

Autonomous work groups are teams of workers, without a formal company-appointed leader, who decide among themselves most decisions traditionally handled by supervisors.[25] The key feature of autonomous work groups is a high degree of empowerment of employees in the management of their day-to-day work. Typically this includes collective control over the pace of work, distribution of tasks, and organization of breaks, along with collective participation in the recruitment and training of new members. Often direct supervision is unnecessary.

Figure 17-4	A Summary of Gaines and Volvo Experiences with Autonomous Work Groups

GAINES PET FOOD

At the Gaines Pet Food plant in Topeka, Kansas, jobs were radically changed. No longer are workers assigned specific tasks in traditional jobs. Instead, teams of workers are held responsible for a group of tasks that previously constituted several separate jobs. For example, the work group is held responsible for packing and storing the completed products instead of each worker having a narrow job that includes only a few tasks in the packaging and storing operations. Employees are assigned to a work group, not a job. They are free to participate in group decision-making processes. Members develop work schedules, interview new employees, perform quality control checks, maintain machinery, and perform other diverse activities. The work-group enrichment led to reduced overhead, higher productivity, better product quality, and lower turnover and absenteeism. And labor costs are 7 percent lower than those at a sister plant in Kankakee, Illinois.

VOLVO'S KALMAR PLANT

Volvo, the Swedish automobile producer, sought to design a more humane car production environment. It built the Kalmar plant around the concept of work teams rather than the traditional assembly line. Again, workers are assigned to teams, not jobs. Teams build subsystems of the car: doors, cooling systems, engines, and other key components. Buffer stocks of partially completed cars reduce the dependence of one group on another. The physical work environment is as quiet as the latest technology permits.

Volvo claims higher satisfaction levels among employees because of the design changes, and production costs are 25 percent lower than those at Volvo's conventional plants. On the basis of the Kalmar experience, the company is building a new plant at Uddevalla.

Classic applications

Two early classic experiments with autonomous work groups occurred at the Gaines Pet Food plant in Topeka, Kansas, and the Volvo plant in Kalmar, Sweden (these experiments are summarized in Figure 17-4).[26] Similar innovations intended to increase employee commitment have been undertaken by Cummins Engine in Jamestown, New York; Procter & Gamble in Lima, Ohio; and General Motors plants in Mississippi, Michigan, and New York. Improving the QWL may mean completely redesigning factories and workplaces, as Volvo and Gaines have done to satisfy the efficiency, environmental, and behavioral requirements of jobs.

QWL is more likely to improve as workers demand jobs with more behavioral elements. These demands will probably emerge from an increasingly diverse and educated workforce that expects more challenges and more autonomy in its jobs, such as worker participation in decisions traditionally reserved for management. Through codetermination, this trend in Europe has lasted more than thirty years and is still growing in popularity. And experiments by

Gaines, Volvo, TRW, and other employers indicate that these new arrangements are economically feasible.

▶ Employee Relations Practices

HR and employee relations

Employee relations activities are shared with supervisors because of the growing complexity of organizations, laws, and union-management relations. Earlier in this century, for example, supervisors were solely responsible for employee relations practices and hiring, which led to unethical practices such as favoritism and kickbacks. Today, with the need for uniform, legal, and corporationwide approaches, HR specialists are given a considerable degree of responsibility for employee relations. The result is a dual responsibility between the HR department and supervisors. Of course, supervisors remain responsible for communicating task-related requirements and for counseling and disciplining their employees within the guidelines established by the department. But when serious problems are uncovered in counseling or a major disciplinary action is planned, HR specialists are commonly involved to ensure fairness and uniformity of treatment.

Virtually everything the manager and the HR department do affects employee relations directly or indirectly. Many activities are largely unnoticed by employees, including recruitment, selection, and benefits administration. Other activities affect employees only periodically, such as performance and salary review sessions. However, managers and HR departments directly affect employee relations through communications, counseling, and disciplinary practices.

Employee Communication

Information flows

Information about the organization, its environment, its products and services, and its people is essential to management and workers. Information is the engine that drives organizations. Without information, managers cannot make effective decisions about markets or resources, particularly human resources. Similarly, insufficient information may cause stress and dissatisfaction among workers. This universal need for information is met through an organization's communication system.[27] *Communication systems* provide formal and informal methods for moving information through an organization so that appropriate decisions can be made. Consider an example from IBM.

IBM

IBM has long excelled in the management of its human resources. Long ago, top management realized that the company's future success rested with the people who developed its technology and sold its products. To tie its various employee relations activities together and facilitate motivation and satisfaction, IBM relies heavily on communication. Some of its approaches include extensive career planning information and assistance, attitude surveys, suggestion systems, open-door policies, daily newspapers at some sites, and bulletins issued nearly every day on educational opportunities and promotions.

"Trolling for open doors"

Beyond these formal methods, informal communication occurs. For example, "management by walking around" is known at IBM as "trolling for open doors." IBM has an *open-door policy* by which employees are free to walk into any manager's office with their problems. However, IBM management realizes that most workers are reluctant to take a problem to their boss's boss.[28] Therefore, HR specialists and line managers leave their offices and go out among the employees to learn what problems exist. As one IBM executive explained, "The only open-door policy that works is one where the manager gets up from the desk and goes through the door to talk to employees."

Most organizations use a blend of formal, systematically designed communication efforts and informal, ad hoc arrangements. For convenience, most of these approaches can be divided into downward communication systems, which exist to get information *to* employees, and upward communication systems, which exist to get information *from* employees.

Downward communication systems.   HR departments operate extensive communication systems to keep people informed. They try to facilitate an open, two-way flow of information, although most messages are of the top-down variety. *Downward communication* is information that begins at some point in the organization and cascades down the organizational hierarchy to inform or influence others. Top-down methods are necessary to execute decisions and give employees knowledge about the organization and feedback on how their efforts are perceived. For example, experts recommend that companies develop and communicate policies about dealing with discrimination, sexual harassment, disabled workers, and AIDS.[29]

Organizations use a variety of downward communications because the diversity of multiple channels is more likely to overcome barriers and reach the intended receivers. Common examples of downward communication include house organs (such as company newspapers), information booklets, employee bulletin boards, prerecorded messages, and jobholder reports and meetings, which inform employees about company developments.

IBM's Boulder, Colorado, facility publishes a daily paper called *Boulder Today,* plus almost daily fliers about promotions and educational opportunities. In addition, the Information Systems Division at the Boulder site prints its own newspaper every two months. These local house organs are supplemented by other divisional and corporate publications that try to keep IBM employees in Boulder informed. Similar house organs are published at other IBM facilities around the world.

IBM

Chevron

At Chevron Corporation, more than sixty newsletters called "blue-tops" were produced during the year after its merger with Gulf Corporation, which at the time was the largest corporate merger in history. In addition, twenty-minute videos, recorded phone updates, seminars, and "town hall" meetings with Chevron's leader, George Keller, were used.[30]

When a firm is operating internationally, communications need to be modified to fit local benefits and programs. Sending publications written in the home-country language, for example, indicates insensitivity to employees who speak only their native language.

Upward communication systems.   Perhaps no area of communication is more in need of improvement than upward communication. *Upward communication* consists of information sent by people who seek to inform or influence those higher up in the organization's hierarchy. The cornerstone of all such messages is the employee and the supervisor. When a free flow of information travels between an employee and the supervisor, informal day-to-day communications are sufficient for most situations. Consider a tragic example of blocked upward communication:

The *Challenger* disaster

> Washington—"If the decision-makers had known all of the facts, it is highly unlikely they would have decided to launch."
> With that sentence, the blue-ribbon commission investigating the explosion of the space shuttle Challenger summed up perhaps the most haunting element in the tragedy: not the fatal flaws in NASA's ultrasophisticated rockets but the human failure to follow one of the oldest rules in the book.
> Despite the weaknesses in Challenger's technology, its seven crew members would probably still be alive today if shuttle officials had only spoken more candidly to their superiors and if their superiors had only been willing to listen.[31]

An employee may have a good, open relationship with the supervisor in regard to job-related matters such as supplies, work performance, and quality of outputs. However, that employee may not be able to discuss interpersonal issues such as peer relations and career expectations. If the HR department is to help build effective communication, it must provide additional channels through which messages can flow, such as IBM's active open-door policy and Xerox's Employee Assistance Program (discussed in Chapter 15).

Although no universal formula exists, a common element of effective upward communications is a genuine concern for employee well-being combined with meaningful opportunities for ideas to flow up the organization's hierarchy. Common upward communication channels include the grapevine, in-house complaint procedures, rap sessions, suggestion systems, and attitude survey feedback.

Informal communication

Grapevine communication is an informal system that arises spontaneously from the social interaction of people in the organization. It is the people-to-people system that arises naturally from the human desire to make friends and share ideas. When two employees chat at the water fountain about their trouble with a supervisor, that is grapevine communication. The HR department has an interest in the grapevine because it provides useful off-the-record feedback from employees if HR specialists are prepared to listen, understand, and interpret the information. According to a study reported in the *Wall Street Journal*, "The office grapevine is 75% to 95% accurate and provides managers and staff with better information than formal communications."[32] Some types of grapevine feedback that come to their department are shown in Figure 17-5.

In-house complaint procedures are formal methods through which an employee can register a complaint. Normally these procedures are operated by the HR department and require the employee to submit the complaint in writing. Then an employee relations specialist investigates the complaint and advises its author of the results.

"Speak Up!"

IBM's program is called "Speak Up!" It uses a confidential form designed as a prepaid envelope. On the inside the employee completes a home address section and then writes the complaint, opinion, or question. When the Speak Up! administrator receives the envelope, the name and address sections are removed and the issue is investigated. Answers are mailed to the employee's home address. If the employee is not satisfied, an interview with an executive from corporate headquarters is arranged regardless of where the employee works.

Managers at IBM "troll for open doors" to avoid Speak Ups! that cause an executive to visit a disgruntled employee. If that employee is dissatisfied with an improper management action and talks to an executive about it, the manager's career with IBM may be adversely affected. What makes IBM's complaint procedure and open comunications so ef-

| Figure 17-5 | Types of Grapevine Feedback to the Human Resource Department |

- Information about the problems and anxieties employees have

- Incorrect feedback that provides evidence of breakdowns in communication

- Insights into goals and motivation of employees

- Identification of job problems that have high emotional content, because intense feelings encourage grapevine communication

- Information about the quality of labor relations, including grievance settlements

- Information about the quality of supervision; complaints about supervision often are brought informally to the attention of personnel specialists with the hope that they will do something

- Information about areas of job dissatisfaction

- Feedback about acceptance of new policies and procedures

fective is that executives support the program with their actions; they are willing to get on an airplane and fly to a meeting with a dissatisfied employee.

Rap sessions

Rap sessions are meetings between managers and groups of employees at which complaints, suggestions, opinions, or questions are discussed. These meetings may begin with some information sharing by management to tell the group about developments in the company. However, the primary purpose is to encourage upward communication, often with several levels of employees and lower-level management in attendance at the same time. When these meetings are face-to-face informal discussions between a higher-level manager and rank-and-file workers, the process may be called *deep-sensing* if it attempts to probe in some depth the issues that are on the minds of employees. These sessions also are called *vertical staffing meetings* because they put higher-level managers directly in touch with employees. Sometimes constructive suggestions emerge, as the president of Hyatt Hotels discovered.

Hyatt Hotels

In one eight-month period, Patrick Foley, president of Hyatt Hotels Corporation, held a dozen meetings with hotel employees. "Sometimes he hears of serious problems that require immediate attention. More often, he hears seemingly trivial complaints—but they concern matters that can make day-to-day life miserable. 'Every time I do one of these meetings, I realize it's the little things that most often affect morale,' Mr. Foley says. 'This is a way to make the employee feel like we care.' "[33]

Suggestion systems are a formal method for generating, evaluating, and implementing employees' ideas. Figure 17-6 shows the key steps in a successful suggestion system. It begins with the employee's idea and a discussion with the supervisor. Once the suggestion form is completed, the supervisor reviews and signs it, indicating awareness of the suggestion but not necessarily approval. The suggestion system office or committee receives the idea and sends an acknowledgment to the employee through company mail. The idea is then evaluated, and the decision is communicated to the employee. If it is a good idea, implementation follows, with the employee receiving recognition and usually an award that is typically equal to 10 percent of the first year's savings.

Success is likely if management provides prompt and fair evaluations, supervisors are trained to encourage employees to make suggestions, and top management actively supports the program. Unfortunately, evaluations often take months to process or supervisors see suggestions as too much work for them with few personal benefits. As a result, many company suggestion plans exist on paper but are not effective.

Attitude surveys and feedback

Attitude surveys are systematic methods of determining what employees think about the organization. These surveys may be conducted through face-to-face interviews but are usually done through anonymous questionnaires. An attitude survey typically seeks to learn what employees think about working

Figure 17-6   **Steps in a Suggestion System**

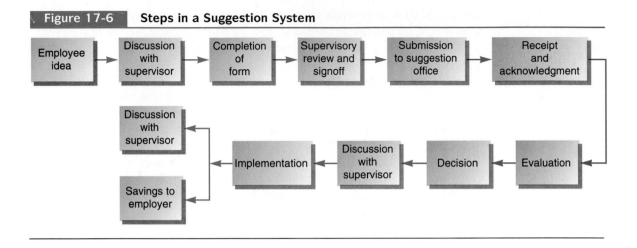

conditions, supervision, and HR policies. Questions about new programs or special concerns of management may also be included. The resulting information can be used to evaluate specific concerns, such as how individual managers are perceived by their employees.

Attitude surveys can be a frustrating experience when employees do not see any results.[34] Therefore, a summary of upward communication should be provided to employees to learn their reactions. When this feedback loop is closed, the overall process is called *attitude survey feedback*. However, feedback is not enough. Action is needed. Employees need to see that the survey resulted in the resolution of problems. Feedback from the results and action on the problem areas make attitude survey feedback a powerful communication tool that can positively affect employee relations and employees' attitudes toward QWL. However, providing feedback in a constructive manner may require considerable assistance from the HR department, especially for first-level supervisors who have little experience in running meetings and listening to employees' criticisms.

Allied-Signal

In the Bendix Automotive Division of Allied-Signal, supervisors are given a workbook to help them analyze the survey. Trained internal facilitators assist the supervisors in interpreting these results. Then the facilitators conduct a role-playing exercise with the supervisors to prepare them for the questions employees are likely to ask.

After the role playing, the supervisor meets with the employees and presents the results. Then problems are identified and solutions are sought. From this meeting a prioritized list is drawn up with completion dates indicated for each action item. The company's approach to attitude survey feedback not only gives employees an explanation of what the results showed but develops an action plan to resolve the problems that emerged from the process.

Employee Counseling

Counseling is a discussion of a problem with an employee that is intended to help the worker resolve or cope with the problem. Stress and personal problems are likely to affect both performance and an employee's general life adjustment; therefore, it is in the best interests of all concerned (employer, employee, and community) to help the employee return to full effectiveness. Counseling is a useful tool for accomplishing this goal. The success rate from counseling programs often is substantial, as at Kimberly-Clark.

Kimberly-Clark

Kimberly-Clark, a paper and forest products firm, compared the records of participants for one year before and one year after their involvement in its program. These workers had a 43 percent reduction in absences and a 70 percent reduction in accidents.[35]

EAPs

Counseling programs usually are administered by the HR department, which uses various combinations of in-house and external counseling services.[36] As discussed in Chapter 15, many companies use a blend of internal and external resources to create an employee assistance program (EAP), which often proves particularly helpful to managers and employees in dealing with sensitive and difficult problems such as AIDS, drug addiction, and family problems.[37]

Counseling is strictly a confidential relationship, and records of it should be restricted to persons directly involved in solving the counseling problem.[38] These practices are necessary to protect employee privacy and protect the employer from possible lawsuits for invasion of privacy or slander. The policy of some firms is to refer all marital and family counseling to community agencies. These companies believe that for reasons of employee privacy, they should not be involved in these problems. Employers also must be certain that their counseling programs comply with EEO regulations by providing equal counseling services to all protected employee groups. When counseling an employee does not resolve performance-related issues, discipline may be the next step.

Discipline

Approaches to discipline

Counseling does not always work. Sometimes the employee's behavior is inappropriately disruptive or performance is unacceptable. Under these circumstances, discipline is needed. *Discipline* is management action that encourages compliance with organizational standards. There are two types of discipline: preventive and corrective.

Preventive discipline is action taken to encourage employees to follow standards and rules so that infractions are prevented. The basic objective is to encourage self-discipline, and the HR department plays an important role. It develops programs to control absences and grievances, communicates standards to employees and encourages workers to follow them, and encourages employee participation in setting standards, since workers give greater support to rules they have helped create. Employees also give more support to standards that are stated positively instead of negatively, such as "Safety first!" rather than "Don't be careless!" Effective discipline is a system relationship, and so the HR department needs to be concerned with all parts of this system.

Corrective discipline is an action that follows a rule infraction. It seeks to discourage further infractions and ensure future compliance with standards. Typically the corrective or *disciplinary action* is a penalty, such as a warning or suspension without pay. These actions are usually initiated by an employee's immediate supervisor but may require approval by a higher-level manager or the HR department, especially when the worker is a union member. Approvals exist to guard against subsequent labor union or legal actions and to assure uniform application of rules throughout the organization. Any appeals then go to higher levels in the company and in the union hierarchy. At Motorola, for example, a senior vice president must approve the discharge of anyone who has worked for the company for ten years.

Progressive discipline

Most employers apply a policy of *progressive discipine,* which means that there are stronger penalties for repeated offenses. The purpose is to give an employee an opportunity to take corrective action before more serious penalties are applied. A typical progressive discipline system is shown in Figure 17-7, and more detailed examples can be found in most labor union contracts. The first infraction leads to a verbal reprimand by the supervisor. The next infraction leads to a written reprimand, with a record placed in the files. Further infractions build up to stronger discipline, leading finally to discharge. Usually the HR department is involved in step 3 or an earlier step to ensure that company policy is followed consistently in all departments. In severe cases, such as fighting, drug use, and stealing, discipline may not be progressive at all: The employee may be fired for the first offense.

Due process

Due process for discipline is required by courts of law, arbitrators, and labor unions, especially in areas where employee handbooks, labor agreements, or even verbal promises apply. *Due process* means that established rules and procedures for disciplinary action are followed and employees have an opportunity to respond to the charges made against them. Compliance with due process rules and procedures usually falls to the HR department.

Figure 17-7	A Progressive Discipline System

1. Verbal reprimand by supervisor

2. Written reprimand, with a record in personnel file

3. One- to three-day suspension from work

4. Suspension for one week or longer

5. Discharge for cause

If challenged on the justification for the discipline or on whether the discipline was handled fairly, the department must have sufficient documentation to support its decisions for all disciplinary actions. Even in employment-at-will states (discussed in Chapter 9), proper documentation should be specific, beginning with the date, time, and location of an incident. Specific rules and regulations that relate to the incident should also be identified. The documentation should state what the manager said to the employee and how the employee responded, including specific words and acts. All documentation must be recorded promptly while the supervisor's memory is still fresh. It should be objective, complete, precise, and accurate and should be based on observations, not impressions. If there were witnesses, they should be identified.

Failure to follow due process and establish just cause for dismissal or another punishment through careful documentation can lead to unjust-dismissal suits, which courts are increasingly willing to entertain.[39] Moreover, if the person disciplined is a member of a protected class under the EEO laws (discussed in Chapter 4), the discipline may become grounds for an EEO complaint.

▶ Emerging Employee Relations Challenges

The growing diversity of the workforce and the increased globalization of many companies present unique employee relations challenges to HR departments. Departmental policies and practices—even those based on experience and sound research—may have to be modified or even discarded in dealing with different groups. Domestic goals of equal opportunity may conflict with laws or cultures in other countries. For example, separation of women from men or members of different ethnic or tribal groups may be a practical and even legal necessity in many developing nations. Domestically and internationally, employee relations may be strained by perceptions of discrimination and "reverse discrimination," which may occur when job assignments, promotions, or rewards favor one group over another. This problem is not limited to North America. Arabs resent being replaced by immigrants in Israel, and many British and French workers resent seeing jobs go to immigrants from former colonies. Moreover, as borders within the European Union present fewer barriers to immigration, resentments are likely to grow throughout Europe, especially in the more industrially advanced nations.

Employee relations specialists will also face growing challenges from employee concerns about AIDS-infected coworkers,[40] exposure to hazardous materials,[41] eyestrain and radiation exposure from work with video display terminals, smoking and air quality at work,[42] and issues of privacy as computers are increasingly used to measure employee productivity.[43] All these challenges can be expected to grow in importance during the remainder of the 1990s. Perhaps even more disturbing, simple answers to these complex workplace issues involve trade-offs that are likely to be unsatisfactory to at least some employees. Communications, counseling, and even discipline may be needed to ensure a work environment that balances employee relations concerns with pressing competitive pressures for productivity and quality performance. Failure of HR practices in general and employee relations in particular can lead to unionization, the subject of Chapter 18.

▶ Summary

Quality of work life efforts are systematic attempts by organizations to give workers a greater opportunity to affect the way they do their jobs and the contributions they make to the organization's overall effectiveness. These efforts are not a substitute for sound HR employee relations practices and policies. Effective employee relations can supplement other departmental actions and provide improved QWL, employee motivation, satisfaction, and productivity. QWL is most commonly improved through involvement that empowers employees. Whether that involvement means solving workplace problems or merely participating in the design of one's job, it empowers people by making them feel that they make a difference.

Many interventions exist that can further employee relations and improve employees' feelings about QWL. Team building and other QWL approaches must have top-management support and be adjusted to the organization's needs and culture. One method is an import from Japan: quality circles, which rely on a small group of employees from the same work area who meet regularly with their supervisor to identify and solve workplace problems. Other forms of team building are similar to quality circles, although different groupings or objectives may be sought. Sociotechnical systems seek to change the human and technical relationship that exists in the workplace. Codetermination gives workers a formal voice in management decisions. Although common in Europe, it is almost nonexistent in North America. Autonomous work groups consist of employees who collectively assume the supervisor's role of making decisions about work schedules, job assignments, and so forth.

In many ways, this entire book has been about employee relations. How well the HR department handles human resource planning, staffing, placement, development, evaluation, compensation, and quality of work life largely determines the state of employee relations. A mistake in any of these areas can harm the employee-employer relationship. However, even when these activities are performed properly, solid employee relations demand careful and continuous attention to organizational communication, employee counseling, and discipline.

▶ Terms for Review

Quality of work life (QWL)	Grapevine communication
Employee involvement (EI)	In-house complaint procedures
Quality circles	Attitude survey feedback
Sociotechnical systems	Suggestion systems
Ergonomics	Preventive discipline
Codetermination	Corrective discipline
Autonomous work groups	Progressive discipline
Open-door policy	

▶ Review and Discussion Questions

1. What forces are causing a growing number of organizations to strive for improved employee relations and QWL?

2. How are HR departments involved in improving employee relations and QWL?

3. Other countries pursue QWL through innovative approaches that are sometimes adopted or adapted in North America. Identify and explain two of these approaches.

4. Suppose you are an operating manager who seeks a high-QWL environment. Why could you not simply order it done and expect a high-QWL environment almost immediately?

5. If TRW and Gaines Pet Food have had success with autonomous work groups, why have so few other employers used this innovative way to manage?

6. Suppose you are assigned to create a companywide employee communications program. What approaches would you use?

7. How do preventive and corrective discipline differ? What examples of either one were applied to you on the last job you had?

8. What is meant by "due process"? What implications does due process have for operating managers and HR managers?

▶ Incident 17-1

Cooperation, QWL, and Space

Psychologists Joseph Brady and Henry Emurian at Johns Hopkins Hospital have been doing research to learn how to increase productivity and reduce friction on future space missions. Under research grants from NASA, they are "studying the psychological and physiological effects of prolonged confinement on two- and three-person 'microsocieties.' Their goal is to develop behavioral guidelines for the most productive individual and group performance, with the least social friction, on future space and underwater missions."[44]

Their studies have revealed the unsurprising conclusion that rewards and incentives are better motivators than are sanctions and controls. Cooperation leads to greater individual performance and greater satisfaction within the group.

Assume for the sake of this incident that these findings are applicable to larger societies called organizations.

1. What implications do you see in these studies for improving the QWL in organizations?

2. If you were a supervisor with six employees working for you, how could these findings make teamwork more effective? On the basis of this brief summary of Brady and Emurian's findings, suggest specific actions you would implement to improve the effectiveness of your team.

▶ References

1. Carla C. Carter, *Human Resources Management and the Total Quality Imperative*, New York: AMACOM, 1994, p. 25.

2. Brian O'Reilly, "Your New Global Work Force," *Fortune*, Dec. 14, 1992, p. 52.

3. Carter, op. cit., pp. 24–42.

4. Anne B. Fisher, "GM Is Tougher Than You Think," *Fortune*, Nov. 10, 1986, p. 58.

5. William B. Werther, Jr., " 'Job 1' at Ford: Employee Cooperation," *Employee Relations*, vol. 7, no. 1, 1985, pp. 10–16.

6. Fisher, op. cit.

7. Ibid.

8. William B. Werther, Jr., and William A. Ruch, "Chief Productivity Officer," *National Productivity Review*, Autumn 1985, pp. 397–410.

9. William A. Ruch and William B. Werther, Jr., "Productivity Strategies at TRW," *National Productivity Review*, Spring 1983, p. 116.

10. William B. Werther, Jr., "Out of the Productivity Box," *Business Horizons,* September–October 1982, p. 56.

11. Ibid., pp. 51–52.

12. Edward E. Lawler III and Lyman W. Porter, "The Effect of Performance on Job Satisfaction," *Industrial Relations,* October 1967, pp. 20–28. See also Lyman W. Porter and Edward E. Lawler, *Managerial Attitudes and Performance,* Homewood, Ill.: Irwin, 1968.

13. William B. Werther, Jr., "Productivity Improvement through People," *Arizona Business,* February 1981, pp. 14–19.

14. Lisa Copenhaver and Robert H. Guest, "Quality of Work Life: The Anatomy of Two Successes," *National Productivity Review,* Winter 1982–1983, p. 5.

15. Ibid.

16. J. Sterling Livingston, "Pygmalion in Management," *Harvard Business Review,* July–August 1969, pp. 81–89.

17. Barbara Presley Noble, "Worker-Involvement Program Violates Labor Law, U.S. Rules," *The New York Times,* National ed., June 8, 1993, p. A11. See also Steve Gunderson, "NLRB Muddies Regulatory Waters," *The Wall Street Journal,* Eastern ed., Feb. 1, 1993, p. A10.

18. Rosabeth Moss Kanter, "The New Workforce Meets the Changing Workplace: Strains, Dilemmas, and Contradictions in Attempts to Implement Participative and Entrepreneurial Management," *Human Resource Management,* vol. 25, no. 4, 1986, pp. 515–537.

19. William B. Werther, Jr., "Quality Circles: Key Executive Issues," *Journal of Contemporary Business,* vol. 11, no. 2, no date, pp. 17–26. See also Frank Shipper, "Quality Circles Using Small Group Formation," *Training and Development Journal,* May 1983, p. 82.

20. "Moving beyond Assembly Lines," *Business Week,* July 27, 1981, pp. 87, 90.

21. Ibid. See also John Hoerr, Michael A. Pollock, and David E. Whiteside, "Management Discovers the Human Side of Automation," *Business Week,* Sept. 29, 1986, pp. 70–75.

22. "Ergonomics" (adapted from *Ergonomics Handbook* of the IBM Corporation), *Personnel Journal,* June 1986, pp. 95–101.

23. Sana Siwolop, "Making the Assembly Line Easier on the Joints," *Business Week,* May 12, 1986, p. 67.

24. Michael H. Belzer, "An American Version of Co-Determination," *Industrial Relations Research Association Dialogues,* November 1993, pp. 1–2.

25. Briane Dumaine, "Who Needs a Boss?" *Fortune,* May 7, 1990, pp. 52–60.

26. Jonathan Kapstein and John Hoerr, "Volvo's Radical New Plant: 'The Death of the Assembly Line'?" *Business Week,* Aug. 28, 1989, pp. 92–93.

27. William Arnold and Lynne McClure, *Communication Training & Development,* New York: Harper & Row, 1989.

28. Walter D. St. John, "Successful Communications between Supervisors and Employees," *Personnel Journal,* January 1983, p. 73.

29. Ron Stodghill et al., "Why AIDS Policy Must Be a Special Policy," *Business Week,* Feb. 1, 1993, pp. 53–54.

30. Cathy Trost, "Labor Letter: Major Changes Put Demands on Corporate Communicators," *The Wall Street Journal,* Western ed., May 20, 1986, p. 1.

31. Gaylord Shaw, "NASA Managers Broke Oldest Rule in the Book," *Los Angeles Times,* June 10, 1986, p. 1.

32. Carol Hymowitz, "Spread the Word: Gossip Is Good," *The Wall Street Journal,* Eastern ed., Oct. 4, 1988, p. B1. See also Alan Zaremba, "Working with the Organizational Grapevine," *Personnel Journal,* July 1988, pp. 38–42.

33. Lawrence Rout, "Hyatt Hotels' Gripe Sessions Help Chief Maintain Communications with Workers," *The Wall Street Journal,* Western ed., July 16, 1981, p. 25.

34. Carter, op. cit., pp. 12–13. See also Paul Sheibar, "The Seven Deadly Sins of Employee Attitude Surveys," *Personnel,* June 1989, pp. 66–71.

35. David Hill, "Employee Assistance Programs: The Helping Hand That's Good for All," *Corporate Fitness and Recreation,* October–November 1982, pp. 43–49.

36. Robert C. Ford and Frank S. McLaughlin, "Employee Assistance Programs: A Descriptive Survey of ASPA Members," *Personnnel Administrator,* September 1981, pp. 29–35.

37. Ron Stodghill II, "Managing AIDS," *Business Week,* Feb. 1, 1993, pp. 48–52.

38. Heather Salt et al., "Confidentiality about Health Problems at Work," *Employee Counseling Today,* vol. 4, no. 4, pp. 10–14. See also Heather Salt and Simon Callow, "AIDS Prevention and Work-Based Counselling," *Counseling Today,* vol. 4, no. 2, 1992, pp. 11–14.

39. Alan B. Krueger, "The Evolution of Unjust-Dismissal Legislation in the United States," *Industrial and Labor Relations Review,* July 1991, pp. 644–660.

40. George D. Stevens, "Understanding AIDS," *Personnel Administrator,* August 1988, pp. 84–88.

41. "Workplace Issues," *Inc.,* March 1990, p. 91.

42. Dexter Hutchins, "The Drive to Kick Smoking at Work," *Fortune,* Sept. 15, 1986, pp. 42–44.

43. Jeffrey Rothfeder, Michele Galen, and Lesa Driscoll, "Is Your Boss Spying on You?" *Business Week,* Jan. 15, 1990, pp. 74–75.

44. For a more detailed explanation of this study, see Berkeley Rice, "Space-Lab Encounters," *Psychology Today,* June 1983, pp. 50–58.

The way for labor to regain the edge is to be proactive, to propose changes.
JOHN STURDIVANT[1]

Union-Management Relations

CHAPTER OBJECTIVES

After studying this chapter, you should be able to:

1. EXPLAIN the relationship between unions, employers, and government.

2. IDENTIFY illegal management and union activities.

3. DISCUSS the impact of unions on managers and human resource professionals.

4. DESCRIBE techniques commonly used to resolve grievances.

5. IDENTIFY the role of the human resource department in dispute resolution.

6. LIST the steps that facilitate cooperation.

Unions do not mean the end of an organization's success or the end of sound human resource practices. Whether a union is present or not, line managers and HR professionals remain responsible for employee relations. Many successful companies have one or more unions and continue to perform the HR activities discussed in this book.

Nevertheless, both managers and HR specialists must comply with new rules that emerge from the union-management framework. Some changes are mandated by law; others come from agreements between the union and management officials. Because unions place constraints on an organization, some companies try to avoid unionization.

Emerson's "southern strategy"

> For many years the Emerson Electric Company was a high-cost producer of fans, motors, tools, and defense equipment. However, during the twenty-year reign of W. R. "Buck" Persons, Emerson became a low-cost manufacturer and consistently outperformed other firms in the electrical and electronics industry.
>
> Part of this transformation was achieved by Persons's "southern strategy," which involved opening new small factories throughout the rural South. (Most of Emerson's 116 plants are in the mid-South.) Also as part of its strategy, the company bases 10 percent of the division managers' bonuses on keeping their plants union-free.[2]

Emerson resists unionization because it hopes to keep labor costs down through lower wages and greater management flexibility in the day-to-day operations of its plants. Union avoidance and workplace diversity have affected the American Federation of Labor and Congress of Industrial Organizations (AFL-CIO), which is the largest association of national and international unions in North America. According to the *Wall Street Journal:*

> . . . the bad news keeps on coming. The AFL-CIO now represents 11% of the U.S. work force, down a third from 16.4% in 1975, despite absorbing the 1.3 million-member Teamsters union several years ago.[3]

> Rutgers University Professor Leo Troy counters that organized labor was a "20th-century phenomenon"; he surmises that membership will decline to 7% by the end of the century, just where it was at the turn of this century.[4]

In industries that are largely unionized, management often takes a more conciliatory view of the union-management relationship. Consider the approach taken by the Communications Workers of America (CWA) and the International Brotherhood of Electrical Workers in reaching an agreement with AT&T:

CWA and AT&T

> In a section called Workplace of the Future, the contract says, "The parties share the goals of establishing a world-class, high-performance organization and protecting employment security through market success." Labor Secretary Robert Reich calls the agreement "a real landmark contract" and says it is a model for the nation.
>
> The unions recognize that today's pace of change makes traditional job security obsolete; jobs are safe only in fast-moving responsive businesses. . . .[5]

Today, the president of the CWA lectures union members about customer service, meets with customers to help close deals, and lobbies state and federal governments for AT&T.[6]

The differences between Emerson Electric and AT&T are common in industry. Some employers view unions as outsiders; others see them as another component of the business environment that must be addressed. This chapter discusses the three major challenges that shape union-management relations: international competition, the labor-management system, and dispute resolution. How each of these challenges is addressed will determine whether organized labor regains the relevance previous generations of workers ascribed to unions.

▶ International Competition

As Elizabeth Dole, a former secretary of labor observed:

> . . . the United States is facing its stiffest economic competition in history. The Pacific Rim nations continue their remarkable economic expansion. Western Europe will . . . be united in one common market with a GNP larger than that of the United States. And the newly emerging free-market economies of Eastern Europe are hoping to take their place at the table.
>
> America's ability to compete in this complex global market may well be determined by our success in providing quality workplaces.[7]

Increased international competition demands higher productivity and quality from North American organizations. Companies such as Emerson Electric seek a competitive advantage by locating in small southern towns, avoiding unions while gaining the benefits of higher productivity and lower wages. Employers such as AT&T and GM have sought greater cooperation, even though competition has forced these firms to drastically reduce their workforces. AT&T, for example, has cut 35,000 CWA workers from its payroll in recent years.[8] Still other firms have relocated operations to lower-wage countries such as Mexico or have simply imported needed parts or products, sparking intense political debate and strong resistance by U.S. unions to *North American Free Trade Agreement* (NAFTA) efforts to reduce trade barriers among the United States, Canada, and Mexico.[9]

International competition has affected the growth of North American unions. The cuts among CWA workers at AT&T were not unusual. The United Auto Workers, for example, lost 500,000 members during the 1980s, or about one-third of its membership, as foreign imports took away jobs. Since the mid-1950s, union membership has declined from about 36 percent of private-sector workers to 11 percent in the mid-1990s. Parallel to the drop in membership has been a drop in the political ability of unions to influence employee relations laws.

HR professionals, however, are badly mistaken if they assume that unions in other countries have suffered the same fate. Though overseas unions also find service and white-collar workers hard to organize, union membership in industrialized countries grew during the 1970s and 1980s, today averaging 53 percent of all workers.[10] Experts attribute this difference to the smaller wage gap between union and nonunion workers abroad. In most industrialized countries the difference between union and nonunion workers is about 10 percent or less; in the United States it is often 20 to 25 percent.[11]

Union and nonunion wage gaps

▶ The Labor-Management System

Unions remain a powerful political and economic force, particularly in highly industrialized regions and in industries with a high percentage of unionized workers. Electric utilities, telecommunicatons, manufacturing, trucking, aerospace, and government are examples. Nevertheless, union-management relations continue to take place within a well-defined system of laws and past practices that consists of three principal actors: workers and their representatives (unions), managerial employees (management), and government representatives in the legislative, judicial, and executive branches (government).[12] Each of these parties depends on the other, as shown in Figure 18-1. For example, the union relies on management to run the business and provide jobs, although in some countries, such as Germany, union officials commonly sit on the equivalent of the board of directors. Management and unions depend on

Union-management framework

| Figure 18-1 | The Interdependence of Unions, Management, and Government |

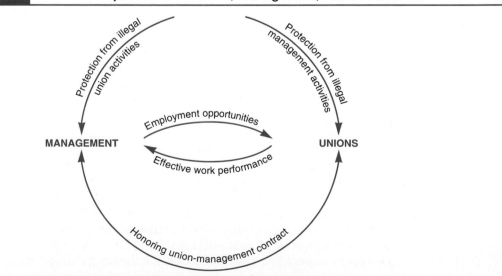

the government for protection of their legal rights. Managers rely on unions to honor their obligations and, increasingly, to assist management in cooperative ventures to increase productivity and quality. In turn, government relies on both of the other parties to meet society's needs through productive organizations.

Unions and Human Resource Management

The presence of unions formalizes employee relations, often leading to greater centralization of employee relations decisions by the HR department to ensure uniformity of treatment among unionized workers. For example, privileges such as overtime or vacation preferences are decided on the basis of a worker's seniority, determined by length of employment. Management must still manage, and the union does not assume the responsibilities of the HR department.

Unions as open social systems

Like other organizations, unions are open social systems that pursue objectives and are influenced by the external environment. The financial strength of the employer, gains of rival unions, inflation and unemployment rates, government, and, as already discussed, international competition influence union objectives. Nevertheless, a core of widely agreed on objectives exists. These objectives were stated by Samuel Gompers, the first president of the American Federation of Labor and are quoted in Figure 18-2. Although published in 1919, Gompers's philosophy remains valid today.[13] He sought to protect workers, increase their pay, and improve their working conditions.

Union objectives

Gompers's approach became known as *business unionism* because he recognized that a union can survive only if it delivers what its members want in a businesslike manner. Gompers also realized that unions must address larger social issues of politics and economics to serve the best interests of their members; this is called *social unionism*. Figure 18-3 contrasts the sometimes conflicting trade-offs: Business unionism focuses on membership or pay, and social unionism addresses the welfare of members or of working people. While business unionism directs its attention to the bargain between the employer and the union, HR departments are affected by social unionism when unions lobby for employment relations laws such as the Occupational Safety and Health Act and the various civil rights acts. And union gains in wages and benefits or other changes must be met by nonunionized employers that wish to remain competitive in the labor market.

Business and social unionism

Union Structure and Functions

Some writers believe that as organizations grew, employees lost direct contact with owners, and so unions emerged to help workers influence workplace decisions.[14] Through unions, workers were able to exert control over "their jobs" and "their work environment."[15] Then, when employers attempted to cut wages, the employees relied on their unions to resist those actions.[16]

Figure 18-2	Union Philosophy and Objectives

The groundwork principle of America's labor movement has been to recognize that first things must come first. The primary essential in our mission has been the protection of the wage-worker, now; to increase his wages; to cut hours off the long workday, which was killing him; to improve the safety and the sanitary condition of the work-shop; to free him from the tyrannies, petty and otherwise, which serve to make his existence a slavery. These, in the nature of things, I repeat, were and are the primary objects of . . . unionism.

Our great Federation has uniformly refused to surrender this conviction and to rush to the support of any one of the numerous society-saving or society-destroying schemes which decade by decade have been sprung upon this country. A score of such schemes . . . have gone down behind the horizon and are now but ancient history. But while our Federation has thus been conservative, it has . . . had its face turned toward whatever reforms in politics or economics could be of direct and obvious benefit to the working class. It has pursued its avowed policy with the conviction that if the lesser and immediate demands of labor could not be obtained now from society as it is, it would be mere dreaming to preach and pursue that will-o'-the-wisp, a new society constructed from rainbow materials—a system of society on which even the dreamers themselves have never agreed.

These demands of organized labor are comprehended in this larger and ultimate ideal—to enrich, enlarge, and magnify humanity. . . .

Source: Samuel Gompers, *Labor and the Common Welfare,* Freeport, N.Y.: Books for Libraries Press, 1919, p. 20.

Early attempts to control the work environment were local efforts because most companies were small operations. As employers—particularly the railroads—began to span city and then state boundaries, labor organizations formed national unions composed of locals from all over the country. When social problems affected several national unions at once, those unions joined together and formed multiunion associations. The most successful of these associations has been the *American Federation of Labor and Congress of Industrial Organizations* (AFL-CIO). A brief review of the three levels—locals, nationals,

AFL-CIO

Figure 18-3	Trade-offs Faced by Unions under Business and Social Unionism

PHILOSOPHICAL APPROACHES	TRADE-OFFS BETWEEN UNION OBJECTIVES		
BUSINESS UNIONISM	Maximize number of employed members.	OR	Maximize pay and benefits of members.
SOCIAL UNIONISM	Maximize welfare of members.	OR	Maximize welfare of working people.

| Figure 18-4 | Organizational Structure of a Typical Local Union |

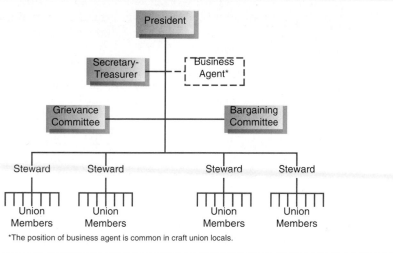

*The position of business agent is common in craft union locals.

and multiunion associations, as represented by the AFL-CIO—illustrates the functions and structure of unions.[17]

Local unions.   For human resource directors, *local unions* are the most important part of the union structure.[18] They provide the members, the revenue, and the power of the entire union movement. There are three types of local unions: craft, industrial, and mixed locals. *Craft unions* are composed of workers who possess the same skills or trades. These include, for example, all the carpenters who work in the same geographic area. *Industrial unions* include the unskilled and semiskilled workers employed at the same location. When an employer has several locations that are unionized, the employees at each location are usually represented by a different local union. Such is the case with the United Automobile Workers, for example. A local may combine both unskilled and skilled employees. This arrangement is common in the electric utility industry, where the International Brotherhood of Electrical Workers includes skilled, semiskilled, and unskilled workers, resulting in a *mixed local.*

Figure 18-4 shows the structure of a typical local. The *steward* represents the first level in the union hierarchy and usually is elected by the workers. Stewards help employees present their problems to management. If the steward of an industrial or mixed local cannot help a worker, the problem is given to a *grievance committee,* which takes the issue to higher levels of management or to the human resource department.[19] In craft unions, the steward—who is also called the representative—usually takes the issue directly to the *business agent,* who may be a full-time employee of the union. This process of resolving employee problems, called the *grievance procedure,* limits HR specialists and line managers because it challenges their decisions. If a challenge is successful, the results may serve as a precedent that limits future decisions.

Craft unions

Industrial unions

Mixed locals
Steward

Grievance committee

HR specialists also find that employees' perceptions of the local union's administration can influence worker attitudes, satisfaction, and even complaints to the department about the union. Yet little is known about how union members view their locals. After surveying 3000 members of nine different locals, one researcher concluded:

Research summary

> Union members were largely satisfied with contract terms, with the communications and informational materials received from officials, and with the opportunity to participate in local union affairs. Members were moderately satisfied with the effectiveness of union leadership, the overall worth of union meetings, and the administration of grievances. The main dissatisfaction uncovered was in the areas of adequacy of union training, the willingness of union leaders to act on personal views of constituents, and the usefulness of union meetings to serve job-related needs.[20]

Bargaining committee

An even more important limitation is the labor contract, which usually is negotiated between the local union's *bargaining committee* and the human resource or industrial relations department. It specifies wages, hours, working conditions, and related issues such as grievance procedures, safety standards, probationary periods, and benefits.

National unions.   Most local unions are chartered by a larger association called the *national union,* which organizes workers into locals and then helps local union officials with their duties. National unions also pursue social objectives of interest to their members and maintain a staff that helps local unions with legal assistance, negotiations, training of local officials, grievance handling, and expert advice. In return, locals share their dues with the national union and must obey its constitution and bylaws. For example, a national union may require that locally bargained contracts receive its approval to ensure consistent treatment among locals and create a floor under wages. The national union may even bargain for a companywide contract, as is the case with the Communications Workers of America and AT&T, which leaves the locals to negotiate issues related to the particular worksite.[21]

Multiunion associations.   The AFL-CIO is the principal multiunion association. It is composed of affiliated national unions, and most major unions are members. The AFL-CIO is not a union but an association of unions. Its primary purpose is to further the social unionism goals of organized labor. Through lobbying, education, and research efforts, it supports new laws and social changes that benefit workers and affect human resource management. In the case of the *North American Free Trade Agreement,* a union may actively resist legislation it believes is harmful to its members.[22] The AFL-CIO's influence over national unions is limited. It charges them a small per capita tax to finance its programs. Any national union that fails to pay the tax or fails to support the AFL-CIO's policies may be removed as a member. At one time the United Automobile Workers union was expelled temporarily for nonpayment of dues, for example.

Government and Labor Relations Law

U.S. Constitution

Government's role comes from its obligation to protect the welfare of society and from the authority in Section VIII of the U.S. Constitution, which states that Congress shall have the power "to regulate commerce . . . among the . . . states." Congress has used that authority several times to regulate union-management relations.

NLRA

National Labor Relations Act.   The *National Labor Relations Act* (NLRA), also known as the Wagner Act, became law in 1935, during the Great Depression, in an attempt to minimize the disruption to interstate commerce caused by strikes.[23] It gives employees the right to engage in collective action free of employer interference, except in government and very small businesses that have little or no impact on interstate commerce. It allows employees to form labor organizations and bargain with management about wages, hours, and working conditions. To prevent employers from interfering with these employee rights, the law prohibits five *unfair labor practices* by management. These legal prohibitions are summarized in Figure 18-5. The act requires that management neither interfere with nor discriminate against employees who undertake collective action.

The law also prohibits employers from discriminating against anyone who brings charges against a company for violating the law. To make the result of unionization meaningful, employers must bargain with the union in good faith over wages, hours, and working conditions. Refusal to do so is a violation of the act, as the National Football League owners discovered.

The NFL owners were charged with a violation of their duty to bargain in good faith, according to a formal complaint issued against them. The complaint stemmed from a strike by the National Football League Play-

| Figure 18-5 | Unfair Labor Practices by Management |

The National Labor Relations Act makes it an unfair labor practice for members of management to:

1. *Interfere,* restrain, or coerce employees who desire to act collectively or refrain from such activities.

2. *Dominate* or interfere with the formation or administration of any labor organization by contributing money or other support to it.

3. *Discriminate* against anyone in hiring, stability of employment, or any other condition of employment because of union activity or lack of involvement.

4. *Discharge,* discipline, or otherwise discriminate against employees who have exercised their rights under the act.

5. *Refuse* to bargain in good faith with employee representatives.

NFL

ers Association. It charged that the players' strike "was caused and has been prolonged by the unfair labor practices of respondents—the NFL management council."[24] The owners had failed to give the union required "information essential to bargaining, changing working conditions . . . coercing players and interfering with their rights, as well as attempting to bypass the union in dealing with individual players."[25]

NLRB

To make the NLRA work, Congress also created the *National Labor Relations Board* (NLRB) to enforce it. This federal agency prosecutes violators and conducts secret-ballot elections among employees. It was the NLRB that filed the complaint against the NFL owners, for example.

The enforcement procedures of the NLRB are summarized in Figure 18-6. This agency does not search for violations until someone files a complaint with one of the local NLRB offices, which are located in major cities.[26] Then the complaint is investigated. If a violation appears to have occurred, a judge from the NLRB hears the case and renders a decision. A guilty employer must refrain from these illegal actions in the future. If an employee was fired as a result of the violation, that person is entitled to back pay plus interest and reinstatement with no loss of seniority.

HR departments become involved when a charge is filed against the employer by assisting the company's attorney in preparing the case. The HR department compiles performance appraisals, attendance records, and other documents that help the company prove its case. Sometimes the department's investigation reveals that the company is guilty. At this point, time and legal costs are saved by admitting guilt and accepting the NLRB's proposed settlement.

HR departments also become involved when the NLRB holds an employee

---

| **Figure 18-6** | **NLRB Procedures to Redress Unfair Labor Practices** |

1. The aggrieved individual or organization contacts the nearest NLRB regional office and explains the alleged violation.

2. If the case appears to have merit, the regional director assigns the case to an NLRB employee for investigation.

3. The investigator determines if the facts are accurate.

4. The NLRB employee reports the findings to the regional director. If a violation appears to have occurred, the wrongdoer is charged with a violation of the act.

5. The local NLRB office prosecutes the alleged violator (who is defended by counsel) before an administrative law judge who renders an opinion after receiving final written arguments from both sides.

6. If innocent, the procedure ends. If guilty, the party may appeal the case to a five-member board in Washington, D.C.

7. If the board's ruling upholds the original finding, the guilty party may appeal to the federal courts.

Figure 18-7	**Unfair Labor Practices by Unions**

The Labor Management Relations Act made it an unfair practice for unions to:

1. *Restrain* or coerce employees or employers in the exercise of their legal rights.

2. *Force* an employer to discriminate against an employee because of that employee's membership or nonmembership in the union.

3. *Refuse* to bargain with an employer in good faith.

4. *Engage* in strikes or threats to force members of management to join a union (usually to collect large initiation fees) or to force an employer to cease doing business with another employer.

5. *Require* an employer to bargain with a union other than the one employees have selected.

6. *Demand* excessive or discriminatory initiation fees.

7. *Picket* an employer to force it to recognize the union as the employees' representative without requesting a government election within a reasonable time period.

Elections

election. This function of the NLRB takes place when a substantial number of employees (at least 30 percent) request a government-supervised election. The election determines whether the workers want a union. Through its local offices, the NLRB conducts a secret-ballot election at the employer's place of business. To win, the union must get a majority of the votes cast. If the union loses, another election among the same employees cannot be held for one year. If the union wins, the HR department must be prepared to bargain with the union to reach a labor agreement.

LMRA

Taft-Hartley

Labor Management Relations Act.   After World War II, the public objected to inflationary conditions, strikes, and the lack of legal constraints on unions. As a result, Congress passed the *Labor Management Relations Act* (LMRA) in 1947. Although most unions did not abuse their power, isolated cases of abuse contributed to the legal restrictions found in the LMRA.

The Taft-Hartley Act, as the LMRA also is called, amended the earlier NLRA by adding unfair labor practices by unions. These prohibitions appear in Figure 18-7. The act makes it illegal for unions to force employees to join or interfere with an employer's selection of its collective bargaining representatives. It also requires unions to bargain with management in good faith and outlaws picketing and strikes under certain circumstances. This law also leaves to the individual states the right to pass "right-to-work" laws. *Right-to-work laws* allow each state to decide whether employees must join an already established union as a condition of retaining their jobs. In states without right-to-work laws, the union and management may agree contractually to create a *union shop,* an arrangement requiring all nonprobationary employees to join the union. Violations of the Taft-Hartley Act are prosecuted by the NLRB.

"Slave labor act"

Although some union leaders called Taft-Hartley the "slave labor act," the law meant that unions had to organize employees on the basis of the merits of unionization, not through unfair economic pressures on workers or their employer. To further minimize the disruptions caused by strikes, the Labor Management Relations Act made two other changes in union-management practices. It created the Federal Mediation and Conciliation Service and authorized Taft-Hartley injunctions.

FMCS

As its name implies, the *Federal Mediation and Conciliation Service* (FMCS) helps union and management bargainers remain friendly (conciliate) during the process of bargaining for a contract. When bargaining leads to a deadlock, the agency suggests compromises (mediates). Although it has no power to force a settlement of disputes, the agency helps both sides reach an agreement without the need for a strike. When serious strikes threaten national security or create a national emergency, the Taft-Hartley Act allows the President of the United States to seek a court-ordered injunction to delay the strike for eighty days. During this eighty-day "cooling-off" period, the government investigates the facts surrounding the dispute. The results of these fact-finding activities are turned over to the parties, and the office of the President urges a negotiated settlement. If a settlement is not reached at the end of eighty days, the strike can resume. Public pressure and the potential for congressional action usually cause both sides to find a solution.

Cooling-off period

Labor-Management Reporting and Disclosure Act.   During the twelve years after the passage of the Taft-Hartley Act, it became evident that a few union leaders were not properly representing their members' interests. To correct this problem, the *Labor-Management Reporting and Disclosure Act* was passed in 1959.[27] Figure 18-8 summarizes the major provisions of the act. In general, the law had two broad objectives. First, it made union officials responsible for properly using union funds by establishing detailed reporting requirements. It backed up these requirements with the possibility of prison sentences for those found guilty of serious violations.

Union members'
"bill of rights"

Second, the act sought to make unions more democratic by providing members with certain rights. In fact, Title I of the law is often referred to as the union members' "bill of rights." If an employee has a complaint about his or her treatment by the union, the human resource department need not get involved. Instead, it can direct workers to the nearest office of the Department of Labor. Specialists within that department then investigate and ensure that employees' rights are not being ignored or abused by the union leaders.[28]

▶ Cooperation and Dispute Resolution

Given the increased competition faced by North American organizations and the growing complexity of labor relations laws, competitive success—even economic survival—depends on the successful resolution of disputes. The actions

Figure 18-8	**Major Provisions of the Labor-Management Reporting and Disclosure Act**

■ *Title I* created a bill of rights for union members in dealing with their union. It assured members equal rights, freedom of speech and assembly, the right to sue the union, and other safeguards.

■ *Title II* imposed detailed reporting requirements on those who handle union funds.

■ *Title III* established safeguards to ensure that the rights of members to elect leaders will not be lost when a national union takes over a local union and creates a trusteeship.

■ *Title IV* requires that fair elections for union officers be held periodically.

■ *Title V* sets forth the fiduciary responsibility of union officers and prohibitions against certain people from holding union office (primarily convicted felons).

■ *Title VI* grants the secretary of labor the right to conduct investigations into possible abuses under this act.

■ *Title VII* includes a series of miscellaneous provisions that limit strikes, picketing, and boycotts.

that employees take depend on the treatment they have received. When that treatment is perceived to be unacceptable by nonunionized employees, a union is one possible outcome. If a union already exists, its members seek to negotiate an agreement that changes the worst features of their relationship. When negotiations fail to resolve the major causes of friction, a strike is likely. Consider the situation surrounding a strike by 11,000 federal employees.

Air Traffic Controllers' strike

After members of the Professional Air Traffic Controllers' Organization (PATCO) went on strike, they were fired and barred from further federal employment because strikes by U.S. government workers are illegal. According to research done by the University of Michigan's Institute for Social Research, the strike "was bred in and precipitated by the deteriorating conditions created by the Federal Aviation Administration's own organizational and management practices."[29] A survey of more than 33,000 FAA employees revealed that morale among air traffic controllers was low from the bottom to the top of the organization. Strikers and nonstrikers alike produced similarly negative assessments of their jobs. "FAA employees holding managerial positions gave relatively high approval to an autocratic, no-questions-asked style of management, while the generally younger technicians and controllers—strikers and nonstrikers alike—strongly rejected such a style."[30]

The principal researcher concluded: "A less directive bureaucratic style would have buffered the problem of the strike. . . . participatory management . . . can go far toward preventing future labor relations disasters like the massive federal strike and employee dismissals suffered by the FAA."[31]

The economic warfare of strikes extends to innocent victims too. The PATCO strike meant restrictions on air traffic during the peak summer flying season. Passengers were inconvenienced, airlines lost money, and many employees were laid off for lack of work. Since the strike was illegal, the Federal Labor Relations Authority (which administers federal-sector labor regulations) decertified PATCO. This meant that the union could no longer represent air traffic controllers. For most PATCO leaders and employees, the strike-caused decertification meant a loss of their jobs too. Since these actions, the air traffic controllers have formed another union.

Although most contract negotiations do not result in strikes, when they do, the strikes can have serious effects on both parties along with those who depend on them, such as the traveling public and the airline industry in the case of the PATCO strike. One spin-off of this strike was a greater use of *permanent replacements* (workers hired to permanently replace strikers) by Greyhound, International Paper, and other employers, which further undermined union strength in the United States during the 1980s and 1990s.[32]

Disputes also arise during the administration of the labor agreement after it has been negotiated. Although these contract interpretation disputes almost never lead to a strike, disruptions can occur while dispute resolution procedures are applied. In truly progressive union-management relations, cooperation can be the basis for improved organizational performance that can benefit management and the union, along with owners, customers, suppliers, and the general public.[33]

Since most disputes arise from the negotiation or administration of the labor agreement, the remainder of this chapter will provide an overview of the collective bargaining process and conclude with discussions of dispute resolution and cooperation.

Collective Bargaining

Contract
negotiations

Figure 18-9 summarizes the collective bargaining process. Preparation for contract negotiations is often an ongoing activity in sophisticated companies such as AT&T. In other organizations, serious preparations begin three to six months before the expiration of the old contract or as soon as it looks like a union will successfully organize a previously nonunionized employer. The HR department starts by studying recent trends in the economy and other labor negotiations. A plan is developed that outlines the company's position on wages, hours, and other terms and conditions of employment. The company's bargaining team may be supplemented by outsiders, most often a labor attorney. Once top management has approved the plan and strike preparations are under way, negotiations begin several weeks or months before the expiration date of the labor agreement.

| Figure 18-9 | Stages of Collective Bargaining |

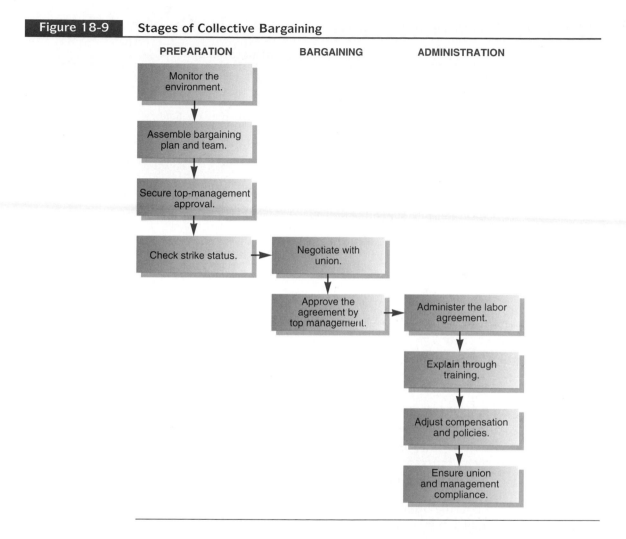

Negotiations with the union bargaining committee continue until a mutually satisfactory agreement is reached. Figure 18-10 identifies some of the traditional guidelines for negotiating a labor contract. If the old contract expires, the union may elect to strike in an attempt to increase the pressure for its position. Once the contract is approved by top management and by a vote of the union members, the contract administration phase begins.

The final contract determines the terms and conditions of employment. Figure 18-11 captures the main topics found in a labor agreement. Although these documents can range from a few photocopied pages to multivolume printed books, most agreements address the topics in Figure 18-11. As the relationship matures, topics are typically defined in greater detail. At Dayton Power and

Dayton Power
and Light

Figure 18-10	Guidelines for Negotiations

THE "DOS" OF NEGOTIATIONS

1. Do seek more (or offer less) than you plan to receive (or give).

2. Do negotiate in private, not through the media.

3. Do let both sides win; otherwise the other side may retaliate.

4. Do start with easy issues.

5. Do remember that negotiations are seldom over when the agreement is concluded; eventually the contract will be renegotiated.

6. Do resolve deadlocks by stressing past progress, another point, or counterproposals.

7. Do enlist the support of the Federal Mediation and Conciliation Service if a strike seems likely.

THE "DON'TS" OF NEGOTIATIONS

1. Do not make your best offer first; that is so uncommon that the other side will expect more.

2. Do not seek unwanted changes; you may get them.

3. Do not say no absolutely unless your organization will back you up absolutely.

4. Do not violate a confidence.

5. Do not settle too quickly; union members may think a quick settlement is not a good one.

6. Do not let the other side bypass your team and go directly to top management.

7. Do not let top management actually participate in face-to-face negotiations; they are often inexperienced and poorly informed.

Light the union agreement grew to 141 pages and was dominated by a "rule-book" mentality that sought to specify rights and responsibilities in increasing detail over the years. However, growing economic pressures led the company and the union to seek a more cooperative relationship, which has resulted in a fourteen-page document that stresses mutual goals and has led to greater trust. As a result, lost-time accidents have dropped by more than half and grievances have fallen by nearly 85 percent. Even in cooperative relationships based on trust, the need for dispute resolution remains.[34]

Dispute Resolution

Grievance
resolution

Contract administration requires the company and the union to abide by the terms and conditions they have negotiated. An alleged violation of the agreement requires a resolution of the resulting complaint, which is called a grievance.

| Figure 18-11 | **Common Provisions in Union-Management Agreements** |

■ *Union recognition.* Normally near the beginning of a contract, this clause states management's acceptance of the union as the sole representative of designated employees.

■ *Union security.* To ensure that the union maintains members as new employees are hired and current employees quit, a union security clause commonly is demanded by the union. Forms of union security include:

    a. *Union shop.* All new workers must join the union shortly after being hired, usually within sixty or ninety days.

    b. *Agency shop.* All new workers must pay to the union an amount equal to dues.

    c. *Checkoff.* Upon authorization, management agrees to deduct the union dues from each union member's paycheck and transfer the moneys to the union.

■ *Wage rates.* The amount of wages to be paid to workers (or classes of workers) is specified in the wage clause.

■ *Cost of living.* Increasingly, unions are demanding and receiving automatic wage increases for workers when price levels go up. For example, a common approach is for wages to go up by 1 cent an hour for each 0.3 or 0.4 percent increase in the consumer price index.

■ *Insurance benefits.* This section specifies which insurance benefits the employer provides and how much the employer contributes toward those benefits. Frequently included benefits are life, hopitalization, and surgical insurance.

■ *Pension benefits.* The amount of retirement income, years of service required, penalties for early retirement, employer and employee contributions, and vesting provisions are described in this section if a pension plan exists.

■ *Income maintenance.* To provide workers with economic security, some contracts give guarantees of minimum income or minimum work. Other income maintenance provisions include severance pay and supplements to the state unemployment insurance.

■ *Time-off benefits.* Vacations, holidays, rest breaks, wash-up periods, and leave-of-absence provisions typically are specified in this clause.

■ *Strike/lockouts.* It is common to find clauses in which the union promises not to strike for the duration of the contract in return for management's promise not to lock employees out of work during a labor dispute.

■ *Seniority clause.* Unions seek contract terms that cause personnel decisions to be made on the basis of seniority. Often senior workers are given preferential treatment in job assignments, promotions, layoffs, vacation scheduling, overtime, and shift preferences.

■ *Management rights.* Management must retain certain rights to do an effective job. These may include the ability to require overtime work, decide on promotions into management, design jobs, and select employees. This clause reserves to management the right to make decisions that management thinks are necessary for the organization's success.

■ *Discipline.* Prohibited employee actions, penalties, and disciplinary procedures are either stated in the contract or included in the agreement by reference to the documents that contain the information.

■ *Dispute resolution.* Disagreements between the union and management are resolved through procedures specified in the contract.

Either management or the union may file a grievance when the contract is violated. But since most decisions are made by management, there are few opportunities for the union to break the agreement. More commonly, unions file grievances because of alleged violations by management. The *grievance procedure* consists of a series of steps to resolve disputes. Figure 18-12 describes the steps through which an employee's grievance typically passes. The actual number of steps in the procedure depends on the size of the organization. A three-step grievance procedure is most common; in very large firms (often in manufacturing) four and even five steps are possible. The extra steps reduce the number of cases reaching top union and company officials.

Types and causes of grievances.   Even though HR specialists may not handle grievances in the early stages, the HR department plays an important role. Each supervisor sees only a small number of complaints, but the HR department has an organizationwide view from which it can identify the types and causes of grievances. With this information, the HR department can create programs to improve grievance handling.[35]

Grievances can be legitimate, imagined, or political. *Legitimate grievances* occur when there is reasonable cause to think that there has been a contract violation. Even in a cooperative environment, contract clauses have different meanings to different people. *Imagined grievances* occur when employees believe that the agreement has been violated even though management is exercising its contract rights in a reasonable manner. Again, misunderstanding is the primary cause of these grievances. A cooperative union can help settle such complaints quickly by explaining management rights. Otherwise, when a manager says that a complaint is without merit, the worker may think that management is trying to save face after making a bad decision. *Political grievances* are

---

Figure 18-12   **Typical Steps in a Union-Management Grievance Procedure**

- *Preliminary discussion.* The aggrieved employees discuss the complaint with the immediate supervisor with or without a union representative.

- *Step 1.* The complaint is put in writing and formally presented to the first-level supervisor. Normally, the supervisor must respond in writing within a contractually specified period, usually two to five days.

- *Step 2.* The union representative or the union grievance committee takes the written complaint to the supervisor's boss or the HR department. A written response is required, usually within a week.

- *Step 3.* The local union president or another high-ranking union official takes the complaint to a member of top management or the HR director. Again, a written response typically is required.

- *Step 4.* The company and the union present their viewpoints to an outside neutral arbitrator who hears the case and renders a decision much as a judge would.

the most difficult to solve. They occur most frequently just before contract negotiations and union elections. They also occur when a complaint is pursued to further someone's political aspirations. For example, a union representative may be reluctant to tell union members that their grievances are without merit. Doing so may mean a loss of political support in the next union election. Instead, the union leader may process a worthless grievance. Likewise, management also files political grievances.[36]

Handling grievances.   Once a grievance is submitted, management should seek to resolve it fairly and quickly. Failure to do so can be seen as disregard for employees' needs. In time, morale, motivation, performance, and company loyalty may be damaged. In adjusting grievances, several precautions should be followed.[37] Most important, grievances should be settled on their merits. Political considerations by either party weaken the grievance system. Complaints need to be carefully investigated and decided on the facts, not on emotions. Otherwise, damaging precedents may result. Second, the cause of each grievance should be recorded. Many grievances coming from one or two departments may indicate personality conflicts or a poor understanding of the contract. Third, employees should be encouraged to use the grievance procedure. Problems cannot be solved unless management and union officials know what they are. But before employees can use the grievance process, it must be explained through meetings, employee handbooks, or bulletin-board notices. Finally, whatever the solution may be, it needs to be explained to those affected. Even though union leaders do this, management should not fail to explain *its* reasoning to the affected supervisor and worker.[38]

Precautions (margin note)

Arbitration

Arbitration is the submission of a dispute to a neutral third party. Both sides of the issue are heard by an arbitrator who acts as judge and jury. After weighing the facts, the arbitrator renders a decision.

In *advisory arbitration,* the arbitrator's opinion is intended to guide the parties toward a fair resolution without compelling them to accept the arbitrator's recommendations. *Last-offer* arbitration is usually binding and requires the arbitrator to select either labor's or management's position, whichever seems more reasonable. Both advisory and last-offer arbitration are more commonly used in resolving disputes that arise during contract negotiations. *Binding arbitration* requires both parties to accept the arbitrator's decision. When a grievance procedure does not result in a mutually acceptable solution, binding arbitration is called for in 96 percent of all labor agreements.[39]

Types of arbitration (margin note)

Arbitration clauses are common because they allow a complaint to be resolved once and for all. Although a court action would have the same result, an arbitrator's ruling usually is not subject to several levels of time-consuming appeals. Since arbitration is private, it is not an open proceeding as court cases are. Perhaps best of all, arbitration is less expensive than a court case.[40]

Arbitration holds two potential problems for HR specialists: costs and unacceptable solutions. Although the employer and the union usually share the expenses, each case may cost several hundred to several thousand dollars. Admittedly, court costs and legal fees usually are higher. Nevertheless, the HR department needs to consider the costs involved. Another potential problem occurs when an arbitrator renders a decision against management's best interests. Since the ruling is binding, it may drastically alter management's rights. For example, if an arbitrator accepts the union's argument of extenuating circumstances in a disciplinary case, those extenuating circumstances may become a precedent that is cited in future cases. Consider what happened in a chain of convenience markets.

The Quick Foods Market had a policy that stealing from the company was grounds for immediate discharge. Sam Anglin, a new employee, took a sandwich and a beer from the cooler and consumed them without paying for them. He was fired when caught by the store manager. The union argued that Sam should get a second chance since he was a new employee. The arbitrator upheld management but added that discharge for such a minor theft might have been too harsh a penalty if Sam had not been a probationary employee. If a senior employee is caught stealing, the union may use this opinion to claim that discharge is the wrong penalty. And another arbitrator might agree.

In cases like Sam's, a prompt arbitration decision is essential. The employee may be reluctant to look for a new job, and the HR department may be reluctant to train a replacement until a final decision is made. To speed up the arbitration process, the company and the union may agree to use *expedited arbitration*. Under this approach the arbitrator usually gives an oral opinion at the end of the hearing or a written decision within a few days. Otherwise, arbitrators usually are allowed thirty days in which to render their decisions, and some arbitrators take considerably longer.[41]

It is important for HR specialists to seek a solution with the union before arbitration. In this manner they avoid additional costs, delays, and the possibility of an unsatisfactory decision. When arbitration is unavoidable, HR specialists should follow the guidelines in Figure 18-13. These suggestions offer the best chance of winning a favorable decision. If these guidelines reveal serious flaws in the employer's case, a compromise solution with the union before arbitration is usually advised.

▶ Union-Management Cooperation

Although dispute resolution techniques stop most complaints from erupting into a strike, they are after-the-fact measures. Even the "winner" of a favorable arbitration decision loses the time and money it took to argue the case. To

| Figure 18-13 | **Preparation Guidelines for Arbitration Hearings** |

1. Study the original grievance and review its history through every step of the grievance machinery.

2. Determine the arbitrator's role. It might be found, for instance, that while the original grievance contains many elements, the arbitrator is restricted by the contract to resolving only certain aspects.

3. Review the collective bargaining agreement from beginning to end. Often, other clauses may be related to the grievance.

4. Assemble all documents and papers you will need at the hearing. Where feasible, make copies for the arbitrator and the other party. If some of the documents you need are in the possession of the other party, ask in advance that they be brought to the arbitration.

5. Make plans in advance if you think it will be necessary for the arbitrator to visit the plant or jobsite for on-the-spot investigation. The arbitrator should be accompanied by representatives of *both* parties.

6. Interview all witnesses. Make certain that they understand the whole case and the importance of their own testimony within it.

7. Make a written summary of what each witness will say. This serves as a useful check-list at the hearing to make certain nothing is overlooked.

8. Study the case from the other side's point of view. Be prepared to answer the opposing evidence and arguments.

9. Discuss your outline of the case with others in your organization. A fresh viewpoint often will disclose weak spots or previously overlooked details.

10. Read as many articles and published awards as you can on the general subject matter in dispute. While awards by other arbitrators for other parties have no binding precedent value, they may help clarify the thinking of parties and arbitrators alike.

Source: Labor Arbitration Procedures and Techniques, New York: American Arbitration Association, 1972, pp. 15–16. Used with permission.

avoid this situation, labor-management relations are experiencing an ongoing trend toward greater cooperation, sometimes in exchange for greater employment stability or guaranteed jobs.[42] Through cooperation, both parties can replace reactive measures with proactive ones. Proactive efforts benefit the union and the company by saving time and expenses. These savings can mean higher profits for the employer and better contracts for the union.[43]

Oregon Logging

As human resource manager for the Oregon Logging Company, Joe Von Kampen spent about 40 percent of his time on some phase of dispute resolution. Although the Teamsters represented only 125 of the employees, there were usually 275 to 300 grievances a year. About 10 percent of those cases went to arbitration. These costs seriously affected the company's profitability, forcing the union to accept the lowest wage rates in the area. To change the situation, the town's mayor offered to help.

• The mayor devised a training program that consisted of the union leader and the HR manager taking turns reading the contract to an audience of supervisors and union representatives. After each paragraph, the HR manager and the union president both summarized what the paragraph meant. The mayor did not let them go on to the next paragraph until both agreed on the meaning of the previous one. After several sessions, the entire contract was reviewed. Lower-ranking union and management officials learned what the contract meant and found out that they were expected to cooperate with each other. The following year, fourteen grievances were filed and only one went to arbitration. The company's profitability improved dramatically, and the local union obtained its largest wage increase in the next negotiations.

Union-Management Attitudes

Severe conflicts between a company and a union often can be traced to the attitudes each holds about the other. In the Oregon Logging example, supervisors felt that the union was intruding on their rights. When the supervisors in turn denied workers their rights, the union fought back with grievances. Sometimes the members of a union get so upset that they conduct a "rules strike" or slowdown by following all the rules literally, as the workers at Caterpillar did.[44] Or workers may resort to a *wildcat strike,* which is a spontaneous act that takes place in violation of the contract, often over the official objections of union leaders. After the strike is over, the underlying problems still have to be settled.[45]

The "rules strike"

Wildcat strikes

Building Cooperation

Proactive HR departments cannot wait for disaster to occur before attempting to build cooperation with the union. Such departments realize that cooperation is not automatic and must be initiated by HR specialists. However, obstacles to cooperation exist.

Obstacles to cooperation.   HR specialists often seek union cooperation to improve the organization's effectiveness. However, effectiveness usually is far less important to union leaders. Quite naturally, these officials are more concerned about the welfare of their members and winning reelection to union office. Thus, when cooperation is not attractive politically, union leaders have little incentive to cooperate. In fact, if leaders do cooperate, they may be accused by workers of forgetting the union's interests. Thus cooperation may not be in a leader's best interest.

Steel industry

For many years negotiations in the steel industry were marked by strikes and threats of strikes. The result was lower profitability and a loss of markets to foreign producers. In turn, many members of the United Steel Workers union were laid off. Both the union and the steel companies were suffering.

Both parties reached a cooperative arrangement called the *Experimental Negotiations Agreement.* This agreement called for concessions from the steel producers and no nationwide strikes by the union. The cooperative move was intended to benefit both the union and the employees. But some members saw it as a loss of rights, particularly the right to strike. In the union's national elections, a splinter group was able to mount a serious challenge to the established leadership by attacking this cooperative agreement.

Besides political obstacles, union leaders may mistrust the HR department. For example, bitter remarks during the organizing drive may convince union officials that HR specialists are antiunion. In this climate cooperative gestures by the HR department may be seen as tricks. If mistrust increases, cooperation usually fails.

Cooperative methods.   Once HR specialists recognize the political concerns and suspicions of union leaders, several cooperative methods can be tried. These techniques are summarized in Figure 18-14 and are explained in the following paragraphs.

One of the most basic actions is *prior consultation* with the union. Not every management decision must be approved by the union, but actions that affect the union or its leaders may cause a grievance unless they are explained before

---

| Figure 18-14 | Methods of Building Union-Management Cooperation |

Managers and personnel specialists can build cooperation between the employer and the union through:

▪ *Prior consultation* with union leaders to defuse problems before they become formal grievances

▪ *Sincere concern* for employee problems and welfare even when management is not obligated to do so by the labor agreement

▪ *Training programs* that objectively communicate the intent of union and management bargainers and reduce biases and misunderstandings

▪ *Joint study committees* that allow management and union officials to find solutions to common problems

▪ *Third parties* who can provide guidance and programs that bring union leaders and managers closer together to pursue common objectives

they are taken. Suppose a senior employee was passed over for promotion because his or her use of profanity could mean a loss of customers. Suppose further that the HR department explains to the union leaders that the use of profanity by the most senior worker could mean a loss of valuable business and jobs for union members. In this case the union leaders might accept the promotion of a junior worker. At least politically, the union president would be less likely to challenge the promotion decision. Some managers even ask union leaders to talk to problem employees before management has to take an action that might lead to a grievance.

Managers and the HR department also can build cooperation through a *sincere concern* for employees. This concern may be shown through the prompt settlement of grievances, regardless of who wins. Or managers can bargain sincerely with the union to reduce the need for a strike. Even when a strike occurs, management can express its concern for workers. For example, during a strike at General Motors, GM continued to pay the strikers' insurance premiums to prevent a lapse in coverage. Ford Motor Company provides another example:

Ford

The president of Ford Motor Company issued a policy letter to all Ford divisions, subsidiaries, and affiliated companies. In that policy letter, entitled "Employee Involvement," he stated: "It is the policy of the Company to encourage and enable all employees to become involved in and contribute to the success of the Company. A work climate should be created and maintained in which employees, at all levels, can achieve individual goals and work satisfaction by directing their talents and energies toward clearly defined Company goals.

■ Methods of managing should encourage employee participation in identifying and solving work-related problems.

■ Communications programs and procedures should be implemented that encourage frequent, timely and constructive two-way communications with employees concerning work-related problems."[46]

Training programs are another way to build cooperation. If the HR department sponsors training for both the union and management, a common understanding of the contract is more likely to occur than it is when training is done separately. The training can be as simple as taking turns paraphrasing the contract, as was done in the Oregon Logging Company example. Or outside neutrals can be hired to do the training. Either way, supervisors and union officials end the training with a common understanding of the contract and a new basis for cooperation.

Joint study committees

When a complex problem confronts the union and the employer, *joint study committees* are sometimes formed. For example, the three largest automobile companies agreed to create separate committees with the United Auto Workers union to study health-care costs. If this is successful, costs will grow more slowly and there will be more money available for other benefits.[47] Productivity committees are another common form of union-management cooperation. According to the Department of Labor, 97 of 1550 contracts surveyed had provisions for union-management committees to study production.[48] And these committees also can improve bargaining prospects.

> Says Buddy Davis, a grizzled, gravelly voiced district director for the USW [United Steel Workers] in St. Louis: "We used to have war on the shop floor. Now 100% of our members are on a committee, and because those committees work out day to day a lot of smaller problems that used to be saved up for the bargaining table, the bargaining goes fast and smooth."[49]

> In return for job guarantees and no concessions, the USW has offered to expand the shop-floor teams and worker empowerment systems that management wants to boost productivity. After Japan's NKK Corp. bought control of the U.S.'s No. 4 steelmaker in 1984, National opened its books to the union and offered profit-sharing and job security. Now, the rest of the union is clamoring for similar deals.[50]

An important caution concerning these committees comes from a pair of cases recently decided by the NLRB.

> In the first, a nonunion employer, Electromation, Inc., of Elkhart, Indiana, established five action committees consisting of six employees and one manager to meet during business hours to address issues such as absenteeism, smoking, an attendance bonus program, and other terms and conditions of employment. The NLRB ruled that the company had established and dominated a labor organization even though no formal union vote was held or contemplated.[51]
>
> A second ruling involved E. I. Du Pont de Nemours & Company, which was ordered "to dismantle seven committees established to deal with safety and recreation issues at the Chambers Works plant in Deepwater, New Jersey, and to bargain in good faith with the plant's union, the Chemical Workers Association."[52]

In both cases—one with a union and one without—the NLRB ruled that management's creation and direction of committees to resolve matters that normally are the subject of union-management negotiations was an unfair labor practice. This ruling does not mean that management cannot use committees; instead, it requires that committees not address issues that are normally subject to labor-management negotiations, which traditionally include wages, hours, and other terms or conditions of employment. As long as members are speaking only for themselves (and not representing others), are merely providing information, or have the authority to implement changes, it appears that violations are unlikely to occur.[53]

A final method of building cooperation is through *third parties,* such as consultants and government agencies, who may act as catalysts. For example, the FMCS has a program entitled *relations by objectives* (RBO).

In a series of meetings, which at first are held separately with labor and management, FMCS staff members determine company and union viewpoints on what the "other party" should do to improve relations and then on what each party should do itself. After these sessions, meetings are held, attended by all management officials—including top executives and line supervisors—and all union officials, including shop stewards. Respective viewpoints are discussed, clarified, and incorporated into mutually acceptable lists of objectives for the improvement of labor-management relations.

The list then is discussed by the two parties separately and jointly. The joint sessions develop an agreement on action steps for attaining each objective, assigning responsibility for starting and completing steps, and implementing a timetable for the achievement of each objective.[54]

Dayton Power and Light Company

Dayton Power and Light Company faced a dramatic slowdown in its growth prospects because of a serious decline in new customers. Hundreds of employees were laid off. The union reacted by filing 450 grievances and unfair labor practices charges with the National Labor Relations Board. Morale and productivity suffered.

The FMCS had previously set up an RBO program that had begun to open communication channels between labor and management. Monthly meetings were set up in forty departments, and 90 percent of the workforce was trained in analytic decision-making approaches. Although hostile relations between the union and management remained, over the following years cooperation and trust emerged and grew. Through the participation of union officials and rank-and-file members along with various levels of management, joint committees attacked mutual problems.

The results have been a dramatic drop in accidents, grievances, and negative attitudes. Productivity and morale have improved. And the detailed 141-page contract that sought to control the relationship in minute detail gave way to a 14-page compact that outlines the new relationship in more positive terms.[55]

Labor-management cooperation grew dramatically during the 1980s and early 1990s in response to international and domestic pressures for greater productivity.[56] And with participative approaches now popular in Japan, North America, and Europe—particularly in Germany—employee participation approaches to cooperation seem to be a common thread in an otherwise diverse world of work.[57] Success with cooperative approaches means that this trend is likely to continue as these innovations are institutionalized and diffused throughout the economy.[58] These trends toward greater cooperation are already appearing in the public sector too.[59] As a member of the Public Employee Department of the AFL-CIO observed, "Generally, whenever there is a fairly sophisticated labor-management relationship, the chances are that the parties have developed some type of cooperative program."[60]

▶ The Challenges to Human Resource Management

HR challenges

Unions are at a crossroads. During recent years they have experienced a steady decline in membership, political power, and prestige. Nevertheless, unions represent a significant challenge to HR professionals and operating managers. At employers with unions, compliance with labor laws, contract provisions, and past practices limit managers' flexibility. Even when a union is not present, proactive employee relations are needed to assure a productive workforce. And if a company wants to remain nonunion, additional pressures fall on employee relations specialists and operating managers, especially supervisors.

Whether unions will rebound and reclaim their role as a powerful actor in the economic and political systems of developed nations is uncertain.[61] It does seem certain, however, that unions will seek innovative approaches to reverse these trends.[62] Some examples include efforts to organize nontraditional groups such as white-collar, service, government, and professional workers. Other examples include offering new services—from charge cards to health-care advice—to supplement more traditional collective bargaining efforts and fringe benefits.[63]

At the same time, many HR managers and union leaders perceive government intervention as a potential threat to the traditional freedoms they have enjoyed. Their common concern arises out of the fear that more government laws will control their affairs. And since current laws are enforced by agencies with the power to "make laws" by interpreting existing ones, regulations are bound to grow.

To meet these challenges from increased union innovation and government intrusion into the workplace, HR professionals need to be proactive. Organizationally, when unions are present, the department is expanded by the addition of a labor relations section. This section allows labor specialists to deal with critical areas such as negotiations and contract administration, while HR professionals attend to their more traditional roles. In fact, HR and labor relations may form two equal divisions within a broader department that typically is called *industrial relations.*

Operationally the HR section seeks sound employee relations through effective practices. The labor relations section has a complementary role. It wants to minimize restrictions on management through diligent negotiations and fair administration of the union contract. To use a sports analogy, the HR department is the offensive team and labor relations is the defensive team.

Effective HR policies and practices provide the best stance for meeting the challenges of a productive workforce, unions, and government involvement. More specifically, HR specialists (within the constraints of organizational effectiveness and efficiency, law, technology, and other challenges) must carefully do the following:

- *Design* jobs that are personally satisfying to workers
- *Develop* plans that maximize individual opportunities and minimize the possibility of layoffs
- *Select* workers who are qualified
- *Establish* fair, meaningful objective standards of individual performance
- *Train* workers and managers to enable them to achieve expected levels of performance
- *Evaluate* and reward behavior on the basis of actual performance

In other words, HR managers should proactively apply the ideas discussed in earlier chapters of this book.

▶ Summary

Unions are open systems—affected by their environment—and political organizations—influenced by the needs and wishes of their members. Increased global competition has put pressure on many firms to reduce costs whether the result is lower wages for employees or lower labor costs through better productivity. Some organizations seek to avoid unions, such as Emerson Electric. Other employers seek ways to prosper with a union through contract negotiations, dispute resolution procedures, and various cooperative approaches.

The labor-management system means additional constraints for operating managers and human resource professionals. However, management remains responsible for the economic success of the firm and its employee relations. Government plays a crucial role by setting the legal rules under which the collective bargaining relationship occurs. It outlaws unfair labor practices and provides mechanisms through the National Labor Relations Board to conduct representation elections and resolve allegations of unfair labor practices.

Dispute resolution relies on contractual terms and the cooperation of labor and management. Grievance procedures culminating in binding arbitration commonly exist to resolve disputes over contract interpretation. Although strikes are rare, they allow both parties to exercise their economic strength to pressure the other side in negotiating a labor agreement. Although cooperation is determined by the nature of the union-management relationship, international and domestic competitive pressures have forced many unions and employers to find ways to cooperate in order to prosper during these turbulent economic times.

▶ Terms for Review

Business unionism	National Labor Relations Board
Social unionism	Union shop
American Federation of Labor and Congress of Industrial Organizations (AFL-CIO)	Federal Mediation and Conciliation Service
Local unions	Labor agreement
Craft unions	Labor-Management Reporting and Disclosure Act
Industrial unions	Grievance procedure
National unions	Seniority
National Labor Relations Act	Management rights
Unfair labor practices	Arbitration

▶ Review and Discussion Questions

1. In your own words, summarize the primary objectives of unions.

2. What distinguishes craft, industrial, and mixed unions from one another?

3. Suppose you are an HR specialist and are having the following problems. For each problem, which government agency would you turn to for assistance?

    a. The union is trying to get the HR department to fire a union critic.

    b. An employee complains to you that the union will not allow members to speak up at the local union's meetings.

    c. The company and the union are deadlocked over the terms of a new labor agreement.

4. In your own words, explain why unions usually file the most grievances.

5. How are local and national unions affected by international competition?

6. When an employee has a complaint about a management action in a unionized operation, how does she or he go about resolving it?

7. What are the advantages and disadvantages of using arbitration?

8. Since labor-management cooperation is important to the economic success of the business and eventually to the union's ability to negotiate wage gains and other benefits for members, what are some of the ways you could recommend to improve labor-management cooperation?

▶ **Incident 18-1**

In-Flight Food Services Company

The In-Flight Food Services Company provides prepared meals for several airlines at a major airport in the Southeast. Food handlers cook and package meals to be reheated in airplane galleys for service to passengers while in flight. Most of the 535 food handlers belong to the Independent Food Handlers Union, which has represented these employees for over five years.

Each year the industrial relations department noticed that the number of grievances filed by members of the union had increased about 15 percent. The time spent by union representatives, employees, and supervisors as a result of those grievances was affecting productivity in the company's cafeteria. The general manager was concerned that the company's costs and the low productivity could lead to a loss of key contracts with major airlines.

The industrial relations department studied all the grievances during the past year and provided the following analysis.

Total grievances filed	803
Number settled at:	
First-level supervision	104
Second-level supervision	483
General manager level	205
Arbitration	11

Although some grievances involved more than one issue, most of them were single-issue matters. When the industrial relations department classified the grievances, the following results were reported:

Tardiness or absence control	349
Overtime disputes	265
Other discipline or discharge	77
Incorrect job schedules	75
Multiple-issue disputes	37

1. How would you approach the local union for help?

2. Assuming the industrial relations director asked you to design a training program to reduce the high number of grievances, who do you think should attend the training sessions?

3. What topics would you cover in the training?

▶ **References**

1. Kevin G. Salwen, "What, Us Worry? Big Unions' Leaders Overlook Bad News, Opt for Status Quo," *The Wall Street Journal,* Eastern ed., Oct. 5, 1993, p. B6.

2. "Emerson Electric: High Profits from Low Tech," *Business Week,* Apr. 4, 1983, p. 60.

3. Salwen, op. cit., p. B1.

4. Kevin G. Salwen, "Labor Letter: Is the Glass 89% Empty or 11% Full? Assessments Vary on the Future of Unions," *The Wall Street Journal,* Eastern ed., Sept. 21, 1993, p. A1.

5. David Kirkpatrick, "Could AT&T Rule the World?" *Fortune,* May 17, 1993, p. 66. Though AT&T seems to have been successful in dealing with the CWA, another perspective is suggested by "Rocking the Boat," *The Economist,* May 8, 1993, p. 71.

6. Kirkpatrick, op. cit.

7. Elizabeth Dole, "Facing Tomorrow Together," *Labor Relations Today,* May–June, 1990, p. 1.

8. Kirkpatrick, op. cit.

9. Stephen Baker, Geri Smith, and Elizabeth Weiner, "The Mexican Worker," *Business Week,* Apr. 19, 1993, pp. 84–92.

10. Gene Koretz, "Why Unions Thrive Abroad," *Business Week,* Sept. 10, 1990, p. 26. See also "Germany Labours On," *The Economist,* Jan. 23, 1993, pp. 63–64. Smaller estimates of the wage gap are suggested by Stephen B. Jarrell and T. D. Stanley, "A Meta-Analysis of the Union–Non-union Wage Gap," *Industrial and Labor Relations Review,* October 1990, pp. 54–67.

11. Koretz, op. cit.

12. John T. Dunlop, *Industrial Relations Systems,* New York: Henry Holt, 1958, pp. 7–8. See also J. W. Miller, Jr., "Power, Politics, and the Prospects for Collective Bargaining: An Employer Viewpoint," in Stanley M. Jacks (ed.), *Issues in Labor Policy,* Cambridge, Mass.: MIT Press, 1971, pp. 144–157.

13. Samuel Gompers, *Labor and the Common Welfare,* Freeport, N.Y.: Books for Libraries Press, 1919.

14. Frank Tannenbaum, *The Labor Movement: Its Conservative Functions and Consequences,* New York: Knopf, 1921.

15. Selig Perlman, *A Theory of the Labor Movement,* New York: Macmillan, 1928.

16. John R. Commons et al., *History of Labor in the United States,* New York: Macmillan, 1918. See also A. H. Raskin, "From Sitdowns to Solidarity," *Across the Board,* December 1981, pp. 22–25.

17. Reed C. Richardson, *American Labor Unions: An Outline of Growth and Structure,* 2d ed., Ithaca, N.Y.: New York State School of Industrial and Labor Relations, Cornell University, 1970, p. 19.

18. Leonard Sayles and George Strauss, *The Local Union,* New York: Harcourt, Brace & World, 1967.

19. Harry Graham and Brian Heshizer, "The Effect of Contract Language on Low Level Settlement of Grievances," *Labor Law Journal,* July 1979, pp. 427–432.

20. George W. Bohlander, "How the Rank and File Views Local Union Administration: A Survey," *Employee Relations Law Journal,* Autumn 1982, p. 232.

21. "Labor's Marriage of Convenience," *Business Week,* Nov. 1, 1982, pp. 28–29.

22. John R. Oravec, "NAFTA Sells Out American Families," *AFL-CIO News,* Sept. 20, 1993, pp. 1, 9.

23. Irving Berstein, *A History of the American Worker, 1933–1941: Turbulent Years,* Boston: Houghton Mifflin, 1971, p. 332.

24. "NLRB Complaint Blames Football Owners," *AFL-CIO News,* Oct. 30, 1982, p. 8.

25. Ibid.

26. John S. Irvin, Jr., "Why Do We Need a Labor Board?" *Labor Law Journal,* July 1979, pp. 387–395.

27. George W. Bohlander and William B. Werther, Jr., "The Labor-Management Reporting and Disclosure Act Revisited," *Labor Law Journal,* September 1979, pp. 528–589.

28. Ibid.

29. "Management vs. Labor," *ISR Newsletter,* Autumn 1982, p. 3.

30. Ibid.

31. Ibid.

32. Marc Levinson and Farai Chideya, "One for the Rank and File," *Newsweek,* July 19, 1993, p. 38.

33. Joel Cutcher-Gershenfeld, Robert B. McKersie, and Kristen R. Wever, *The Changing Role of Union Leaders,* Washington, D.C.: U.S. Department of Labor, 1988.

34. Phil Farish, "HRM Update: New-Style Pact," *Personnel Administrator,* October 1988, p. 12.

35. Debra J. Mesch and Dan R. Dalton, "Unexpected Consequences of Improving Workplace Justice: A Six-Year Time Series Assessment," *Academy of Management Journal,* vol. 35, no. 5, 1992, pp. 1009–1114. See also William B. Werther, Jr., "Reducing Grievances through Effective Contract Administration," *Labor Law Journal,* April 1974, pp. 211–216.

36. Ross Stagner and Hjalmar Rosen, *Psychology of Union-Management Relations,* Belmont, Calif.: Wadsworth, 1965, pp. 110–111.

37. Thomas F. Gideon and Richard B. Peterson, "A Comparison of Alternate Grievance Procedures," *Employee Relations Law Journal,* Autumn 1979, pp. 222–233. See also "The Antiunion Grievance Play," *Business Week,* Feb. 12, 1979, pp. 117, 120; George W. Mauer and Jeanne Flores, "From Adversary to Advocate," *Personnel Administrator,* June 1986, pp. 53–58.

38. George W. Bohlander, "Fair Representation: Not Just a Union Problem," *Personnel Administrator,* March 1980, pp. 36–40, 82.

39. *Basic Patterns in Union Contracts,* Washington, D.C.: Bureau of National Affairs, 1975, p. 37.

40. William B. Werther, Jr., and Harold C. White, "Cost Effective Arbitration," *MSU Business Topics,* Summer 1978, pp. 59–64. See also Mollie H. Bowers, "Grievance-Mediation: Another Route to Resolution," *Personnel Journal,* February 1980, pp. 132–136, 139.

41. Werther and White, op. cit.

42. Peter Nulty, "Look What the Unions Want Now," *Fortune,* Feb. 8, 1993, pp. 128–133.

43. *Labor-Management Cooperation: 1989 State-of-the-Art Symposium,* Washington, D.C.: U.S. Department of Labor, 1989. See also Steve Donahue, "New Ways to Divide the Pay Pie," *Labor Relations Today,* October–November–December 1988, pp. 1–2; Allan D. Gilmour, "Union-Management Cooperation," *Proceedings of the 1992 Spring Meeting, Industrial Relations Research Association,* May 6–9, 1992, pp. 513–517.

44. Louis Uchitelle, "Stop the Line in Decatur," *The New York Times,* June 13, 1993, pp. 3-1, 3-6.

45. "In Wildcat Strikes, Court Rules: Union Leaders Safe from Discipline," *Resource,* May 1983, pp. 1, 10. See also David P. Swinehart and Mitchell A. Sherr, "A Systems Model of Labor-Management Cooperation," *Personnel Administrator,* Apr. 1, 1986, p. 87.

46. Phillip Caldwell, "Policy Letter 13-14, Subject: Employee Involvement," Ford Motor Company (internal document), Nov. 5, 1979, p. 1. See also Denise Tanguay and Gregory E. Huszczo, *Forging a Partnership through Employee Involvement: The Case of the GM Hydra-Matic Willow Run Plant and UAW Local 735 Joint Activities,* Washington, D.C.: U.S. Department of Labor, 1988.

47. Allan D. Gilmour, "Union-Management Cooperation," *Labor Law Journal,* August 1992, pp. 513–517.

48. Edgar Weinberg, "Labor-Management Cooperation: A Report on Recent Initiatives," *Monthly Labor Review,* April 1976, p. 3. See also David C. Mowery and Bruce E. Henderson, *The Challenge of New Technology to Labor-Management Relations,* Washington, D.C.: U.S. Department of Labor, 1989.

49. Nulty, op. cit., p. 132.

50. Steven Baker and Thomas Buell, "Buddy-Buddy at the Steel Smelter," *Business Week,* Apr. 5, 1993, pp. 26–27.

51. Nulty, op. cit., p. 132.

52. Barbara Presley Noble, "Worker-Involvement Program Violates Law, U.S. Rules," *The New York Times,* June 8, 1993, p. A-11.

53. "Law Prohibits Employer-Created Committees," *Bulletin* (from Godwins Book & Dickenson), August 1993, pp. 1–3.

54. National Center on Productivity and Quality of Working Life, *Recent Initiatives in Labor-Management Cooperation,* Washington, D.C.: U.S. Government Printing Office, 1976.

55. Phyllis Lehmann McIntosh, "Labor Compact Key to New Employee-Management Partnership at Dayton Power and Light," *Labor-Management Cooperation Brief,* January 1988, pp. 1–7. See also Farish, op. cit.

56. Richard Shore, "Regaining the Productive Edge," *Labor Relations Today,* September–October 1989, pp. 1–2.

57. Sarosh Kuruvilla et al., "Union Participation in Japan: Do Western Theories Apply?" *Industrial and Labor Relations Review,* April 1990, pp. 374–387.

58. Thomas A. Kochan and Joel Cutcher-Gershenfeld, *Institutionalizing and Diffusing Innovations in Industrial Relations,* Washington, D.C.: U.S. Department of Labor, 1988.

59. Donna St. John, "A Unique Labor-Management Partnership Has Made Dade County Public Schools a Model in Education Reform," *Labor-Management Cooperation Brief,* June 1989, pp. 1–7.

60. John R. Stepp, "Making Public Service Work Better," *Labor Relations Today,* April–May 1989, p. 1. See also Jan Abott, "New Approaches to Collective Bargaining and Workplace Relations: Do They Work?" *Readings on Labor-Management Relations,* Washington, D.C.: U.S. Department of Labor, 1990.

61. Peter T. Kilborn, "Labor Seeking to Reverse Decline, Turns to Hungry Young Organizers," *The New York Times,* National ed., June 3, 1993, p. A10. See also Agis Salpukas, "Labor's Showdown at Federal Express," *The New York Times,* National ed., Feb. 7, 1993, pp. 3-1, 3-6.

62. Richard B. Peterson, Thomas W. Lee, and Barbara Finnegan, "Strategies and Tactics in Union Organizing Campaigns," *Industrial Relations,* Spring 1992, pp. 370–381.

63. Jonathan Tasini and Jim Hurlock, "Big Labor Tries the Soft Sell," *Business Week,* Oct. 13, 1986, p. 126. See also Cathy Trost, "Rejuvenating Organized Labor Is the Aim of a Three-State Pilot Project," *The Wall Street Journal,* Western ed., July 16, 1986, p. 1; "Unions Must Adapt, Labor Leader Says," *Resource,* October 1986, p. 7; and Cathy Trost, "What They Preach to Cut Health-Care Costs," *The Wall Street Journal,* Eastern ed., Aug. 12, 1986, p. 1.

19

"Do more and spend less" is one example of the paradoxes in HR management. As difficult as it may be, the art of managing in the '90s may lie in embracing— rather than choosing between—both sides of the paradox.

PETER STROH and WYNNE W. MILLER[1]

Assessment and Prospects

CHAPTER OBJECTIVES

After studying this chapter, you should be able to:

1. EXPLAIN the value of a human resource audit.

2. IDENTIFY common approaches to audits.

3. DESCRIBE the role of research in a human resource audit.

4. DISCUSS the future challenges facing human resource practitioners.

5. DESCRIBE the impact third parties have on human resource management.

6. IDENTIFY major workplace innovations that are likely to emerge in the coming years.

More than ever before, the HR function is expected to make a strategic contribution to a firm's competitive advantage. At the same time, growing diversity of the workforce, complex legal and ethical issues, and global and domestic competition are reshaping the role of HR management.[2] At the core of these pressures for change are the HR department's multiple objectives, which were set forth in Chapter 1 and are shown in Figure 19-1.

Besides furthering the organizational objective of competitive advantage, the HR department must address societal, functional, and personal objectives. Societal objectives—often in the form of laws—must be met to ensure fair treatment and legal compliance. Functional objectives add professional and ethical challenges to the department's constraints. And the personal objectives of employees gain in importance and complexity as the workforce slows its growth and becomes more diverse, especially as HR professionals encounter increased executive expectations.

CEOs and HR

> Top executives say that people are an increasingly important factor in distinguishing one company from another. As a result, many now consider the human resource function . . . critical to business success.
>
> CEOs . . . are looking to their human resource departments for help on such "people" issues as productivity improvement, succession planning and culture change. . . .
>
> Some CEOs are attempting to reshape the mandate of the human resource function according to their companies' future business needs.[3]

As a result of these forces, the HR function has grown dramatically more important and is likely to continue to gain in importance in the future.

Strategic contribution

For modern HR departments to make a strategic contribution and meet other objectives, their efforts must respect the importance and dignity of human beings; this was called the "human resource approach" in Chapter 1. At the same time, specialists must not lose sight of the systems approach, which *subordinates* the departmental subsystem to the larger system of the organization. The organization's success, not the HR department's, is the first priority. Achieving success requires service to managers and employees through a proactive approach. The department does not usurp each manager's HR responsibilities. Instead, a professional management approach assumes a dual responsibility between the worker's immediate supervisor and the HR department, with the department playing a major and proactive role in the areas outlined in Figure 19-1.

Self-audits

Nevertheless, errors happen. Policies and practices become outdated. By auditing itself as a first step toward continuous improvement, the HR department finds and corrects problems before they become serious.[4] When done correctly, the evaluation process can build rapport between the HR department and operating managers. Also, it can reveal outdated assumptions that can be changed to meet the organization's objectives and future challenges. Of course, any self-audit assumes that department members are objective when they evaluate their performance and line management's compliance.

The scope of the HR department's responsibilities is broad, as suggested by this book and Figure 19-1. Through a comprehensive audit, HR departments assess the subsystems of the overall model in Figure 19-1. But an effective audit

Figure 19-1	The Human Resource Management Model

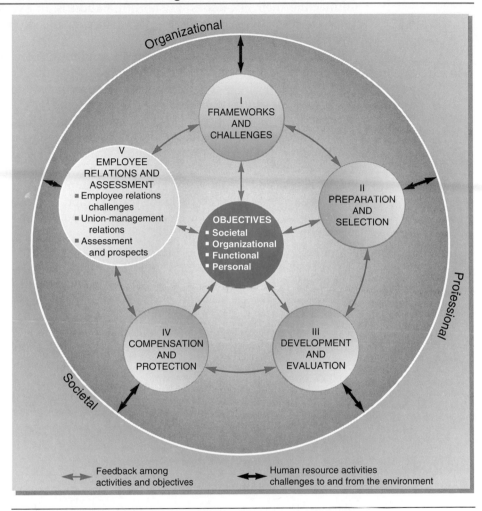

does more than assess the subsystems; it ensures that the subsystems mesh to form a rational approach to the creation and delivery of services.

This chapter examines the scope, approaches, and tools used in HR audits and research. It concludes with a review of future challenges that are likely to confront HR professionals.

▶ The Scope of Human Resource Audits

HR audits

A *human resource audit* evaluates the HR activities in an organization with the intent of improving those activities. The audit may include one division or an entire company. It provides feedback about the HR function to operating managers and HR specialists. It also provides feedback about how well managers are meeting their HR duties. In short, the audit is an overall quality control check on HR activities in a division or company and on how those activities support the organization's strategy.[5]

Several benefits associated with an HR audit are listed in Figure 19-2. An audit reminds members of the HR department and others of its contribution, creating a more professional image of the department among managers and specialists. The audit helps clarify the department's role and leads to greater uniformity, especially in the geographically scattered and decentralized HR functions of large firms. Perhaps most important, it finds problems and ensures compliance with a variety of laws and the strategic plans of the organization.

The scope of an audit extends beyond the HR department's actions. The department's success depends on how well it performs *and* how well its programs are carried out by others in the organization. For example, consider how supervisors at the American Guard Agency reduced the effectiveness of the performance appraisal process.

American Guard Agency

To become a sergeant at the American Guard Agency, employees need two years of good or superior performance evaluations. The agency uses a critical incident appraisal form; this means that supervisors should record both positive and negative incidents as they occur. In practice, supervisors stressed employees' mistakes when they recorded incidents. As a result, few guards received good enough ratings to qualify for sergeant. Many of them blamed the department's appraisal process for their lack of promotion.

An audit uncovered the misuse of the program and recommended additional training for supervisors in the use of the critical incident

---

| Figure 19-2 | Benefits of a Human Resource Management Audit |

■ *Identifies* the contributions of the HR department to the organization.

■ *Improves* the professional image of the HR department.

■ *Encourages* greater responsibility and professionalism among members of the HR department.

■ *Clarifies* the HR department's duties and responsibilities.

■ *Stimulates* uniformity of personnel policies and practices.

■ *Finds* critical personnel problems.

■ *Ensures* timely compliance with legal requirements.

■ *Reduces* human resource costs through more effective personnel procedures.

■ *Creates* increased acceptance of needed changes in the HR department.

■ *Requires* a thorough review of the HR department's information system.

method. If the audit had not uncovered this problem, employee dissatisfaction might have grown worse.

As this example illustrates, people problems seldom are confined to the HR
department. Thus audits should be broad in scope to be effective and evaluate
the use of HR procedures by managers and the impact of those activities on
employees.

In recent years, however, this "inward-looking perspective" has become insufficient. HR professionals find that the scope of the audit must transcend the
concerns of the department and operating managers. Although not all HR audits review corporate strategy and its fit with the external environment, these
broader concerns merit mention.

Audit of Corporate Strategy

Corporate strategy is not set by HR professionals, but they strongly determine
its success. Corporate strategy concerns how the organization is going to gain a
competitive advantage. By assessing the firm's internal strengths and weaknesses and external opportunities and threats, for example, senior management devises ways of gaining an advantage. Whether the company stresses superior marketing channels (State Farm), service (IBM), innovation (3M),
low-cost production (Emerson Electric), or another approach, HR management
is affected.[6] Understanding the strategy has strong implications for planning,
staffing, compensation, employee relations, and other HR activities, which can
be deemed "effective" only if they contribute to the organization's strategic
goals.

Strategy-
environment fit

The strategy-environment fit cannot be ignored. Members of the HR department can learn about the firm's strategy through interviews with key executives, reviews of long-range business plans, and systematic environmental
scans designed to uncover changing trends.[7] They must audit their function,
managerial compliance, and employee acceptance of HR policies and practices
in relation to the firm's strategic plans. For example, high turnover in entry-
level jobs may keep wages near the bottom of the rate range, lowering labor
costs. Thus, employee turnover in a "Big Six" accounting firm may be a low-
cost way to keep overall labor costs competitive. An audit, however, may reveal considerable dissatisfaction among recent accounting graduates about the
number of billable hours required of them each week. Knowledge of the firm's
strategy (to hire excess entry-level accountants) affects the value of audit information (about employee satisfaction, for example).

Audit of the Human Resource Function

Audits logically review the HR department's work.[8] Figure 19-3 lists the major
areas covered. An audit touches on virtually every subject discussed in this
book. Reviewing only a few aspects of the HR management system may ignore

| Figure 19-3 | **Major Areas Covered by a Human Resource Functions Audit** |

HUMAN RESOURCE INFORMATION SYSTEM

AFFIRMATIVE ACTION PLANS
- Underutilization and concentration
- Affirmative action goals
- Progress toward goals

HUMAN RESOURCE PLANS
- Supply and demand estimates
- Skills inventories
- Replacement charts and summaries

JOB ANALYSIS INFORMATION
- Job standards
- Job descriptions
- Job specifications

COMPENSATION ADMINISTRATION
- Wage, salary, and incentive levels
- Fringe benefit package
- Employer-provided services

STAFFING AND DEVELOPMENT

RECRUITING
- Sources of recruits
- Availability of recruits
- Employment applications

SELECTION
- Selection ratios
- Selection procedures
- Equal opportunity compliance

TRAINING AND ORIENTATION
- Orientation program
- Training objectives and procedures
- Learning rates

CAREER DEVELOPMENT
- Internal placement success
- Career planning program
- Human resource development effort

ORGANIZATION CONTROL AND EVALUATION

PERFORMANCE APPRAISALS
- Standards and measures of performance
- Performance appraisal techniques
- Evaluation interviews

LABOR-MANAGEMENT RELATIONS
- Legal compliance
- Management rights
- Dispute resolution problems

HUMAN RESOURCE CONTROLS
- Employee communications
- Disciplinary procedures
- Change and development procedures

HUMAN RESOURCE AUDITS
- Human resource function
- Operating managers
- Employee feedback on personnel

topics that affect the department's performance. For each item in the figure, the audit team should:

Audit teams

- *Identify* who is responsible for each activity

- *Determine* the objectives sought by each activity

- *Review* the policies and procedures used to achieve those objectives

- ▪ *Sample* the records in the HR information system to learn if policies and procedures are being followed correctly

- ▪ *Prepare* a report commending proper objectives, policies, and procedures

- ▪ *Develop* an action plan to correct errors in objectives, policies, and procedures

- ▪ *Follow up* on the action plan to see if it solved the problems found through the audit[9]

Obviously, audits are time-consuming. As a result, small firms use ad hoc arrangements that often limit the evaluation to selected areas. Very large organizations have *audit teams* similar to those used to conduct financial audits. These teams are especially useful when the department is decentralized into regional or field offices, as is the case at the State Farm Insurance Companies. Through the use of audits, the organization maintains consistency in its practices even though there are several offices in different locations. And the mere existence of a corporate audit team encourages compliance and self-audits by the regional offices between visits.[10]

Cliff Swain, a regional HR manager, realized that his chances for promotion to corporate headquarters depended on how well his region's offices performed. The corporate audit team reviewed his region's performance every June. In preparation for the audit, he had each HR office in the southwest region conduct a self-audit in April. Then, in early May, the administrators from the four branches met in Phoenix to review the results. Errors uncovered through the audit were corrected if possible. When the corporate audit team completed its review in June, it always gave Cliff's region high marks for compliance with company policies and employment laws.

Audit of Managerial Compliance

Auditing management compliance

How well do managers comply with HR policies and procedures? If managers ignore policies or violate employee relations laws, the audit should uncover these errors so that corrective action can be started. Compliance with laws is especially important. When equal opportunity, safety, compensation, or labor laws are violated, the government holds the company responsible.

Besides ensuring compliance, the audit can improve the department's image and contribution to the company. Operating managers may have more respect for the department when an audit team seeks their views. If the comments of managers are acted on, the department will be seen as being more responsive to their needs. And since it is a service department, these actions may improve its contribution to organizational objectives. For example, consider what an audit team learned when it talked to managers of local claims offices.

After several interviews with claims office managers, the audit team discovered a pattern to their comments. Most managers believed that the HR department filled job vacancies quickly. The major criticism was that the department did not train recruits before assigning them to a claims office. The day-to-day pressures in the claims office caused training to be superficial and led to many errors by the new adjusters. Most managers felt that the training should be done by the HR department at the regional office.

After reading the team's report, the regional HR manager felt confident that the selection process was satisfactory. To resolve the complaints about field training, she created a two-week program for claims adjusters with her next budget increase.

Audit of Employee Satisfaction

Auditing employees' perceptions

Effective departments meet both the company's objectives and employees' needs. When employee needs are unmet, turnover, absenteeism, and union activity are more likely to occur. To learn how well employee needs are met, the audit team gathers data from workers. The team collects information about wages, benefits, supervisory practices, career planning assistance, and the feedback employees receive about their performance.

The audit team of an automobile parts distributor received one common complaint from employees: they felt isolated because they worked in retail stores or in warehouses all over the Midwest. They had little sense of belonging to the large company of which they were a part. To bolster sagging morale and help employees feel that they were members of a fast-growing and dynamic organization, the department started a biweekly "Payroll Action Newsletter." The two-page letter was put into every pay envelope each payday. It gave tips on new developments at headquarters and at different field locations. In this way, the department used the audit to make the firm more responsive to its employees' needs.

▶ Research Approaches to Audits

HR research

Research is also used to evaluate HR activities. At times the research may be advanced, relying on sophisticated designs and statistics. But whether informal or rigorous, research seeks to improve the department's performance. Applications-oriented research efforts are called *applied research.* The most common

| Figure 19-4 | Research Approaches to a Human Resource Audit |

■ *Comparative approach.* The audit team compares its firm (or division) with another firm (or division) to uncover areas of poor performance. This approach commonly is used to compare the results of specific activities or programs. It helps detect areas of needed improvement.

■ *Outside authority approach.* The audit team relies on the expertise of a consultant or published research findings as a standard against which activities or programs are evaluated. The consultant or research findings may help diagnose the cause of problems.

■ *Statistical approach.* From existing records, the audit team generates statistical standards against which activities and programs are evaluated. With these mathematical standards, the team may uncover errors while they are still minor.

■ *Compliance approach.* By sampling elements of the human resource information system, the audit team looks for deviations from laws and company policies or procedures. Through its fact-finding efforts, the team can determine whether there is compliance with company policies and legal regulations.

■ *MBO approach.* When an MBO approach is applied to the human resource area, the audit team can compare actual results with stated objectives. Areas of poor performance can be detected and reported.

forms of applied HR research are described in Figure 19-4 and explained in the following paragraphs.

Perhaps the simplest form of research is the *comparative approach*, in which another division or company that has better practices or results is chosen as a model. The audit team then compares its results or procedures with the "best practices" of the other organization. This "best practices" approach often is used with absence, turnover, staffing levels, and salary data. It also makes sense when a procedure is being tried for the first time. For example, if a company installs an alcohol rehabilitation program, it may copy a successful program at another firm or division. Then the results of both programs are compared. IBM conducts a "Common Staffing Study" to compare employment levels among its various plants and facilities, for example.

The use of an *outside authority* is another approach. Standards set by a consultant or taken from published research findings serve as a benchmark for the audit team. For example, the consultant or industrywide research may indicate that the HR budget is usually about three-fourths of 1 percent of gross sales. This figure then serves as a rough guidepost in evaluating the department's overall budget.

A *stratistical approach* relies on performance measures drawn from the company's existing information system. For example, company records often track turnover and absenteeism rates from one period to another. Changes in these data may be helpful in identifying how well HR activities and operating managers control these problem areas. Often this approach is supplemented with comparative data from external sources such as other firms or industry sources such as industry association surveys. This information often is expressed as ratios that are easy to compute and use. For example, if 8 employees in a workforce of 200 miss work on a particular day, the absenteeism rate is 4 percent. Likewise, a company that averages 200 employees during the month and has 12 quit finds that its turnover rate is 6 percent per month, or 72 percent a year.

Roy Rogers Restaurants

Roy Rogers Restaurants, a major division of Marriott Corporation, operates 657 restaurants, primarily in the northeastern part of the United States. Entry-level managers are drawn largely from workers age 20 to 24. However, that age cohort will experience a decline throughout the 1990s. Making matters worse, company audits reveal an annualized turnover rate of 80 to 90 percent, the costs of which are conservatively estimated at $3 million a year.

A survey of field managers who oversee groups of restaurants revealed that 58 percent of the turnover is seen as being beyond their control and that 31 percent of the reasons for turnover lie with the HR department. Armed with this knowledge, the department was able to address the managers' perceptions and begin addressing the turnover problem before the targeted labor pool of workers 20 to 24 years old shrank further.[11]

Another audit strategy is the *compliance approach*, which reviews past practices to determine if those actions followed legal requirements and company policies and procedures. Often the audit team examines a sample of employment, compensation, discipline, and employee appraisal forms. The purpose of the review is to ensure that field offices and operating managers comply with internal rules and legal regulations, such as EEO requirements and minimum-wage laws.

A final approach is for specialists and operating managers to set objectives in their areas of responsibility. This *MBO* (management by objectives) *approach* creates specific goals against which performance can be measured. Then the audit team researches actual performance and compares it with the previously set objectives. For example, field managers at Roy Rogers may set a goal of reducing turnover to below 50 percent in one year. Then the audit evaluates the trends in this area.

No one of these audit approaches can be applied to all parts of HR management.[12] More commonly, audit teams use several of these strategies, depending on the specific activities under evaluation. Then, as Figure 19-5 suggests, the audit team gives feedback on activities to those in the department, to operating managers, and to employees. Unfavorable feedback leads to corrective action that improves the contribution of HR activities.

Figure 19-5	An Overview of the Human Resource Management Audit Process

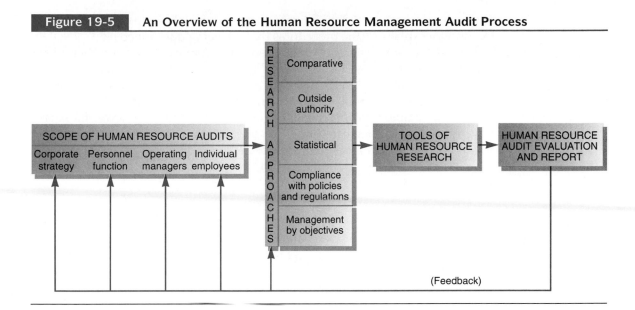

▶ Tools of Human Resource Research

Data-gathering tools

Several information-gathering tools help collect data about the firm's HR activities. Each tool provides partial insight into the firm's activities. If these tools are used skillfully, the audit team can weave the insights into a clear picture of the organization's HR activities. The tools include:

- Interviews
- Surveys
- Historical analysis
- External information
- Human resource experiments
- International audits

Interviews

Interviews of employees and managers offer audit teams a powerful tool for collecting information about HR activities and identifying areas that need improvement. For example, when the turnover problem at Roy Rogers was identified, the director of resources and a consultant conducted interviews with field managers to learn about the issue. Criticisms and comments from interviews can help pinpoint perceptions and causes that can form the basis for departmental action. Likewise, suggestions by managers may reveal ways to provide them with better service. When the criticisms are valid, changes should be made. But when the HR department is correct, it may have to educate others in the firm by explaining the procedures that are being questioned.[13]

Exit interviews

Exit interviews are conducted with departing employees to learn their views of the organization. Figure 19-6 shows the types of questions that are asked. The workers' comments are recorded and later reviewed during the audit to find the causes of employee turnover, dissatisfaction, and other problems. Since many employees are reluctant to criticize, the exit interviewer must take time to probe and listen carefully. Then the results must be studied to uncover trends among departments, divisions, or managers.[14]

Surveys

Since interviews are time-consuming and costly and often are limited to only a few people, many HR departments use questionnaires to broaden the scope of their research. Also, questionnaires may lead to more candid answers than do face-to-face interviews. As discussed in Chapter 17, attitude survey feedback can find answers to the concerns listed in Figure 19-7. Of particular importance

---

Figure 19-6	**An Exit Interview Form**

Employee's Name _____   **Date Hired** _____

Interviewed by _____   **Interviewed on** _____

Supervisor's Name _____   **Department** _____

1. Were your job duties and responsibilities what you expected?   _____
   If not, why not?_____

2. What is your frank and honest opinion of: _____
   a. Your job? _____
   b. Your working conditions? _____
   c. Your orientation to your job? _____
   d. Your training provided by the company? _____
   e. Your pay? _____
   f. Your company-provided benefits and services? _____
   g. Your treatment by your manager? _____

3. What is your major reason for leaving the company? _____
   _____

4. What could we have done to keep you from leaving? _____
   _____

5. What could be done to make this a better place to work? _____
   _____
   _____

Figure 19-7	Critical Concerns to Be Answered by Attitude Surveys

EMPLOYEE ATTITUDES ABOUT SUPERVISORS

- Are some supervisors' employees exceptionally satisfied or dissatisfied?

- Do specific supervisors need training in supervisory and human relations skills?

- Have attitudes improved since the last survey?

EMPLOYEE ATTITUDES ABOUT JOBS

- What are common elements of jobs that cause negative attitudes? Positive attitudes?

- Can jobs that cause poor attitudes be redesigned to improve satisfaction?

- Can jobs that cause poor attitudes be given alternative work schedules (such as shorter workweeks or flextime)?

PERCEIVED EFFECTIVENESS OF THE HUMAN RESOURCE DEPARTMENT

- Do employees think they work for a good or a bad employer?

- Do employees think they merely have a job or a career?

- Do employees think they have someplace to turn to solve problems besides their immediate superior?

- Do employees feel informed about company developments?

- Do employees know what is expected of them in their jobs?

- Are employees satisfied with the amount and type of feedback they get about their performance?

- Are employees satisfied with their pay? Benefits?

are trends revealed through the repeated administration of questionnaires. Research-based trends suggest challenges that are becoming more or less important to those surveyed.

Historical Analysis

Sometimes insight can be obtained by means of an analysis of historical records, which is often done to ensure compliance with laws and company procedures. Figure 19-8 lists the records normally reviewed by an audit team.[15]

Safety and health

Safety and health audits.   Compliance with the Occupational Safety and Health Act is evidenced through an analysis of safety and health records. Under the record-keeping requirements of OSHA, the audit team should find detailed records of all safety and health violations. Patterns of accidents by job

Figure 19-8	Records Commonly Reviewed as Part of a Human Resource Audit

SAFETY AND HEALTH RECORDS

- Determine differences before and after programs aimed at lowering accident rates.
- Are there patterns or discernible causes? By jobs? By shift?
- Is the firm in compliance with OSHA record-keeping requirements?

GRIEVANCE RECORDS

- Are there patterns to grievances arising from specific contract clauses or supervisors?
- Are there sections of the agreement that are unclear to union or management officials?

COMPENSATION STUDIES

- Are wages externally and internally equitable?
- Are fringe benefits understood by employees?
- Does the fringe benefits package compare favorably with local firms and national competitors?

AFFIRMATIVE ACTION PLANS

- Is the firm in compliance with all equal employment laws?
- Does the affirmative action plan address those areas where the firm is not in compliance?
- Has the firm made acceptable progress toward meeting its affirmative action goals?

PROGRAM AND POLICY STUDIES

- Does each human resource program meet its stated goals?
- Are policies and procedures being followed by the human resource department and line managers?

SCRAP RATES

- Determine if training, bonuses, and other programs have reduced scrap rates.

classification, location, supervisor, employee seniority, age, sex, and type of violation may uncover targets for additional safety training or equipment. Insurance companies or private consultants may assist the audit team in analyzing these statistics.

Grievance audits. The audit team also may be able to uncover a pattern to employee grievances brought through the company's in-house complaint

TURNOVER / ABSENTEEISM

- Are there patterns or discernible causes? By age? Sex?
- How do these records compare with those of other employers?
- Determine differences before and after programs aimed at lowering turnover or absenteeism.

PRETEST / POSTTEST SCORES

- Determine if orientation or training programs improve test scores or job performance.
- How well do test scores relate to job performance?

INTERNAL PLACEMENT RECORDS

- What percentage of jobs are filled internally?
- How well do internally promoted candidates perform?
- Do replacement charts / summaries indicate sufficient promotable talent?

SELECTION RECORDS

- Is the performance of recruits better according to the source from which they were recruited?
- Are recruitment and selection costs comparable with those of other firms?

EMPLOYEE FILES

- Are employee files in order, properly completed?
- Do records contain accurate information for making employee decisions?
- Is this employee making reasonable career progress?
- Is this employee a source of discipline or interpersonal problems?

SPECIAL PROGRAMMING REPORTS

- Are special programs achieving the desired results?
- Is the firm in compliance with COBRA for medical coverage of former employees and dependents?
- Is the firm in compliance with citizenship requirements under immigration reform?

process (discussed in Chapter 17) or through the union-management grievance procedure (discussed in Chapter 18). Patterns may emerge by job classification, supervisor, union representative, age group, or contract provision. If patterns are detected, HR specialists seek the causes of grievances. And if union officials participate in finding such patterns, they may support management's suggested changes, which usually involve training or the rewording of the union-management agreement.

Compensation audits. Audit teams carefully review the HR department's compensation practices. Primarily, they study the level of wages, incentives, benefits, and services provided. If jobs have been priced properly through job evaluations and salary surveys, pay levels are fair. Benefits and services also are studied to learn if they are cost-effective, competitive with those of other employers, and in compliance with government regulations.

Affirmative action

Affirmative action audits. The audit team also reviews the firm's compliance with equal opportunity laws, paying particularly close attention to concentration and underutilization of protected classes of workers. Although most large employers have a compliance officer to monitor the affirmative action program, the audit team serves as a further check. It usually focuses on hiring, developmental, placement, and compensation practices as they are applied to protected groups. Of particular concern is the progress being made by the company compared with the goals in its affirmative action plan. If discrimination exists, the team informs management of the need for corrective action.[16]

Program and policy audits. Besides safety, grievance, compensation, and affirmative action programs, audits evaluate many other programs and policies to determine if they are doing what was intended.

Seafood Canners

Two years after Seafood Canners, Inc., adopted a "promotion-from-within" policy, most supervisors still were recruited from outside the firm. Few workers applied for supervisory openings, even though those jobs were posted throughout the plant and employees were encouraged to apply. The audit team learned that during peak seasons, production workers earned more money than did supervisors because of overtime pay and the incentive system. Many employees viewed supervisory jobs as having more responsibility with less pay. To remedy the problem, supervisors were given a percentage of the department's production bonus. A year later, 90 percent of the supervisory openings were filled internally.

As this example illustrates, policies (promote from within) may conflict with other programs (the incentive system) and legal requirements (overtime pay) may conflict with the department's goals. Virtually every policy or program affects others. Thus, a thorough audit needs to include all the major human resource policies and programs and a study of how they relate to one another.

External Information

Checking the environment

Information is the central tool of the audit team. Outside comparisons give the team a perspective against which the firm's activities can be judged. Some needed information is readily available, while other data may be difficult to find. Perhaps the most significant source of external information is the federal government. Through the Department of Labor, numerous statistics and reports are compiled. This department regularly publishes information about future employment opportunities, employee turnover rates, workforce projections, area wage and salary surveys, and severity and frequency rates of accidents that can serve as benchmarks for comparing internal information.

State unemployment offices and industrial development commissions often provide information that also can be used for comparative purposes. Workforce demographics—age, sex, education, and racial composition—are commonly available from state agencies and are useful in evaluating affirmative action programs.

Industry associations usually make specialized data available to their members. Of most use to audit teams are statistics on industry norms such as turnover rates, absenteeism rates, standard wage rates, growth rates, standardized job descriptions, accident rates, fringe benefit costs, and sample union-management agreements.

Professional associations often provide similar information to members of the profession. Studies conducted by the association may include salary and benefit surveys, demographic profiles, and other data that can serve as standards against which the department's efforts are measured. Consultants and university research bureaus may be able to provide information as well.

Human Resource Research

The final tool available to HR departments and audit teams is the research experiment, particularly the *field experiment,* which compares an experimental group with a control group under realistic conditions. Experimentation is used to research absenteeism, turnover, job satisfaction, compensation, safety, and other activities. For example, the department may implement a safety training program for half the supervisors. This half is the experimental group; the control group contains the supervisors who are not given training. The subsequent safety records of both groups are compared several months after the program has been completed. If the experimental group has a significantly lower accident rate, there is evidence that the safety training program was effective. Then a *cost-benefit analysis* can be conducted by comparing the *costs* of the training with the *benefits* to the company to determine if the training is cost-effective.

Cost-benefit
analysis

Experimentation does have drawbacks. Many managers are reluctant to experiment with workers because of morale problems and potential dissatisfaction among those who were not selected. Employees involved in the experimental group may feel manipulated. And the experiment may be confounded by changes in the work environment or simply by the two groups talking to each other about the experiment.

International Audits

HR audits of international organizations are more complex and more important. The complexity of auditing HR activities across foreign borders is compounded by differences in laws, languages, cultures, traditional practices, and expectations. The tendency for an audit team from the home country is to use its experiences and standards as a benchmark against which the evaluation is conducted. Variations may seem wrong merely because they differ from the experiences of the auditors. For example, discrimination by sex, race, tribal grouping, social status, religion, caste, or another nonmeritorious criterion may violate company policies but may also be an expected and even necessary practice in some foreign countries.

The greatest difficulty for the audit team lies in identifying areas of variation from company practices that are not justified by the foreign context. On the one hand, the HR function seeks uniformity in practices and procedures across all operations to ensure compliance with company policies and assure a uniform corporation culture. On the other hand, competition, laws, culture, and employee satisfaction may demand variations from company policies, practices, and procedures. Variations should be noted so that policy makers can decide whether such differences should be allowed to continue. Probing into the purpose of the variations may reveal appropriate justification or poor management practices. Of particular importance are variations that violate home-country laws even though those actions are accepted practice in the foreign country. For example, bribing government officials is a common practice in some countries, but when done by U.S. firms, those actions violate the *Foreign Corrupt Practices Act.*

Foreign Corrupt
Practices Act

International audits are of particular importance precisely because of the wide variability in a global operation. Differences in education, experience, culture, and other factors may lead to different HR practices that are at best inefficient and at worst ineffective. Unless business necessity justifies differences, the goal should be uniformity in policies, practices, and procedures throughout the organization. This is not uniformity for its own sake. Instead, uniformity facilitates ease of administration and reassignment of personnel and makes research into intracompany comparisons easier and more accurate.

▶ The Audit Report

Performance
feedback

The *audit report* is a comprehensive description of HR activities that includes both commendations for effective practices and recommendations for improving practices that are less effective. A recognition of both good and bad practices is more balanced and encourages wider acceptance of the report.

Often an audit report contains several sections. One part is for line managers, another is for managers of specific HR functions, and the final part is for the HR manager. For line managers, the report summarizes their HR objectives, responsibilities, and duties. Examples of duties include interviewing applicants, training employees, evaluating performance, motivating workers, and satisfying employees' needs. The report also identifies people problems. Violations of policies and employee relations laws are highlighted. Poor management practices are revealed in the report along with recommendations.

The specialists who handle employment, training, compensation, and other activities also need feedback. The audit report they receive isolates areas of good and poor performance within their functions. For example, one audit team observed that many jobs did not have qualified replacements. This information was given to the manager of training and development along with the recommendation for more programs to develop promising supervisors and managers. The report also may provide other feedback, such as attitudes of operating managers about the HR specialists' efforts.

HR manager's report

The HR manager's report contains all the information given to both operating managers and staff specialists. In addition, the manager gets feedback about:

- Attitudes of operating managers and employees about the department's benefits and services

- A review of the department's objectives and plans to achieve them

- HR problems and their implications

- Recommendations for needed changes and the priority for their implementation

With the information contained in the audit report, the HR manager can take a broad view of the function. Instead of solving problems in a random manner, the manager can focus on those which have the greatest potential for improving the department's contribution to the firm. Perhaps most important, the audit serves as a map for future efforts and a reference point for future audits. With knowledge of the department's current performance, the manager can make long-range plans to upgrade crucial activities. These plans identify new goals for the department, which serve as standards for future audit teams.

▶ Human Resource Prospects for the Future

Audits are necessary but backward-looking. They only uncover the results of past decisions. Although past performance should be evaluated, HR departments also should look to the future. Without a future orientation, the department becomes reactive, not proactive. And reactive approaches allow minor problems to become major ones. Challenges that are likely to affect HR management are briefly discussed here to increase awareness of their potential importance. The major categories of concern include:

Future challenges

- Globalization, diversity, and the environmental context

- Employee rights

- Employee performance and productivity

- The challenging role of HR management

Globalization, Diversity, and the Environmental Context

The United States, Canada, and Mexico are virtually eliminating all barriers to free trade, creating through the North American Free Trade Act a North American trade bloc. At the same time, the European Union is becoming more closely integrated, creating another zone of free trade. Brazil, Argentina, Uruguay, and Paraguay are working steadily toward the creation of yet another trade bloc. And east Asia, led by Japan, contains some of the world's leading exporters. At the same time, deregulation of transportation, airlines, and financial institutions within the United States has increased the intensity of competition in those industries. Even governments at the federal, state, and local levels are under considerable budgetary pressures to perform with limited resources. These and other trends have placed growing pressures on organizations to perform better in terms of productivity, quality, time, and service.

Although technology, capital, materials, and energy are vital inputs in any organization, improved performance ultimately rests with the people who use those resources. But just as the demands on employees are increasing, HR experts and managers in the United States, Canada, and many European countries are confronted by a rapidly diversifying workforce. Consider these trends and their potential impact on HR management:

- In the United States, "an estimated 14.5 million employees work nonstandard hours—evenings, overnight, rotating shifts and split shifts—and in an economy gone global and a culture hungry for 24-hour *everything*, the numbers are growing."[17]

- By the year 2000, 63 percent of all women over age 16 will be in the workforce, up from 57 percent in 1990.[18]

- The black workforce is projected to increase twice as fast and the Hispanic labor force is expected to increase four times as fast as the white workforce.[19]

- Annual immigration into the United States will average 600,000 a year during the 1990s.[20]

- "Non-Caucasians, women and immigrants are projected to make up more than five-sixths, or 83%, of the new additions to the work force between now and the next century."[21]

- More than 85 pecent of those who will be working in 2001 are already in the workforce today, and most will need training and retraining.[22]

- Half of children under age 1 live in families where both parents work.[23]

- The workforce in the United States will grow only 1.2 percent a year during the 1990s, down from 2.9 percent as recently as the 1970s.[24]

- The number of people employed by temporary-help firms has increased 400 percent.[25]

- Part-time workers represent 20 percent of the workforce in Denmark, Norway, Sweden, and the Netherlands, with 17.4 percent of the U.S. workforce composed of part-timers.[26]

- Mandatory retirement ages in the United States have been abolished.[27]

- "People ages 50 to 60, though still energetic, are being passed over, pushed out, or shot with the so-called silver bullet of early retirement in extraordinary numbers."[28]

- According to one study, 85 percent of employers will conduct drug tests on at least some employees.[29]

- The number of AIDS cases is growing rapidly. More workers are likely to die from AIDS in the 1990s than from automobile accidents; already AIDS has killed more U.S. citizens than did the Vietnam conflict.[30]

- The United States has posted the slowest productivity growth among all major industrialized nations.

To put some of these statistics in perspective, consider what a plant manager at Digital Equipment Corp. faces:

> Harold Epps, who runs the Digital Equipment Corp. plant that makes computer keyboards, manages the work force of the future. The Boston factory's 350 employees come from 44 countries and speak 19 languages. When the plant issues written announcements, they are printed in English, Chinese, French, Spanish, Portuguese, Vietnamese, and Haitian Creole.[31]

The implications of increased competition and workforce diversity are countless. One obvious implication is that HR departments will be pressured for additional employment flexibility and additional child-care *and* elder-care assistance by their workers. This flexibility probably will be achieved through flexible benefits, flextime schedules, part-timers, temporary workers, and telecommuting. Rapid rises in health-care costs and slow productivity growth rates will put *downward* pressure on *real* (inflation- and tax-adjusted) wage increases, causing compensation almost certainly to be tied more closely to performance.[32]

Employee Rights

WARN

Beginning in 1842, when the supreme court of the Commonwealth of Massachusetts ruled that joining a union was not a criminal conspiracy, judicial opinions and legislation have expanded employees' rights. Even the employer's right to lay off workers has been limited by the *Worker Adjustment and Retraining Act* (WARN).[33] Likewise, employee terminations have been constrained by EEOC, OSHA, NLRB, and court rulings that have limited the "employment-at-will" doctrine. And experience suggests that legislative and judicial efforts will expand employment-related rights even further.[34] Although no one argues against protecting workers in a society of wage earners, the result of these growing limitations is increased responsibility and complexity for HR managers. In Europe, mandated benefits and services are credited with contributing to high and persistent unemployment rates during the 1980s and 1990s. Government-mandated employment requirements and fears about the cost of health-care reform in the United States are believed to have contributed to employer reluctance to hire new workers during the economic expansion of 1992–1995.

The list of current and future challenges continues to grow. The rights of smokers and nonsmokers provide an example that is part of a larger concern about workplace safety and health. Included here are concerns about radiation exposure from video display terminals and radon gas in the office and from chemicals and solvents in the factory. HR professionals also are involved with fearful employees and AIDS-infected coworkers.[35] Another long-simmering issue is comparable worth.[36] Should comparable work be paid equally? Or should "market rates" based on supply and demand prevail? Explosive medical costs and health-care reform are likely to put additional demands on employers beyond the extended coverage requirements of COBRA. And concerns over employee privacy—which have already caused many employee assistance programs to use outside counselors—are likely to grow as employees' records become more readily accessible electronically.[37]

Employee Performance and Productivity

Real wages cannot go up faster than productivity does. The wealth and well-being of society depend on the productivity of its workforce. No major industrial nation has had *worse* productivity improvement than the United States during the last two decades: not Great Britain, not Italy, not France, and certainly not Japan or Germany. Although the United States remains the worldwide productivity leader (both total and per capita), the effects of losing that leadership in industries such as automobiles, shipbuilding, steel, and consumer electronics have led to serious economic dislocations for employers and employees. These dislocations will spread unless productivity improves relative to that of our trading partners.

Competitive advantage

Competitive advantage increasingly is found in the creativity of employees. Tapping that wellspring may be the best hope for both emerging and mature industries. As a sign in a Union Carbide plant observed: "Assets make things possible; people make things happen." Improved productivity through people is ultimately the fountainhead of all human progress. And HR professionals are key players in improving people productivity. Through pay and incentive systems geared to increased productivity, the department can help align labor costs with performance. Pay for performance, however, assumes measurable performance. Improved appraisal systems are likely to be demanded by cost-conscious executives seeking to identify and reward top performers. In turn, those top performers will need sophisticated career planning assistance, training, flexible working hours, and flexible compensation systems—systems that proactive professionals are already designing and testing.

The Challenging Role of Human Resource Management

"Downsizing" used to be associated with a contracting economy. Today, however, downsizing occurs even when the economy is expanding. By reengineering workplace practices and procedures, many firms are gaining increased efficiencies that allow them to compete in the global marketplace. Unfortunately, those efficiencies often result from reductions in a firm's workforce, placing considerable emotional and financial strains on the workers who are affected.[38] The inevitable result for HR management will be more challenges and more importance attached to HR effectiveness. This additional importance will also mean additional responsibilities. The traditional duties of obtaining, maintaining, and retaining a qualified workforce will be expanded by additional roles that will demand even greater professionalism from the department leader and support staff.

Strategic contribution

Increasingly, HR managers are expected to contribute to the organization's strategic thinking. Marketing, production, and finance strategies depend on the abilities of the firm's people to execute these plans. To assist with the "people side" of implementation, HR directors will be forced to continuously uncover, through audits and research, the causes of and solutions to people-related problems. Their diagnostic ability to assess current and potential human issues will be needed as they and their staffs increasingly serve as internal consultants to others who are facing HR-related challenges. Then they will be called on to facilitate changes in the organization that maximize the human contribution. In short, the traditional administrative skills associated with HR management must grow to accommodate diagnostic, assessment, consultative, and facilitative skills.[39]

At the same time, HR professionals must continue to address societal, organizational, functional, and personal objectives that challenge the organization.

Societal challenges.   Modern societies prosper or decline through the productive contribution of their organizations. It is therefore not surprising that society takes an active interest in these engines of wealth. Legislative and judicial trends increasingly put individual rights above those of organizations. The success of this trend during the last sixty years has led to employers becoming vehicles of social policy. Equal employment laws and the affirmative action plans they spawned, for example, caused organizations to achieve more racial equality in one generation than did a civil war and a century of "separate but equal" policies. More needs to be done, but social planners, legislators, and judges have learned to use modern organizations as instruments of social policy. This trend is likely to continue.

Organizational and functional challenges. The HR function exists to further organizational effectiveness. Sometimes this entails pursuing societal objectives because doing otherwise may be illegal. Organizational challenges also mean that the department's goals—goals of efficiency or professionalism, for example—must be balanced against the organization's strategy and objectives. The HR department is a service department. When its members forget that, they cease serving the objectives of the organization.

Personal challenges. People have personal goals that HR professionals help them attain, at least insofar as those goals enhance the person's contribution to the organization. Many times HR professionals go further, helping people attain goals that have little relationship to the job. They create employee assistance programs, for example, because as a former vice president of human resources at State Farm Insurance observed, "we look at the employee as a *whole* person, not just a worker,"[40] As a result, more companies are adding positions with titles such as "Work and Family Program Manager" to oversee flextime, telecommuting, and dependent care programs and "Wellness Program Manager" to foster programs intended to promote employee health and fitness.[41]

State Farm
Insurance

> The most successful companies of all will be those that elevate their level of creativity and commitment to human resource issues before it is necessary. . . . Companies that do not change before they must will be defeated by their competitors who do. Economic power is not a zero-sum game. Even when power shifts, there can be many winners. The winners will be those companies and governments who welcome people-power, and do not resist it as a challenge to their own.[42]

Often the humanistic view means becoming an advocate for employees. This is not an advocacy intended to conflict with the organization but one that realizes that people are the ultimate resource in any organization. Economic advancement requires people who add greater value per hour worked regardless of where they work. By advocating employee needs, operating managers and HR professionals help our organizations—those most inventive developments of the twentieth century. By undertaking the challenge of making our organizations more productive and satisfying places, HR professionals assure that the wealth and well-being of society increase—now and into the twenty-first century.

▶ Summary

A human resource audit evaluates the HR activities used in an organization. Its purpose is to ensure that operating managers and HR specialists are following policies and maintaining an effective workforce.

The scope of the audit includes HR specialists, operating managers, employees, and the external environment. Inputs are sought from all four sources because each has a unique perspective. And to be truly effective, HR activities must do more than meet the wishes of experts. They also must meet the needs of employees and operating managers as well as challenges from the environment and the company's strategic plans.

The audit team uses a variety of research approaches and tools. Along with internal comparisons, the team compares the firm's efforts with those of other companies or with standards developed by external authorities and internal statistics. It may also evaluate compliance with laws or objectives set by management.

Research tools include interviews, questionnaires, surveys, internal records, external sources, and experimentation. Through these tools, the audit team is able to compile an audit report. The audit report gives feedback to top management, operating managers, HR professionals, and the HR manager. Armed with this information, the HR manager can then develop plans to ensure that activities make an effective contribution to the organization. If HR management is to be responsible, it needs to review its past performance through audits and research. At the same time, it needs a future orientation to anticipate upcoming challenges. Finally, a proactive view encourages HR professionals to contribute to both employee and company goals.

With all the challenges facing HR professionals, their role is sure to grow in scope and importance. The key to this growth is how well they can help employees make a better contribution to their organizations. It is through their contribution that an organization prospers. And it is through these life-giving and life-sustaining organizations that we prosper as individuals and as a society.

▶ Terms for Review

Human resource audit	Exit interviews
Audit teams	Field experiment
Applied research	Audit report
MBO approach	

▶ Review and Discussion Questions

1. "Human resource audits are unneeded because mistakes in HR practices should be corrected immediately and not wait until a periodic audit occurs. Besides, employees, managers, government agencies, and unions will all report errors." Do you agree or disagree? Explain.

2. If you were asked to assess (*a*) an evaluation of an employee assistance program, (*b*) an evaluaton of employee absenteeism, (*c*) the appropriateness of the current advertising budget for recruiting, what approaches would you use?

3. Assume that voluntary turnover increased dramatically and a review of the exit interviews showed that more than 90 percent of the people gave as their reason for leaving "more money elsewhere." What actions would you take? Would you modify the exit interview form or process?

4. Design an experiment to determine which fringe benefits employees are aware of and the relative importance of those benefits.

5. How does an HR audit of an overseas operation differ from an audit of a domestic operation? What considerations would you want to discuss with your boss before you left for the assignment?

6. What types of information should be put in an audit report for (*a*) an employment manager, (*b*) an assistant plant manager, and (*c*) a human resource director?

7. In the last two decades many cultural values have changed, some rather drastically. Briefly describe how human resource management might be affected by (*a*) a trend toward smaller families, (*b*) increased participation of women in the workforce, and (*c*) the aging of the workforce and the general population.

8. Most of your career will be spent in the twenty-first century. What changes in the closing years of the twentieth century do you think will have the greatest impact on the management of people in the coming decades of your career? Why?

▶ Incident 19-1

The Changing Face of Global Employment

More than 3 billion members of developing countries want the good life enjoyed in the triad nations of North America, Japan, and the European Union. The men and women of China, India, Russia, Indonesia, Brazil, Nigeria, Mexico, and smaller nations outside the triad represent billions of mostly unskilled or semiskilled workers. For one dollar (U.S.), you can get an unskilled Indian, Indonesian, or Nigerian to work ten-hour days with no fringe benefits—no paid vacations, no paid holidays, no private insurance coverage. And that worker will be grateful for the job and work diligently to prove it. In other developing nations the cost is not much higher. Yet for most workers in the postindustrialized triad nations, one dollar would not even cover lunch.

As *Business Week* observed:

The fundamental force . . . is integration into the global economy of the new capitalist nations and much of the developing world. With more than 3 billion inhabitants, many of them hungry for a better life, these new free-market adherents are competing as never before with the industrialized world.

> In just three years, the developing nations' share of world exports has jumped by some three percentage points, to 20%. . . . a new global trading system is emerging.
>
> To stay competitive, companies are locating more facilities abroad, eliminating jobs, and investing in technologies to boost productivity.[43]

To compete and prosper in the face of a tidal wave of third-world workers, advanced nations must tap the creativity and enthusiasm of their workers. Work must be both productive and fun. If it is not productive, layoffs, stagnant wages, and even bankruptcy become likely in a global economy ruled by efficiency; if the work is not enjoyable, the wellspring of employee creativity is apt to run dry as workers withdraw physically by quitting or psychologically by "retiring" on the job behind a bureaucratic facade of legal or union rules.

Creating a productive and enjoyable work environment is the dual responsibility of managers and human resource experts. Managers are responsible for marshaling the organization's human and nonhuman resources to achieve business objectives. Human resource professionals provide the "people expertise," procedures, and systems that enable managers to meet their challenges.

Ultimately, the organization has a competitive advantage in the way it adds value or it fails. Human resource management is one way to gain a sustainable competitive advantage that is not easily duplicated, as in the case of technology or capital.

After reviewing the concepts presented in this book, answer the following questions.

1. What are the ways in which an effective HR department contributes to providing the employer with a sustainable competitive advantage?

2. Select three topics in this book and explain how their proper utilization enables the HR function to contribute to a firm's competitive advantage.

▶ References

1. Peter Stroh and Wynne W. Miller, "HR Professionals Should Thrive on Paradox," *Personnel Journal*, May 1993, p. 132.

2. Brian O'Reilly, "Your New Global Work Force," *Fortune*, Dec. 14, 1992, pp. 52–66.

3. *Positioning Corporate Staff for the 1990s*, New York: Towers, Perrin, Forster & Crosby, 1986, p. 9.

4. Bruce R. Ellig, "Improving Effectiveness through an HR Review," *Personnel*, June 1989, pp. 56–63.

5. George E. Biles and Randall S. Schuler, *Audit Handbook of Human Resource Practices: Auditing the Effectiveness of the Human Resource Function*, Alexandria, Va.: American Society for Personnel Administration, 1986.

6. Thomas J. Peters and Robert H. Waterman, Jr., *In Search of Excellence: Lessons from America's Best-Run Companies*, New York: Harper & Row, 1982.

7. John A. Hooper, Ralph F. Catalanello, and Patrick L. Murray, "Showing Up the Weakest Link," *Personnel Administrator,* April 1987, p. 53.

8. Alfred H. Lievertz, "Developing Your Functional Fingerprint," *Personnel Administrator,* January 1987, pp. 61–65.

9. Dean F. Berry, *The Politics of Personnel Research,* Ann Arbor: Bureau of Industrial Relations, Graduate School of Business Administration, University of Michigan, 1967.

10. Robert O. Hansson, Nancy D. Smith, and Pamela S. Mancinelli, "Monitoring the HR Job Function," *HRMagazine,* February 1990, pp. 76–78.

11. Barbara Whitaker Shimko, "All Managers Are HR Managers," *HRMagazine,* January 1990, pp. 67–68, 70.

12. Anne S. Tsui, "Defining the Activities and Effectiveness of the Human Resource Department: A Multiple Constituency Approach," *Human Resource Management,* Spring 1987, pp. 35–69.

13. Lievertz, op. cit.

14. Walter Kiechel III, "The Art of the Exit Interview," *Fortune,* Aug. 13, 1990, pp. 114–115.

15. Hooper, Catalanello, and Murray, op. cit.

16. Joel Dreyfuss, "Get Ready for the New Work Force," *Fortune,* Apr. 23, 1990, pp. 165–181.

17. Michele Ingrassia and Karen Springen, "Living on Dracula Time," *Newsweek,* July 12, 1993, p. 68.

18. Diane Crispell, "Workers in 2000," *American Demographics,* March 1990, p. 36.

19. Ibid., p. 38.

20. Robert W. Goddard, "Work Force 2000," *Personnel Journal,* February 1989, p. 68.

21. Ibid.

22. "Pace of Change Is Challenge for HRM, Analyst Says," *Resource,* October 1986, p. 4.

23. Ibid.

24. Goddard, op. cit.

25. "New BNA Report Details Changes in Work Patterns," *Resource,* December 1986, p. 3.

26. John Naisbitt and Patricia Aburdene, *Megatrends 2000,* New York: William Morrow, 1990, p. 534.

27. The 1986 amendments to the Age Discrimination in Employment Act extend coverage to those over 40; previously, the act applied only to those between 40 and 70. Executives are excluded from coverage.

28. Stratford Sherman, "A Brave New Darwinian Workplace," *Fortune,* Jan. 25, 1993, p. 56.

29. Lee Smith, "What the Boss Knows about You," *Fortune,* Aug. 9, 1993, p. 90.

30. Jeff Miller and William B. Werther, Jr., "An American Perspective on AIDS: Executive and HR Implications for the Second Decade," *EAP International,* vol. 1, no. 3, 1993, pp. 14–18.

31. Dreyfuss, op. cit., p. 165.

32. Ibid.

33. Betty Southard, Wayne E. Barlow, and D. Diane Hatch, "Employers Must Notify Employees of Plant Closure," *Personnel Journal,* October 1988, p. 22.

34. James Fraze and Martha I. Finney, "Employee Rights between Our Shores," *Personnel Administrator,* March 1988, pp. 50–54.

35. Phyllis Schiller Myers and Donald W. Myers, "AIDS: Tackling a Tough Problem through Policy," *Personnel Administrator,* April 1987, pp. 95–108, 143.

36. "U.S. Comp Worth Bill Draws Fire in Hearing," *Resource,* May 1987, pp. 1, 9.

37. Joe Pasqualetto, "Staffing, Privacy and Security Measures," *Personnel Journal,* September 1988, pp. 84–89. See also Morton E. Grossman and Margaret Magnus, "The Growing Dependence on HRIS," *Personnel Journal,* September 1988, pp. 53–59.

38. Samuel Greengard, "Don't Rush Downsizing: Plan, Plan, Plan," *Personnel Journal,* November 1993, pp. 64–76.

39. James W. Walker, "Human Resource Roles for the '90s," *Human Resource Planning,* vol. 12, no. 1, 1989, pp. 55–61.

40. State Farm Insurance Companies, *Operation Understanding,* Bloomington, Ill., April–May 1983, p. 1.

41. Edward L. Hansen, "Companies Add Work /Family Managers and Other New Positions," *William M. Mercer News Release,* July 14, 1993, p. 1. See also Allen I. Kraut, "Some Lessons on Organizational Research Concerning Work and Family Issues," *Human Resource Planning,* June 1990, pp. 109–118.

42. Frank P. Doyle, "People-Power: The Global Human Resource Challenge for the '90s," *Columbia Journal of World Business,* Summer 1990, p. 45.

43. Christopher Farrell, Michael J. Mandel, Bill Javetski, and Stephen Baker, "What's Wrong?" *Business Week,* Aug. 2, 1993, p. 55.

GLOSSARY

Absentees   Absentees are employees who are scheduled to be at work but are not present.

Accident and sickness policies   Accident and sickness policies usually provide a minimum-care stipend for several weeks up to six months to help employees defray the loss of income while they are sick or recovering from an accident.

Accreditation   Accreditation is a process of certifying the competence of a person in an area of capability. The Society for Human Resource Management (SHRM) operates an accreditation program for human resource professionals.

Active listening   Active listening requires the listener to stop talking, remove distractions, be patient, and empathize with the talker.

Adverse selection   Adverse selection occurs when an insurance company has a disproportionately high percentage of insureds who will make claims in the future. Adverse selection often results when people are given a chance to buy insurance without prescreening, which often means that a higher than normal proportion have a condition that is likely to cause them to be frequent claimants.

Advisory authority   See *Staff authority.*

Affirmative action programs   Affirmative action programs are detailed plans developed by employers to undo the results of past employment discrimination or ensure equal opportunity in the future.

Age Discrimination in Employment Act of 1967 (as amended)   This act prohibits discrimination in employment because of age against those who are 40 years old or older.

American Federation of Labor and Congress of Industrial Organizations (AFL-CIO)   The AFL-CIO is a federation of most national unions. It exists to provide a unified focal point for the labor movement, assist national unions, and influence government policies that affect members and working people.

American Society for Personnel Administration (ASPA)   See *Society for Human Resource Management.*

Americans with Disabilities Act   The Americans with Disabilities Act makes it unlawful to discriminate against the qualified handicapped. Employers are required to make reasonable accommodations to enable a person to do the job.

Applied research   Applied research is a study of practical problems, the solutions to which will lead to improved performance.

Arbitration   Arbitration is the submission of a dispute to a neutral third party.

Assessment centers   Assessment centers are a standardized form of employee appraisal that relies on multiple types of evaluation and multiple raters.

Associate membership   Associate membership in a labor organization allows people who are not employed under a union contract to affiliate with a union by paying fees and dues in return for union-supported benefits.

Attitude surveys   Attitude surveys are systematic methods of determining what employees think about the organization. The surveys are usually done through questionnaires. Attitude survey feedback results when the information collected is reported back to the participants. This process then is usually followed by action planning to identify and resolve specific areas of employee concern.

Attrition   Attrition is the loss of employees who leave an organization's employment.

Audit report   The audit report is a comprehensive description of human resource activities. It includes both commendations for effective practices and recommendations for improving practices that are ineffective.

Audit team   An audit team consists of people who are responsible for evaluating the performance of the human resource department.

Authorization cards   Authorization cards are forms that prospective union members sign. The cards indicate their wish to have an election to determine whether a labor organization will represent the workers in their dealings with management.

Autonomous work groups   Autonomous work groups are teams of workers without a formal company-appointed leader who decide among themselves most decisions traditionally handled by supervisors.

Autonomy   Autonomy is having control over one's work.

Bargaining book   A bargaining book is a compilation of the negotiation team's plans for collective bargaining with labor or management. Increasingly, the bargaining book is being replaced by information stored in a company or union computer.

Bargaining committee   The union bargaining committee consists of union officials and stewards who negotiate with management's representatives to determine the wages, hours, and working conditions that will be embodied in the labor agreement.

Barriers to change   Barriers to change are factors that interfere with employee acceptance and implementation of change.

Barriers to communication   Barriers to communication are interferences that may limit the receiver's understanding.

Behaviorally anchored rating scales (BARs)   BARs rate employees on a scale that includes specific behavioral examples to guide the rater.

Behavior modeling   Behavior modeling relies on the initiation or emulation of a desired behavior. A repetition of behavior modeling helps develop appropriate responses in specified situations.

Behavior modification Behavior modification states that behavior depends on its consequences.

Blind ads Blind ads are want ads that do not identify the employer.

Bona fide occupational qualifications (BFOQ) A BFOQ occurs when an employer has a justified business reason for discriminating against a member of a protected class. The burden of proving a BFOQ generally falls on the employer.

Bottom-line test The bottom-line test is applied by the Equal Employment Opportunity Commission to determine if a firm's overall selection process is having an adverse impact on protected groups. Even though individual steps in the selection process may exhibit an adverse impact on a protected group, the firm will be considered in compliance if the overall process does not have an adverse effect.

Boulwarism Boulwarism is a negotiation strategy developed by General Electric. Using this approach, the company made its "best" offer to the union at the beginning of negotiations and then remained firm unless the union could find where management had erred in the calculations used to arrive at the offer. This strategy was ruled an unfair labor practice by the National Labor Relations Board and the federal courts.

Brainstorming Brainstorming is a process by which participants provide their ideas on a stated problem during a freewheeling group session.

Buddy system The buddy system of orientation exists when an experienced employee is asked to show a new worker around the jobsite, conduct introductions, and answer the newcomer's questions.

Burnout Burnout is a condition of mental, emotional, and sometimes physical exhaustion that results from substantial and prolonged stress.

Business agent A business agent is a full-time employee of a local (usually craft) union. The business agent helps employees resolve their problems with management.

Business unionism Business unionism describes unions that seek to improve the wages, hours, and working conditions of their members in a businesslike manner. (See *Social unionism*.)

Buyback Buybacks occur when an employee who attempts to resign is persuaded to stay in the employment of the organization. Normally the person is "bought back" with an offer of increased wages or salary.

Cafeteria benefit programs Cafeteria benefit programs (also called flexible benefits) allow employees to select the fringe benefits and services that satisfy their individual needs.

Career A career consists of all the jobs held during one's working life.

Career counseling Career counseling assists employees in finding appropriate career goals and paths.

Career development Career development consists of the experiences and personal improvements one undertakes to achieve a career plan.

Career goals   Career goals are the future positions one strives to reach. These goals serve as benchmarks along one's career path.

Career path   A career path is the sequential pattern of jobs that form one's career.

Career planning   Career planning is the process by which one selects career goals and paths to those goals.

Career plateau   A career plateau occurs when an employee is in a position that he or she does well enough not to be demoted or fired but not well enough to be promoted.

Cause-and-effect diagrams   Cause-and-effect, or fishbone, diagrams begin with a known effect such as a defective part. From that effect, an individual or group attempts to brainstorm the various possible contributing factors—usually people, machines, materials, and methods. Then each element that could be contributing toward this effect undergoes further scrutiny.

Change agents   Change agents are people who stimulate and coordinate change within a group.

Checkoff   A checkoff provision in a union-management labor agreement requires the employer to deduct union dues from employees' paychecks and remit those moneys to the union.

Civil Rights Act of 1964   This act was passed to make various forms of discrimination illegal.

Closed shop   A closed shop is a workplace where all employees are required to be members of the union *before* they are hired. These arrangements are illegal under the National Labor Relations Act.

Codetermination   Codetermination is a form of industrial democracy first popularized in West Germany. It gives workers the right to have representatives vote on management decisions.

Cognitive dissonance   Cognitive dissonance results from a gap between what one expects and what one experiences.

Cognitive models of motivation   Cognitive models of motivation depend on the thinking or feeling (that is, cognition) within each individual.

Coinsurance clause   A coinsurance clause is a provision in an insurance policy that requires the employee to pay a percentage of the insured's expenses.

Communication   Communication is the transfer of information and understanding from one person to another.

Communication overload   Communication overload occurs when employees receive more communication inputs than they can process or more than they need.

Communication process   A communication process is the method by which a sender reaches a receiver. It requires that an idea be developed, encoded, transmitted, received, decoded, and used.

Communication system   A communication system provides formal and informal methods for moving information throughout an organization so that appropriate decisions are made.

Comparable worth   Comparable worth is the idea that a job should be evaluated in regard to its value to the organization and then paid accordingly. Thus jobs of comparable worth would be paid equally. For example, two people with widely different jobs would both receive the same pay if the two jobs were of equal value to the employer.

Comparative evaluation approaches   Comparative evaluation approaches are a collection of different methods that compare one person's performance with that of coworkers.

Compensation   Compensation is what employees receive in exchange for their work, including pay and benefits.

Comprehensive Employment and Training Act of 1973 (CETA)   CETA was a broad-ranging act designed to provide job training, employment, and job-hunting assistance to less advantaged persons. It has been replaced by the *Job Training Partnership Act.*

Concentration in employment   Concentration exists when an employer (or a subdivision such as a department) has a higher proportion of employees from a protected class than is found in the employer's labor market. (See *Underutilization.*)

Concessionary bargaining   Concessionary bargaining occurs when labor-management negotiations result in fewer employer-paid fringe benefits or wage concessions, such as a freeze or wage cut.

Conciliation agreement   A conciliation agreement is a negotiated settlement agreeable to the EEOC and all the parties involved. Its acceptance closes the case.

Consolidated Omnibus Budget Reconciliation Act of 1986 (COBRA)   COBRA requires employers to extend medical-related insurance availability to employees who leave employment and to extend coverage to the employee's dependents when their status changes and they are no longer eligible as dependents. (This change may occur because of divorce, college graduation, or the marriage of a child dependent, for example.)

Constructs   Constructs are substitutes for actual performance. For example, a score on a test is a construct for actual learning.

Content theories of motivation   Content theories of motivation describe the needs or desires within people that initiate behavior.

Contract labor   Contract labor consists of people who are hired (and often trained) by an independent agency that supplies companies with needed human resources for a fee.

Contributory plans   Contributory plans are fringe benefits that require both the employer and the employee to contribute to the cost of the insurance, retirement plan, or other employer benefit.

Coordinated organizing   Coordinated organizing occurs when two or more unions pool their resources to organize a targeted employer or group of employees.

Corrective discipline   Corrective discipline is an action that follows a rule infraction and seeks to discourage further infractions so that future acts are in compliance with standards.

Counseling   Counseling is the discussion of an employee's problem with the general objective of helping the worker cope with it.

Counseling functions Counseling functions are the activities performed by counselors. They include advice, reassurance, communication, release of emotional tension, clarified thinking, and reorientation.

Craft unions Craft unions are labor organizations that seek to include all workers who have a common skill, such as carpenters or plumbers.

Critical incident method The critical incident method requires the rater to report statements that describe extremely good or extremely bad employee behavior. These statements are called critical incidents and are used as examples of good or bad performance in rating the employee.

Decision-making authority See *Line authority.*

Deductible clause A deductible clause is a provision in an insurance policy that requires the insured to pay a specified amount of a claim before the insurer is obligated to pay.

Deep-sensing meeting At a deep-sensing meeting a manager or human resource specialist uses probing questions to understand the issues on employees' minds.

Deferral jurisdictions Deferral jurisdictions are areas in the United States where the EEOC will refer a case to another, usually state or local, agency.

Deferred stock incentive systems These incentives award stock that becomes owned by an executive gradually over several years.

Delegation Delegation is the process of getting others to share a manager's work. It requires the manager to assign duties, grant authority, and create a sense of responsibility.

Delphi technique The Delphi technique solicits predictions from a panel of experts about specified future developments. The collective estimates are then reported back to the panel so that the members may adjust their opinions. This process is repeated until a general agreement on future trends emerges.

Demographics Demographics is the study of population characteristics.

Demotions Demotions occur when an employee is moved from one job to another that is lower in pay, responsibility, and organizational level.

Development Development represents activities that prepare an employee for future responsibilities.

Dictionary of Occupational Titles (DOT) The *Dictionary of Occupational Titles* is a federal government publication that provides detailed job descriptions and job codes for most occupations in government and industry.

Differential validity Differential validity is used to demonstrate that tests or other selection criteria are valid for different subgroups or protected classes.

Directive counseling Directive counseling is the process of listening to an employee's emotional problems, deciding with the employee what should be done, and then telling and motivating the employee to do it. (See *Nondirective counseling.*)

Discipline Discipline is management action to encourage compliance with the organization's standards.

Dismissal   Dismissal is the ultimate disciplinary action because it separates the employee from the employer for a cause.

Disparate impact   Disparate impact occurs when the results of an employer's actions have a different effect on one or more protected classes.

Disparate treatment   Disparate treatment occurs when members of a protected class receive unequal treatment.

Downsizing   Downsizing means a scaling back of an organization's employment level, usually through attrition, early retirement programs, or layoffs.

Downward communication   Downward communication is information that begins at some point in the organization and then feeds down the hierarchy to inform or influence others in the firm.

Dual responsibility (for human resource management)   Since both line and staff managers are responsible for employees, production, and quality of work life, a dual responsibility for human resource management exists.

Due process   Due process means that established rules and procedures for disciplinary action are followed and that employees have an opportunity to respond to the charges made against them.

Early retirement   Early retirement occurs when a worker retires from an employer before the "normal" retirement age.

Employee assistance programs (EAPs)   EAPs are company-sponsored programs to help employees overcome their personal problems through direct company assistance, counseling, or outside referral.

Employee handbook   The employee handbook explains key benefits, policies, and general information about the employer.

Employee involvement (EI)   Employee involvement consists of a variety of systematic methods that enable employees to participate in decisions that affect them.

Employee Retirement Income Security Act (ERISA)   ERISA was passed by Congress to ensure that employer pension plans meet minimum participation, vesting, and funding requirements.

Employment freeze   An employment freeze occurs when an organization curtails future hiring.

Employment function   The employment function is the aspect of the human resource department that is responsible for recruiting, selecting, and hiring new workers. This function is usually handled by the employment section or employment manager of a large human resource department.

Employment references   Employment references are evaluations of an employee's work performance provided by past employers.

Employment tests   Employment tests are devices that assess the probable match between applicants and job requirements.

Equal Employment Act of 1972   This act strengthened the role of the Equal Employment Opportunity Commission by amending the Civil Rights Act of 1964. The 1972 law empowered the EEOC to initiate court action against noncomplying organizations.

Equal employment opportunity   Equal employment opportunity means giving people a fair chance to succeed without discrimination based on factors unrelated to job performance, such as age, race, or national origin.

Equal Employment Opportunity Commission (EEOC)   The EEOC is the federal agency responsible for enforcing Title VII of the Civil Rights Act, as amended.

Equal employment opportunity laws   Equal employment opportunity laws are a family of federal and state acts that seek to ensure equal employment opportunities for members of protected groups.

Equal Pay Act of 1963   This act prohibits discrimination in pay because of a person's sex.

Equifinality   Equifinality means that there are usually multiple paths to an objective.

Equity theory   Equity theory suggests that people are motivated to close the gap between their efforts and the perceived amount and appropriateness of the rewards they receive.

Ergonomics   Ergonomics is the study of biotechnical relationships between the physical attributes of workers and the physical demands of the job. The object of the study is to reduce physical and mental strain in order to increase productivity and the quality of work life.

Error of central tendency   The error of central tendency occurs when a rater evaluates employee performance as neither good nor poor even when some employees perform exceptionally well or poorly. Instead, the rater rates everyone as average.

Evaluation interviews   Evaluation interviews are performance review sessions that give employees feedback about their past performance or future potential.

Executive orders   Executive orders are presidential decrees that normally apply to government contractors or managers in the executive branch of the federal government.

Exit interviews   Exit interviews are conversations with departing employees to learn their views of the organization.

Expatriate   An expatriate is a person who lives and works in a foreign country.

Expectancy   Expectancy is the strength of a person's belief that an act will lead to a particular outcome.

Expectancy theory   Expectancy theory states that motivation is the result of the outcome one seeks and one's estimate that action will lead to the desired outcome.

Expedited arbitration   Expedited arbitration is an attempt to speed up the arbitration process. It may include an arrangement in which the arbitrator is available on short notice (one or two days) and renders a quick decision at the conclusion of the hearings (sometimes an oral decision is used in these cases).

Experience rating   Experience rating is a practice by which state unemployment offices base an employer's unemployment compensation tax rate on that employer's previous experience in providing stable employment.

Experiential learning   Experiential learning means that participants learn by experiencing in the training environment the kinds of problems they face on the job.

Exposure   Exposure means becoming known by those who decide on promotions, transfers, and other career opportunities.

Extrapolation   Extrapolation involves extending past rates of change into the future.

Facilitator   A facilitator is someone who assists quality circles and the quality circle leader in identifying and solving workplace problems.

Factor comparison method   The factor comparison method is a form of job evaluation that allocates part of each job's wage to key factors of the job. The result is a relative evaluation of the organization's jobs.

Fair employment practices   Fair employment practices are state and local laws that prohibit employer discrimination in employment against members of protected classes.

Fair Labor Standards Act of 1938 (FLSA)   FLSA is a comprehensive federal law affecting compensation management. It sets minimum-wage, overtime pay, equal pay, child labor, and record-keeping requirements.

Family and Medical Leave Act of 1993   The Family and Medical Leave Act requires employers with fifty or more employees to grant up to twelve weeks' leave within a twelve-month period after the birth or adoption or placement of a child in foster care in the employee's family; for the care of employee's spouse, child, or parent; or because of a serious health condition.

Federal Mediation and Conciliation Service (FMCS)   The FMCS was created by the Labor Management Relations Act of 1947 to help labor and management resolve negotiation impasses peacefully through mediation and conciliation without resort to a strike. The FMCS also is a source of qualified labor arbitrators.

Feedback   Feedback is information that helps evaluate the success or failure of an action or system.

Field experiment   A field experiment is research that allows researchers to study employees under realistic conditions to learn how experimental and control subjects react to new programs and other changes.

Field review method   The field review method requires skilled representatives of the human resource department to go into the "field" and assist supervisors with their ratings. Often it is the human resource department's representative who actually fills out the evaluation form after interviewing the supervisor about employee performance.

Flextime   Flextime is a scheduling innovation that abolishes rigid starting and ending times for each day's work. Instead, employees are allowed to begin and end the workday at their discretion, usually within a range of hours.

Flexyear   Flexyear is a scheduling concept that allows workers to be off the job for part of the year. Employees usually work a normal work year in less than twelve months.

Forced choice method   The forced choice method of employee performance evaluation requires the rater to choose the most descriptive statement in each pair of statements about the employee being rated.

Foreign Corrupt Practices Act   The Foreign Corrupt Practices Act outlaws the use of bribes or bribelike payments in dealing overseas under a variety of conditions.

Foreign national   A foreign national is a person who is a citizen of one country livng and working in another country.

Four-fifths rule   The four-fifths rule is a test used by the EEOC. When the selection ratio of protected-class applicants is less than 80 percent (or four-fifths) of the selection ratio for majority applicants, an adverse impact is assumed.

Fully insured workers   Fully insured workers are employees who have contributed forty quarters (ten years) to social security.

Functional authority   Functional authority allows staff experts to make decisions in specified circumstances that are normally reserved for line managers.

Funded plan   Funded plans require an employer to accumulate moneys in advance so that the organization's contribution plus interest will cover its obligation.

Funded retirement plans   A funded retirement plan is one in which the employer sets aside enough money to meet future payout requirements.

Gainsharing   Gainsharing matches an improvement (gain) in company performance with some distribution (sharing) of the benefits to employees.

Glass ceiling   A glass ceiling refers to the idea that people can see higher-level positions but are blocked from attaining those positions by a real but unseen barrier such as discrimination. The term is most often applied to the careers of women who are blocked from achieving the seniormost positions in a company. It also applies to foreign nationals who may be blocked from the seniormost positions in a company based in another country.

Golden parachutes   Golden parachutes are agreements by the company to compensate executives with bonuses and benefits if they are displaced by a merger or acquisition.

Grapevine communication   Grapevine communication is an informal system that arises spontaneously from the social interaction of people in an organization.

Grievance procedure   A grievance procedure is a multistep process that the employer and union jointly use to resolve disputes that arise under the terms of the labor agreement.

Griggs v. Duke Power Company   The U.S. Supreme Court held that when an employment criterion disproportionately discriminates against a protected class, the employer is required to show how that criterion is job-related.

Guaranteed annual wage   A guaranteed annual wage assures workers of receiving a minimum amount of work or pay during the course of a year.

Guest workers   Guest workers are foreign nationals allowed to work in another nation, generally to alleviate a labor shortage or provide desired skills, knowledge, or ability.

Halo effect   The halo effect is a bias that occurs when a rater allows some information to disproportionately prejudice the final evaluation.

Harassment   Harassment occurs when a member of an organization treats an employee in a disparate manner because of the worker's sex, race, religion, age, or another protected classification.

Hazard communication   A hazard communication, required under Occupational Safety and Health Act rules and regulations, is issued by an employer to inform employees about the nature of hazardous materials being used at work.

Health maintenance organizations (HMOs)   HMOs are a form of health insurance in which the insurer provides the professional staff and facilities needed to treat insured policyholders for a predetermined monthly fee.

Hot-stove rule   The hot-stove rule states that disciplinary action should have the same characteristics as the penalty a person receives after touching a hot stove. That is, the discipline should be with warning, immediate, consistent, and impersonal.

House organs   A house organ is any regularly published organizational magazine, newspaper, or bulletin directed to employees.

Human resource audit   A human resource audit evaluates the human resource activities used in an organization.

Human resource forecasts   Human resource forecasts predict an organization's future demand for employees.

Human resource planning   Human resource planning systematically forecasts an organization's future supply of and demand for employees.

Human resources   Human resources are the people who are ready, willing, and able to contribute to organizational goals.

Imminent danger   An imminent danger is a situation that is likely to lead to death or a serious injury if allowed to continue.

Improshare plans   Improshare plans are a form of gainsharing that focuses on reducing the labor hours used to produce a given level of output, with part of the savings shared with the employees.

Incentive systems   Incentive systems link compensation and performance by paying employees for actual results, not for seniority or hours worked.

Indexation   Indexation is a method of estimating future employment needs by matching employment growth with an index, such as sales growth.

Industrial democracy   Industrial democracy involves giving employees a larger voice in making the work-related decisions that affect them.

Industrial unions   Industrial unions are labor organizations that seek to include all of an employer's eligible workers whether they are skilled, semiskilled, or unskilled.

In-house complaint procedures   In-house complaint procedures are organizationally developed methods for employees to register complaints about various aspects of the organization.

Job analysis   Job analysis systematically collects, evaluates, and organizes information about jobs.

Job analysis schedules   Job analysis schedules are checklists or questionnaires that seek to collect information about jobs in a uniform manner. (They are also called job analysis questionnaires.)

Job banks   Job banks exist in state employment security offices. They are used to match applicants with job openings.

Job code   A job code uses numbers, letters, or both to provide a quick summary of a job and its content.

Job description   A job description is a written statement that explains the duties, working conditions, and other aspects of a specified job.

Job enlargement   Job enlargement means adding more tasks to a job to increase the job cycle.

Job enrichment   Job enrichment means adding more responsibilities, autonomy, and control to a job.

Job evaluations   Job evaluations are systematic procedures for determining the relative worth of jobs.

Job families   Job families are groups of different jobs that require similar skills.

Job-flo   Job-flo is a monthly report of frequently listed openings from job banks throughout the country.

Job grading   Job grading is a form of job evaluation that assigns jobs to predetermined classifications according to a job's relative worth to the organization. This technique is also called the job classification method.

Jobholder reports   Jobholder reports are reports to employees about the firm's economic performance.

Job information service   The job information service is a feature of state employment security agencies that enables job seekers to review job bank listings in their efforts to find employment.

Job instruction training   Job instruction training is training received directly on the job. It is also called on-the-job training.

Job performance standards   Job performance standards are the work requirements that are expected from an employee on a particular job.

Job-posting program   Job posting informs employees of unfilled job openings and the qualifications for those jobs.

Job progression ladder   A job progression ladder is a particular career path where some jobs have prerequisites.

Job ranking   Job ranking is a form of job evaluation that subjectively ranks jobs according to their overall worth to the organization.

Job rotation   Job rotation is the process of moving employees from one job to another to allow them more variety in their jobs and provide the opportunity to learn new skills.

Job satisfaction   Job satisfaction is the favorableness or unfavorableness with which employees view their work.

Job sharing   Job sharing is a scheduling innovation that allows two or more workers to share the same job, usually by having each working part-time.

Job specifications   A job specification describes what a job demands of the employees who do it and the human skills that are required.

Job Training Partnership Act of 1983   This act provides federal funds to authorized training contractors, often city or state government agencies. These moneys are used to train people in new, employable skills. (It replaces the Comprehensive Employment and Training Act of 1973.)

Joint study committees   Joint study committees include representatives from management and the union who meet away from the bargaining table to study some topic of mutual interest in the hope of finding a solution that is mutually satisfactory.

Juniority   Juniority provisions require that layoffs be offered first to senior workers, who may accept or refuse them. If enough senior workers do not accept the layoffs, management is free to lay off the least senior workers.

Key jobs   Key jobs are jobs that are common in the organization and in its labor market.

Key subordinates   Key subordinates are employees who are crucial to a manager's success in a particular job.

Labor agreement   A labor agreement, which is also called a labor contract, is a legal document that is negotiated between the union and the employer. It states the terms and conditions of employment.

Laboratory training   Laboratory training is a form of group training primarily used to enhance interpersonal skills.

Labor Management Relations Act of 1947 (LMRA)   The LMRA, also known as the Taft-Hartley Act, amended the National Labor Relations Act of 1935 by designating specific union actions that were considered unfair labor practices. The act also created the Federal Mediation and Conciliation Service and enabled the President of the United States to call for injunctions in national emergency strikes.

Labor-Management Reporting and Disclosure Act of 1959 (LMRDA)   The LMRDA, also called the Landrum-Griffin Act, amended the National Labor Relations Act. It created the union members' "bill of rights" by giving union members certain rights in dealing with a union. The law also established detailed reporting requirements for those who handle union funds.

Labor market   The labor market is the area in which an employer recruits.

Labor market analysis   Labor market analysis is the study of the employer's labor market to evaluate the current or future availability of workers.

Labor shortages Labor shortages occur when there is a scarcity of people to fill job openings.

Landrum-Griffin Act See *Labor-Management Reporting and Disclosure Act of 1959.*

Law of effect The law of effect states that people learn to repeat behaviors that have favorable consequences and avoid behaviors that have unfavorable consequences.

Layoffs Layoffs are separations of employees from an organization for economic or business reasons.

Learning curve A learning curve is a visual representation of the rate at which one learns given material over time.

Learning principles Learning principles are guidelines to the ways in which people learn most effectively.

Legal insurance Legal insurance is usually a group insurance plan provided by the employer that reimburses insureds when they have specified legal expenses or provides insureds with access to legal assistance at predetermined (usually low) rates.

Leniency bias A leniency bias occurs when employees are rated higher than their performance justifies.

Leveraging Leveraging refers to resigning to further one's career with another employer.

Life plan A life plan is an often ill-defined series of hopes, dreams, and personal goals that each person carries through life.

Lifetime employment Lifetime employment refers to employer guarantees, stated or implied, that assure the worker employment for his or her lifetime.

Line authority Line authority allows managers to direct others and make decisions about the organization's operations.

Listening Listening is a receiver's positive effort to understand a message transmitted by sound.

Local unions Local unions are the smallest organizational unit of a union. They are responsible for representing the members at the worksite.

Long-term disability insurance Long-term disability insurance provides a proportion of a disabled employee's wages or salary. These policies typically have long waiting periods and seldom allow the employee to attain the same income level that existed before the disability.

Lost-time accidents These are severe job-related accidents that cause an employee to lose time from his or her job.

Maintenance factors Maintenance factors are the elements in the work setting that lead to employee dissatisfaction when they are not adequately provided. These factors are also called hygiene factors or dissatisfiers. They include working conditions and fringe benefits.

"Make-whole" remedies   When an individual is mistreated in violation of employment laws, the wrongdoer usually is required to make up the losses the employee suffered because of the wrongdoing.

Management by objectives (MBO)   MBO requires an employee and a superior to jointly establish performance goals for the future. Employees are subsequently evaluated on how well they have attained these agreed-upon objectives.

Management inventories   Management inventories summarize the skills and abilities of management personnel. (See *Skills inventories*, which are used for nonmanagement employees.)

Management rights   Management rights are the rights and freedoms an employer needs to manage the enterprise effectively. These areas of discretion usually are reserved by management in the labor agreement.

Maturity curves   Maturity curves are used to compensate workers based on their seniority and performance. Normally, these compensation plans are limited to professional and technical workers.

Mentor   A mentor is someone who offers informal career advice.

Merit-based promotions   Merit-based promotions occur when an employee is promoted because of superior performance in the current job.

Merit raises   Merit raises are pay increases given to individual workers according to an evaluation of their performance.

Motivation   Motivation is a person's drive to take action because that person wants to do so.

Motivational factors   Motivational factors are the elements in the work environment that motivate the individual. They are sometimes called motivators and satisfiers.

National Institute of Occupational Safety and Health (NIOSH)   NIOSH was created by the Occupational Safety and Health Act to conduct research and develop additional safety and health standards.

National Labor Relations Act of 1935 (NLRA)   The NLRA, also known as the Wagner Act, was passed by Congress to ensure that covered employees could join (or refrain from joining) unions for the purpose of their own mutual aid and protection and for negotiating with employers. The act also created the National Labor Relations Board.

National Labor Relations Board (NLRB)   The NLRB was created by the National Labor Relations Act to prevent unfair labor practices and conduct union representation elections.

National unions   National unions are the parent body that helps organize, charter, guide, and assist affiliated local unions.

Needs assessment   Needs assessment diagnoses current problems and future challenges that can be met through training and development.

Net benefit   Net benefit means that there will be a surplus of benefits after all costs are included.

Nominal group techniques (NGT)   NGT is a group method of drawing out ideas from people on a specified topic. It requires participants to list their ideas and then share them in round-robin fashion with the group and a facilitator. Once all the ideas of the group are vented, duplicate ideas are eliminated and clarification follows. Then the members of the group vote on what they believe to be the best or the most important items uncovered through the NGT process.

Noncontributory benefit plans   Noncontributory benefit plans are fringe benefits that are paid entirely by the employer. (See *Contributory plans.*)

Nondeferral jurisdictions   Nondeferral jurisdictions are areas where the EEOC finds no qualified agency to which it may defer cases.

Nondirective counseling   Nondirective, or client-centered, counseling is the process of listening to an employee and encouraging him or her to explain bothersome problems, understand them, and determine appropriate solutions.

Nonmonetary incentives   Nonmonetary incentives, such as recognition, reward employees for desired performance without the use of money.

Nonverbal communication   Nonverbal communication is action that communicates without spoken words.

Obsolescence   Obsolescence results when an employee no longer possesses the knowledge or ability to perform successfully.

Occupational Outlook Handbook   The *Occupational Outlook Handbook* is published by the U.S. Department of Labor. It indicates the future need for certain jobs.

Occupational Safety and Health Act of 1970 (OSHA)   OSHA is a broad-ranging law that requires employers to provide a work environment free of recognized safety and health hazards.

Occupational Safety and Health Administration   The Occupational Safety and Health Administration is located in the U.S. Department of Labor and is responsible for enforcing the Occupational Safety and Health Act.

Occupational Safety and Health Review Commission   The Occupational Safety and Health Review Commission is the federal agency that reviews on appeal the fines given to employers by the Occupational Safety and Health Administration for safety and health violations.

Open communication   Open communication exists when people feel free to communicate all relevant messages.

Open-door policy   An open-door policy encourages employees to go to their manager or even to higher management with any problem that concerns them.

Open system   See *System.*

Operating authority.   See *Line authority.*

Organizational climate   The organizational climate is the favorableness or unfavorableness of the environment for people in the organization.

Organization culture An organization's culture is the product of all the organization's features, such as its people, objectives, technology, size, age, unions, policies, successes, and failures. It is the organization's "personality."

Organization development (OD) OD is an intervention strategy that uses group processes to focus on the whole organization to bring about planned changes.

Organization development process The OD process is complex and difficult to implement. It consists of seven steps: initial diagnosis, data collection, data feedback and confrontation, action planning and problem solving, team building, intergroup development and evaluation, and follow-up.

Organizing committee An organizing committee consists of employees who guide the efforts needed to organize their fellow workers into a labor organization.

Orientation programs Orientation programs familiarize primarily new employees with their roles, the organization, its policies, and other employees.

Outplacement Outplacement occurs when an organization assists its current employees in finding jobs with other employers.

Pareto analysis Pareto analysis is a means of collecting data about the types or causes of production problems in descending order of frequency.

Participation rates Participation rates are the percentages of working-age men and women in the workforce.

Participative counseling Participative counseling seeks to find a balance between directive and nondirective counseling techniques, with the counselor and the counselee participating in the discussion and solution of the problem.

Part-time layoffs Part-time layoffs occur when an employer lays off workers without pay for a part of each week, such as each Friday. (Some states allow employees to collect partial unemployment benefits under these types of layoffs.)

Paternalism Paternalism exists when management assumes that it alone is the best judge of employee needs and therefore does not seek or act on employees' suggestions.

Pattern bargaining Pattern bargaining occurs when the same or essentially the same contract is used for several firms, often in the same industry.

Patterns and practices When discrimination is found to exist against a large number of individuals who are in a protected class, a pattern and practice case exists.

Pay-for-knowledge compensation systems These systems give employees higher pay as an incentive for each new skill or job they learn.

Payout standards Payout standards are the benchmarks or triggers that determine whether an incentive or gainsharing award has been earned.

Performance appraisal Performance appraisal is the process by which organizations evaluate employees' performance.

Performance measures Performance measures are the ratings used to evaluate employee performance.

Performance standards Performance standards are the benchmarks against which performance is measured.

Perks "Perks" stand for prerequisites, which are associated with the fringe benefits of a given job. The term "perks" is often used as shorthand or human resource slang for fringe benefits.

Personal leave days Personal leave days are normal workdays an employee is entitled to take off. (In some firms personal leave days are used instead of sick days.)

Personnel management Personnel management is the study of how employers obtain, develop, utilize, evaluate, maintain, and retain the right numbers and types of workers. Its purpose is to provide organizations with an effective workforce. (It is also called human resource management.)

Peter Principle The Peter Principle states that in a hierarchy, people tend to rise to their level of incompetence.

Piecework Piecework is a type of incentive system that compensates workers for each unit of output.

Placement Placement is the assignment of an employee to a new or different job.

Point system The point system is a form of job evaluation that assesses the relative importance of a job's key factors to arrive at the relative worth of jobs.

Political grievances Political grievances are filed or supported because of their political implications, not their merits.

Portability clauses Portability clauses allow workers to transfer accumulated pension rights to the subsequent employer when they change jobs.

Position analysis questionnaire (PAQ) The PAQ is a standardized, preprinted form that collects specific information about jobs.

Precedent A precedent is a new standard that arises from past practices of either the company or the union.

Preferential quota systems Preferential quota systems exist when a proportion of the job openings, promotions, or other employment opportunities is reserved for members of a protected class who previously were discriminated against.

Pregnancy Discrimination Act of 1978 This act prevents discrimination in employment against women who are pregnant and able to perform their jobs. It amends the Civil Rights Act of 1964.

Prevailing wage rates Prevailing wage rates are the rates most commonly paid for a given job in a specific geographic area. They are determined by a wage and salary survey.

Preventive discipline Preventive discipline is action taken to encourage employees to follow standards and rules so that infractions are prevented.

Private placement agencies Private placement agencies are for-profit organizations that help job seekers find employment.

Proactive human resource management Proactive human resource management exists when decision makers anticipate problems and take affirmative steps to minimize those problems rather than wait until a problem occurs before taking action.

Problem-solving interviews   These types of interviews rely on questions that are limited to hypothetical situations or problems. The applicant is evaluated on how well the problems are solved.

Production bonuses   Production bonuses are a type of incentive system that provides employees with additional compensation when they surpass stated production goals.

Production-sharing plans   Production-sharing plans are gainsharing approaches that reward employees for exceeding predetermined production levels.

Productivity   Productivity is the ratio of a firm's output (goods and services) divided by its input (people, capital, materials, energy).

Professional associations   Professional associations are groups of workers who voluntarily join together to further their profession and their professional development. When these associations negotiate for their members, they are also labor organizations.

Profit sharing   Profit sharing exists when an organization shares a proportion of its profits with the workers, usually on an annual basis.

Profit-sharing plans   Profit-sharing plans enable eligible employees to receive a proportion of the organization's profits.

Progressive discipline   Progressive discipline requires strong penalties for repeated offenses.

Promotion   A promotion occurs when an employee is moved from one job to a job that is higher in pay, responsibility, and/or organizational level.

Protected groups   Protected groups are classes of people who are protected from discrimination under one or more laws.

Psychic costs   Psychic costs are the stresses, strains, and anxieties that affect a person's inner self during a period of change.

Pygmalion effect   The Pygmalion effect occurs when people live up to the highest expectations others hold of them.

Qualifiable worker   A qualifiable worker is one who does not currently possess all the requirements, knowledge, skills, or abilities to do the job but will become qualified through additional training and experience.

Qualified handicapped   The qualified handicapped are mentally or physically handicapped individuals who, with reasonable accommodations, can perform successfully.

Quality circles   Quality circles are small groups of employees who meet regularly with a common leader to identify and solve work-related problems.

Quality of work life   Qualty of work life means having good supervision, good working conditions, good pay and benefits, and an interesting, challenging, and rewarding job.

Quality of work life efforts   Quality of work life efforts are systematic attempts by an organization to give workers a greater opportunity to affect their jobs and their contributions to the organization's overall effectiveness.

Rap sessions Rap sessions are meetings between managers and groups of employees to discuss complaints, suggestions, opinions, or questions.

Rate ranges Rate ranges are pay ranges for each job class.

Rating scale A rating scale requires the rater to provide a subjective evaluation of an individual's performance along a scale from low to high.

Rational validity Rational validity exists when tests include reasonable samples of the skills needed to perform successfully or when there is an obvious relationship between performance and other characteristics that are assumed to be necessary for successful job performance.

Reactive human resource management Reactive human resource management exists when decision makers respond to problems instead of anticipating problems before they occur. (See *Proactive human resource management*.)

Realistic job preview (RJP) An RJP allows the job applicant to see the type of work, equipment, and working conditions involved in the job before the hiring decision is finalized.

Recency effect The recency effect is a rater bias that occurs when a rater allows recent performance to sway the overall evaluation.

Recruitment Recruitment is the process of finding and attracting capable applicants for employment.

Red-circle rates Red-circle rates are wages or salaries that are inappropriate for a given job according to the job evaluation plan.

Reengineering Reengineering seeks to radically revise the way work is performed with the objective of restructuring work and work processes to attain significantly better performance.

Regulations Regulations are legally enforceable rules developed by government agencies to ensure compliance with laws that an agency interprets and administers.

Rehabilitation Act of 1973 This act prohibits discrimination against those who are handicapped but qualified to perform work. It applies to employees who receive federal moneys and to federal agencies. (See *Americans with Disabilities Act*.)

Reinforcement schedules Reinforcement schedules are the different ways behavior reinforcement can be given.

Relations by objectives Relations by objectives is a program created by the Federal Mediation and Conciliation Service to improve labor-management cooperation between participating parties.

Reliability Reliability means that a selection device (usually a test) yields consistent results each time an individual takes it.

Relocation policies Relocation policies are company guidelines used to determine the benefits and other assistance that will be provided to employees who must move domestically or internationally in connection with their jobs.

Relocation programs Relocation programs are company-sponsored fringe benefits and assistance that aid employees who must move in connection with their jobs.

Repatriation programs   Repatriation programs are company-sponsored efforts to relocate an employee back to the home country.

Repetition   Repetition facilitates learning through repeated review of the material to be learned.

Repetitive strain injury   A repetitive strain (or stress) injury occurs when a worker's job requires constant repetition of movement that leads to some form of strain on the body. For example, "tennis elbow" occurs when people play tennis; typists and word processors are sometimes afflicted with carpal-tunnel syndrome, which is an inflammation of the nerves in the wrist.

Replacement charts   Replacement charts are visual presentations of who will replace whom in an organization when a job opening occurs.

Resistance to change   Resistance to change arises from employee opposition to change.

Résumé   A résumé is a brief listing of an applicant's work experience, education, personal data, and other information relevant to the applicant's employment qualifications.

Reverse discrimination   Reverse discrimination occurs when an employer seeks to hire or promote a member of a protected class over an equally (or better) qualified candidate who is not a member of a protected class.

Reward-performance model   The reward-performance model combines the strengths of other motivational approaches. It argues that properly reinforced behavior enhances an individual's self-image and therefore that individual's self-expectations. These self-expectations lead to greater effort, and the rewards for this effort continue to reinforce the behavior.

Role ambiguity   Role ambiguity results when people are uncertain of what is expected of them in a given job.

Role playing   Role playing is a training technique that requires the trainee to assume different identities to learn how others feel under different circumstances.

Rucker plans   Rucker plans are cost reduction gainsharing approaches used to reduce labor and material costs by sharing a proportion of the savings with employees.

Sandwich model of discipline   The sandwich model suggests that a corrective comment should be sandwiched between two positive comments to make the corrective comment more acceptable.

Scanlon Plan   The Scanlon Plan is an incentive program that compensates eligible employees for improvement in labor costs that are better than the previously established company norms.

Search firms   Search firms are private for-profit organizations that help employers locate hard-to-find applicants.

Selection interviews   Selection interviews are a step in the selection process in which the applicant and the employer's representative have a face-to-face meeting.

Selection process   The selection process is a series of specific steps used to decide which recruits should be hired.

Selection ratio   The selection ratio is the ratio of the number of applicants hired to the total number of applicants.

Self-actualization   See *Self-fulfillment needs*.

Self-fulfillment needs   Self-fulfillment needs are the needs people have that make them feel they are becoming all they are capable of becoming. This need also is called self-actualization.

Self-funding   Self-funding occurs when an organization agrees to meet its insurance obligations out of its own resources.

Seniority   Seniority means the length of a worker's employment in relation to that of other employees.

Seniority-based promotions   Seniority-based promotions result when the most senior employees are promoted into new positions.

Severance pay   Severance pay is a payment made to workers when they are dismissed from the company. Employees who are terminated because of poor performance or behavior are usually not eligible.

Shelf-sitters   "Shelf-sitters" is a slang term for upwardly immobile managers who block promotion channels.

Shorter workweeks   Shorter workweeks are employee scheduling variations that allow full-time workers to complete a week's work in less than the traditional five days. One variation is forty hours of work in four days.

Skills inventories   Skills inventories are summaries of each employee's skills and abilities. (Skills inventories usually are used for nonmanagement workers. See *Management inventories*.)

Socalization   Socialization is the ongoing process by which an employee adapts to an organization by understanding and accepting the values, norms, and beliefs held by others in the firm. Orientation programs—which familiarize primarily new employees with their role, the organization, its policies, and other employees—speed up the socialization process.

Social Security Act of 1935   This act established the social security program of the federal government, which taxes workers and employers to create a fund from which medicare, retirement, disability, and death payments are made to covered workers and their survivors.

Social unionism   Social unionism describes unions that seek to further their members' interests by influencing the social, economic, and legal policies of government at all levels—city, county, state, and federal. (See *Business unionism*.)

Society for Human Resource Management (SHRM)   SHRM is the major association for professional human resource specialists and administrators.

Sociotechnical systems   Sociotechnical systems are interventions in the work situation that restructure the work, the work groups, and the relationship between the workers and the technology they use to do their jobs.

Specialization   Specialization occurs when a very limited number of tasks are grouped into one job.

Sponsor   A sponsor is a person in an organization who can create career development opportunities for others.

Staff authority   Staff authority is the authority to advise, not direct, others.

Staffing table   A staffing table lists anticipated employment openings for each type of job.

State employment security agency   A state employment security agency (or unemployment office) matches job seekers with employers who have job openings.

Steering committee   The steering committee is part of a quality circle or another employee involvement effort and usually includes the top manager of the worksite (such as a plant manager) and his or her direct staff.

Steward   A union steward is elected by workers (or appointed by local union leaders) to help covered employees present their problems to management.

Stock options   Stock options are fringe benefits that give the holder the right to purchase the company's stock at a predetermined time.

Strategic plan   A strategic plan identifies a firm's long-range objectives and proposals for achieving those objectives.

Stress   Stress is a condition of strain that affects one's emotions, thought processes, and physical condition.

Stress interviews   Stress interviews rely on a series of harsh rapid-fire questions that are intended to upset the applicant and show how the applicant handles stress.

Stressors   Stressors are conditions that tend to cause stress.

Stress-performance model   The stress-performance model shows the relationship between stress and job performance.

Stress threshold   A stress threshold is the level of stressors a person can tolerate before feelings of distress begin.

Strictness bias   A strictness bias occurs when employees are rated lower than their performance justifies.

Structural unemployment   Structural unemployment occurs when people are ready, willing, and able to work but their skills do not match the jobs available.

Structured interviews   Structured interviews use a predetermined checklist of questions that usually are asked of all applicants.

Suggestion systems   Suggestion systems are a formal method for generating, evaluating, and implementing useful employee ideas.

Suitable employment   Suitable employment means employment for which the person is appropriate as a result of education, training, or experience.

Supplemental unemployment benefits (SUB)   SUB is an employer-provided fringe benefit that supplements state unemployment insurance when an employee is laid off.

System   A system is two or more parts (or subsystems) that work together as an organized whole with identifiable boundaries. An open system is one that is affected by the environment.

Taft-Hartley Act   See *Labor-Management Act of 1947.*

Taft-Hartley injunctions   Taft-Hartley injunctions allow the President of the United States to seek a court order to delay a labor strike for eighty days. During this cooling-off period, the government investigates the facts surrounding the dispute.

Task identity   Task identity means doing an identifiable piece of work, thus enabling the worker to have a sense of responsibility and pride.

Task significance   Task significance means knowing that the work one does is important to others in the organization and outside of it.

Time studies   Time studies are measurements of how long a job takes to perform.

Title VII   Title VII refers to the part of the Civil Rights Act of 1964 that requires equal employment opportunities without regard to race, color, religion, sex, pregnancy, or national origin.

Training   Training represents activities that teach employees how to perform their current jobs.

Transference   Transference refers to how applicable training is to actual job situations, as evaluated by how readily the trainee transfers the learning to the job.

Transfers   Transfers occur when an employee is moved from one job to another that is relatively equal in pay, responsibility, and organizational level.

Turnover   Turnover is the loss of employees by an organization. It represents employees who depart for a variety of reasons.

Two-tiered orientation program   A two-tiered orientation program exists when both the human resource department and the immediate supervisor provide an orientation for new employees.

Two-tiered wage rate   This is a pay structure that occurs when one group of employees (usually new hires) receives a different wage rate than do other employees. The employer achieves lower labor costs by paying new workers less while previously hired union members usually are able to retain their existing wage rates.

Two-way communication   Two-way communication means that a sender and a receiver are exchanging messages so that a regular flow of communication is maintained.

Underutilization   Underutilization occurs when a department or an entire organization has a smaller proportion of members of a protected class than is found in the firm's labor market. (See *Concentration in employment.*)

Unemployment compensation   Unemployment compensation is payment to those who lose their jobs, are unemployed, are seeking new employment, and are willing and able to work.

Unfair labor practices (ULPs)   ULPs are violations of the National Labor Relations Act, as amended. These unfair practices are specific activities that employers and labor organizations are prohibited from doing.

Union-management agreement   See *Labor agreement.*

Union members' bill of rights   The union members' bill of rights refers to Title I of the Labor-Management Reporting and Disclosure Act of 1959, which established the specific rights of union members in dealing with their unions.

Union organizers   Union organizers are people who assist employees in forming a local union.

Union shop   A union shop is a workplace where all employees are required to join the local union as a condition of employment. New employees are usually given thirty, sixty, or ninety days in which to join.

Unstructured interview   An unstructured interview uses few, if any, planned questions to enable the interviewer to pursue the applicant's responses in depth.

Upward communication   Upward communication is communication that begins at some point in the organization and then proceeds up the hierarchy to inform or influence others.

Validity   Validity means that the selection device (usually a test) is related significantly to job performance or to another relevant criterion.

Variety   Variety in jobs means being able to use different skills and abilities.

Vertical staffing meetings   Vertical staffing meetings occur when managers meet with two or more levels of subordinates to learn about their concerns.

Vestibule training   Vestibule training occurs off the job on equipment or methods that are highly similar to those used on the job. This technique minimizes the disruption of operations caused by training activities.

Vesting   Vesting is a provision in retirement plans that gives workers rights to retirement benefits after a specified number of years of service even if an employee quits before retirement.

Vietnam Era Veterans Readjustment Act of 1974   This act prohibits certain government contractors from discriminating in employment against Vietnam-era veterans.

Wage and salary surveys   Wage and salary surveys are studies made by an organization to discover what other employers in the same labor market are paying for specific key jobs.

Wage compression   Wage compression occurs when the difference between higher- and lower-paying jobs is reduced. This compression usually results from giving larger pay increases to lower-paying jobs.

Wagner Act   See *National Labor Relations Act of 1935.*

Walk-ins   Walk-ins are job seekers who arrive at the human resource department in search of a job without any prior referrals and not in response to a specific ad or request.

Want ads   Want ads describe a job and its benefits, identify the employer (or employment agency), and tell those who are interested how to apply.

Weighted checklist A weighted checklist requires the rater to select statements or words to describe an employee's performance or characteristics. After those selections are made, different responses are given different values or weights to determine a quantified total score.

Weighted incentive systems These systems reward executives on the basis of improvements in multiple areas of business performance. Depending on the weights used, part of the incentive bonus can be tied to improvements in market share, profit margin, return on assets, cash flow, or other indexes.

Welfare secretary The welfare secretary was a forerunner of the modern human resource specialist. Welfare secretaries existed to help workers meet their personal needs and minimize any tendency of workers to join unions.

Well pay Well pay is a fringe benefit provided by some employers that pays employees for unused sick leave.

Wildcat strikes Wildcat strikes are spontaneous work stoppages that take place in violation of the labor contract and are officially against the wishes of union leaders.

Workers' compensation Workers' compensation is payment made to employees for work-related injuries or to their families in the event of a worker's job-caused death.

Work flow Work flow is the sequence of jobs in an organization needed to produce the firm's goods or service.

Work measurement techniques Work measurement techniques are methods for evaluating what a job's performance standards should be.

Work practices Work practices are set ways of performing work in an organization.

Work sampling Work sampling means using a variety of observations on a particular job to measure the length of time devoted to certain aspects of the job.

Work simplification Work simplification means simplifying jobs by eliminating unnecessary tasks or reducing the number of tasks by combining them.

Write-ins Write-ins are people who send in a written inquiry, often seeking a job application.

INDEXES

Name Index

Subject Index